ADVANCES IN FOOD RESEARCH

VOLUME 31

ADVANCES IN
FOOD RESEARCH

VOLUME 31

Edited by

C. O. CHICHESTER
University of Rhode Island
Kingston, Rhode Island

E. M. MRAK
University of California
Davis, California

B. S. SCHWEIGERT
University of California
Davis, California

Editorial Board

F. CLYDESDALE
E. M. FOSTER
J. HAWTHORNE
J. F. KEFFORD

H. MITSUDA
E. SELTZER
V. G. SGARBIERI
W. M. URBAIN

ACADEMIC PRESS, INC.
Harcourt Brace Jovanovich, Publishers
San Diego   New York   Berkeley   Boston
London   Sydney   Tokyo   Toronto

ACADEMIC PRESS, INC.
1250 Sixth Avenue
San Diego, California 92101

United Kingdom Edition published by
ACADEMIC PRESS INC. (LONDON) LTD.
24-28 Oval Road, London NW1 7DX

LIBRARY OF CONGRESS CATALOG CARD NUMBER: 48-7808

ISBN 0-12-016431-0 (alk. paper)

PRINTED IN THE UNITED STATES OF AMERICA
87 88 89 90   9 8 7 6 5 4 3 2 1

CONTENTS

Chocolate

Robert A. Martin, Jr.

Endogenous Proteolytic Enzymes in Skeletal Muscle: Their Significance in Muscle Physiology and during Postmortem Aging Events in Carcasses

A. Asghar and A. R. Bhatti

Olive Oil: A Review

A. Kiritsakis and P. Markakis

CONTENTS

In Memoriam

EMIL M. MRAK
1901–1987

CARCINOGEN RISK ASSESSMENT

R. NICHOLS HAZELWOOD

International Technology Corporation
17461 Derian Ave.
Irvine, California 92714
and
University of California, Irvine
University Extension
Program in Toxic and Hazardous Materials
Irvine, California 92716

I.   Introduction
   A.   Why Assess Risks?
   B.   Legal and Regulatory Reasons
   C.   Cancer Prevention
   D.   Avoiding Hazards
   E.   Relationships
II. Basic Notions of Risk Assessment
   A.   Risk and Rare Events
   B.   Risks to Individuals
   C.   Regulatory Efforts
   D.   Critique of Early Approaches
   E.   The National Academy Report
   F.   Other Developments
   G.   Types of Problems
   H.   The IARC Approach
III. Cancer Statistics and Risk
   A.   Cancer Is Caused by Specific Agents
   B.   Statistical Considerations
   C.   Causes of Human Cancers
   D.   Proportionate Risk
   E.   Industrial Exposure
   F.   Food and Cancer Risks
   G.   Dietary Risk Factors
IV. Laboratory Data on Risk
   A.   Animal Data on Carcinogens
   B.   Long-Term Animal Bioassays
   C.   Short-Term Tests

1

I. INTRODUCTION

A. WHY ASSESS RISKS?

Why should anyone be interested in assessing the risks from carcinogens? We all understand that cancer, in its various forms, has been known for thousands of years. At present, it seems that more people are getting cancer, but more are being cured. Besides, except for some people who are exposed in the workplace, much of the causes of cancer seem to be due to "bad habits," such as cigarette smoking, overeating, too much sun, X rays, or breathing contaminated air. Of course, none of us wants to be exposed to any excess risks. But we learned a decade ago that almost everything can cause cancer—at least everything that was fun or necessary for living. Some people, of course, claim that there are lots of carcinogens in the environment, but they can be eliminated by forcing the polluters to clean up the air, or water, or soil, or the workplace, or consumer products, or whatever.

B. LEGAL AND REGULATORY REASONS

At the time the Toxic Substances Control Act (TSCA) was passed in 1976, the national crusade to find a cure for cancer had been underway for 5 years. Progress did not meet expectations. The need for TSCA was not clear to the public. There seemed, however, to be ample evidence among regulatory groups that cancer could be reduced by control of public exposure to carcinogens. Estimates, taken out of context, and with precious little attention paid to accurate reflection of what was said, asserted that up to 90% of all cancers were "environmental'' in origin. Never mind that the word environmental was used to contrast to ''genetic'' in origin. So we saw the parade of ''carcinogen of the week'' in the press, until it became clear that the public had reacted with indifference. The action then shiftted to the regulatory arena, with workplace exposures leading the way.

C. CANCER PREVENTION

A number of influences converged in the late 1970s. The scientific community began to express the view that many cancers were, in principle, preventable. Cairns (1977), for example, pointed out that there was little evidence then that a ''cure'' was about to be discovered. However, there was good reason to believe that prevention could be effective in reducing the incidence of cancer. The analogy with the major reduction in infectious disease through general improvements in public health and sanitation was cited. Thus, Cairns stated, ''. . . we are forced to concentrate on prevention as the only plausible route open to us at present for the conquest of cancer.'' He added that prevention requires some understanding of origins.

D. AVOIDING HAZARDS

If we are to prevent cancer, then we must understand how the disease works. The implicit model underlying Cairns' statement is that cancer can be attributed to some exogenous agents that induce the disease. The agents do not always cause cancer whenever someone is exposed, otherwise there would be nearly 100% incidence in the United States and other advanced countries. From clinical observations that go back at least to the eighteenth century, cancer can be related to exposure to substances found in the workplace. This was the famous finding by Percival Pott in 1775. Other strong associations between agent and clinical disease included X-rays, cigarette smoking, sunlight, and heredity. Cancer, then, could be associated with a variety of chemical, physical, and biological agents. Clearly, we cannot begin to find ways to prevent a disease if there are numerous different and apparently independent causes, unless we can sort out the relationships.

E. RELATIONSHIPS

Risk assessment of carcinogens, then, depends on being able to relate the action of known agents that produce cancer to the clinical appearance of the disease. We have to have some means of comparing the potency of agents. We need an overall assessment of the relative impact of various possible causes. Prevention implies some pro-active measures. With an always limited amount of resources to devote to prevention, some way of setting priorities is desirable. Fundamental to all this is a model of carcinogenesis. How does a substance induce cancer? What is the shape of the dose–response curve? How do we screen for the property of inducing cancer? If we use animal tests, how can bioassays be extrapolated to humans? Finally, what do we think we know now about the causes of human cancers? These are subjects of carcinogen risk assessment as it has evolved today.

II. BASIC NOTIONS OF RISK ASSESSMENT

A. RISK AND RARE EVENTS

Intuitively, one thinks about rare events in terms of the probability of the event happening, and the consequences of such a happening. Risk is the resultant of both ideas. However, where the probability becomes very small, approaching zero, and the consequences very large, ultimately approaching infinity, the mathematical result, zero times infinity, is indeterminate. A more useful way to think about risks of low probability–high consequence events is to define risk as the result of hazard and exposure. This is most useful for risks associated with carcinogens, because it is clear that the hazard can be thought of as an intrinsic property of the substance(s) in question. Exposure, in this risk equation, is an extrinsic property of the process. To produce a risk, there must be both hazard and exposure.

The use of probability times consequences has a long and useful history in risk assessment. For acute events, the results of some low probability but potentially catastrophic accident can be estimated. Given a variety of possible accidents, the associated consequences can be calculated. All the possibilities can be combined with the consequences to produce a risk assessment. This kind of analysis is derived from a variety of engineering techniques useful in studying the reliability of complex electronic and mechanical systems. Such methods are thoroughly documented in the literature of various professions dealing with large complex systems. The same basic techniques have been applied to nuclear power plant safety, handling and storage of hazardous materials such as toxic or flammable chemicals, and transportation accidents, for example. Indeed, probability times consequences underlies some of the oldest risk assessment and management methods known to society—the basic principles of insurance underwriting.

When we turn to low probability events that may affect one or a few individuals, that have long periods between the exposure event and any manifestation of the results of the exposures, and where the consequences are dire for the individuals, the idea of risk as the result of hazard and exposure becomes more relevant. Cancer is such a process. The hazard term includes all of the biological information about a substance: short- and long-term animal bioassays; human epidemiology; dose–response relationships; scaling factors to relate animal data to human physiology: and the pharmacological properties of the material *in vivo*. The hazard term clearly includes all the intrinsic properties of the potential carcinogen. The exposure term, in contrast, contains the external information, the extrinsic processes that are involved. Exposure data are derived from a combination of ambient measurements of concentrations in various media (air, water, soil, food), measures or other estimates of intake or contact, and the temporal changes in the exposure factors. Because we often lack detailed measurements about exposure, estimates of one kind or another are used. These exposure models are the source of much controversy and misunderstanding in risk assessment. There is no reasonable alternative to these models at present.

B. RISKS TO INDIVIDUALS

For many purposes, the assessment and management of risks are closely intertwined. A physician treating a patient will determine various risk factors and prescribe ways to alleviate, avoid, or minimize future risk. The process is in part intuitive and based on training and experience (what computer people are beginning to try to emulate with "expert systems") and in part based on analytical and deductive methods of identifying hazards and exposures (although the clinician may use different words to describe these factors). An epidemiologist investigating a sudden outbreak of some illness proceeds similarly. The source of the disease is found, and it is removed (when possible). Exposure to the vector is eliminated, reduced, or protective and remedial measures undertaken. In a clinical setting, where the physician is treating an individual patient, or in the classic epidemiologist/outbreak situation, there are few problems with finding the hazards and eliminating exposures. There are limits here, however. Economics may prevent a person from changing jobs to eliminate exposure to some hazard in the workplace, or personal preferences may make it very difficult to change a life-style.

When we move from the small-scale doctor/patient relationship to the larger area of public policy and the regulatory process, the simple notion of "find a hazard and eliminate all possible exposure to it" breaks down. A whole set of new players and new interests comes into the process. Where before, the relationship was personal, with a physician or other practitioner interacting directly with his/her patients, the regulatory system is far more impersonal. Even the simple introduction of economics has major consequences. In fact, Ibsen's play *An Enemy of the People* illuminated this exact dilemma a hundred years ago. Dr. Thomas Stockmann finds that the town spa is a source of disease for the tourists who visit it. The cure is apparent—close it until the tannery wastes contaminating the spa waters can be diverted. His brother, the mayor, and most of the townspeople are not so quick to want to shut down the major source of livelihood for the town. Eventually, the Doctor is branded an enemy of the people for his proposal. Here, the public health benefits of an action would accrue to outsiders, and the economic costs to the town. This is seen in the play as a far different situation. Many reasons are found to rationalize keeping the spa open. Other reasons are found to attack the motives of both the doctor and the mayor, and their respective followers. In the end, no one emerges a winner, and the fight seems destined to go on.

C. REGULATORY EFFORTS

In the 1970s, a serious and concerted effort began to reduce the toll that cancer was taking on human life in the United States. Major increases in funding were made available by Congress, both for fundamental research on cancer and for attempts to find/develop cures of existing disease. For many decades prior to this, there had been a public recognition that some substances found in nature or made artificially could cause cancer. The first pure food laws were passed in the early part of this century. Regulation of pesticides began shortly after World War II, with passage of the Federal Insecticide, Fungicide and Rodenticide Act (FIFRA). The Delaney Clause, which prohibits addition of carcinogens to food, was enacted in 1958. Laws dealing with clean water and air pollution appeared in the sixties and seventies. The Toxic Substances Control Act (TSCA) and the Resource Conservation and Recovery Act (RCRA) both were enacted in 1976. So in addition to the scientific efforts, a series of major regulatory bills were in place to support the "War on Cancer."

The regulatory effort seemed obvious enough at the start. We needed to identify those substances that posed a carcinogenic risk to humans and bar them from all sources of exposure. It seemed that all we had to do was analyze, for example, food and water, consumer and industrial products, and determine which contained carcinogens. These would be barred from sale or use until "safe substitutes" could be found, or the offending material removed from the product. We didn't anticipate that analytical chemists would rise to the challenge and come up with methods to determine parts per billion and lower concentrations of all sorts of things. In addition, a number of short-term bioassays were introduced. These, while not offering the same assurances of accuracy that conventional animal bioassays do give, were cheap and quick, and of high enough accuracy to allow evaluation of many more substances.

One result of all this was that every week seemed to bring new announcements of the discovery that almost everything we ate, drank, breathed, wore, or touched had some unacceptable level of carcinogens or possible carcinogens. Government reacted by attempting to regulate carcinogens in generic fashion (this often meant publishing a list of proscribed materials and banning them, or publishing a set of criteria by which substances were determined to be carcinogens and banning those that met the tests). Congress added to the confusion by establishing different criteria for regulation in different laws. The Delaney clause, for example, imposes an absolute ban on any carcinogen added to a food (but "natural" carcinogens in the food are not banned, e.g., aflatoxins in corn and peanut products are allowed because they are not additives). The FIFRA procedures, on the other hand, require explicit balancing of risks and the economic benefits of using pesticides.

This situation created a natural arena of conflict. It pitted farmer against environmentalist, labor against management, public interest groups against government, and most often put the regulators in between the regulated community, various special interest and advocacy groups, the Congress, and the courts. One reason, of course, was much of the legal foundation for regulation was new, without firm precedent, and ambiguous. Naturally, parties who did not prevail in the regulatory arena went to court. Many efforts to "implement a toxics policy" or to take rapid action by issuing emergency regulations were blocked by the courts. Agencies that moved too deliberately, on the other hand, found themselves under court orders to issue regulations by a date certain. Finally, as the regulation of "toxics" bogged down in this swamp of conflicting rules and policies, lawmakers began to set deadlines or make rules in bills that did not always reflect the limitations of the scientific knowledge available.

D. CRITIQUE OF EARLY APPROACHES

A few scholarly studies and critiques of the regulatory process have emerged. Lave (1982) has edited a collection of essays that critique the process and use of risk assessment in regulation. Studies include revisions of air pollutant standards for ozone, workplace standards for benzene and for coke oven emissions, ionizing radiation regulations, and food additive standards. The basic conclusion of these studies is that the federal government did not do a very effective job of formulating regulations in the 1970s, and that use of quantitative risk assessment methods would have improved the process. However, the very process of selecting substances for evaluation of risks is heavily weighted toward political and social factors. Douglas and Wildavsky (1983) describe the polarization of attitudes among the various interested groups and caution that much of the process of selecting which risks are of concern is political. In such a situation, purely scientific considerations may well be relegated to a low place on the list of topics considered in regulatory decisions.

When the environment for making decisions becomes a complex mixture of social, political, economic, and scientific issues, the conflict that results tends eventually to lead to some consensus. Often, this comes about slowly, and may result simply because all the conflicting parties realize that no one can prevail while all have veto power. Sometimes, a few important meetings or documents trigger this. In other cases, exhaustion and lack of new ideas or ways to argue a point lead to acceptance of a consensus. Finally, a few individuals may present some important new insights, and these trigger a rethinking and covergence of ideas. All of these processes seem to have occurred in the past few years. A few seminal reports, a gradual acceptance of some ideas that were controversial earlier, and some keen insights have all happened. We are now closer to some general acceptance of the ideas of risk assessment and the ways to do it. At the same time, a number of scientific developments in mechanisms of carcino-genesis, identification of carcinogens, and the associated biology of the diseases called cancer have opened up the possibility that we can carry out risk assess-ments with a better degree of confidence in the science underlying what we do.

E. THE NATIONAL ACADEMY REPORT

In 1983, the National Research Council/National Academy of Sciences (NRC/NAS, 1983) issued a report, "Risk Assessment in the Federal Govern-ment, Managing the Process." This truly was one of those seminal documents that appeared at the right time and the right place. Major changes in the political climate regarding regulations had started in both Washington and the various state capitals. Court decisions had slowed or changed regulatory thrusts initiated in an earlier time, when attitudes were different (and perhaps more naive). The NRC/NAS report provided a review of the process of risk assessment, described various inference guidelines used by agencies for carcinogen risk assessment and compared the conflicts found between them, and outlined the process and organi-zational arrangements for doing such work. Finally, the separation of risk assess-ment and risk management was stressed.

The report indicated that there were four basic steps in the risk assessment process:

1. Hazard Identification. Is a substance linked causally to a health effect?
2. Dose–Response Assessment. The relation between the magnitude of ex-posure and the probability of health effects occurring.
3. Exposure Assessment. The extent of human exposure before or after con-trols are imposed.
4. Risk Characterization. The nature, magnitude, and uncertainty of risk to humans.

The report stresses that the risk management process is a separate and distinct part of regulation. Assessing risk involves the factual base used to define the health effects of human exposure to specified hazards. Risk management is the process of weighing and selecting policy alternatives and deciding how to regu-late and what to regulate. The risk management process not only uses risk assessment information but also includes engineering data and social, economic, and political concerns. In one sense, risk assessment is part of a long series of quantitative aids to decision making that began with the introduction of Operations Research in World War II and evolved in government and industry over the next four decades. If so, one could apply the same definitions to risk assessment as were used for operations research: "To provide quantitative information to decision makers about operations under their control"; or, in a more modest vein, "The art of giving bad answers to questions that would otherwise be given worse answers." The first says it accurately, the second warns us about undue hubris.

The NRC/NAS report established two important things about risk assessment: we need to have some consistency in how we do it (i.e., inference guidelines should be consistent among all regulatory agencies), and risk management is a separate process and should be separated organizationally from risk assessment. This latter finding has been seized by some and used to argue that assessment requires "good science," while risk management is not appropriately done by these "good scientists."

F. OTHER DEVELOPMENTS

Certain other important notions have developed about risk. In 1975, Lowrance posed the response to, "How safe is safe enough?" as, "When the risk is acceptable." It remained for Starr to formulate the appropriate definition of acceptable as "public acceptance of a risk depends on public confidence in its effective management" (Starr, 1985). Although a semanticist would probably criticize the circular nature of the words, the notion is clear: safe means that the level of risk can be kept to an acceptable level. Interestingly, the notion of a safe level for incremental risks seems to have arrived almost by silent acceptance. Milvy (1986) has noted that a risk of one in a million seems to be an acceptable level for incremental risks from carcinogens. He points out that a number of regulatory proceedings have settled on that value as an appropriate and acceptable level for risk management. There is not universal acceptance of 1×10^{-6} by any means. It seems, though, the idea that there needs to be some level of risk other than zero has pretty well been adopted. This in itself is a significant step from the time when zero risk was both thought to be possible and seriously pursued.

G. TYPES OF PROBLEMS

How, then, do we assess risks in this complex and confrontational world? The answer is, "It depends." The methods depend on the kind of data we have and our confidence in it. Is a substance a carcinogen? How potent is it? Who is at risk, and through what pathways? How much trust can we place in the data? These are the kinds of questions that roll around the minds of risk assessors.

These relate back directly to the four steps outlined in the NRC/NAS report—identifying the hazards, finding a dose–response relationship, assessing exposure, and characterizing the risk involved. There are three different situations that obtain in the real world:

1. Substances/processes for which there is valid epidemiological evidence of a cause–effect relationship, including dose–response data.
2. Substances/processes which have been in public use for many years (at least long enough for clinical cases of cancer to have been seen) and for which there is evidence from laboratory studies, usually animal bioassays, of carcinogenicity, but where there is no good clinical, statistical, or epidemiological evidence of a carcinogenic effect in humans.
3. Substances/processes that are found to be carcinogenic in laboratory tests, but where there has been no human exposure, or so little as to be considered none.

For the first group, the controversies, if any, deal with the technical issues of the human evidence. There is a very large body of evidence, and this will be discussed in Section III. The third group poses another set of technical issues, and also becomes entangled in policy questions. Should we take the risk of letting the material "out of the bottle" as it were? Or should prudent public health policy dictate that such materials should not be allowed to be released? Is there some overriding benefit that might be obtained? (This is not a straw man, because many cancer chemotherapy agents are themselves carcinogens. X-Ray therapy for some tumors also increases cancer risks.) The most difficult and acrimonious problems have been generated by the second group. Some of the chemicals have been widely used for many decades and have real advantages over earlier materials. The evidence for carcinogenicity in the laboratory ranges from fairly solid, in some cases, to ambiguous and arguable in others.

Perhaps the most complete review of the scientific basis for carcinogen risk assessment was prepared by the Interagency Staff Group on Chemical Carcinogens. It was originally published in the *Federal Register* in 1985, and later reprinted in 1986. The California Department of Health Services also prepared a review (DOHS, 1985) of the scientific basis for carcinogen risk assessments. Both documents summarize the epidemiological and statistical methods used, discuss long-term animal bioassays as ways to identify carcinogenic hazards and dose–response relationships, describe the problems associated with extrapolating from animal data to human exposures, and review various other bioassays. The Interagency Staff Group review also discusses exposure assessment briefly.

H. THE IARC APPROACH

With this plethora of data, with conflicting viewpoints, and with so much at stake, how can one sort out the ideas and reach conclusions? One approach has been that taken by the International Agency for Research on Cancer (IARC). The IARC procedure has been to convene a panel of experts who review all the evidence available on a particular substance or process. The IARC staff and panel members prepare reviews and summaries of the evidence. These are discussed, and the panel eventually reaches a conclusion on the degree of evidence for a carcinogenic risk to humans. Periodically, IARC publishes monographs about specific chemicals, groups of chemicals, industrial processes, and industries associated with cancer in humans. Every few years, the results of all the IARC panels are collected and published as a supplement to the IARC Monograph series. The supplement (see IARC, 1982) provides a list of chemicals, processes, and industries associated with cancer and an assessment of the nature and degree of risk. This "IARC List" has become one of the major reference documents for regulating possible carcinogens. IARC classifies chemicals in one of three groups. Group 1 substances and processes are those for which ". . . there was sufficient evidence from epidemiological studies to support a causal association between the exposure and cancer." Group 2 lists those which are judged ". . . probably carcinogenic to humans." This group is further subdivided into Groups 2A and 2B. In 2A substances had at least limited evidence of carcinogenicity in humans. Group 2B had good evidence in animals, but insufficient evidence in human exposures. Finally, IARC Group 3 is defined as: "The chemical, group of chemicals, industrial process or occupational exposure cannot be classified as to its carcinogenicity to humans."

The IARC nomenclature has generally been adopted in the risk assessment field. IARC considers evidence as "sufficient," "limited," or "inadequate," and makes this evaluation for the evidence in humans, in animals, and for activity in short-term tests. Thus, evidence in each of three areas will be given one of three evaluations. To be in Group 1, evidence must be sufficient in humans, and that is all that is needed. For Group 2A, evidence must be limited in humans and sufficient in animals. For Group 2B, sufficient evidence in animals and in short-term tests is needed. If there is inadequate human evidence, and limited animal evidence, the classification would probably always be Group 3. This general scheme has largely carried over into other proposals for classifying chemical carcinogens. To decide that a substance is a potential carcinogen requires positive long-term animal bioassay results plus evidence from short-term tests. To confirm that a substance is a carcinogen in humans, epidemiological data relating human exposure are needed. The strongest confirmation in humans is when a dose–response relationship can also be demonstrated.

There are two quite different problems with the IARC list: not every substance that is or might be of concern has been evaluated by IARC; and the results, in the final analysis, depend on the collective judgment and voting of a small group of "experts". The first issue can be alleviated somewhat by developing similar lists from other sources, applying the same set of standards as used by IARC. In general, IARC has not examined many of the pesticides either registered or proposed for registration in the United States. A number of food additives and other chemicals involved in processing and packaging have not been studied by IARC. However, the regulatory procedures required for pesticides under FIFRA, the evaluations required under TSCA, and the Food and Drug Administration procedures, including the Generally Regarded as Safe (GRAS) requirement, provide a basis for expanding the IARC list.

The complaint that IARC is, in the end, merely the votes of a small group of experts, is harder to dismiss. However, in nearly every aspect of our lives, we are subject to the same kind of rule by small groups of experts. Certainly the legal system, culminating in the U.S. Supreme Court, is an "expert system." The editor and peer reviewers for any given professional journal are such a system, and we all have had our disappointments there. Tenure decisions, job promotions, and so on depend on such procedures. Further, as in any of the processes of science, if the collective belief of a large body of peers differs from a published finding, there are mechanisms for correction, based on a continuing reevaluation of the evidence.

In the context of pure science, then, the problem with IARC methods are not serious. For people who might get cancer from an exposure to a substance that was classified in Group 3, that is little consolation. To protect public health, and to provide a basis for rapid regulatory response, many groups have argued for a "generic" set of rules for identifying and controlling carcinogens. The proposals, usually, take the form of regulating all chemicals and processes that would fall in IARC Groups 1, 2A, and 2B. Rules are set for the number and kind of animal bioassays and short-term tests that must be positive. In general, no data on human evidence for carcinogenicity are required. Needless to say, the arguments over how many, how much, what kind, etc. can be endless in such proposals. In the end, such decisions are not science and are not necessarily best made by scientists. "Policy makers," whoever they might be, have to decide. Risk assessment is a process by which information and insights on the science can be brought to the attention of those who make policy.

III.   CANCER STATISTICS AND RISK

A.   CANCER IS CAUSED BY SPECIFIC AGENTS

The idea that cancer can be associated with specific risk factors goes back at least to Percival Pott's report on the association between workplace exposure (in this case, to soot in chimneys) and cancer in the exposed population (scrotal cancer among chimney sweeps). In fact, medicine and public health are founded on the notion that almost all diseases are due to exposure to some agent. A relatively few types of illness are believed to be genetic in origin. Over the past several decades, ideas about the nature and causes of cancer have varied considerably. Today, we believe the evidence is overwhelming that most cancer, if not all, is the result of exogenous agents that trigger and promote the course of the disease. Some genetic linkages are believed to exist in the process, although the genetic penetrance is thought to be incomplete (so that not everyone with the genes will develop the disease). Agents involved in triggering and promoting cancer include chemicals, of course, radiation (sunlight as well as nuclear), viruses, other biological entities such as hormones, and certain "physical agents" such as asbestos. Exposure to these agents is correlated with various behavioral, social, and occupational factors. An enormous body of statistical analysis on cancer has been produced. The interpretation of such data has led to a series of generally accepted beliefs about the causes and risks of cancer in the population. While much of what follows refers to the U.S. population, similar findings are observed elsewhere.

B.   STATISTICAL CONSIDERATIONS

For the past half century or more, cancer death rates have been falling or remaining constant, with the notable exception of lung cancer. However, the total number of cancer deaths, and the proportion of all deaths, has been increasing steadily. This apparent conflict is readily resolved by noting that death *rates* are age- adjusted, while overall cases are not so corrected. The life expectancy of a person at birth has increased by over 25 years in this century. As the population bears a greater proportion of older persons, diseases that seem to be more frequent in the elderly are seen more often. The observed rate of new cancer cases increases as some power of age—from age 20 to 80, for example, the incidence of colorectal cancer increases by a factor of 1000 (Cairns, 1975). Typically, the cancer rate is proportional to the third or fourth power of age. If we analyze a population with a growing proportion of older members, we expect to see what is in fact observed.

There is some controversy about the actual statistical meaning of the cancer data available. Problems of reporting accuracy, better diagnosis, and other technical statistical issues leave room for some important disagreements. When one steps back from these issues and looks at the actual data, the picture still emerges that when the changing age composition of the population is considered, cancer is not increasing in any epidemic proportions. Indeed, the only striking increases are seen in lung cancers, and these are overwhelmingly related to smoking. The annual publication *Cancer Facts and Figures,* by the American Cancer Society, provides statistics on new cases and deaths, by site and sex. Additional data on historical trends, geographical patterns, and racial/ethnic differences are provided. The 1984 edition (American Cancer Society, 1984) presents a summary of

25-year trends in the age-adjusted cancer death rates by sex and site. Clear increases in lung cancer deaths (167% of males, 276% in females) are seen. A 34% increase (over the 25 years) is seen for male kidney cancers. Slight increases in prostate and esophageal cancers are found in males. Earlier increases, with later leveling off, are shown for leukemias and pancreatic cancers in both sexes.

Periodically, the technical arguments among statisticians break out in the popular press. These receive headlines such as, "War on Cancer: New Study Disputes Claims of Progress" (*Wall Street Journal,* May 7, 1986). Generally, the news stories recast arcane debates about relatively small issues, or knock over some straw man. Unfortunately, the straw men often are set up by the statisticians themselves. The statistical and epidemiological literature does not support a conclusion that cancer is being conquered, or that some "war" is being won or lost. In contrast, analyses of all the vital statistics on cancer show that lung cancer is the major cause of an observed increase in cancer, once the changing age of the population is considered. A second finding is that new "cures" for cancer have not been forthcoming. As measured by 5-year survival, most of the cancers that show real improvement in cure rates are relatively rare varieties. Nevertheless, there has been some significant clinical progress in treatment. There has been a tremendous increase in our understanding of the biology of cancer.

Finally, epidemiological studies have given us a very clear picture of the causes of cancer, and the possibilities for prevention. This latter point is extremely important, because the major increases in life expectancy have not come so much from cures of disease, but prevention. The massive reduction in infectious disease rates has come about by a combination of sanitary engineering, protection of water supplies, food and drug laws, health education, and better tools for treating infections early in their course. There is every reason to believe that strenuous efforts to reduce the risk of contracting cancer will pay off. Indeed, there are those who think the significant reduction in smoking by males is beginning to show a leveling off in new lung cancer cases. So let us turn to what is known about the causes of cancer in humans.

C.   CAUSES OF HUMAN CANCERS

The landmark study of the causes of cancer in humans is the Doll and Peto report "The Causes of Cancer" (Doll and Peto, 1981). This study was originally commissioned by the Office of Technology Assessment, U.S. Congress. It was first published in the *Journal of the National Cancer Institute,* and later as a separate monograph. When it appeared, the Doll and Peto study aroused heated emotions and substantial rhetoric. Because its conclusions tended to negate some widely reported views by members of the federal regulatory establishment, there were strong criticisms offered. At the same time, many in the regulated community viewed the study as a vindication of their views, and embraced it whole-heartedly. It did not seem to matter that the report was an honest scientific attempt to sort out a number of conflicting sets of data. By the time it was published, emotions had become so involved that almost no rational discussion of the scientific issues was possible. One must remember that in 1981 the Carter administration had just left office, and the Reagan administration, dedicated to reform of the regulatory process, had just taken office.

In the period from the end of World War II to 1970, there was a huge growth in the production of man-made chemicals. Earlier studies, going back to Pott and the chimney sweeps, had linked chemical exposures to increased cancer risks. Greenwald and Greenwald (1983) have provided a concise history of such stud-ies and give additional references. Some important names, in addition to Pott, include Rigoni-Stern, who found a relation between breast cancer and celibacy (in nuns), between cancer and age, and between marital status and uterine can-cer. Ramazzini also detected the breast cancer relationship in 1713. Harting and Hesse found a relationship between occupation (miners in the Black Forest region) and lung cancer, in 1879: 75% of the miners died of lung cancer! Undoubtedly, this was due to radioactivity from uranium. In 1895, Rehn re-ported a relation between bladder cancer and occupational exposure for workers in the aniline dye industry, with aromatic amines, especially naphthylamines, implicated. Tales of the relationship between exposure to radium, to X-rays, and to paints containing radium and thorium isotopes are well known. In 1761, John Hill reported nasal cancer in snuff users, while Soemmering reported soon after a relationship between lip cancer and pipe smoking. By the early 1950s, several studies had linked cigarette smoking and lung cancer. Finally, dermatologists, led by Thiersch, had come to believe that skin cancer was linked to chronic exposure to sunlight. (The previous information is taken from Greenwald and Greenwald, 1983.)

In a 1949 review, Conklin listed an impressive variety of associations between industrial products and processes and cancer. He discussed ionizing radiation and sunlight (ultraviolet); inorganics such as arsenic, asbestos, chromates, nickel carbonyl, and beryllium; and biological agents such as viruses and bacteria. He also discussed an impressive list of organic compounds, including aniline and azo dyes, estrogens, polycyclic aromatic hydrocarbons, soots, tars, and oils, carbon black, creosote, and benzene. The remarkable thing about Conklin's list is that it includes almost all the substances now believed to be human car-cinogens. Only the synthetic organochlorine compounds [pesticides, dioxins, polychlorinated biphenyls (PCBs), cancer chemotherapy agents, and the methyl- and ethylhalocarbons] that were introduced largely in the 1930s or later are not included in Conklin's list, which was published in 1949. Not enough time would have elapsed between widespread commercial use of these substances and the normal 20–30 years required for tumor induction.

In the 30 years following Conklin's paper, statisticians and epidemiologists identified a number of what are now called "life-style" associations with cancer. These include cigarette smoking, diet (particularly caloric intake), and alcohol use. Interactions between these factors and workplace exposures have been reported. Smokers, for example, have an elevated risk of lung cancer about 10 times the nonsmokers' risk. Asbestos workers who are nonsmokers show an elevated lung cancer risk of about 5, while asbestos workers who smoke have a cancer risk 50 times that of nonexposed nonsmokers (American Cancer Society, 1984). Similar effects have been reported for miners who are at elevated risk from ionizing radiation at work. The life-style cancer problem is one that transcends purely technical issues, and it has become a sociological and political issue as well. The so-called life-style cancers are, in theory, avoidable by reducing exposure. So, however, are cancers caused by industrial or other exposures. An important part of risk assessment is to try to estimate the proportions of human cancers due to various causes, and the possibility of risk reductions by various means.

Doll and Peto first set out some basic findings about the incidence of cancer in various parts of the world. They listed a large variety of cancers and compared rates for various parts of the world. For the same kind of cancer, in the same sex and site of the disease, incidence rates varied among different populations by, in some cases, one to two orders of magnitude. Esophageal cancer in males, for example, was 300 times as common in northeast Iran as in Nigeria. The Iranian population shows a cumulative incidence of about 20% for this cancer. Colon cancer affects about 3% of U.S. males in Connecticut, a rate 10 times the Nigerian rate. The range of variation was never less than 6-fold for any given cancer.

Next, populations that, living in one area, show a high or low incidence of specific cancers will show changes in these rates after migration. Black Americans show a cancer incidence far more like the pattern shown by white Americans than the pattern seen in Nigeria, for example. Similar findings are reported for Japan and Japanese immigrants to Hawaii. Finally, as noted earlier, changes with time are seen in populations living in the same area. Worldwide, there has been a decline of 40–60% in stomach cancer mortality in the quarter century from 1950 to 1975. In the same period, lung cancer mortality grew by up to 400% in some countries (although the increase was closer to 90–150% in most countries). Doll and Peto also noted temporal decreases in such things as bladder cancer in chemical industry workers, which they attribute to a cessation of manufacture of 2-naphthylamine.

Cancer is thus seen to be an avoidable disease, at least in part. Smoking, diet, consumption of alcohol, exposure to sunlight and to ionizing radiation, and industrial exposure may all lead to cancer. Risk can therefore be reduced by a combination of eliminating the use of hazardous substances and reducing or eliminating exposures. The problem is not simple, however. As a graduate student at the Donner Laboratory in Berkeley, I recall a seminar by Hardin Jones in the mid 1950s. He had been studying the effect on life expectancy of what he called "physiological insults"—smoking, use of alcohol, rich foods, sexual activity, and various diseases and vaccinations. One of the others present said, "If I understand what you said, I could live to 120 by cutting out smoking, drinking, good food, and sex, right?" The answer Professor Jones gave was, "Well, you may only live to 70, but it will seem like 120."

D. PROPORTIONATE RISK

At this time, about 25% of the U.S. population develops cancer, and 20% dies from it. There were an estimated 870,000 new cases in 1984, and 450,000 deaths. Approximately 35% of male deaths and 18% of female deaths are due to lung cancer. Table I shows cancer deaths for 1984, by site and sex. The most important causes of death, in addition to lung cancers, are breast cancer in women, colorectal cancers for both sexes, ovarian and uterine cancers in women, prostate cancer in men, and leukemias and lymphomas in both sexes (American Cancer Society, 1984). How are the causes we identified earlier related to this pattern?

It is possible to relate the causes of cancer to various physical, chemical, or biological actions through clinical observations, epidemiology, or through laboratory tests. The problem of identifying a substance or agent as a carcinogen is complex. Clinical observations, backed up by laboratory and/or epidemiological studies, permit reliable associations. Epidemiology provides valid relations between causes and outcomes (although from time to time the findings of specific

TABLE I

CANCER DEATHS (%) BY SITE AND SEX, 1984[a]

Site	Males	Females
Skin	2	1
Oral	3	1
Lung	35	18
Breast	—	18
Colorectal	12	15
Pancreas	5	5
Prostate	10	—
Ovary	—	6
Uterus	—	5
Urinary	5	3
Leukemias and lymphomas	8	9
All other	20	19

[a] Source: American Cancer Society (1984).

studies may be challenged as "statistical associations but not proof"). Laboratory results alone pose greater problems because tests with animal models or *in vitro* systems cannot be correlated completely with findings in humans.

Much of the controversy between regulators and the regulated community is the result of differing viewpoints about the degree of confidence that can be placed in laboratory tests as predictors of human cancers. The extremes are perhaps best exemplified by Peto's recent critique of the "hygienists" (Peto, 1985), on the one side, and the study produced by the U.S. Occupational Safety and Health Administration proposing a "generic" policy for identifying and regulating carcinogens, particularly in the workplace (Bridboard *et al.*, 1978). Peto argues that the most promising hypotheses for risk reduction involve infectious, nutritional, or hormonal factors rather than exposure to synthetic chemicals. Thus, ". . . the industrial hygienists' interests may be irrelevant or diversionary to the epidemiologist." The alternate view may be summarized by the common phase, "We can't wait for a body count." If the introduction of new chemicals in commerce can lead to the proliferation of a host of new carcinogens, public health requires that potential public exposure be minimized, if not eliminated. If the only data available are laboratory tests, then control must be based on those data.

Table II, based on Doll and Peto (1981), is derived from a substantial body of analysis. While a number of criticisms of the work have been offered, the ensuing years since publication have not produced any valid, serious challenges to the conclusions. Other studies cited by Doll and Peto, and subsequent works

TABLE II

PROPORTION OF CANCER DEATHS (%) DUE TO VARIOUS FACTORS[a]

Factor	Estimate	Range
Tobacco	30	25–40
Alcohol	3	2–4
Diet	35	10–70
Food additives	<1	0–2
Reproductive and sexual behavior	7	1–13
Occupation	4	2–8
Pollution	2	<1–5
Industrial products	<1	<1–2
Medicine and medical procedures	1	0.5–3
Geophysical factors[b]	3	2–4
Infection	10?	1–?
Unknown	?	? ?

[a] Source: Doll and Peto (1981).
[b] Ionizing radiation and sunlight.

such as Reif (1981), Knowlden *et al.* (1981), Greenwald and Greenwald (1983), Speizer (1983), Spratt and Greenberg (1984), and Zeigler *et al.* (1986), support the estimates. The conclusions are clear—at least 75% of cancers in the United States are avoidable. The principle causes of cancer are smoking, diet, reproductive and sexual behavior, and alcohol use. It is not clear, however, that changes in behavioral patterns can be expected to achieve all the potential reductions implied by these results. The smoking link is clear, and evidence exists to support the belief that stopping smoking will reduce risks but not eliminate them. It appears that smokers who quit remain at higher risk than those who have never smoked. Former smokers eventually have a relative risk double the never smoked group, while smokers have a 10-fold or greater excess risk over those who never smoked.

For other risks, either the evidence is less clear or the behavioral changes so great that one cannot expect the dramatic reductions possible by not smoking. The dietary issues, for example, are still unclear. If some component of the risk is simply due to excess calories, regardless of their nature, we are faced with the same problem of overweight, in another form. Changes in reproductive and sexual behavior are hard to achieve, as evidenced by the current AIDS epidemic, which was not even a consideration in Doll and Peto's work. Similar ambiguities exist with alcohol habits. After all, who wants to live for 70 years and have it seem to be 120 years?

It is clear, however, that one additional cancer risk can be avoided, one not mentioned by Doll and Peto or others. As a rule, non-melanoma skin cancers are excluded from most statistical compilations. The estimated number of new cases for 1984 was 400,000 (American Cancer Society, 1984). This represents about 45% of the total of all other new cancer cases reported for the year. About 0.5% of the non-melanoma skin cancers are listed as causes of death in the ACS report. Avoiding skin cancer, as with other life-style cancers, requires some behavioral changes that are not simple or easy to achieve. However, the economic cost of so many cases, and the impact of the 1900 preventable deaths, seem now to have encouraged more publicity and attention. Skin cancer probably is the largest occupationally linked cancer in the United States.

E.   INDUSTRIAL EXPOSURE

It is equally important to notice that Doll and Peto estimate that about 4% of U.S. cancer deaths are the result of industrial exposures. Presumably, a significant fraction of these cases results from exposure to synthetic chemicals, as opposed to natural products. Conklin's (1949) report dealt entirely with what might be considered "natural" chemicals rather than synthetic ones. In many cases, new chemicals have been introduced to reduce the perceived risks from other, older substances. Pentachlorophenols (PCPs), for example, were intended to replace creosote as a wood preservative. Later evidence of dioxin contamination has made PCPs suspect. New pesticides were introduced to replace the arsenicals widely used at the beginning of this century. Polychlorinated biphenyls (PCBs) were introduced to replace petroleum oils that posed fire hazards in electrical apparatus. Perchlorethylene replaced the very flammable Stoddard Solvent in dry cleaning. Trichloroethylene replaced various other volatile, flammable hydrocarbons in metal degreasing applications. All the substances just listed are now on one or another list of potential human carcinogens. The question of setting priorities for reducing cancer risks is intimately related to the degree to which any agent or action may induce cancer and may be controllable.

F. FOOD AND CANCER RISKS

For readers of this publication, the relationship, if any, of diet, food additives, and other substances involved in food production, processing, packaging, and marketing is of particular interest. Until recently, the relationship between diet components and cancer was not part of the mainstream of cancer research. In fact, most discussions of diet and cancer were the province of what can only be described as the lunatic fringe. Despite this, a number of studies showed a firm link between diet and cancer. Nearly every review of cancer risks (except this one) contains a graph plotting the female breast cancer rate on the ordinate and some measure of calories or fat intake in the diet on the abscissa, for several dozen countries. The correlation is very striking—high caloric intake, or better, high fat intake is strongly related to the breast cancer rate, worldwide. Thailand, for example, shows an average daily fat intake of about 25 grams, and a breast cancer death rate of about 1 per 100,000 population. At the other extreme, countries such as the Netherlands, Denmark, the United Kingdom, New Zealand, the United States, and Canada all have average daily fat intakes of 140–160 grams and a death rate of about 25 per 100,000. A similar plot of daily meat consumption per capita and colon cancer rate shows another strong relationship (see Doll and Peto 1981, figure 1A and 1B, for an example).

Popular belief, reinforced by some legitimate research results, led to continuing congressional pressure on various federal agencies to study and report on diet and cancer. As a result, a study was commissioned from the National Research Council, National Academy of Sciences. Their Committee on Diet, Nutrition, and Cancer produced a major report, "Diet, Nutrition, and Cancer" (NRC/NAS, 1982). This study collected and critically reviewed a large number of previous studies. Subsequently, Creasey (1985) published an updated review of the subject. Spratt (1984a) and Spratt and Greenberg (1984) have provided additional reviews specifically related to colorectal cancer and diet. Ziegler et al. (1986) also have reviewed the epidemiology of colorectal cancer. To illustrate how far the subject of diet and cancer has progressed, Hennekens (1986) recently reported on current research on prevention of cancer with vitamin A analogs. He describes, among other subjects, a National Cancer Institute randomized trial of the use of β-carotene in cancer prevention, where the subjects are U.S. physicians. We all have probably noticed with interest the advertising campaign conducted by cereal companies, promoting high fiber diets as a potential cancer preventative, with the approval of the National Cancer Institute. Who would have imagined such developments a decade or two ago? At best, such proposals would have been politely ignored. But as we saw from Doll and Peto's work, diet may be involved in up to 35% of cancer cases. So things have changed greatly.

The magnitude of the change in attitudes is seen most clearly in Hennekens' review. He discusses the Physicians' Health Study and also lists a number of other ongoing dietary projects. These include measurement of serum retinol levels in cancer and control groups, questionnaire studies of dietary β-carotene and several different cancer sites, and clinical trials in several places, both in the United States and abroad. The questionnaire studies as well as other epidemiological efforts are very strongly suggestive that high intake of β-carotene

TABLE III

EFFECT OF DIETARY COMPONENTS ON SITE-SPECIFIC CANCERS[a]

Site	Effect[b]	Comments
Esophagus	+ +	Synergistic with cigarette smoke
	+	Mouldy foods
	+	Trace mineral deficiency
	+	Very hot beverages
	− −	Fresh fruits/vegetables
Stomach	+ +	Smoked/salt-pickled/high NO_3/NO_2 foods
Colon/rectum	+ +	Fat
	0	Alcohol (but suspicious)
	− −	Fiber and cruciferous vegetables
Liver	+ +	Aflatoxins
	+ +	Hepatitis B infection
	0	Alcohol
Pancreas	+	Alcohol, coffee, meat
Gall bladder	+	Total caloric intake
Lung	+	Low vitamin A intake
Bladder	+ (weak)	Coffee
Kidney	0	No effect established
Breast	+ +	Early life fat intake
Endometrium	0	(Possible + for calories)
Ovaries	0	Inconclusive, but possible link to high fat intake
Prostate	+	High fat/protein intake
	−	Vitamin A precursors

[a] Source: National Research Council (1982).

[b] + +, Strong positive; +, positive; − −, strong negative; 0, no; −, negative association.

and retinoids has a general protective effect against cancer. The effect may extend well beyond cancers of the digestive system. Reduced risks are seen for lung, bladder, breast, cervix, and prostate cancers. Clinical trials are underway to relate micronutrient intake (of such substances as vitamins B6 and E, selenium, various synthetic retinoids, and β-carotene) to a whole spectrum of different cancers. It will take perhaps another decade before the results of the clinical trials are in. Until then, we shall have to draw conclusions from the major epidemiological studies, supplemented where possible by laboratory data and animal bioassays.

The National Research Council (NRC/NAS, 1982) analyzed the evidence from the viewpoint of both specific effects of specific dietary components on site-specific cancers and general effects of diet constituents on the overall risk of cancer to humans. Table III shows the NRS/NAS findings on effects of diet components on specific cancers. As might be anticipated from existing folklore, diet has a significant effect on cancers involving the digestive tract. In addition, evidence connects diet with a variety of cancers in other organs. Intake of fat, total calories, use of alcohol and coffee, and some food contaminants (or processing chemicals) seem to be implicated with developing a variety of tumors. Beneficial effects of some diet components are seen as well. Fresh fruits, cruciferous vegetables, and fiber, as well as constituents of these, seem to reduce tumor incidence in some organs.

The contributions of diet to enhancing or reducing the risk of cancer are summarized in Table IV, also based on the NRC/NAS report. Factors related to increased risks of cancer include salted and smoked foods, calories per se, fats, alcohol, and sweeteners added to foods. Diet factors showing a beneficial or protective effect include low fat diets, high intakes of fruits and vegetables, low doses of selenium, antioxidants added to food, and vitamins A and C. Perhaps of equal significance is the NRC committee's comments on constituents that have no apparent effect on cancer risks. No effects were found for food packagings or animal growth promoters. Environmental contaminants, despite labatory test results, could not be shown to affect risks as dietary constituents. (No assessment regarding other sources of these substances was attempted.) The NRC/NAS study claimed that no protective effect could be associated with vitamins B and E, and data on protection from dietary fiber was inconclusive. The fiber result is somewhat surprising, because work going back at least to Burkitt's studies in the early 1970s suggested a strong protective effect related to a high fiber diet. Creasey (1985) has provided a recent review of the fiber question. He concludes that the evidence for a direct protective effect from dietary fiber intake is weak. Some of the early findings may be due to a low fat intake that seems to be related to the high fiber diet life-style. Some writers suggest that cholesterol and/or bile salts may be implicated in colon cancer, and that fiber absorbs these compounds, with a resulting protective effect. The observed speedup in transit time for

TABLE IV

EFFECTS OF DIETARY CONSTITUENTS ON CANCER RISKS[a]

Factors	Effects[b]	Comments
Diet patterns and components of food	+ +	Salted and smoked foods
	− −	Low fat, high fruits and vegetables
Total caloric intake	+	Evidence stronger in animals than humans
Lipids	+ +	Particularly breast and colon cancer
Proteins and carbohydrates	+	Related to total caloric intake
Dietary fiber	0	Inconclusive data
Vitamins		
A	− −	Protective
B	0	No conclusion
C	−	Some protection
E	0	No conclusion
Minerals		
Se	− −	At low doses only (in diet only)
Fe, Cu, Zn, Mo	0	
I, As, Cd, Pb	0	
Alcohol	+	May be synergistic with smoking
Food additives		
Antioxidants	−	
Sweeteners	+	
Packagings	0	
Animal growth promoters	0	
Environmental contaminants (PCBs, pesticides, polynuclear hydrocarbons)	0	No epidemiological data, despite animal tests
Inhibitors of cancer (carotene-rich and cruciferous vegetables)	− −	

[a] Source: National Research Council (1982).
[b] See footnote to Table III for definition of symbols.

intestinal contents with higher fiber diets may also contribute, if the cholesterol/bile acids theory is correct.

G. DIETARY RISK FACTORS

To summarize the recent studies on diet, diet constituents, and cancer risks, it is clear that some food constituents increase the likelihood that individuals will develop cancer. Other constituents are clearly beneficial, exerting a protective effect. Finally, indirect evidence seems to support the idea that environmental contaminants and food additives cannot be shown to be causing a problem (with the exception of "sweeteners," where public policy seems to have judged the risks to be acceptable). Cyclamates have been banned, saccharin risks seem to have been discounted, and no generally accepted evidence exists for aspartame risks. Earlier additives, particularly dyes, have been banned. There are working hypotheses that attempt to explain the observed results, with some degree of success.

Salted, smoked, and nitrite/nitrate-preserved foods are believed to have trace contamination with known chemical carcinogens—nitrosamines from the nitrite/nitrates, polynuclear aromatic hydrocarbons from smoked foods. The protective effects of β-carotene, retinoids, antioxidants, selenium, and vitamin C are believed to be related to their ability to interrupt free radical processes, which are associated particularly with oxygen radicals and oxidizers. The adverse effect of high fat diets is hypothesized to relate to the propensity of lipids to participate in free radical processes. As part of a larger discussion, Ames (1983) points out that lipids are easily oxidized in cooking, and that the peroxidation chain reaction, or rancidity, leads to various epoxides, hydroperoxides, aldehydes, and alkoxy radicals. The production of oxygen radicals in the interaction of tissue with ionizing radiation and the subsequent role of these processes in radiation carcinogenesis should be recalled (see the review by Coggle, 1985, for example).

There are additional reasons to believe that diet and diet components are significant in cancer. Certainly, the nutritional state of cancer patients is of clinical concern. Cachexia, a loss of appetite and wasting of the cancer patient's body, is a major concern. There are as yet unexplored relationships between diet and the state of the immune system. A number of unproven or frank quackeries have been promoted as cancer cures (laetrile, various herb potions that actually contain carcinogens, macrobiotic diets, and megavitamin treatments). Above all, the relationship of food and cancer has become respectable in the research community. New discoveries plus rediscoveries are leading to important approaches to our fundamental understanding of cancer. Food and diet approaches suggest major possibilities for the prevention of cancer.

IV. LABORATORY DATA ON RISK

A. ANIMAL DATA ON CARCINOGENS

So long as one assesses risks based on data derived from human exposure and human disease, there is little controversy about the basic facts of the hazard and dose–response data. When risks are assessed based on data derived from animal experiments and other laboratory procedures, however, major controversies arise. At one extreme, the Bridboard et al. (1978) paper estimated that industrial exposures could be the cause of as much as 35% of all cancers, based largely on laboratory data. On the other hand, Peto (1985) has expressed extreme reservations about what he calls the hygienists approach, arguing that epidemiological methods have identified the major causes of cancer in man, and that the occupational exposure problem is very small compared to smoking and diet. The debate is certainly not going to be settled in this article. The debate is not over whether or not something should or can be done to prevent cancer. The issue is about priorities—what are the best ways, from a public health standpoint, to proceed?

Laboratory data on carcinogen hazards take two forms: the so-called long-term bioassays and the short-term *in vivo* or *in vitro* tests. There is also a whole area of study that relates the physical structure of chemicals to their potential carcinogenic hazard. Reviews of both long- and short-term testing methods can be found in the Interagency Staff Group report (1985) and in the California Department of Health Services "Guidelines" (DOHS, 1985). No really adequate review of structure–activity relationships has been published recently. Both laboratory techniques are attempts to provide information on carcinogenic hazards and on the dose–response relationships that exist. Strictly, the data obtained in the laboratory have to be extrapolated from the test systems to humans. Most laboratory work is done at concentrations much higher than anticipated environmental exposure levels. Data must be extrapolated downward from high doses to low doses. Doses in animal systems must be extrapolated to human systems. Finally, human exposure to the substance must be presumed to give a similar result—the formation of tumors.

There have been major efforts devoted to animal testing. The federal government has consolidated a number of efforts in various agencies under the National Toxicology Program. Private laboratories are operated both as part of the research and development activities of chemical, food, and pharmaceutical companies and as contract agents. The chemical industry has recently established the Chemical Industry Institute of Toxicology to perform such work. The results of these efforts are published in the scientific literature. The National Toxicology Program issues an annual report on carcinogens, listing substances in much the same manner as the IARC. The NTP list, however, is based primarily on animal bioassay results rather than the weighting and grading of evidence approach used by IARC.

Short-term testing has an even greater volume of literature than long-term bioassays. Many of the short-term tests are relatively inexpensive, as well as requiring much simpler interpretation to reach a conclusion. The major problem with the short-term tests has been to correlate the observed results with animal and human observations. The endpoints of human or animal exposure to suspect carcinogens are the production of tumors—usually malignant but certainly life-threatening. Short-term bioassays sometimes have similar endpoints, but more often do not. Instead, the outcome may be mutations in bacterial systems, chromosomal changes in cells, DNA damage, or altered cell morphology. Comparisons between these tests and bioassays almost always show far less than

100% correspondence. This is not surprising, given the wide variety of test systems. It does mean that short-term tests, while useful for screening, cannot alone be used to identify carcinogenic hazards. Positive results in any single test system raise red flags. Positive results in more than one test, when the tests are based on different biological phenomena, are clear warnings of potential serious hazards.

B. LONG-TERM ANIMAL BIOASSAYS

Typical bioassays use inbred strains of rats and mice. To keep the numbers of test animals low, administered doses are high. Preliminary toxicology tests for acute responses are used to develop a "maximum tolerated dose" (MTD). This is based on a 90-day test. Male and female rodents are then given a dose equal to the MTD and usually two lower doses, and a zero-dose control is included. The animals are exposed through diet, water, or inhalation for their lifetimes. In some protocols, a few animals in each test group may be sacrificed at some fixed fraction of their life span. Some earlier bioassays used only two doses, typically the MTD and 0.5 MTD. Current practice has been to choose three or more doses. In many cases, the MTD proved to be toxic during long exposures to a significant fraction of the test group. The use of at least three dose levels also provides better information on the shape of the dose–response curve.

Animals that die or are sacrificed early are examined for macroscopic and microscopic evidence of tumors. Controls are important in this kind of work because the rodent strains used are inbred. Most commonly, the Fischer inbred (F344) rat and the B6C3F1 hybrid mouse are the strains chosen. There is a long history of data on both strains, both for known positive carcinogens and for control zero-dose groups. The B6C3F1 mouse poses continuing problems, despite its history. The mice are particularly sensitive to extraneous stimuli, and show a significant rate of tumor development in negative controls. Further, the strain is susceptible to developing proliferative liver lesions, which complicate the interpretation of many bioassays. In fact, a major unresolved controversy has raged for several years over the meaning of liver damage in these mice when exposed to chlorinated solvents. IARC (1982) rates both trichloroethylene and tetrachloroethylene as group 3, judging the animal bioassay evidence to be limited and the human evidence inadequate. Later assessments and reviews of the data by the Environmental Protection Agency (EPA) have been equivocal. The problem continues to be that mouse liver data are the only really strong evidence for carcinogenicity of these compounds.

A major assumption is built into all animal bioassay interpretations. In the absence of any plausible biological or physical reasons, a substance found to be a carcinogen in well-conducted rodent bioassays is presumed to be carcinogenic to humans. Again, the debate over this point has been heated, but there is really no alternative. One must stress, however, the rule, "in the absence of any plausible biological or physical reasons." Philosophically, one cannot prove a negative, and statistically the same is true. If there is no evidence, we are at best able to say only that—there is no evidence. As more and more negative results are obtained, our confidence is strengthened. Eventually, we are quite sure that something is not a carcinogen in humans. But in the regulatory climate of the past two decades, it seems unlikely that very many substances that test positive in animal bioassays in two species, and with repeated tests, have ever been allowed into widespread use in commerce. The "carcinogen of the week" press releases of 1976–1977 were the result of new analytical chemistry methods, not new clinical cases.

At present, there are several chemicals that give positive results in animal bioassays but where carcinogenicity in humans is questioned. Two examples provide the greatest contrast—dioxin and saccharin. Both have been found to be carcinogens in long-term animal bioassays. Short-term assays have been negative or equivocal. As yet, the epidemiological evidence has not been strong. The two substances are just about at the opposite ends of the potency spectrum, with dioxin (technically, 2,3,7,8-tetrachlorodibenzo-p-dioxin) extremely potent and saccharin of very low potency. Table V shows the distribution of potency values for over 500 chemicals, both natural and synthetic (Peto et $al.$, 1984). The TD_{50} is the dose that will produce tumors in half the animals tested. Saccharin may not have shown clinical carcinogenicity in humans simply because it is not very potent, and so exposure levels have not been large enough to produce detectable results. In fact it may not be a carcinogen for humans. Dioxin, on the other hand, is extremely potent, in the 1–10 μg/kg range, or six orders of magnitude greater than saccharin. As interest in dioxin has grown, it has been found to be widely distributed in the environment. Dioxin is a combustion product, a contaminant in

TABLE V

CARCINOGEN POTENCIES[a]

TD_{50} Range[b]	Number of compounds
100 ng–1 μg	2
1–10 μg	4
10–100 μg	11
100 μg–1 mg	42
1–10 mg	138
10–100 mg	157
100 mg–1 g	127
1–10 g	30

[a] Source: Gold et $al.$ (1984).
[b] TD_{50}, Dose per kilogram body weight to produce tumors in 50% of animals tested.

wood preservatives and in some herbicides. A recent review of the dioxin controversy (Tschirley, 1986) argues that while there is ample evidence that dioxin has
acute effects in humans, it is not carcinogenic.

C.   SHORT-TERM TESTS

Without question, the best known short-term test used for carcinogenic screening is the Ames test (see Ames, 1979, for a discussion of the earlier development
of the test). The Ames test measures the mutagenic potential of a substance. It
uses a histidine-requiring strain of *Salmonella* bacteria and a liver homogenate
(from rodent livers). The test substance is added, and the number of revertant
bacterial colonies measured after incubation for 2 days. The liver homogenate is
present to provide enzyme systems that can activate substances being tested. A
number of known carcinogens (e.g., vinyl chloride) must undergo metabolic
transformation before they are capable of inducing tumors. The revertants are
strains that have mutated so that they no longer require added histidine in the
nutrient gel. By testing at different doses, a dose–response curve can be generated. The Ames test, and variations of it, have been used on literally thousands of
chemicals and chemical mixtures from both laboratory and natural sources.

The Interagency Staff Group (1985) has reviewed a number of short-term
tests. They classify the tests by the nature of the assay and the observable
endpoint. The Ames test, for example, is a mutation assay, using a microbial
system, and has as its endpoint histidine reversion. Other mutation systems
include tryptophan reversion in *Escherichia coli* and several mammalian cell
systems, using mouse, hamster, or human cells. Chromosome effects can be
tested in a variety of cell types, with chromosome aberrations, sister chromatid
exchanges, translocations, chromosome gain or loss, or presence of micronuclei
being the endpoint indicating a significant result. Measures of DNA damage
from exposure to carcinogens are sometimes used in test systems. Other tests
result in alterations to cell morphology and growth patterns. Finally, a number of
test systems have been used to directly measure tumor induction on animal skin.
Rodents and rabbits have been used commonly. Measured doses of test substances are applied repeatedly to the skin surface. Growth of skin tumors is a
common endpoint. The skin-painting tests have found wide use in studying the
relationship of tumor promoters to carcinogenesis. Promoters are substances that
are not in themselves initiators of tumors in rodents, but will promote tumor
growth when applied following treatment with an initiator.

The finding that some chemicals are initiators, while others are promoters, has
had important implications in studying the mechanisms of carcinogenesis. In the
skin test system, certain chemicals are found to be initiators, but require addition
of a promoter to produce tumors. Promoters that do not act as initiators are also
well known. Finally, some substances are complete carcinogens, capable of both
initiation and promotion. If skin is first painted with a promoter, followed by an

initiator, no tumor develops. In some cases, a single application of an initiator is sufficient to start the tumor process; however, multiple application of a promoter is needed. Therefore, initiation is considered an irreversible process, but promotion is reversible, up to at least a certain point. Some clinical arguments have been advanced that seem to support such a process in humans. Smokers who stop seem to have a significantly lower risk for lung cancer over time, compared to continuing smokers. This suggests that cigarette smoke may act as a promoter, and at least up to a certain point tumor induction is reversible.

Further discussions of tumor promotion can be found in the reviews by Phillips (1985) and Sugimura (1986). Hathway (1986) has provided a monograph that reviews the chemical mechanisms of carcinogenesis.

D. EXTRAPOLATION OF DOSE–RESPONSE DATA

The basic data used in most risk assessments result from long-term animal bioassays. One measure of potency, described earlier, is the TD_{50}, the dose at which 50% of the test animals develop tumors. Such doses are orders of magnitude greater than the dose levels we expect to see in the environment. We expect to be able to assess risks of producing tumors in the range of one chance in a thousand to less than one in a million. So the extrapolation of dose levels over three to five orders of magnitude is a major problem. The well-known "law of large numbers" in statistics tells us the futility of trying to do experiments that will give us data in the low dose range. Indeed, the "Megamouse Experiment," the largest controlled experiment on dose–response, was aimed at determining the 1% response level. The ED_{01} experiment (the proper name for the megamouse study) involved over 24,000 mice. That number is massive by laboratory standards, yet is a long way from the implied million of the megamouse name. And to extend it down to the one in ten or one hundred thousand level would truly require a "Gigamouse" experiment.

Dose–response extrapolation means using a mathematical model, since there are not enough data over a large enough range to use statistical fitting of points to a curve. If one argues that zero dose must give zero tumors in test animals, the curve-fitting exercise is somewhat easier. However, this raises the issue of whether or not there is a threshold dose below which no tumor is produced. Just as there are no good extremely low-dose data points in animal bioassays, there are no really convincing, consistent data to either support or negate the idea that a threshold dose exists for any carcinogen. Most of the opinions offered on thresholds fall on the "no threshold" side of the debate. Experimental evidence for a threshold is nonexistent. This is not surprising, because the statistical precision of long-term animal bioassays is much lower than that needed to demonstrate that a threshold is even possible.

Claus and Bolander (1982) predicted that the threshold dose for benzene would be about 10^4 molecules per cell. There are about 3×10^{13} blood cells in a human. The threshold dose for benzene-induced cancer of the blood cell system would be about 39 μg. To exceed this in drinking water, with an average daily 2-liter intake, would mean a 20-ppb benzene concentration. Gravitz (1984) indicates that 1 ppb benzene in water is equal to a lifetime incremental risk of 2×10^{-6}, or two cases per million exposed. At 20 ppb, the incremental risk would be 40×10^{-6} without a threshold, or 2×10^{-6} if there is a threshold. This difference would seem to be detectable. However, going back to the bioassay process, we would be looking at doses that produce perhaps 20–50% cancers in animals. This result comes from dose levels of 10^4 times the ''threshold'' value. Clearly, we cannot expect to be able to show this kind of precision in extrapolating from laboratory levels to possible human threshold levels.

The next issue is what kind of dose–response curve best depicts what the data show and is consistent with what we believe about the biology, chemistry, and physics of carcinogenesis. The phrase, ''cancer is a multistage process,'' appears in almost every discussion of carcinogensis. Taken literally, it means that the only applicable class of model is the multistage model first described by Armitage and Doll. Armitage (1985) has reviewed the history of such models. There are other extensive reviews available (Crump, 1985; Crump et al., 1985; Crump and Howe, 1984; Interagency Staff Group, 1985; and DOHS, 1985). The multistage model postulates that cancer is produced by a sequential series of steps. The number of steps, or stages, is at least two and may extend up to as many as can be argued from whatever biological information we have. For risk assessment work, however, the number of stages to be used in a multistage model has to be a function of what we can observe, either in the laboratory or clinically. As Armitage points out (Armitage, 1985), only the initiator/promoter steps have been observed and quantified. We can justify only a two-stage model. The Moolgavkar (1983) model also describes a two-stage model of carcinogenesis. Thorslund et al. (1987) describe how such models could be applied to laboratory data.

In many cases, we do not even have the data to choose a two-stage over a single-stage model. Figure 1 shows why this happens. All of our data points are clustered somewhere in the high-dose end of the scale, and we have the presumed zero response at zero dose. We cannot distinguish between a one- or two-stage model statistically. Obviously, the two-stage model yields a lower probability of tumor at any of the intermediate to low doses. For regulatory purposes, the argument is made that in the absence of data, one should use the most conservative (i.e., health protective) approach. This justifies the use of a single-stage model in such cases, as shown in the figure. There is an abundance of data on both sides of this issue. For some experiments, a simple straight line through the point (0,0) gives the best fit. For others, an equation with an exponential term in dose squared gives a better fit.

The basic equation for the two-stage dose–response relationship is

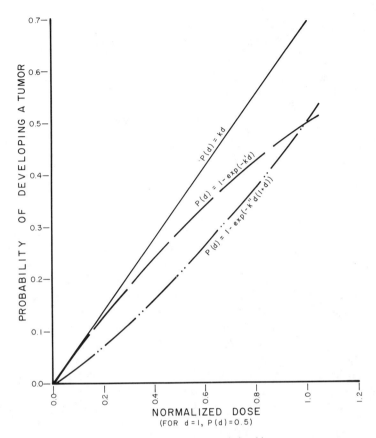

FIG. 1.   Dose–response relationships.

$$P(d) = 1 - \exp[-kd(1 + d)] \qquad (1)$$

where $P(d)$ is probability of tumor at dose d and k a constant. At low doses, so that $P(d)$ is close to zero, Eq. (1) reduces to

$$P(d) = kd \qquad (2)$$

At low doses, then, it does not matter whether a linear, a one-, or a two-stage model is used for estimating the shape and slope of the dose–response curve. All the models reduce to the same mathematical expression. The question, however, cannot be dismissed so easily. The point at which Eq. (1) simplifies to Eq. (2) is somewhere below where the exponent is 0.1 or so. If the animal data stop at a place where $P(d)$ is 0.3 or 0.5, which is common in bioassays, the choice of a single-stage model over a two-stage model would overestimate the low dose risks somewhat. Table VI compares the models and the overestimation involved. For

TABLE VI

COMPARISON OF DOSE–RESPONSE MODELS

Probability of tumor	Relative dose		
	Linear model	$P = f(d)$	$P = f(d, d^2)$
0.50	0.73	1.0	1.0
0.30	0.43	0.5	0.63
0.20	0.31	0.31	0.44
0.10	0.14	0.14	0.24
0.05	0.07	0.065	0.13
0.01	0.014	0.014	0.03
10^{-3}	0.0014	0.0014	0.003
10^{-4}	1.4×10^{-4}	1.4×10^{-4}	3×10^{-4}
10^{-5}	1.4×10^{-5}	1.4×10^{-5}	3×10^{-5}
10^{-6}	1.4×10^{-6}	1.4×10^{-6}	3×10^{-6}

the particular model used, the two-stage model predicts a probability of tumor that is half as much as that predicted either by a single-stage model or by the simple linear extrapolation. The data for this table were prepared by assuming that we have data that provides a good estimate of the 50% tumor dose (i.e., the TD_{50} value) and by solving Eq. (1) for either the one- to two-stage case or Eq. (2) for the linear case. As noted above, the single-stage model and the linear case give almost the same values when the dose is down in the 0.1 probability range.

If, instead of the TD_{50} value as a starting point, we take something like a "TD_{10}" or "TD_{01}" value, all three models will give substantially the same result. Our earlier discussion fo the megamouse experiment showed why it is not practical to perform animal bioassays to determine the 1% response level. With modifications to current protocols, it should be possible to determine the doses corresponding to the 10 or 20% tumor response levels, without a quantum increase in the size of the animal population tested. Alternatively, one could use the two-stage model assumption with data at the TD_{50} level, to estimate a value in the 10–20% response range, then use a linear trend down to zero dose. In any case, if one has real data to estimate a dose that produces a tumor frequency of 10–20% in animal bioassays, the choice of model is not important in extrapolation to low doses.

E.   WHAT IS THE DOSE TO USE?

For extrapolation from laboratory doses down to the low dose levels used in risk assessments, some substances do not seem to follow any orderly relationship between dose and result. This has been shown to be due to a metabolic transformation of the material fed (or otherwise administered) to the test animals. The dose used in developing a dose–response curve should be the "effective dose" of the material. The metabolic change will produce another substance that is in fact the carcinogen. From this, it is clear that knowledge of the pharmacology of the substance being tested is important. Obviously, if the pharmacology of the material is different in different rodent species, or between rodents and primates, these findings must be accounted for in the development of a risk assessment.

F. ANIMAL TO HUMAN DOSE CONVERSIONS

When we try to convert dose data from laboratory animals to humans, there are several issues to consider: scaling for differences in size, life span, and metabolism; differences in routes of exposure and absorption; differences in biochemistry and pharmacokinetics; and differences in susceptibility between species (DOHS, 1985). The scaling factor is, normally, the only one of these issues where any real effort is made to resolve the outstanding questions. Because little or no data are available on human pharmacology and metabolism of new substances, little can be done. The assumption is made that humans and rodents behave in the same way. Differences in susceptibility are often the subject of inconsequential debates, again in the absence of any real experimental data. Where data have been advanced, there tends to be disagreements about what it means. The California Department of Health Services (DOHS, 1985) reprinted some data from a paper by Crouch and Wilson and indicated that the information showed, "Empirically, there is evidence that humans are approximately as sensitive as the most sensitive animal species. . . ." In fact, examination of the data shows just the opposite; humans turn out to be less sensitive than both rats and mice in 4 of 10 cases, less sensitive than one of the two animal species in 2, equally sensitive in 1, and more sensitive in 3 cases. Humans are more sensitive to benzene, radiation, and vinyl chloride, by at most a factor of 2. Where humans are less sensitive, the data show factors of 2–80 times lower sensitivity. Further, as noted previously, there are substances such as chlorinated dioxins for which there is apparently growing evidence of no carcinogenic effect in humans, despite animal bioassays that do show carcinogenicity in rodents.

Ames has been prominent in the debate about relative susceptibility. He has pointed out that when substances were tested against both rats and mice, ". . . 42% of the chemicals were positive in the mouse and negative in the rat, or vice versa." (Ames, 1985). This is based on the TD_{50} data base published by Gold et al. (1984, 1986). There may some reason to expect that a small fraction of the data base would show such results. It is hard to believe that over 500 tested chemicals would show such a lack of correlation, if we can believe that "a carcinogen is a carcinogen in all species." The problem for risk assessment, however, is the impossibility of proving a negative—i.e., that something is not a carcinogen. Nevertheless, one useful criterion for deciding that something is a carcinogen is to require that it be established as such in well-conducted bioassays in at least two species. That is the IARC criterion, and it seems to be upheld by Ames' observations of the Gold database.

Adjusting for differences in routes of exposure and routes of absorption has much the same problems. In the absence of data on humans, one has to assume that absorption is the same as in the animal bioassays. Exposure routes, unless they are grossly different (such as skin painting in animals and inhalation in humans), are most often assumed to be comparable. Thus, risk can be assessed for human exposure through ingestion, inhalation, or dermal absorption routes only when ingestion or inhalation or dermal absorption experiments have been done in animals. Since this is not often the case, most risk assessments assume that if the route of exposure in an animal experiment allows systemic distribution of the substance, the route of human exposure is not an important consideration. In fact, exposure analysis should be able to correct for such differences. (This assumes that good exposure data and analyses have been done. In practice, this is seldom the case.)

Scaling for size differences, etc., may be done by scaling for differences through relative body surface areas, through total dose corrected for relative body weights, or for dose per day. The common factors proposed are mg/kg/day, mg/kg/lifetime, mg/m^2/day, ppm in diet. There is little evidence, in most cases, to decide which is preferable. As a rule, the use of mg/kg/day is most common. It is believed to give accurate results for slowly metabolized compounds. Different regulatory agencies use different values. The California Department of Health Services (DOHS, 1985) suggested using the mg/m^2/day scale factor as perhaps a compromise choice. Both the DOHS and the Interagency Staff Group (1985) point out that use of surface area predicts the highest human risk. In keeping with the health protective philosophy advanced by some agencies, the factor that predicts the greatest human risk is often chosen as a default condition.

G.   RISK ASSESSMENT FROM LABORATORY DATA

In the absence of epidemiological data about the relationship between exposure and tumor response in humans, we need to be able to estimate the risks from laboratory data. In most cases, this means estimating from long-term animal bioassays of the kind described in Section IV,B, above. The steps used in the real world are

1. Determining that the substance is a carcinogen.
2. Developing a dose–response relationship in the test species used.
3. Converting the animal dose levels to human doses.
4. Relating dose effects to human exposure.

Although this appears fairly simple, all of the problems indicated in the previous sections do come into play. We have shown that the identification of a substance as a carcinogen depends on a number of what are, at best, debatable findings. As we have seen, there are enough questions about the whole bioassay process to require some minimal assurance that we can avoid false positives. To do so, IARC and others have suggested that positive bioassays in at least two animal species are required. This seems to be a minimum, but more research focused directly on the question of interspecies relationships is needed. Short-term bioassays can provide valuable clues about carcinogenic potential of substances. Alone, short-term tests do not provide sufficient proof in a new substance. Short-term tests may, however, prove to be the most powerful set of research tools leading to a better understanding of the mechanism of carcinogenesis.

The dose–response relationship has been the subject of heated debates among concerned people in the risk assessment community. From the analysis given above, there is less than meets the eye in this field. One can simply take data from some source such as Gold et al. (1984) and extrapolate to very low doses and low responses (to tumor probabilities in the one in a million range), using simple models–linear, nonthreshold, passing through zero dose and response.

Ames et al. (1987) have concluded that there are not enough sound biological data to carry out these calculations of human cancer risk. Data bases such as the TD_{50} list are a way to compare the hazards of substances to humans. Ames and colleagues developed an index called HERP (human exposure dose/rodent potency dose). The HERP is the average daily human exposure dose expressed as a percentage of the rodent TD_{50} dose in the most sensitive species. The human exposure data have to be calculated on an average lifetime exposure basis to match the TD_{50} dose rates. The HERP allows for simple comparisons of various human exposures. Such comparisons are intended to be ". . . only a way of setting priorities for concern . . ." (Ames et al., 1987).

The conversion of animal to human doses depends on making assumptions about the biology of carcinogenesis. We do not have enough basic information to state that such and so is the most plausible mechanism that we know. At present, we can compare a few known substances in both animal and human systems. Benzene is an example. Good human epidemiological studies exist, and there are animal bioassays as well. When we lack the luxury of such good data, we must compare the results of different models for conversion. Perhaps more studies comparing epidemiology and bioassays will help. In the meantime, we need to compute risks using alternative models for dose conversion.

All of this can appear to be a never-never land. From animal data measured at high doses, we extrapolate down to extremely low doses—from levels that produce, say, fifty–fifty chances of developing tumors over lifetime, to one or ten in a million chances. Extrapolation is over a five orders of magnitude range!

To compound the problem, we then have to find a way of converting from doses given to rodents that have lifetimes of 1–2 years, and convert these to equivalents for humans with a nominal 70-year life. At the same time, we extrapolate from creatures that weigh a few hundred grams to humans weighing 50 to over 100 kg. This is another two or three orders of magnitude change. Faced with these problems, perhaps we should not even try to estimate human risks from animal bioassays. But the overriding consideration is that cancer is a disease that affects one in four Americans, and will kill some 450,000 people each year. As crude as our predictions from laboratory data are, there is a need to do more than wring our hands and complain that the "hygienists" are worried about small things, the deaths of only a few percent of the cancer cases each year. Instead, we need to try to improve our ability to assess risks when we don't have epidemiological data.

The final step in risk assessment is to estimate human exposure to the carcinogen and predict risk from the combination of the hazard and the exposure. For many purposes, it has been the practice to standardize on one level of exposure, say, parts per million in drinking water or micrograms per cubic meter in air, and compute the "risk factor" for a nominal 70-kg male or 50-kg female drinking 2 liters of water per day or inhaling some standard volume of air per day. An alternative is to compute the dose, in air, water, food, or whatever exposure route, that would produce tumors in some fraction of the exposed population. These exercises produce one or another variation of a "potency index," such as the TD_{50} values of Peto et al. (1984). Such indexes are useful for making population-wide comparisons of the effect of, for example, alternative regulatory strategies. One can calculate the statistically expected incremental lifetime human cancers from various exposure levels produced by different regulations. Presumably, such information can help in setting regulatory priorities. It provides little of value to assessing the real risks to humans if we lack real exposure data.

It is disappointing to look into a file of reprints and reports on carcinogen risk assessment and compare the volume of papers on animal bioassays and short-term tests with the volume dealing with exposure data. The Interagency Staff Group (1985) defines chemical exposure assessment as ". . . that process which seeks to define the quantity of a chemical which comes into contact, or may come into contact, with human populations." Their brief chapter provides an excellent review of the field; it covers a little over 10 pages and cites 168 references. Much of the material describes what various agencies do, or how they would do exposure analysis. Many of the references cited are to contractor reports, internal working drafts, and other unpublished sources. There are precious few published descriptions of exposure analysis. Perhaps this is indeed the "art" of the practitioner of risk assessment. One can certainly list the elements of an exposure assessment easily enough. They include the following:

1. Ambient levels of the carcinogen in air, water, soil, food, and any other carrier (such as cigarette smoke).
2., Quantity inhaled, ingested, contacted by skin, etc.
3. Biological handling of the substance by the body, e.g., is some fraction exhaled, absorbed, transformed (and to what)?
4. Calculating the received dose that could affect the target human.
5. Estimating the different doses received during different activities and stages of life, over the entire life of the human (currently taken as 70 years).
6. Adding up the doses received and estimating the *incremental* risk of cancer to that individual.
7. Repeating the process for as many different kinds of people as may undergo different exposures to the same carcinogen.

Conceptually, the steps are easy. In the real world, they are rarely done at all, much less done well.

Because it is so difficult to develop the information listed above, some short cuts may be taken. If ambient air levels are known for some pollutants, in some locations, it may be possible to estimate average exposures over time. Generally, this approach simplifies such subtleties as differences in activity levels indoors or outdoors, workplace exposures, and changing patterns of work and home locations. Nevertheless, if the data are available on ambient levels, some useful insights may be possible. The next section of this article will discuss such an analysis.

In summary, human risk assessment from laboratory data is a process that involves many assumptions and leaps of faith. Animal bioassays at high doses have to be extrapolated downward by four to six orders of magnitude to reflect doses that are likely in the environment. Corrections from small, short-lived rodents to large, long-lived humans are needed. The corrections include not only size and age, but possible biological differences. A major uncertainty exists in that substances shown to be carcinogens for one rodent species frequently are not active in another species. Once all the extrapolation is complete, we are left with a list of substances that are ranked in some manner by potency. The data are based on experiments in rodents, and the relative potency reflects only rodent potencies, which are assumed, in the absence of other evidence to be comparable in humans. The final step, analyzing human exposures and estimating human risk, is rarely done well because data are not often available. Relative potencies combined with some measure of exposure can be used to compare relative risks. This is useful in comparing and evaluating proposals for alternative regulatory policies. While one might wish that the results from such laboratory testing would have more powerful uses, it is no mean thing to be able to compare different policies and procedures in a systematic, quantitative way. Where the danger comes is in thinking that the data represent absolute truth. To achieve that, we need to be able to somehow "calibrate" the calculations from laboratory data. This must be done using actual statistical data of human disease—the process and results of human epidemiology studies. There is no way to evade or escape the need to test the statistical, computational, and biological hypotheses involved in doing risk assessments.

V. COMPARING EPIDEMIOLOGY AND LABORATORY RESULTS

A. THE NEED FOR TESTING HYPOTHESES

Any effort that considers itself to be based on science must test methods and hypotheses. Carcinogen risk assessment is no exception. As seen earlier, there are two ways to approach the evaluation of carcinogenic risks: through the analysis of human morbidity and mortality data; and through the development of risks from laboratory data on various biological test systems, exposure data, and models to allow extrapolation to humans. Peto (1985), in his critique, in fact splits the first into two parts: epidemiological studies of disease at doses of comparable intensity in nature; and evidence from much higher doses. Examples of the latter are predictions made about the effects of much lower ambient dose levels from workplace exposures or the effects of passive smoking (exposure to the cigarette smoke of others, by nonsmokers).

The epidemiological data reported by Doll and Peto (1981), and by a number of subsequent analysts, seem to provide data by which some risk assessments from animal bioassays can be tested. In theory, this should be simple. Merely compare the known human epidemiology data with some well-conducted bioassays that have been combined with good exposure data. Unfortunately, most of the bioassay data are for substances where we have little or no good epidemiology, and vice versa. While smoking has certainly been the subject of extensive epidemiological work, the active elements in smoke are not well enough known as yet to compare bioassay data. Rodent tests using smoke inhalation have several problems that preclude a reasonable comparison. Although diet is clearly related to cancer in humans, the carcinogens and the protective elements have not been isolated and tested in the laboratory. Perhaps the only place where both bioassay and exposure data exist along with good epidemiological studies is in the area of air pollution. There may also be some good data relating water pollution to carcinogenesis, but that problem is made more difficult by the much greater diversity of natural constituents, pollutant levels, and consumption patterns.

B. AIR POLLUTION EPIDEMIOLOGY

The relation between air pollution and respiratory illness has been known for many years. A treatise on the "Smoakes" of London written two centuries ago quotes Pliny the Elder on the same subject. Since then, a huge literature has developed. Under current U.S. practices, air pollutants are grouped into "primary pollutants" and "hazardous air pollutants." The primary pollutants include ozone, oxides of nitrogen and sulfur, carbon monoxide, and particulate matter. As part of the strategy for reducing ozone emissions, controls have been placed on emissions of volatile organic compounds, since these are known to be ozone precursors in the atmosphere. Hazardous air pollutants include asbestos, benzene, and vinyl chloride. Hazardous air pollutants are regulated by many state and/or local agencies under the name of toxic air pollutants or "air toxics."

Speizer (1983) has reviewed the major air pollution epidemiology studies of the years since World War II. There have been consistent findings that there is a rural–urban gradient in lung cancer, after correcting for smoking. Some of this may be attributed to air pollution in general, some to specific occupational exposures. Much of the urban–rural difference, however, seems to be more related to significant differences between the age of starting smoking. The older a person is at the start of regular smoking, the lower the risk, at constant dose (cigarettes smoked per day). Apparently, subtle differences in smoking habits account for most of the rural–urban gradient of lung cancer. The small number of cases remaining may indeed be considered as "air pollution-related lung cancers." Speizer lists a series of estimates of the fraction of lung cancer cases attributable to air pollution. The higher estimates, generally made earlier, were up to 5% of the cases. By the time of the Doll and Peto study (1981), estimates were in the range of 1–2%. Speizer then concludes that less than 2% of lung cancers, and less than 1% of *all cancers,* are due to air pollution. Based on the American Cancer Society estimate (1984), there are about 870,000 new cases and 450,000 deaths annually. For lung cancer, there are 139,000 new cases and 121,000 deaths per year. Thus, Speizer's estimate translates into 2400 lung cancer deaths and 4500 total cancer deaths due to air pollution annually.

C. ESTIMATES FROM LABORATORY-BASED RISK ASSESSMENTS

In 1985, an EPA group published what is known as the "Six-Month Study" (Haemisegger *et al.,* 1985). The study used laboratory bioassay data to develop carcinogen potencies—the so-called unit risk values. The unit risk value is defined as the estimated excess probability of developing cancer as a result of a 70-year exposure to a concentration of 1 $\mu g/m^3$ of a substance in ambient air. (In some cases, laboratory data were combined with human epidemiology to produce unit risk values.) Exposure data were obtained from three different EPA projects. Estimates for all pollutants were not available for all locations. The results, based on data for 15–45 pollutants were that toxic air pollutants might account for some 1300 to 1700 cancer cases annually. Further, it was possible to identify the pollutants that had the greatest effect on producing cancer. These included metals, particularly arsenic and chromium; asbestos; benzene, gasoline vapors, and chlorinated organics; and products of incomplete combustion. Finally, an estimate was made that the number of cancer cases attributable to the toxic air pollutants was about 3000 in 1970 and dropped below 1800 in 1980. The reduction was attributed mostly to efforts to control primary pollutants, particularly ozone precursors, rather than to control efforts aimed at toxic air pollutants as such. (There were few programs other than those related to occupational exposure that could claim to have reduced ambient air ievels of nonpriority hazardous air pollutants in the 1970s. Only asbestos controls were widely in place.)

The comparison of the results from the Six-Month Study and the estimates derived by Speizer show relatively good agreement. Epidemiological estimates predict something less than 2400 lung cancer deaths per year from air pollution, while the risk assessment calculation yields 1300–1700 annual deaths. It is appropriate to compare the lung cancer deaths rather than the all-causes deaths because the route of ingestion is known and the biology of inhalation is consistent with lung cancer. It is not very plausible to connect inhalation of carcinogens with cancers of major digestive organs (117,300 deaths), or the breast and genital organs (85,750 deaths). These and other implausible relations would eliminate at least 50% of all cancers as not relevant to inhalation of air pollutants. Then Speizer's estimate would yield approximately 2250 cancer deaths from all causes as a plausible upper limit.

Clearly, one study agreeing with another does not constitute proof that all the assumptions, hypotheses, and models used in assessing risks are true and valid. On the other hand, these results provide at least one small bit of evidence that risk assessment methods may have some value. Further, these findings provide a standard for judging other risk assessment processes. If the calculations from any set of data and methodologies cannot match the agreement found here, some significant explaining is needed. When risks differ by one or two orders of magnitude, strong justification is needed. As long as most risk predictions from bioassay data were not compared to epidemiological findings, arcane debates about processes and calculations were the only forum. The comparison between Speizer's work and the Six-Month Study calculations has provided at least one anchor point for validating methodologies.

VI. SUMMARY AND CONCLUSIONS

1. In the opinion of most epidemiologists, clinicians, and other research analysts, cancer is largely a preventable disease. The causes of cancer can be identified from clinical, statistical, and laboratory work. One major purpose of risk assessment is to convert an understanding of "risk factors" into identification of carcinogenic hazards. A second goal is evaluation of human exposures to these hazards. Risk is a function of both hazard and exposure. One must have both hazard and exposure to have risk.

2. From statistical and epidemiological studies, reinforced by clinical data, the major identifiable factors related to cancer in the United States are cigarette smoking, diet, reproductive and sexual behavior, infections, ultraviolet and ionizing radiation, and alcohol consumption. Occupational exposures and air and water pollutants each account for no more than 1–2% of the cases. Most of the dire predictions about epidemic outbreaks of cancer have not come true. Debate over the reasons for these findings will surely continue, but the evidence grows stronger each year.

3. Among the risk factors cited above, some hazards have been identified—the overwhelming association between smoking and lung cancer, confirmed in laboratory tests, or the link between vinyl chloride exposure and angiosarcoma. For such hazards, dose–response relations have been worked out, and risks due to specified levels of exposure can be calculated. In many other cases, however, we have been unable to identify the specific substance or stimulus that accounts for the specific hazard—links between diet and various cancers are still being studied.

4. Laboratory methods for identifying carcinogenic hazards include both short-term tests, using relatively simple cells or organisms, and long-term animal bioassays. Short-term tests have proven to be fairly accurate, although not perfect predictors of carcinogenicity. In systematic comparisons, 90–95% of the compounds shown to be carcinogenic in long-term animal bioassays give positive test results in short-term tests. Long-term bioassays are always needed to confirm carcinogenic hazards in animals. Such tests are not, however, entirely convincing as predictors of a cancer hazard for humans. Even between rodent species, there is not good correlation; in one evaluation of over 500 chemicals, less than half were carcinogens in *both* rats and mice, although every one was positive in one of the two species and good dose–response data were available. Both short- and long-term test methods can provide dose–response data for use in risk assessments.

5. One of the major concerns in use of dose–response data from animal bioassays or short-term tests has been the shape of the dose–response curve.

Extensive mathematical and statistical efforts fill the literature, exploring many possibilities. *For purposes of risk assessment,* there is much *less* than meets the eye here. The accuracy of the laboratory results, the extrapolation required (three to five orders of magnitude), and the limitations of mathematical models of carcinogenesis lead to choosing a simple linear dose–response relationship. Similarly, there are no experimental data and few biological, chemical, or physical reasons to believe that there is a threshold dose for carcinogen activity. A linear, nonthreshold dose–response curve is sufficiently accurate and biologically defensible for risk assessment of carcinogenic hazards.

6. Very little validation of risk assessment methods has been attempted. In part, the results from an inability to identify the hazards responsible for the risk factors associated with human cancer. There are few good exposure data for cases where hazards have been identified. This article compared some epidemiological results (for toxic air pollutants) with risk assessments from laboratory data. The agreement was remarkably good for this single case. Much more work is needed before we can be confident that current methods are valid for estimating human cancer risks from laboratory tests and exposure measurements.

VII. RESEARCH NEEDS

A. GENERAL

Whenever one discusses as broad a topic as "Research Needs," there is a major risk (no pun intended). Primarily, the ability to predict what research ought to be done is very close to predicting the stock market, the possibility of major natural disasters, or the winner of the World Series. Further, the hallmark of great scientists has been their ability to select those projects that are both important and successful. Small wonder, then, that a reviewer approaches the listing of research with trepidation. No matter what fields are mentioned, some important ones will surely be omitted. One not only appears foolish, but runs the risk of angering colleagues whose work is not mentioned.

As a general disclaimer, any basic research that provides better understanding of the disease and the process called cancer is important. Our best hope for being able to do a better job of assessing carcinogenic risks depends on being able to model the mechanisms involved accurately. Being specific about where the payoffs seem to lie is, as noted, a gamble. Personally, I see the following areas as most needed and most promising: use of a suitable *in vitro* human cell model system to explore the process of carcinogenesis; further study of the role of the immune system in both the initiation/promotion of neoplastic transformations at the molecular level and the growth and metastasis of neoplastic cells; better collection of exposure data; better modeling of exposures; and a serious effort to "tease out" the more subtle relationships of exposure to hazards and actual cases of cancer through epidemiological methods. Each of these is discussed further below.

B. MODEL SYSTEMS

The recent report by Rhim *et al.* (1986) offers what appears to be one of the most exciting prospects in many years. The system described apparently is a true *in vitro* model of human neoplasia. Human foreskin cells are infected with adenovirus 12 and simian virus 40 (Ad 12–SV 40). This system seems to act as an initiated cell line that can be transformed to tumor cells on exposure to chemical carcinogens. The transformed cells can produce squamous cell carcinoma when injected into mice. The possibilities of this model are enormous. Rhim and colleagues have correctly suggested that the system might be used for screening possible chemical carcinogens. While there are a number of short-term screening systems available, all have some shortcomings as screening tools. The Rhim model system, however, may overcome some of the most serious. Other screens use nonhuman cells, the end point of the test is something other than development of transformed cancerous cells, or the system fails to provide confidence that the carcinogen may affect humans.

A model system would allow other important research. It is a truism that people describe the development of cancer as a multistage process, according to the Armitage–Doll model. However, the number of stages involved is not known with any degree of confidence. No one suggests that one stage is sufficient. The Rhim model certainly establishes that there are at least two stages involved in the neoplastic transformation. Some estimates have speculated that the number of stages may be as high as five or six. Such estimates seem to be based on general biological principles. From time to time, statistical evidence of three, four, or more stages is offered. On close examination, however, the statistical result is an artifact of "curve fitting" exercises. For example, if there are five doses used in an animal bioassay, a polynomial equation of fifth power may give a good statistical "fit" to the dose–response data. However, goodness of fit is not a sufficient criterion for judging the number of stages involved in carcinogenesis.

Perhaps the Rhim model can be used to evaluate the number of steps involved in cell transformation. In their initial report, six or seven subcultures after the initial exposure were required before morphological alterations were seen in the cultures. This suggests that examination of the subculture at each step after exposure may reveal the changes, probably in the genome of these cells, necessary for complete development of a neoplastically transformed cell line. Such a process, alone, however, probably does not reflect all the actual *in vivo* steps involved. It seems clear that the body's immune system has a way of dealing with most transformed cells. Otherwise, a single initiating event acting on a single cell followed by a finite, probably small (surely less than ten) number of promotional events affecting that same cell would lead to an irreversible malignant transformation of the single human cell. This process, repeated frequently enough, would surely overcome whatever immune system defenses were marshaled, leading to a fairly early, fatal course of cancer. This is observed in less than the whole population and, where observed, seems to increase only with advanced age.

A system using human epithelial cells (which are the cell systems involved in at least 90% of human cancers) is certainly to be preferred over a rodent bioassay that is consistent only two times in five. One of the constant criticisms of animal bioassays relates to the locus of cancers induced by tested substances. It may be perfectly sound scientifically to estimate the risks of a rat developing tumors of the zymbal gland, but it is virtually impossible to convince an elected official or a judge of the relevance of such a finding to humans. It would make life a lot simpler if a model system using human cells could be validated. Efforts to develop and validate a test based on the Rhim model would help remove some of the current uncertainty. Ways to do this seem clear—demonstrate that known human carcinogens will "infect" (to use Rhim et al.'s words) the cell line. Then test a variety of questionable human carcinogens. The best candidates would be the chlorinated solvents per- and trichloroethylene. These are ambiguous as to their carcinogenic hazard, based on rodent bioassays, and show no evidence in human epidemiological studies. If these ambiguous substances tend to sort out in interesting and different ways, we may be on to a better test method. At worst, we will have some more data on hazards in another, hopefully independent test system.

C. IMMUNE SYSTEM

The whole field of tumor immunology has been growing explosively. One of the side effects of the huge international research effort on problems associated with acquired immune deficiency syndrome (AIDS) has been a growing realization that the immune systems of all mammals are even more complex than we thought. Still, so much has been learned about tumor immunology in the past few years that a comprehensive review would fill far more pages than are available for this entire volume. Nevertheless, such a review, by a person who really understands the field and who can write for the nonspecialist, is desperately needed.

From the perspective of carcinogen risk assessment, once cell materials are altered at the molecular level, the immune system comes into play. How, and in what places, may not yet be clear. Some insight can be gained from the reviews by Barbacid, Rosenberg, Yunis, Ozols and Cowan, Haseltine and others, and Golomb *et al.* (in DeVita *et al.*, 1986). Reviews reprinted from *Scientific American* in a book edited by Friedberg (1986), particularly those by Bishop, Weinberg, and Old, provide a broader view for the nonspecialist.

Can the Rhim test system contribute here? Obviously, any model that uses human cells and (apparently) causes changes in the genetic materials of the cell when stressed by chemical carcinogens will affect the immune system. The Rhim model may also provide a mechanism for exploring how the processes of chemical carcinogenesis change critical aspects of the immune systems. The Rhim model does not include components of the human immune system; however, it seems clear that cellular changes in the model system would be amenable to analysis by immunochemical methods. Genetic changes to DNA, alterations to surface antigens, and effects on reverse transcriptase copying could all, in principle, be probed. Once again, the impact of such genetic effects would be seen directly in the multistage model of carcinogenesis used to quantify the hazard of specific amounts of specific carcinogens. What is not known, as yet, is how immunological processes might affect the multistage model that we think is the best representation of carcinogenesis.

Very specifically, one might be able to provide test materials for immunological study by isolating cells at the various subculture stages in the Rhim model system. The first paper indicates that treatment of the basic cell line with Ad 12–SV 40 results in expression of the *ras* oncogene. Following promotion with a chemical carcinogen, the *ras* oncogene seems to disappear. What other cellular oncogenes might appear? What are the surface antigens that form and disappear in this process? The report by Spits and others (1986) indicates that cytolytic T-cell lymphocytes will form nonspecific adducts with target cells, but that the adducts detach without the target being harmed in the absence of specific surface antigens. Are such surface antigens altered by the processes elucidated in the Rhim model system? What does all this mean for carcinogenic hazards?

D. EXPOSURES

The literature of the industrial hygiene field is full of pleas for better exposure data and full of excellent suggestions about how to obtain such information. The problem of defining exposures in a realistic way, however, is far from solved. Most risk assessments of carcinogens tend to dodge the issue entirely, or to hide behind excuses of lack of data. Perhaps the most misleading risk assessments are the result of attributing more to the exposure data than can reasonably be expected.

In California, a whole set of risk assessments are being conducted to determine how "Toxic Air Pollutants" should be regulated. Various volatile organic compounds are selected for evaluation. The State Department of Health Services performs hazard evaluations based on literature reviews of epidemiological and toxicological data. These studies result in a hazard estimate that, for example, might be of the form, ''There is one chance in one million that a person exposed to a concentration of one microgram per cubic meter of hexachloro-chicken wire in ambient air for 70 years will develop cancer.'' The staff of the California Air Resources Board, in parallel to the health assessment, gathers data from the literature about ambient air concentrations. Since there are rarely many data points, and few of these extending over any period of time, statistical models are used to project some average exposure level to an urban (usually) population in some part of the state. (Most often, this is done for the Los Angeles area, apparently because it is the only place where many real monitoring data have been collected in the state.) The average exposure is then multiplied by the hazard estimate calculated by the Health Department. The resulting number is supposed to represent the risk to some population of developing cancer from the particular toxic pollutant in question. To satisfy various criticisms, the results are expressed in terms of a best estimate (although not necessarily a maximum likelihood estimate in the usual statistical sense) and an upper confidence limit, usually something like a 95 percentile value. The estimates then come out in the form, ''Therefore, hexachloro-chicken wire at ambient air levels in the South Coast Air Basin may be causing 236 cases of cancer per million people exposed, with an upper limit estimate of 1027 cases per million people.''

Exposure to ambient outdoor air fails to reflect the reality that most people spend 85% or more of their time indoors. The usual quick rejoinder to this criticism is that indoor air concentrations of many toxic air pollutants are higher than outdoors. This is the case sometimes, but one would surely expect to see a little evidence of this. For example, is this true for hexavalent chromium or chlorinated dibenzodioxins indoors? It is one thing to compare measured pollutants both in- and outdoors, but it is not valid to assume that because some are found in higher concentrations indoors, all will be. Basic chemistry and physics suggest otherwise. Better indoor air pollutant level data are clearly needed. Where data are not available, a little consideration of sources of the pollutants may give some better insight into exposures. At least a modest effort ought to be devoted to modeling the exposure of target populations.

Probably one of the real obstacles to getting better exposure information is the lack of any real rewards for making such measurements. Unless some legal, regulatory, or economic requirement (such as to obtain insurance coverage) exists, there is not much glory in collecting and trying to publish the data. Often, in legal or other situations, the data are closely held for all the obvious competitive and tactical reasons. It is probably too much to hope that the offices and agencies interested in regulating carcinogens will spend resources to collect and publish negative data on exposure. Probably, the regulated community will need to find ways to fund and publish such information. There are other precedents, such as the Chemical Industry Institute of Toxicology, but these are usually for more fundamental research than the somewhat more applied work suggested here. Nevertheless, such information is badly needed.

Examples of needed exposure data include comparisons of indoor and outdoor pollutant levels of a variety of toxic inorganic and organic compounds. Controlling for obvious variables is essential—smoking versus nonsmoking households, type of cooking and heating systems (including fireplaces) used, recreational habits, and many more. There is no escaping the reality that we know very little about human exposure to carcinogens in air, water, and soil. We have a few more data on food and drinking water, sunlight, and radioactive decay as sources of carcinogens. The need for more and better data are reinforced by the demands of performing better epidemiological studies to learn more about the relationships between multiple sources of possible carcinogens and actual human disease.

E. EPIDEMIOLOGY

For many, the only totally valid evidence about cause and effect must come from data on human cancers. Even among rodents, there is at best a weak relationship between induction of cancer in one species and in another. Acute toxicological data should remind us that there are tremendous differences in the response of various mammalian species to the same substance. The example of 2,3,7,8-tetrachlorodibenzodioxin is perhaps the most dramatic. There are at least three orders of magnitude difference in the LD_{50} for the most sensitive species (the guinea pig) and the least (hamster). Similar differences in response to carcinogens can and should be expected.

The basic problem with epidemiology is its relative lack of sensitivity. This means that relatively small but real risks from exposure to carcinogens may not be detectable. In fact, if a lengthy exposure to some substance were to cause an excess risk of 30%, it is unlikely that it could be detected in a sample population much smaller than the entire United States, some 220,000,000. Even sorting out the effects of heavy cigarette smoking on lung cancer took a few decades of intensive research, with a test population (of male smokers) that numbered in the tens of millions. On the other hand, where the picture was less confused by complex side issues, epidemiology has worked well. The standard example is the induction of angiosarcoma from vinyl chloride exposure. A rare tumor type, combined with a well-defined exposed population and the support of animal bioassays, led quickly to the characterization of the risk due to exposure to the vinyl chloride hazard.

Many almost trivial epidemiological studies are offered as "negative evidence" about the carcinogenicity of substances in humans. Based on the model of carcinogenesis we defined earlier in this article, any epidemiological study must have several characteristics:

1. The population studied must have had some exposure to the substance in question.
2. The exposure must have been for some plausible time to allow development of cancer.
3. The test and control populations must have been large enough to permit detection of an effect of exposure to the hazard.

These seem obvious enough, but many so-called epidemiological studies that supposedly "prove" that something is not a human carcinogen fail one or more of these simple tests. Lord Rutherford once said, "If your experiment needs statistics, you should have done a better experiment." In contrast, epidemiological studies could benefit by keeping in mind the need to provide convincing statistical evidence, and for designing a better experiment to begin with.

In contrast to Peto's views about risk assessment and the choice of priorities, I believe that we are going to need more attempts to define what substances are carcinogens in humans. For all the reasons expressed earlier, particularly Ames' incisive criticism of depending on animal bioassays alone, both laboratory systems using human cell systems (as discussed above) and micro-sized but well-designed human epidemiological studies will be needed to improve our ability to assess human risk from carcinogens. Further, these are precisely the kinds of techniques that will be needed to evaluate the effectiveness of treatment methods. Without better epidemiological studies, we might not be able to determine what does not work in cancer therapy. We seem to be on the verge of having model cell systems; there is great and justifiable enthusiasm that we are getting closer to a deeper understanding about immune systems and cellular genetics, and there is some optimism that the long hunt for therapeutic agents is beginning to show a return. What we must learn is how to identify human hazards and how to evaluate their effect on carcinogen risks.

REFERENCES

American Cancer Society. 1984. "Cancer Facts and Figures 1984." American Cancer Society, New York.

Ames, B. N. 1979. Identifying environmental chemicals causing mutations and cancer. *Science* **204**, 587–593.

Ames, B. N. 1983. Dietary carcinogens and anticarcinogens. *Science* **221**, 1256–1264; and ensuing correspondance in 1984. *Science* **224**, 658–760.

Ames, B. N. 1985. Testimony, California Senate Committee on Toxics and Public Safety Management, Nov. 11.

Ames, B. N. Magaw, R., and Gold, L. S. 1987. Ranking carcinogenic hazards. *Science* **236**, 271.

Armitage, P. 1985. Multistage models of carcinogensis. *Environ. Health Perspect.* **63**, 195–201.

Barbacid, M. 1986. Human oncogenes. *In* "Important Advances in Oncology 1986" (V. T. DeVita, S. Hellman, and S. A. Rosenberg, eds.), pp. 3–22. Lippincott, Philadelphia.

Bridboard, K., Decoufle, P., Fraumeni, J. F., *et al.* 1978. Estimates of the fraction of cancer in the United States related to occupational factors. National Cancer Institute, National Institute of Environmental Health Sciences, and National Institute for Occupational Safety and Health, Bethesda, Maryland.

Cairns, J. 1975. The cancer problem. *In* "Cancer Biology (Readings from *Scientific American*)" (E. C. Friedberg, ed.), pp. 4–14. Freeman, San Francisco, 1986.

Cairns, J. 1977. Some thoughts about cancer research in lieu of a summary. *In* "Origins of Human Cancer" (H. H. Hiatt, J. D. Watson, and J. A. Winsten, eds.), pp. 1813–1820. Cold Spring Harbor Laboratory, Cold Spring Harbor, N.Y.

Cannon, J. A. 1986. The regulation of toxic air pollutants. *J. Air Pollut. Control Assoc.* **36**, 562–573.

Claus, G., and Bolander, K. 1982. Environmental carcinogenesis: The threshold principle: A law of nature. *In* "Pollution and Water Resources" (G. J. Halasi-Kun, ed.), pp. 153–182. Pergamon, New York.

Coggle, J. E. 1985. Radiation carcinogenesis. *In* "The Molecular Basis of Cancer" (P. B. Farmer and J. M. Walker, eds.), pp. 71–98. Wiley, New York.

Conklin, G. 1949. Cancer and environment. *In* "Cancer Biology (*Readings from Scientific American*)" (E. C. Friedberg, ed.), pp. 19–23, Freeman, San Francisco, 1986.

Creasey, W. A. 1985. "Diet and Cancer." Lea & Febiger, Philadelphia.

Crump, K. S. 1985. Methods for carcinogenic risk assessment. *In* "Principles of Health Risk Assessment" (P. F. Ricci, ed.), pp. 279–320. Prentice-Hall, New York.

Crump, K. S. and Howe, R. B. 1984. The multistage model with a time-dependent dose pattern: Applications to carcinogenic risk assessment. *Risk Anal.* **4**, 163–176.

Crump, K. S., Silvers, A., Ricci, P. F., and Wyzga, R. 1985. Interspecies comparison for carcinogenic potency to humans. *In* "Principles of Health Risk Assessment" (P. F. Ricci, ed.), pp. 321–372. Prentice-Hall, New York.

DeVita, V. T., Hellman, S., and Rosenberg, S. A. eds. 1986. "Important Advances in Oncology 1986." Lippincott, Philadelphia.

DOHS—California Department of Health Services. 1985. Guidelines for chemical carcinogen risk assessments and their scientific rationale.

Doll, R., and Peto, R. 1981. "The Causes of Cancer." Oxford Univ. Press, New York (reprinted from 1981. *J. Natl. Cancer Inst.* **66**, 1197–1312).

Douglas, M., and Wildavsky, A. 1983. "Risk and Culture." Univ. of California Press, Berkeley.

Farmer, P. B., and Walker, J. M., eds. 1985. "The Molecular Basis of Cancer." Wiley, New York.

Friedberg, E. C., ed. 1986. "Cancer Biology (Readings from *Scientific American*)." Freeman, San Francisco.

Gold, L. S., Sawyer, C. B., Magaw, R., Backman, G. M., deVeciana, M., Levinson, R., Hooper, N. K., Havender, W. R., Bernstein, L., Peto, R., Pike, M. C., and Ames, B. N. 1984. A carcinogenic potency database of the standardized results of animal bioassays. *Environ. Health Perspect.* **58**, 9–319.

Gold, L. S., de Veciana, M., Backman, G. M., Magaw, R., Lopipero, P., Smith, M., Blumenthal, M., Levinson, R., Bernstein, L., and Ames, B. N. 1986. Chronological supplement to the carcinogenic potency database: Standardized results of animal bioassays published through December 1982. *Environ. Health Perspect.* **67**, 161–200.

Gravitz, N. 1984. Models of Carcinogenesis. *Science* **226**, 1022.

Greenberg, P., and Lanza, E. 1986. Role of dietary fiber in the prevention of cancer. *In* "Important Advances in Oncology 1986" (V. T. DeVita, S. Hellman, and S. A. Rosenberg, eds.), pp. 37–54. Lippincott, Philadelphia.

Greenwald, E. D., and Greewald, E. S. 1983. "Cancer Epidemiology." Medical Examination Publ. New Hyde Park, New York.

Haemisegger, E., Jones, A., Steigerwald, R., and Thompson, V. E. 1985. The air toxics problem in the United States: An analysis of cancer risks posed by selected air pollutants. U.S. Environmental Protection Agency, Washington, D.C.

Hathway, D. E. 1986. "Mechanisms of Chemical Carcinogenesis." Butterworths, London.

Hennekens, C. H. 1986. Vitamin A analogues in cancer chemoprevention. *In* "Important Advances in Oncology 1986" (V. T. DeVita, S. Hellman, and S. A. Rosenberg, eds.), pp. 23–36. Lippincott, Philadelphia.

IARC–International Agency for Research on Cancer. 1982. IARC monographs on the evaluation of the carcinogenic risk of chemicals to humans (Suppl. 4). IARC, Lyon.

Interagency Staff Group on Chemical Carcinogenesis. 1985. Chemical carcinogens: A review of the science and its associated principles. *Fed. Register* 10371–10442; 1986. *Environ. Health Perspect.* **67**, 201–282.

Knowlden, N. F., Burack, W. R., and Burack, T. S. 1981. Cancer: I. Analysis of recent new case incidence reports. *Fundam. Appl. Toxicol.* **1**, 458–468.

Lave, L. B., ed. 1982. "Quantitative Risk Assessment in Regulation." Brookings Institution, Washington, D.C.

Milvy, P. 1986. A general guideline for management of risk from carcinogens. *Risk Anal.* **6**, 69–79.

Moolgavkar, S. H. 1983. Model for human carcinogenesis: Action of environmental agents. *Environ. Health Perspect.* **50**, 285.

NRC/NAS—National Research Council/National Academy of Sciences, Committee on Diet, Nutrition and Cancer. 1982. "Diet, Nutrition and Cancer." National Academy Press, Washington, D.C.

NRC/NAS—National Research Council/National Academy of Sciences, Committee on the Institutional Means for Assessment of Risks to Public Health. 1983. "Risk Assessment in the Federal Government: Managing the Process." National Academy Press, Washington, D.C.

Peto, R. 1985. Epidemiological reservations about risk assessment. *In* "Assessment of Risk from Low-Level Exposure to Radiation and Chemicals" (A. D. Woodhead, C. J. Shellabarger, and V. Pond, eds.). Plenum, New York.

Peto, R., Pike, M. C., Bernstein, L., Gold, L. S., and Ames, B. N. 1984. The TD_{50}: A proposed general convention for the numerical description of the carcinogenic potency of chemicals in chronic-exposure animal experiment. *Environ. Health Perspect.* **58**, 1–8.

Phillips, D. H. 1985. Chemical carcinogenesis. *In* "The Molecular Basis of Cancer" (P. B. Farmer and J. M. Walker, eds.). Wiley, New York.

Reif, A. E. 1981. The causes of cancer. *Am. Sci.* **69**, 437–447.

Rhim, J. S., Fujita, J., Arnstein, P., and Aaronson, S. A. 1986. Neoplastic conversion of human keratinocytes by adenovirus 12–SV40 virus and chemical carcinogens. *Science* **232**, 385–388.

Speizer, F. E. 1983. Assessment of the epidemiological data relating lung cancer to air pollution. *Environ. Health Perspect.* **47**, 33–47.

Spratt, J. S., ed. 1984a. "Neoplasms of the Colon, Rectum, and Anus." Saunders, Philadelphia.

Spratt, J. S. 1984b. Good health and avoidance of cancer. *In* "Neoplasms of the Colon, Rectum, and Anus" (J. S. Spratt, ed.), pp. 430–448. Saunders, Philadelphia.

Spratt, J. S., and Greenberg, R. A., 1984. Epidemiology and etiology. *In* "Neoplasms of the Colon, Rectum, and Anus" (J. S. Spratt, ed.), pp. 1–23. Saunders, Philadelphia.

Starr, C. 1985. Risk Management, assessment, and acceptability. *Risk Anal.* **5**, 97–102.

Sugimura, T. 1986. Studies on environmental chemical carcinogenesis in Japan. *Science* **233**, 312–318.

Thorslund, T. W., Brown, C. C., and Charnley, G. 1987. Biologically motivated cancer risk models. *Risk Anal.* **7,** 109.

Tschirley, F. H. 1986. Dioxin. *Sci. Am.* **254,** 29–35.

Zeigler, R. G., Devesa, S. S., and Fraumeni, Jr., J. F. 1986. Epidemiologic patterns of colorectal cancer. *In* "Important Advances in Oncology 1986" (V. T. DeVita, S. Hellman, and S. A. Rosenberg, eds.), pp. 209–232. Lippincott, Philadelphia.

A REVIEW OF CURRENT LITERATURE ON *N*-NITROSO COMPOUNDS IN FOODS

JOSEPH H. HOTCHKISS

Institute of Food Science
Department of Food Science
Cornell University
Ithaca, New York 14853

I. INTRODUCTION

The occurrence and formation of N-nitroso compounds in foods has received considerable research attention throughout the world over the last 10–15 years. These efforts have resulted in changes in the way several foods are processed in order to decrease human exposure to these carcinogens. The occurrence of N-nitroso compounds in foods and other consumer products has prompted action by regulatory agencies in several countries. N-Nitroso compounds have also become important experimental carcinogens, and an extensive literature concerning the unusual biological action of this class of compounds has developed. And most recently, the study of N-nitroso compounds in foods has lead to the discovery that dietary amines (and likely amides) are nitrosated *in vivo,* possibly producing a constant low level exposure to carcinogens.

This article will concentrate on literature published since 1975 relating to N-nitroso compounds in foods. The literature up to 1975 has been reviewed in detail and will only be mentioned as it pertains to more recent work. The chemistry, biological activity, and analysis of foods will be briefly discussed. In-depth reviews of these subjects have been published. Nearly all western foods have been analyzed for volatile N-nitrosamines. This permits us to classify the occurrence of N-nitrosamines in food by sources of contamination or mechanism of formation. It is now possible to generalize about how N-nitrosamines get into the food supply and to quantitatively put human exposure from foods into perspective with other known routes of exposure. The occurrence of volatile N-nitrosamines in foods has become of less research interest while more recent interests have shifted to nonvolatile compounds and the endogenous formation of N-nitroso compounds in general.

HISTORICAL

Outside of the field of chemical carcinogenesis, N-nitroso compounds received little attention until the mid 1960s. N-Nitrosodimethylamine was investigated in the 1930s as an industrial solvent because it is miscible with both hexane and water and is anticorrosive. The acute toxicity of N-nitrosodimethylamine was first discovered in humans. Two research chemists who were investigating the properties of the compound were poisoned. Both suffered severe symptoms of liver failure with the more acutely poisoned individual dying of liver necrosis approximately 7 weeks after exposure. The ability of N-nitrosodimethylamine to cause liver necrosis was confirmed by exposing mice and dogs to vapors (Freund, 1937). A more thorough investigation of the acute effects of N-nitrosodimethylamine was presented by Barnes and Magee (1954). Acute human toxicity has been further supported by the apparent use of N-nitrosodimethylamine to commit homicide (Fussaenger and Ditschuneit, 1980). Again, liver failure was the cause of death. Other work with human tissues and N-nitrosodimethylamine have demonstrated DNA alkylation (Harris *et al.*, 1979). In all of these cases, the level of exposure was orders of magnitude above that possible through environmental or dietary routes. The concern about human exposure to N-nitroso compounds is due to their chronic rather than acute effects.

The first suspicion that foods might be contaminated with N-nitroso compounds resulted from an incident in Norway in the late 1950s. Domestic animals that were fed fish meal preserved with nitrite were dying from severe liver disorders. N-Nitrosodimethylamine was later isolated and shown to be the causative factor, and it was proposed that the added nitrite reacted with dimethyl- and trimethylamines endogenous to fish meal to form the N-nitroso derivative (Ender *et al.*, 1964). Ender *et al.* (1967) later undertook the first experiments designed to study the formation of N-nitrosamines in a food, albeit an animal food. They demonstrated that drying nitrite-preserved fish meal (6.3 g $NaNO_2$/ kg meal) at higher temperatures resulted in a more toxic meal. Mink fed meal dried at 50°C lived nearly 3 times as long as those fed meal dried at 175°C. Aged meals resulted in more N-nitrosodimethylamine production than fresh meals, presumably because the concentration of free amines increased during storage. The amount of nitrite added was also a determining factor; more nitrite gave more N-nitrosodimethylamine and shorter survival times. Also studied were the effects of pH and temperature on the nitrosation of di- and trimethylamine, and trimethylamine oxide in model systems containing rice starch. This early work raised questions regarding the ''general risk'' of using nitrite as a food preservative and stimulated researchers in other countries to investigate the occurrence of N-nitrosamines in human foods, especially those to which nitrite had been intentionally added.

Probably the first report that a human food contained an N-nitroso compound was that of Herman (1961) who identified N-nitroso-4-methylamino-benzaldehyde as a metabolite of an edible mushroom. Assuming that the compound was correctly identified, the parent amine was probably nitrosated through the microbiological reduction of the substantial amount of nitrate added to the synthetic culture medium. It is unlikely that this or other N-nitrosamines would occur in cultivated mushrooms.

The latter half of the 1960s saw a number of reports indicating the presence of N-nitrosamines in human foods. One of the most disturbing was the report by Devik (1967) that the heat-induced reactions between reducing sugars and amino acids resulted in the formation of one or more N-nitrosamines. These thermal reactions are one of the most common changes occurring in foods and are responsible for the brown pigments formed during cooking. The chemistry of heat-induced browning has been studied in detail and is commonly termed Maillard browning. If true, the report of Devik would have meant that the cooking process resulted in the formation of N-nitroso compounds. Heyns and Roper (1970) and Scanlan and Libbey (1971) investigated the Maillard reaction using mass spectrometry to determine structures and found that the nonspecific nature of Devik's polarographic method had misidentified the N-nitrosamines. Kadar and Devik (1970) later showed that pyrazines have half-wave potentials which are similar to dialkyl N-nitrosamines.

The nonspecific nature of thin-layer and polarographic detection techniques have led to other reports of N-nitroso compounds in foods which have not been confirmed by unequivocal methods such as mass spectrometry. Ender and Ceh (1968) reported that mushrooms contained N-nitrosamines at levels ranging from 0.4 to 14 μg/kg. They also reported that fish and cured meats contained N-nitrosamines. Analyses were by TLC with reduction to hydrazine (Preussmann et al., 1964). Hedler and Marquardt (1968) qualitatively "confirmed" N-nitrosodiethylamine in wheat plants (stalks and leaves), wheat grain, flour, milk, and cheese by TLC with detection as prescribed by Preussmann et al. (1964). Thewlis (1967) later refuted these findings. McGlashan et al. (1968) reported that certain African beverages contained 2 mg/kg N-nitrosamines, using polarography and TLC; later, however, when analyzing British alcoholic beverages they found that furfural gave the same half-wave potential as dialkyl N-nitrosamines. They also failed to confirm the presence of the N-nitrosamine by mass spectrometry. Sen et al. (1969) published one of the first articles which critically investigated the methods used to detect volatile N-nitrosamines in foods. They found many of the previously published methods unreliable or otherwise inadequate. A large majority of the earlier positive findings were not supported by improved analytical methods. Other, now suspect, positive findings were also reported during the late 1960s. For example, N-nitrosamines were reported in fresh meats up to 250 μg/kg (Mohler and Mayrohfer, 1968) and cheese up to 120 μg/kg (Freimuth and Glaser, 1970). Neither finding has been substantiated.

The large number of unconfirmable reports appearing in the literature prompted the International Agency for Research on Cancer (IARC) to hold meetings in 1969 and again in 1971 for the small group of researchers working in the area of N-nitrosamines. Reports from the second conference were published (Bogovski et al., 1972). The initial objective was to foster improved analytical techniques so that exposure to N-nitrosamines, primarily through foods, could be quantified. These data were considered necessary to complement the epidemiological data which suggested that N-nitroso compounds may be related to human cancer etiology, especially cancer of the esophagus. Chief among the recommendations resulting from these meetings was that analytical methods be further improved, studied collaboratively, and that large surveys of foods for N-nitrosamines be undertaken on a worldwide basis.

Because many of the early positive reports could not be substantiated (Thewlis, 1968) the necessity for an unequivocal confirmatory method became apparent (Crosby *et al.*, 1972). One of the first reports which confirmed the presence of *N*-nitrosamines in foods was that of Fazio *et al.* (1971). These workers examined 51 cured meat products and confirmed 5 μg/kg *N*-nitrosodimethylamine in one ham sample, using mass spectrometry, although few details of the procedure were given. Other reports which used mass spectrometry as a confirmatory technique began to appear at about the same time. Telling *et al.* (1971) developed a high-resolution gas chromatography–mass spectrometry technique but was unable to confirm *N*-nitrosamines in cured and uncured meats at a sensitivity of 25–65 μg/kg. Sen (1972) used gas chromatography–mass spectrometry to confirm *N*-nitrosodimethylamine in three cured meats at levels of 10–80 μg/kg, and Crosby *et al.* (1972) used high-resolution mass spectrometry to confirm *N*-nitrosodimethylamine in several samples of fried bacon, fish, and cheese at levels ranging from 1 to 40 μg/kg.

While methods to unequivocally confirm the presence of *N*-nitrosamines in foods were being developed, other laboratories were working on finding more reliable and rapid screening procedures so that larger numbers of samples could be analyzed. Most of this work centered around developing more selective gas chromatography detectors. For example, Howard *et al.* (1970) described a modification of the alkali flame ionization detector to determine *N*-nitrosamines in foods, and Gadbois *et al.* (1975) used a Coulson Electrolytic Conductivity Detector in the analysis of fish for *N*-nitrosodimethylamine. Goodhead and Gough (1975) used the same detector to screen samples prior to confirmation by mass spectrometry. Electron capture detectors have also been used to detect the nitramine resulting from the intentional oxidation of the corresponding *N*-nitrosamine (Althorp *et al.*, 1970).

The search for more selective detectors ultimately led to the commercial introduction of the thermal energy analyzer (TEA) as a gas chromatographic detector. This unique instrument was a watershed in *N*-nitrosamine research because it became possible to screen large numbers of samples (12 or more per day per analyst) with only a minimum of preparation. The selectivity of the instrument for the *N*-nitroso group was far beyond anything available, and the sensitivity was below 1 μg/kg for most samples. It was still necessary to confirm positive findings by mass spectrometry for unequivocal identification. The operation and principles of the TEA have been described in detail elsewhere (Fine *et al.*, 1975a).

The above brief history does not include many significant works, especially from the early 1970s. The literature up to 1975 has been reviewed in detail. Reviews by Scanlan (1975), Crosby (1976), Mirvish (1975), Fiddler (1975), Foreman and Goodhead (1975), and Swann (1975) are recommended.

II. FUNDAMENTALS

A. CHEMISTRY

All N-nitroso compounds have the N—N=O functional group in common and can be divided into two classifications: the N-nitrosamines and the N-nitrosamides. N-Nitrosamines are N-nitroso derivatives of secondary amines while the N-nitrosamides are derivatives of substituted amides, ureas, carbamates, or guanidines (Fig. 1). N-Nitroso compounds can also have additional functional groups, resulting in a wide range of physical and chemical properties. The generalized structures of several of the N-nitroso compounds discussed in this article are given in Fig. 1. The basic chemistry of N-nitroso compounds has been reviewed by Fridman et al. (1971) and recently updated by Challis (1981).

N-Nitrosamines are, as a rule, quite stable compounds under most conditions found in foods. For example, Fan and Tannenbaum (1972) studied the decomposition of several N-nitrosamines including dialkyl, heterocyclic, and carboxylic substituted and found all tested compounds to be relatively stable. The stability of N-nitrosamides, on the other hand, decreases as the pH is raised above 2. Decomposition is rapid at pHs above 7. This may explain why N-nitrosamines have been found as environmental and food contaminants while N-nitrosamides have not. Kakuda and Gray (1980a,b) demonstrated that N-nitrosamides would likely be destroyed by common cooking procedures. However, substituted amides are relatively stable and could serve as precursors to N-nitroso compounds formed in vivo (Mirvish et al., 1980). The occurrence of N-nitrosamides in foods has not been exhaustively studied, in large part because of inadequate analytical methods.

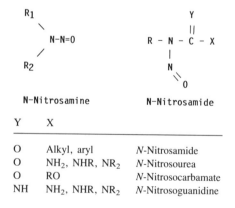

Y	X	
O	Alkyl, aryl	N-Nitrosamide
O	NH_2, NHR, NR_2	N-Nitrosourea
O	RO	N-Nitrosocarbamate
NH	NH_2, NHR, NR_2	N-Nitrosoguanidine

FIG. 1.   Generalized structures of N-nitroso compounds.

B. CHEMISTRY OF NITROSATION

Detailed discussions of the chemistry of the nitrosation reaction have been presented (Ridd, 1961; Ingold, 1969; Challis and Butler, 1968; Mirvish, 1975). In nitrosation reactions a nitrosating agent X—N=O, must first be generated from nitrous acid and a catalytic nucleophile where X is NO_2, H_2O^+, SCN^-, or Cl^-. This nitrosating species reacts with an unprotonated amine or amide giving the N-nitroso derivative. Secondary amines and substituted amides form stable compounds, but primary amines and unsubstituted amides decompose to molecular nitrogen and a carbonium ion. Aromatic primary amines form stable diazonium salts. Tertiary amines can also form N-nitrosamines but usually only after dealkylation to form a secondary amine. At moderate acidities, the nitrosation step is rate limiting. The reaction is first order in amine and second order in nitrous acid in aqueous systems because nitrous acid, as pointed out above, must first be converted to one or more nitrosating species. In the absence of very high acidities or catalysts nitrous acid itself becomes the nucleophile forming nitrous anhydride (N_2O_3) which is a potent nitrosating species. The overall aqueous reaction can be described by the following equations:

$$2 \ HNO_2 \overset{fast}{\rightleftarrows} N_2O_3 + H_2O \tag{1}$$

$$N_2O_3 + R_2NH \overset{slow}{\rightarrow} R_2NN{=}O + HNO_2 \tag{2}$$

$$\text{rate} = k_1[R_2NH][HNO_2]^2$$

$$\text{rate} = k_2[\text{amine}][\text{nitrite}]^2$$

As the above equations suggest, nitrosation is pH dependent because only unprotonated amine reacts. Thus, k_2 is pH dependent but independent of reactant concentrations, while k_1 is independent of pH but the concentration of the unprotonated amine and nitrous acid change with pH. Lower pHs favor the formation of nitrous acid and, hence, more nitrous anhydride, but as the pH decreases more amine is protonated and rendered unreactive. This results in a maximum rate of nitrosation at some pH, on either side of which the rate falls off. This maxima depends on basicity of the amine; more basic amines (higher pK_as) have maximal rates of nitrosation at lower pHs than less basic amines. At a given pH, amines with lower pK_as will be nitrosated faster than amines with higher pK_as. For example, morpholine (pK_a 8.7) is nitrosated at a faster rate than dialkylamines ($pK_a > 10$). Mirvish (1970) showed that the maximum reaction rate for the nitrosation of dimethylamine occurred at pH 3.4 and that the rate decreased on either side of this value.

Amides and related compounds do not have an optimum pH for nitrosation and react more rapidly as the pH is decreased (Mirvish, 1975). The reaction rate is first order in both amide and nitrous acid but third order overall because of the necessity for H^+. In general, the formation of N-nitrosamides is less facile than the formation of N-nitrosamines. N-Nitrosation can also occur without the formation of nitrous acid in the presence of certain oxides of nitrogen (NO_x). Challis and Kyrtopoulos (1978) found very rapid nitrosation rates at basic pHs with N_2O_3 and N_2O_4; the former being more reactive. N-Nitroso compounds can be formed at basic pHs because oxides of nitrogen, unlike nitrous acid, are direct nitrosating agents. As will be pointed out below, nitrosation by NO_x is an important reaction in the environmental formation of N-nitrosamines.

C.   CATALYSIS AND INHIBITION

In addition to nitrite and amine concentration, the rate of N-nitrosation is influenced by a number of other chemical species that commonly occur in foods and the environment. The quantity of N-nitroso compound formed and, hence, the total exposure can depend on the presence of these catalysts and inhibitors. Archer (1984) has briefly reviewed the chemistry of nitrosation catalysis and inhibition.

Nucleophilic anions such as halides and pseudohalides are catalytic toward amine nitrosation. In general, the stronger the nucleophile, the greater the catalysis. Amides and related compounds are not catalyzed. Catalysis by chloride (Cl^-) and thiocyanate (SCN^-) are of particular interest in foods and endogenous synthesis because the former occurs in most foods and the latter is found in saliva in significant concentrations. Fan and Tannenbaum (1973a) found a 7-fold increase in the initial rate of nitrosation of 10 mM morpholine by 5 mM NO_2^- when 2.5 mM KSCN was present. Thiocyanate was 15,000 times more catalytic than chloride. In addition, the pH maximum for the nitrosation of morpholine was shifted from 3.4 to 2.5. High concentrations of chloride can also be inhibitory at pHs below 3, presumably due to secondary salt effects (Hildrum et al., 1975).

Certain carbonyl-containing compounds also catalyze nitrosation, but their role in foods is unclear. Keefer and Roller (1973), first showed that formaldehyde and chloral were effective catalysts for the nitrosation of dialkyl amines, even at pHs as high as 11. The catalytic effect is dependent on the structure of the carbonyl compound; neither acetone nor dimethylpropionaldehyde were catalytic. Archer et al. (1976) confirmed these data and extended the number of carbonyl compounds that were catalytic to include benzaldehyde derivatives and pyridoxal. Casado et al. (1984a) have investigated the mechanism for the catalysis and suggested the formation of the iminium ion $(R_2N{=}CH_2)^+$ from the formaldehyde and the amine as the initial step which subsequently reacts directly with nitrite to form the N-nitrosamine.

Simple as well as polyphenolic compounds can be inhibitors or catalysts of nitrosation depending on the structure of the phenolic, the relative concentrations of the phenolic and nitrosating agent, and the pH. The overall effect of poly-phenolics may be important in foods and endogenous nitrosation because they occur in substantial quantities in many foods (Maga, 1978). Challis (1973) reported that phenol was nitrosated 1000 times faster than dialkylamines and that phenol should be inhibitory. Davies and McWeeny (1977) showed that, while phenol is C-nitrosated at a faster rate, the resulting nitrosophenol can catalyze N-nitrosation. In systems where both dialkylamines and phenol are present the overall result is an increase in the rate of N-nitrosamine formation. The mechanism (Fig. 2) likely involves the C-nitrosation of the ring with subsequent tautormerization of the p-nitrosophenol to the quinone monoxime which is itself O-nitrosated. The resulting O-nitroso compound, in turn, may nitrosate any amine present while regenerating the p-nitrosophenol (Davies et al., 1978). High nitrite to phenol ratios favor catalysis while low ratios favor inhibition because the nitrite is consumed in the initial formation of p-nitrosophenol.

Catalysis has been extended to several other more complex polyphenolics which occur in foods, and the mechanism has been studied in detail (Pignatelli et al., 1980). For example, 1,3-dihydroxyphenol (and related natural derivatives) are catalytic by the same mechanism, but 1,2- and 1,4-dihydroxyphenols are inhibitory because they reduce N_2O_3 to NO with the formation of the quinone. Catalysis and inhibition of endogenous nitrosation by polyphenolics has been demonstrated in vivo in rats (Pignatelli et al., 1982). Caffeic and ferulic acids have each inhibited hepatotoxicity when dimethylamine and nitrite where co-fed to rats, presumably by inhibiting the endogenous formation of N-nitrosodimethylamine (Kuenzig et al., 1984).

Other foods or food components have been shown to affect N-nitrosation. For example, wheat bran increased the rate of N-nitrosation of dipropylamine while there was no effect on morpholine or pyrrolidine N-nitrosation (Wishnok and Richardson, 1979). Several common soy-based food products inhibited the formation of dialkylnitrosamines by 44–74% (Kurechi et al., 1981). Alcohols were reported to be inhibitory at pH 3.0 but enhanced N-nitrosation at pH 5.0 (Kurechi et al., 1980). Inhibition at the lower pH may be attributed to the formation of alkyl nitrites which, under most circumstances, do not N-nitrosate (Casado et al., 1984b). Thiol-containing compounds can similarly inhibit N-nitrosation by forming thionitrite esters (Williams and Aldred, 1982). Inhibition can be effective at low pHs, but at pHs greater than 5 thionitrite esters can become nitrosating agents (Dennis et al., 1979).

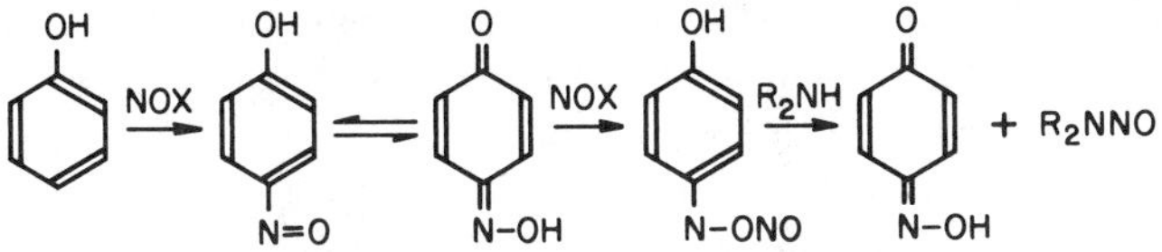

FIG. 2. Mechanism of nitrosation catalysis by phenol.

Lipid-containing foods have been shown to inhibit N-nitrosation by removing available nitrosating agent (Kurechi and Kikugawa, 1979). Mirvish *et al.* (1978) have shown that oxides of nitrogen react facilely with unsaturated fatty acids to form unknown compounds. We have extended these studies to show that at temperatures above 80°C these compounds will react with amines to form *N*-nitrosamines (Ross *et al.*, 1987). These lipid–nitrite compounds may be responsible for the formation of *N*-nitrosamines in fried bacon. In biphasic systems, the formation of micelles can be catalytic to the formation of *N*-nitroso derivatives of longer chain dialkyl *N*-nitrosamines by concentrating the amine and the N-nitrosating agent.

Juice extracted from kiwi fruit has been shown to inhibit N-nitrosation beyond what would be expected from the vitamin C content (Normington *et al.*, 1986). Ascorbic acid is capable of inhibiting aqueous N-nitrosation reactions and has been studied in detail because of its suitability as a food additive and as dietary supplement. The reaction between ascorbic acid and nitrite has been known for several years, but its potential in reducing human exposure to *N*-nitroso compounds was not recognized until 1972 (Mirvish *et al.*, 1972). Both ascorbic acid and ascorbate anion react stoichiometrically with nitrosating agents in a redox reaction. Dehydroascorbic acid and nitric oxide, which is a poor nitrosating agent, are formed (Fig. 3). Nitric oxide can be oxidized by molecular oxygen to nitrogen dioxide (NO_2) which combines with NO or NO_2 to form N_2O_3 or N_2O_4 which are N-nitrosating agents. Therefore, in the presence of oxygen, inhibition is not stoichiometric and an excess of ascorbic acid or ascorbate must be used. Oxygen can also oxidize ascorbate to dehydroascorbate which eliminates its ability to inhibit N-nitrosation. Archer *et al.* (1975) have studied the reaction between nitrite and ascorbate in aerobic and anaerobic systems. At pH 4 the combination of nitrite and oxygen (air) decreased available ascorbate from 10 m*M* to undetectable levels in 30 min. The pH of the solution can also affect the inhibition by influencing the equilibrium between ascorbate ion and ascorbic acid, each of which reacts with nitrosating agents at different rates (Dahn *et al.*, 1960). The lower the pH, the less effective ascorbate is in inhibiting nitrosation and the higher the ascorbate to nitrite ratio must be to give complete inhibition (Fan and Tannenbaum, 1973b).

Ascorbic acid has been shown to inhibit the endogenous formation of *N*-nitroso compounds in laboratory animals (Mirvish, 1975) and humans (Ohshima and Bartsch, 1981). Mirvish *et al.* (1972) have suggested that N-nitrosatable drugs be formulated with ascorbic acid to prevent endogenous N-nitrosation. As is discussed below, ascorbic acid and related compounds have been investigated as a means of blocking *N*-nitrosamine formation in foods, and, in the United States, cured meat products are required to be formulated with ascorbic acid or its isomer erythorbic acid. Kim *et al.* (1981) have correctly pointed out that the effects of ascorbic acid on N-nitrosation in a given system will depend on several complex factors including the pK_a of the amine, the pH of the reaction, whether

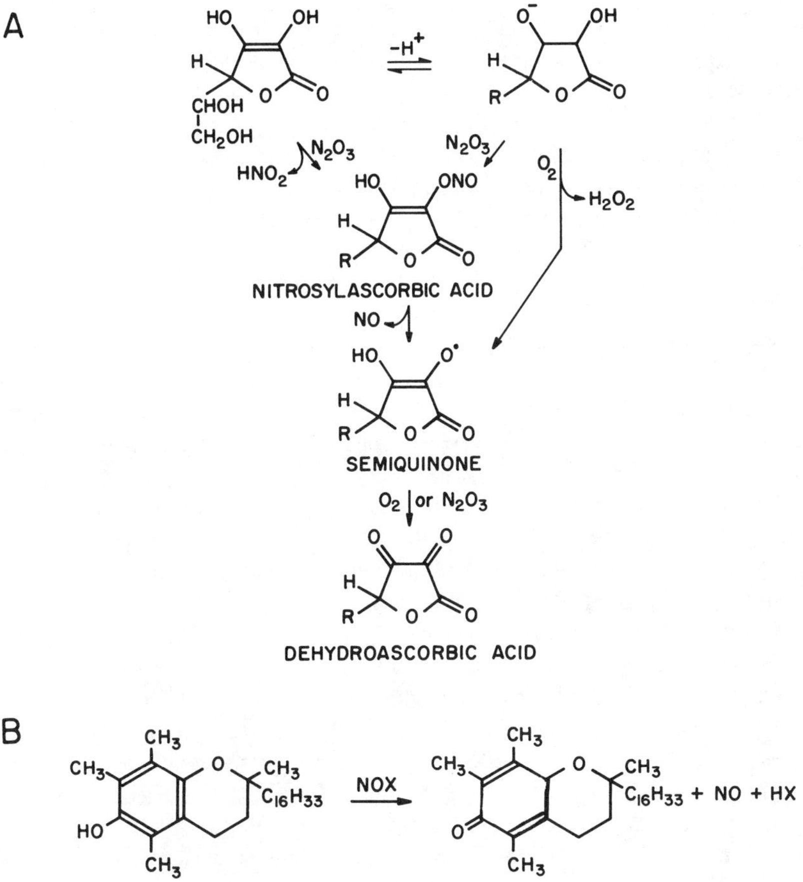

FIG. 3. Reduction of dinitrogen trioxide (N_2O_3) to nitric oxide (NO) by ascorbic acid (A) or tocopherol (B).

the reaction is aerobic or anaerobic, and the presence or absence of catalysts or inhibitors. The result of all these factors cannot be predicted at present and each situation must be empirically determined.

N-Nitrosation reactions can occur at very rapid rates in lipophilic systems such organic solvents (Mirvish *et al.*, 1978) or the lipid phase of cured meats (Hotchkiss and Vecchio, 1985). This has lead to research into lipid-soluble N-nitrosation inhibitors. Vitamin E is the most studied lipophilic inhibitor (Mergens and Newmark, 1980). Tocopherols react with oxides of nitrogen in a manner analogous to ascorbic acid; the tocopherol is oxidized to the quinone while the oxides of nitrogen are reduced to nitric oxide (Fig. 3). In most commercial forms of vitamin E, the tocopherol is esterified and incapable of inhibiting N-nitrosation because the alcohol group is unavailable for the redox reaction. Not all antioxidants are effective nitrosation inhibitors. For example, butylated hy-droxyanisole (BHA) and butylated hydroxytoluene (BHT) are not inhibitors but gallic acid is (Astill, 1978). This difference may be related to the ability of some antioxidants to reduce oxides of nitrogen to nitric oxide. As is discussed in a later section, several lipid-soluble compounds have been investigated as a means to inhibit N-nitrosamine formation in cured meats, and tocopherols are approved for use in products such as bacon (Gray et al., 1982).

D. BIOLOGICAL ACTIVITY

Were it not for the biological activity of N-nitroso compounds they would be of little scientific interest. As a class, they are among the most widely studied toxic compounds. More than 90% of the 300 individual N-nitroso compounds assayed in animals have proven to be capable of producing carcinomas. While little direct evidence exists showing that they are human carcinogens, much indirect evidence indicates that N-nitroso compounds may be involved in the etiology of certain human cancers. Ironically, several N-nitrosamides and N-nitrosoureas have become important therapeutic agents in treating human cancer (Serrou and Schein, 1981). The biological activity of N-nitroso compounds has been reviewed in detail (Preussmann and Stewart, 1984; Olajos and Coulston, 1978), and only a few salient points will be made here.

An important distinction must be made between the biological activities of N-nitrosamines and N-nitrosamides. While both may result in the same adverse outcome (i.e., carcinogenesis) N-nitrosamines are not inherently active but must first be enzymically activated by the organism. Organisms such as bacteria which do not possess the activating enzymes are not mutated by N-nitrosamines. N-Nitrosamides, on the other hand, derive their biological activity from their inherent chemical instability, especially at higher pHs. N-Nitrosamides are direct-acting mutagens and produce tumors at the site of application (as well as others), while N-nitrosamines produce tumors at sites that are usually distant from the point of application.

The acute toxicity of N-nitroso compounds has not been extensively studied because environmental exposure at acutely toxic levels is unlikely; N-nitroso compounds have little direct commercial use outside of therapeutic uses of some N-nitrosamide compounds. Those compounds for which LD_{50} values have been determined show a remarkably wide acute toxicity range, from a low of 22 to a high of 7500 mg/kg for N-nitrosomethyl-2-chloroethylamine and N-nitro-sodiethanolamine, respectively. The primary but not the only effect of N-nitro-samines is acute liver necrosis and hemorrhaging. N-Nitrosamides, on the other hand, cause tissue damage primarily at the site of application.

The major interest in N-nitroso compounds relates to their possible role in the etiology of human cancer and their use as experimental carcinogens. It is gener-ally accepted that N-nitrosamines are metabolically activated to carcinogens by the hydroxylation of a carbon atom α to the nitrosamino nitrogen. The resulting α-hydroxyalkylnitrosamine is chemically unstable and spontaneously rearranges to an aldehyde and a primary alkyldiazohydroxide structure. The latter compound loses a hydroxide ion forming a alkyldiazonium ion. This ion further decomposes to molecular nitrogen and a carbonium ion which, in turn, serves as the alkylating agent and reacts with proteins, nucleic acids, water, or other nucleophiles (Archer, 1982). Lijinsky *et al.* (1968) have clearly shown the importance of the α-hydroxylation *in vivo*. They substituted deuteriums for the α hydrogens, which resulted in a marked decrease in the potency owing to the increased difficulty in abstracting the deuterium. This hydroxylation is carried out by the mixed-function oxidase system. Alkylnitrosamines that have more than one carbon atom on at least one side can be hydroxylated in the other positions resulting in stable hydroxyalkylnitrosamines (Bauman *et al.*, 1985).

One of the most studied aspects of *N*-nitrosamine carcinogenesis is the relationship between the structure of a given *N*-nitrosamine and the organ in which tumors develop. For example, symmetrical dialkylnitrosamines are primarily liver carcinogens while unsymmetrical dialkylnitrosamines are esophageal carcinogens. With only a few exceptions, this organotropism is independent of route of administration or species of animal. Very small changes in structure can cause a change in the target organ. Target organs for cyclic *N*-nitrosamines are less predictable, but for a given structure the target organ is often the same regardless of dose or route. Lijinsky and co-workers have spent considerable time studying the relationship between structure and biological activity for *N*-nitroso compounds.

Nitrosamides produce tumors primarily at the sight of application, but several structures demonstrate neurotropism. The C_1 through C_6 *N*-nitrosoureas are particularly potent neurocarcinogens and are used experimentally (Preussmann and Stewart, 1984).

The potency of *N*-nitroso compounds is evidenced by the fact that the dose required to produce statistically significant numbers of tumors in laboratory animals is remarkably low and in some cases near the concentrations seen in environmental exposures. For example, Crampton (1980) reported that a daily dose of *N*-nitrosodimethylamine of 130 μg/kg of food produced significant tumors in rats. Anderson *et al.* (1979) found that the lowest effective dose of *N*-nitrosodimethylamine was 10 μg/kg of diet in mice. As is discussed below, these levels are within the same order of magnitude of concentration that *N*-nitrosodimethylamine has been reported to occur in some human foods.

N-Nitroso compounds can also produce tumors in experimental animals after a single dose, particularly if given to very young animals. Single doses of *N*-nitrosodimethylamine or *N*-nitrosodiethylamine in the lower mg/kg body weight range have produced tumors in several species. *N*-Nitroso compounds can also act transplacentally. Tomatis *et al.* (1975) have studied multigeneration carcinogenesis by *N*-nitroso compounds after exposure *in utero* and have shown significant tumor development in animals two generations after exposure to the carcinogen. It is evident from the above brief discussion that N-nitroso compounds are undesirable and that exposure should be minimized to the lowest levels feasible whenever possible.

E. ANALYTICAL METHODS

Interest in analytical methods related to N-nitroso compounds in foods has focused on three areas: (1) precursors, including nitrate, nitrite, and nitrosatable amines and amides; (2) volatile N-nitrosamines; and (3) nonvolatile N-nitroso compounds. Volatile N-nitrosamines consist of those compounds which are stable enough to be chromatographed by gas chromatography without derivatization. Nonvolatile N-nitroso compounds are either not stable enough for gas chromatography or have too high of a boiling point. N-Nitrosamines that do not have functional groups and that have up to 12–14 carbon atoms as well as some low molecular weight compounds containing a hydroxy group can be separated by gas chromatography. N-Nitrosamines with polar functional groups must first be derivatized to increase volatility.

The distinction between volatile and nonvolatile is of practical importance because methods to isolate and detect volatile N-nitrosamines in a variety of matrices have been developed over the last 15 years. Detailed reviews of these procedures have been published and will not be dealt with in depth here (Hotchkiss, 1981; Issenberg, 1981). In general, the first step in these procedures is to isolate the N-nitrosamine from the sample matrix by atmospheric steam distillation (Goodhead and Gough, 1975), vacuum distillation (Fine *et al.*, 1975b), or direct solvent extraction using solid-phase techniques (Pensabene *et al.*, 1982). The vacuum distillation method is the most widely used procedure and works for a variety of sample types. Owens and Kinast (1980) have developed a modification of the procedure that allows nonaqueous substrates to be analyzed. Samples are placed in a round distilling flask along with mineral oil and N-nitrosation inhibitors to prevent artifact formation, and the contents are distilled under a strong vacuum while being heated to 100–110°C. The distillate is trapped in one or two vacuum vapor traps cooled in liquid nitrogen and subsequently extracted with methylene chloride. The disadvantage of the vacuum procedure is the time and equipment required. Simpler procedures based on solid-phase extraction methods have replaced the vacuum procedure for many substrates such as cooked bacon, dried milk, beverages, and malt. These methods usually involve mixing a finely ground sample (or liquid sample) with water and a support material such as diatomaceous earth (Celite), packing a column with the material, and eluting the N-nitrosamine with methylene chloride or other appropriate solvent. In the case of samples containing lipids, a prewash with hexane can be utilized. These methods have the advantage of speed and simplicity but are not adaptable to all substrates.

After separating the volatile *N*-nitrosamines from the substrate, the solvent must be concentrated by at least 10- to 100-fold. This step requires care because considerable loss of *N*-nitrosodimethylamine can occur due to its volatility. The Kuderna–Danish apparatus is used for the initial concentration to 4–5 ml. Final concentration to 0.5–1.0 ml is accomplished under a stream of nitrogen at room temperature. Aliquots of 1–8 μl are injected into the gas chromatograph.

In the early 1970s, considerable effort was directed at finding a highly specific detector in order to increase both the speed and reliability of analyses. Improvements in the alkali flame ionization and electrolytic conductivity detectors were reported, but these methods were overshadowed by the commercial introduction of the thermal energy analyzer (TEA) (Fine *et al.*, 1975a). This detector is based on the fact that the N—N bond in a *N*-nitrosamine is considerably weaker than other bonds and can be cleaved by heating to 500–600°C yielding a nitrosyl (NO) radical (Fig. 4). When the nitrosyl radical is reacted with ozone, excited NO_2^* is produced in a reaction chamber under vacuum. The NO_2^* decays to ground state with the emission of photons which are detected in the near IR by a photomultiplier tube and amplified. This chemiluminescence detector is highly specific for the R_2N—N=O group and, hence, very little cleanup of samples is required. Many food samples can be analyzed after only an extraction and concentration procedure. While the specificity of the TEA is very high, positive samples must still be confirmed by mass spectrometry. Several reviews and reports have been published which provide details of cleaning up samples sufficiently for mass spectrometry (Gough, 1978).

Recent research in the analysis of *N*-nitroso compounds has focused on nonvolatile methodology. The TEA detector can be interfaced to an HPLC, but this combination has not been widely used. The HPLC–TEA can be used for normal-phase chromatography, but mobile phases that contain water, such as are used in reverse-phase chromatography, cause an unpredictable response over time. Unfortunately, many if not most of the nonvolatile *N*-nitroso compounds of interest are water soluble and are chromatographed by reverse-phase chromatography. Several authors have proposed solutions to this dilemma. One of the most prom-

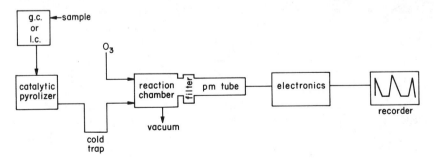

FIG. 4.   Schematic diagram of the thermal energy analyzer (TEA).

ising is that of Shuker and Tannenbaum (1983). They have developed a detector in which the effluent stream of an HPLC is irradiated in a narrow-bore Teflon tube by a high-intensity discharge lamp. This results in the cleavage of the N—NO bond, generating nitrite in the aqueous stream. A reagent is added postcleavage which forms a chromophore with nitrite that is subsequently detected in the visible region by a spectrophotometric detector. This system has been used to analyze N-nitrosoureas, N-nitrosoguanidine, and N-nitrosoglycocholic acid in gastric fluid and urine (Shuker and Tannenbaum, 1983).

Other approaches have focused on interfacing the TEA to reverse-phase HPLC. Massey *et al.* (1982a) have interfaced a microbore HPLC to the TEA in order to detect an ionic N-nitrosamine, using ion-pair chromatography and a methanol–water mobile phase. Later Ruhl and Reusch (1985) used a nonaqueous microbore HPLC–TEA combination to analyze dialkyl-N-nitrosamines in rubber products. Microbore systems have the disadvantage of using small sample loadings, thus limiting the sensitivity of the analysis. Typical injection volumes of $4\mu l$ are common. Massey *et al.* (1982b) later reported a procedure for extracting and analyzing polar N-nitrosamines from food extracts by conventional normal-phase HPLC–TEA.

Sen and Seaman (1984) reported a method of interfacing a HPLC to the TEA which bypasses the pyrolyzer, thus eliminating the major source of the problem in reverse-phase HPLC–TEA. The method is based on the total N-nitroso compound procedure developed by Walters and co-workers (Walters *et al.*, 1979a). The effluent of the HPLC is directed into a round-bottomed flask containing refluxing ethyl acetate. The top of the condenser is connected to the vacuum of the TEA after passing through a cold trap. Acetic acid containing 15% hydrogen bromide is added to the flask, and argon gas is bubbled through the ethyl acetate. As N-nitroso compounds elute the column, the N-nitroso group is cleaved by the HBr–acetic acid in a well-known reaction (Eisenbrand and Preussmann, 1970), resulting in nitric oxide. The NO is swept into the TEA by the argon and detected by the chemiluminescence reaction. The peak widths in the system as reported were up to 4 min wide probably because of the excessive dead volume in the system. Analyses of real samples were not reported nor were aqueous mobile phases used. Water inhibits the HBr–acetic acid cleavage of N-nitroso compounds.

The TEA has been of little use to date for direct analysis of N-nitrosamides. Thermal decomposition of N-nitrosamides results in the formation of N_2 rather than nitrosyl radicals (Mirvish *et al.*, 1979). Fine *et al.* (1984) reported that a proprietary modification to the TEA detector had been developed that overcame these shortcomings. The apparent modifications involved replacement of the standard pyrolyzer catalyst with a new material and the placement of a flow restrictor after the pyrolyzer. A fused silica capillary column allowed certain N-nitrosamides to be chromatographed by gas chromatography. The above preliminary report has not been described in detail nor has a commercial instrument been introduced.

The International Agency for Research on Cancer has published a compendium of methods for the analysis and confirmation of volatile *N*-nitrosamines in a variety of substrates and should be consulted when questions concerning *N*-nitrosamine analysis occur (Egan, 1983).

F. MAJOR SURVEYS OF FOODS

The introduction of the TEA made it possible to conduct large surveys of human foods for volatile *N*-nitrosamines. Several of these studies are summarized in Table I. The most extensive surveys are those of Spiegelhalder *et al.* (1980) and Gough *et al.* (1977). The former workers systematically analyzed nearly 3000 food samples including meat and meat products, cheeses and related

TABLE I

SELECTED INTERNATIONAL SURVEYS OF FOODS FOR VOLATILE NITROSAMINES (VNA)

Survey and food	Number positive/ number analyzed	VNA found[a]	Range[b]	Country
Havery *et al.* (1976)				
Fried bacon	22/22	NPYR	7–139	U.S.
Pork products	0/4	—	—	U.S.
Baby foods	0/2	—	—	U.S.
Variety meats	1/6	NPYR	6– —	U.S.
Fats and oils	0/2	—	—	U.S.
Cheese	0/10	—	—	U.S.
Gough *et al.* (1977)				
Fried bacon	33/56	NDMA, NPYR	ND[c]–200	U.K.
Canned, cured meats	9/34	NDMA	ND–10	U.K.
Other meats	0/73	—	—	U.K.
Fish	28/112	NDMA	ND–10	U.K.
Cheese	10/58	NDMA	ND–15	U.K.
Yogurts, desserts	0/16	—	—	U.K.
Eggs	0/25	—	—	U.K.
Vegetables/fruits	0/30	—	—	U.K.
Baby foods	0/16	—	—	U.K.
Soups	0/20	—	—	U.K.
Prepared meals	0/7	—	—	U.K.
Pastry based	0/36	—	—	U.K.
Salads	0/NR[d]	—	—	U.K.
Miscellaneous	0/31	—	—	U.K.
Cured meats	25/64	NDMA, NDEA, NPYR, NPIP	ND–8.6	U.K.
Baby foods	0/10	—	—	U.K.

(*Continued*)

TABLE I (*Continued*)

Survey and food	Number positive/ number analyzed	VNA found[a]	Range[b]	Country
Kawabata *et al.* (1980)				
Salt-fermented vegetables	6/49	NDMA, NPYR	ND–5	Japan
Beers	27/29	NDMA, NPYR	ND–5	Japan
Other alcoholic beverages	2/31	NDMA, NPYR	ND–<5	Japan
Miscellaneous	3/14	NDMA, NPYR	ND–<5	Japan
Maki *et al.* (1980)				
Cured meats	72/81	NR	ND–1	Japan
Canned meats, fish	3/29	NR	ND–10	Japan
Dried fish	18/18	NR	ND–>10	Japan
Smoked fish	13/14	NR	ND–>10	Japan
Dairy products	0/23	NR	—	Japan
Broiled dried fish	9/9	NR	ND–>10	Japan
Spiegelhalder *et al.* (1980)				
Meat products	127/395	NDMA, NPYR	0.5–>5	Germany
Cheese	49/209	NDMA	0.5–5	Germany
Beer	142/215	NDMA	ND–68	Germany
Other	NR/2000	—	—	Germany
Sen *et al.* (1980b)				
Cured meats	77/118	NDMA, NDEA, NPYR, NPIP	ND–55	Canada
Cooked pizza	1/12	NDMA, NDEA	ND–trace	Canada
Milk products	11/26	NDMA	ND–0.7	Canada
Alcoholic beverages	23/50	NDMA	ND–4.9	Canada

[a] Abbreviations: NDMA, *N*-nitrosodimethylamine; NDEA, *N*-nitrosodiethylamine; NPYR, *N*-nitrosopyrrolidine; NPIP, *N*-nitrosopiperidine.

[b] In μg/kg.

[c] Not detected.

[d] Not reported.

products, beer, and a variety of other foods, all available in the German market. Of the 395 meat and sausage products tested, 127 had >0.5 μg/kg *N*-nitrosodimethylamine and 51 had >0.5 μg/kg *N*-nitrosopyrrolidine. The highest values were 12 and 45 μg/kg *N*-nitrosodimethylamine and *N*-nitrosopyrrolidine, respectively. Of the 209 cheeses tested, 49 were >0.5 μg/kg in *N*-nitrosodimethylamine, but only one had >5 μg/kg. Of the 215 beer samples tested, 66% had >0.5 μg/kg *N*-nitrosodimethylamine. A mean value of 2.5 and a maximum value of 68 μg/kg were found. The remaining 2000 samples of breads, cereals, fish, milk and milk products, potatoes, vegetables, fruit, and beverages only occasionally gave positive results, usually at the detection limit. An estimate of the daily exposure to *N*-nitrosodimethylamine from the diet of 1.1

μg/person was made, with the greatest contribution coming from beer (64%) and 10% from cured meats.

Gough *et al.* (1977) analyzed over 500 foods available in the United Kingdom including meats, poultry, fish, dairy products, and sundry other products including cooked whole meals. Only *N*-nitrosodimethylamine and *N*-nitrosopyrrolidine were found with any regularity and then only in fried bacon. *N*-Nitrosodimethylamine was found in some cheese and meat samples, usually at levels below 5 μg/kg. Interestingly, none of the 23 complete meals contained detectable *N*-nitrosamines, even when they were prepared with cured meats. These workers estimated that the average diet in the United Kingdom contained 1 μg of *N*-nitrosamine per week. Beer was not included in this survey.

Ellen *et al.* (1986) have recently surveyed Dutch cured meats. Of the 140 samples analyzed, 33% did not contain detectable volatile *N*-nitrosamines while the remainder contained low levels of one or more volatile *N*-nitrosamines. They concluded that the *N*-nitrosamine content of Dutch cured meats had declined since the 1970s.

Several workers have reported surveys of Japanese foods for volatile *N*-nitrosamines. Maki *et al.* (1980) analyzed 370 samples available in Japan including some alcoholic beverages, seasonings, spices, and pickled vegetables. *N*-nitrosodimethylamine was found with the greatest regularity and in the highest concentration. Nearly all fish products contained detectable levels of *N*-nitrosodimethylamine, with the highest levels being found in dried fish (38 μg/kg). All beers examined contained *N*-nitrosodimethylamine. These workers concluded that the typical Japanese diet contained 1.8 μg *N*-nitrosodimethylamine per day based on the survey. Yamamoto *et al.* (1984) analyzed only foods suspected of containing volatile *N*-nitrosamines and concluded that the major source for Japanese consumers was from seafoods, especially if they were prepared by gas broiling. Kawabata *et al.* (1980) also conducted a large survey of Japanese foods, with similar results.

Stephany and Schuller (1980) surveyed 206 Dutch foods and beverages which were consumed by volunteers in order to assess their daily exposure to volatile *N*-nitrosamines from dietary sources. As in other studies, *N*-nitrosodimethylamine was found in the greatest frequency and at the highest levels. Beer contributed up to 90% of the daily *N*-nitrosodimethylamine exposure with cured meats being responsible for most of the remainder. It must be noted that these studies were conducted before process modifications were instituted to lower the *N*-nitrosodimethylamine content of beer.

Large comprehensive surveys of North American foods have not been reported. The Health Protection Branch of the Canadian government has reported on limited surveys of a number of products including cured meats, cheeses, and beer (Sen *et al.*, 1977b, 1979; Sen and Seaman, 1981a–c). Workers at the U.S. Food and Drug Administration have made similar surveys (Havery *et al.*, 1976) in which meat products, baby foods, fats and oils, cheeses, and total diet samples were analyzed. Only fried bacon consistently contained volatile N-nitrosamines. These reports were recently summarized by Havery and Fazio (1985), who concluded that the N-nitrosamine content of the American diet has declined over the last decade. Additional surveys of several products including fried bacon, beverages containing malt, dried milk and soy products, and baby bottle rubber nipples and pacifiers have been conducted. Many of these studies have been repeated over time and have quantified a decline in volatile N-nitrosamines. An industry trade group has reported a large survey of cured meat products available in the United States and has concluded that only dry-cured hams consistently contain volatile N-nitrosamines (Nitrite Safety Council, 1980).

Foods consumed in the People's Republic of China have not been extensively surveyed for volatile N-nitrosamines. This is unfortunate because there is an indication that the local diet may play a role in the etiology of certain cancers such as esophageal cancer. Singer *et al.* (1986) recently reported that of five vegetable-based foods tested (28 samples), all but one contained one or more volatile N-nitrosamine at levels of less than 1 µg/kg.

Several generalizations can be made based on the above data. First is that, on the average, diet contributes no more than 1 µg of volatile N-nitrosamine per day per person, and recent evidence indicates that this figure has decreased in recent years. When compared to other known sources of human exposure to preformed volatile N-nitrosamines, especially tobacco products, foods represent a minor exposure (see below). Because the foods which are known to contain trace amounts of volatile N-nitrosamines are widely consumed, more people are probably exposed to N-nitrosamines through foods than through the other known sources. As the National Academy of Sciences committee recently concluded (NAS–NRC, 1981), N-nitrosamines are potent carcinogens, and, where possible, human exposure should be minimized. The second generalization is that, with some exceptions, volatile N-nitrosamines are found in a relatively few products such as fried bacon, products containing malt or other ingredients which are dried by direct flame-heated air, and foods in contact with materials that contain N-nitrosamines. It is also apparent that the N-nitrosamine content of the food supply is decreasing due to changes in processing techniques.

III. *N*-NITROSO COMPOUND FORMATION DUE TO NITRITE/NITRATE ADDITION

A. NITRITE/NITRATE FUNCTION

Nitrite and/or nitrate salts (potassium as well as sodium) are added to meats, poultry, and fish in the low hundreds of milligrams per kilogram range as functional ingredients. This has been a common preservation method for meats for many centuries (Binkard and Kolari, 1975). The use of nitrite in meat preservation has been reviewed in detail (Cassens *et al.*, 1978). Nitrate salts are added to certain products as a source of nitrite, which is the active substance. Nitrate is reduced to nitrite by microbial enzymes and so nitrate can serve as a continuous reservoir of nitrite in products which are fermented or stored over long periods. Nitrite serves three major functions in meat products: (1) addition to red meats results in the characteristic pink–red color common to cured meats; (2) it acts as an antioxidant, preventing rancidity from developing under normal storage; and (3) nitrite effectively inhibits toxigenesis by *Clostridium botulinum*. Each of these important functions has been reviewed in detail and will not be dealt with in depth here. Readers are directed to reviews on flavor/antioxidant activity (Gray *et al.*, 1981b), on control of *C. botulinum* (Woods and Wood, 1982; Pierson and Smoot, 1982; Sofos *et al.*, 1979), and on the pigments associated with nitrite use (Clydesdale and Francis, 1971). Chapter 3 of the National Academy of Sciences (NAS–NRC, 1981) report is an especially thorough review of the chemistry and microbiology of nitrate and nitrite in foods. Part 2 of the National Academy of Sciences report (NAS–NRC, 1982) deals with possible alternatives to the use of nitrite in foods, as does the recent review by Sofos and Busta (1980).

The U.S. Department of Agriculture requires that 120 mg/kg of sodium nitrite (or equivalent potassium salt) be added to bacon. However, detectable nitrite is reduced to less than 50% of that value shortly after the curing process and continues to decline during storage. Woolford and Cassens (1977) showed that during the smokehouse treatment of bacon, residual nitrite dropped from an original 156 mg/kg to 45 and that levels fell to nearly undetectable after 7 weeks of storage. The reactions that nitrite undergoes have not been elucidated, but the reactive nature of nitrite would suggest that several products are formed. Nitrite is reduced by ascorbic acid, which also must be added to bacon, to nitric oxide. The nitric oxide can further react with several components or escape as a gas (Frouin, 1977). Nitrite is also in equilibrium with nitrous acid at the pH of meat, which is in turn in equilibrium with oxides of nitrogen such as dinitrogen trioxide. This substance is chemically reactive and may readily react with proteins (Ito *et al.*, 1983), thiols (Kanner and Juven, 1980), cholesterol (Kobayashi and Kubota, 1980), hemoproteins (Bonnett *et al.*, 1980), and lipids (Goutefongea *et al.*, 1977). The chemistry of nitrite in meats has been reviewed (Cassens *et al.*, 1979). Workers at the University of Wisconsin have studied the chemistry of meat curing for several years, using ^{15}N stable isotopes of nitrite. Woolford *et al.* (1976) found that the largest portion of the nitrite was chemically bound to protein and heme fractions. Cassens *et al.* (1977) have summarized the fate of nitrite as follows: 5–15% in myoglobin, 1–10% oxidized to nitrate, 5–10% as free nitrite, 1–5% as NO gas, 5–15% bound to sulfhydryl groups, 1–5% bound to lipids, and 20–30% bound to the protein fraction. Nitrite also reacts to form minor volatile components such as aliphatic nitriles and nitrates (Mottram, 1984).

B. FRIED BACON

A large majority of the research into the occurrence of N-nitrosamines in foods has involved cooked bacon because it was the only food, with the later exception of beer, that consistently contained volatile N-nitrosamines. While the N-nitrosamine content of fried bacon appears to have declined over the last 10–15 years (Havery and Fazio, 1985), this product still consistently contains detectable levels of volatile N-nitrosamines. Very recent evidence indicates that in the United States the levels of N-nitrosopyrrolidine in fried bacon may be increasing (Canas et al., 1986; Vecchio et al., 1986).

The chemistry of the formation of N-nitrosamines in fried bacon has been studied in detail and reviewed through 1978 (Gray, 1976; Gray and Randall, 1979). The regulation of N-nitrosamines in bacon by the U.S. Department of Agriculture has also been reviewed (McCutcheon, 1984). Two volatile N-nitrosamines can be consistently detected in nitrite-cured fried bacon, N-nitrosodimethylamine and N-nitrosopyrrolidine. The latter compound usually occurs in somewhat higher amounts. In 1982 another volatile N-nitrosamine, N-nitrosothiazolidine, was found to occur in many fried bacon samples. This compound was not detected by most analytical procedures used previously to that time. Other volatile N-nitrosamines have been reported with less frequency in fried bacon, especially N-nitrosopiperidine. The occurrence of this N-nitrosamine was found to result from the use of spice-curing premixes that contained nitrite. The N-nitrosopiperidine was formed in the dry mix prior to addition to the meat (Sen et al., 1974). A few reports have indicated the presence of nonvolatile N-nitrosamines, primarily N-nitrosamino acids, in both raw and fried bacon.

Table II lists some recent studies in which the volatile N-nitrosamine content of commercial bacon samples was investigated. These studies show that N-nitrosopyrrolidine occurs in nearly all fried samples in concentrations of 1–20 µg/kg while N-nitrosodimethylamine occurs with somewhat less frequency and at levels of <1–10 µg/kg. N-Nitrosothiazolidine occurs in levels of 1–20 µg/kg. Other volatile N-nitrosamines such as N-nitrosomorpholine, N-nitrosodiethylamine, and N-nitrosopiperidine have been reported on occasion but most often at levels of 1 µg/kg or less. N-Nitrosodimethylamine and N-nitrosopyrrolidine are both animal carcinogens, with the former being among the most potent N-nitroso carcinogens. N-Nitrosothiazolidine has not been tested for carcinogenicity but has been reported to be both mutagenic (Mihara and Shibamoto, 1980) and nonmutagenic (Miller et al., 1985); the discrepancy may be due to the impurities in the preparation of the N-nitrosothiazolidine.

The occurrence of nonvolatile N-nitrosamines in fried bacon has not been studied in the detail that volatiles have. Lee et al. (1978) identified N-nitroso-3-

TABLE II

COMMERCIAL FRIED BACON RASHERS AND FRIED-OUT FAT[a]

Sample	Number tested	NDMA	NPYR	NTHZ	Other	Comment	Reference
Edible	18	NR[b]	20.0 (4–75)	NR	NR	U.S., 1977 data	Havery et al. (1978)
Edible	17	NR	NR (5–63)	NR	NR	U.S.	Pensabene et al. (1979b)
Edible	12	3.4 (ND[c]–17.2)	9.3 (1.7–21.8)	NR	1.0 (NDEA)	Canadian	Sen et al. (1979)
Fried-out fat	10	6.4 (2.6–11.9)	21.9 (15.1–24.0)	NR	0.6 (NDEA, 1 sample)	Canadian	Sen et al.(1979)
Edible	NR	NR (0.1–5)	NR (1–20)	NR	NPIP (<1.0)	U.K.	Webb and Gough (1980)
Edible	21	NR	NR (3.4–11.8)	NR	NR	U.S.	Kimoto and Fiddler (1982)
Edible	7	NR	NR	21 (13–32)	NR	U.S.	Kimoto et al. (1982)
Raw bacon	7	NR	NR	2.8 (ND–7.5)	NR	Canadian	Sen et al. (1985a)
Fried bacon	22	NR	NR	6.3 (ND–241)	NR	Canadian	Sen et al. (1985a)
Fried-out fat	6	NR	NR	1.0 (ND–2.5)	NR	Canadian	Sen et al. (1985a)
Edible	18	7 (ND–44)	21 (1–65)	NR	NPIP (ND–1)	U.S.	Canas et al. (1986)
Fried-out fat	18	4 (ND–11)	27 (<1–75)	NR	NPIP (ND–1)	U.S.	Canas et al. (1986)
Edible	39	4.0 (trace–23)	17 (ND–130)	8.9 (ND–30)	NPIP	Consumer cooked	Vecchio et al. (1986)
Fried-out fat	39	5.3 (ND–33)	32 (ND–120)	3.4 (ND–17)	NPIP	Consumer cooked	Vecchio et al. (1986)

[a] In μg/kg, average (range). Abbreviations: NDMA, N-nitrosodimethylamine; NPYR, N-nitrosopyrrolidine; NTHZ, N-nitrosothiazolidine; NDEA, N-nitrosodiethylamine; NPIP, N-nitrosopiperidine.
[b] Not reported.
[c] Not detected.

hydroxypyrrolidine in fried bacon and fried-out fat at mean concentrations of 2.2 and 1.6 μg/kg, respectively. Sen *et al.* (1977a) found 2 of 13 fried bacons contained 8 and 12 μg/kg of *N*-nitrosohydroxyproline. Gray *et al.* (1977) studied the formation of this *N*-nitrosamine in model systems. Kushnir *et al.* (1975) reported that raw bacon contained 0.38–1.18 mg/kg *N*-nitrosoproline, but this same group later failed to detect the same compound in any samples analyzed using improved methodology (Pensabene *et al.*, 1979a). Sen *et al.* (1976) and Hansen *et al.* (1977) also failed to detect *N*-nitrosoproline in raw bacon. Tricker *et al.* (1985a) analyzed several cured meats for six *N*-nitrosamino acids and consistently found *N*-nitrosothiazolidine-4-carboxylic acid at levels of not detected to 520 μg/kg in smoked bacons. Bacons which were not smoked contained either nondetectable or very low levels. *N*-Nitrosoproline and *N*-nitrosohydroxyproline were found with less frequency in levels of not detected to 90 μg/kg. Sen *et al.* (1986a) similarly found *N*-nitrosothiazolidine-4-carboxylic acid in both fried and raw bacon at levels up to 14,000 μg/kg with an average of 85 μg/kg in fried bacon. Massey *et al.* (1985) reported that smoked bacon also contained 2-(hydroxymethyl)-3-*N*-nitrosothiazolidine-4-carboxylic acid in levels up to 2 mg/kg. The toxicological significance, if any, of these *N*-nitrosamino acids in bacon is unknown, but *N*-nitrosoproline is not a carcinogen and is excreted unchanged (Chu and Magee, 1981).

Analytical methods to detect *N*-nitrosamides in foods have not been developed and so their presence in bacon or other foods has not been directly addressed. However, Gray and co-workers have published a series of reports which have indirectly investigated the formation and stability of *N*-nitrosamides in model systems and foods. Kakuda and Gray (1980a,b) and Kakuda *et al.* (1980) showed that α-amino acids can react with fatty acids to form substituted amides which can then be N-nitrosated. However, the temperatures and time necessary for amide formation are higher than those normally encountered in food processing or preparation and well above the thermal decomposition temperature *N*-nitrosamides. Fooladi *et al.* (1983) concluded that it is unlikely that *N*-nitrosamides would be present in thermally processed foods such as bacon.

The nature of the precursors to *N*-nitrosamines, especially *N*-nitrosopyrrolidine, in fried bacon has been investigated in depth and reviewed (Gray, 1977). Several amines naturally present in tissue have been shown to produce small amounts of *N*-nitrosopyrrolidine when treated with nitrite in model systems. Bills *et al.* (1973) demonstrated the formation of *N*-nitrosopyrrolidine from *N*-nitrosoproline, pyrrolidine, spermidine, proline, and putrescine in yields of 2.6, 1.0, 1.0, 0.4, and 0.04%, respectively. Glutamic acid, glutamine, and hydroxyproline did not produce *N*-nitrosopyrrolidine. Huxel *et al.* (1974) showed collagen to be a potential precursor but only after heating for 2 hr. Others have discounted the role of collagen (Patterson *et al.*, 1976). Hwang and Rosen (1976) used ^{14}C-labeled amines to show that greater amounts of *N*-nitrosopyrrolidine formed from proline than from spermidine or putrescine in fried bacon. N-Nitrosoproline gave the largest yields, which led the authors to suggest that proline was first nitrosated then decarboxylated during frying. Gray and Collins (1977) found the free proline content of whole green pork bellies was 11.8 μmol/100 g tissue and increased to 35.6 μmol/100 g tissue after 28 days of storage at 2°C. Coleman (1978), working with rendered bacon fat and with bacon, found that the addition of free proline greatly increased the yield of N-nitrosopyrrolidine at 170°C.

These reports have led most workers to agree that proline is the major precursor of N-nitrosopyrrolidine in fried bacon, but the mechanism of formation has been debated. Because N-nitrosopyrrolidine is not found in raw bacon, a thermally induced mechanism is likely. Two mechanisms seem possible; proline may first be nitrosated then decarboxylated during frying or proline could be first decarboxylated and the resulting pyrrolidine N-nitrosated. Hwang and Rosen (1976) added ^{14}C-labeled N-nitrosoproline to bacon and recovered ^{14}C-labeled N-nitrosopyrrolidine after frying. The yield of N-nitrosopyrrolidine was greater from N-nitrosoproline than from proline and nitrite. Gray and Collins (1978) rehydrated freeze-dried bacon with water containing nitrite and proline or N-nitrosoproline and heated the samples to 100–200°C. Up to 2.2% of the N-nitrosoproline was converted to N-nitrosopyrrolidine while only 0.33% of the proline–nitrite was converted. Using a 0.33% conversion factor and a proline content of 23.8 μM, these authors concluded that 90 μg/kg N-nitrosopyrrolidine would be formed in fried bacon.

Several authors have studied the kinetics of N-nitrosopyrrolidine formation in both bacon and model systems in order to determine the sequence by which N-nitrosopyrrolidine is formed during frying. Nakamura et al. (1976) added pyrrolidine, proline, or N-nitrosoproline to bacon and measured yields of N-nitrosopyrrolidine over temperatures of 100–225°C. At temperatures between 100 and 150°C, both pathways gave similar amounts of N-nitrosopyrrolidine, but at temperatures between 175 and 225°C decarboxylation followed by nitrosation gave higher yields. Coleman (1978) working with model systems suggested that proline is first decarboxylated, based on the thermal instability of N-nitrosoproline. In an extensive investigation, Bharucha et al. (1979) found by differential scanning calorimetric studies that the decarboxylation of N-nitrosoproline was more facile than proline decarboxylation and that the amount of free proline in raw bacon was orders of magnitude more than necessary to account for the N-nitrosopyrrolidine found. Lee et al. (1983a) carefully studied the kinetics in adipose model systems over a temperature range of 80–160°C and found that proline is nitrosated faster than pyrrolidine over the entire temperature range studied and that decarboxylation of N-nitrosoproline has a lower energy of activation than decarboxylation of proline. These data further support the intermediacy of N-nitrosoproline.

Both nitrosation and decarboxylation occur during the frying process because raw bacon does not contain sufficient N-nitrosoproline to account for the N-nitrosopyrrolidine found upon frying (Baker and Ma, 1978; Hansen et al., 1977). Tricker et al. (1985b) have recently repeated similar experiments to those described above and have come to the similar conclusion that proline is the major precursor to N-nitrosopyrrolidine in fried bacon. Lakritz et al. (1976) have shown that the free proline content of pork bellies increases on storage at 2°C, which supports the observation that the N-nitrosamine content of bacon increases with increasing storage time.

The majority of the N-nitrosopyrrolidine occurs in the fat portion of the edible rasher, the fried-out fat, and the vapors but not in the lean edible. Fiddler et al. (1974) could not detect any N-nitrosamine when the lean portion of bacon was fried separately from the fat but did find N-nitrosopyrrolidine in the fried fat solids and the fried-out fat. Mottram et al. (1977) and Coleman (1978) observed a similar preference for formation in the adipose portion. Different authors have offered different explanations. Fiddler et al. (1974) suggested that the chemical precursors exist in the fat but not in the lean portions. Mottram et al. (1977) suggested that the precursors occur in both portions, but the nonpolar environment in the lipid phase was more conducive to nitrosation. They found that freeze-dried lean did yield N-nitrosamine when heated in corn oil. Scanlan (1975) speculated that the preferential formation in the fat may be related to the higher temperature which the fat could reach during frying due to its lower water content and higher heat capacity. Using micro-thermal couples, Mottram et al. (1977) demonstrated that the fat did reach a temperature of as much as 50°C higher than the lean. Bharucha et al. (1979) suggested that the reaction proceeds by a free radical mechanism and N-nitrosation would, therefore, be favored by the nonaqueous lipid phase. Their experimental evidence which showed that water and free radical scavengers inhibited N-nitrosamine formation strongly supports this hypothesis.

The precursors to N-nitrosodimethylamine have not been investigated in detail. Gray et al. (1978) studied several possible precursors including dimethylamine, trimethylamine, sarcosine, and choline. Sarcosine, in their system, proved to be the most likely precursor. Archer et al. (1971) had previously shown that N-nitrososarcosine could be formed from the reaction between nitrite and creatinine. Pensabene et al. (1975) demonstrated the formation of N-nitrosodimethylamine from lecithin in model systems.

While the precursor amine and mechanism to N-nitrosopyrrolidine formation in fried bacon have been determined with reasonable certainty, the nature of the N-nitrosating agent has not been investigated to the same extent. Nitrite is the source of nitrosating agent, but as noted above residual nitrite decreases rapidly during storage while N-nitrosamine formation increases. Most authors have assumed that dissolved oxides of nitrogen are the nitrosating agents, based, in part, on the preferential formation of N-nitrosamines in the lipid phase (Bharucha *et al.*, 1979) and the fact that N-nitrosation by oxides of nitrogen in nonpolar solvents is very rapid (Mirvish *et al.*, 1978).

We have shown that both the fat rendered from fried bacon and lipids extracted from raw bacon contain the capacity to form 2–3 orders of magnitude more N-nitrosamine than is normally found in fried-out fat (Hotchkiss and Vecchio, 1985). This N-nitrosation capability results from a lipid-bound nitrite compound (Hotchkiss *et al.*, 1986). While the structure of this compound has not been determined, we have recently confirmed the earlier work of Walters *et al.* (1979b) showing that oxides of nitrogen react with unsaturated lipids to form several compounds which are capable of N-nitrosating amines (Ross *et al.*, 1987). The compound formed by the nitro–nitroso addition across the double bond of methyl oleate gave the highest degree of N-nitrosation. The energy of activation and kinetics of N-nitrosation by the lipid-bound nitrite were similar to those reported N-nitrosamine formation in bacon. This mechanism also explains why there is not sufficient N-nitrosoproline in raw bacon to account for the N-nitrosopyrrolidine formed during frying. These lipid-derived compounds are likely responsible for N-nitrosation during bacon frying.

Several studies indirectly support this possibility. Goutefongea *et al.* (1977) demonstrated that nitrite reacts with unsaturated fatty acids and suggested that this may play a role in N-nitrosamine formation. Mirvish *et al.* (1983) showed that nitrogen dioxide reacts with methyl esters of fatty acids to form compounds capable of N-nitrosation, and Gray *et al.* (1983) demonstrated that increased N-nitrosamine formation in bacon correlates with a higher degree of unsaturation in the fatty acids in the bacon. This thermal nitrosation reaction could be either a direct transfer of a nitrosyl radical (transnitrosation) or the thermally induced formation of nitric oxide (NO) which is oxidized to a nitrosating agent by molecular oxygen. Dennis *et al.* (1982) have shown that the formation of N-nitrosamines during frying is oxygen dependent; N-nitrosamine formation is inhibited by up to 90% when oxygen is excluded from the environment. This observation has been confirmed by Skrypec *et al.* (1985). Transnitrosation reactions are, however, also possible. Dennis *et al.* (1980) have formed N-nitrosothiol compounds which are capable of transnitrosation under conditions similar to frying bacon. Peptides and polypeptides can also form stable N-nitroso derivatives which may be capable for forming N-nitrosamines during frying (Kubacka and Scanlan, 1984). Challis *et al.* (1984) have presented evidence that the peptide bond can be nitrosated.

In addition to ingoing or residual nitrite, several factors such as bacon composition, processing procedures, cooking methods and temperatures, and the addition of N-nitrosation inhibitors to the cure mix may affect the quantity of N-nitrosamine formed in a given bacon sample. As pointed out above, N-nitrosamine formation occurs primarily in the fat portion of fried bacon so bacons with higher fat to lean ratios are likely to form more N-nitrosamine. Amundson *et al.* (1981) compared the N-nitrosamine content of two bacons having initial fat contents of 51 and 57%. The bacon with higher fat content resulted in 2–5 times more N-nitrosodimethylamine and N-nitrosopyrrolidine than was formed in the leaner bacon after frying under similar conditions. Pensabene *et al.* (1979b) also found a correlation between N-nitrosamine content of fried bacon and fat content. Gray *et al.* (1983) have extended these findings by altering the degree of saturation in pork bellies by modifying the source of dietary lipids fed to the animals prior to slaughter. Fried bacon from animals consuming coconut oil (high saturation) was significantly lower in N-nitrosamines than bacon from animals fed corn oil (more unsaturated). The authors speculated that adipose tissue serves as a reservoir for potential nitrosating agents. As mentioned above, aging increases the free proline content of bellies, and hence, the N-nitrosopyrrolidine content after frying (Pensabene *et al.*, 1980; Lakritz *et al.*, 1976).

The curing mix composition is one of the most controllable factors in N-nitrosamine formation. Theiler *et al.* (1981a) investigated the effects of several cure ingredients and found that sucrose and tripolyphosphate had no effect on N-nitrosamine content but that sodium chloride and sodium ascorbate were inhibitory. Later work by the same group found that a combination of glucose, liquid smoke, and tocopherol reduced N-nitrosamine content of fried bacon by as much as 80% (Theiler *et al.*, 1984).

The inhibition of N-nitrosamine formation in cured bacon has been investigated in depth by several groups. Fiddler *et al.* (1973) demonstrated that 550 and 5500 mg/kg sodium ascorbate would inhibit the formation of N-nitrosodimethylamine in heated frankfurters, and Herring (1973) demonstrated similar effects in bacon; the degree of inhibition, however, was not consistent. The inconsistencies may have resulted from the fact that ascorbate is hydrophilic and the formation of N-nitrosamines occurs predominantly in the fat portion. Mottram and Patterson (1977) found that in a lipid–water system, ascorbate can actually increase N-nitrosation rates by 5- to 25-fold. This was likely related to the formation of oxides of nitrogen, which migrated to the lipophilic portion where N-nitrosation was accelerated. Sen *et al.* (1976) tested a number of inhibitory agents including sodium ascorbate and confirmed the erratic inhibition, but because sodium ascorbate was approved for addition to bacon the authors called for its continued use. Propyl gallate, piperazine, and ascorbyl palmitate were more effective in inhibiting N-nitrosamine formation. U.S. Department of Agriculture regulations now require the addition of ascorbate (or its equivalent isomer, erythorbate) to be added to cured bacon, primarily as a N-nitrosamine inhibitor.

Walters *et al.* (1976) recognized that N-nitrosamine formation occurred in the fat phase of bacon and that fat-soluble inhibitors would be more effective. They determined that the inclusion of α-tocopherol in their model system at levels of 500 mg/kg resulted in no detectable levels of N-nitrosopyrrolidine. Fiddler *et al.*

(1978) extended these findings to a commercial type of cure. Formulation of the curing mix with either 500 mg/kg each of sodium ascorbate and α-tocopherol or 500 mg/kg α-tocopherol alone were more inhibitory than ascorbate alone. The tocopherol was solubilized in the cure mix with Polysorbate 20 in order to achieve distribution of the inhibitor. Coleman (1978) demonstrated a similar inhibition by other fat-soluble antioxidants in model systems. The greatest inhibition was by ethoxyquin, but some inhibition was also seen with BHT and BHA. Mergens and Newmark (1980) have reviewed the literature up to 1980 on the effects of antioxidants on *N*-nitrosamine formation and have listed the effectiveness and side effects of several potential inhibitors.

Bharucha *et al.* (1980) have proposed that effective N-nitrosation inhibitors for fried bacon should meet several requirements: (1) they should serve as traps for NO· radicals; (2) they should be fat soluble; (3) they must not be carried off with the steam during frying; and (4) they must be thermally stable up to 174°C. These workers synthesized the C_{12} through C_{18} and C_{18-1} acetals of ascorbic acid and tested each for ability to inhibit *N*-nitrosamine formation in fried bacon. The C_{12} acetal was effective in inhibiting N-nitrosation but imparted a soaplike aftertaste. The C_{16} acetal was 97% inhibitory and did not present off flavors. This substance is not approved for addition to foods, however. These same workers applied similar techniques to demonstrate the effectiveness of ethoxyquin, dihydroethoxyquin, and several analogs in inhibiting N-nitrosation (Bharucha *et al.*, 1985). These compounds are effective inhibitors at levels of as little as 20 mg/kg. As would be predicted from the work with the ethoxyquins, these same workers found that *N*-alkylanilines with a *p*-alkoxy substituent were effective inhibitors of *N*-nitrosamine formation in bacon. A series of related compounds was tested, and several gave 100% inhibition (Bharucha *et al.*, 1986).

The requirement that effective inhibition can only be achieved with lipid-soluble compounds presents a practical problem in that curing solutions are water based, thus making it difficult to achieve an even distribution of the blocking agent. Gray and co-workers have investigated a dispersing system in which α-tocopherol is first coated onto the curing salt prior to addition to the brine. This results in an aqueous suspension of the tocopherol and a more even mixing with the bacon. This has been reported to be effective with both dry-cured (Reddy *et al.*, 1982) and pump-cured (Bernthal *et al.*, 1986) bacons. A commercial product has been developed (Gray *et al.*, 1982).

Lower levels of nitrite could be used in bacon if lactic acid-producing bacteria and fermetable sugar were added with the curing mixture. The lower nitrite would reduce the formation of *N*-nitrosamines, and the lactic acid bacteria would reduce the pH by forming lactic acid if the bacon were temperature abused. The lower pH would inhibit toxigenesis by *Clostridium botulinum*. (Collins-Thompson and Rodriguez-Lopez, 1981). Recently, the U.S. Department of Agriculture has permitted the use of only 40 mg/kg ingoing nitrite in bacon if accompanied by inoculation with active lactic acid bacterial cultures and a fermentable sugar (*Federal Register* **51,** 21731, 1986). Trials using this method of curing have been reported to be effective in lowering the *N*-nitrosamine content of the bacon while not compromising the safety of the resulting bacon (Tanaka *et al.*, 1985).

The method used to cook bacon as well as the temperature and time of cooking influence the amount of *N*-nitrosamine formed. Pensabene *et al.* (1974) fried a randomized lot of bacon to the same degree of doneness at temperatures ranging from 99 to 204°C for times of 4–105 minutes. The higher temperatures for shorter time resulted in more *N*-nitrosamine formation than did lower frying temperatures for longer times. They also showed that microwave cooking resulted in nearly undetectable levels. Lee *et al.* (1983b) also found that higher pan temperatures resulted in more *N*-nitrosamine formation. Theiler *et al.* (1981b) fried bacons of different thicknesses and found that the *N*-nitrosamine content was dependent on the frying time; thicker slices formed less *N*-nitrosamine when fried for 3 min per side but more when fried at 5 min per side. This probably resulted from differences in internal temperature reached during frying. We have found that the maximum amount of total *N*-nitrosamine (edible + fried-out fat + steam) was formed after frying for 3–4 min per side in a preheated pan at 171°C (Hotchkiss and Vecchio, 1985). The *N*-nitrosamine content of fried bacon acquired from consumers who reported that they fried at higher pan temperatures was slightly greater than that of samples from consumers who reported using lower temperatures (Vecchio *et al.*, 1986).

The occurrence of *N*-nitrosothiazolidine in fried bacon deserves special mention. Researchers at the U.S. Department of Agriculture (Kimoto *et al.*, 1982) and at Michigan State University (Gray *et al.*, 1982) independently found that, in a majority of cases, fried bacon contained this *N*-nitrosamine. This had been overlooked previously either because of *N*-nitrosothiazolidine's long retention time compared to *N*-nitrosopyrrolidine on Carbowax 20M or the fact that the compound is not stable on columns containing base. Kimoto *et al.* (1982) reported levels up to 700 μg/kg but concluded that the majority of this resulted from artifactual formation during sample work up and that levels of 13–32 μg/kg were actually present in the fried bacon. They speculated that the parent amine, thiazolidine, was formed from cysteamine and formaldehyde, which originated from the smoking process. Pensabene and Fiddler (1982) suggested that a Celite column extraction procedure be used to limit the formation of positive artifacts, but others have found the vacuum mineral oil procedure satisfactory if sufficient precautions are used (Hotchkiss and Vecchio, 1985). Gray *et al.* (1982) reported average levels of 4.1 μg/kg in laboratory-prepared bacon using such a modified vacuum mineral oil procedure.

The mechanism by which *N*-nitrosothiazolidine is formed has not been determined. Some evidence indicates that it is formed from the N-nitrosation of thiazolidine during the smoking of raw bacon, while other reports suggest that the decarboxylation during frying of the precursor N-nitrosamino acid, which can be found in raw bacon, is the major route of formation. Pensabene and Fiddler (1983a) found that the N-nitrosothiazolidine content of raw bacon was greater than the amount found in the fried bacon and concluded that N-nitrosothiazolidine was not formed during frying. They suggested that the formation was associated with the smoking process. Pensabene and Fiddler (1983b) also reported that 23 of 70 cured products other than bacon contained 1.7–19 μg/kg of N-nitrosothiazolidine. The average levels were slightly below those found for bacon products. Mandagere et al. (1984) used a model system containing nitrite, cysteamine, cysteine, or cystine along with wood smoke condensate to investigate the role of the smoking process. This work confirmed that the smoking process gave the highest levels of N-nitrosothiazolidine and indicated that formaldehyde derived from the smoke probably reacted with cysteamine to form the precursor amine. They also suggested that cysteine could react with formaldehyde to form thiazolidine carboxylic acid which could then be nitrosated to form N-nitrosothiazolidine carboxylic acid.

Sen et al. (1985a) confirmed the presence of this N-nitrosamino acid in both raw and fried bacon at levels ranging from 20 to 14,000 μg/kg and suggested that at least part of the N-nitrosothiazolidine in fried bacon could result from decarboxylation of N-nitrosothiazolidine carboxylic acid in a manner analogous to the formation of N-nitrosopyrrolidine. As evidence for this suggestion, they spiked raw bacon with N-nitrosothiazolidine carboxylic acid and found a 1.5–3.1% conversion rate to N-nitrosothiazolidine. Mandagere et al. (1984) suggested that decarboxylation could occur during frying if sufficiently high temperatures were reached but that this mechanism does not explain the finding of N-nitrosothiazolidine in raw bacon. Fiddler et al. (1986) separated pork bellies into lean and adipose fractions and cured, smoked, and analyzed each for N-nitrosothiazolidine. Only the lean fraction contained the N-nitrosamine, which was interpreted as evidence that the precursors must be hydrophilic.

Pensabene and Fiddler (1985) analyzed several cured meat products for N-nitrosothiazolidine carboxylic acid and found all samples positive at levels ranging from 8 to 1400 μg/kg. Using model systems these workers concluded that decarboxylation mechanisms did not contribute significant amounts of N-nitrosothiazolidine formation and that the most likely mechanism is the reaction of formaldehyde with cysteamine followed by nitrosation of the resulting thiazolidine. Sen et al. (1986a), on the other hand, recently found that the level of N-nitrosothiazolidine in fried bacon correlated with the concentration of N-nitrosothiazolidine carboxylic acid but not N-nitrosothiazolidine in the raw bacon. They interpreted this as evidence that decarboxylation of N-nitrosothiazolidine carboxylic acid during frying was the primary mechanism of formation of N-nitrosothiazolidine. They suggested that procedural differences in frying or analysis might be responsible for the discrepancy. It may be that N-nitro-sothiazolidine can be formed by both mechanisms and that the predominating mechanism depends on the relative concentration of the two precursors.

Massey *et al.* (1985) confirmed the presence of hydroxyalkyl derivatives of N-nitrosothiazolidine carboxylic acid in smoked bacon. Ikins *et al.* (1986) have shown that higher homologs of formaldehyde can result in alkylnitro-sothiazolidine formation. This group also showed that incorporation of liquid smoke into the cure mix reduced the overall formation of N-nitrosamines when compared to the traditional wood smoke process.

C.   REGULATION OF NITRITE AND NITRATE IN FOODS

The U.S. Department of Agriculture has issued regulations concerning the N-nitrosamine content of fried bacon and has set requirements for the addition of nitrite, ascorbate, and other additives. The N-nitrosamine content of fried bacon is not permitted to be above 10 $\mu g/kg$. In practice, the Food Safety and Inspection Service of the U.S. Department of Agriculture takes action when samples reach 17 $\mu g/kg$. This is the level at which there is statistical confidence that the sample is at least 10 $\mu g/kg$ based on the precision of the analyses. These regulations were published in 1978 (*Federal Register*, **43**, 20992) and require the addition of 120 mg/kg of sodium nitrite (or equivalent potassium nitrite) along with 550 mg/kg of sodium ascorbate.

More recently, the U.S. Department of Agriculture promulgated new regulations which gave bacon producers more latitude in their formulations (*Federal Register*, **51**, 21731, 1986). These regulations permit a reduction in the level of sodium nitrite to 100 mg/kg if the manufacturer participates in a quality control program. A further reduction in the ingoing sodium nitrite (or equivalent potassium nitrite) to 40 mg/kg along with the addition of sugar and lactic acid bacteria cultures is also available. This so-called Wisconsin Process has been shown to reduce the residual nitrite content and, hence, the N-nitrosamine content of the fried bacon while continuing to provide protection against botulism. It is not clear at this time how many producers will adopt this program.

D.   OTHER CURED MEATS

The N-nitrosamine content of cured meats other than fried bacon has been investigated. Most investigators have concluded that these products do not routinely contain volatile N-nitrosamines, even when fried. Fazio *et al.* (1973) suggested that N-nitrosamines might be formed during the frying of cured meats but that they would be carried off with the vapor. Fiddler *et al.* (1974) analyzed fried ham, Canadian bacon, and beef bacon and did not find N-nitrosopyrrolidine in the edible or fried-out fat portions. They suggested that these products contained lower amounts of the precursors to *N*-nitrosopyrrolidine and that this might explain the failure to form *N*-nitrosamines when fried. This same group expanded this work to include other cured meats and found most, with the exception of dry-cured ham and bacon, to be essentially free of *N*-nitrosamines.

Sen *et al.* (1979) conducted a more extensive study in which 64 various cured meats were analyzed before and after cooking. Only 8 samples had volatile *N*-nitrosamine contents above 1 μg/kg, and frying increased the *N*-nitrosamine content in only 2 samples. The authors concluded that only fried bacon contains significant levels of *N*-nitrosamines but did not explain why similar products such as fried ham do not contain *N*-nitrosamines. Ellen *et al.* (1986) recently surveyed 140 samples representing 16 types of cured meat products available in the Dutch market. Only a few samples had *N*-nitrosamine levels above 1 μg/kg. A meat industry trade group (Nitrite Safety Council, 1980) surveyed several cured products beside bacon and concluded that cooking does not cause volatile *N*-nitrosamine formation in products such as sausages and that only a few dry-cure products contain significant levels of *N*-nitrosamines.

We have investigated the formation of *N*-nitrosamines in cured products during frying by trapping the vapors above the pan (Hotchkiss and Vecchio, 1985). Most cured products formed volatile *N*-nitrosamines; up to 4,000 ng/100 g of raw product, when fried. However, virtually all of the *N*-nitrosamine was carried off with the vapor during frying, leaving only trace amounts behind. We suggested that bacon represents a unique example in that it is the only product that continues to be fried well after all of the water has been driven off. Other cured meats form *N*-nitrosamines, but the water vapor removes them from the edible portion during frying. This difference can also be explained in part by the fact that water may partially inhibit nitrosation.

E.   CHEESE

Nitrate is added to certain cheeses in order to inhibit the growth of *Clostridia* bacteria which produce gas and a defect in ripened cheese known as late blowing (Vos, 1948). While not permitted in the United States, nitrate is more commonly used in some European cheeses, particularly Gouda and Edam types. This has lead to the possibility that *N*-nitrosamines might be formed (Gray *et al.*, 1979). Crosby *et al.* (1972) found *N*-nitrosodimethylamine in 6 of 12 cheeses analyzed, but Goodhead *et al.* (1976) could not confirm *N*-nitrosodimethylamine in 9 European Gouda cheeses at a sensitivity of 1 μg/kg. This same group later reported that 9 of 58 cheeses contained *N*-nitrosodimethylamine in the range of 1–5 μg/kg. Havery *et al.* (1976) could not detect volatile *N*-nitrosamines in 17 cheeses analyzed at a sensitivity of 10 μg/kg. Sen *et al.* (1978) reported that cheeses available in Canada contained small amounts of volatile *N*-nitrosamines. They surveyed 31 imported and 31 domestic varieties that included 5 Edam/

Gouda types. Of the imported cheeses, 21 contained one or more N-nitrosamines while 5 of the domestic cheeses were positive. There was no clear correlation between nitrite levels or nitrate use and the N-nitrosamines. Elgersma *et al.* (1978) came to a similar conclusion after a collaborative study. The National Food Institute of Denmark (NFI, 1980) has made an extensive study of N-nitrosamines in cheese made in Denmark. Of the nearly 400 samples analyzed, 17% contained volatile N-nitrosamines above 1 μg/kg. No apparent correlation between the use of nitrate and the occurrence of the N-nitrosamine could be made.

The above studies lead to the conclusion that cheese sporadically contains very small amounts of volatile N-nitrosamines, but there does not appear to be a strong correlation with the practice of adding nitrate to prevent late blowing. While the source of the N-nitrosamines is unclear, as is pointed out below, drying dairy products by direct-heated flame can result in N-nitrosamine formation. If dried ingredients such as powdered milk were used in cheese, then N-nitrosamines might be present.

F.   FISH PRODUCTS

U.S. Food and Drug Administration regulations (CFR 172.160; 172.170; 172.175; 172.177) permit the use of nitrate and/or nitrite as curing agents for certain fish products such as cod roe and several types of smoked fish. These same regulations permit the sale of meat-curing preparations containing nitrite/nitrate that are intended for home curing. This practice should, however, be discouraged in light of the original finding that this led to liver disease in animals (see above). Pedersen and Meyland (1981) surveyed pickled herring products to which nitrate had intentionally been added and found that several samples contained volatile N-nitrosamines but at levels of less than 1 μg/kg and only 6 of 34 samples had more than 1 μg/kg. No correlation with residual nitrite or nitrate was apparent.

IV.   OCCURRENCE RELATED TO PROCESSING

A.   MALT AND MALT BEVERAGES

For several years it was believed that N-nitrosamines occurred in foods primarily as a result of the intentional addition of nitrite (Scanlan, 1975). However, in 1979 Spiegelhalder *et al.* reported that several brands of beer available in Germany contained an average of 2.7 μg/kg of N-nitrosodimethylamine. This concentration of N-nitrosamine is lower than that found in fried bacon, but overall exposure from beer could be much greater because a larger mass of beer may be consumed compared to bacon. For example, a single serving of beer (500 ml, 2.8 μg/kg) could contain 1,400 ng of N-nitrosamine while a single serving (25 g, 10 μg/kg) of bacon might contain 250 ng. Spiegelhalder *et al.* (1980) concluded that beer represented 64% of the dietary exposure to preformed N-nitrosamines in the German diet. Walker *et al.* (1979) have similarly concluded that the major source of dietary N-nitrosamine exposure in Normandy, France, was due to alcoholic beverage consumption. This finding led to the conclusion that certain food processing operations, especially drying, could lead to the formation of volatile N-nitrosamines in foods. McWeeny (1983) has briefly reviewed N-nitrosamines in beverages.

Several surveys of beers from throughout the world have been reported. These reports are summarized in Table III. They have confirmed that N-nitrosodimethylamine was present in beers produced throughout the world and that all types of beer were contaminated. In the first report, Spiegelhalder *et al.* (1979) speculated that the N-nitrosamine was formed during the brewing process and that malt may provide the precursor amine. Scanlan *et al.* (1980) suggested, on the basis of preliminary data, that the malt was the source of the N-nitrosamine but that it was formed during the kilning or drying process used in malt manufacture and not during the brewing process. Several investigations have confirmed this suggestion (Hotchkiss *et al.*, 1980).

Preussmann *et al.* (1981) investigated the brewing process and determined that malt was the only source of N-nitrosodimethylamine and that contaimination resulted from the addition of N-nitrosamine with the malt, not the formation of N-nitrosamine during the brewing process. They also determined that the N-nitrosamine was formed as a result of the kilning process. Pale malts which were dried in kilns in which the air was heated by a direct open flame had as much as 80 times more N-nitrosodimethylamine than malts dried in indirectly heated kilns. Darker malts, which are kilned to higher temperatures, had as much as 160 times more N-nitrosamine than malt from indirectly heated kilns. These findings were confirmed by Kann *et al.* (1980) in the Soviet Union and by the brewing industry in the United States (Hardwick *et al.*, 1982).

The U.S. Food and Drug Administration conducted a large survey of malts produced and imported into the United States in 1980. These malts were collected after the industry had taken significant measures to reduce the N-nitrosamine content of malt. A total of 120 domestic samples representing 32 manufacturers and 78 lots of imported malt were analyzed (Havery *et al.*, 1981). The average N-nitrosamine content of the domestic and imported samples were 5 and 6 μg/kg, respectively. The highest sample was a domestic sample at 86 μg/kg. Malt is normally used in beer at a 1 : 10 (w/v) dilution which means that beer made from these malts would contain on the average less than 1 μg/kg N-nitrosodimethylamine. Several samples contained trace amounts of N-nitrosopyrrolidine. Similar results have been reported for malt and beer available in New

TABLE III

VOLATILE NITROSAMINES IN BEERS

Survey and type of beer	Origin	Number positive/ number analyzed	NDMA[a]	
Goff and Fine (1979)				
Light	I[b]	7/7	2.5	(0.5–5.2)
Dark	I	3/3	2.1	(0.4–5.3)
Lager	I	1/1	1.8	(NR[c])
Ale	I	1/1	6.4	(NR)
Light	U.S.	4/4	3.5	(0.9–7)
Dark	U.S.	2/2	2.3	(1.4–3.1)
Scanlan et al. (1980)				
Lager	U.S.	14/15	7.7	(ND[d]–14)
Low-calorie	U.S.	2/3	4.0	(ND–7)
Ale	U.S.	2/2	5.0	(3–7)
Dark	U.S.	2/2	0.7	(0.5–0.8)
Malt liquor	U.S.	3/3	2.8	(0.5–5)
Spiegelhalder et al. (1979)				
Lager	—	47/76	1.2	(ND–6.5)
Ales	—	1/8	0.2	(NR)
Strong lager	—	18/23	2.0	(ND–5.0)
Dark	—	19/21	6.8	(ND–47)
Alcohol-free	—	4/6	1.6	(ND–4.0)
Special	—	22/24	6.8	(ND–68)
Walker et al. (1979)				
Beer	European	63/75	1.8	(ND–11)
Kann et al. (1980)				
Ale	U.S.S.R.	58/89	6.5	(ND–45)
Porter	U.S.S.R.	25/55	17	(ND–56)
Kawabata et al. (1980)				
Beer	—	27/29	—	(ND–>5.0)
Sen et al. (1980a)				
Regular	I	5/6	1.4	(ND–3.3)
Regular	Canada	10/10	1.6	(0.6–4.9)
Dark	Canada	3/3	1.8	(1.6–2.6)
Dark	I	3/3	2.3	(0.5–4.3)
Havery et al. (1981)				
Lager	U.S.	78/105	<1	(ND–9)
Light	U.S.	26/36	<1	(ND–4)
Malt liquor	U.S.	9/13	<1	(ND–3)
Nonalcoholic	U.S.	2/6	<1	(ND–3)
Bock	U.S.	4/5	<1	(ND–<1)
Dark	U.S.	2/4	1	(ND–3)
Ale	U.S.	7/11	<1	(ND–2)
Lager	I	51/59	1	(ND–4)
Dark	I	10/11	2	(ND–8)
Ale	I	5/6	3	(ND–13)
Malt liquor	I	1/2	<1	(ND–1)
Bock	I	2/2	<1	(ND–1)

[a] N-Nitrosodimethylamine in μg/kg, average (range).
[b] Imported into the United States.
[c] Not reported.
[d] Not detected.

Zealand (Weston, 1983a). Other workers have subsequently shown that malt also contains *N*-nitrosamino acids. Sen *et al.* (1983) have found that direct flame-dried malt contains *N*-nitrosoproline at a mean concentration of 24 μg/kg and that beer contains one-tenth this amount, as expected.

Scanlan and co-workers have extensively studied the formation of *N*-nitro-sodimethylamine during the kilning process. They compared the *N*-nitrosamine content of barley before and after conversion into malt and found an increase of up to 54 μg/kg in direct-fired kilns (Mangino *et al.*, 1981). It is now clear that oxides of nitrogen (NO_x) are produced during combustion and that these oxides can readily N-nitrosate amines which are endogenous to the malt (Wainright, 1986a). O'Brien *et al.* (1980) have sampled a single lot of malt during the kilning process and have found that over half of the *N*-nitrosodimethylamine was formed during the last 6 hr of a 42-hr kilning cycle, when the moisture content was the lowest.

Several reports detailing analytical methods for volatile *N*-nitrosamines in malt and malt-containing products have been published. Hotchkiss *et al.* (1980) found that water must be added to dried malt in order to achieve adequate recoveries of *N*-nitrosodimethylamine by the mineral oil distillation procedure, and Weston (1983a) has detailed an extraction method using water as the solvent with subsequent solvent extraction and analysis by HPLC. Sen and Seaman (1981b) investigated an atmospheric distillation from alkaline solution to determine *N*-nitrosamines in beer. Havery *et al.* (1981) published a rapid column elution method in which *N*-nitrosamines were extracted from beer after mixing with diatomaceous earth and packing the semidry material into a glass column. Several of these methods have been collaboratively tested (Marinelli, 1980). Nearly all methods rely on the TEA for detection of the *N*-nitrosamine.

Brewing organizations throughout the world have undertaken research programs to find ways to reduce the *N*-nitrosamine content of malt without changing the character of the beer and have suggested several methods. Three of these methods have proven feasible. The first is to alter the construction of the kiln so that the drying gases are not directly heated by the open flame but are instead heated in a heat exchanger. This means that the by-products of combustion do not directly contact the malt. This is the most effective and widely adopted method and has resulted in very low to nondetectable *N*-nitrosamine levels in malt. However, malt houses located in areas where there is atmospheric pollution can still produce malts with detectable levels of *N*-nitrosamines due to the residual NO_x in the air and the very large volumes of gas drawn through the malt bed in a normal drying cycle. This method also has the disadvantage of cost arising from capital investment and higher operating costs owing to lower fuel efficiency.

Low temperature gas burners which produce lower levels of NO_x in the heated air have been commercially introduced (Altemark *et al.*, 1980). These burners are designed to burn oxygen rich and at temperatures lower than the 1500–

1800°C found in the conventional burners. Lower temperatures favor a reduction in the formation of nitrogen oxides and, hence, lower the N-nitrosamine content of the dried malt (Wainwright, 1981).

The third method to reduce the N-nitrosamine content of malt is to treat the malt with sulfur dioxide during the kilning process. Sulfur dioxide had been used in the malting process on a limited basis for several years to increase the yield during brewing (Hough et al., 1971). When investigating the occurrence of N-nitrosamines in malt, Preussmann et al. (1981) noted that malts which had been treated with sulfur dioxide were generally lower in N-nitrosamine content. They suggested that this might be an effective way to reduce N-nitrosamine formation. Sulfur dioxide may be added either by burning sulfur or sulfur compounds in the flame or by directly adding sulfur dioxide gas from a compressed gas bottle to the heated gases prior to contacting the malt. The latter method affords more precise control of application rates. Lukes et al. (1980) determined that a residual sulfur dioxide content of 30 mg/kg in the malt resulted in an N-nitrosamine level of less than 10 µg/kg and that residual levels of less than 30 mg/kg gave a proportionately higher N-nitrosamine content. There is also a relationship between the time of sulfur application and the amount of N-nitrosamine formed; application during the first few hours of kilning has been reported to be the most effective (Wainwright, 1986b). Two mechanisms of N-nitrosamine inhibition may be operating simultaneously; first, the pH at the surface of the malt may be lowered, and, second, sulfur dioxide reduces nitrogen dioxide (NO_2) to the much poorer N-nitrosating agent nitric oxide (NO). The use of sulfur dioxide has at least two disadvantages; it is itself an atmospheric pollutant, and it is corrosive.

Malt contains at least four amines which might serve as precursors to N-nitrosodimethylamine formation: dimethylamine, trimethylamine, hordenine, and gramine. The last two compounds are alkaloids formed during the germination process (Kirkwood and Marion, 1950). Mangino and Scanlan (1985) have studied the nitrosation of these two alkaloids in detail and have shown that gramine was N-nitrosated at a rate equivalent to dimethylamine, even though gramine is a tertiary amine. Hordenine was nitrosated at a rate equivalent to trimethylamine. These authors concluded that both gramine and hordenine must be considered as potential precursors to N-nitrosodimethylamine in malt, but others (Slack and Wainwright, 1980) have considered hordenine to be the most likely precursor based on its higher concentration in malt. These workers have shown that hordenine could form N-nitrosodimethylamine on treatment with oxides of nitrogen.

Mangino and Scanlan (1985) have correctly pointed out that the relative contribution of each amine to N-nitrosamine formation will depend not only on their relative concentrations in malt but on their relative rates of reaction. Haley and Palmer (1985) have presented evidence that the N-nitrosodimethylamine content of malt does not correlate with the hordenine content and that insufficient amounts of gramine are present to account for the N-nitrosamine formed. They suggest an unknown intermediate in amine metabolism may be the precursor. Gramine is biosynthesized from tryptophan, and, after nitrosation to form N-nitrosodimethylamine, the possibility exists that the indole ring might be N-nitrosated to form a nonvolatile N-nitroso compound. Ahmad et al. (1985) have presented evidence that in a model system gramine does form N-nitroso-3-nitro-methylindole. These authors point out that this nonvolatile compound would not be detected in beer by current analytical methods.

In addition to beer, a few other foods containing malt and additional alcoholic beverages have been surveyed for volatile N-nitrosamines. Goff and Fine (1979) analyzed 53 wines, sherries, liqueurs, gins, brandies, vodkas, rums, and whiskys for volatile N-nitrosamines with the result that all were negative except for the Scotch whiskys. The finding of N-nitrosodimethylamine in Scotch whiskys is not surprising in that it contains malt. Sen et al. (1980a) made similar observations for other alcoholic beverages. Walker et al. (1979) found low levels (<1 μg/kg) of several volatile N-nitrosamines in alcoholic beverages including distilled spirits, ciders, and brandies. Havery et al. (1981) surveyed 44 samples (28 brands) of Scotch whisky and found 28 positive with a N-nitrosodimethylamine content below 1 μg/kg. Weston (1984) analyzed several foods that contained barley malt such as vinegar, breakfast cereal-type products, malt concentrates, and baked products. Only occasionally were volatile N-nitrosamines found and at levels less than 1 μg/kg in most cases.

B. DRIED PRODUCTS

The knowledge that the drying process could lead to the formation of carcinogenic N-nitrosamines in malt attracted attention to other dried foods. In addition to malt, Sen and Seaman (1981a) analyzed dried soups, nonfat milk powder, instant coffee, powdered infant formulas, and dried baby cereals. All 11 nonfat milk powders analyzed were positive as were 5 of 10 instant coffees and 3 of 10 infant formulas, all at levels of 1 μg/kg or less. Libbey et al. (1980) found 8 of 9 dried dairy products positive for N-nitrosodimethylamine, which were confirmed by mass spectrometry. Levels ranged from not detectable to 4.5 μg/kg. Havery et al. (1982) made similar observations on a U.S. nationwide survey that included 57 samples, 48 of which were positive for N-nitrosodimethylamine at an average concentration of 0.6 μg/kg. Weston (1983b) observed only traces of N-nitrosamine in milk powders manufactured in New Zealand. Most authors have suggested that the low levels of N-nitrosamines result from the drying process and that the difference between malt and dairy products relates to the temperatures reached during drying and to the initial amine content of each product. However, Lakritz and Pensabene (1981) claimed that pasteurized fluid, but not raw, milk products contained sufficient N-nitrosamine to account for the N-nitrosamine levels seen in dried products. This finding has not been confirmed.

Occasional reports that other foods contain N-nitrosamines as result of processing or preparation have appeared. Fazio and Havery (1982) found 0.3 and <0.1 μg/kg N-nitrosodimethylamine in soy protein isolates and concentrates that had been dried by direct-flame techniques. N-nitrosomorpholine was confirmed in one sample. Several soy-containing products were also analyzed and a few found to contain volatile N-nitrosamines at levels of less than 1 μg/kg. Dried cheeses were analyzed with similar results. Weston (1984) found dried maize meal and wheaten corn flour samples to contain 2.6 and 4.2 μg/kg of N-nitrosodimethylamine, respectively, presumably from the drying process. Gray *et al.* (1981a) suggested that the use of steam during the smoking process can result in the formation of N-nitrosomorpholine after finding this N-nitrosamine in a chicken frankfurter. Morpholine is a common additive to boiler steam.

C.   DRIED OR COOKED FISH PRODUCTS

Several reports have indicated that processed and/or cooked fish products can contain trace amounts of volatile N-nitrosamine due to processing or preparation. Using an electrolytic conductivity detector, Gadbois *et al.* (1975) investigated the N-nitrosamine content of fish which had been treated with 0–530 mg/kg of sodium nitrite prior to smoking. N-Nitrosodimethylamine increased from not detectable to 8.2 μg/kg as the level of nitrite increased. Huang *et al.* (1977, 1981) analyzed several samples of traditional salt-preserved fish products before and after cooking. In their first study, 8 of 11 salted fish products contained N-nitrosodimethylamine, with the highest sample being an anchovy at 35 μg/kg. In the later work, raw, steamed, and fried Chinese-type salted fish were analyzed. All samples contained N-nitrosodimethylamine either before or after cooking, but with only three exceptions were the levels above 1 μg/kg.

Havery and Fazio (1977) did not detect volatile N-nitrosamines in 78 samples of 26 different varieties of finfish products. The limit of their detection was 10 μg/kg, however, and unconfirmable peaks were seen at or near this level. Iyengar *et al.* (1976) found volatile N-nitrosamines in 15 of 29 raw and cooked fish products, but most were at levels too low to confirm. Later this same group surveyed 63 fish products including smoked, dried and salted, canned, and fresh samples (Sen *et al.*, 1985b). N-Nitrosodimethylamine was found in 85% of the smoked samples, while most canned and all fresh samples were negative. Only seven samples contained >1 μg/kg; the highest was 4.2 μg/kg. The authors concluded that N-nitrosamines are more likely to form in dried and salted fish, albeit at very low levels.

Kawabata *et al.* (1980) have demonstrated that broiling fish under a gas flame can result in an increase in the N-nitrosodimethylamine and N-nitrosopyrrolidine content of the fish. The highest levels were found when dried squid was broiled, up to 313 μg/kg. Further studies by this same group have indicated that the mechanism may be analogous to malt in that oxides of nitrogen react with amines derived from the fish (Matsui *et al.*, 1984). Key *et al.* (1982) compared the *N*-nitrosodimethylamine content of several fish products before and after cooking in gas or electrically heated ovens and concluded that while there was a small (<0.5 μg/kg in most cases) increase in the *N*-nitrosamine content of the gas-cooked fish, it was not significant compared to the variation in the *N*-nitrosamine content of the raw fish. These findings are contradictory to those of Kawabata *et al.* (1980) and could be explained by differences in cooking procedures or in the sulfur content of natural gas in Japan and the United Kingdom.

The above-cited studies lead to the conclusion that food processing, particularly drying in a direct-heated flame, can result in the formation of low μg/kg amounts of volatile and possibly nonvolatile *N*-nitrosamines in foods. The amount of *N*-nitrosamine formed appears to depend on the temperature of the flame, the amine content of the product, and the time that the product contacts the hot gases. Processes in which foods are exposed to directly heated gases should be considered as potential sources of dietary *N*-nitrosamines. This is especially true for foods with relatively high amine contents.

V. INDIRECT CONTAMINATION

A. RUBBER PRODUCTS

Recently it has become apparent that preformed *N*-nitrosamines can become food contaminants through indirect addition to the food as opposed to formation during processing. This is a relatively new discovery, and considerably less work has been conducted in the area of the migration *N*-nitrosamines to foods and beverages including water.

It has been known for several years that potentially toxic substances can migrate from food contact surfaces to foods (Crosby, 1981), but this was not thought to be a route by which *N*-nitroso compounds contaminated foods. The first information indicating that a food contact surface might contain *N*-nitrosamines came from Yeager *et al.* (1980). They found that several elastomer products contained volatile *N*-nitrosamines in the high hundreds of μg/kg range and that these *N*-nitrosamines migrated to the air around rubber processing equipment. Earlier, Fajen *et al.* (1979) had found airborne *N*-nitrosamines in rubber tire plants. Shortly after their report on the *N*-nitrosamine content of elastomers, this same group found that the *N*-nitrosamines could be extracted from common rubber products including baby bottle nipples and determined that the source of the *N*-nitrosamine was the dialkylamino vulcanization accelerators used to manufacture rubber products (Ireland *et al.*, 1980). This lead to the possibility that human foods might be contaminated as a result of contacting rubber products. These findings were confirmed by Preussmann *et al.* (1981), who found that dialkyl-*N*-nitrosamines migrated from rubber to a synthetic saliva mixture containing nitrite and suggested that *N*-nitrosamines could also be formed in the saliva from the dialkylamines. They further suggested that such rubber products be reformulated with accelerators that do not form stable *N*-nitrosamines, such as primary amines.

Workers at the U.S. Food and Drug Administration have published several reports that clearly demonstrate the migration of *N*-nitrosamines to foods in contact with rubber products, especially baby bottle nursing nipples (Havery and Fazio, 1982). This report demonstrated that sterilizing milk in contact with a rubber nursing nipple resulted in the migration of *N*-nitrosamines to the milk. Even 2 hr of contact with a nipple at room temperature resulted in migration. This led the Food and Drug Administration to conduct a small survey of rubber nipples (Havery and Fazio, 1983). Several volatile *N*-nitrosamines were found at levels up to 387 µg/kg. These values are similar to those reported by Babish *et al.* (1983), who also confirmed that the *N*-nitrosamines would migrate to water in contact with the rubber. The Food and Drug Administration later promulgated regulations requiring that the sum of the volatile *N*-nitrosamine content of nursing nipples be below 60 µg/kg (*Federal Register* **48,** 57014, 1983). A large compliance survey found that by April 1984 only 1 of 189 samples did not meet this requirement (Havery *et al.*, 1985). Later, the requirement was reduced to 10 µg/kg (*Federal Register* **49,** 26149, 1984). Similar regulations were issued in the United States for infant rubber pacifiers (*Federal Register* **48,** 56988, 1983). Analytical methods to quantify volatile *N*-nitrosamines in nursing nipples have been collaboratively tested (Gray and Stachiw, 1987).

Workers in the Health Protection Branch of Health and Welfare Canada have documented a similar decrease in the *N*-nitrosamine content of nipples and pacifiers available in Canada (Sen *et al.*, 1985c). This group used an *in vitro* method to demonstrate that several common foods might serve to inhibit the formation of *N*-nitrosamines in the stomach from amines ingested as a result of using rubber nursing nipples. The *in vitro* system used did not take into account the fact that an infant's stomach pH is considerably higher than an adult's and often colonized by bacteria which are capable of forming nitrite.

Recently, Sen *et al.* (1986b) have shown that hams and other cured meats which are held in rubber netting during the smoking process can contain low levels of *N*-nitrosodibutylamine arising from migration. The outer layer of the product can contain higher levels than inner layers. In addition, dibutylamine may migrate from the rubber and subsequently be nitrosated during processing (Sen *et al.*, 1986b).

B. PACKAGING

Hoffmann *et al.* (1982) and Hotchkiss and Vecchio (1983) independently demonstrated that many paper-based packaging materials are contaminated with morpholine and N-nitrosomorpholine. Hoffmann *et al.* (1982) suggested that this might be the source of N-nitrosomorpholine in tobacco snuff and that the morpholine came from the wax used on the paperboard snuff container. They also found that certain foods including butter, cream cheese, yogurt, cottage cheese, frozen vegetables, and semi-soft cheeses contained traces of N-nitrosomorpholine as a result of migration from the packaging material. The containers contained up to 17,000 μg/kg of morpholine. Hotchkiss and Vecchio (1983) examined 34 different paper-based food packages and found 9 to be contaminated with trace to 33 μg/kg levels of N-nitrosomorpholine. All materials analyzed contained morpholine up to 800 μg/kg. Migration of both the amine and the N-nitroso derivative were demonstrated.

Sen and Baddoo (1986) have recently presented evidence that migration may explain why certain edible oils occasionally contain volatile N-nitrosamines. This followed earlier work of Hedler *et al.* (1979) which indicated that edible oils contained N-nitrosodimethylamine and N-nitrosodiethylamine up to 28 μg/kg. Fiddler *et al.* (1981) made a similar survey and found N-nitrosodimethylamine in several samples but all at levels of 1 μg/kg or less. They suggested that the results of Hedler *et al.* (1979) were due to artifactual formation during analysis. Sen and Seaman (1981c) also repeated the work of Hedler *et al.* (1979) and found all samples to be negative with the exception of one butter and five margarine samples which contained up to 3.8 μg/kg of N-nitrosomorpholine. As Sen and Baddoo (1986) have pointed out, N-nitrosomorpholine in margarine and butter likely results from migration from waxed paper packaging. Differences in the packaging material may explain the discrepancies in the literature.

C. OTHER INDIRECT SOURCES

Other indirect routes of possible contamination of foods by N-nitroso compounds have been investigated and should be considered. For example, Ross *et al.* (1977) published data which demonstrated that certain pesticides used on food crops contained up to 150 mg/kg of volatile N-nitrosamines. This was of concern because these compounds might expose applicators to undue risks and residues of N-nitrosamines might remain on edible portions of the plants. The possibility also exists that pesticides containing an N-nitrosatable amine or amide function might be nitrosated in the environment or *in vivo*. Oliver (1981) has discussed these possibilities in detail. While the environmental formation of N-nitroso compounds has been demonstrated (Oliver and Kontson, 1978), the compounds are also susceptible to environmental decomposition by several mechanisms including photolysis, microbial degradation, and plant metabolism. These factors appear to limit the environmental consequences of pesticide-derived N-nitroso compounds. Ross et al. (1978) examined a tomato field for dialkyl-N-nitrosamines after applying a dinitroaniline-type herbicide that was contaminated with 154 mg/kg N-nitrosodipropylamine. No residues of the N-nitrosamine could be detected in the air, soil, irrigation water, or crops immediately after application. The authors suggested that the N-nitrosamine might have been volatilized on application. The N-nitrosamine contamination of commercial pesticide formulations has been reduced considerably through process modifications (Probst, 1981). To date, no food product has been shown to contain a N-nitroso compound as a result of the application of pesticides.

Kimoto et al. (1980) have shown that the treatment of water with ion-exchange resins can result in the addition of small amounts (<1 μg/kg) of N-nitrosodimethylamine. If this water were used in foods, then the food might contain detectable N-nitrosamines. In most cases, however, the levels would likely be too low for detection.

D.   MICROBIAL ACTIVITY

Exposure to N-nitroso compounds as a result of microbial activity has also been of research interest. This indirect route of exposure may be of more importance in the endogenous formation of N-nitroso compounds and less important as a route by which foods are contaminated. There is little doubt that active bacteria cultures can facilitate N-nitrosation by reducing nitrate to nitrite, by lowering the pH of the medium, or by producing compounds which are catalytic to N-nitrosation. Direct catalysis of N-nitrosation by microorganisms is less straightforward. Several early workers in this area claimed a direct role for bacteria in N-nitrosation. Ralt and Tannenbaum (1981) and Archer (1984) have reviewed several of these reports and point out that in most cases controls were not properly established, the decrease in pH of the medium as a result of the growth of the organisms was not accounted for, or the methods used to detect the formation of the N-nitrosamines were not specific. They concluded that the major role of bacteria in N-nitrosation was to reduce nitrate to nitrite and to lower the pH of the medium.

More recently, Leach et al. (1985) used short-term experiments with resting cells of Escherichia coli in pH 7 buffer to demonstrate catalytic formation of N-nitrosamines from the corresponding amine and nitrite. They concluded that catalysis had occurred, on the basis of the kinetic data which were not characteristic of normal N-nitrosation chemistry and the fact that the pH optima were near neutrality and not as acid as would be expected. They suggested that the data could best be explained by enzymatic catalysis. Whether or not bacteria play a role in the indirect exposure to N-nitroso compounds requires further research.

VI. RELATIVE HUMAN EXPOSURE FROM FOODS

Humans are exposed to N-nitroso compounds from a surprisingly large number of sources in addition to foods (Table IV), and in order to put exposure through foods in perspective the relative exposures from these sources should be considered. Preussmann and Eisenbrand (1984) have divided these exposures into two main categories; exogenous exposure and endogenous exposure. The first group covers intake of N-nitroso compounds due to life-style sources including food, tobacco, cosmetics, drugs, pesticides, indoor room air, and household goods. All of these substances had been shown to contain N-nitroso compounds at one time. Exogenous exposure also occurs as a result of occupational exposure, particularly from such industries as rubber manufacturing, leather tanning, chemical manufacture using amines, and metalworking. Exposure from these sources has been quantitatively reduced by modifying life-styles and occupational habits and through regulatory action. Endogenous exposure results from the ingestion of both N-nitrosating agents and amines/amides or their precursors. Recent evidence suggests that N-nitrosating agents may be themselves endogenously synthesized. These precursors can combine within the body

TABLE IV

ESTIMATED DAILY EXPOSURE TO VOLATILE NITROSAMINES FOR U.S. RESIDENTS[a]

Source	Nitrosamine[b]	Route	Daily intake[c]
Occupational	NDMA, NDELA	Inhalation/dermal	Up to 440[d]
Cigarettes	NDMA, NDEA, TSN, NDELA, NPYR	Inhalation	17
Automobile interiors	NDMA, NMOR	Inhalation	0.2–0.5
Beer	NDMA	Ingestion	0.34
Fried bacon	NDMA, NPYR	Ingestion	<0.17
Scotch whisky	NDMA	Ingestion	<0.03

[a] Adapted from NAS–NRC (1981).

[b] Abbreviations: NDMA, N-nitrosodimethylamine; NDEA, N-nitrosodiethylamine; NDELA, N-nitrosodiethanolamine; NPYR, N-nitrosopyrrolidine; NMOR, N-nitrosomorpholine: TSN, tobacco-specific nitrosamines.

[c] In μg/day/person.

[d] Only for persons working in selected industries.

to form N-nitroso compounds (Ohshima and Bartsch, 1981). The significance of any one of these exposures will depend on the amount and type of N-nitrosamine to which an individual is exposed. While precise data on the amount and structure of N-nitrosamine exposure by source are not available, an ordering of the degree of exposure from each source is possible. The report of the National Academy of Sciences deals in depth with the relative levels of human exposure for each known route of exposure (Table IV). Tannenbaum (1983) has pointed out in a recent discussion of the various sources of human exposure, that assessment of an individual's overall exposure must take into account life-style, workplace, and endogenous factors.

Developments in analytical methods have allowed a comprehensive survey of human exposure to preformed volatile N-nitrosamines, but nonvolatiles are beyond the capability of current methods so such data are not available. Occupational exposures, for those individuals working in such environments, represents the highest levels of exposure. For example, McGlothin et al. (1981) found N-nitrosomorpholine levels of up to 250 $\mu g/m^3$ in the air of rubber tire processing plants. Spiegelhalder and Preussmann (1982) have found levels as high as 4700 $\mu g/m^3$. Rounbehler et al. (1979) found up to 47 $\mu g/m^3$ N-nitrosodimethylamine in the ambient air of several leather tanneries. Fine et al. (1980) estimated that this results in a maximum daily exposure of up to 440 μg/person/day for people working in such settings. The lubricating oils used in machine shops have been shown to contain up to 3% N-nitrosodiethanolamine (Spiegelhalder and Preussmann, 1984) which could result in an extremely high exposure for those who had their hands in such fluid daily.

Tobacco products contain considerable amounts of N-nitroso compounds and as such represent the highest level of human exposure with the possible exception of the occupational environments listed above. For example, Brunnemann et al. (1985) found that chewing tobacco routinely contained volatile N-nitrosamines in the 10–100 $\mu g/kg$ range as well as tobacco-specific N-nitrosamines, which are also potent animal carcinogens, in the 1,000–10,000 $\mu g/kg$ range. Other tobacco products, including cigarette smoke, contain substantial amounts of carcinogenic N-nitrosamines. The committee of the National Academy of Sciences (NAS–NRC, 1981) estimated that cigarette smoking contributed a total exposure of 17 μg/person/day for those who smoke, based on the data of Hoffmann et al. (1981). This is greater than 10 times the estimated exposure from fried bacon.

Beer has been estimated to be the next highest source of N-nitrosamine exposure at just under 1 μg/person/day, based on the N-nitrosodimethylamine levels reported in 1979. As has been pointed out above, however, changes in the manufacture of malt have resulted in substantial reductions in the N-nitrosamine content of beer. While no large surveys have been reported since the early 1980s, it is likely that the N-nitrosamine content of beer is well below 1 $\mu g/kg$ which would result in a current exposure of less than 0.2 μg/person/day. Scotch whisky probably does not now contribute significant amounts of volatile N-nitrosamines for similar reasons.

The National Academy of Sciences committee estimated that for a cosmetic user, the average daily exposure to N-nitrosodiethanolamine is 0.41 μg/person/day, based on an N-nitrosamine content of 11 μg/kg and a cosmetic usage of 2 g/day. However, the N-nitrosamine content of cosmetics varies by at least an order of magnitude in both directions (Spiegelhalder and Preussmann, 1984).

As pointed out above, the principle source of volatile N-nitrosamines from foods (excluding beer) is fried bacon. There is some dispute about the contribution of fried bacon to dietary N-nitrosamine exposure. The National Academy of Sciences committee estimated that bacon contributes 0.17 μg/person/day. We have suggested that the procedures used to calculate this number were incorrect and that the number is less than one-half this value (Vecchio et al., 1986). The American Meat Institute has estimated that fried bacon contributes even less N-nitrosamine to the diet. Other foods would contribute a relatively small fraction of that found in bacon. The National Academy of Sciences committee estimated that beer and cured meats were the principal sources of dietary N-nitrosamines and that, combined, they contributed a daily exposure of 0.51 μg/person/day. This number probably overestimates current exposure to volatile N-nitrosamines because of reductions in the N-nitrosamine content of beer and fried bacon. This is approximately 8% of the daily exposure from cigarette smoking and approximately the same level estimated for a daily exposure from new car interiors (NAS–NRC, 1981).

It is not possible to estimate exposure to N-nitrosamines that may be endogenously formed. This results from the extraordinarily rapid metabolism of dialkylnitrosamines. Gombar et al. (1986) have recently shown that the mean systemic clearance of N-nitrosodimethylamine from blood at a dose of 1 mg/kg was 57 ml/min/kg. This means that N-nitrosamines formed in the gut would be metabolized at a rate equal to their formation and, therefore, may not be detectable in blood or urine. Ohshima and Bartsch (1981) have developed a method which does allow some insight into the endogenous formation of N-nitrosamines. This method is based on the excretion of the N-nitrosamino acid N-nitrosoproline. This N-nitrosamine is not metabolized and is quantitatively excreted in the urine and can thus be taken as a measure of the extent of endogenous N-nitrosation (Wagner and Tannenbaum, 1985). This work has shown that normal healthy adults excrete a basal level of over 3 μg of N-nitrosoproline/day which cannot be accounted for in the diet. We have recently confirmed these findings (Leaf et al., 1987) and have suggested that this results from endogenous nitrosation and represents a significant exposure. This exposure appears to be at least 10 times the exposure to preformed N-nitrosamines in foods.

VII. FUTURE RESEARCH TRENDS

Considerable literature on the occurrence of volatile N-nitrosamines in foods is available. Most western foods have been analyzed for the presence of volatile N-nitrosamines, and an understanding of the mechanisms by which they become part of some foodstuffs has emerged. It is now possible to estimate mean daily exposures. There is little question that this has resulted in a decrease in exposure. Unfortunately, it is not possible to quantify total exposure because analytical methods for nonvolatile N-nitroso compounds have not been developed. This area has been sorely neglected. It is possible that nonvolatile compounds make up a greater exposure than the volatiles. If screening methods for nonvolatile compounds were developed as they are for volatiles, it would be possible to assess total human exposure. As Scanlan and Reyes (1985) have pointed out, analytical procedures for nonvolatile N-nitroso compounds must first be developed and refined before quantitative data can be gathered. Of particular importance is the development of methods for N-nitrosamides.

The second related area in need of further research concerns the effect of general diet and specific foods on the endogenous formation N-nitroso compounds. It has been established that N-nitrosamino acids are formed *in vivo*, but whether other carcinogenic compounds are formed and in what quantity is unknown. Neither reliable qualitative nor quantitative data are available. These data must be available before the importance, if any, of endogenous N-nitrosation in the development of human cancer can be assessed. An improved animal model for studying the endogenous formation of N-nitroso compounds, particularly carcinogenic N-nitrosamides, will have to be developed along with analytical methods. These two areas present the greatest research challenges related to N-nitroso compounds and foods over the next several years.

ACKNOWLEDGMENT

The assistance of T. J. Fowler in preparing the manuscript is gratefully acknowledged as is the research support of the U.S. Department of Agriculture and the National Cancer Institute (Grant 1 R01 CA40833).

REFERENCES

Ahmad, M. U., Libbey, L. M., Barbour, J. F., and Scanlan, R. A. 1985. Isolation and characterization of products from the nitrosation of the alkaloid gramine. *Food Chem. Toxicol.* **23,** 841.
Altemark, V. D., Hess, R., and Sommers, H. 1980. Wege zum nitrosaminfreien Bier. *Monatsschr. Brau.* **Nov.,** 415.

Althorpe, J., Goddard, D. A., Sissons, D. J., and Telling, G. M. 1970. The gas chromatographic determination of nitrosamines at the picogram level by conversion to their corresponding nitramines. *J. Chromatogr.* **53**, 371.

Amundson, C. M., Sebranek, J. G., Rust, R. E., Kraft, A. A., Wagner, M. K., and Robach, M. C. 1981. Effect of belly composition on sorbate-cured bacon. *J. Food Sci.* **47**, 218.

Anderson, L. M., Priest, L. J., and Budinger, J. M. 1979. Lung tumorigenesis in mice after chronic exposure in early life to a low dose of dimethylnitrosamine. *J. Natl. Cancer Inst.* **62**, 1353.

Archer, M. C. 1982. Reactive intermediates from nitrosamines. *In* "Biological Reactive Intermediates—II. Chemical Mechanisms and Biological Effects" (R. Snyder, D. V. Park, J. J. Kocsis, D. J. Jollow, C. G. Gibson, and C. M. Witmer, eds.), p. 1027. Plenum, New York.

Archer, M. C. 1984. Catalysis and inhibition of N-nitrosation reactions. *In* "*N*-Nitroso Compounds: Occurrence, Biological Effects and Relevance to Human Cancer" (I. K. O'Neill, R. C. Von Borstel, C. T. Miller, J. Long, and H. Bartsch, eds.), p. 263. International Agency for Research on Cancer, Sci. Publ. No. 57, Lyon.

Archer, M. C., Clarke, S. D., Thilly, J. E., and Tannenbaum, S. R. 1971. Environmental nitroso compounds: Reaction of nitrite with creatine and creatinine. *Science* **174**, 1341.

Archer, M. C., Tannenbaum, S. R., Fan, T. Y., and Weisman, M. 1975. Reaction of nitrite with ascorbate and its relation to nitrosamine formation. *J. Natl. Cancer Inst.* **54**, 1203.

Archer, M. C., Tannenbaum, S. R., and Wishnok, J. S. 1976. Nitrosamine formation in the presence of carbonyl compounds. *In* "Environmental *N*-Nitroso Compounds. Analysis and Formation" (E. A. Walker, P. Bogovski, and L. Griciute, eds.), p. 141. International Agency for Research on Cancer, Sci. Publ. No. 14, Lyon.

Astill, B. D. 1978. Antioxidants and *N*-nitrosamine formation. *J. Am. Oil Chem. Soc.* **55**, 248A.

Babish, J. G., Hotchkiss, J. H., Wachs, T., Vecchio, A. J., Guntenmann, W. H., and Lisk, D. J. 1983. *N*-Nitrosamines and mutagens in rubber nursing nipples. *J. Toxicol. Environ. Health* **11**, 167.

Baker, J. K., and Ma, C. Y. 1978. Determination of *N*-nitrosoproline in meat samples. *J. Agric. Food Chem.* **26**, 1253.

Barnes, J. M., and Magee, P. N. 1954. Some toxic properties of dimethylnitrosamine. *Br. J. Ind. Med.* **11**, 167.

Bauman, P. A., Hotchkiss, J. H., and Parker, R. S. 1985. Metabolism of *N*-nitroso-*n*-propylamine and *N*-nitrosodiallylamine by isolated rat hepatocytes. *Cancer Lett.* **28**, 229.

Bernthal, P. H., Gray, J. I., Mandagere, A. K., Ikins, W. G., Cuppett, S. L., Booren, A. M., and Price, J. F. 1986. Use of antioxidant-coated salts as *N*-nitrosamine inhibitors in dry- and brine-cured bacon. *J. Food Protect.* **49**, 58.

Bharucha, K. R., Cross, C. K., and Rubin, L. J. 1979. Mechanism of *N*-nitrosopyrrolidine formation in bacon. *J. Agric. Food Chem.* **27**, 63.

Bharucha, K. R., Cross, C. K., and Rubin, L. J. 1980. Long-chain acetals of ascorbic and erythrobic acid as antinitrosamine agents for bacon. *J. Agric. Food Chem.* **28**, 1274.

Bharucha, K. R., Cross, C. K., and Rubin, L. J. 1985. Ethoxyquin, dihydroethoxyquin, and analogues as antinitrosamine agents for bacon. *J. Agric. Food Chem.* **33**, 834.

Bharucha, K. R., Cross, C. K., and Rubin, L. J. 1986. *p*-Alkoxyanilines as antinitrosamine agents for bacon. *J. Agric. Food Chem.* **34**, 814.

Bills, D. D., Hildrum, K. I., Scanlan, R. A., and Libbey, L. M. 1973. Potential precursors of *N*-nitrosopyrrolidine in bacon and other fried foods. *J. Agric. Food Chem.* **21**, 876.

Binkerd, E. F., and Kolari, O. E. 1975. The history and use of nitrate and nitrite in curing of meat. *Food Cosmet. Toxicol.* **13**, 655.

Bogovski, P., Preussmann, R., and Walker, E. A., eds. 1972. "*N*-Nitroso Compounds—Analysis and Formation." International Agency for Research on Cancer, Sci., Publ. No. 3, Lyon.

Bonnett, R., Chandra, S., Charalam, A. A., Sales, K. D., and Scourides, P. A. 1980. Nitrosation and nitrosylation of hemoproteins and related compounds. *J. Chem. Soc. Perkin 1,* 1706.

Brunnemann, K. D., Genoble, L., and Hoffman, D. 1985. *N*-Nitrosamines in chewing tobacco: An international comparison. *J. Agric. Food Chem.* **33**, 1178.

Canas, B. J., Havery, D. C., Joe, F. L., and Fazio, T. 1986. Current trends in levels of volatile *N*-nitrosamines in fried bacon and fried-out bacon fat. *J. Assoc. Off. Anal. Chem.* **69**, 1020.

Casado, J., Mosquera, M., Paz, L. C., Prieto, M. F. R., and Tato, J. V. 1984a. Nitrite ion as a nitrosating reagent. Nitrosation of morpholine and diethylamine in the presence of formaldehyde. *J. Chem. Soc. Perkin 2*, 1963.

Casado, J., Lorenzo, F. M., Mosquera, M., and Prieto, M. F. R. 1984b. A kinetic study of the influence of alcohols on the nitrosation of morpholine in acid media. Equilibrium constants for the formation of alkyl nitrites. *Can. J. Chem.* **62**, 136.

Cassens, R. G., Woolford, G., Lee, S. H., and Goutefongea, R. 1977. Fate of nitrite in meat. *Proc. Int. Symp. Nitrite Meat Prod., 2nd PUDOC, Wageningen*, p. 95.

Cassens, R. G., Ito, T., Lee, M., and Buege, D. 1978. Use of nitrite in meat. *Bioscience* **28**, 633.

Cassens, R. G., Greaser, M. L., Ito, T., and Lee, M. 1979. Reactions of nitrite in meat. *Food Technol.* **33**, 46.

Challis, B. C. 1973. Rapid nitrosation of phenols and its implications for health hazards from dietary nitrites. *Nature (London)* **244**, 466.

Challis, B. C., 1981. The chemistry of formation of *N*-nitroso compounds. *In* "Safety Evaluation of Nitrosatable Drugs and Chemicals" (G. G. Gibson, and C. Ioannides, eds.), pp. 16–55. Taylor & Francis, London.

Challis, B. C., and Butler, A. R. 1968. Substitution at an amino nitrogen *In* "The Chemistry of the Amino Group" (S. Patai, ed.), p. 277. Wiley (Interscience), New York.

Challis, B., and Kyrtopoulos, S. A. 1978. The chemistry of nitroso compounds. Part 12. The mechanism of nitrosation and nitration of aqueous piperidine by gaseous dinitrogen tetroxide and dinitrogen trioxide in aqueous alkaline solutions. Evidence for the existence of molecular isomers of dinitrogen tetroxide and dinitrogen trioxide. *J. Chem. Soc. Perkin 2*, 1296.

Challis, B. C., Milligan, J. R., and Mitchell, R. C. 1984. Synthesis and stability of *N*-nitrosodipeptides. *J. Chem. Soc., Chem. Commun.*, 1050.

Chu, C., and Magee, P. N. 1981. Metabolic fate of nitrosoproline in the rat. *Cancer Res.* **41**, 3653.

Clydesdale, F. M., and Francis, F. J. 1971. Color measurement of foods. XXVII. Chemistry of meat color. *Food Prod. Dev.* **5**, 81, 87.

Coleman, M. H. 1978. A model system for the formation of *N*-nitrosopyrrolidine in grilled or fried bacon. *J. Food Technol.* **13**, 55.

Collins-Thompson, D. I., and Rodriguez-Lopez, G. 1981. Depletion of sodium nitrite by lactic acid bacteria isolated from vacuum-packaged bologna. *J. Food Prot.* **44**, 593–595.

Crampton, R. F. 1980. Carcinogenic dose-related response to nitrosamines. *Oncology* **37**, 251.

Crosby, N. T. 1976. Nitrosamines in foodstuffs. *Residue Rev.* **64**, 77.

Crosby, N. T. 1981. Food packaging materials. Aspects of analysis and migration of contaminants. *Appl. Sci. (London)*, 190.

Crosby, N. T., Forman, J. K., Palframan, J. F., and Sawyer, R. 1972. Estimation of steam-volatile nitrosamines in foods at the µg/kg level. *Nature (London)* **238**, 342.

Dahn, H., Loewe, L., and Bunton, C. A. 1960. Uber die Oxydation von Ascorbunsäure durch salpetrige Säure. Teil VI: Ubersicht und Diskussion der Ergebnisse. *Helv. Chim. Acta* **43**, 320.

Davies, R., and McWeeny, D. J. 1977. Catalytic effect of nitrosophenols on *N*-nitrosamine formation. *Nature (London)* **266**, 657.

Davies, R., Massey, R. C., and McWeeny, C. 1978. Study of rates of competitive *N*-nitrosation of pyrrolidine, *para*-cresol and *L*-cysteine. *J. Sci. Food Agric.* **29**, 62.

Dennis, M. J., Davis, R., and McWeeny, D. J. 1979. The transnitrosation of secondary amines by *S*-nitrosocysteine in relation to *N*-nitrosamine formation in cured meats. *J. Sci. Food Agric.* **30**, 639.

Dennis, M. J., Massey, R. C., and McWeeny, D. J. 1980. The transnitrosation of *N*-methylaniline by a protein-bound nitrite model system in relation to *N*-nitrosamine formation in cured meats. *J. Sci. Food Agric.* **31,** 1195.

Dennis, M. J., Massey, R. C., and McWeeny, D. J. 1982. The effect of oxygen on nitrosamine formation in bacon. *Z. Lebensm. Unters. Forsch.* **174,** 114.

Devik, O. G. 1967. Formation of *N*-nitrosamines by the Maillard reaction. *Acta Chem. Scand.* **21,** 2302.

Egan, H. 1983. "Environmental Carcinogens Selected Methods of Analysis," Vol. 6, p. 508. International Agency for Research on Cancer, Lyon.

Eisenbrand, G., and Preussmann, R. 1970. Eine neue Methode zur kolorimetrischen Bestimmung von Nitrosaminen nach Spaltung der N-Nitrosagruppe muit Bromowasserstoff in Eisessig. *Arzneim. Forsch.* **20,** 1513.

Elgersma, R. H. C., Sen, N. P., Stephany, R. W., Schuller, P. L., Webb, K. S., and Gough, T. A. 1978. A collaborative examination of some Dutch cheeses for the presence of volatile nitrosamines. *J. Neth. Milk Dairy* 32, 125.

Ellen, G., Egmond, E., and Sahertian, E. T. 1986. *N*-Nitrosamines and residual nitrite in cured meats from the Dutch market. *Z. Lebensm. Unters. Forsch.* **182,** 14.

Ender, F., and Ceh, L. 1968. Occurrence of nitrosamines in foodstuffs for human and animal consumption. *Food Cosmet. Toxicol.* **6,** 569.

Ender, F., Harve, G., Helgebostad, A., Koppang, N., Madsen, R., and Ceh, L. 1964. Isolation and identification of a heptatotoxic factor in herring meal produced from sodium nitrite preserved herring. *Naturwissenschaften* **51,** 637.

Ender, F., Havre, G. N., Madsen, R., Ceh, L., and Helgebostad, A. 1967. Studies on conditions under which *N*-nitrosodimethylamine is formed in herring meal produced from nitrite-preserved herring. *Z. Tierphysiol. Tierernaehr. Futtermittelkd.* **22,** 181.

Fajen, J. M., Carson, G. A., Rounbehler, D. P., Fan, T. Y., Vita, R., Goff, U. E., Wolff, M. H., Edwards, G. S., and Fine, D. H. 1979. *N*-Nitrosamines in the rubber and tire industry. *Science* **205,** 1262.

Fan, T. Y., and Tannenbaum, S. R. 1972. Stability of *N*-nitroso compounds. *J. Food Sci.* **37,** 274.

Fan, T. Y., and Tannenbaum, S. R. 1973a. Factors influencing the rate of formation of nitrosomorpholine from morpholine and nitrite: Acceleration by thiocyanate and other anions. *J. Agric. Food Chem.* **21,** 237.

Fan, T. Y., and Tannenbaum, S. R. 1973b. Natural inhibitors of nitrosation reactions: The concept of available nitrite. *J. Food Sci.* **38,** 1067.

Fazio, T., and Havery, D. C. 1982. Volatile *N*-nitrosamines in direct flame dried processed foods. *In* "*N*-Nitroso Compounds: Occurrence and Biological Effects" (H. Bartsch, M. Castegnaro, I. K. O'Neill, and M. Okada, eds.), p. 277. International Agency for Research on Cancer, Sci. Publ. No. 41, Lyon.

Fazio, T., White, R. H., and Howard, J. W. 1971. Analysis of nitrite- and/or nitrate-processed meats for *N*-nitrosodimethylamine. *J. Assoc. Off. Anal. Chem.* **54,** 1157.

Fazio, T., White, R. H., Dusold, L. R., and Howard, J. W. 1973. Nitrosopyrrolidine in cooked bacon. *J. Assoc. Off. Anal. Chem.* **56,** 919.

Fiddler, W. 1975. The occurrence and determination of *N*-nitroso compounds. *Toxicol. Appl. Pharmacol.* **31,** 352.

Fiddler, W., Pensabene, J. W., Piotrowski, E. G., Doerr, R. C., and Wasserman, A. E. 1973. Use of sodium erythorbate to inhibit formation *N*-nitrosodimethylamine in frankfurters. *J. Food Sci.* **38,** 1084.

Fiddler, W., Pensabene, J. W., Fagan, J. C., Thorne, E. J., Piotrowski, E. G., and Wasserman, A. E. 1974. The role of lean and adipose tissue in the formation of nitrosopyrrolidine in fried bacon. *J. Food Sci.* **39,** 1070.

Fiddler, W., Pensabene, J. W., Piotrowski, E. G., Phillips, J. G., Keating, J., Mergens, W. J., and Newmark, H. L. 1978. Inhibition of formation of volatile nitrosamines in fried bacon by the use of cure-solubilized α-tocopherol. *J. Agric. Food Chem.* **26**, 653.

Fiddler, W., Pensabene, J. W., and Kimoto, W. I. 1981. Investigations of edible oils for volatile nitrosamines. *J. Food Sci.* **46**, 603.

Fiddler, W., Pensabene, J. W., and Gates, R. A. 1986. Role of lean tissue on the formation of *N*-nitrosothiazolidine in raw bacon. *J. Food Sci.* **51**, 514.

Fine, D. H., Rufeh, F., Lieb, D., and Rounbehler, D. P. 1975a. Description of the thermal energy analyzer (TEA) for trace determination of volatile and nonvolatile *N*-nitroso compounds. *Anal. Chem.* **47**, 1188.

Fine, D. H., Rounbehler, D. P., and Oettinger, P. E. 1975b. A rapid method for the determination of sub-part per billion amounts of *N*-nitroso compounds in foodstuffs. *Anal. Chim. Acta* **78**, 383.

Fine, D. H., Fan, S., and La Fleur, A. 1980. *N*-Nitroso compounds as air pollutants. *AIChE Symp. Ser.* **76**, 305.

Fine, D. H., Rounbehler, D. P., Yu, W. C., and Goff, E. U. 1984. A new thermal energy analyzer for direct high-performance liquid chromatographic and gas chromatographic analysis of *N*-nitrosamides. *In* "*N*-Nitroso Compounds: Occurrence, Biological Effects and Relevance to Human Cancer" (I. K. O'Neill, R. C. Von Borstel, C. T. Miller, J. Long, and H. Bartsch, eds.), p. 121. International Agency for Research on Cancer, Sci. Pub. No. 57, Lyon.

Fooladi, M. H., Gray, J. I., Pearson, A. M., and Mandagere, A. K. 1983. An investigation into the potential formation of N-substituted amides and their nitrosated derivatives during the frying of bacon. *J. Agric. Food Chem.* **31**, 527.

Foreman, J. K., and Goodhead, K. 1975. The formation and analysis of *N*-nitrosamines. *J. Sci. Food Agric.* **26**, 1771.

Freimuth, U., and Glaser, E. 1970. Zum Auftreten von Nitrosamune in Lebensmitteln. *Nahrung* **14**, 357.

Freund, H. A. 1937. Clinical manifestations and studies in parenchymatous hepatitis. *Ann. Intern. Med.* **10**, 1144.

Fridman, A. L., Mukahametshin, F. M., and Novikou, S. S. 1971. Advances in the chemistry of aliphatic *N*-nitrosamines. *Russ. Chem. Rev.* **40**, 34.

Frouin, A. 1977. Nitrates and nitrites: Reinterpretation of analytical data by means of bound nitric oxide. *Proc. Int. Symp. Nitrite Meat Produ., 2nd, PUDOC, Wageningen* p. 115.

Fussaenger, R. D., and Ditschuneit, H. 1980. Lethal exitus of a patient with *N*-nitrosodimethylamine poisoning 2.5 years following the first ingestion and signs of intoxication. *Oncology* **37**, 273.

Gadbois, D. F., Ravesi, E. M., Lundstrom, R. C., and Maney, R. S. 1975. *N*-Nitrosodimethylamine in cold-smoked sablefish. *J. Agric. Food Chem.* **23**, 665.

Goff, E. U., and Fine, D. H. 1979. Analysis of volatile *N*-nitrosamines in alcoholic beverages. *Food Cosmet. Toxicol.* **17**, 569.

Gombar, C. T., Harrington, G. W., Pylypiw, H., Bevill, R. F., Thurman, J. C., Nelson, D. R., and Magee, P. N. 1986. Pharmacokinetics of dimethylnitrosamine in swine. *Pan Am. Assoc. Cancer* **27**, 108.

Goodhead, K., and Gough, T. A. 1975. The reliability of a procedure for the determination of nitrosamines in food. *Food Cosmet. Toxicol.* **13**, 307.

Goodhead, K., Gough, T. A., Webb, K. S., Stadhouders, J., and Elgersma, R. H. C. 1976. The use of nitrate in the manufacture of Gouda cheese. Lack of evidence of nitrosamine formation. *J. Neth. Milk Dairy* **30**, 201.

Gough, T. A. 1978. Determination of *N*-nitroso compounds by mass-spectrometry. A review. *Analyst* **103**, 785.

Gough, T. A., McPhail, M. F., Webb, K. S., Wood, B. J., and Coleman, R. F. 1977. An examination of some foodstuffs for presence of volatile nitrosamines. *J. Sci. Food Agric.* **28**, 345.

Goutefongea, R., Cassens, R. G., and Woolford, G. 1977. Distribution of sodium nitrite in adipose tissue during curing. *J. Food Sci.* **42**, 1637.

Gray, J. I. 1976. *N*-Nitrosamines and their precursors in bacon: A review. *J. Milk Food Technol.* **39**, 686.

Gray, J. I. 1977. *N*-Nitrosamine precursors in bacon. Review. *J. Can. Inst. Food Sci. Technol.* **10**, A15.

Gray, J. I., and Collins, M. E. 1977. The development of free proline during the storage of green pork bellies. *J. Can. Inst. Food Sci. Technol.* **10**, 97.

Gray, J. I., and Collins, M. E. 1978. Formation of *N*-nitrosopyrrolidine in fried bacon. *J. Food Protect.* **41**, 36.

Gray, J. I., and Randall, C. J. 1979. The nitrite/*N*-nitrosamine problem in meats: An update. *J. Food Protect.* **42**, 168.

Gray, J. I., and Stachiw, M. A. 1987. Gas chromatographic thermal energy analysis method for determination of volatile *N*-nitrosamines in baby bottle rubber nipples—A collaborative study. *J. Assoc. Off. Anal. Chem.* **70**, 64.

Gray, J. I., Collins, M. E., and Russell, L. F. 1977. Formation of *N*-nitrosohydroxypyrrolidine in model and cured meat systems. *J. Can. Inst. Food Sci. Technol.* **10**, 36.

Gray, J. I., Collins, M. E., and MacDonald, B. 1978. Precursors of dimethylnitrosamine in fried bacon. *J. Food Protect.* **41**, 31.

Gray, J. I., Irvine, D. M., and Kakuda, Y. 1979. Nitrates and *N*-nitrosamines in cheese. *J. Food Protect.* **42**, 263.

Gray, J. I., Bussey, D. M., Dawson, L. E., Price, J. F., and Stevenson, K. E. 1981a. An investigation into the formation of *N*-nitrosamines in heated chicken frankfurters. *J. Food Sci.* **46**, 1817.

Gray, J. I., MacDonald, B., Pearson, A. M., and Morton, I. D. 1981b. Role of nitrite in cured meat flavor: A review. *J. Food Protect.* **44**, 302.

Gray, J. I., Reddy, S. K., Price, J. F., Mandagere, A., and Wilkens, W. F. 1982. Inhibition of *N*-nitrosamines in bacon. *Food Technol.* **36**, 39.

Gray, J. I., Skrypec, D. J., Mandagere, A. K., Booren, A. M., and Pearson, A. M. 1983. Further factors influencing nitrosamine formation in bacon. *In* "*N*-Nitroso Compounds: Occurrence, Biological Effects and Relevance to Human Cancer" (I. K. O'Neill, R. C. Von Borstel, C. T. Miller, J. Long, and H. Bartsch, eds.), p. 301. International Agency for Research on Cancer, Sci. Publ. No. 57, Lyon.

Haley, J., and Palmer, G. 1985. Factors affecting *N*-nitrosodimethylamine development in germinated barley. *J. Sci. Food Agric.* **36**, 471.

Hansen, T., Iwaoka, W., Green, L., and Tannenbaum, S. R. 1977. Analysis of *N*-nitrosoproline in raw bacon—Further evidence that nitrosoproline is not a major precursor of nitrosopyrrolidine. *J. Agric. Food Chem.* **25**, 1423.

Hardwick, W. A., Hickman, D. H., Jangaard, N. O., Ladish, W. J., and Meilgaard, M. C. 1982. *N*-Nitrosodimethylamine in malt beverages—Anticipatory action by the brewing industry. *Reg. Toxicol. Pharmacol.* **2**, 38.

Harris, C. C., Autrup, H., Stoner, G. D., Trump, B. F., Hillman, E., Schafer, P. W., and Jeffrey, A. M. 1979. Metabolism of benzo[*a*]pyrene, *N*-nitrosodimethylamine, and *N*-nitrosopyrrolidine and identification of the major carcinogen–DNA adducts formed in cultured human esophagus. *Cancer Res.* **39**, 4401.

Havery, D. C., and Fazio, T. 1977. Survey of finfish and shellfish for volatile nitrosamines. *J. Assoc. Off. Anal. Chem.* **60**, 517.

Havery, D. C., and Fazio, T. 1982. Estimation of volatile *N*-nitrosamines in rubber nipples for babies' bottles. *Food Chem. Toxicol.* **20**, 939.

Havery, D. C., and Fazio, T. 1983. Survey of baby bottle rubber nipples for volatile *N*-nitrosamines. *J. Assoc. Off. Anal. Chem.* **66**, 1500.

Havery, D. C., and Fazio, T. 1985. Human exposure to nitrosamines from foods. *Food Technol.* **39,** 80.

Havery, D. C., Kline, D. A., Miletta, E. M., Joe, Jr., F. L., and Fazio, T. 1976. Survey of food products for volatile N-nitrosamines. *J. Assoc. Off. Anal. Chem.* **59,** 540.

Havery, D. C., Fazio, T., and Howard, J. W. 1978. Trends in levels of N-nitrosopyrrolidine in fried bacon. *J. Assoc. Off. Anal. Chem.* **61,** 1379.

Havery, D. C., Hotchkiss, J. H., and Fazio, T. 1981. Nitrosamines in malt and malt beverages. *J. Food Sci.* **46,** 501.

Havery, D. C., Hotchkiss, J. H., and Fazio, T. 1982. A rapid method for the determination of volatile N-nitrosamines in nonfat dry milk. *J. Dairy Sci.* **65,** 182.

Havery, D. C., Perfetti, G. A., Canas, B. J., and Fazio, T. 1985. Reduction in levels of volatile N-nitrosamines in rubber nipples for baby bottles. *Food Chem. Toxicol.* **23,** 991.

Hedler, L., and Marquardt, P. 1968. Occurrence of diethylnitrosamine in some samples of food (Review). *Food Cosmet. Toxicol.* **6,** 341.

Hedler, L., Schurr, C., and Marquardt, P. 1979. Determination of volatile N-nitroso compounds in various samples of edible vegetable oils and margarine (commercially available products). *J. Am. Oil Chem. Soc.* **56,** 681.

Herman, H. 1961. Identifizierung eines Stoffwechselproduktes von *Clitocybe* suaveolens als 4-methylnitrosamino-benzaldehyd. *Hoppe-Seylers Z. Physiol. Chem.* **326,** 13.

Herring, H. K. 1973. Effect of nitrite and other factors on the physio-chemical characteristics of nitrosamine formation bacon. *Proc. Meat Ind. Res. Conf., Am. Meat Inst., Chicago,* p. 47.

Heyns, K., and Roper, H. 1970. Ein spezifisches analytisches Nachweisverfahren für Nitrosamine durch Kombination von Gaschromatographie mit der Massenspecktrometrie. *Tetrahedron Lett.* **10,** 737.

Hildrum, K. I., Williams, J. L., and Scanlan, R. A. 1975. Effect of sodium chloride concentration on the nitrosation of proline at different pH levels. *J. Agric. Food Chem.* **23,** 439.

Hoffmann, D., Adams, J. D., Brunnemann, K. D., and Hecht, S. S. 1981. Formation occurrence, and carcinogenicity of N-nitrosamines in tobacco products. *In* "N-Nitroso Compounds" (R. A. Scanlan and S. R. Tannenbaum, eds.), p. 247. American Chemical Society, Washington, D.C.

Hoffmann, D., Brunnemann, K. D., Adams, J. D., Rivenson, A., and Hecht, S. S. 1982. N-Nitrosamines in tobacco carcinogenesis. *In* "Nitrosamines and Human Cancer," Banbury Report No. 12, p. 211 (P. N. Magee, ed.). Cold Spring Harbor Laboratory, Cold Spring Harbor, New York.

Hotchkiss, J. H. 1981. Analytical methodology for sample preparation, detection, quantitation, and confirmation of N-nitrosamines in foods. *J. Assoc. Off. Anal. Chem.* **64,** 1037.

Hotchkiss, J. H., and Vecchio, A. J. 1983. Analysis of direct contact paper and paperboard food packaging for N-nitrosomorpholine and morpholine. *J. Food Sci.* **48,** 240.

Hotchkiss, J. H., and Vecchio, A. J. 1985. Nitrosamines in fried-out bacon fat and its use as a cooking oil. *Food Technol.* **39,** 67.

Hotchkiss, J. H., Barbour, J. F., and Scanlan, R. A. 1980. Analysis of malted barley for N-nitrosodimethylamine. *J. Agric. Food Chem.* **28,** 680.

Hotchkiss, J. H., Vecchio, A. J., and Ross, H. D. 1986. N-Nitrosamine formation in fried-out bacon fat: Evidence for nitrosation by lipid bound nitrite. *J. Agric. Food Chem.* **33,** 5.

Hough, J. S., Briggs, D. E., and Stevens, R. 1971. "Malting and Brewing Science," p. 623. Chapman & Hall, London.

Howard, J. W., Fazio, T., and Watts, J. O. 1970. Extraction and gas chromatographic determination of N-nitrosodimethylamine in smoked fish: Application to smoked nitrite-treated chub. *J. Assoc. Off. Anal. Chem.* **53,** 269.

Huang, D. P., Ho, J. H. C., Gough, T. A., and Webb, K. S. 1977. Volatile nitrosamines in some traditional southern Chinese food products. *J. Food Safety* **1,** 1.

Huang, D. P., Ho, J. H. C., Webb, K. S., Wood, B. J., and Gough, T. A. 1981. Volatile nitrosamines in salt-preserved fish before and after cooking. *Food Cosmet. Toxicol.* **19,** 167.

Huxel, E. T., Scanlan, R. A., and Libbey, L. M. 1974. Formation of *N*-nitrosopyrrolidine from pyrrolidine ring containing compounds at elevated temperatures. *J. Agric. Food Chem.* **22,** 698.

Hwang, L. S., and Rosen, J. D. 1976. Nitrosopyrrolidine formation in fried bacon. *J. Agric. Food Chem.* **24,** 1152.

Ikins, W. G., Gray, J. I., Mandagere, A. K., Booren, A. M., Pearson, A. M., and Stachiw, M. A. 1986. *N*-Nitrosamine formation in fried bacon processed with liquid smoke preparations. *J. Agric. Food Chem.* **34,** 980.

Ingold, C. K. 1969. Substitution at hetero-elements. *In* "Structure and Mechanism in Organic Chemistry," 2nd. Ed., p. 611. Cornell Univ. Press, Ithaca, New York.

Ireland, C. B., Hytrek, F. P., and Lasoski, B. A. 1980. Aqueous extraction of *N*-nitrosamines from elastomers. *J. Am. Ind. Hyg. Assoc.* **41,** 895.

Issenberg, P. 1981. Analytical methods for nitrosamines. *In* "*N*-Nitroso Compounds" (R. A. Scanlan and S. R. Tannenbaum, eds.), p. 331. American Chemical Society, Washington, D.C.

Ito, T., Cassens, R. B., Greaser, M. L., Lee, M., and Izumi, K. 1983. Lability and reactivity of nonheme protein-bound nitrite. *J. Food Sci.* **43,** 1204.

Iyengar, J. R., Panalaks, T., Miles, W. F., and Sen, N. P. 1976. Survey of fish products for volatile *N*-nitrosamines. *J. Sci. Food Agric.* **27,** 527.

Kadar, R., and Devik, O. G. 1970. Pyrazines as interfering substances in the determination of nitrosamines in roasted foods. *Acta Chem. Scand.* **24,** 2943.

Kakuda, Y., and Gray, J. I. 1980a. *N*-Nitrosamides and their precursors in food systems. 1. Formation of N-substituted amides. *J. Agric. Food Chem.* **28,** 580.

Kakuda, Y., and Gray, J. I. 1980b. *N*-Nitrosamides and their precursors in foods. 2. Kinetics of the nitrosation reaction. *J. Agric. Food Chem.* **28,** 584.

Kakuda, Y., Gray, J. I., and Man, L. L. 1980. *N*-Nitrosamines and their precursors in food systems. 3. Influence of pH and temperature on stability of *N*-nitrosamides. *J. Agric. Food Chem.* **28,** 588.

Kann, J., Tauts, O., Kalve, R., and Bogovski, P. 1980. Potential formation of *N*-nitrosamines in the course of technological processing of some foodstuffs. *In* "*N*-Nitroso Compounds: Analysis, Formation, and Occurrence" (E. A. Walker, M. Castegnaro, L. Griciute, and M. Borzsonyi, eds.), p. 319. International Agency for Research on Cancer, Sci. Publ. No. 31, Lyon.

Kanner, J., and Juven, B. J. 1980. *S*-Nitrosocysteine as an antioxidant, color developing, and anticlostridial agent in comminuted turkey meat. *J. Food Sci.* **45,** 1105.

Kawabata, T., Uibu, J., Ohshima, H., Matsui, M., Hamano, M., and Tokiwa, H. 1980. Occurrence, formation and precursors of *N*-nitroso compounds in Japanese diet. *In* "*N*-Nitroso Compounds: Analysis, Formation and Occurrence" (E. A. Walker, M. Castegnaro, L. Griciute, and M. Borzonyi, eds.), p. 481. International Agency for Research on Cancer, Sci. Publ. No. 31, Lyon.

Keefer, L. K., and Roller, P. O. 1973. N-Nitrosation by nitrite ion in neutral and basic medium. *Science* **181,** 1245.

Key, P. E., Baylor, J. M., Massey, R. C., and McWeeny, D. J. 1982. Nitrosodimethylamine levels in fish cooked by natural gas and by electricity. *J. Food Technol.* **17,** 703.

Kim, Y. K., Tannenbaum, S. R., and Wishnok, J. S. 1981. Effects of ascorbic acid on the nitrosation of dialkyl amines. *In* "Ascorbic Acid: Chemistry, Metabolism, and Uses" (P. A. Seib and B. M. Tolbert, eds.), p. 571. American Chemical Society, Washington, D.C.

Kimoto, W. I., and Fiddler, W. 1982. Confirmatory method for *N*-nitrosodimethylamine and *N*-nitrosopyrrolidine in food by multiple ion analysis with gas chromatography—Low resolution mass spectrometry before and after ultraviolet photolysis. *J. Assoc. Off. Anal. Chem.* **65,** 1162.

Kimoto, W. I., Dooley, C. J., Carre, J., and Fiddler, W. 1980. Role of strong ion exchange resins in nitrosamine formation in water. *Water Res.* **14,** 869.

Kimoto, W. I., Pensabene, J. W., and Fiddler, W. 1982. Isolation and identification of *N*-nitrosothiazolidine in fried bacon. *J. Agric. Food Chem.* **30,** 757.

Kirkwood, S., and Marion, L. 1950. The biogenesis of alkaloids. 1. The isolation of *N*-methyltyramine from barley. *J. Am. Chem. Soc.* **72,** 2522.

Kobayashi, K. T., and Kubota, K. 1980. The reaction of nitrogen dioxide with lung surface components: The reaction with cholesterol. *Chemosphere* **9**, 777.

Kubacka, W., and Scanlan, R. A. 1984. Kinetics of nitrosation of four dipeptides N-terminal in proline. *J. Agric. Food Chem.* **32**, 404.

Kuenzig, W., Chau, J., Norkus, E., Holowaschenko, H., Newmark, H., Mergens, W., and Conney, A. H. 1984. Caffeic and ferulic acid as blockers of nitrosamine formation. *Carcinogenesis* **5**, 309.

Kurechi, T., and Kikugawa, K. 1979. Nitrite–lipid reaction in aqueous system: Inhibitory effects on *N*-nitrosamine formation. *J. Food Sci.* **44**, 1263.

Kurechi, T., Kikugawa, K., and Kato, T. 1980. Effect of alcohols on nitrosamine formation. *Food Cosmet. Toxicol.* **18**, 591.

Kurechi, T., Kikugawa, K., Fukuda, S., and Hasunuma, M. 1981. Inhibition of *N*-nitrosamine formation by soya products. *Food Cosmet. Toxicol.* **19**, 425.

Kushnir, I., Feinberg, J. I., Pensabene, J. W., Diotrowski, E. G., Fiddler, W. F., and Wasserman, A. E. 1975. Isolation and identification of nitrosoproline in uncooked bacon. *J. Food Sci.* **40**, 427.

Lakritz, L., and Pensabene, J. W. 1981. Survey of some fluid and nonfat dry milks for *N*-nitrosamines. *J. Dairy Sci.* **64**, 371.

Lakritz, L., Spinelli, A. M., and Wasserman, A. E. 1976. Effect of storage on the concentration of proline and other free amino acids in pork bellies. *J. Food Sci.* **41**, 879.

Leach, S. A., Challis, B. C., Cook, A. R., Hill, M. J., and Thompson, M. H. 1985. Bacterial catalysis of the *N*-nitrosation of secondary amines. *Biochem. Soc. Trans.*, 380.

Leaf, C. D., Vecchio, A. J., Roe, D. A., and Hotchkiss, J. H. 1987. Influence of ascorbic acid dose on *N*-nitrosoproline formation in humans. *Carcinogenesis* **8**, 791.

Lee, J. S., Libbey, L. M., Scanlan, R. A., and Bills, D. D. 1978. Identification and quantification of 3-hydroxy-*N*-nitrosopyrrolidine in fried bacon. *Bull. Environ. Contam. Toxicol.* **19**, 511.

Lee, M. L., Gray, J. I., Pearson, A. M., and Kakuda, Y. 1983a. Formation of *N*-nitrosopyrrolidine in fried bacon: Model system studies. *J. Food Sci.* **48**, 820.

Lee, M. L., Gray, J. I., and Pearson, A. M. 1983b. Effects of frying procedures and compositional factors on the temperature profile of bacon. *J. Food Sci.* **48**, 817.

Libbey, L. M., Scanlan, R. A., and Barbour, J. F. 1980. *N*-Nitrosodimethylamine in dried dairy products. *Food Cosmet. Toxicol.* **18**, 459.

Lijinsky, W., Loo, J., and Ross, A. 1968. Mechanisms of alkylation of nucleic acids by nitroso dimethylamine. *Nature (London)* **218**, 1174.

Lukes, B., O'Brien, T. J., and Scanlan, R. A. 1980. Residual sulfur dioxide in finished malt: Colorimetric determination and relation to *N*-nitrosodimethylamine. *J. Am. Soc. Brew. Chem.* **38**, 146.

McCutcheon, J. W. 1984. Nitrosamines in bacon: A case study of balancing risks. *Public Health Rep.* **99**, 360.

McGlashan, N. D., Walters, C. L., and McLean, A. E. M. 1968. Nitrosamines in African alcoholic spirits and oesophageal cancer. *Lancet 2*, 1017.

McGlothin, J. D., Wilcox, T. C., Fajen, J. M., and Edwards, G. S. 1981. A health hazard evaluation of nitrosamines in a tire manufacturing plant. *In* "Chemical Hazards in the Workplace" (G. Choudhary, ed.), p. 283. American Chemical Society, Washington, D.C.

McWeeny, D. J. 1983. Nitrosamines in beverages. *Food Chem.* **11**, 273.

Maga, J. A. 1978. Simple phenol and phenolic compounds in food flavor. *CRC Crit. Rev. Food Sci. Nutr.* **18**, 323.

Maki, T., Tamura, Y., Shimamura, Y., and Naoi, Y. 1980. Estimate of the volatile nitrosamine content of Japanese food. *Bull. Environ. Contam. Toxicol.* **25**, 257.

Mandagere, A. K., Gray, J. I., Skrypec, D. J., Booren, A. M., and Pearson, A. M. 1984. Role of woodsmoke in *N*-nitrosothiazolidine formation in bacon. *J. Food Sci.* **49**, 658.

Mangino, M., and Scanlan, R. 1985. Nitrosation of the alkaloids hordenine and gramine. Potential precursors of *N*-nitrosodimethylamine in barley malt. *J. Agric. Food Chem.* **33**, 699.

Mangino, M. M., Scanlan, R. A., and O'Brien, T. J. 1981. *N*-Nitrosamines in beer. *In* "*N*-Nitroso Compounds" (R. A. Scanlan and S. R. Tannenbaum, eds.), p. 229. American Chemical Society, Washington, D.C.

Marinelli, L. 1980. *N*-nitrosamines in malt and beer. *J. Am. Soc. Brew. Chem.* **38**, 111.

Massey, R. C., Crews, C., McWeeny, D. J., and Knowles, M. E. 1982a. Analysis of a model ionic nitrosamine by microbore high-performance liquid chromatography using a thermal energy analyzer chemiluminescence detector. *J. Chromatogr.* **236**, 527.

Massey, R. C., Crews, C., and McWeeny, D. J. 1982b. Method for high-performance liquid chromatographic measurement of *N*-nitrosamines in food and beverages. *J. Chromatogr.* **241**, 423.

Massey, R. C., Crews, C., Dennis, M. J., McWeeny, D. J., Startin, J. R., and Knowles, M. E. 1985. Identification of a major new involatile *N*-nitroso compound in smoked bacon. *Anal. Chim. Acta* **174**, 327.

Matsui, M., Ishibashi, T., and Kawabata, T. 1984. Precursors of *N*-nitrosodimethylamine formed in dried squid upon broiling. *Bull. Jpn. Soc. Sci. Fish.* **50**, 155.

Mergens, W. J., and Newmark, H. L., 1980. Antioxidants as blocking agents against nitrosamine formation. *In* "Autoxidation in Food and Biological Systems" (M. G. Simic and M. Karel, eds.), p. 387. Plenum, New York.

Mihara, S., and Shibamoto, T. 1980. Mutagenicity of products obtained from cysteamine–glucose browning model systems. *J. Agric. Food Chem.* **28**, 62.

Miller, A., Pensabene, J. W., Doerr, R., and Fiddler, W. 1985. Apparent mutagenicity of *N*-nitrosothiazolidine caused by a trace contaminant. *Mutat. Res.* **157**, 129.

Mirvish, S. S. 1970. Kinetics of dimethylamine nitrosation in relation to nitrosamine carcinogenesis. *J. Natl. Cancer Inst.* **44**, 633.

Mirvish, S. S. 1975. Formation of *N*-nitroso compounds: Chemistry, kinetics and *in vivo* occurrence. *Toxicol. Appl. Pharmacol.* **31**, 325.

Mirvish, S. S., Wallcave, L., Eagen, M., and Shubik, P. 1972. Ascorbate–nitrite reaction: Possible means of blocking the formation of carcinogenic *N*-nitroso compounds. *Science* **177**, 65.

Mirvish, S. S., Karlowski, K., Sams, J. P., and Arnold, S. C. 1978. Studies related to nitrosamide formation: Nitrosation in solvent: water and solvent systems, nitrosomethylurea, formation in the rat stomach and analysis of a fish product for ureas. *In* "Environmental Aspects of *N*-Nitroso Compounds" (E. A. Walker, M. Castegnaro, L. Griciute, and R. E. Lyle, eds.), p. 283. International Agency for Research on Cancer, Sci. Publ. No. 19, Lyon.

Mirvish, S. S., Sams, J. P., and Arnold, S. D. 1979. Spectrophotometric method for determining ureas applied to nitrosoureas, nitrosocyanamides and a cynamide. *Fresenius Z. Anal. Chem.* **298**, 408.

Mirvish, S. S., Karlowski, K., Cairnes, D. A., Sams, J. P., Abraham, R., and Nielsen, J. 1980. Identification of alkylureas after nitrosation–denitrosation of a bonito fish product, crab, lobster, and bacon. *J. Agric. Food Chem.* **28**, 1175.

Mirvish, S. S., Sams, J. P., and Issenberg, P. 1983. The nitrosating agent in mice exposed to nitrogen dioxide: Improved extraction method and localization in the skin. *Cancer Res.* **43**, 2550.

Mohler, K., and Mayrohfer, U. L. 1968. Detection and determination of nitrosamines in food. *Z. Lebensm. Unters. Forsch.* **135**, 313.

Mottram, D. S. 1984. Organic nitrates and nitrites in the volatiles of cooked cured pork. *J. Agric. Food Chem.* **32**, 343.

Mottram, D. S., and Patterson, R. L. S. 1977. The effect of ascorbate reductants on *N*-nitrosamine formation in a model system resembling bacon fat. *J. Sci. Food Agric.* **28**, 352.

Mottram, D. S., Patterson, R. L., Edwards, R. A., and Gough, T. A. 1977. Preferential formation of volatile *N*-nitrosamines in fat bacon. *J. Sci. Food Agric.* **28**, 1025.

NAS–NRC. 1981. "The Health Effects of Nitrate, Nitrite, and N-Nitroso Compounds." National Academy Press, Washington, D.C.

NAS–NRC. 1982. "Alternatives to the Current Use of Nitrite in Foods." National Academy Press, Washington, D.C.

Nakamura, M., Baba, N., Nakaoka, T., and Wada, Y. 1976. Pathways of formation of N-nitrosopyrrolidine in fried bacon. J. Food Sci. **41**, 874.

NFI. 1980. "Investigations on Formation and Occurrence of Volatile Nitrosamines in Danish Cheese." The National Food Institute, Copenhagen.

Nitrite Safety Council. 1980. A survey of nitrosamines in sausages and dry-cured meat products. Food Technol. **34**, 45.

Normington, K. W., Baker, I., Molina, M., Wishnok, J. S., Tannenbaum, S. R., and Puju, S. 1986. Characterization of a nitrite scavenger, 3-hydroxy-2-pyranone, from Chinese wild plum juice. J. Agric. Food Chem. **34**, 215.

O'Brien, T. J., Lukes, B. K., and Scanlan, R. A. 1980. Control of N-nitrosodimethylamine in malt through the use of liquid/gaseous sulfur dioxide. Mast. Brew. Assoc. Am. Tech. Q. **17**, 196.

Ohshima, H., and Bartsch, H. 1981. Quantitative estimation of endogenous nitrosation in humans by monitoring N-nitrosoproline excreted in the urine. Cancer Res. **41**, 3658.

Olajos, E. J., and Coulston, F. 1978. Comparative toxicology of N-nitroso compounds and their carcinogenic potential to man. Ecotoxicol. Environ. Saf. **2**, 317.

Oliver, J. E. 1981. Pesticide-derived nitrosamines: Occurrence and environmental fate. In "N-Nitroso Compounds" (R. A. Scanlan and S. R. Tannenbaum, eds.), p. 349. American Chemical Society, Washington, D.C.

Oliver, J., and Kontson, A. 1978. Formation and persistence of N-nitrosobutralin in soil. Bull. Environ. Contam. Toxicol. **20**, 170.

Owens, J. L., and Kinast, O. E. 1980. An improved procedure for the determination of volatile N-nitrosamines in bacon grease by using the mineral oil distillation–thermal energy analyzer method. J. Agric. Food Chem. **28**, 1262.

Patterson, R. L. S., Taylor, A. A., Mottram, D. S., and Gough, T. A. 1976. Localized occurrence of N-nitrosopyrrolidine in fried bacon. J. Sci. Food Agric. **27**, 257.

Pedersen, E., and Meyland, I. 1981. Nitrate, nitrite, and volatile nitrosamines in pickled fish prepared with addition of nitrate. Z. Lebensm. Unters. Forsch. **173**, 359.

Pensabene, J. W., and Fiddler, W. 1982. Dual column chromatographic method for determination of N-nitrosothiazolidine in fried bacon. J. Assoc. Off. Anal. Chem. **65**, 1346.

Pensabene, J. W., and Fiddler, W. 1983a. Factors affecting the N-nitrosothiazolidine content of bacon. J. Food Sci. **48**, 1452.

Pensabene, J. W., and Fiddler, W. 1983b. N-Nitrosothiazolidine in cured meat products. J. Food Sci. **48**, 1870.

Pensabene, J. W., and Fiddler, W. 1985. Effect of N-nitrosothiazolidine-4-carboxylic acid on formation of N-nitrosothiazolidine in uncooked bacon. J. Assoc. Off. Anal. Chem. **68**, 1077.

Pensabene, J. W., Fiddler, W., Gates, R. A., and Fagan, J. C. 1974. Effect of frying and other cooking conditions on nitrosopyrrolidine formation in bacon. J. Food Sci. **39**, 314.

Pensabene, J. W., Fiddler, W., Doerr, R. C., Lakritz, L., and Wasserman, A. E. 1975. Formation of dimethylnitrosamine from commercial lecithin and its components in a model system. J. Agric. Food Chem. **23**, 979.

Pensabene, J. W., Feinberg, J. I., Piotrowski, E. G., and Fiddler, W. 1979a. Occurrence and determination of N-nitrosoproline and N-nitrosopyrrolidine in cured meat products. J. Food Sci. **44**, 1700.

Pensabene, J. W., Feinberg, J. I., Dooley, C. J., Phillips, J. G., and Fiddler, W. 1979b. Effect of pork belly composition and nitrite level on nitrosamine formation in fried bacon. J. Agric. Food Chem. **27**, 842.

Pensabene, J. W., Fiddler, W., Miller, A. J., and Phillips, J. G. 1980. Effect of preprocessing procedures for green bellies on *N*-nitrosopyrrolidine formation in bacon. *J. Agric. Food Chem.* **28**, 966.

Pensabene, J. W., Miller, A. J., Greenfield, E. L., and Fiddler, W. 1982. Rapid dry column method for determination of *N*-nitrosopyrrolidine in fried bacon. *J. Assoc. Off. Anal. Chem.* **65**, 151.

Pierson, M. D., and Smoot, L. A. 1982. Nitrite alternatives, and the control of *Clostridium botulinum* in cured meats. *CRC Crit. Rev. Food Sci. Nutr.* **17**, 141.

Pignatelli, B., Friesen, M., and Walker, E. A. 1980. The role of phenols in catalysis of nitrosamine formation. *In* "*N*-Nitroso Compounds: Analysis, Formation and Occurrence" (E. A. Walker, M. Castegnaro, L. Griciute, and M. Borzsonyi, eds.), p. 95. International Agency for Research on Cancer, Sci. Publ. No. 31, Lyon.

Pignatelli, B., Bereziat, J. C., Descotes, G., and Bartsch, H. 1982. Catalysis of nitrosation *in vitro* and *in vivo* in rats by catechin and resorcinol and inhibition by chlorogenic acid. *Carcinogenesis* **3**, 1045.

Preussmann, R., and Eisenbrand, G. 1984. *N*-Nitroso carcinogens in the environment *In* "Chemical Carcinogens" (C. E. Searle, ed.), 2nd Ed., p. 829. American Chemical Society, Washington, D.C.

Preussmann, R., and Stewart, B. W. 1984. *N*-Nitroso carcinogens. *In* "Chemical Carcinogens" (C. E. Searle, ed.), 2nd Ed. American Chemical Society, Washington, D.C.

Preussmann, R., Neurath, G., Wulf-Lorentzen, G., Daiber, D., and Hengy, H. 1964. Methods of colour formation and thin layer chromatography for organic *N*-nitroso compounds. *Fresenius Z. Anal. Chem.* **202**, 188.

Preussmann, R., Spiegelhalder, B., and Eisenbrand, G. 1981. Reduction of human exposure to environmental *N*-nitroso compounds. *In* "*N*-Nitroso Compounds" (R. A. Scanlan and S. R. Tannenbaum, eds.), p. 217. American Chemical Society, Washington, D.C.

Probst, G. W. 1981. Reduction in nitrosamine impurities in pesticide formulations. *In* "*N*-Nitroso Compounds" (R. A. Scanlan and S. R. Tannenbaum, eds.), p. 363. American Chemical Society, Washington, D.C.

Ralt, D., and Tannenbaum, S. R. 1981. The role of bacteria in nitrosamine formation. *In* "*N*-Nitroso Compounds" (R. A. Scanlan and S. R. Tannenbaum, eds.), p. 157. American Chemical Society, Washington, D.C.

Reddy, S. K., Gray, J. I., Price, J. F., and Wilkens, W. F. 1982. Inhibition of *N*-nitrosopyrrolidine in dry cured bacon by α-tocopherol-coated salt systems. *J. Food Sci.* **47**, 1598.

Ridd, J. H. 1961. Nitrosation, diazotisation and deamination. *Q. Rev. Chem. Soc. London* **15**, 418.

Ross, R. D., Morrison, J., Rounbehler, D. P., Fan, T. Y., and Fine, D. H. 1977. *N*-Nitroso compound impurities in herbicide formulations. *J. Agric. Food Chem.* **25**, 1416.

Ross, R., Morrison, J., and Fine, D. H. 1978. Assessment of dipropylnitrosamine levels in a tomato field following application of Treflan EC. *J. Agric. Food Chem.* **26**, 455.

Ross, H. D., Henion, J., Babish, J. G., and Hotchkiss, J. H. 1987. Nitrosating agents from the reaction between methyl oleate and dinitrogen trioxide: Identification and mutagenicity. *Food Chem.* **23**, 207.

Rounbehler, D. P., Krull, I. S., Goff, E. U., Mills, K. M., Morrison, J., Edwards, G. S., and Fine, D. H. 1979. Exposure to *N*-nitrosodimethylamine in a leather tannery. *Food Cosmet. Toxicol.* **17**, 487.

Ruhl, C., and Reusch, J. 1985. Analysis of volatile nitrosamines by microbore high-performance liquid chromatography and thermal energy analyzer detection. *J. Chromatogr.* **328**, 362.

Scanlan, R. A. 1975. *N*-Nitrosamines in foods. *CRC Crit. Rev. Food Technol.* **5**, 357.

Scanlan, R. A., and Libbey, L. M. 1971. *N*-Nitrosamines not identified from heat induced D-glucose/alanine reactions. *J. Agric. Food Chem.* **19**, 570.

Scanlan, R. A., and Reyes, F. G. 1985. An update on analytical techniques for *N*-nitrosoamines. *Food Technol.* **39**, 95.

Scanlan, R. A., Barbour, J. F., Hotchkiss, J. H., and Libbey, L. M. 1980. N-Nitrosodimethylamine in beer. *Food Cosmet. Toxicol.* **18,** 27.

Sen, N. P. 1972. The evidence for the presence of dimethylnitrosamine in meat products. *Food Cosmet. Toxicol.* **10,** 219.

Sen, N. P., and Seaman, S. 1981a. Volatile N-nitrosamines in dried foods. *J. Assoc. Off. Anal. Chem.* **64,** 1238.

Sen, N. P., and Seaman, S. 1981b. Gas–liquid chromatographic–thermal energy analyzer determination of N-nitrosodimethylamine in beer at low parts per billion level. *J. Assoc. Off. Anal. Chem.* **64,** 933.

Sen, N. P., and Seaman, S. 1981c. An investigation into the possible presence of volatile N-nitrosamines in cooking oils, margarine and butter. *J. Agric. Food Chem.* **29,** 787.

Sen, N. P., and Seaman, S. 1984. On-line combination of high-performance liquid chromatography and total N-nitroso determination of N-nitrosamides and other N-nitroso compounds, and some recent data on N-nitrosoproline in foods and beverages. *In* "N-Nitroso Compounds: Occurrence, Biological Effects and Relevance to Human Cancer" (I. K. O'Neill, R. C. Von Borstel, C. T. Miller, J. Long, and H. Bartsch, eds.), p. 137. International Agency for Research on Cancer, Sci. Publ. No. 57, Lyon.

Sen, N. P., and Baddoo, P. A. 1986. Origin of N-nitrosomorpholine contamination in margarine. *J. Food Sci.* **51,** 216.

Sen, N. P., Smith, D. C., Schwinghamer, L., and Morleau, J. J. 1969. Diethylnitrosamine and other N-nitrosamines in foods. *J. Assoc. Off. Anal. Chem.* **52,** 47.

Sen, N. P., Donaldson, B., Charbonneau, C., and Miles, W. F. 1974. Effect of additives on the formation of nitrosamines in meat curing mixtures containing spices and nitrites. *J. Agric. Food Chem.* **22,** 1125.

Sen, N. P., Donaldson, B., Seaman, S., Iyengar, J. R., and Miles, W. F. 1976. Inhibition of nitrosamine formation in fried bacon by propyl gallate and L-ascorbylpalmitate. *J. Agric. Food Chem.* **24,** 397.

Sen, N. P., Coffin, D. E., Seaman, S., Donaldson, B., and Miles, W. F. 1977a. Extraction, cleanup, and estimation as methyl ether of 3-hydroxy-1-nitrosopyrrolidine, a nonvolatile nitrosamine in cooked bacon at mass fractions of μg/kg. *Proc. Int. Symp. Nitrite Meat Produ., 2nd, PUDOC, Wageningen,* p. 179.

Sen, N. P., Donaldson, B., Seaman, S., Collins, B., and Iyengar, J. R. 1977b. Recent nitrosamine analysis in cooked bacon. *J. Can. Inst. Food Sci. Technol.* **10,** A13.

Sen, N. P., Donaldson, B., Seaman, S., Iyengar, J. R., and Miles, W. F. 1978. Recent studies in Canada on the analysis and occurrence of volatile and non-volatile N-nitroso compounds in foods. *In* "Environmental Aspects of N-Nitroso Compounds" (E. A. Walker, M. Castegnaro, L. Griciute, and R. E. Lyle, eds.), p. 373. International Agency for Research on Cancer, Sci. Publ. No. 19, Lyon.

Sen, N. P., Seaman, S., and Miles, W. F. 1979. Volatile nitrosamines in various cured meat products: Effect of cooking and recent trends. *J. Agric. Food Chem.* **27,** 1354.

Sen, N. P., Seaman, S., and McPherson, M. 1980a. Nitrosamines in alcoholic beverages. *J. Food Safety* **2,** 13.

Sen, N. P., Seaman, S., and McPherson, M. 1980b. Further studies on the occurrence of volatile and non-volatile nitrosamines in foods. *In* "N-Nitroso Compounds: Analysis, Formation and Occurrence" (E. A. Walker, M. Castegnaro, L. Griciute, and M. Borzsonyi, eds.), p. 457. International Agency for Research on Cancer, Sci. Publ. No. 31, Lyon.

Sen, N. P., Tessier, L., and Seaman, S. W. 1983. Determination of N-nitrosoproline and N-nitrososarcosine in malt and beer. *J. Agric. Food Chem.* **31,** 1033.

Sen, N. P., Seaman, S. W., and Baddoo, P. A. 1985a. N-Nitrosothiazolidine and nonvolatile N-nitroso compounds in foods. *Food Technol.* **39,** 84.

Sen, N. P., Tessier, L., Seaman, S. W., and Baddoo, P. A. 1985b. Volatile and nonvolatile nitrosamines in fish and the effect of deliberate nitrosation under simulated gastric conditions. *J. Agric. Food Chem.* **33**, 264.

Sen, N. P., Kushwaha, S. C., Seaman, S. W., and Clarkson, S. G. 1985c. Nitrosamines in baby bottle nipples and pacifiers: Occurrence, migration and effect of infant formulas and fruit juices on *in vitro* formation of nitrosamines under simulated gastric conditions. *J. Agric. Food Chem.* **33**, 428.

Sen, N. P., Baddoo, P. A., and Seaman, S. W. 1986a. *N*-Nitrosothiazolidine and *N*-nitrosothiazolidine-4-carboxylic acid in smoked meats and fish. *J. Food Sci.* **51**, 821.

Sen, N. P., Baddoo, P. A., and Seaman, S. W. 1986b. Volatile nitrosamines in cured meats packaged in elastic rubber nettings. *J. Agric. Food Chem.* **35**, 346.

Serrou, B., and Schein, P. 1981. "Nitrosoureas in Cancer Treatment." Elsevier, Amsterdam.

Shuker, D. E. G., and Tannenbaum, S. R. 1983. Determination of nonvolatile *N*-nitroso compounds in biological fluids by liquid chromatography with postcolumn photohydrolysis detection. *Anal. Chem.* **55**, 2152.

Singer, G. M., Chuan, J., Roman, J., Min-Hsin, L., and Lijinsky, W. 1986. Nitrosamines and nitrosamine precursors in foods from Linxian, China, a high incidence area for esophageal cancer. *Carcinogenesis* **7**, 733.

Skrypec, D. J., Gray, J. I., Mandagere, A. K., Booren, A. M., Pearson, A. M., and Cuppett, S. L. 1985. Effect of bacon composition and processing on *N*-nitrosamine formation. *Food Technol.* **39**, 74.

Slack, P. T., and Wainwright, T. 1980. Hordenine as the precursor of NDMA in malt. *J. Inst. Brew.* **87**, 259.

Sofos, J. N., and Busta, F. F. 1980. Alternatives to the use of nitrite as an antibotulinal agent. *Food Technol.* **34**, 244.

Sofos, J. N., Busta, F. F., and Allen, C. E. 1979. Botulism control by nitrite and sorbate in cured meats: A review. *J. Food Prot.* **42**, 739.

Spiegelhadler, B., and Preussmann, R. 1982. Nitrosamines and rubber. *In* "*N*-Nitroso Compounds: Occurrence and Biological Effects" (H. Bartsch, M. Castegnaro, I. K. O'Neill, and M. Okada, eds.), p. 231. International Agency for Research on Cancer, Sci. Publ. No. 41, Lyon.

Spiegelhalder, B., and Preussmann, R. 1984. Contamination of toiletries and cosmetic products with volatile and nonvolatile *N*-nitroso carcinogens. *J. Cancer Res. Clin. Oncol.* **108**, 160.

Spiegelhalder, B., Eisenbrand, G., and Preussmann, R. 1979. Contamination of beer with trace quantities of *N*-nitrosodimethylamine. *Food Cosmet. Toxicol.* **17**, 29.

Spiegelhalder, B., Eisenbrand, G., and Preussmann, R. 1980. Volatile nitrosamines in food. *Oncology* **37**, 211.

Stephany, R. W., and Schuller, P. L. 1980. Daily dietary intakes of nitrate, nitrite, and volatile *N*-nitroso amines in the Netherlands using the duplicate portion sampling technique. *Oncology* **37**, 203.

Swann, P. F. 1975. The toxicology of nitrate, nitrite and *N*-nitroso compounds. *J. Sci. Food Agric.* **26**, 1761.

Tanaka, N., Meske, L., Doyle, M. P., Traisman, E., Thayer, D. W., and Johnston, R. W. 1985. Plant trials of bacon made with lactic acid bacteria, sucrose and lowered sodium nitrite. *J. Food Prot.* **48**, 679.

Tannenbaum, S. R. 1983. *N*-Nitroso compounds: A perspective on human exposure. *Lancet* 19 March, 629.

Telling, G. M., Bryce, T. A., and Althorpe, J. 1971. Use of vacuum distillation and gas chromatography–mass spectrometry for determining low levels of volatile nitrosamines in meat products. *J. Agric. Food Chem.* **19**, 937.

Theiler, R. F., Sato, K., Aspelund, T. G., and Miller, A. F. 1981a. Model system studies on *N*-nitrosamine formation in cured meats: The effect of curing solution ingredients. *J. Food Sci.* **46**, 996.

Theiler, R. F., Aspelund, T. G., Sato, K., and Miller, A. F. 1981b. Model system studies on *N*-nitrosamine formation in cured meats: The effect of slice thickness. *J. Food Sci.* **46**, 691.

Theiler, R. F., Sato, K., Aspelund, T. G., and Miller, A. F. 1984. Inhibition of *N*-nitrosamine formation in a cured ground pork belly model system. *J. Food Sci.* **49**, 341.

Thewlis, B. H. 1967. Testing of wheat flour for the presence of nitrite and nitrosamines. *Food Cosmet. Toxicol.* **5**, 333.

Thewlis, B. H. 1968. Nitrosamines in wheat flour. *Food Cosmet. Toxicol.* **6**, 822.

Tomatis, L., Hilfrich, J., and Turusov, V. 1975. Occurrence of tumors in F_1, F_2, and F_3 descendants of BD rats exposed to *N*-nitrosomethylurea during pregnancy. *Int. J. Cancer* **15**, 385.

Tricker, A. R., Perkins, M. J., Massey, R. C., McWeeny, D. J. 1985a. Some nitrosamino acids in bacon adipose tissue and their contribution to the total *N*-nitroso compound concentration. *Z. Lebensm. Unters. Forsch.* **180**, 379.

Tricker, A. R., Perkins, M. J., Massey, R. C., and McWeeny, D. J. 1985b. *N*-Nitrosopyrrolidine formation in bacon. *Food Add. Contamin.* **2**, 247.

Vecchio, A. J., Hotchkiss, J. H., and Bisogni, C. A. 1986. Ingestion of *N*-nitrosamines from fried bacon: A consumer survey. *J. Food Sci.* **51**, 754.

Vos, E. A. 1948. The influence of potassium nitrate on butyric acid fermentation of cheese. *J. Neth. Milk Dairy* **2**, 223.

Wagner, D. A., and Tannenbaum, S. R. 1985. *In vivo* formation of *N*-nitroso compounds. *Food Technol.* **39**, 89.

Wainwright, T. 1981. Nitrosodimethylamine: Formation and palliative measures. *J. Inst. Brew.* **87**, 264.

Wainwright, T. 1986a. The chemistry of nitrosamine formation: Relevance to malting and brewing. *J. Inst. Brew.* **92**, 49.

Wainwright, T. 1986b. Nitrosamines in malt and beer. *J. Inst. Brew.* **92**, 73.

Walker, E. A., Castegnaro, M., Garren, L., Toussaint, G., and Kowalski, B. 1979. Intake of volatile nitrosamines from consumption of alcohols. *J. Natl. Cancer Inst.* **63**, 947.

Walters, C. L., Edwards, M. W., Elsey, T. S., and Martin, M. 1976. The effect of antioxidants on the production of volatile nitrosamines during the frying of bacon. *Z. Lebensm. Unters. Forsch.* **162**, 377.

Walters, C. L., Hart, R. J., and Perse, S. 1979a. Determination of nitrate at low level without prior extraction and its differentiation from nitrite. *Z. Lebensm. Unters. Forsch.* **169**, 1.

Walters, C. L., Hart, R. J., and Perse, S. 1979b. Possible role of lipid pseudo-nitrosites in nitrosamine formation in fried bacon. *Z. Lebensm. Unters. Forsch.* **168**, 177.

Webb, K. S., and Gough, T. A. 1980. Human exposure to preformed environmental *N*-nitroso compounds in the U.K. *Oncology* **37**, 195.

Weston, R. J. 1983a. *N*-Nitrosamine content of New Zealand beer and malted barley. *J. Sci. Food Agric.* **34**, 1005.

Weston, R. J. 1983b. Trace amounts of nitrosamines in powdered milk and milk proteins. *J. Sci. Food Agric.* **34**, 893.

Weston, R. J. 1984. Analysis of cereals, malted foods and dried legumes for *N*-nitrosodimethylamine. *J. Sci. Food Agric.* **35**, 782.

Williams, D. L. H., and Aldred, S. E. 1982. Inhibition of nitrosation of amines by thiols alcohols and carbohydrates. *Food Chem. Toxicol.* **20**, 79.

Wishnok, J. S., and Richardson, D. P. 1979. Interaction of wheat bran with nitrosamines and with amines during nitrosation. *J. Agric. Food Chem.* **27**, 1132.

Woods, L. F. J., and Wood, J. M. 1982. The effect of nitrite inhibition on the metabolism of *Clostridium botulinum*. *J. Appl. Bacteriol.* **52**, 109.

Woolford, G., and Cassens, R. G. 1977. Fate of sodium nitrite in bacon. *J. Food Sci.* **42**, 586.

Woolford, G., Cassens, R. G., Greaser, M. L., and Sabranek, J. G. 1976. The fate of nitrite: Reaction with protein. *J. Food Sci.* **41**, 585.

Yamamoto, M., Iwata, R., Ishiwata, H., Yamada, T., and Tanimura, A. 1984. Determination of volatile nitrosamine levels in foods and estimation of their daily intake in Japan. *Food Chem. Toxicol.* **22,** 61.

Yeager, F. W., VanGulick, N. N., and Lasoski, B. A. 1980. Dialkylnitrosamines in elastomers. *J. Am. Ind. Hyg. Assoc.* **41,** 148.

DIETARY FIBER: CHEMISTRY, ANALYSIS, AND PROPERTIES

R. R. SELVENDRAN, B. J. H. STEVENS, AND M. S. DU PONT

AFRC Institute of Food Research
Norwich Laboratory
Colney Lane
Norwich NR4 7UA
England

I. INTRODUCTION

A. DIETARY FIBER HYPOTHESIS AND DEFINITION OF DIETARY FIBER

Following the hypothesis of Trowell (1960, 1972a, 1976), Cleave *et al.* (1969), and Burkitt (1973a,b) that the consumption of low fiber diets is a common etiological factor in many metabolic and gastrointestinal diseases of the Western world, there has been a revival of interest in the fiber content of foods and the effects of its intake on man. For a comprehensive list of references on dietary fiber up to 1977 see Trowell (1977). Although the amount of fiber ingested is small in relation to the total diet, fiber appears to exert a major influence on the metabolism of the gastrointestinal tract, and these effects are dictated by the physicochemical properties of the fiber and its components (Kelsay, 1978; Eastwood and Kay, 1979; Anderson, 1985; Southgate, 1986).

Southgate (1982) has made the following two primary statements about the "dietary fiber hypothesis," and these are based on the postulates of Burkitt and Trowell (1975) and Trowell (1976):

1. A diet that is rich in foods which contain plant cell walls (e.g., high-extraction cereals, fruits, and vegetables) is protective against a range of diseases, in particular those prevalent in affluent Western communities (e.g., constipation, diverticular disease, large bowel cancer, coronary heart disease, diabetes, obesity, and gall stones).

2. In some instances a diet providing a low intake of plant cell walls is a causative factor in the etiology of the disease and in others it provides the conditions under which other etiological factors are more active.

The hypothesis, as stated, implies that the essential difference between protective diets and nonprotective diets is the amount of plant cell wall material they provide and that the protection is, or is derived from, the plant cell walls in the diet.

Dietary fiber (DF) was initially defined as the skeletal remains of plant cells, in our diet, that are resistant to hydrolysis by the digestive enzymes of man (Trowell, 1972b, 1974, 1976). The above definition implied that DF is derived primarily from plant cell walls. However, as this definition did not include polysaccharides present in some food additives, such as plant gums, algal polysaccharides, pectins, modified celluloses, and modified starches, Trowell *et al.* (1976) extended the definition to include all the polysaccharides and lignin in the diet that are not digested by the endogenous secretions of the human digestive tract. Accordingly, for analytical purposes, the term DF refers mainly to nonstarchy polysaccharides and lignin in the diet (Southgate, 1976). While the revised definition is generally accepted, it should be borne in mind that the polysaccharides of food additives generally constitute only a very small proportion (<2%) of the DF component of most diets. However, the food additives are commercially available and have structural features similar to those of cell wall components and have therefore served as useful model components in studies on the mode of action of DF. Hence, plant cell walls are the main source of DF, and most of our DF intake comes from the cell walls in foods such as vegetables, fruits, cereal products, and seeds other than cereals. In this context, it should be borne in mind that the composition of plant cell walls depends on the stage of maturity at which the plant organ is harvested.

The principal components of DF are complex polysaccharides, some of which are associated with polyphenolics (which include lignin) and proteins. The noncarbohydrate components of cell walls, such as polyphenolics, protein, cutin, waxes, suberin, phenolic esters, and inorganic constituents, are quantitatively minor constituents of most plant foods, but some of them (e.g., lignin and phenolic esters in lignified tissues of wheat bran, cutin and waxes in leafy vegetables, and suberin in roots and tubers) have significant effects on the properties and physiological effects of DF. Attention will be drawn to these aspects and the digestibility characteristics of crystalline and retrograded starches. Although most of the DF constituents may survive digestion in the proximal gastrointestinal tract, a significant proportion of them are degraded by microorganisms of the human colon (Stephen and Cummings, 1980a,b; Salyers, 1979).

B. SOME GENERAL CONSIDERATIONS AND SCOPE OF THE REVIEW

Understanding of the structure and properties of cell walls from edible plant organs was restricted before the early 1970s by three main factors: (1) cell walls and products derived from them were regarded as nutritionally unimportant and therefore very little encouragement was given for work on cell walls of edible plant tissues; (2) as most plant foods are rich in starch and proteins, the preparation and analysis of cell walls from plant foods proved to be a difficult task; and (3) relatively large amounts of polysaccharides (>100 mg) were required for detailed structural work. This scene has, however, changed over the past 15–20 years because (1) fiber in food is considered to be more important than hitherto; (2) there have been improved methods for the isolation, fractionation, and analysis of cell wall material (CWM) from starch- and protein-rich foods; and (3) the use of improved methods of methylation analysis of polysaccharides, coupled with gas chromatography–mass spectrometry (GC–MS) of the derived products permits the scale of experiments to be reduced so drastically that a few milligrams of material can be made to yield much more information than could be gained previously from work with quantities hundreds of times larger.

Our research group has been actively involved in (1) defining the chemistry of cell walls from a range of plant foods, and also of DF preparations used in clinical feeding trials, (2) analyzing DF by simplified methods, and (3) studying the relevant properties of DF, particularly with reference to adsorption characteristics and bacterial degradation of DF. In view of all these factors, in this article we shall concentrate on the following: (1) developments in the chemistry of cell walls from edible plant organs, (2) improved methods for effectively removing starch to obtain an accurate estimate of the nonstarch polysaccharide content of foods, (3) reassessment of some of the past work on the properties of DF in the light of recent findings (special emphasis will be given to how the recent knowledge enhances our understanding of the fate of DF in the human alimentary tract, particularly the colon), and (4) some aspects of DF which warrant future research. As we have reviewed at length the analysis of cell walls from edible plant organs (Selvendran et al., 1985; Selvendran and O'Neill, 1986) and developments in the analysis of DF (Selvendran and Du Pont, 1984), these aspects, particularly the former, are not discussed at any length, but the relevant developments are referenced throughout the text. The uneven treatment given to the different aspects is partly a reflection of the amount of research in these areas and is partly due to our own research interests.

II. THE MAIN COMPONENTS OF CELL WALLS AND DIETARY FIBER (DF)

The main components which make up DF are summarized in Table I; this lists the types of polymer that can be obtained from the cell walls of parenchymatous, lignified, and cutinized tissues of fruits, vegetables, cereal products, seeds (other than cereals), and also some food additives. The parenchymatous tissues are particularly important in connection with DF, because the walls of these tissues comprise the bulk of the DF from fruits, vegetables, the cotyledons of seeds, and the endosperm of cereals. The parenchymatous tissues have (mainly) thin primary cell walls, whereas the lignified tissues have cell walls which have ceased to grow and have undergone secondary thickening. Although significant amounts of tissues capable of undergoing lignification are present in the leaves (e.g., cabbage), pods (e.g., runner beans), stems (e.g., asparagus), and roots (e.g., carrots), most of these organs are consumed in a relatively immature condition, therefore the vascular bundles, parchment layers, etc. in them are only slightly lignified. Small lignified seeds are consumed when certain fruits (e.g., strawberries) are eaten, but the contribution of the lignified seeds to the total DF of the fruits is generally small. Lignified tissues are, however, of greater importance with some cereal products, e.g., wheat bran and bran-based products and dehulled oat products.

TABLE I

COMPONENTS OF DIETARY FIBER

Main components of a mixed diet	Tissue types	Main constituent groups of DF polymers[a]
Fruits and vegetables	Mainly parenchymatous	Pectic substances (e.g., arabinans and methyl esterified rhamnogalacturonans), cellulose, hemicellulosic polymers (e.g., xyloglucans), and some proteins[b] and phenolics
	Partially lignified vascular tissues	Cellulose, hemicelluloses (e.g., glucuronoxylans), lignin, and some pectic substances and proteins[b]
	Cutinized epidermal tissues	Cutin and waxes
Cereals and products	Parenchymatous (endosperm and aleurone layer)	Hemicelluloses (e.g., arabinoxylans and/or β-D-glucans) and some cellulose, proteins,[b] and phenolics
	Partially lignified seed coats	Hemicelluloses (e.g., glucuronoarabinoxylans), cellulose, lignin, and phenolics and some proteins[b]
Seeds other than cereals (e.g., legume seeds)	Parenchymatous (e.g., pea cotyledons)	Cellulose, pectic substances, hemicelluloses (e.g., xyloglucans) and some proteins[b]
	Cells with thickened endosperm walls (e.g., guar seed splits)	Galactomannans and some cellulose, pectic substances, and proteins[b]
Seed husk of *Plantago ovata* (ispaghula husk)	Mucilage of epidermal cells	Mainly highly branched acidic arabinoxylans
Polysaccharide food additives	—	Food gums—gum arabic, alginates, carrageenan, guar gum, carboxymethylcellulose, modified starches, etc.

[a] The polymers are listed in approximately decreasing order of amounts.

[b] Most of the proteins are present as components of glycoproteins or proteoglycans.

In order to understand the structure and properties of the cell wall, we have to have some idea of the process of wall formation. The mode of formation of cell walls is as follows: On cell division, a cell plate is formed, separating the cells. Pectic substances, particularly calcium salts of pectins, are deposited on this plate to form the middle lamella, and then cellulose, hemicelluloses, additional pectic substances, glycoproteins, proteoglycans, and phenolics are deposited to form the primary cell wall. The primary cell wall is more highly organized than the middle lamella. The pectic material in the middle lamella cements the cells together. The newly formed cells usually increase in length 10- to 20-fold before growth stops. The cellulose is deposited as microfibrils, which are the main structural elements, and these are embedded in an amorphous matrix of closely associated and interlinked macromolecules of pectic substances, hemicellulosic polymers, and glycoproteins, which are bathed in an aqueous medium. In the microfibrils parallel linear chains of cellulose molecules are closely packed by hydrogen bonding into bundles, forming highly ordered structures. Interspersed with these ordered crystalline regions are somewhat disordered amorphous regions in which the chains of cellulose molecules are not closely packed and in which other sugars or polysaccharides may be found. The cellulose microfibrils show wide variations in orientation from predominantly longitudinal in the first formed (outer) layers to predominantly transverse in the last formed (innermost) layers. This arrangement gives what is known as a multinet structure.

Such walls of undifferentiated cells are a major component of DF from edible plant organs. Cells in some regions of the plant, vascular tissues, become differentiated into specialized structures such as the xylem and phloem bundles; these form the veins and ribs of leaves, and continue into the petioles and stems. The xylem cells become thickened and hardened by lignification, as the plant organ matures. Lignification begins in the primary wall region and then extends outward to the middle lamella and inward into the developing secondary wall, the final lignin concentration increasing from the outside to the inside wall. The lignified walls have cellulose microfibrils dispersed in hemicelluloses and lignin. Their structure is roughly analogous to man-made composite systems such as reinforced concrete or glass reinforced plastics, in which the steel and glass are the main structural elements embedded in an amorphous matrix of concrete and plastic, respectively. However, man-made systems are static whereas cell walls are dynamic structures. The relevant information on the biochemical processes that transform primary walls into secondary walls has been summarized in reviews by Northcote (1963, 1969).

The main cell wall polymers of parenchymatous tissues of dicotyledons are pectic substances, hemicelluloses (e.g., xyloglucans), and cellulose, whereas those of lignified tissues are lignin, hemicelluloses (e.g., glucuronoxylans), and cellulose; usually different types of hemicellulosic polysaccharides occur in the cell walls of the two types of tissue. So, while pectic substances predominate in the cell walls of parenchymatous tissues, lignin is a major component of the cell walls of lignified tissues. In contrast to the cell walls of parenchymatous tissues of dicotyledons, those of cereal grains (wheat, barley, etc.) contain very few or no pectic substances (Mares and Stone, 1973a,b; Fincher, 1975; Ballance and Manners, 1978). The primary cell walls of most cereal grains have cellulose microfibrils, which are closely associated with glucomannan, and these fibrillar structures are embedded in an amorphous matrix of hemicelluloses, which consist mainly of arabinoxylans and/or β-D-glucans, some of which are cross-linked by phenolic esters and/or proteins. Rice endosperm walls seem to be intermediate in character between these and parenchyma of dicotyledons in that they contain about 10% of pectic substances and a substantial amount of cellulose

(Shibuya and Iwasaki, 1978; Shibuya and Misaki, 1978). These differences in organization of the cell wall structure are reflected in their overall composition.

The constituents of cell walls therefore fall into three groups: the fibrillar polysaccharides, the matrix polysaccharides, and the encrusting substances (Northcote, 1963, 1972). Fibrillar and matrix polysaccharides are formed simultaneously during wall formation, whereas the encrusting substances, namely, lignins, are formed during secondary thickening of specialized cells. The fibrillar polysaccharides, which are the basic structural units of microfibrils, are made up mainly of cellulose.

The matrix polysaccharides are made up of both linear and slightly branched polymers, which are present at all stages of the development of the wall, and also of highly branched polysaccharides that are deposited at particular stages of growth. At the surface of the microfibril these polysaccharides may be incorporated into its structure. There are two major fractions in the matrix polysaccharides. (1) The pectic substances, which were defined as those polysaccharides that are solubilized from the cell walls by hot aqueous solutions of chelating agents such as ethylenediaminetetraacetate or ammonium oxalate. However, recent work with a range of soft tissues has shown that a significant amount of pectic substances is insoluble in chelating agents, and most of this appears to be held in the cell walls by phenolic and ester cross-links (Selvendran, 1985). (2) The hemicelluloses, which are those polysaccharides solubilized by alkali from the depectinated (and delignified) cell walls. Recent work suggests that some of the alkali-soluble polymers are polysaccharide–protein–polyphenol complexes (O'Neill and Selvendran, 1985a; Selvendran, 1985). In addition to polysaccharides, small amounts of glycoproteins, both hydroxyproline-rich and hydroxyproline-poor, are also present, and the associated sugars in the former are mainly arabinose and galactose (O'Neill and Selvendran, 1980a; Selvendran and O'Neill, 1982).

Water is also an important component of the cell wall, and is present in various amounts, high in the primary cell walls of most tissues, except mature dry seeds, but low in secondary walls. This is because the amount of water within the wall matrix can be partly controlled by the deposition of matrix polysaccharides which form close, intermolecular associations, or by the deposition of a "hydrophobic filler" such as lignin. During the late stages in the development of walls which undergo secondary thickening, the space occupied by water in the wall becomes progressively filled by lignin–polysaccharide complexes. The overall compositions (w/w) of cell walls from parenchymatous and lignified tissues of mature runner bean pods are as follows: primary cell walls—water 70%, cellulose 10%, pectic substances 12%. hemicelluloses 6%, and glycoproteins 2%; secondary cell walls—water 15%, cellulose 35%, lignin 18%, hemicelluloses 25%, pectic substances 5%, and proteins 2% (R. R. Selvendran, unpublished results).

Because the nature of the carbohydrate polymers associated with various types of tissue from dicotyledonous and monocotyledonous plants are different, the polymers present in these species will be discussed separately, with the main emphasis on the cell walls of edible plant organs. The cell walls of mono- cotyledonous plants rich in pectic substances (e.g., immature tissues of onions) are discussed under dicotyledons, because they are highly comparable with them. As several reviews dealing with the chemistry of cell wall polysaccharides are available (Northcote, 1972; Albersheim, 1976; Aspinall, 1980; Darvill *et al.*, 1980; Stephen, 1983; Selvendran, 1983), the chemistry of the individual poly- saccharides will not be described in any detail. However, attention will be drawn to (1) recent developments in the chemistry (and biochemistry) of pectic and hemicellulosic polymers, and (2) certain structural features and properties of the polymers which may be of interest in the context of the analysis of DF, or its mode of action in the human alimentary tract. Where necessary, the cell wall composition of selected tissues (or organs) and DF preparations are discussed briefly to illustrate certain special aspects of DF composition. The structural features of a range of cell wall polysaccharides from edible plant organs are given in Selvendran (1983).

A.   CELL WALLS OF DICOTYLEDONOUS PLANTS

1.   Parenchymatous and Growing Tissues

The dry matter of the cell walls of parenchymatous and growing soft tissues is composed of α-cellulose (35–40%), pectic substances (35–40%), hemicellulosic polymers (10–15%), proteins (5%), and polyphenolics (5–10%); the proteins are present as components of glycoproteins and proteoglycans. Our recent work has focused attention on the occurrence of the polyphenolics, which are present essentially as components of polysaccharide–protein–polyphenolic complexes (Selvendran, 1985). The investigations with suspension culture tissues of spin- ach leaves have served to emphasize the importance of ferulic and *p*-coumaric acids as integral components of the cell wall matrix (Fry, 1982a, 1983), and these findings have been confirmed with studies on the cell walls of sugar beet (Selvendran, 1985).

The relative proportions of the different types of cell wall polymers vary with the type and maturity of the tissue, and a fairly good indication of the nature and amount of polysaccharides present in the cell walls can be obtained from their overall carbohydrate composition (Table II). In this connection see also the tables given in the following references (Ring and Selvendran, 1981; O'Neill and Selvendran, 1983; Stevens and Selvendran, 1984a–d; Aspinall and Fanous, 1984; Redgwell and Selvendran, 1986), which describe the results of purifying cell walls and of chemical fractionation studies. From Table II, columns 2–5, it

TABLE II

CARBOHYDRATE COMPOSITIONS OF CELL WALLS FROM SOME NONLIGNIFIED TISSUES[a]

Sugar[b]	Potatoes[1] (parenchyma)	Apples[2] (parenchyma)	Cabbage[3] (immature leaves)	Onion bulbs[4] (immature tissues)	Potatoes[5] (culture)	Sycamore[6] (culture)	Pea[7] (cotyledons)	Soybean[7] (cotyledons)	Guar[8] seed (whole)	Guar[8] seed (dehusked)
6-Deoxyhexose	2.0	2.0	3.0	1.5	1.5	4.4	2.3	3.6	0.9	0.5
Arabinose	4.6	12.3	12.5	2.0	10.1	21.0	35.0	13.2	3.6	1.9
Xylose	1.7	3.3	4.5	2.3	2.3	7.6	3.7	3.8	5.4	0.4
Mannose	Trace	4.3	2.5	1.2	1.0	0.3	—	—	32.6	50.6
Galactose	28.4	5.7	6.7	26.7	4.1	12.8	4.4	25.4	19.8	30.1
Glucose[c]	31.5	22.7	35.5	24.2	16.2	23.0	21.2	10.2	15.6	2.3
Uronic acids[d]	27.0	32.8	27.8	27.9	17.0	13.4	15.3	16.5	7.8	4.2
Carbohydrate (%, w/w)	(95.2)	(83.1)	(92.5)	(85.8)	(52.2)	(82.5)	(81.9)	(72.7)	(85.7)	(90.0)

[a] References: (1) Ring and Selvendran (1981); (2) Stevens and Selvendran (1984); (3) Stevens and Selvendran (1984); (4) Redgwell and Selvendran (1986); (5) R. R. Selvendran and P. Ryden (unpublished results); (6) Talmadge et al. (1973); (7) Brillouet and Carré (1983); (8) Selvendran (1984).

[b] Values are g anhydrosugar/100 g dry cell walls.

[c] The bulk (~85–90%) of the glucose arises from cellulose, except in the case of peas where it is apparently only ~50%.

[d] The bulk (>90%) of the uronic acid is D-galacturonic acid from pectic material.

can be inferred that the cell walls of parenchymatous and growing tissues contain mainly cellulose, pectinic acid as well as other pectic substances, and small amounts of xyloglucans. The validity of these statements depends on the following: (1) the bulk of the neutral sugars from pectic substances and hemicelluloses are released by hydrolysis with 1 M H_2SO_4 [to release glucose from cellulose, Saeman hydrolysis conditions are required, in which the cell walls are first dispersed in 72% (w/w) H_2SO_4 at 20°C to "solubilize" and partially depolymerize the cellulose, and the slurry is then diluted to 1 M acid strength and heated at 100°C to complete the hydrolysis of cellulose and other polysaccharides]; (2) a large proportion of the uronic acid arises from the galacturonic acid (Gal$p$A) of acidic pectic substances; (3) the pectic substances of potatoes and onion bulbs are rich in galactose, whereas those of apples and cabbage are rich in arabinose; (4) parenchyma cell walls have little or no "free" glucuronoxylans, which are the predominant hemicelluloses of secondary walls; much of the xylose of parenchyma cell walls arises from xyloglucans. It should be noted that the cell walls of suspension culture tissues (Table II, columns 6 and 7) contain much less pectic acid because cultured tissues are virtually devoid of the middle lamellae. Further, the cell walls of suspension culture tissues of dicotyledons contain, in general, much higher levels of pectic arabinans, polyphenolics, and hydroxyproline-rich glycoproteins compared with those of parenchymatous tissues (Selvendran, 1985), and are therefore not particularly relevant as model types in the DF context. We shall now discuss briefly the main types of polymers present in the cell walls of parenchymatous and immature tissues.

    a.   The Microfibrillar Component—Cellulose.   Cellulose is the major structural polysaccharide of the cell walls of all higher land plants. Because of its importance in the paper and textile industry, cellulose has been extensively studied, and most of the available information on cellulose comes from studies on wood and cotton although it is generally assumed to be applicable to cellulose from other sources. There are extensive reviews on the chemistry of cellulose (Jones, 1964; Teng and Whistler, 1973), and the following account is a summary of cellulose chemistry that is relevant to the DF context.

    Cellulose is a linear polymer characterized by long chains of β-(1→4)-linked D-glucopyranose residues, whose degree of polymerization is of the order of 10,000. Because of the high molecular chain length and the considerable capacity of the three hydroxyl groups to hydrogen bond, both inter- and intramolecularly, cellulose forms fibers of remarkable strength. In nature, cellulose molecules are arranged in an ordered manner within the microfibrils, and these microfibrils are a remarkably distinctive feature of the cell walls of all higher plants. Crystalline regions of the microfibrils may reach lengths of 800–1200 Å and have a diameter of 50–100 Å; the crystallite core has a diameter of about 40 Å. The length of the individual chains is probably very much longer than this because the degree of polymerization ranges from 8,000 to 12,000, which corresponds to a chain length of 40,000–60,000 Å and a molecular weight of more than a million. Therefore, it is conceivable that cellulose chains pass repeatedly through highly ordered crystalline and amorphous regions of a low degree of order (see Northcote, 1969). Since the molecules in the crystalline regions are tightly held together by hydrogen-bonding and other secondary forces, these regions are difficult to penetrate by reagent molecules, and are (probably) less susceptible to acid and enzymatic hydrolysis. In contrast, the amorphous regions can be penetrated more readily by reagent molecules and react with the molecules therein. Thus, on heating with acid, an initial rapid rate of hydrolysis in the amorphous regions is followed by a relatively slow rate of hydrolysis of molecular segments in the crystalline regions.

The proportion of cellulose in crystalline and amorphous regions is probably of considerable importance in explaining the differences in proportions between cellulose in the primary and secondary cell walls, and also between the cellulose of different cell types. This aspect may be relevant to the varying properties of the cell walls of fruits, vegetables, and cereals, although it has been little studied and warrants further investigation. Although molecules such as xyloglucans, which contain a cellulosic β-D-glucan backbone, hydrogen bond to the crystalline regions of cellulose microfibrils, it is probable that other carbohydrate polymers are incorporated into the microfibrillar structures within the amorphous regions (see Selvendran, 1983). These noncellulosic polymers give rise to sugars other than glucose on acid hydrolysis of the α-cellulose residue. All the α-cellulose fractions which we isolated from parenchymatous or very immature tissues of runner bean pods (O'Neill and Selvendran, 1983), cabbage leaves (Stevens and Selvendran, 1980), apples (Stevens and Selvendran, 1984d), potatoes (Ring and Selvendran, 1981), and onions (Redgwell and Selvendran, 1986) contained significant amounts (~20–25%) of noncellulosic polymers, mainly of pectic origin. Similar observations have been made with α-cellulose from cambial tissues (Thornber and Northcote, 1962) and pear fruits (Jermyn and Isherwood, 1956). In the case of α-cellulose from parenchymatous tissues of runner bean pods (Selvendran, 1975a) and suspension culture sycamore cells (Heath and Northcote, 1971), the bulk of the hydroxyproline-rich glycoproteins were associated with the α-cellulose residue. The α-cellulose fraction from beeswing wheat bran, which consists of the outer layers of the wheat grain which are lignified, contained a significant amount of acidic arabinoxylan, but the α-cellulose from the parchment layers of mature runner bean pods was only slightly contaminated with acidic xylan (Selvendran, 1984). A proportion (up to 50–60%) of the associated polymers could be solubilized by treating the α-cellulose fractions with sodium chlorite/acetic acid at 70°C for 2 hr, suggesting the involvement of phenolic cross-links in the complexes. This association of cellulose with other polysaccharides might occur during the preparation of the material by some adsorption effects, or it might form part of the essential organization of the polysaccharides within the wall. If the latter is true, then the associated polysaccharides, polyphenolics, and glycoproteins probably serve as linking compounds for the entanglement of the cellulose microfibrils with the matrix polymers.

   b. Hemicellulosic Polymers.   The major hemicellulosic polymers of parenchymatous tissue are xyloglucans, glucomannans, and proteoglycan complexes. The xyloglucans and proteoglycans constitute approximately 7–10% and about 5% of the dry weight of the cell walls, respectively (Selvendran, 1985). It should be noted, however, that in the case of tamarind seeds xyloglucan is the major cell wall storage polysaccharide and therefore constitutes the bulk of the dry weight of the cell walls of the cotyledons (Meier and Reid, 1982).

   Xyloglucans.   Xyloglucans have been isolated from seeds (Meier and Reid, 1982), suspension culture tissues (Bauer *et al.,* 1973), extracellular medium of suspension culture cells (Aspinall *et al.,* 1969), cambial tissues (Simson and Timell, 1978), and parenchymatous and immature tissues of a range of vegetables (Ring and Selvendran, 1981; O'Neill and Selvendran, 1983; Stevens and Selvendran, 1984b) and fruits (Stevens and Selvendran, 1984d). Xyloglucans contain a cellulosic β-D-glucan backbone to which short side chains are attached at C-6 of at least one-half of the glucose residues. α-D-Xylopyranose residues appear to be directly linked to glucose residues, but these side chains may be extended by the apposition of β-D-galactopyranose, L-arabinofuranose, or β-L-fucopyranosyl-(1→2)-β-D-galactopyranosyl residues. The major structural features of the xyloglucan from parenchymatous tissues of runner bean pods are shown in Fig. 4 of O'Neill and Selvendran (1983). In subsequent work the relative distribution of the side chains on the glucan backbone was obtained from a detailed analysis of the products of cellulase degradation of the xyloglucan (O'Neill and Selvendran, 1985b). Recently we have shown that apple xyloglucans exhibit heterogeneity (Ruperez *et al.,* 1985).
   In the case of parenchymatous tissues, the bulk of the xyloglucans could be solubilized from the depectinated cell walls using only 4 M KOH, which is in accord with the xyloglucans being strongly hydrogen bonded to the cellulose microfibrils (Selvendran, 1983). The available evidence suggests that most of the xyloglucans hydrogen bond to cellulose microfibrils and thus serve to disperse the microfibrils within the primary cell wall matrix. In addition to their structural role, xyloglucans are also implicated in auxin-induced growth (McNeil *et al.,* 1984; Darvill *et al.,* 1985), and a nonasaccharide from the xyloglucan of suspension culture sycamore cells has been shown to exhibit anti-auxin activity (York *et al.,* 1984).

   Proteoglycan Complexes.   Evidence for the occurrence of proteoglycan complexes (pectic–hemicellulose, pectic–hemicellulose–protein, and pectic–hemicellulose–protein–polyphenol complexes) was provided by our studies on immature cabbage leaves (Stevens and Selvendran, 1984b), immature carrots (Stevens and Selvendran, 1984c), apples (Stevens and Selvendran, 1984d), runner beans (O'Neill and Selvendran, 1985a), and immature tissues of onion bulbs (Redgwell and Selvendran, 1986). The bulk of the proteoglycan complexes was solubilized by 1 M KOH from the depectinated cell walls. The major carbohydrate moieties in the complexes were arabinoxylan, xylan, xyloglucan, pectic arabinan, and pectic arabinogalactan. The relative amounts of the polysaccharides in the complexes depended on the type of tissue, and the amounts of the individual complexes ranged from 0.1 to 2.5% of the dry weight of the cell walls. For a summary of the results, the reader should consult Selvendran (1985).

All the purified complexes from runner bean cell walls, and some of the complexes from the other tissues, contained proteins with relatively low levels of hydroxyproline and high levels of aspartic and glutamic acids. This showed that the proteins associated with the complexes were distinct from the hydroxyproline-rich cell wall glycoproteins (Lamport, 1965; Lamport and Catt, 1981; Selvendran and O'Neill, 1982). It is probable that some of the proteins in the complexes are cell wall enzymes that have been immobilized by phenolic and/or glycosidic linkages and located at specific sites within the walls. Other proteoglycan complexes may serve as linking components within the wall matrix. This latter property is important in the DF context, because it may influence the solubility characteristics of cell wall polymers and hence the physiological activity of DF.

c. Pectic Substances. The pectic substances are a complex mixture of colloidal polysaccharides, which can only be partially extracted from the cell walls with hot water or with hot aqueous solutions of chelating agents such as ethylenediaminetetraacetate (EDTA), ammonium oxalate, or sodium hexametaphosphate. Hot water can only partially solubilize some of the pectic substances of the primary cell walls and middle lamellae. The pectic substances of the latter are complexed with relatively higher concentrations of Ca^{2+} (and Mg^{2+}) and therefore require the action of a chelating agent. In the 1950s and early 1960s the duration of extraction was around 10–12 hr on a boiling water bath (Jermyn and Isherwood, 1956). Subsequent work has shown that these conditions result in considerable breakdown of pectic substances by autohydrolysis and also by transeliminative degradation. Above pH 5, breakdown by transelimination becomes significant at elevated temperatures (Albersheim *et al.*, 1960). Prolonged exposure to hot aqueous solutions was done in the belief that most of the pectic substances could be solubilized by such treatments. However, it is now clear that insoluble pectic material, possibly held by covalent linkages, is present in all types of cell walls, the amount depending on the type of tissue. With runner beans ~80% of the total pectic material is extractable with chelating agents (O'Neill and Selvendran, 1983), whereas with apples it is ~50% (Stevens and Selvendran, 1984d), and with sugar beet ~30% (Selvendran, 1985). Some of the insoluble pectic material is extractable with alkali, but the bulk is found in close association with other cell wall constituents, particularly the α-cellulose fraction. A significant amount of this pectic material could be solubilized by treatment with sodium chlorite/acetic acid at 70°C for 2 hr, suggesting the involvement of phenolic cross-links (R. R. Selvendran, unpublished results).

Rhamnogalacturonans are the major constituents of pectic substances. Those in which a proportion of the galacturonic acid residues are present as methyl esters are designated pectinic acids, and those devoid of ester groups are called pectic acids, which usually exist as the salts (pectates). In some pectins (e.g., from sugar beet) a proportion of the free hydroxyl groups of galacturonic acid residues are acetylated. The rhamnogalacturonan backbone consists of chains of α-(1→4)-D-GalpA residues interspersed with (1→2)-linked L-Rhap residues. Attached to the main chains are side chains consisting of D-galactose, L-arabinose, D-xylose, D-glucose, and, less frequently, D-mannose, L-fucose, D-glucuronic acid, and the rather rare sugars 2-O-methyl-D-xylose, 2-O-methyl-L-fucose, and D-apiose. The methylated sugars occur exclusively as end groups (Aspinall, 1980). Darvill et al. (1978, 1980) have shown that in suspension culture sycamore cells the rare sugars are concentrated in a certain pectic fraction (rhamnogalacturonan II, RG-II), which constitutes approximately 3–4% of the dry weight of the cell walls. In subsequent work, RG-II has also been shown to contain the unusual sugars 3-C-carboxy-5-deoxy-L-xylose, which has been given the name aceric acid (Spellman et al., 1983), and 3-deoxy-D-manno-D-octulosonic acid (York et al., 1985).

The nonmethylated sugars occur in short one- to three-unit side chains mainly at O-4 of (1→2,4)-linked Rhap, and at O-3 of some of the GalpA residues, but the more common neutral sugars, D-galactose and L-arabinose, are also present as part of oligosaccharide chains linked to O-4 of L-Rhap residues. Where the oligosaccharide chains have been adequately characterized, the sugar residues in these moieties have been shown to be linked as in galactans, arabinans, and arabinogalactans type 1 (Aspinall, 1980). In the oxalate-soluble pectic polysaccharides of cabbage cell walls, the arabinan was shown to be linked to O-4 of L-Rhap residues, directly or through a short chain of (1→4)-linked Galp residues (Stevens and Selvendran, 1984a). In rhamnogalacturonan I (from the cell walls of suspension culture sycamore cells), seven differently linked glycosyl residues were shown to be attached to O-4 of the (1→2,4)-linked Rhap residues (McNeil et al., 1982). These side chains help to form a hydrophilic network that can hold water within the matrix of the walls.

The distribution of (1→2)- and (1→2,4)-linked L-Rhap residues in the rhamnogalacturonan backbone is variable, but there is evidence from studies using mild acid hydrolysis of citrus fruit pectin, in which the rhamnose content is small, that the acid-labile L-Rhap residues may occur at regular intervals. This evidence is based on the isolation, after mild hydrolysis, of polygalacturonic acid blocks containing ~25 residues (Powell *et al.*, 1982). The polygalacturonic acid blocks on adjacent chains, when aligned in a parallel manner, form stable ionic bonds by enclosing calcium ions, giving rise to the egg-box junction zones (Grant *et al.*, 1973; Rees, 1982). The Rha*p* residues in the backbone give rise to irregularities in the structure, which give some degree of flexibility to the chains. This factor, coupled with the esterification of the Gal*p*A residues, the occasional acetylation of its hydroxyl groups, and the presence of substituents on the backbone, may give rise to the pectin structure shown in Fig. 1A of Selvendran (1985). For an account of the physical properties of pectins and related polysaccharides, the reader should consult Rees (1969) and Morris (1986).

Our recent work on the pectic polymers from the middle lamellae and primary cell walls of parenchymatous tissues of potatoes (R. R. Selvendran and A. R. Bushell, unpublished results; Selvendran, 1985) and immature tissues of onion bulbs (Redgwell and Selvendran, 1986) has shed additional light on the nature and distribution of the pectic polymers within the walls of parenchymatous tissues (see Selvendran *et al.*, 1985, and Redgwell and Selvendran, 1986, for experimental details to isolate pectic polymers with minimum degradation). The main conclusions are as follows: (1) The pectic polymers of the middle lamellae are highly methyl esterified, and a significant proportion of them can be solubilized by a dilute solution of cyclohexanediaminetetraacetate (CDTA), sodium salt, at 20°C. (2) The bulk of the pectic polymers of primary cell walls could only be solubilized (after extraction of cell walls with CDTA) under alkaline conditions which suggested that, in addition to removing the "bridging" Ca^{2+}, the ester cross-links between the Gal*p*A residues and hydroxyl groups of sugar residues elsewhere in the wall matrix had to be hydrolyzed. (3) The ratio of Rha*p* to Gal*p*A was ~1 : 45–50 for the bulk of the pectic polymers from the middle lamellae and ~1 : 10–15 for the pectic polymers from the primary cell walls. (4) The relative amount of branched rhamnose residues was much higher in the pectic polymers of primary cell walls. A diagramatic representation of some of the structural features of the pectic polymers from the middle lamellae and primary cell walls are shown in Fig. 1 of Selvendran (1985).

Neutral Pectic Polysaccharides.   Neutral pectic polysaccharides that are essentially pure arabinans, galactans, and arabinogalactans types 1 and 2 (mainly the former) have been isolated from a number of soft tissues (Aspinall, 1980; Selvendran, 1983). In view of the fact that the pectic polymers, particularly those of primary cell wall origin, are esterified and highly branched, it has been argued that a large proportion of the neutral pectic polysaccharides may be products of β-eliminative degradation of more complex pectic polysaccharides (Selvendran, 1985). Our recent work with pectic polymers of onions, in which special precautions were taken to minimize β-eliminative degradation, suggests that small

amounts of neutral pectic arabinogalactans (in which the galactans are the dominant carbohydrate moieties) are native to the walls (Redgwell and Selvendran,
1986). However, it would appear that a large proportion of the "neutral" pectic
polysaccharides obtained on extraction of cell walls of potatoes, cabbage, and
onions with hot water are artifacts of extraction (Selvendran, 1985).

   d.   Cell Wall Glycoproteins.   The cell walls of parenchymatous tissues contain approximately 3–6% of the dry weight of the walls as proteins (Selvendran,
1975b). These proteins are usually present in the glycosylated form. Two main
types of glycoproteins have been isolated; one rich in hydroxyproline (hyp) and
the other relatively poor in hydroxyproline (Selvendran, 1975a; O'Neill and
Selvendran, 1980a, 1985a)—the latter type has been briefly discussed under
proteoglycans. The relative amounts of the two glycoproteins vary in the cell
walls of tissues. Parenchymatous tissues of runner bean pods contain significant
amounts of both glycoproteins, whereas in potato tubers the hyp-poor component
is the predominant one (Ring and Selvendran, 1981). The hyp-rich glycoproteins
(extensin) have been shown to be particularly rich in hyp, serine, arabinose, and
galactose (Lamport and Catt, 1981; Selvendran and O'Neill, 1982). Partial alkaline hydrolysis studies have shown that the hyp is O-glycosidically linked to
arabinose-containing oligosaccharides (1 to 4 Ara residues). The galactose residues are linked to serine residues. It is interesting to note that the glycopeptide
moieties of potato lectin have many structural features in common with hyp-rich
glycoproteins (Allen and Neuberger, 1973; Allen *et al.*, 1978; Selvendran and
O'Neill, 1982).
   The wall glycoproteins have generally been regarded as structural although
some of them may be enzymes (e.g., peroxidase). The exact role of these
glycoproteins in the formation of cross-links within the wall matrix is not well
established, but the hyp-rich component has been shown to be associated with
the α-cellulose fraction (Selvendran, 1975a; O'Neill and Selvendran, 1983). The
presence of an oxidatively coupled dimer of tyrosine (isodityrosine) in plant cell
walls has been described (Fry, 1982b). The bulk of the isodityrosine is presumably associated with the hyp-rich glycoproteins, because the amount of isodityrosine in the cell wall appears to be proportional to the amount of hyp.
Isodityrosine has been suggested to function as a cross-linking agent in primary
cell walls. The cell wall glycoproteins are important in the DF context because
they influence the solubility characteristics of the constituent DF polymers.

2.   Lignified Tissues (Secondary Cell Walls)

   The differentiation of the primary wall into secondary wall involves considerable thickening of the wall and profound changes in its chemical composition.
During the growth of secondary wall, α-cellulose, hemicelluloses (mainly acidic

xylans and small amounts of glucomannan), and lignin are deposited, and the thickening results more from the cellulose than the hemicellulose deposition (Northcote, 1963). Lignin occurs to the extent of 15–35% of most supporting structures and seems to form covalent linkages with some of the hemicelluloses (Azuma *et al.*, 1981), and possibly even with cellulose, cementing together the wall polymers into a unified rigid matrix and stratifying the wall.

Acidic xylans have backbones containing β-(1→4)-linked D-Xyl*p* residues with side chains of 4-*O*-methyl-D-glucuronic acid or D-glucuronic acid linked to C-2 of about 10% of the Xyl*p* residues (Timell, 1964); the ratio of 4-*O*-Me-D-Glc*p*A to D-Glc*p*A in the purified xylan from parchment layers of runner bean pods was approximately 2 : 1 (R. R. Selvendran, unpublished results). The 4-*O*-methylglucuronoxylan isolated from birch, under conditions which prevent deacetylation, was shown to have acetyl groups attached to C-3 of ~70% of the xylose residues (Bouveng and Lindberg, 1960). Native larchwood xylans contain about 150–200 xylose residues per molecule (Timell, 1964). The carbohydrate compositions and lignin content of the cell wall preparations from lignified tissues ("strings" and "parchment layers") of mature runner bean pods, veins of mature cabbage leaves, beeswing wheat bran, and some of the component polysaccharide fractions are shown in Table III; also included in the table are the carbohydrate compositions of soy bran and pea hulls. The carbohydrate compositions show that the CWM of "strings" and "parchment layers" is rich in cellulose and acidic xylans and contains very small amounts of pectic substances. These inferences are corroborated by the carbohydrate compositions of the hemicellulose and α-cellulose fractions. In contrast, the CWM of veins, from which the loosely adhering parenchyma cells were removed, contained significant amounts of acidic pectic material and cellulose. The CWM of seed hulls also contained significant amounts of pectic material in addition to cellulose (and acidic xylans), which presumably help the seed coats to imbibe water during germination; the seed hulls, however, contained relatively few phloroglucinol/HCl-staining lignified elements. A significant amount of the xylose in seed hulls arises from acidic xylans (Aspinall *et al.*, 1967; Brillouet, 1982), and these polysaccharides are usually associated with tissues that have undergone secondary thickening. Therefore the lignified elements from different tissues are likely to be degraded to different extents by colonic bacteria; this point will be discussed later.

3. Seeds

The seeds of dicotyledonous plants can be classified into those which are free of an endosperm (i.e., nonendospermic, e.g., pea, bean) and those which have an endosperm (i.e., endospermic, as in certain leguminous species, e.g., guar, locust bean). The former type of seeds usually has starch as the main storage

TABLE III

CARBOHYDRATE COMPOSITIONS OF CELL WALLS AND SOME POLYSACCHARIDE FRACTIONS FROM SOME LIGNIFIED TISSUES AND SEED HULLS[a]

Sugar[b]	Runner beans[1c] Strings (CWM)	Runner beans[1c] Parchment (CWM)	Runner beans[1c] Parchment (1M KOH soluble)	Runner beans[1c] Parchment (α-cellulose)	Cabbage[2] lignified veins (CWM)	Soy bran[1d]	Pea hulls[1]	Beeswing wheat bran[3e] CWM	Beeswing wheat bran[3e] 1M KOH soluble	Beeswing wheat bran[3e] α-Cellulose
6-Deoxyhexose	0.5	0.7	0.7	0.2	2.0	1.3	1.6	—	—	—
Arabinose	0.7	1.1	0.4	1.6	4.4	6.1	2.7	21.6	28.0	7.3
Xylose	25.0	24.0	81.0	0.7	6.0	10.7	11.8	16.8	27.0	5.3
Mannose	0.9	0.6	Trace	0.3	1.8	5.5	0.3	Trace	—	—
Galactose	0.4	1.6	Trace	Trace	2.5	2.4	1.1	1.2	1.5	—
Glucose[f]	43.0	42.0	0.7	92.0	22.6	47.2	57.0	20.4	0.9	65.7
Uronic acid[g]	4.0	8.0	9.4	—	33.2	16.8	15.4	4.0	6.0	2.0
Carbohydrate (%, w/w)	(74.5)	(78.0)	(92.2)	(94.8)	(72.5)	(90.0)	(89.9)	(64.0)	(63.4)	(80.3)

[a] References: (1) Selvendran (1984); (2) B. J. H. Stevens and R. R. Selvendran (unpublished results); (3) Ring and Selvendran (1980). The Klason lignin contents (% w/w) of the cell wall material (CWM) from strings, parchment layers, and beeswing wheat bran are 17.2, 16.9, and 12.0, respectively.

[b] Values are g anhydrosugar/100 g dry material.

[c] "Strings" and "parchment layers" of mature runner bean pods and the polysaccharides solubilized from the holocellulose by 1 M KOH, and α-cellulose residue.

[d] Soy bran contains mainly tissues from the seed hulls.

[e] Cell walls of beeswing wheat bran, the polysaccharides solubilized by 1 M KOH, and α-cellulose residue.

[f] The bulk of the glucose (~95%) arises from cellulose.

[g] The uronic acid from the lignified tissues of runner beans and beeswing wheat bran is mainly glucuronic acid and 4-O-methylglucuronic acid.

polysaccharide, and their cell walls are derived mainly from the tissues of the cotyledons with some contribution from the testa. The cell wall polysaccharides of the cotyledons are similar to those of parenchymatous tissues and are mainly pectic substances, cellulose and hemicelluloses (e.g., xyloglucans), and glycoproteins. The notable difference is that arabinans (in the case of peas) and arabinogalactans (in the case of soybeans) both free and linked to the rhamnogalacturonans tend to predominate in the seeds (Siddiqui and Wood, 1974; Aspinall and Cottrell, 1971). The presence of these polysaccharides can be inferred from the carbohydrate compositions of the cell walls of the cotyledons (Table II, colums 8 and 9).

In contrast to nonendospermic seeds, all the endospermic leguminous seeds contain galactomannans, which are located in the endosperm cell walls (Meier and Reid, 1982). The galactomannans are deposited on the cell walls of the endosperm during seed development and are later mobilized during germination of the seeds. From the carbohydrate compositions of the starch-free alcohol-insoluble residues of guar seeds and dehusked guar seeds, it can be inferred that galactomannans are the major cell wall polysaccharides of the dehusked seeds (Table II, columns 10 and 11). The bulk of the glucose and xylose in the cell walls of the whole seeds is derived from cellulose and xylans of the husk. The galactomannans are essentially linear molecules but are highly substituted on C-6 of the β-(1→4)-linked D-Man$p$ residues with single Gal$p$ residues, which confer on them properties which are quite different from those of unbranched, cellulose-like, water-insoluble mannans and glucomannans. In galactomannans, the ratio of galactose to mannose varies within the limits 1 : 1 to 1 : 5 (McCleary et al., 1976). Galactomannans are somewhat comparable with xyloglucans (amyloids) which can also serve as storage polysaccharides in some seeds (e.g., tamarind). Galactomannans are hydrophilic and are usually obtained from the crushed seeds (or endosperms) by extraction with hot water (Glicksman, 1962). The interactions of galactomannans with water and other polysaccharides form the basis of the widespread industrial uses of galactomannans from guar and locust bean seeds (Goldstein et al., 1973). Because guar gum forms very viscous solutions in water, it appears to slow glucose absorption in the small intestine by interacting with intestinal mucosae (Johnson and Gee, 1981); this aspect will be discussed later.

B. CELL WALLS OF MONOCOTYLEDONOUS PLANTS (CEREALS)

The cell walls of certain organs of monocotyledonous plants, particularly those of cereal grains, are an important source of DF. Cereal grains are used for the production of flour required for bread, cakes, biscuits, etc. The amounts of DF provided by cereal products depend on the type of cereal and particularly on the extent of its refinement; high extraction wheat products (e.g., wholemeal bread, wholemeal breakfast cereals) contain more DF than products from low extraction white flours. Products derived from grains are also commonly used as breakfast foods in the form of bran-based products, flakes, or porridge. All cereals have endospermous seeds; the endosperm of wheat, for example, represents about 80–85% of the grain and is the source of white flour. To obtain white flour, almost pure endosperm must be separated and ground. Thus the milling process for wheat is a complex operation, involving separation into three main fractions: bran or pericarp, with the attached testa and aleurone layer (in all about 12–17%), the endosperm itself (about 80–85%), and the wheat germ (about 3%). The removal of the bran may result in a loss of up to 75% of the total DF content of the grain. Therefore a knowledge of the cell walls of the different types of tissues of the grain is important. In this section we shall consider the cell wall polymers from parenchymatous and lignified tissues of some important cereals: wheat, barley (which is comparable to oats), and rice.

1. Endosperm and Aleurone Layer

Chemical extraction studies coupled with electron microscopy have shown that the endosperm (and aleurone layer) cell walls of wheat and barley consist of an amorphous matrix in which microfibrillar structures are dispersed (Mares and Stone, 1973a,b; Bacic and Stone, 1981a,b). The matrix polymers consist of mainly arabinoxylans in the case of wheat endosperm and β-glucans and arabinoxylans in the case of barley endosperm, and the fibrillar structures contain cellulose in close association with glucomannans. Some of the matrix polymers are cross-linked, and the others are "loosely" held on the surface of the walls; the removal of the latter with hot water or dilute alkali partially revealed the microfibrillar network of the walls. Unlike the cell walls of parenchymatous tissues of dicotyledons, the microfibrillar component consisted of only a small proportion (<5%) of the dry weight of the walls, and pectic substances were virtually absent. The absence of the intercellular cementing layer of pectins may account for the apparent ease with which the individual cells of cereal endosperms separate. The above points are reflected in the overall carbohydrate compositions of the cell walls and some of the hemicellulosic fractions (see Table 7 of Selvendran, 1984). In contrast to the endosperm cell walls, the carbohydrate compositions of the aleurone layers of both wheat and barley are comparable, and these layers contain significant amounts of arabinoxylans and β-glucans and small amounts of cellulose and glucomannans. The matrix polymers of aleurone cell walls are highly cross-linked by ferulic acid and ferulic acid types of compounds, which exhibit UV fluorescence (Fulcher, 1982).

The preponderant polysaccharides of wheat endosperm cell walls are arabinoxylans (88%), of which one-third are soluble in water; alkaline agents are needed to dissolve the remaining two-thirds (Mares and Stone, 1973b). The cellulose content of the walls is $\sim2\%$, and it is notable that the β-glucan content is only $\sim1\%$. In contrast, the endosperm cell walls of barley (Fincher, 1975; Ballance and Manners, 1978) contain unusually high levels of mixed-linkage β-glucans which account for the bulk of the glucose present, the cellulose content being (very) small. The β-glucans of barley endosperm walls can be revealed by calcofluor staining (Wood and Fulcher, 1978). The requirement of alkaline conditions to solubilize the bulk of the arabinoxylans suggests the possible involvement of phenolic ester cross-linkages in the wall. The involvement of phenolic ester cross-linkages receives support from the work of Neukom and colleagues (Neukom *et al.*, 1964; Markwalder and Neukom, 1976), who demonstrated the formation of a diferulic acid–arabinoxylan complex when a solution of water-soluble arabinoxylan (containing ferulic acid) from wheat flour was oxidized with H_2O_2 in the presence of peroxidase.

The investigations of Fincher (1975) and Ballance and Manners (1978) have shown that approximately 70% of barley endosperm cell walls is composed of mixed-linkage β-glucans. The ratio of $(1\rightarrow3)$- to $(1\rightarrow4)$-linkages was essentially $3:7$ for both warm water-soluble (glucan-I) and alkali-soluble (glucan-II) fractions (Ballance and Manners, 1978). This work has further shown that the difference in extractability could not be attributed to the degree of polymerization (DP) of the β-glucan chains, because the DP of glucan-I was 405 and that of the less soluble glucan-II was 258. These results suggested that glucan-II was probably covalently linked to other wall compounds via proteins and/or, phenolics. Supporting evidence for the occurrence of covalent linkages between β-glucans and proteins was provided by the work of Forrest and Wainwright (1977) and Bamforth *et al.* (1979), and the available evidence to date has been summarized by Selvendran (1983). The solubility characteristics of β-glucans from barley and oat endosperm cell walls are comparable (Englyst and Cummings, 1986a), and the soluble β-glucans are known to exhibit gastrointestinal effects that are beneficial (Anderson, 1985).

Unlike wheat and barley endosperm cell walls, rice endosperm cell walls contain appreciable amounts of cellulose ($\sim48\%$) and some galacturonic acid-containing pectic substances rich in arabinose and xylose ($\sim10\%$), acidic and neutral arabinoxylans, and a complex containing xyloglucan, β-glucan, and arabinoxylan (Shibuya and Iwasaki, 1978; Shibuya and Misaki, 1978). The rice β-glucan contains 80% $(1\rightarrow3)$- and 20% $(1\rightarrow4)$-linkages. It therefore appears that the composition of rice endosperm cell walls is intermediate between those of parenchymatous tissues of dicotyledons and those of wheat and barley.

2. Lignified Tissues of Wheat Grain

Beeswing wheat bran consists mainly of the outer coating of the grain and is about three cells thick, containing the cuticle, epidermis, and hypodermis. The studies of various groups of workers have shown that the CWM of beeswing wheat bran consists of hemicelluloses (acidic arabinoxylans), cellulose, lignin and phenolic esters, and proteins (Adams, 1955; Ring and Selvendran, 1980; Selvendran, 1983). The observations are borne out by the carbohydrate compositions of the CWM and one of the alkali-soluble hemicellulosic fractions (Table III, columns 9 and 10). The Klason lignin and protein contents of the CWM were 12 and 6% (w/w), respectively (Ring and Selvendran, 1980).

Our recent studies on the sequential extraction of the CWM from beeswing wheat bran with 1 M KOH at 2°C, followed by 1 and 4 M KOH at 20°C showed that only ~70% of the wall acidic arabinoxylans could be solubilized by direct extraction with alkali. The dialysates of the alkaline extracts were shown to contain significant amounts of phenolics, including ferulic and p-coumaric acids, by paper and thin-layer chromatography. A large proportion of the remaining acidic arabinoxylans was solubilized with alkali after delignification of the residue. This study helped us to distinguish between arabinoxylans held in the walls by phenolic ester cross-links and those encrusted with lignin. Fractionation of the alkali-soluble polymers by graded alcohol precipitation followed by anion-exchange chromatography showed that the major hemicellulosic polymers were a range of acidic arabinoxylans, a proportion (~20%) of which were associated with appreciable amounts of polyphenolics and some proteins. Methylation analysis and partial acid hydrolysis studies showed that the major hemicelluloses were a range of glucurono- and 4-O-methylglucuronoarabinoxylans, and most of the terminal residues were Ara$f$, Xyl$p$, and Gal$p$ residues (Du Pont and Selvendran, 1987; R. R. Selvendran and M. S. Du Pont, unpublished results). The solubility characteristics of the acidic arabinoxylans are important because they influence the mode of degradation of fiber from wheat bran by the microorganisms of the human colon.

The chemistry of the cell walls from parenchymatous tissues of wheat, barley, and rice, and those of beeswing wheat bran, has been discussed at some length because of their intrinsic importance in the DF context. In fact, fiber from wheat bran and bran-based products, and that of wheat flour and wheat flour-based products, make a major contribution to the cereal fiber of most Western nations, while fiber from rice endosperm is of importance in the Near and Far East.

C.   MINOR CONSTITUENTS OF CELL WALLS AND DF

1.   Lignins of Secondary Cell Walls

Lignin has a very complex structure which varies with the type of plant; therefore it is probably more correct to discuss the "lignins" from different sources. Lignins may be described as high molecular weight aromatic polymers, which are formed by the enzymatic dehydrogenation and subsequent polymerization of coniferyl, sinapyl, and p-coumaryl alcohols; the monomeric units derived from these alcohols are called guaiacyl (3-methoxy-4-hydroxyphenylpropane), syringylpropane (3,5-dimethoxy-4-hydroxyphenylpropane), and p-coumaryl (4-hydroxyphenylpropane) residues, respectively (Freudenberg, 1968; Sarkanen and Hergert, 1971). Thus lignins consist for the most part of variously condensed substituted phenylpropane residues. Phylogenetic origin determines the relative proportions of the phenylpropane residues in the lignins. The lignins can be divided into three broad classes, which are called softwood (gymnosperm), hardwood (dicotyledonous angiosperm), and grass (monocotyledonous angiosperm) lignins. Of these the softwood lignins contain mainly guaiacyl residues, with small amounts of p-coumaryl and syringylpropane residues; the hardwood lignins contain comparable amounts of guaiacyl and syringylpropane residues, with only small amounts of p-coumaryl residues; and the grass lignins are composed of approximately equal amounts of all three residues. The angiosperm lignins, which are the ones of interest in the DF context, demonstrate considerable variation from species to species.

Lignin is formed in the middle lamella region and infiltrates the wall matrix, causing the wall to expand. When the cell wall is fully lignified, the cell itself is usually dead. Lignification serves two main functions. It cements and anchors the cellulose microfils and other matrix polysaccharides, and, because the lignin–polysaccharide complexes are hard, they stiffen the walls, thus preventing biochemical degradation and physical damage to the walls. The properties are important in the DF context, because they minimize the bacterial degradation of the lignified walls in the human colon. The implications of these properties are discussed later.

2. Skins and Protective Coverings of the Wall

The outer walls of the epidermal cells of leaves, fruits, and many other aerial organs of plants are covered with a protective layer of waxes and cutin (Martin and Juniper, 1970; Kolattukudy, 1980). Where the walls themselves are impregnated with cutin, they are said to be cutinized; where the cuticle occurs as a discrete layer, the surface is said to be cuticularized. Generally the cutin penetrates and intermingles with the outer polysaccharides of the wall. Underground organs, e.g., tubers, are protected by another type of lipid-derived polymeric material, called suberin. Both cutin and suberin are embedded in and overlaid with a complex mixture of relatively nonpolar lipids, which are collectively called waxes.

Phenolic compounds have been found to be present in very small amounts in cutin ($<1\%$ of the weight of the cutin). The major phenolic acid esterified to cutin is p-coumaric acid (e.g., tomato, apple, and pear), but small amounts of ferulic acid have also been detected in the cutins from pear and peach. In the case of suberin, the predominant phenolic compound is ferulic acid (Riley and Kolat-tukudy, 1975).

Because cutin and waxes are resistant to bacterial degradation, cutinized tissues may serve an important role in restricting the access of intestinal bacteria (and bacterial enzymes) to the cell wall polysaccharides of some vegetables and fruits, especially when they are not cooked. This phenomenon may be particularly significant in the case of leafy vegetables (e.g., lettuce and cabbage), which have spongy parenchyma cells sandwiched between cutinized layers.

3. Inorganic Constituents

Plant cell walls contain calcium, potassium, and magnesium deposits, and calcium plays an important role in intercellular adhesion by "bridging" the pectins of the middle lamella. Removal of the bridging Ca^{2+} by intracellular chelating agents (e.g., citrate) during cooking of vegetables leads to cell separation and subsequent softening of the tissue (Selvendran, 1985). Small amounts of silicates are associated with the cell walls of all land plants, but significantly larger amounts are associated with the cell walls of cereals, particularly rice and oats (Jones, 1978). The extent to which silica influences the colonic bacterial degradation of cereal-based foods is not known, but, in ruminants, the amount of silica in the cell wall of the forage is known to influence the rate of degradation in the rumen (Dekker and Richards, 1973; Van Soest, 1973).

4. Polysaccharide Food Additives: Gums and Mucilages

a. Food Gums.   A range of polysaccharides, the majority of which are heteroglycans with branched structures, are used in small amounts in the food industry to give the desired texture to the finished product. The food gums are included under the broader definition of the term DF, but their overall contribution to the total DF intake is not significant, except in certain special cases, e.g., guar-based breads for diabetics. The chemistry and properties of food gums have been extensively reviewed, and the reader should consult Klose and Glicksman (1972) and the book *Industrial Gums,* edited by Whistler and BeMiller (1973), for details. Southgate (1976) and Southgate and Englyst (1985) have drawn together some of the information on food gums, and for an account of the chemistry of gums and mucilages, see Aspinall (1969).

The technical definition of a food gum is a polymeric material that can be dissolved or dispersed in water to give a thickening and/or a gelling effect (Klose and Glicksman, 1972). Among the leading materials, in decreasing order of use in food, are pectins, gum arabic, alginates, guar gum, carboxymethylcellulose (CMC), carrageenan, locust bean gum, and modified starches. The major structural features of some of these gums are given in Table 5 of Selvendran (1984), and, with the exception of modified starches and gum arabic, all the polymers listed above are derived from plant cell walls. For example, the cell wall polysaccharides and mucilaginous material of some seaweeds (certain species of brown algae) are important sources of alginates and carrageenans. CMC is derived from cellulose by replacing the hydroxy groups on C-6 of the glucose residues by carboxylic acid groups. This alteration in structure profoundly decreases the hydrogen bonding between the polymer chains, so that the molecule becomes more readily dispersible in water. Some of the useful properties of food gums are listed below: (1) High methoxy pectins gel in sugar solutions at low pH, whereas low methoxy pectins form gels with Ca^{2+} in dilute solution (pectins are widely used in jams, jellies, and desserts). (2) Alginates form salts with varying solubility characteristics and have found widespread use in many foods (milk, puddings, dairy products, ice cream, beers, and confectionery). (3) Guar gum forms viscous solutions and is generally used as a thickening agent, e.g., in soups. More recently guar-based breads have been used to lower blood glucose levels in diabetics (Jenkins et al., 1980a). (4) κ-Carrageenans form brittle gels with K^+ (Morris and Chilvers, 1983), exhibit synergistic effects with proteins, and are used in a range of foods. Usually the amount of polymer required to produce the desired change in texture in the food product is about 1% of its fresh weight.

b. Seed Mucilage. The mucilage from the seed husk of *Plantago ovata* Forsk. (usually referred to as ispaghula husk) is obtained by milling the seeds and extracting with water. The mucilage is located in the "thick" mucilage cells which form the outer epiderm of the spermoderm. The mucilage has important physiological effects on large bowel action and is widely used for treating large bowel disorders such as diverticular disease (Godding, 1972). The mucilage forms a gel in water, retaining many times its own weight of water (Kennedy et al., 1979; Sandhu et al., 1981). This property of the mucilage (coupled with the fact that the constituent polysaccharide has a highly substituted xylan backbone and is therefore not readily degraded by colonic bacteria) is probably one of the factors responsible for its laxative action. The major sugars obtained on acid hydrolysis of the mucilage polysaccharide were D-xylose, L-arabinose, and L-rhamnose in the ratio 10:3.2:1. The overall structural features of the polysaccharide were first elucidated by Laidlaw and Percival (1950), and more recently the fine structure of the polysaccharide (Kennedy et al., 1979) and some of its properties have been described (Sandhu et al., 1981). The major structural features of the polysaccharide are given in Fig. 10 of Selvendran (1983).

III. ANALYSIS OF DF AND SOME VALUES FOR DF FROM FRESH AND PROCESSED FOODS

Over the past decade a number of simplified methods have been developed for the analysis of DF, and as these have been reviewed recently (Selvendran and Du Pont, 1984; Asp and Johansson, 1984) we shall not deal at length with the large amount of work in this area. The information which such methods can provide about the constituent DF polymers is very limited, and there is little doubt that over the next decade more detailed information will be sought about the structure, mode of occurrence, solubility and adsorptive characteristics, viscosity, degradability by colonic bacteria, and related properties of DF polymers from a range of plant foods. Such information can be obtained by isolating and fractionating gram quantities of relatively pure DF from a range of plant foods. For a detailed account of the methods available for the isolation and analysis of cell walls, mostly from edible plant organs, the reader should consult Selvendran *et al.* (1985) and Selvendran and O'Neill (1987). For an account of the applications of mass spectrometry for the examination of pectic polysaccharides, see Selvendran and Stevens (1986).

A.   ANALYSIS OF DF

In the following discussion we shall consider the principles underlying the methods available for the analysis of DF and draw attention to the improvements in the methods that have made possible reasonably accurate estimates of the DF content of a range of plant foods. As the term DF refers mainly to the nonstarch polysaccharides (NSP) and lignin in the diet, we shall consider these two components from an analytical point of view.

NSP. In order to obtain accurate estimates of the NSP the starch should be removed "completely," preferably by enzymatic hydrolysis. Incomplete removal of starch results in inflated values for DF, and this is particularly so for starch-rich products such as potatoes and oats (as well as other cereals) in which the starch to cell wall ratios are about $15-20:1$ and $8:1$, respectively (Selvendran and Du Pont, 1980a). Incomplete hydrolysis of starch could be attributed to a number of factors. (1) Insufficient mixing of the enzyme and substrate; continuous mixing during the incubation period is required. (2) The starch in starch granules (e.g., fresh potato and unripe banana) exists in the crystalline form and therefore offers considerable resistance to hydrolysis with α-amylase. Gelatinization of the starch granules, which results in disruption of the crystalline structure, makes the starch more susceptible to enzymatic degradation. (3) The retrograded starch in processed starch-rich products (e.g., cornflakes) is resistant to enzymatic hydrolysis, because of the modifications undergone by the starch molecules. This could be due to the interactions between closely aligned starch molecules (which sometimes results in the elimination of water molecules between adjacent hydroxy groups of the starch molecules, e.g., in extrusion cooking) and also due to interactions between starch, proteins, lipids, other intracellular compounds, and even some of the cell wall components. The net effect is to render the starch less soluble and therefore less degradable. Inclusion complexes between amylose and polar lipids occur naturally in some cereals, and can also be found during extrusion cooking (Mercier, 1980; Mercier *et al.*, 1980). Amylose–lipid complexes are resistant to amylase, but can be degraded slowly on prolonged incubation. A proportion of the retrograded starch can, however, be estimated, and this will be discussed later. (4) The presence of α-amylase inhibitors in some foods and food additives inhibit starch degradation. (5) The starch may be in less available form as in partially broken grains and seeds; the bulk of such starch may escape digestion in the small intestine.

The main steps involved in the analysis of DF by two procedures that have given good values for the nonstarch polysaccharide content of a range of plant foods are shown in Figs. 1 and 2. For an account of the gravimetric method for the analysis of DF, see Asp *et al.* (1983) and Asp and Johansson (1984); the values for DF obtained by Asp and co-workers compare favorably with those obtained by more detailed carbohydrate analysis of the starch-depleted food samples. The procedure outlined in Fig. 1 was developed by Faulks and Timms (1985) and is based on the procedure of Theander and Aman (1979). In this method the starch is removed in two steps. The bulk of the starch is removed by treating the gelatinized material with Termamyl at 100°C for 15 min. Termamyl contains appreciable β-glucanase activity at 40°C, but this activity is preferentially inhibited by carrying out the enzymatic degradation at 100°C; the starch-degrading activity is apparently not impaired by the high temperature. The remaining starch in the residue (Residue 1) is removed by dispersing it in aqueous dimethyl sulfoxide (DMSO) and treating with amyloglucosidase at 37°C for 35 min. The sugars in the residue (Residue 2) are hydrolyzed with acid and analyzed by colorimetry and also, after derivatization, by GLC. The main advantage of this procedure is that the removal of starch can be accomplished in a very short time. This is because Termamyl is a powerful enzyme, which can degrade the bulk of the starch rapidly at 100°C. The values for DF obtained by Faulks and Timms (1985) are highly comparable with those obtained by the somewhat longer procedure of Englyst *et al.* (1982), and anyone interested in DF analysis is advised to consult the method.

The procedure outlined in Fig. 2 was proposed by Englyst *et al.* (1982). In this procedure the finely ground sample is gelatinized in acetate buffer and rendered free of starch by incubation with α-amylase and pullulanase; α-amylase and pullulanase hydrolyze α-$(1\rightarrow4)$- and α-$(1\rightarrow6)$-glucosidic linkages, respectively.

Sample

1. Gelatinize in buffer at 100°C for 10 min and treat
   with Termamyl at 100°C for further 15 min.

2. Cool mixture, precipitate with absolute ethanol to
   give 80% (v/v) alcohol, centrifuge, and remove
   supernatant.

Residue 1

3. Disperse the residue in DMSO, add buffer, and
   incubate with amyloglucosidase at 37°C for 35 min.

4. Treat with alcohol as before and dry precipitate in
   the oven at 100°C.

Residue 2

5. Disperse the residue in 12 M H_2SO_4 at 35°C for 1
   hr, dilute to 1 M acid strength and hydrolyze at
After 1 hr remove   100°C for 2 hr.
aliquot for uronic acid
assay.   6. Determine the sugars by
                       (a) colorimetric assay and
                       (b) GLC as alditol acetates.

FIG. 1. The main steps in the procedure of Faulks and Timms (1985), based on the method of Theander and Aman (1979).

The use of α-amylase and pullulanase for the effective removal of starch from starch-rich food samples was recommended by Selvendran and Du Pont (1980a,b). It should be noted that during the incubation period the contents of the tube should be continuously mixed to ensure "complete" removal of starch. The suspension is then cooled and treated with ethanol and the precipitate washed with solvents by centrifugation, dried and analyzed for the constituent sugars. Hydrolysis with sulfuric acid, under the two conditions shown in Fig. 2, is essentially based on the procedure of Selvendran *et al.* (1979), and this has been applied to various cell wall and DF samples (Ring and Selvendran, 1978; O'Neill and Selvendran, 1980b; Selvendran and Du Pont, 1980a,b).

The procedure of Englyst *et al.* is an improvement on the colorimetric method for the analysis of unavailable carbohydrates proposed by Southgate (1969), who pioneered the work on DF analysis (Southgate *et al.*, 1978). Considering the fact that the complete removal of starch is difficult, the values for DF obtained by Southgate (1978a), Southgate *et al.* (1976) are to be commended.

In the procedure of Englyst *et al.*, the starch resistant to α-amylase and

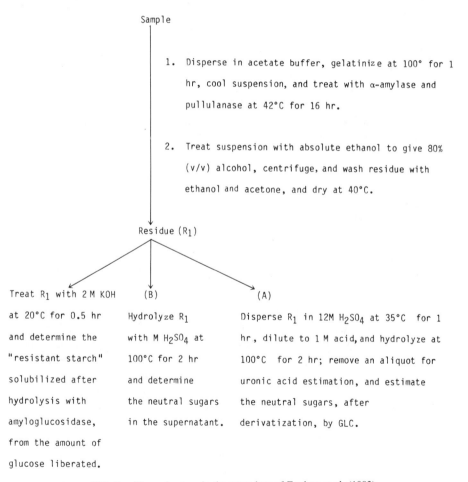

Sample

1. Disperse in acetate buffer, gelatinize at 100° for 1 hr, cool suspension, and treat with α-amylase and pullulanase at 42°C for 16 hr.

2. Treat suspension with absolute ethanol to give 80% (v/v) alcohol, centrifuge, and wash residue with ethanol and acetone, and dry at 40°C.

Residue (R_1)

Treat R_1 with 2 M KOH at 20°C for 0.5 hr and determine the "resistant starch" solubilized after hydrolysis with amyloglucosidase, from the amount of glucose liberated.

(B)
Hydrolyze R_1 with M H_2SO_4 at 100°C for 2 hr and determine the neutral sugars in the supernatant.

(A)
Disperse R_1 in 12M H_2SO_4 at 35°C for 1 hr, dilute to 1 M acid, and hydrolyze at 100°C for 2 hr; remove an aliquot for uronic acid estimation, and estimate the neutral sugars, after derivatization, by GLC.

FIG. 2.   The main steps in the procedure of Englyst *et al.* (1982).

pullulanase treatment was solubilized with 2 M KOH and subsequently estimated after hydrolysis with amyloglucosidase (pH 4.5, 65°C for 1 hr); this starch is referred to as "resistant starch." In subsequent work Englyst and Cummings (1984) have slightly modified the procedure by first dispersing the food sample in DMSO at 100°C for 1 hr, before treatment with the acetate buffer; the DMSO treatment apparently solubilizes the bulk of the "resistant starch." The authors claim that this modification has enabled them to hydrolyze all the starch (including the "resistant starch"), and thus obtain values for NSP that are more meaningful, particularly for starch-rich processed products.

B. THE NONSTARCH POLYSACCHARIDE CONTENT OF SOME PLANT FOODS

The NSP content of some vegetables, apples, seeds, and cereal products is given in Tables IV and V. As the major cell wall polymers present in most of the products have been discussed earlier, attention will be drawn only to some of the distinctive features. The comments on the solubility characteristics and structural features of the polymers are based on detailed chemical fractionation studies of the purified cell wall preparations, and the original papers should be consulted for a better appreciation of these points. Additional information on the NSP content of a range of plant foods can be obtained from Englyst and Cummings (1986a), Southgate and Englyst (1985), Theander and Aman (1979), Schweizer and Wursch 1979), Chen and Anderson (1981), Bittner et al. (1982), and Selvendran (1984).

1. Vegetables and Fruits

The NSP contents of potatoes, apples, cabbage, and carrot are highly comparable on a fresh weight basis (Table IV); these organs contain mainly parenchymatous and some slightly lignified tissues. The NSP content of mature runner bean pods is considerably higher than that of the above products, because they contain a significant amount of lignified tissue; this is reflected in the relatively high level of xylose derived from acidic xylans. The types of pectic polymers present in the products are different. The major pectic polymers of potatoes are galactans covalently linked to the rhamnogalacturonans, and these are comparable with the pectic polymers of onions (Redgwell and Selvendran, 1986); in cabbage and apples, however, pectic arabinans and arabinogalactans preponderate (Stevens and Selvendran, 1984a,d; Aspinall and Fanous, 1984; De Vries et al., 1983). Immature carrots are also rich in pectic arabinogalactans (Stevens and Selvendran, 1984c), but these have structural features different from those of the pectic polymers of apples and cabbage. In this connection it is interesting to note that the cell walls of sugar beet roots are also rich in pectic

TABLE IV

CARBOHYDRATE COMPOSITIONS OF THE STARCH-DEPLETED ALCOHOL-INSOLUBLE RESIDUES AND NONSTARCH POLYSACCHARIDES OF SOME PLANT FOODS[a]

Sugar[b]	Potatoes[1]	Apples[1]	Cabbage[1]	Carrot[2]	Runner bean pods[3]	Soy flour[1]	Dried peas[4]	Chick peas[5]	Haricot beans[4]	Butter beans[5]
6-Deoxyhexose	1.0	2.3	1.8	2.8	1.1	1.0	0.2	0.2	0.4	0.2
Arabinose	3.8	12.8	4.7	6.5	2.9	3.7	3.5	4.2	6.0	5.2
Xylose	1.2	4.9	3.1	1.1	6.8	1.4	0.9	0.5	1.9	2.0
Mannose	1.0	1.9	1.5	2.0	1.5	1.1	0.1	0.1	0.5	1.2
Galactose	20.4	5.7	3.0	10.8	7.1	6.6	0.5	0.5	0.7	0.5
Glucose[c]	24.0	30.0	27.9	24.1	32.3	4.6	10.1	2.1	4.5	4.2
Uronic acid	15.9	33.1	23.5	35.1	22.0	7.0	3.3	2.3	3.1	2.6
NSP (% w/w)[d]	(1.8)	(1.9)	(2.2)	(2.1)	(4.0)	(14.0)	(18.6)[e]	(9.9)[e]	(17.1)[e]	(15.9)[e]

[a] References: (1) Selvendran (1984); (2) B. J. H. Stevens and R. R. Selvendran (unpublished results); (3) Selvendran and Du Pont (1980); (4) Englyst and Cummings (1984); (5) Southgate and Englyst (1985).

[b] Sugar values for potatoes, apples, to soy flour are as g anhydrosugar/100 g dry starch-depleted alcohol-insoluble residues, whereas for dried peas to butter beans the values are as g anhydrosugar/100 g dry original product. Note that all the sugar and DF values have been corrected to the first decimal place.

[c] The bulk (~90%) of the glucose is derived from cellulose.

[e] These products contain "resistant starch": values, not included in the glucose and NSP values, are dried peas (4.4), chick peas (0.3), haricot beans (0.8), and butter beans (0.5).

[d] The NSP content of potatoes to runner bean pods are on a fresh weight basis, whereas those for soy flour to butter beans are on a dry weight basis.

arabinans and arabinogalactans, and a large proportion of these are not soluble in hot water or hot oxalate. The insolubility of the beet pectic material in chelating agents is due to cross-linking by phenolics and phenolic esters (B. J. H. Stevens and R. R. Selvendran, unpublished results; Selvendran, 1985), and it is probable that the same is true of carrot and apple pectic polymers; fluorescence micros-copy has shown that the cell wall polymers of beet root are also highly cross-linked by phenolics (R. R. Selvendran and P. Ryden, unpublished results).

The solubility characteristics of the pectic polymers is important, because a significant proportion of the pectic polymers in apples, carrot, and beet root may not be in the soluble form when the digesta from these products reaches the small intestine. Therefore some caution has to be exercised when extrapolating the results of nutritional studies on commercially available citrus and apple pectins to the situation one encounters with pectins in normal food products. It is also important to note that pectins in cooked vegetables, which have much less intercellular adhesion (Selvendran, 1985), can be rendered more soluble by intestinal fluids compared with those of uncooked vegetables and fruits.

2.   Seeds

The NSP content of the seeds shown in Table IV, columns 7–11, shows considerable variation on a dry weight basis. Dried peas, chick peas, haricot beans, and butter beans are rich in arabinose and uronic acid, indicating the presence of significant amounts of pectic arabinans. Soy flour has a significantly higher level of galactose compared with arabinose showing that it is rich in pectic arabinogalactans. The bulk of the glucose is derived from cellulose of the cotyledons and seed hulls, and a significant proportion of the xylose is derived from the acidic xylans of the seed hulls. The "resistant starch" contents of the seed preparations show considerable variation, and there is a significant amount of "resistant starch" in dried peas.

3.   Cereal Products

From the carbohydrate compositions of the nonstarch polysaccharides, the values for buffer-soluble and buffer-insoluble NSP content of the products, and a knowledge of the background literature, the following points can be inferred from Table V. (1) The NSP of white flour are derived mainly from the primary cell walls which are rich in (neutral) arabinoxylans but are relatively poor in cellulose and β-glucans. (2) Whole wheat flour contains much higher levels of arabinose, xylose, and glucose relative to white flour, and a significant propor-tion of these sugars are derived from acidic arabinoxylans and cellulose of the bran layers. (3) Whole wheat flour bread contains some "resistant starch" which is formed during the baking process. (4) In contrast to white flour the major DF

TABLE V

CARBOHYDRATE COMPOSITIONS OF NONSTARCH POLYSACCHARIDES IN SOME CEREAL PRODUCTS[a]

Sugar[b]	White flour[1]	Whole wheat flour[1]	Whole wheat bread[1c]	Porridge oats[2]	Pearl barley[1]	Rye flour[1]	Wheat bran[2]	Wheat bran product[1d]	Corn flakes[1c]	Brown rice[2]
Arabinose	0.9	2.7	2.6	1.0	1.2	3.6	9.8	5.9	0.1	0.4
Xylose	1.4	4.3	4.2	1.2	1.6	5.8	18.8	9.7	0.1	0.5
Mannose	0.1	0.2	0.2	0.1	0.3	0.3	0.2	0.3	—	—
Galactose	0.2	0.3	0.3	0.2	0.1	0.3	0.7	0.5	—	0.1
Glucose[e]	0.7 (0.2)	2.6 (1.6)	2.4 (1.6)	4.5 (0.3)	4.5 (0.4)	3.7 (1.5)	11.0 (8.0)	6.8 (4.7)	0.4 (0.2)	0.9 (0.7)
Uronic acid	—	0.3	0.3	0.1	0.1	0.2	1.2	0.7	0.1	0.2
NSP (% w/w)	(3.3)	(10.4)	(10.0)	(7.1)	(7.8)	(13.9)	(41.7)	(23.9)	(0.7)	(2.1)

[a] References: (1) Englyst et al. (1982); (2) Southgate and Englyst (1985).

[b] Sugar and NSP values are expressed on a g/100 g dry original product basis, and all the values have been corrected to the first decimal place.

[c] These products contained a significant amount of "resistant starch"; the "resistant starch" values for whole wheat bread and corn flakes, which are not included in the values for glucose and NSP, were 0.8 and 2.9 g/100 g dry original product, respectively.

[d] The NSP content of this wheat bran product (All-Bran, Kelloggs Company, Manchester, U.K.) is somewhat low; most commercial wheat bran samples have NSP values between 40 and 50 g/100 g dry original product.

[e] Glucose released by a modified Saeman hydrolysis procedure; the glucose values in parentheses are from cellulose only.

polymers of porridge oats and pearl barley are β-glucans, and a significant proportion of these are soluble in the acetate buffer. (5) The rye flour used for making rye biscuits (e.g., Ryvita) is also relatively rich in β-glucans but contains significant amounts of cellulose and (acidic) arabinoxylans derived from the lignified bran layers of the grain. (6) The main DF polymers of wheat bran are acidic arabinoxylans and cellulose. Commercial wheat bran also contains some neutral arabinoxylans and β-glucans which are derived from the endosperm and aleurone layers, respectively. The NSP content of a typical wheat bran product (e.g., All-Bran, Kelloggs Co., Manchester, U.K.) is only half that of commerical wheat bran. (7) In addition to cellulose and acidic arabinoxylans, cornflakes contain an appreciable amount of "resistant starch." (8) Brown rice contains significant amounts of arabinoxylans, cellulose, and some acidic polymer, the bulk of which is probably of pectic origin.

The solubility characteristics of the constituent polymers of cereal fibers show considerable variation. A significant proportion of the buffer-insoluble arabinoxylans could be solubilized with alkali. The buffer-soluble β-glucans of porridge oats, which can form viscous solutions, probably influence the transfer of molecules across the mucosae in the small intestine (Johnson and Gee, 1981). Although most of the "resistant starch" of cornflakes would survive into the large intestine, to be degraded by colonic bacteria, this starch is not likely to modify the architecture of the cell wall matrix in the same manner as cell wall polyphenolics and lignin.

The average intake of DF in the United Kingdom is about 20 g/person/day, and of this about a third comes from cereal sources (Bingham et al., 1979). The approximate breakdown of DF intake is as follows: vegetables and fruits (12 g)—this would be derived from about 2–3 potatoes or comparable vegetable (6 g) and 3 apples (6 g); cereal products (7 g)—wheat bran-based products (2–3 g), which is roughly equivalent to 1 tablespoon of wheat bran, and six slices of white bread (5 g). As yet there is no official recommendation on a desirable level of DF intake, but 30 g/person/day might be suggested. This intake is best derived equally from vegetables and fruits (15 g) and cereal sources (15 g). The intake from cereal sources could easily be enhanced by consuming more wheat bran-based products. The above is an approximate but useful guide.

C. LIGNIN CONTENT OF DF PREPARATIONS

The quantitative estimation of lignin is beset by a number of problems (Browning, 1967), and these are compounded for starch- and protein-rich plant foods (Selvendran and Du Pont, 1984). The problems arise from the following. (1) There is uncertainty in the detailed chemistry of lignins from different sources. (2) There are differences in the chemical nature of materials associated with lignin; for example, lignin is covalently linked to some hemicelluloses and is therefore difficult to separate from these polysaccharides—hydrolysis with dilute acid to remove the associated polysaccharides results in the loss of acid-soluble lignin. (3) There are differences in the solubility characteristics of lignin in acid. (4) There are chemical reactions of lignin with accompanying materials (e.g., proteins) during cooking and processing of food products (Hartley, 1978). Hence there is no satisfactory method for the quantitative estimation of lignin in DF preparations. The situation is much better for woods (e.g., conifer) used in the paper industry, because one is dealing with defined species, and also because much more research has been done on the lignin content of woods. For a critical account of the methods used for the estimation of lignin in woods, see Browning (1967).

Because most plant organs, with the exception of a few cereal products (e.g., wheat bran- and whole oats-based products), are harvested and eaten before much lignification has taken place, lignin is regarded as a minor component of most plant foods. However, it should be borne in mind that the cell walls of parenchymatous tissues contain ~5–10% of the dry weight of the walls as polyphenolic material. This material appears to cross-link the matrix polysaccharides (Selvendran, 1985)and therefore influences the solubility characteristics of the cell wall polymers. The amount of cell wall polyphenolic material (including lignin) in organs which are partially lignified is probably much higher, about 10–20% of the dry weight of the walls. Because lignified tissues are not readily degraded by colonic bacteria, it is clear that estimates of cell wall polyphenolics (including lignin) in DF preparations should be obtained for a better understanding of the fate of DF in the human alimentary tract, particularly the large intestine.

The most generally used methods for lignin determination are (1) the sulfuric acid hydrolysis method, which gives "Klason lignin" (Browning, 1967; Pearl, 1967); (2) the permanganate oxidation methods (Browning, 1967; Van Soest and Wine, 1968; Robertson and Van Soest, 1981); and (3) the acetyl bromide method (Johnson *et al.,* 1961; Morrison, 1972a,b). The principles underlying these methods, their relative merits, and their applications for the estimation of lignin content of a range of well-purified cell wall preparations, from edible plant organs, have been given by Selvendran and Du Pont (1984). Our view is that the acetyl bromide method is to be preferred for dietary fiber preparations, because it can be scaled down for very small samples (5–10 mg).

D. SOME COMMENTS ON THE DETERMINATION OF DF CONSTITUENTS USING DETERGENT-EXTRACTED RESIDUES

1. Neutral Detergent Fiber (NDF) and Modified NDF

Briefly, the NDF method of Van Soest and Wine (1967, 1968) consists of extracting the fresh or air-dried tissue with 3% (w/v) sodium lauryl sulfate, containing 0.5% (w/v) sodium sulfite, and boiling under reflux for 1 hr. The mixture is then filtered and washed with hot water and acetone. In the original method, the dried residue was either treated with amylase to get an estimate of the modified NDF, or ashed and reweighed, with the loss on ignition taken as a measure of NDF. The method was initially developed for the analysis of forages (mainly grasses) and has given satisfactory results. This is because in grasses (1) the pectic polysaccharide content is low (~5–6% of the dry weight of the cell walls); (2) the matrix polysaccharides (hemicelluloses) are not readily solubilized by hot aqueous solutions at neutral pH, because they are cross-linked by lignin and phenolic esters; and (3) the starch content is low. Application of the NDF method to plant foods, however, has not proved to be successful, and we shall discuss the merits of the method when applied to cereal- and vegetable-based foods, and fecal samples.

a. Cereal Products. Cereal-based foods generally have high levels of starch which impede filtration rates considerably, and the NDF is usually heavily contaminated with starch, some of which may be modified. Attempts have been made to improve the filtration rates and also to remove the residual starch by treatment with starch-degrading enzymes (Robertson and Van Soest, 1977; Mc-Queen and Nicholson, 1979; Schaller, 1981), to give the modified NDF, but these modifications have not really proved to be particularly effective (Selvendran and Du Pont, 1984). The modified NDF procedure gives a reasonably good estimate of the DF content of wheat bran (a product which contains much lignified tissues and relatively little starch). However, application of the method to dehulled oats and brown bread has given DF values which are numerically of the same order as total DF values obtained by the procedure of Selvendran and Du Pont (1980a), but carbohydrate analysis showed that this agreement is fortuitous (Selvendran and Du Pont, 1984). Therefore the application of the modified NDF method to starch-rich cereal products is not recommended.

b. Vegetable Products. The modified NDF method underestimates the DF content of vegetables and fruits significantly, because a large proportion of the pectic polysaccharides is solubilized (Englyst, 1981; Selvendran and Du Pont, 1984). We have compared the modified NDF values of some food products with the total DF values (Selvendran and Du Pont, 1984), and the results should be consulted for a better appreciation of the deficiencies of the modified NDF method.

c. Fecal Samples. The NDF method has been used to obtain partial fractionation of fecal samples (Holloway *et al.*, 1978; Gramstorff Fetzer *et al.*, 1979). It is difficult to comment on the relative merits of the method for such fractionations, because most workers have not given the carbohydrate and protein compositions of the fractions. The bulk of the fecal protein is derived from colonic bacteria, which adhere to the undegraded fiber components. Therefore, fractionation studies on fecal samples may not be particularly meaningful unless the carbohydrate and protein contents of the fractions are also given.

2. Acid Detergent Fiber (ADF)

The ADF procedure consists in extracting the fresh or air-dried tissue with 2% cetyltrimethylammonium bromide in 0.5 M H_2SO_4 and then boiling under reflux for 1 hr. The mixture is then filtered, washed, dried, and weighed (Van Soest and Wine, 1968). The ADF is used to determine the cellulose and lignin content of the sample. Cellulose is obtained from the loss in weight on treatment with 72% H_2SO_4, and lignin is obtained from the loss in weight of the 72% H_2SO_4 residue on ashing. Alternatively the lignin content can be obtained from the loss in weight of the ADF on treatment with potassium permanganate (Robertson and Van Soest, 1981). It should be noted that the loss in weight of the ADF and not the whole cell wall material on treatment with permanganate gives an estimate of the lignin content. This is because some of the hemicelluloses in the cell walls are associated with the lignin by covalent linkages, or are held in the cell wall matrix by phenolic ester cross-linkages which are also solubilized on treating the cell walls with permanganate see Selvendran and Du Pont (1984).

During the preparation of the ADF, the acid hydrolysis is restricted to 1 hr, presumably to minimize loss of acid-soluble lignin. However, the conditions used may not result in the quantitative hydrolysis of all the hemicelluloses and pectins as shown by our studies on wheat bran and mature runner bean pods. The carbohydrate compositions (% w/w dry ADF) of the ADF of wheat bran and mature runner bean pods are as follows: wheat bran—Ara 0.8, Xyl 8.8, Man 2.5, Glc 62.0, and uronic acid 3.1; mature runner bean pods—Rha 0.3, Ara 0.4, Xyl 7.4, Man 5.7, Gal 2.2, Glc 77.3, and uronic acid 7.8 (R. R. Selvendran and M. S. Du Pont, unpublished results). Other workers have also reported that ADF preparations contain residual hemicelluloses (Morrison, 1980) and pectin (Belo and de Lumen, 1981), which would affect the values for "cellulose" and "lignin."

IV. PROPERTIES OF DF: GENERAL CONSIDERATIONS

Plant foods that provide fiber are derived from a range of organs that have various tissues and cell types. Therefore, it is difficult to make generalizations about the physiocochemical properties of DF preparations from various sources. Further, it should be borne in mind that diets rich in fiber exhibit characteristic properties depending on (a) the structure of the tissue types, (b) the nature of the intracellular compounds, and (c) the form in which the food is taken—fresh, cooked, or processed. The texture of starch-rich foods is dependent on the capacity of starch to absorb water and produce gels, and the structure of flour-based baked foods is largely due to starch. Food additives and modified starches influence the physical characteristics of processed foods. An example will be given to illustrate the above points mainly with a view to showing the effects of cell wall structure on the properties of the diet.

If dried peas are soaked in water at 20°C overnight and swallowed without mastication, the chances are that a large proportion of the peas will go through the gastrointestinal tract with minimum change, and can be recovered in the feces. This is because of the protective action of the intact hard seed hulls, which would resist even bacterial degradation in the human colon. If the pea hulls are carefully removed from the soaked peas, and the cotyledons and hulls are swallowed without mastication, a small proportion of the constituents of the cotyledons would be degraded by colonic bacteria, but the virtually intact hulls would be only very slightly degraded. However, in the above case, if the cotyledons and hulls are thoroughly masticated before swallowing then a proportion of the starch would be degraded by intestinal enzymes; significant degradation of the starch by pancreatic α-amylase is only possible when the starch is gelatinized (Snow and O'Dea, 1981; Englyst and Cummings, 1985). The enzymatically undegraded starch (in the granules) and a large proportion of the cell walls of the cotyledons would be degraded by colonic bacteria. If the cotyledons and hulls from soaked peas are cooked for 20 min in boiling water and well masticated before swallowing, then the effects in the gastrointestinal tract, particularly the small and large intestines, would be profound. This is because the starch within the cells of the cotyledons would have been gelatinized and a significant proportion of it would be released during the cooking and mastication due to the rupture of the parenchyma cell walls. The gelatinized starch (and proteins, etc.) would be degraded by intestinal enzymes and absorbed in the small intestine. The starch-depleted digesta from the cotyledons would be largely degraded by bacteria in the colon and a significant proportion of the broken pieces of the hulls would also be degraded. Finally, if the soaked peas (cotyledons and hulls) are thoroughly blended in water to disrupt the tissue structure, cooked for 20 min, and eaten, then (1) most of the starch (and proteins) would be degraded and absorbed in the small intestine, (2) the soluble pectic polysaccharides of the cotyledons would exert a greater influence on the properties of the digesta in the small intestine, and (3) most of the cell wall constituents of the cotyledons would be degraded by colonic bacteria and a large proportion of the cell wall constituents of the hulls would also be degraded. The effects produced by different forms of peas in the above illustration are obviously oversimplified, but they serve to show the importance of the physical state, including particle size, of the food product when assessing the role of dietary fiber.

During the preparation of plant foods for consumption a variable degree of disruption of the cellular structure occurs. The cell walls which act as physical barriers for the diffusion of cell contents and the entry of digestive secretions therefore determine the fate of the food in the gastrointestinal tract to a significant extent. During boiling of starch-rich materials, e.g., legume seeds, and potatoes, considerable cell separation and sloughing of the cells takes place, making the tissue soft. This softening process is partly due to (1) the gelatinization of the starch and the consequent swelling of the granules, which forces the cells to become spherical and to separate, (2) the diffusion of the intracellular chelating agents (e.g., citrate ions) into the middle lamella region where they complex with the Ca^{2+} (which cements the pectins of adjacent cells), and (3) the β-eliminative degradation of the pectins—these processes also help cell separation (Selvendran, 1985). Cellular disruption is enhanced on mastication and continues in the intestinal tract.

Further, when considering the role of DF, one has to bear in mind the characteristics of the diet as a whole, and the physical and chemical nature of the components of DF and the range of possible interactions; in fact, all the polysaccharides in the diet influence the consistency of the digesta in the stomach and in the small intestine. The structure of a plant organ is destroyed by cooking, mastication, and digestion, although most of the properties of the fiber components are retained, modified by the particular environment in the gastrointestinal tract. The physiological effects of the fiber components *in vivo* may therefore differ from those observed in *in vitro* studies. Starch is probably more important during the initial stages of digestion, and as the starch is hydrolyzed the dietary fiber components may exert a greater influence on the propulsive movement of the digesta. The access of digestive enzymes to the constituents present in thick-walled cells (e.g., the aleurone layer) is restricted, consequently the proteins in such cells seem to be digested slowly (Schaller, 1978). Of the DF components, the soluble polymers such as pectins, β-glucans, and galactomannans may be more important initially because they influence the mucosal absorption of some nutrients. However, it should be borne in mind that as the digestible materials are removed, more "pores" will be formed within the insoluble cellular matrix of the fiber, which can entrap some of the intestinal compounds and thus impede their diffusion out of the digesta. Most of the DF components of cereal-based foods and "resistant starch" survive into the large intestine (Englyst and Cummings, 1985), but there is evidence to suggest that in some individuals a small proportion of DF from vegetables and fruits may be metabolized in the small intestine, possibly by bacteria (Holloway *et al.,* 1978; Sandberg *et al.,* 1981). Some of these aspects are summarized in Fig. 3. However bacterial degradation of the digesta (which includes significant amounts of DF components) occurs in the colon, absorption of compounds and the ease of defecation is dependent on the amount of undergraded DF components, the bacterial biomass, and associated water.

Some of the properties of DF that may be of importance in relation to gastroin-

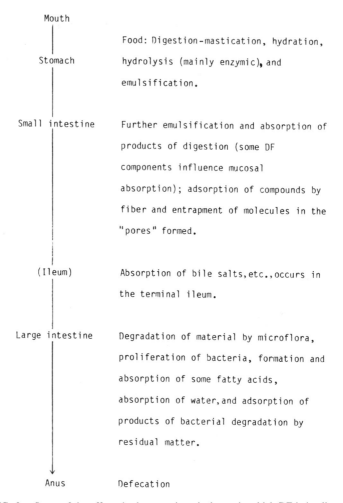

FIG. 3.   Some of the effects in the gastrointestinal tract in which DF is implicated.

testinal function are discussed below. These include particle size, water holding capacity, ion binding capacity, bile salt binding capacity, viscosity enhancing characteristics, influence on digestibility of starch, and inhibition of intestinal enzymes; the properties of DF which determine its fate in the human colon, particularly the bacterial degradation of DF, are discussed separately.

A.   PARTICLE SIZE

The sizes of cellular fragments from plant foods will depend on (1) the type of food, (2) whether it is eaten fresh or cooked, and (3) the steps involved in food processing. Boiling in water generally results in loss of turgor in leafy vegetables and the collapse of various tissues, but in potatoes boiling disrupts intercellular adhesion and allows fragmentation of the tissues to occur. Cooked carrots and apples, for example, fragment far more readily on mastication than the uncooked products. The (particle) size of cereal products (e.g., wheat bran) depends on the degree of milling and the type of mill used. Among other things, the particle size of food components determines (1) their water holding and binding capacities, (2) the amount of surface area of the cell wall accessible to intestinal secretions and colonic bacteria, and (3) the ease with which intracellular compounds (e.g., starch, proteins, and lipids) may be degraded by digestive secretions; for example, the starch in unmilled grains and partially broken seeds is in a less available form.

B. WATER HOLDING CAPACITY

The water holding capacity (WHC) of a fiber preparation is taken as a measure of its ability to immobilize water within its matrix. When a DF preparation is placed in water, some of the water molecules are adsorbed by the exposed regions of the fiber polymers, some held within the hydrated wall matrix, and some "fill" the "dehydrated" as well as partially broken cells. Water is also held in the interstitial spaces as "trapped" water. On finely subdividing the fiber preparations more DF polymers would be exposed to adsorb water, but the number of "dehydrated" cells which can "imbibe" water would decrease as would the interstitial spaces available for the retention of water. Water outside the matrix can be removed by filtration or by centrifugation, and is referred to as "free" water.

Methods for measuring WHC usually involve saturating the fiber with excess water and removing the "free" water by centrifugation or filtration (McConnell et al., 1974; Eastwood and Mitchell, 1976). The resultant WHC is a measure of the extent to which a DF preparation is capable of holding water within its matrix under the defined conditions. Using suction pressure, "trapped" water can also be removed (Robertson and Eastwood, 1981a).

Several factors influence the WHC of DF as measured by centrifugation or filtration. These include the particle size of the preparation, the chemical composition of the fiber and the nature of the associated compounds, the preparation of the food product, and possibly the pH and osmolarity of the surrounding medium. Some of these factors have been determined by Robertson and Eastwood (1981b,c), and the implications of their results have been discussed (Eastwood, 1978, 1983). We shall make some pertinent comments based on the above and related studies (Stephen and Cummings, 1979), as well as our own work on the WHC of well-defined cell wall preparations.

The water molecules that adsorb to the DF polymers hydrogen bond at positions not otherwise involved in intra- and intermolecular bonding of the polysaccharide molecules. When a (partially) soluble polysaccharide (e.g., pectin) is placed in water, the water molecules penetrate the amorphous regions and bind to available sites, greatly reducing interpolysaccharide associations. Parts of the polysaccharide become solvated, and other regions associate with each other through formation of Ca^{2+} bridges and also by hydrogen bonding, thus forming a loose ''gel'' network within which a significant amount of water can be held. On the other hand, perfectly linear polysaccharides, e.g., cellulose microfibrillar structures, do not dissolve in water because the polysaccharide chains associate laterally by intermolecular hydrogen bonds. However, the glucan chains at the surface of the cellulose microfibrils hydrogen bond with water molecules and can retain some water. In the case of carboxymethylcellulose (sodium salt), the hydrogen bonding between the linear chains is much weaker compared with cellulose, and again a significant amount of water can be retained within the loose ''gel'' network. The above factors probably account for the reported WHC of pectin (80.9), α-cellulose (5.3), and sodium CMC (60.5); the WHC was determined by a dialysis bag method, and is expressed as g water/g dry polymer after exposure to water for 48 hr (Stephen and Cummings, 1979).

We have used the dialysis bag procedure of Stephen and Cummings (1979) to determine the WHC of apple cell walls and commercial citrus pectin (rapid set) and obtained values of 23.1 and 45.3, respectively, after 48 hr exposure at 37°C (B. J. H. Stevens and R. R. Selvendran, unpublished results). In the above studies the water in the interstitial spaces (''trapped'' water) makes a significant contribution to the WHC. Application of known suction pressures to fiber and gel preparations, however, showed that with a relatively low suction pressure (between 1 and 2 atm) much of the ''trapped'' water could be readily removed. Suction pressure is the pressure that must be applied to pure water, at the same temperature, to create an equilibrium between pure water and test solution. The water binding capacity determined using suction pressure of 2 atm gave the following values: gum arabic, 4.7; potato fiber preparation, 2.8; and wheat bran, 1.4 (Robertson and Eastwood, 1981a). These values have to be compared with those obtained by filtration (i.e., equivalent to zero suction pressure): potato fiber preparation, 16.5, and wheat bran, 4.0 (Robertson and Eastwood, 1981a). The potato fiber preparation used in the above studies was (probably) only slightly contaminated with starch.

The WHC of a range of ''fiber'' preparations (acetone-extracted residues) are given below: lettuce (23.7), carrot (23.4), cucumber (20.9), celery (16.2), potato (2.0), banana (2.9), and wheat bran (3.0); the values are expressed as g water/g acetone powder and were obtained by the centrifugation method (McConnell *et al.*, 1974). The products listed above can be grouped as follows: (1) organs poor in intracellular starch (e.g., lettuce to celery), (2) organs rich in starch (potato and banana), and (3) wheat bran, which contains relatively little starch compared to maize and oatmeal. Such grouping helps one to understand better the significance of the results. This is because in the preparation of the 'fiber' samples and in the interpretation of the results, the authors have not taken into account the presence of contaminating starch.

The results show that WHC of the acetone-dried powder is very much influenced by the presence of contaminating starch. Thus organs which are relatively free of starch, and have similar amounts of DF per gram of acetone-dried preparation, have comparable WHC. However, the acetone powders of potato and banana, which would have significant amounts of (ungelatinized) starch and very little DF, exhibit little WHC. In the above preparations, if the starch was gelatinized (by boiling) then the WHC of the acetone powders would have been significantly higher, but the method of McConnell *et al.* would not have been suitable for such a preparation, because of the solubility characteristics of starch. The values obtained for the WHC of cell wall preparations of potatoes, parenchyma of runner beans, and cortical tissues of apples were 21.2, 23.7, and 22.6 g water/g CWM, respectively. On depectination, the water holding capacity of the CWM of apples decreased to 18.4 (B. J. H. Stevens and R. R. Selvendran, unpublished results). In the above studies, the filtration method was used to obtain estimates of WHC, and it has been shown that the values for WHC obtained by the centrifugation and filtration methods are comparable (Robertson and Eastwood, 1981b; Stevens and Selvendran, unpublished results).

The WHC of fiber from bran is low compared with those of vegetable preparations, and this could be attributed to (1) the presence of significant amounts of lignified fibers in the tissues comprising bran—lignin is hydrophobic therefore lignified tissues bind water poorly, (2) the cells comprising bran are much smaller compared with those of parenchymatous tissues of dicotyledons, and therefore "imbibe" much less water on hydration. There may well be other factors, but the above points should be borne in mind when interpreting the results on water holding capacity of fiber preparations.

C. BILE SALT BINDING CHARACTERISTICS

Fiber preparations from different sources have been shown to have variable capacity to bind bile salts (Eastwood and Hamilton, 1968; Kritchevsky and Story, 1974; Balmer and Zilversmit, 1974; Eastwood *et al.*, 1976; Story and Kritchevsky, 1976), and the binding was estimated from the change in bile salt concentration on exposure of the solution (usually 1–5 mM) to the adsorbent. Based on these and other related studies, it has been suggested that DF binds bile salts and other steroids in the intestine and thus inhibits cholesterol absorption (Balmer and Zilversmit, 1974; Morgan *et al.*, 1974; Eastwood, 1983). The adsorption studies suggested that deconjugated bile salts are more strongly bound than conjugated bile salts, and the binding was shown to be dependent on time of exposure and pH of the medium; maximal binding occurred at acidic pH, and the binding was considerably reduced at alkaline pH. In the work of Eastwood and Hamilton (1968) alcohol-insoluble residues (AIR) of cereals and vegetables were used as fiber sources, whereas Kritchevsky and Story (1974) used detergent-extracted residues as the adsorbents. These studies suggested that there is a component in fiber preparations which is capable of binding bile salts, but the nature of the component was not clear. Initially, Eastwood and Hamilton (1968) suggested that lignin (in the AIR) was the major bile salt binding polymer, because "Klason lignin" exhibited significant bile salt binding characteristics. However, it should be borne in mind that the preparation of Klason lignin involved treatment of the AIR with strong sulfuric acid, which could have altered the structure of lignin.

Oakenfull and Fenwick (1978) were unable to demonstrate any ability of fiber to bind salts unless the fiber was associated with saponins. This conclusion was based on the ability of fiber from lucerne, soybeans, mung beans, chick peas, spinach, and sunflower seeds to bind detectable amounts of bile salts, whereas fiber from apple, sawdust, and wheat bran did not bind the bile salts tested, namely, sodium cholate and sodium deoxycholate in the concentration range 1–5 mM, pH 6.74, at 25°C; the first group of fiber preparations differ from the second group in that they have saponins associated with them. It should be noted that fiber from sawdust and wheat bran contain significant amounts of lignified tissues, which would suggest that lignin-impregnated fibers bind bile salts poorly. Supporting evidence for the role of saponins in bile salt binding was provided by the following experiments: (1) a preparation from wheat bran treated with lucerne saponins adsorbed a significant amount of sodium cholate, and (2) the preparations from lucerne, soyabeans, etc. lost their ability to bind sodium cholate when they were exhaustively extracted with ethanol–water (80 : 100, v/v), in a Soxhlet apparatus, to remove the associated saponins. The binding capacity of lucerne fiber decreased from 17.2 to <0.2 μmol/g fiber, whereas in the case of soybeans the decrease was from 11.3 to 1.2 μmol/g fiber. The binding capacity of the untreated fiber preparations should be compared with that of cholestyramine, which was tested in the study and was 570 μmol/g resin; cholestyramine is an anion-exchange resin which strongly binds bile salts and is used medicinally to control hypercholesterolemia (Kuksis, 1971). Because saponins are strongly surface-active molecules, the binding of bile salts to fiber associated with saponins was attributed to the hydrophobic interactions between the bile salts and saponins. Subsequent work by Calvert and Yeates (1982) failed to substantiate the conclusions of Oakenfull and Fenwick on the role of saponins in the binding of bile salts by fiber.

In view of the conflicting opinions on the nature of the fiber components responsible for the binding of bile salts, one of us (R.R.S.) investigated the binding of sodium cholate (NaCh) and sodium taurocholate (NaTCh) by a range of well-defined cell wall preparations (Selvendran, 1978, 1979). The materials used included: (1) whole, depectinated, and delignified cell wall material (CWM) from parenchymatous and lignified tissues of mature runner bean pods, together with the H and Na forms of some of the preparations; (2) CWM of runner bean pods at different stages of maturity; (3) CWM from lignified tissues of runner bean pods (parchment layers) with different particle sizes; (4) CWM of whole and decutinized leeks and cutinized tissues of leeks; and (5) carboxymethylcellulose and Amberlite resin. The CWM from the various tissues was prepared by sequentially extracting the triturated and wet ball-milled tissues with 1% (w/v) sodium deoxycholate and phenol/acetic acid/water (PAW, 2:1:1, w/v/v) (Selvendran, 1975b); for the merits of the above procedure for preparing CWM, see Selvendran et al. (1985) and Selvendran and O'Neill (1987). Experiments with labeled sodium deoxycholate showed that the final preparations contained negligible amounts of adsorbed deoxycholate; this is because the PAW treatment effectively removed the adsorbed deoxycholate. The overall particle size of the cell wall preparations, with the exception of those used in (3) above, varied from 25 to 50 μm. The binding of the bile salts was measured by a modification of the procedure of Kritchevsky and Story (1974), and the concentration of the bile salt solutions was 1–2 mg/ml, i.e., 2.3–4.6 mM. For the chemical composition of the cell wall preparations, see Selvendran (1978, 1979); some of the compositions have been discussed earlier in the article. Some of the results from the above investigations are given in Table VI. These results will be

TABLE VI

BINDING OF SODIUM CHOLATE (NaCh) AND SODIUM TAUROCHOLATE (NaTCh) BY CELL WALL PREPARATIONS FROM PARENCHYMATOUS AND LIGNIFIED TISSUES OF MATURE RUNNER BEAN PODS AT DIFFERENT pH VALUES[a]

Sample	pH values			
	pH 4	pH 5	pH 6	pH 7
Parenchyma CWM/NaCh	180	50	32	39
Parchment CWM/NaCh	66	33	15	10
Parchment holocellulose/NaCh	36	18	9	5
Parchment α-cellulose/NaCh	14	7	4	4
Mature runner bean pods CWM/NaCh	—	86	15	16
Parenchyma CWM/NaTCh	41	44	45	—
Parchment CWM/NaTCh	28	25	26	29

[a] Results are expressed as μmol bound/g preparation.

discussed briefly because they throw light on the nature of the bile salt binding sites in vegetable cell walls, and also help one to assess the results of other workers.

In Table VI the bile salt binding capacities of a range of cell wall preparations of pH values 4, 5, 6, and 7 are listed. Below pH 4 NaCh precipitated out of solution, and the binding of NaCh at pH 7 was not significantly different from that at pH 6. Because the pK of cholic acid is 5.0, a significant proportion of the NaCh molecules would have remained in the unionized form in the pH range 4–5. Taurocholic acid differs from cholic acid in having a sulfonic acid group which confers on it higher acidity (pK 1.5) and solubility. NaTCh is very soluble and would have remained in the fully ionized form in the pH range 4–7 used for the binding experiments; the binding of NaTCh by the fiber preparations did not change significantly with pH. For a fuller account, the original papers should be consulted.

The experiments on the effect of pH on the binding of NaCh, by the various preparations, showed that the binding capacity was very much dependent on the pH. The binding increased as the pH decreased. These experiments were complicated by the precipitation of cholic acid at pHs below 4; nevertheless it was clear that an interaction between cholate and CWM persisted in the pH range 4–5. In this connection, it is useful to point out that even if precipitation of cholic acid was a factor to be reckoned with at pH 4, it is still highly significant that the binding capacity of the preparations at pH 4 showed the following trend: parenchyma CWM $\gg$ parchment CWM $>$ parchment holocellulose (delignified CWM) $>$ parchment α-cellulose. Therefore the NaCh/fiber interactions in the pH range 4–5 were genuine. The binding capacity of the preparations from parenchymatous tissues was higher than that of lignified tissues in the pH range 5–7.

The above studies were extended by investigating the binding capacities of some cell wall preparations in the H and Na forms. The binding capacities (μmol/g CWM) of parenchyma CWM, depectinated parenchyma CWM (which contained a significant amount of residual pectic material), and parchment CWM in the H and Na forms were as follows: parenchyma CWM (H), 345; parenchyma CWM (Na), <5; depectinated parenchyma CWM (H), 135; depectinated parenchyma CWM (Na), <5; parchment CWM (H), 35; parchment CWM (Na), 15. These results suggested that (1) in the case of preparations which have a high density of carboxylate groups (COO$^-$), the negatively charged cholate ions are repelled and have very little chance of entering the cell wall matrix, (2) the binding of NaCh is greatest under conditions in which the ionization of cholic acid and the acidic groups of the cell wall polymers is at its lowest, and (3) removal of pectic material from the CWM (H) resulted in significant loss of binding capacity.

The results on the effect of particle size of lignified tissues on binding capacity showed that there was only a slight increase in binding capacity on decreasing the particle size of the fibers (Selvendran, 1979). Binding capacities of the preparations from leeks showed that the binding capacity at pH 5 of cell walls from parenchymatous tissues (53 μmol/g) was considerably more than that of cutinized tissues (14 μmol/g). Comparison of the binding capacities of the cell wall preparations with some weak cation-exchange resins showed that there are factors other than the number of free carboxyl groups (e.g., conformation of the macromolecule and "space" within the fiber matrix) which determine the ability of a polymer to bind NaCh (Selvendran, 1979).

From the above results the following conclusions may be drawn: (1) pectins and not lignin are the major binding sites for NaCh; (2) for maximum binding the acidic groups of the cell wall polymers and NaCh must be in the unionized form; therefore, hydrogen bonding plays a major role in the binding process; (3) the binding capacity of the CWM from runner bean pods, in the pH range 6–7, is of the same order of magnitude as the binding capacity of the fiber preparations from lucerne, at pH 6.74, reported by Oakenfull and Fenwick (1978); (4) although the binding of NaTCh by the fiber preparations did not change with pH, the amount of NaTCh bound was comparable with the amount of NaCh bound in the pH range 6–7; (5) it is probable that the main mammalian bile acids which exist as conjugates in the small intestine, and have pK values in the range 1.5–3.5, would be bound by vegetable fiber to the same extent as NaTCh in the intestinal pH range 6.5–7; (6) in the overall binding process two main factors are involved, binding of the bile salts to the surface molecules of the fiber and diffusion of the bile salts into the cell wall matrix (and also into the unbroken cells) and then being loosely held within the matrix—when considering the physiology of the digesta in the small intestine the molecules within the fiber matrix may not be readily available for reabsorption in the terminal ileum. The entrapment of bile salts within the "loose" gel network formed by high methoxy pectins may be a factor responsible for the reduction of plasma cholesterol level observed in pectin feeding experiments (Kay and Truswell, 1977; Judd and Truswell, 1982). The effect of the viscosity of the fiber polymers on intestinal absorption is discussed later.

No doubt the physiological factors and mechanisms involved in the lowering of blood lipids and fecal steroid excretion in humans are very complex, and the reader should consult the following papers for an appreciation of the research trends in this area (Stasse-Wolthuis, 1980, 1981; Judd and Truswell, 1982, 1985). Nevertheless, the comments on the adsorption characteristics of bile salts by well-defined cell wall preparations are useful, because most nutritionists have (1) used ill-defined fiber preparations, (2) removed significant amounts of cell wall constituents in an attempt to remove associated components; and (3) used fiber from organs which have a range of tissue types, which makes interpretation of the results difficult.

D. CATION EXCHANGE CAPACITY

The main functional groups of cell wall polymers that can bind cations are the carboxyl groups of uronic acids, which are known to bind calcium *in vitro* (James *et al.,* 1978). However, the nature of the uronic acid-containing polymers, their mode of occurrence within the cell wall complex, and the form in which the food is taken (fresh, cooked, or processed) are important considerations when assessing the cation exchange capacity (CEC) of DF. A few examples will be given to illustrate the above point.

1. Vegetable fiber, e.g., cell walls of parenchymatous tissues of runner beans, apples, and immature tissues of onions are rich in pectic substances, and the major pectic polymers that are of interest in this context are the rhamnogalacturonans. The rhamnogalacturonans of the middle lamella region are highly esterified, and the nonesterified regions are involved in the formation of "egg-box" junction zones (see Fig. 1a of Selvendran, 1985). The highly branched rhamnogalacturonans of primary cell walls are also esterified and are held together by Ca^{2+}, but most of these polymers are also linked to other matrix polymers by ester linkages (see Fig. 1b of Selvendran, 1985). The CEC of a parenchyma cell wall preparation, based on the titratable carboxyl groups after exposing the fibre to 2 M HCl for 24 hr at room temperature (McConnell *et al.,* 1974), is primarily determined by the number of nonesterified carboxyl groups, most of which are involved in the formation of junction zones, and to a lesser extent on the number of esterified carboxyl groups and the residual traces of hydrochloric acid, which are difficult to remove completely. Because the Ca^{2+} in the junction zones is strongly chelated, treatment with 2 M HCl for extended periods is required for "complete" removal. However, it should be borne in mind that prolonged treatment with acid may cause some deesterification of the pectins, therefore some of the esterified galacturonic acid residues may also contribute to the CEC. Determination of CEC based on the titratable carboxyl groups does not strictly reflect the cation-retaining property of DF in the human alimentary tract for the following reasons: (1) Not all the Ca^{2+} in the middle lamella region is likely to be displaced by the acidity and the retention time of the diet in the stomach (~2–3 hr); the undisplaced Ca^{2+} is more likely to be released into the large intestine when the fiber is degraded by colonic bacteria. (2) The metallic ions (and other low molecular weight intestinal components) that diffuse into the cell wall matrix and pectin gel network may diffuse out more slowly, because the ester groups of the galacturonic acid residues of pectins may undergo slow deesterification by the slightly alkaline conditions that prevail within the small intestine. (3) In the case of cooked foods, e.g., cooked apples, the intercellular adhesion is considerably reduced, therefore more pectin molecules would be available for binding cations. However, the pectin gel network

available for the retention of metallic ions is reduced at the same time. Also, during cooking, transeliminative degradation of pectins takes place, and this would influence the CEC of the fiber in an indefinable manner.

2. Cell walls of lignified tissues of dicotyledons (e.g., parchment layers of runner bean pods) contain relatively small amounts of pectin, and as the middle lamella region is impregnated with lignin it is difficult to get an estimate of the titratable carboxyl groups of the fiber after exposure to acid. For example, the titratable carboxyl groups of the CWM of parenchymatous tissues of runner bean pods were 3.2 meq/g CWM, whereas those of parchment layers were <0.1 meq/g CWM (Selvendran, 1979; R. R.Selvendran, unpublished results). The uronic acids associated with the hemicelluloses (e.g., glucurono- and 4-O-methylglucuronoxylans) would not contribute to the CEC because the hemicelluloses are impregnated with lignin, and also because the uronic acids exist in the esterified form. Although the DF from vegetables and fruits contains relatively small amounts of lignified fibers, the above comments were made (1) because reliable values for the uronic acid content and titratable carboxyl groups of CWM from parchment layers were available, and (2) because the comments are highly relevant when one is considering the CEC of cereal-based foods, particularly those which have significant amounts of lignified tissues (e.g., wheat bran and bran-based products).

3. When considering the ability of wheat bran to retain cations the following factors should be borne in mind: (1) the amount of titratable carboxyl groups is negligible and is in fact comparable with that of parchment layers of runner bean pods (R. R. Selvendran, unpublished results); (2) a small amount of phytin is present in the lignified bran layers, but it is unlikely that the acidic phosphate groups of calcium phytate would normally be available for cation exchange; however, the acidic groups of potassium phytate would be available for exchange provided the molecules are exposed, which could take place during bacterial degradation of fiber in the colon; (3) the structure of the various cell types of bran, which would largely remain intact until the digesta reaches the colon, may, however, play a role in retaining cations—when the intestinal secretions mix with the fibrous tissues of bran those molecules which diffuse into the (relatively small) cells may be partially retained, and the number of available cells would increase as the starch and proteins are digested. A proportion of the entrapped electrolytes may be carried into the large intestine to be (partially) released when the bran layers are degraded by colonic bacteria. It is therefore not surprising that fecal excretion of a range of minerals shows a significant increase when wheat fiber is added to the diet (Jenkins et al., 1975; Cummings et al., 1976; Cummings, 1978a,b).

Estimates of the maximum cation exchange capacities of cell wall preparations from vegetables can be obtained from their total uronic acid contents. Thus the total uronic acid content of the CWM from parenchymatous tissues of runner beans and apples are 370 and 330 μg/mg CWM. Assuming that most of the uronic acid is galacturonic acid, the CEC of the CWM from runner beans and apples would be 2.1 and 1.9 meq/g CWM; this is the maximum estimate because an appreciable proportion of the uronic acid residues would be in the esterified form. The maximum CEC of the fibers from apples, carrots, and cabbage (organs relatively poor in starch) based on the total uronic acid content of the AIR is 2.3, 2.2, and 2.2 meq/g AIR, respectively (Stevens and Selvendran, 1981). The uronic acid contents of the starch-depleted AIR from wheat bran and dehulled oats were 70 and 90 mg/g (Stevens and Selvendran, 1981), and the maximum CEC, assuming that all the uronic acid residues are available for cation exchange would be only 0.4 and 0.5 meq/g material. However, as mentioned before, most if not all the glucuronic and 4-O-methylglucuronic acid residues exist in the esterified form and are therefore not available for cation exchange. McConnell et al. (1974), using the acetone-extracted residues, have determined the CEC of "fibers" from a range of edible plant organs, and some of the values which they have reported are potato 0.3, winter cabbage 1.5, apple 1.9, carrot 2.4 (meq/g acetone powder). It is interesting to note that the CEC of starch-poor organs such as cabbage, apples, and carrot are comparable with the values obtained from the total uronic acids of the CWM or AIR. The CEC of the acetone powder from potato is very low because no allowance was made for the contaminating starch.

The ability of fiber to bind cations, more correctly retain cations, influences mineral absorption in the gastrointestinal tract. For an account of the various effects, see Cummings (1978a,b), James (1980), and Dintzis et al. (1985). Various studies have shown that enhancement of the fiber content of a diet is associated with increased excretion of fecal electrolytes. This has caused some concern, although other studies have shown that a high fiber diet increases the intake of electrolytes (for a review of this topic, see James, 1980). Other possible physiological consequences of cation binding are altered heavy metal toxicity, due to irreversible binding. These effects will depend to a certain extent on the action sites available for binding the ions after colonic bacterial degradation.

E.   VISCOSITY ENHANCING AND GEL FORMING PROPERTIES

Viscosity enhancing and gel forming properties of certain DF components, e.g., guar gum and pectins, are important for two main reasons: (1) viscous components can, under appropriate conditions, delay gastric emptying (Holt et al., 1979), and (2) viscous components possibly reduce absorption rates in the small intestine (Taylor, 1979; Leeds, 1979). It should also be borne in mind that mixing viscous polymers with food may modify the release of gastrointestinal hormones involved in insulin release, gastrointestinal motility, and morphology.

These properties are probably responsible for some of the potential therapeutic applications of guar gum in the management of hyperglycemia (in diabetics) and hypercholesterolemia (Jenkins *et al.*, 1978; Johnson, 1984). Studies with human subjects have shown that glucose absorption is reduced by the simultaneous ingestion of food gums such as guar gum, pectin, or carboxymethylcellulose, and this effect has been shown to increase with the viscosity enhancing properties of the ingested gum (Jenkins *et al.*, 1976, 1978).

In recent years, a number of studies have been made to investigate the mechanisms underlying the effects of viscous fiber polymers on glucose absorption in the small intestine. Johnson and Gee (1981, 1982) have demonstrated substantial reduction in glucose transport *in vitro*, by using everted sacs of rat jejeunum incubated with low concentrations (0.25–0.70% w/v) of guar gum and sodium carboxymethylcellulose. Because comparable changes were effected by polysaccharides having very different chemical structures, it is argued that specific biochemical inhibition of glucose transport by the polysaccharides is an unlikely mechanism. Based on the evidence that (1) glucose transport with and without the addition of guar gum was found to be sensitive to mucosal stirring (in fact glucose transport in the presence of guar gum was largely restored to control levels by increased stirring) and (2) the apparent thickness of the unstirred fluid layer overlying the mucosa increased (guar-free thickness, 317 ± 15 μm; guar-treated thickness, 468 ± 25 μm; and CMC-treated thickness 402 ± 12 μm), it is suggested that the presence of a polysaccharide gum in the fluid surrounding the villi increases its viscosity, and thus gives rise to a thickening of the rate-limiting unstirred layer. The authors, therefore, propose that the inhibition of glucose transport observed in their studies is best explained by an increase in the resistance of the mucosal diffusion brought about by the greater viscosity of incubation media containing food gums.

A point to note in the above study is that the polysaccharides need not be in the bulk phase to exert their effect but need only be present in the layer overlying the mucosa. This may result in some degree of interaction between the gums and the mucopolysaccharides of the mucosal surface, which probably help to retain the surface layer for a period. Therefore the physicochemical properties of food gums may influence their effectiveness in modifying the intestinal transport of glucose. If the above effect occurs *in vivo*, it may restrict the diffusion of solutes in the lumen of the small intestine, and hence influence the rates of digestion and absorption of nutrients (Johnson, 1984), and contribute to the diminished postprandial glycemia observed in human subjects fed with guar gum.

Supporting evidence for the above hypothesis is provided by the work of several researchers: (1) Elsenhans and colleagues (1980a,b) have reported reversible inhibition of monosaccharide and amino acid transport in rat small intestine treated with guar, pectin, tragacanth, carubin, or carrageenan *in vitro* and *in vivo*. (2) Ebihara *et al.* (1981) have observed reduced rates of glucose absorption in perfused segments of rat jejunum *in vivo* in the presence of konjac mannan. (3) Rainbird *et al.* (1982a,b) have reported that guar gum reduces the rate of glucose absorption in isolated loops of jejeunum in conscious pigs. (4) Blackburn and Johnson (1981) and Blackburn (1984) have studied the effect of guar gum on the viscosity of the gastrointestinal contents of rats and on glucose uptake from the perfused jejeunum in the rat, and their results showed that ingestion of guar gum increased the apparent viscosity of the contents of the stomach and small intestine and decreased the rate of glucose absorption in segments perfused with guar solution (6 g guar gum/liter).

The above experiments showed that in the rat the presence of viscosity enhancing components of DF in the small intestine resulted in reduced rates of glucose absorption. Recent studies by Blackburn *et al.* (1984a,b) using guar gum suggested that similar mechanisms may be responsible for the hypoglycemic action of viscous fiber polymers in humans. Because guar gum lowers blood glucose level (Jenkins *et al.,* 1977), guar-enriched breads have been tested on diabetics (Jenkins *et al.,* 1980c), and the results are encouraging.

Another apparently useful property of viscosity enhancing polymers is that they inhibit intestinal uptake of cholesterol (and possibly other steroids, e.g., bile salts), and thus reduce plasma cholesterol level in man (Kay and Truswell, 1977, 1980; Anderson, 1985; Anderson and Chen, 1979). Comparatively recent studies have suggested that guar gum (Jenkins *et al.,* 1980a; Khan *et al.,* 1981), citrus pectin (Kay and Truswell, 1977; Judd and Truswell, 1982), rolled oats (Judd and Truswell, 1981), and oat bran (Anderson *et al.,* 1984; Kirby *et al.,* 1981) may be of therapeutic value in the treatment of hypercholesterolemia. The major water-soluble cell wall polysaccharides of rolled oats and oat bran are β-D-glucans and these can form viscous solutions in water. Johnson and co-workers (Johnson, 1984; Gee *et al.,* 1983) studied the uptake of cholesterol from preformed solutions by everted sacs of rat proximal small intestine and the effect of a guar layer, adsorbed to the mucosal surface, on cholesterol absorption *in vivo*. Based on these results they have suggested that the mechanism of action of guar in inhibiting intestinal cholesterol uptake is similar to that proposed by them in relation to actively absorbed sugars (Johnson and Gee, 1981). However, the interaction between guar gum and lipid micelles and the effect of reduced fluid movement in the presence of guar gum may also be important considerations, and these need further study.

The importance of the interactions between pectins and secretions of the bile duct is shown by the work of Judd and Truswell (1985) on the hypocholesterolemic effects of pectins in rats. It is suggested that the highly viscous gut contents (in pectin-fed rats) may retain the bile salts, fat, and cholesterol within a "loose" gel network and thus minimize absorption and also present a barrier to efficient lipolytic activity. Such effects would result in the increased fecal excretion of lipids, cholesterol, and bile acids (Lin *et al.,* 1957) and reduction of serum cholesterol levels (Tsai *et al.*, 1976; Judd and Truswell, 1985) observed with rats. Effects, similar to those of pectin, on steroid excretion and plasma cholesterol have been reported for other food gums such as guar gum (Jenkins *et al.*, 1975) and psyllium seed mucilage (Stanley *et al.*, 1973). The fact that these food gums are chemically dissimilar but have the ability to form gels and viscous solutions suggests that these properties are important and probably determine their mode of action in the small intestine.

F. EFFECTS OF DF AND OTHER FACTORS ON THE DIGESTIBILITY OF STARCH

In Section III,A the factors that influence the enzymatic degradation of starch *in vitro* were discussed, mainly in connection with the analysis of DF. In this section, some comments will be made on the particle size of the preparations, cooking and processing conditions, and the role of the cell wall matrix on the degradability of starch in plant foods by intestinal enzymes.

a. Particle Size.   Because starch is encapsulated within the cell walls, the walls restrict the accessibility of the starch to intestinal enzymes. Decreasing the particle size, by grinding, greatly increases the amount of starch available for degradation, and results in much more rapid digestion of starch and absorption of the products formed. Haber *et al.* (1977) have shown that disruption of the cell walls of food to be ingested resulted in reduced satiety, more rapid absorption of the carbohydrates, and greater insulin responses. *In vitro* studies on the enzymatic degradation of rice starch has shown that the starch in the ground rice was hydrolyzed more rapidly than that in the unground rice; similar observations were made with rolled oats and rolled wheat (Snow and Dea, 1981). O'Dea *et al.* (1980) have shown that in the case of rice, the postprandial glucose and insulin responses to equal ingestion of ground and unground white and unpolished (brown) rice correlate very closely with the *in vitro* rates of starch hydrolysis.

b. Cooking and Processing Conditions.   Cooking results in gelatinization of the starch (within the granules) and increased cell separation, and thus greatly increases the percentage of starch hydrolyzed. Ungelatinized starch granules are resistant to α-amylase (Palmer, 1972; Fleming and Vose, 1979), but the presence of α-amylase inhibitors in some foods (Shainkin and Birk, 1970; Wolever *et al.*, 1983) and the complexing of starch with other food components such as lipids (Holm *et al.*, 1983) and proteins (Anderson *et al.*, 1981) are also factors to be borne in mind. Snow and Dea (1981) have shown that the hydrolysis of starch in rolled oats and rolled wheat was greatly enhanced by cooking. Using human ileostomy subjects, Englyst and Cummings (1985) have shown that the breakdown of starch in unprocessed cereal foods (rolled and steamed oats) was complete but that in processed foods (white bread and cornflakes) some "resistant starch" escaped digestion by the enzymes of the small intestine. During food processing, part of the gelatinized starch, especially the amylose fraction, retrogrades to material resistant to hydrolysis with α-amylase. In another investigation, Englyst and Cummings (1986b) studied the digestibility of starch in unripe and ripe bananas by the ileostomy subjects. Among other things their results showed that the amount of starch not hydrolyzed and absorbed from the small intestine, and therefore passing into the colon, may be up to eight times more than the NSP present in unripe bananas and was hydrolyzed to a lesser extent than that of the ripe fruit.

c.   Cell Wall Structure.   Throughout the text, the protective role of the cell walls has been alluded to, but some recent work by Gee and Johnson (1985) calls for comment. Gee and Johnson have studied the rates of starch hydrolysis and changes in viscosity in a range of plant foods subjected to simulated digestion *in vitro.* The foods studied included potato and maize starch, white rice, white bread, porridge oats, potatoes, peas, lentils, butter beans, and red kidney beans. Their results showed the following: (1) Different foods exhibited marked differences in rates of starch hydrolysis. The fastest rates were associated with starch preparations and high starch, low fiber foods (e.g., potato and rice); the intermediate rates were associated with bread and porridge; while the slowest rates were observed with the legumes (baked beans, butter beans, lentils, and kidney beans). (2) On simulated digestion (mainly to degrade starch) all the foods underwent a marked fall in viscosity during the first 60 min, and this decline was more prolonged in the case of rice and bread. After 2 hr the relative viscosities of the samples showed the following trend: potatoes > porridge oats > baked beans > bread = white rice. Based on these results the authors suggest that the observed variation in the human glycemic response to various starch-rich foods (Jenkins *et al.,* 1980b, 1984) probably depends primarily on differences in the rate of starch hydrolysis. In this context, it should be noted that the presence or absence of intact cell walls, which are likely to slow the release of starch from the gelatinized granules and thus impede the access of pancreatic enzymes, is probably of greater significance than the total DF content; although there is some relationship between the two which is governed by several factors discussed earlier.

G.   EFFECTS OF DF ON THE ACTIVITY OF INTESTINAL ENZYMES

There is evidence to suggest that the activity of certain pancreatic enzymes, namely, amylase, lipase, trypsin, and chymotrypsin, can be altered *in vitro* by incubation with (1) DF polymers such as cellulose, xylans, pectins, and guar gum and (2) preparations containing significant amounts of DF such as material from alfalfa, oat bran, and wheat bran (Schneeman, 1978; Dunaif and

Schneeman, 1981; Isaksson *et al.*, 1982). The enzymes were dissolved in buffer, incubated with varying amounts of the preparations for 5 min at 37°C, and filtered, and the (total) activity of the enzymes in the filtrate was determined as a percentage of the control. The results showed that (1) cellulose and xylan reduced the activity of amylase, lipase, trypsin, and chymotrypsin to less than half the original activity (Dunaif and Schneeman, 1981); (2) citrus pectin slightly increased the activity of the enzymes tested (Schneeman, 1978; Dunaif and Schneeman, 1981); (3) guar gum decreased the activity of amylase and lipase (Isaksson *et al.*, 1982); and (4) alfalfa, wheat bran, and oat bran decreased the activity of the enzymes to varying degrees (Dunaif and Schneeman, 1981). Schneeman and Gallaher (1985) have attributed the reductions in enzyme activity to nonspecific binding of the enzymes by the fiber polymers, and in the case of nonpurified fiber sources specific enzyme inhibitors are also implicated.

We are of the opinion that it is difficult to draw any firm conclusions from the above studies because (1) the cell wall polysaccharides were (apparently) not further purified before testing, and, since significant amounts of polysaccharides were used relative to the amounts of enzymes tested, the presence of inhibitors in the commercial preparations should not be overlooked; and (2) the alfalfa and bran preparations may have had specific inhibitors. In addition, in the absence of information on the DF content of the preparations, the nature of the constituent DF polymers, and the particle size of the preparations, the results are not particularly meaningful. Also, some work should be done using the purified DF preparations before one can speculate about the role of DF and DF polymers in altering pancreatic enzyme activity. It is possible that the inhibitory effects of DF on the activity of the intestinal enzymes may not have significant effects on the digestibility of food in the small intestine, because of the very large excess of enzyme activity present in pancreatic secretions. Even so, the interactions between DF and pancreatic enzymes warrant further study to clarify the points raised above.

V.   THE ACTION OF THE INTESTINAL BACTERIA ON DF

A.   GENERAL CONSIDERATIONS

1.   Physical and Chemical Properties

The well-established properties of dietary fiber are those of increasing fecal bulk and reducing transit time, and many studies have been made which showed that cereal fiber is very effective and vegetable fiber less so. The earlier studies have been reviewed by Spiller and Amen (1975), and the results have been summarized by Stasse-Wolthuis (1981).

In a mixed diet, increase in fecal weight is probably the result of a combination of three main factors: (1) increased mass of undegraded fiber, (2) an increase of bacterial mass as a result of utilization of the fiber, and (3) increase in water retained by the degraded fiber/bacteria complex. This component will contain water entrapped by the degraded fiber and bacterial cells, but an appreciable proportion of the water will be contained within the bacterial cells, which are ~80% water (Luria, 1960) and on a typical British type of diet account for about 55% of the total mass of fecal solids (Stephen and Cummings, 1980a). This value was obtained from the control groups in a study by Cummings *et al.* (1978) on the effects of various fiber supplements (~20 g/day) on fecal weight and transit time. They found that transit time was reduced and that increases in fecal weight correlated with increases in the pentose content of the noncellulosic polysaccharides and was greatest for bran (127% increase in fecal weight) followed by cabbage (69%), carrot (59%), apple (40%), and guar gum (20%). The correlation of fecal weight versus pentose content remained remarkably good when the results of studies with other cereal fibers were included (Cummings, 1978b). In the above study bacterial mass accounted for a large proportion (25–35%) of the increase in fecal weight with the more fermentable carrot and cabbage, which were 90% degraded, but for only 10–15% of the increase in fecal mass weight with the bran, which was 45% degraded (Stephen and Cummings, 1980b; Cummings, 1984a).

In order to obtain a better understanding of the extent of fermentation and the fecal weight versus pentose correlation observed by Cummings and co-workers, we have carried out a series of detailed studies on the composition and structural features of CWM of the materials used by them, together with studies on the CWM of fresh tissues (Stevens and Selvendran, 1980, 1984a–d). The important conclusions (summarized by Selvendran, 1984) were as follows: (1) During preparation of the CWM appreciable proportions of pectic substances were solubilized by cold aqueous solvents from cabbage, carrot, and apple compared with a small proportion of arabinoxylan from wheat bran. (2) The amounts of pectic substances rich in arabinose extracted by hot water and oxalate were greatest for apple (27%) followed by carrot and cabbage. (3) Some of the pectic polymers remained to be further extracted with alkali which indicated that these were linked through alkali-labile ester groups either directly or via phenolic acid groups to other cell wall polymers. (4) Whereas the pentose in vegetable and apple CWM is in the form of arabinans, arabinogalactans, and xyloglucans, in wheat bran the pentosans are acidic arabinoxylans which are ester cross-linked to other polymers, including lignin, by phenolic ester groups and thus requires 1 or 4 M potassium hydroxide to release them. These results account for the greater degradation of the vegetable and apple fiber in which the fermentable pectic substances are either easily solubilized or are more readily accessible because they are free of lignin. Therefore the composition and solubility characteristics of the cell wall polymers and no doubt the numbers of bacteria present in the colon as well as their metabolic activities are important factors when considering the properties and effects of dietary fiber.

2. Metabolic Activities of the Bacteria

The metabolic activity of the bacteria in the intestine is important in relation to: (1) the extent of degradation of dietary fiber; (2) the production of metabolites of physiological importance to the host; and (3) the modification of potentially toxic components of the diet. Overall, the numbers of bacteria in the small intestine are relatively small. The upper part is essentially sterile, and the count does not become appreciable until the distal end where it rises to the order of $10^6/$ ml (Gorbach et al., 1967; Drasar and Hill, 1974; Berghouse et al., 1984). In feces the total count is approximately $10^{11}–10^{12}/g$ dry wt, (Moore and Holdeman, 1974; Finegold et al., 1983), and studies with ileostomy patients (Sandberg et al., 1981, 1983; Englyst and Cummings, 1985) have revealed that dietary fiber is relatively undegraded on leaving the small intestine. Therefore most of the bacterial activity occurs in the colon.

Dietary fiber and bacteria have been implicated with colorectal cancer. We will not discuss this in detail, but some of the possible factors are as follows: (1) The extra fecal bulk due to fiber may dilute potential carcinogens and exert a protective effect by virtue of decreased transit time resulting in their quicker removal, allowing less time for bacterial production of carcinogens from these compounds and reducing the duration of contact with the intestinal epithelium (Burkitt, 1973b), although this hypothesis has not been supported by experimental evidence. (2) An alteration in the route of nitrogen metabolism, including greater utilization of ammonia which is reputedly toxic and greater production of short chain fatty acids (SCFA) some of which, e.g., butyrate, may exert a protective effect (Cummings et al., 1981; van Soest, 1981). For further discussion the following publications are useful: *Role of Dietary Fibre in Health* (1978), *Banbury Report, 7* (1981), and the report by the Committee on Diet, Nutrition and Cancer (1982).

B. FERMENTATION OF DF COMPONENTS

1. Numbers and Types of Bacteria in the Large Intestine

The numerous surveys of the predominately anaerobic human fecal flora up to 1976 have been reviewed by Brown (1977). Since then Finegold (1978) and Hentges (1978) have published further papers on the effect of diets. One of the most extensive surveys has been that of Moore and Holdeman (1974) on the flora of 20 elderly Japanese–Hawaiian males. One hundred and thirteen distinct types of organisms were isolated; the 20 most abundant species accounted for 69% of the isolates and 66.5% comprised five genera: *Eubacterium* (21.9% of the total), *Bacteroides* (18.7%), *Bifidobacterium* (9.8%), *Peptostreptococcus* (8.9%), and *Fusobacterium* (7.2%). Although there have been several studies on the effect of dietary changes in the human fecal flora, the conclusions were that in adults the composition of the flora remains remarkably constant. Studies have been complicated, however, by significant differences which exist between individuals in the ranking of the species in their "normal" flora (Moore *et al.*, 1981). The fecal flora may not reflect changes in flora which may occur in the colon, and although the ranking of species does not alter with changes of diet the metabolic characteristics of the flora may do so. The problems of studying the colonic microflora have been discussed by Finegold *et al.* (1983) and Hill (1982). Dietary fiber supplements of bran (Fuchs *et al.*, 1976) and of guar (Bayliss and Houston, 1985) have been shown to increase the total anaerobe count. With the use of enrichment techniques for isolation of bacteria, Wyatt *et al.* (1986) have shown that the proportion of fecal organisms able to ferment gum arabic rose from 6.5 to 50% of the total flora during the time the gum was fed and subsequently returned to the control level. Species of *Bacteroides* and *Bifidobacterium* were the principal gum arabic fermenters. These genera produce SCFA from the fermentation of glucose.

The abilities of many of these organisms, in pure culture, to utilize various polysaccharides of plant origin as growth substrates have been extensively studied, but in the case of incompletely degraded substrates very little work has been done to determine the structural features which are resistant to attack. Most of the *in vitro* studies have been made with isolated polysaccharides as substrates and with single strains of bacteria, but more recently some studies have been made with mixed cultures from fecal inocula (Jeraci, 1981; Van Soest *et al.*, 1983). In the rumen the "nylon bag" technique has been used in which the substrate is contained in a nylon bag of fine mesh to prevent mixing with the bulk of the rumen contents. As with studies on the plant cell wall, initially it is convenient to study the degradation of isolated, (fairly) well-defined fractions, and these will be considered before discussing the degradation of the whole cell wall. Although the studies with rumen bacteria may serve as a useful guide to the type of degradation which might occur in the human colon it is important to bear in mind that many species of bacteria previously thought to be common to the ovine rumen and man are now considered to be distinct species specific to the species of host animal (Barnes, 1986).

2. Mode of Fermentation

Polysaccharides are degraded by the bacterial enzymes to their component monosaccharides which can then be used as energy sources by the bacteria. Most of the enzymes are cell associated, but in some instances, e.g., in the fermentation of guar gum by *Bacteroides ovatus* (Balascio *et al.*, 1981), extracellular enzymes are produced. The biochemistry and pathways of monosaccharide fermentation as well as the catabolism of polysaccharides has been adequately reviewed elsewhere, e.g., Prins (1977), so only the main pathways and variations are outlined below. The schemes given by Lin *et al.* (1985) also provide a useful summary of the pathways of catabolism and product formation in the rumen, while the chapter by Wolin and Miller (1983) gives more detail, points out differences in the rumen and human systems and draws attention to the interactions between bacteria (e.g., utilization of hydrogen by methanogens, further fermentation of lactate and succinate by other organisms). Most rumen and intestinal bacteria ferment hexoses by the Embden–Meyerhof–Parnas (EMP) pathway to pyruvate. An exception is *Bifidobacterium* which by means of phosphoketolase cleaves fructose 6-phosphate (F-6-P) to acetyl phosphate and erythrose 4-phosphate (Ery-4-P). The F-6-P and Ery-4-P are then converted to their pentose phosphates and glyceraldehyde-3-phosphate (de Vries *et al.*, 1967). Arabinose, xylose, and galacturonic acid are usually fermented via xylose to F-6-P and the glycolytic pathway, but a proportion can be converted directly to glyceraldehyde 3-phosphate by the pentose phosphate, phosphoketolase pathway. Rhamnose is fermented via ribulose 1-phosphate to lactaldehyde and dihydroxyacetone and thence to 1,2-propanediol and intermediate pyruvate.

3.   Degradation of Polysaccharides

  a.   Pectic Substances.   Pectin is almost completely degraded during its passage through the colon (Werch and Ivy, 1941; Gramstorff-Fetzer *et al.*, 1979). Cummings *et al.* (1979) failed to detect uronic acid in the feces of subjects who had consumed 36 g/day of pectin (24 g total uronic acid) added to a control diet, and Olson *et al.* (1983) also concluded that added pectin was largely metabolized, although the uronic acid content of the feces was not estimated.

During the degradation (B. J. Stevens, R. R Selvendran and C. Bayliss, unpublished) of apple AIR by a human fecal inoculum *in vitro* the uronic acid was the first sugar to be depleted to the extent of 37% after 6 hr and 90% after 12 hr for the apple and in the beet 55% after 12 hr, but only 62% after 24 hr, which was an indication of the lower degradability of the beet pectic substances *in situ*, possibly owing to the presence of linkages through phenolic ester groups (Selvendran *et al.*, 1985). The arabinans were also degraded as indicated by losses of 17% of the apple arabinose after 6 hr and 92% after 12 hr, with values for the beet of 18% after 12 hr and 37% after 24 hr. Chesson and Monro (1982) found that in the rumen, hot water- and oxalate-soluble polysaccharides of clover and lucerne were degraded faster and to a greater extent than other cell wall components. The rate of loss of uronide was lower from the residue which probably contained some residual pectic polysaccharides in addition to acidic hemicelluloses. They concluded that the degradation of pectin in the hot water and oxalate extracts was not related to acetyl or neutral sugar content.

Thomsen *et al.* (1982) reported that when pectin was added to the diet of rats, isobutyrate, isovalerate, and *n*-valerate, which were present in the control diet, were not detected. Some of these SCFA are essential for the growth of some species of bacteria (Bryant, 1974). There is evidence that butyrate may have some protective effect against colon cancer (Cummings, 1984a; Cummings *et al.*, 1981).

b. *Arabinans and Arabinogalactans.* Our own studies (Stevens, Selvendran and Bayliss, unpublished) show that with apple CWM and sugar beet substrates referred to above arabinans and arabinogalactans (type I) are largely fermented along with the pectic substances. To investigate the ability of colonic bacteria to utilize polysaccharides at the low specific growth rates likely to be encountered at the distal end of the colon, Salyers *et al.* (1981a) used larch arabinogalactan as the limiting substrate in continuous culture of *Bacteroides thetaiotaomicron.* Larch arabinogalactan is of type II (Aspinall, 1973) with (1→3)-linked galactose units in the backbone, whereas in the pectic arabinogalactans of type I the galactose residues are (1→4)-linked.

The larch arabinogalactan was not completely degraded, and of the two major molecular (weight) species initially present the lower was degraded most; the proportions of arabinose to galactose, however, remained similar to those in the undegraded substrate. With decreasing specific growth rate the concentration of acetate and propionate produced increased while that of succinate decreased.

Bacteria capable of utilizing larch arabinogalactan were also isolated by enrichment techniques from human feces by Bayliss and Houston (1984) and were mainly *Bifidobacterium* spp. and *Eubacterium* spp. Organisms capable of utilizing citrus pectin and apple CWM were also isolated and were mainly *Bacteroides* spp. Nilsson *et al.* (1984) have provided evidence that some type II arabinogalactans inhibit the adhesion of pathogenic *Escherichia coli* bacteria.

c. *Hemicelluloses*

Vegetables and Fruit. As discussed earlier, xyloglucans are the main hemicellulosic polysaccharides in the majority of edible vegetables and fruits. The bacterial degradation of isolated xyloglucans has not (to our knowledge) been studied, but from *in vitro* experiments with CWM of apples (B. J. H. Stevens and R. R. Selvendran, unpublished) it appears that some degradation occurs, probably by cellulases degrading the glucan 'backbone' to leave branched oligosaccharide fragments as occurs with action of fungal cellulases (Bauer *et al.*, 1973; O'Neill and Selvendran, 1985b).

Cereals. As with vegetable hemicelluloses most of the studies have been made with unfractionated plant material. The ability of rumen bacteria, including those of the genus *Bacteroides,* to utilize xylans, which form the bulk of ruminant forage hemicelluloses, has been extensively studied (Dehority, 1965, 1967; Bailey and Macrae, 1970). Salyers *et al.* (1977a,b, 1981b) found that several strains of bacteria of the genera *Bacteroides, Bifidobacterium,* and *Peptostreptococcus,* which were among the most abundant in the Moore and Holdeman study, were able to utilize larchwood xylan. *Bacteroides* species are among the most active and "versatile" fermenters, and a more detailed study was carried out with some of these species fermenting larchwood xylan (Salyers *et al.,* 1981b). Only the soluble, low molecular weight fraction (65–70% of the total) of the xylan was fermented to a range of xylose oligomers, although these could be degraded to xylose by sonically disrupted cells. In a further study (1982) Salyers *et al.* concluded that the enzymes were probably cell associated and not constitutive. Insoluble xylan was not utilized, and not more than 60% of the soluble xylan was degraded even after repeated enzyme treatments. Removal of arabinose side groups decreased the solubility but did not render the soluble xylan more degradable. It was concluded that the extent of degradation was mainly limited by the extent of hydration. With soluble and insoluble fractions of larchwood (and oat spelts) xylans *in vitro* with fecal inocula, B. J. H. Stevens and R. R. Selvendran (unpublished) found that, although the sugar compositions of the soluble and insoluble fractions were similar, the insoluble xylans were degraded to a lesser extent than the soluble fractions. As with Salyers' results this may have been due to a greater degree of association in the insoluble fractions. Estimation of the proportion of terminal xylose residues by methylation analysis revealed no significant difference in the DP of the insoluble and soluble fractions.

Reddy *et al.* (1983) studied the degradation of wheat straw xylan by strains of *Bacteroides ovatus* which were able to ferment a commercial xylan (Salyers *et al.,* 1977a). Six of the seven strains tested could ferment the hemicellulose A and B fractions but were unable to ferment milled (<1 mm screen) wheat straw. Because there was very little activity in the extracellular enzyme fraction, only the intracellular enzymes from one of the most active strains were studied further (Reddy *et al.,* 1984). The activity was largely inducible with slightly different proportions of xylose and arabinose products depending on whether the inducing substrate was crude hemicellulose or hemicellulose A or B. Crude hemicellulose was the most effective inducer, overall, with the enzyme releasing 22% of the total sugars from crude hemicellulose in 18 hr compared with 4% from hemicellulose A, 19% from hemicellulose B, and only 2% from the milled wheat straw. Xylanases, producing xylooligosaccharides, were most active during the first 4 hr of incubation whereas arabinose was mainly released after this time.

Among the possible causes for the lower degradation of hemicellulose A (of similar sugar composition to B) were solubility (details not given) and the presence of inhibitors such as metal ions or phenolics.

d. Cellulose. There is appreciable breakdown of cellulose in the rumen, and several species of cellulolytic bacteria have been isolated, the preponderant species being *Bacteroides succinogenes, Ruminococcus albus, R. flavefaciens,* and *Butyrivibrio fibrosolvens* (for references see Prins, 1977). Most of the enzymes studied are constitutive, and many are extracellular but closely associated with the cell surface. These and other properties are reviewed by Prins (1977), and more recently Pettipher and Latham (1979a,b) have studied the cellulases of *R. flavefaciens,* Wood *et al.* (1982) have studied the cellulases of *R. albus* strain SY3, and Groleau and Forsberg (1981, 1983) have partially characterized the cellulase enzymes of *Bacteroides succinogenes.*

The breakdown of cellulose by bacteria from the human colon is less well documented, but the studies described below provide evidence that degradation does occur. Cellulolytic bacteria of *Bacteroides* spp., occurring in numbers of at least $10^8/g$ wet wt, have been isolated from the feces of 1 in 5 subjects by Betian *et al.* (1977) and from 2 out of 6 persons by Bryant (1978). The organism isolated by Bryant only slowly fermented ball-milled filter paper, a substrate which is fairly rapidly degraded by rumen cellulolytic bacteria. There are numerous reports of cellulose breakdown, *in vivo,* but many of the early studies were with unfractionated vegetable or cereal materials, the methods of analysis employed may have measured some hemicellulose, lignin, and cellulose-associated pectic substances as cellulose, and fine particles of degraded cellulose may have escaped recovery. However, more recent studies do provide evidence for appreciable cellulose breakdown in the large intestine. In the studies of Cummings *et al.* (1978) with vegetable and cereal fiber, the degradation of cabbage and carrot AIR to the extent of ~90% (Cummings, 1984a) implied that approximately 50% of the cellulose was degraded. The cellulose content of the preparations used was about 20% (Stevens and Selvendran, 1981, 1984c). Holloway *et al.* (1978) reported that only 22.4% of the cellulose from a mixed diet was recovered in feces from "normal" subjects compared with 84.5% from ileostomy patients.

Ehle *et al.* (1982) conducted a study in which bran, Solka floc, and cabbage AIR substrates were inoculated with feces from subjects who had been on a dietary regime which included the same substrates as dietary supplements (12 g additional "cell wall" per day). A maximum of 88% of the cabbage AIR was degraded after 48 hr compared with only 6% of the Solka floc. Van Soest *et al.* (1983), using a human fecal inoculum, reported the fermentability of Solka floc as 23%. In edible vegetable tissue the cellulose is mainly in the primary cell walls and is more amorphous than wood cellulose such as Solka floc which also contains hemicellulose and lignin (Van Soest *et al.,* 1983). In a parallel *in vivo* study (Van Soest, 1984), in one subject 60% of finely ground Solka floc was fermented initially, but with increasing time on the diet (~21 g/day) fermentation decreased and was zero after 6 weeks. This was probably due to a "washout" effect owing to the growth rate of the bacteria being slower than the transit time resulting in a decrease in the numbers of cellulolytic bacteria. However, no attempt was made to isolate these bacteria or to determine their growth rates. In the rumen, cellulose- and hemicellulose-degrading bacteria adhere strongly to the fiber substrates (Akin and Amos, 1975; Dinsdale *et al.*, 1978) and examination by electron microscopy of CWM of wheat bran after *in vitro* degradation has revealed that human intestinal bacteria do likewise (Figs. 4 and 5). Therefore these bacteria are particularly susceptible to loss by excretion, especially since transit times are likely to be reduced with these substrates. In the Van Soest study the subject did not regain bacteria capable of degrading crystalline cellulose over a further 2-year period, and two other subjects tested initially showed no cellulose-degrading ability.

In a study on the fermentation of apple CWM *in vivo* by human fecal bacteria Stevens *et al.* (1987) found that the 93% depletion of glucose after 24 hr was more than could be accounted for by degradation of the xyloglucan present and,

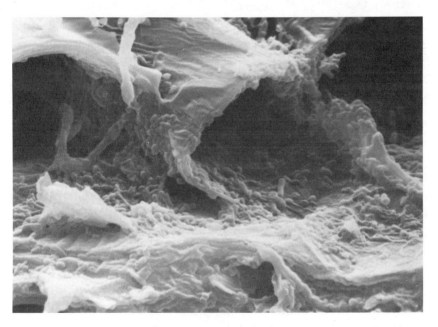

FIG. 4. Scanning electron micrograph of wheat bran CWM after degradation for 24 hr *in vitro* by human fecal bacteria and subsequent treatment with 1% sodium dodecyl sulfate–phenol (1 : 9 v/w) at 65–70°C. Insoluble residue was dialyzed and freeze-dried (3500×). Note bacteria adhering mainly to the damaged edges of the cross cells and tube cells.

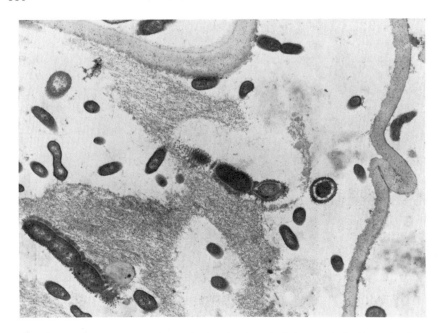

FIG. 5. Transmission electron micrograph of section through alkali-treated wheat bran after degradation for 40 hr *in vitro* by human fecal bacteria (12,600×). Some bacteria are closely associated with the degraded cell walls.

together with the loss of 93% of the initial carbohydrate, concluded that the cellulose was extensively degraded. Gramstorff-Fetzer *et al.* (1979) found an apparent degradation of 46% of an α-cellulose powder (based on NDF and ADF − lignin estimations) in adolescent boys, but no details of transit times were given. In a later study Kies *et al.* (1984) recovered 74, 78, and 75% of cellulose added to a liquid diet at levels of 20, 30, and 40 g/day, respectively.

Slavin *et al.* (1981) reported that with a daily intake of 5.4 g cellulose from fruits, vegetables, and grains the mean digestibility of cellulose by seven women over 1 month was 69.2%. When Solka floc was added to increase the cellulose intake to 19.3 g/day, digestibility fell to a mean value of 14.4% with some subjects showing negative digestibility. NDF digestibility also decreased. In a separate experiment, with four women, in which Solka floc (16 g/day) was added to a semipurified liquid diet, the digestibility of cellulose ranged from 0.5 to 14.1% (mean 8.1%). Cellulose was estimated by the Crampton and Maynard (1938) procedure, using acetic/nitric acid, and the Solka floc contained ~6.3% hemicellulose and <1% lignin (method unspecified). The authors also drew attention to errors in the use of NDF by other workers.

In many of these studies cellulose was measured nonspecifically as ADF minus lignin. In an earlier section we have already drawn attention to the deficiencies of the detergent fiber methods when applied to vegetable CWM. Morrison (1980) pointed out that ADF, especially from lignified tissues, often contains hemicellulose and that the Crampton and Maynard (1938) method for estimation of cellulose is preferable even though a small proportion of hemicellulose is estimated as cellulose. Even in our own studies, using well-defined substrates and specific sugar analysis, complications are caused by the presence of bacteria which adhere strongly to the insoluble substrates. An attempt has been made by Kelleher et al. (1984) to measure cellulose breakdown specifically from ingestion of [^{14}C]cellulose prepared from Cana inidica leaves which were allowed to photosynthesize in the presence of $^{14}CO_2$. As received the cellulose contained starch which could not be entirely removed and may have contributed to the early recovery of $^{14}CO_2$ in the breath (Cummings, 1984b). A mean value of 57% of the ingested ^{14}C was recovered in the feces and 7.5% of this was soluble so that 53% was probably from undegraded, or only slightly degraded, cellulose, although the chemical form of the ^{14}C recovered was not examined.

Carryer et al. (1982) used cellulose iodinated with ^{131}I in the form of the iodobenzhydryl derivative as a marker for rate of transit and from the feces recovered 87% of the ^{131}I. However, this was not a study on degradation per se, and the ability of the cellulolytic bacteria to degrade this derivative has not, to our knowledge, been examined.

   e. Seed Polysaccharides and Polysaccharide Food Additives. As stated earlier the storage polysaccharides in nonendospermic seeds such as peas and beans are similar to those in the parenchymatous tissues, but the storage polysaccharides in the cell walls of endospermic leguminous seeds contain galactomannans which are used as food additives, e.g., guar. Other food additives are exudate gums such as gum arabic.

   The abilities of anaerobic bacteria to utilize many of these materials have been examined. Although strains of *Bacteroides* spp. (not all from human sources) fermented most of the materials (Salyers, 1977a), gum arabic and gum ghatti were fermented only by strains of *Bifidobacterium longum*. However, it is probable that, by the use of an enrichment technique, more species capable of degrading gum arabic could have been isolated. In this way Wyatt et al. (1986) isolated bacteria, capable of fermenting gum arabic, from the feces of volunteers who had consumed a diet supplemented with gum arabic. After a short period of adaptation the gum arabic was apparently completely fermented in the human intestine. The organisms isolated were species of *Bacteroides* and *Bifidobacterium*.

   The mucilage polysaccharides from the husk of *Plantago ovata* is used medicinally as a stool moistener and is a xylan with mixed (1→3)- and (1→4)-xylose linkages with Gal$p$A-(1→2)-Rha$p$, arabinose, and xylose substituents (Kennedy et al., 1979). Strains of *Bacteroides ovatus* were able to utilize this as a gowth substrate and produced an extracellular enzyme capable of markedly reducing its viscosity (Salyers *et al.*, 1978). Strains of other genera of bacteria abundant in the colon were unable to utilize the mucilage, but selective isolation techniques were not used.

The degradation of guar gum has been studied in more detail. Balascio *et al.* (1981) isolated, from human feces, a strain of *Bacetoides ovatus* which was capable of fermenting guar gum and found that an induced extracellular enzyme rapidly reduced the viscosity of the gum. Fragments of approximately one-third of the original molecular size were quickly produced, and slow cleavage to small oligomers of about DP 6 occurred. Gherardini and Salyers (1982) found that there was also a membrane-bound mannanase which produced a trisaccharide.

Polydextrose is a polymer composed mainly of randomly cross-linked glucose molecules prepared from glucose, sorbitol, and citric acid (Torres and Thomas, 1981). It has applications in the food industry as a low calorie replacement for sucrose. It is undigested by the human alimentary enzymes, but Figdor and Bianchine (1983) found that it was partially fermented to SCFA and CO_2 by human colonic bacteria.

4. *Degradation of Whole Cell Wall Material*

Although isolated polysaccharides may be fermented by bacteria, the components may be much less accessible to attack when present in the cell wall or in fractions therefrom. Even with pectic substances, which are the most readily extractable polymers, with many tissues (Selvendran, 1985), there remains a substantial proportion which is not readily extractable. As stated earlier some of the pectic polysaccharides may also be complexed with other polysaccharides, protein, and polyphenolics (Selvendran, 1985). Hemicelluloses, especially in cereal tissues such as bran, may be cross-linked by phenolic ester groups and, in lignified tissues, also complexed with lignin. Many fruit and vegetable products contain differentiating vascular tissue which at an early stage shows the onset of lignification as revealed by staining with acid phloroglucinol.

There have been few *in vitro* studies on the degradation of cell wall material by human intestinal bacteria and, until recently (B.J.H. Stevens, R. R. Selvendran, and C. Bayliss, unpublished) none very detailed. *In vivo* studies have generally used unfractionated plant material and have been concerned mainly with physiological effects and products of degradation such as SCFA and residue weights rather than detailed compositional and structural changes to the fiber. The early study by Williams and Olmsted (1936) showed that wheat bran was much less degradable than vegetable fiber preparations. From this and similar, more recent studies, and from our present knowledge of cell wall chemistry, it can be assumed that most edible vegetable leaf, stem, and root tissues are more readily degradable than bran.

Dekker and Palmer (1981) studied the degradation of fiber prepared from defatted roasted peanuts by an enzymatic treatment to simulate the human digestive process. An organism capable of degrading this substrate was isolated from human feces and identified as a member of the genus *Bacteroides*. Inducible intracellular enzymes, mainly xylanase and polygalacturonase, degraded 11% of the fiber in 18 hr.

Miller and Wolin (1981) used a semicontinuous fermentation system with a human fecal inoculum in an attempt to simulate fermentation in the human large intestine. Comminuted lettuce, celery, carrots, and apple sauce were used without prior enzyme treatment to simulate the human digestive process. The concentrations of SCFA (mainly acetate), the major products, were similar to those found in feces, and species of *Bacteroides, Fusobacterium, Ruminococcus,* and *Clostridium* were isolated from the system. Because the aim of the study was to develop a semicontinuous *in vitro* system, no detailed studies were carried out on degradation of the substrates.

Bayliss and Houston (1984) isolated strains of *Bacteroides* spp. which were capable of degrading apple CWM and wheat bran AIR, and Slade *et al.* (1987) have examined the changes in populations which occurred during the *in vitro* fermentation of these substrates, together with xylans and sugar beet pulp, and found that the most marked change was an increase in the proportion of *Bacteroides* species with all the substrates tested. As part of the same study Stevens *et al.* (1987), using a human fecal inoculum, studied the degradation of the same apple CWM and wheat bran CWM. The carbohydrate content of the apple CWM was only 12% depleted after 6 hr which was an indication of the lag time taken for the induction of enzymes and multiplication of the bacteria capable of utilizing this substrate to an extent where an appreciable rate of degradation could occur. The losses were mainly in pectic substances. After 12 hr the carbohydrate content was 76% depleted, and after 24 hr 93% had been utilized (Figs. 6 and 7). The wheat bran carbohydrate was 46% depleted after 24 hr with little further degradation after 72 hr. With the exception of starch, which was absent in the CWM, these results are comparable with those obtained by Dintzis *et al.* (1979a,b) in studies on human gastrointestinal action on wheat bran although no indication of transit time was given. On examination by scanning electron microscopy (SEM) of particles recovered from the feces they observed that the aleurone layer and adhering endosperm had disappeared, leaving the pericarp containing the lignified cross cells largely intact.

Williams *et al.* (1978) had also reported the presence of relatively undegraded particles of bran in human feces. In our study examination by SEM of the bran after bacterial action yielded similar results to those of Dintzis *et al.,* but in some particles some aleurone cells remained. Schel *et al.* (1980) also observed that the endosperm disappeared but that some damaged aleurone cells remained. They

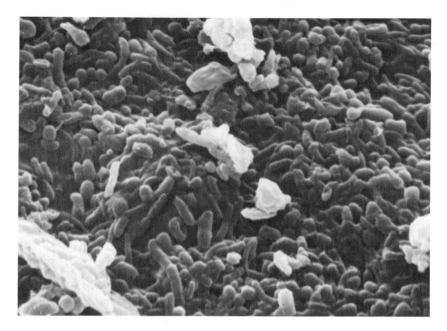

FIG. 6.   Scanning electron micrograph of apple CWM after degradation for 24 hr *in vitro* by human fecal bacteria (7000×). Extensive degradation of the CWM has taken place with only traces of the CWM visible under the mass of bacteria.

found the same structural changes in bran recovered from feces of subjects on a low fiber diet with bran-enriched bread as in that recovered from the feces of subjects on a high fiber intake with a supplement of coarse bran. Bacteria adhered mainly to the broken edges of the cross cells with fewer on the outer surfaces. Akin and Burdick (1981) observed that rumen bacteria generally neither adhered to nor degraded tissues which stained strongly with acid phloroglucinol, which reacts with coniferyl aldehyde groups in the lignin (Vance *et al.*, 1980). SEM has been used extensively in the examination of the attack on forages and cereal strains by rumen bacteria [see reviews by Akin (1979) and Akin and Burton (1983), and papers by Latham *et al.* (1978a,b)]. However, apart from the studies by Williams *et al.* and Dintzis *et al.*, referred to above, and recent studies by us and colleagues, this technique has not been utilized in the study of fiber breakdown in humans; possibly because most of the fiber materials are from predominantly parenchymatous tissues or from amorphous processed foods.

In addition to wheat bran, Dintzis *et al.* (1979a) also examined the breakdown of corn (maize) bran and soy hull bran and found that corn bran was more resistant to degradation than wheat bran and that the extent of degradation of the soy hull bran depended on the individual. Where extensive degradation had occurred, examination by SEM showed considerable disruption of the tissues. Dintzis' analysis showed that, whereas wheat bran contained 40% apparent hemicellulose and 8.8% cellulose, the corresponding values for corn bran were 70 and 22% and for soy hull bran 33 and 53%, respectively. For the monosaccharide composition of soy hull bran, see Selvendran (1984). Olson *et al.* (1983) also studied the degradation of corn bran and found that the hemicellulosic xylose : arabinose ratio of 1.8 : 1 was unaltered by human gastrointestinal action.

In studies with rats fed with fractions of wheat bran and native oat bran, Bertrand *et al.* (1981) reported that the β-glucans were degraded most readily and that the xylose from the arabinoxylans was apparently utilized more than the arabinose. Cellulose degradability was about 15% and, contrary to the results of Fahey (1979), was not increased by a delignification treatment. Fleming and Rodriguez (1983) and Fleming *et al.* (1983) found that corn bran was only slightly degraded in the human colon but the excretion of SCFA was increased and gas production lowered, compared with pectin, xylan, or cellulose.

Although not normally a component of the human diet, sugar beet CWM possesses interesting features that could affect its degradability by intestinal bacteria. (1) Pectic substances are difficult to extract from the CWM, possibly

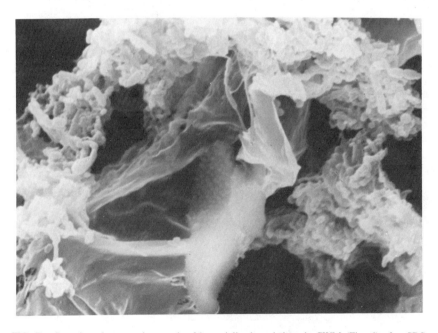

FIG. 7.   Scanning electron micrograph of bacterially degraded apple CWM (Fig. 6) after SDS–phenol treatment, as for Fig. 4, to remove the bulk of the bacteria. The "fibrous" interface layer was dialyzed and freeze-dried (3500×).

because they are cross-linked, or linked to other polysaccharides, by phenolic groups, mainly ferulic acid (Rombouts *et al.*, 1983; Selvendran *et al.*, 1985; Michel *et al.*, 1985); (2) a proportion of the galacturonic acid units in the pectin are esterified with acetyl groups (for references see Pippen *et al.*, 1950); and (3) the pulp which remains after sugar extraction shows evidence of the onset of secondary thickening and lignification. In recent studies *in vitro* using a human fecal inoculum B.J. H. Stevens and R. R. Selvendran (unpublished) found that the carbohydrate content of sugar beet pulp AIR was 25% depleted after 12 hr and 39% depleted after 24 hr; mainly pectic substances were being utilized.

5. Degradation of Cooked and Processed Foods

Much of the dietary fiber we consume has been subjected to cooking or other types of processing in which heat is often involved, e.g., baking, extrusion cooking, and during which complex chemical reactions with other ingredients can occur (e.g., formation of Maillard products). Domestically, many vegetables are rendered more palatable by boiling in water, which extracts some of the pectic substances which may be partially degraded (Anderson and Clydesdale, 1980). In the AIR of cabbage used in the experiments by Cummings *et al.* (1978) the air drying and ethanol extraction rendered the pectic substances much less extractable (Stevens and Selvendran, 1980).

In baking, starch can retrograde and become resistant to attack by the alimentary tract enzymes (Englyst *et al.*, 1982; Selvendran and Du Pont, 1984). This resistant starch thus behaves as a dietary fiber component (Englyst *et al.*, 1985; Björck *et al.*, 1986) and becomes a possible substrate for fermentation by the colonic bacteria. Björck *et al.* (1986) found that 0.6–0.9% of the starch in white wheat bread after baking became resistant to degradation by starch enzymes but was fermented in the hindgut of rats.

Maillard products, associated with brown coloration, are often formed during certain cooking procedures. The end products are complex polymers insoluble in 72% w/v H_2SO_4 and, therefore, are often estimated as "lignin" (Van Soest, 1965). Such products are formed when wheat cereal products are toasted (Anderson and Clydesdale, 1980) and are probably not degraded by the colonic bacteria. However, a range of simpler products can be formed by the interaction of sugars and amino acids, and the fermentability of some of these has been studied. Van Soest *et al.* (1983) reported that a Maillard product was not fermented *in vitro* by a human fecal inoculum, and Salyers *et al.* (1983) found that neither *Bacteroides ovatus* nor *B. thetaiotaomicron* utilized fructosylglycine but *B. thetaiotaomicron* utilized the galactose but not the isomaltose in isomaltolgalactoside. At a relatively high concentration, higher than would occur in the colon, fructosylglycine and isomaltol were inhibitory to these organisms.

C. FACTORS AFFECTING THE RESISTANCE OF DF COMPONENTS TO BACTERIAL DEGRADATION

1. Solubility and Degree of Bonding

Some of the factors such as extent of hydration, solubility, and degree of substitution have already been mentioned. Particle size is an obvious factor because of the increase of surface area as diameter decreases and the relatively greater extent of penetration by enzymes. However, Heller et al. (1980) reported that grinding wheat bran to a small particle size only slightly increased the degradation of the cellulose. Van Soest (1984) and Van Dokkum et al. (1983) found virtually no difference in the degradabilities of coarse and fine bran. In all three studies, transit time was lower with the coarse bran.

Solubility is largely governed by the extent of substitution with side chains or groups which prevent hydrogen bonding between the main chains of molecules with suitable conformations, e.g., xyloglucans, arabinoxylans (Andrewartha et al., 1979). The extent to which the substitution of xylans with arabinose side groups influences enzymatic attack remains uncertain. Some of the conflicting observations on the degradation of grass xylans have been summarized by Gordon et al. (1983). As stated earlier, Salyers et al. (1982) concluded that the presence of arabinose side groups did not in themselves limit the degradation of larchwood xylan.

Substitution of contiguous main chain units of a polysaccharide might restrict attack by specific enzymes (Dekker and Richards, 1976; Andrewartha et al., 1979; de Vries et al., 1982). However, in the large intestine, the combined versatility of bacterial enzymes, particularly those of Bacteroides spp., would be expected to eventually degrade these products.

2. Acetyl Groups

In xylans from wheat straw many of the xylose residues are esterified with acetyl groups at C-2 and/or C-3 (Chesson et al., 1983), and in several fruits, e.g., pears (McCready and McComb, 1954), and in sugar beet some of the galacturonic acid groups in the pectins are also esterified with acetyl groups. The presence of the acetyl groups was originally thought to impede degradation of straw and grasses in the rumen (Bacon et al., 1975; Morris and Bacon, 1976). Increases of degradability following deacetylation treatments could have been due to the cleavage of other alkali-labile linkages such as those of phenolic esters (Morris and Bacon, 1977). Later studies have indicated that acetyl groups do not impede the breakdown of legume, grass, and cereal straw cell wall fractions in the rumen (Chesson and Monro, 1982; Chesson et al., 1983; Lindberg et al., 1984).

3. Lignin

It is well known that in the rumen lignified tissues are resistant to complete degradation and that lignified tissues, e.g., seed coats and pericarps such as bran, that are consumed by man are also resistant to degradation. Various vague theories have been proposed for the mechanism of its resistance. The earlier suggestions of encrustation of the hemicellulose by lignin have given way to suggestions of chemical bonds, between the carbohydrate and phenolic moieties, which are resistant to degradation or which sterically hinder enzyme binding. Chesson (1983) has suggested that during the degradation of the cell walls polyphenolic material might accumulate at exposed surfaces and block adhesion sites of whole organisms or their insoluble enzyme complexes. The inability of many bacteria to adhere to the surfaces of lignified tissues has already been referred to and could well be a contributory factor (Richards, 1976). However, this would be expected to affect only the primary attack.

In the rumen some degradation occurs, resulting in the release of soluble lignin–carbohydrate complexes (LCC) (Gaillard and Richards, 1975) which can amount to 50% of the lignin intake (Richards, 1984). The presence of these soluble complexes suggests a chemical or structural resistance to complete degradation. The LCC from the rumen of steers fed with spear grass was found to have glucose, xylose, and rhamnose glycosidically linked to the lignin with some of the glucose residues carrying other 1→4-linked glucose units and some of the xylose residues carrying 1→4-linked xylose and/or 1→3-linked arabinose residues (Neilson and Richards, 1982). Brice and Morrison (1982) examined the degradation by a rumen hemicellulase complex of LCC from grass varieties and found that the extent of degradation decreased as the lignin content increased.

In their studies on the degradation of grass and cereal straw cell walls by rumen microorganisms, Chesson et al. (1983) found that in the residues which were resistant to further degradation 40–60% of the arabinose residues were linked through C-5 by alkali-labile bonds and were resistant to chlorite delignification. The extent of substitution correlated highly with the proportion of nonacid phenolics (i.e., total phenols minus phenolic acid) so that polyphenolic material from lignin breakdown was linked through the arabinose residues. They concluded that the increase of ovine digestibility of cereal straw following alkali treatment is more likely to be due to the cleavage of such lignin–carbohydrate linkages than to the cleavage of phenolic acid–carbohydrate bonds since the proportion of phenolic acid present is relatively low. Recently, B. J. H. Stevens and R. R. Selvendran (unpublished), using a human fecal inoculum, have found that the in vitro degradation (on a carbohydrate basis) of alkali-treated wheat bran was 72% after 36 hr compared with 35% for the untreated bran.

In connection with chlorite delignification Ford (1986) has reported that many structural modifications can occur including the possibility, in the degradation of phenolic acid esters, of the production of structures susceptible to polymerization.

Arabinoxylan oligosaccharides with ferulic acid esterified to C-5 of arabinose have recently been isolated from wheat bran by Smith and Hartley (1983), from *Zea* shoots by Kato and Nevins (1985), and from barley aleurone cell walls by Gubler *et al.* (1985). *Zea* shoots and barley aleurone cell walls are not lignified and provide further examples of the (cross)-linkage of polysaccharides through phenolic ester groups. In nonlignified tissues these structures are also resistant to degradation, a property which has enabled their isolation by the use of potent enzyme complexes such as Driselase to extensively degrade the non-phenolic-linked structures (Kato and Nevins, 1985; Fry, 1982a; Selvendran, 1985).

Akin (1982), Chesson *et al.* (1982), and Jung (1985) have studied the effect of free phenolic acids on the growth and cellulolytic activity of rumen bacteria. Akin found that *p*-coumaric acid was more inhibitory to growth and cellulolytic activity than ferulic acid. A level of 0.1% *p*-coumaric acid caused significant reduction in the rate of filter paper degradation by a mixed culture of rumen microorganisms. Jung found that the rate of hemicellulose degradation was un-altered but the rate of cellulose degradation by rumen fluid was decreased and that ferulic acid was slightly more inhibitory than *p*-coumaric acid. Chesson and co-workers found that ferulic acid was generally as inhibitory, or even more so, than *p*-coumaric to specific strains tested.

The cellulolytic activities of *Bacteroides succinogenes, Ruminococcus flavefaciens,* and *R. albus* were seriously affected only at levels of 10 mM (~0.2%) of *p*-coumaric acid, and although ferulic acid was more inhibitory to *B. succinogenes* and *R. flavefaciens* it had little effect on *R. albus*. Strains of *Ruminococcus* spp. showed ability to hydrogenate *p*-coumaric and ferulic acids to the corresponding, less toxic phloretic and 3-methoxyphenolic acids. However, in the sheep rumen neither the hydroxycoumaric acids nor their hydrogenated products could be detected other than in trace amounts when the expected concentration was 10 mM, so some other mechanism exists for their removal. Akin (1980) isolated a facultative anaerobe which could attack lignified Bermuda grass tissue and utilize ferulic, *p*-coumaric, and syringic acids as growth substrates.

4. Cutins, Suberins, and Silica

The cutinous waxy coverings of fruits and the suberin in underground tissues are generally assumed to be resistant to degradation by rumen and related bacteria, but the authors are not aware of any specific studies on this. The presence of these compounds would also hinder the degradation of tissues associated with them. The presence of the cutinized seed coat in wheat bran (Bradbury *et al.*,

1956) might contribute to the resistance to degradation observed by Schel *et al.* (1980).

Hartley (1983) has summarized some of the studies on the effects of silica which probably occurs only in animal forages at sufficient levels to possibly impede degradation.

D.   AREAS FOR FUTURE WORK AND POTENTIAL FOR MODIFICATION OF DF

The structural features, such as types of substituent, distribution, and linkage patterns, that are resistant to bacterial degradation remain to be defined, and even less is known about the mechanisms of hypocholesterolemic activity and possible cancer prevention. There is potential for modifying dietary fiber products to enhance these features once they have been identified. Alkali treatments have been used to improve the digestibility of rumen forage feedstuffs, and there could be a case for utilizing similar treatments to render more lignified cereal (or vegetable) products slightly more degradable should they possess particular structural features that are found to be important. The possibility already exists of cross-linking sugar beet pectins through phenolic acid groups (Rombouts *et al.,* 1983) to improve their physical properties and the esterification of guar with phenolic acids (Pilnik and Rombouts, 1985). The use of modified starches and polydextrose has already been referred to. The use of chemical syntheses to introduce specific groups into a polymer or to produce specific oligosaccharides is also a possibility although such products would be considered as food additives or pharmaceuticals and would require extensive and expensive safety testing.

VI.   CONCLUDING REMARKS

An attempt has been made in this article to describe the chemistry of some of the better characterized cell wall polymers of edible plant organs with special emphasis on how this knowledge enhances our understanding of (1) the chemical and physical properties of DF, (2) the analysis of DF, and (3) the mode of action of DF in the human alimentary tract, particularly the large intestine. Throughout, aspects that need further investigation have been indicated.

As it is becoming increasingly clear that the nature of the cell wall polymers associated with various tissue types are different, an effort has been made to describe, where possible, the chemistry of cell walls of different tissues. This aspect is clearly demonstrated in the case of the wheat grain, where the cell wall polymers associated with the parenchymatous tissues of the endosperm and the aleurone layer are shown to be different from those of the lignified outer layers. The same is of course true of parenchymatous and lignified tissues of vegetables, except that phenolic ester cross-links are less abundant in most vegetable and fruit cell walls. Attention has been drawn to the importance of (phenolic) ester cross-links in influencing the solubility characteristics of cell wall polymers of nonlignified tissues. Although lignin is a minor component of most diets, lignin and phenolic ester cross-links influence the resistance of lignified cell walls to bacterial degradation. This property, coupled with the acidic arabinoxylan content of DF, appears to correlate with the greater capacity of (bran-enriched) cereal fiber to increase fecal weight, compared with vegetable/fruit fiber. Most of the pectic polymers, and a significant proportion of the hemicelluloses and cellulose of vegetable fiber, are degraded by colonic bacteria and thus serve to increase bacterial biomass. There is obviously a clear need to know more about the detailed structure of the cell walls of various edible plant organs, particularly those of nonendospermic leguminous seeds, and the recent developments in cell wall structure (Selvendran, 1985) and analysis (Selvendran et al., 1985; Selvendran and O'Neill, 1987) have been discussed elsewhere. Our appreciation of the properties of DF has been very much enhanced by our fractionation studies on the cell walls of a range of edible plant organs. It should be emphasized that the information which the simplified methods for the analysis of DF provide about the constituent DF polymers is very limited, and the scientists interested in the physiological effects of DF should become better acquainted with detailed fractionation studies.

There is increasing evidence from animal studies showing that DF influences the growth, structure, and physiological activities of tissues throughout the gastrointestinal tract. For example, using isolated polysaccharides incorporated into otherwise fiber-free semisynthetic diets, it has been shown that viscous gums cause an increase in the length of the small intestine and increases in the size and weight of tissues in the large bowel. These changes are accompanied by increased rates of cell proliferation, and by changes in the activity of mucosal enzymes (Johnson et al., 1984). However, materials such as guar gum and carboxymethylcellulose, which have apparently similar physical properties in vitro, lead to significantly different gastrointestinal effects (Johnson and Gee, 1986). More work is required to clarify the relationship between the physical and chemical properties of such materials and their biological effects in the gut. Further, there is virtually no information of this kind about the influence of the different constituents of DF on the structure and function of the human gut. The fermentation of DF provides substrates for the nutrition of the colonic epithelium (Roediger, 1986), and absence of such substrates can lead to a serious loss of colonic function in grossly malnourished children. However, the importance of DF for the long-term "health" of the colonic mucosa in well-nourished subjects is not yet known and warrants study.

Finally, a full understanding of the chemistry of DF and its physiological effects in man requires an interdisciplinary approach, combining cell wall structure and biochemistry, microbiology, human physiology and biochemistry (with special reference to effects in the small and large intestine), and the nutritional sciences. The conventional segregation of scientific disciplines and the lack of positive effort on the part of those concerned with DF studies to encourage dialogue between scientists working in different fields have been some of the factors impeding progress in this important area.

ACKNOWLEDGMENTS

We wish to thank the following members of the AFRC Institute of Food Research, Norwich Laboratory. Dr. I. Johnson for helpful discussion on the effects of DF in the small intestine. Mrs. C. Bayliss for her help with the *in vitro* studies with human fecal inocula. Mr. N. King and Mr. R. Turner for electron microscopy, and Linda Dunn for typing so conscientiously from the manuscript. This work was partly funded by the Ministry of Agriculture, Fisheries and Food.

REFERENCES

Adams, G. A. 1955. Constitution of a hemicellulose from wheat bran. *Can. J. Chem.* **33,** 56–67.
Akin, D. E. 1979. Microscopic evaluation of forage digestion by rumen microorganisms—A review. *J. Anim. Sci.* **48,** 701–710.
Akin, D. E. 1980. Attack on lignified grass cell walls by a facultatively anaerobic bacterium. *Appl. Environ. Microbiol.* **40,** 809–820.
Akin, D. E. 1982. Forage cell wall degradation and *p*-coumaric, ferulic, and sinapic acids. *Agron. J.* **74,** 424–428.
Akin, D. E., and Amos, H. E.1975. Rumen bacterial degradation of forage cell walls investigated by electron microscopy. *Appl. Microbiol.* **29,** 692–701.
Akin, D. E., and Burdick, D. 1981. Relationships of different histochemical types of lignified cell walls to forage digestibility. *Crop. Sci.* **21,** 577–581.
Akin, D. E., and Burton II, F. E. 1983. Forage ultrastructure and the digestion of plant cell walls by rumen microorganisms. *In* "Wood and Agricultural Residues" (J. Soltes, ed.), pp. 33–57. Academic Press, New York.
Albersheim, P. 1976. The primary cell wall. *In* "Plant Biochemistry" (J. Bonner and J. E. Varner, eds.), pp. 225–272. Academic Press, New York.
Albersheim, P., Neukom, H., and Deuel, H. 1960. Splitting of pectin chain molecules in neutral solutions. *Arch. Biochem. Biophys.* **90,** 46–51.
Allen, A. K., and Neuberger, A. 1973. The purification and properties of the lectin from potato tubers, a hydroxyproline containing glycoprotein. *Biochem. J.* **135,** 307–314.
Allen, A. K., Desai, N. N., Neuberger, A., and Creeth, J. M. 1978. Properties of potato lectin and the nature of its glycoprotein linkages. *Biochem. J.* **93,** 91–104.
Anderson, I. H., Levine, A. S., and Levitt, M. D. 1981. Incomplete absorption of the carbohydrate in all-purpose wheat flour, *N. Engl. J. Med.* **304,** 891–892.
Anderson, J. W. 1985. Physiological and metabolic effects of dietary fiber. *Fed. Proc., Fed. Am. Soc. Exp. Biol.* **44,** 2902–2906.

Anderson, J. W., and Lin Chen, W.-J. 1979. Plant fiber, carbohydrate and lipid metabolism. *Am. J. Clin. Nutr.* **32**, 346–363.

Anderson, J. W., Story, L., Sieling, B., Lin Chen, W.-J., Petro, M. S., and Story, J. 1984. Hypocholesterolemic effects of oat-bran or bean intake for hypocholesterolemic men. *Am. J. Clin.Nutr.* **40**, 1146–1155.

Anderson, N. E., and Clydesdale, F. M. 1980. Effects of processing on the dietary fiber content of wheat bran, pureed green beans, and carrots. *J. Food Sci.* **45**, 1533–1537.

Andrewartha, K. A., Phillips, D. R., and Stone, B. A. 1979. Solution properties of wheat-flour arabinoxylans and enzymically modified arabinoxylans. *Carbohydr. Res.* **77**, 191–204.

Asp, N.-G., and Johansson, C.-G. 1984. Dietary fibre analysis. *Rev. Clin. Nutr.* **54**, 735–752.

Asp, N.-G., Johansson, C.-G., Hallmer, H., and Siljestrom, M. 1983. Rapid enzymatic assay of insoluble and soluble dietary fibre. *J. Agric. Food Chem.* **31**, 476–482.

Aspinall, G. O. 1969. Gums and mucilages. *Adv. Carbohydra. Chem. Biochem.* **24**, 33–379.

Aspinall, G. O. 1973. Carbohydrate polymers of plant cell walls. *In* "Biogenesis of Plant Cell Wall Polysaccharides" (F. Loewus, ed.), pp. 95–115. Academic Press, New York.

Aspinall, G. O. 1980. Chemistry of cell wall polysaccharides. *In* "The Biochemistry of Plants", (J. Preiss, ed.), Vol. 3, pp. 473–500. Academic Press, New York.

Aspinall, G. O., and Cottrell, I. W. 1971. Polysaccharides of soybeans. VI. Neutral polysaccharides from cotyledon meal. *Can. J. Chem.* **49**, 1019–1022.

Aspinall, G. O., and Fanous, H. K. 1984. Structural investigations on the non-starchy polysaccharides of apples. *Carbohydr. Polymers* **4**, 193–214.

Aspinall, G. O., Hunt, K., and Morrison, I. M. 1967. Polysaccharides of soybeans. V. Acidic polysaccharides from the hulls. *J. Chem. Soc. C,* 1080–1086.

Aspinall, G. O., Molloy, J. A., and Craig, J. W. T. 1969. Extracellular polysaccharides from suspension-cultured sycamore cells. *Can. J. Biochem.* **47**, 1063–1070.

Azuma, J.-I., Takahashi, N., and Koshijima, T. 1981. Isolation and characterisation of lignin-carbohydrate complexes from the milled-wood lignin fraction of *Pinus densiflora* Sieb et Zucc. *Carbohydr. Res.* **93**, 91–104.

Bacic, A., and Stone, B. A. 1981a. Isolation and ultrastructure of aleurone cell walls from wheat and barley. *Aust. J. Plant Physiol.* **8**, 453–474.

Bacic, A., and Stone, B. A. 1981b. Chemistry and organisation of aleurone cell wall components from wheat and barley. *Aust. J. Plant Physiol.* **8**, 475–495.

Bacon, J. S. D., Gordon, A. H., Morris, E. J., and Farmer, V. C. 1975. Acetyl groups in cell-wall preparations from higher plants. *Biochem. J.* **149**, 485–487.

Bailey, R. W., and Macrae, J. C. 1970. The hydrolysis by rumen and caecal microbial enzymes of hemicellulose in plant and digesta particles. *J. Agric. Sci.* **75**, 321–326.

Balascio, J. R., Palmer, J. K., and Salyers, A. A. 1981. Degradation of guar gum by enzymes produced by a bacterium from the human colon. *J. Food Biochem.* **5**, 271–282.

Ballance, G. M., and Manners, D. J. 1978. Structural analysis and enzymic solubilization of barley endosperm cell walls. *Carbohydr. Res.* **61**, 107–118.

Balmer, J., and Zilversmit, D. B. 1974. Effects of dietary roughage on cholesterol absorption, cholesterol turnover, and steroid excretion in the rat. *J. Nutr.* **104**, 1319–1328.

Bamforth, C. W., Martin, H. L., and Wainwright, T. 1979. A role for carboxypeptidase in the solubilization of barley β-glucan. *J. Inst. Brew.* **85**, 334–338.

Banbury Report 7. 1981.Gastrointestinal cancer: Endogenous factors. (W. R. Bruce, P. Correa, M. Lipkin, S. R. Tannenbaum, and T. D. Wilkins, eds.) Cold Spring Harbor Laboratory, Cold Spring Harbor, New York.

Barnes, E. M. 1986. Anaerobic bacteria of the normal intestinal microflora of animals. *in* "Anaerobic Bacteria in Habitats Other than Man" (E. M. Barnes and G. C. Mead, eds.). *Soc. Appl. Bacteriol. Symp. Ser.* **13**, 225–238.

Bauer, W. D., Talmadge, K. W., Keegstra, K., and Albersheim, P. 1973. The structure of plant cell walls. II. The hemicellulose of the walls of suspension-cultured sycamore cells. *Plant Physiol.* **51**, 174–187.

Bayliss, C. E., and Houston, A. P. 1984. Characterization of plant polysaccharide—and mucin—fermenting anaerobic bacteria from human feces. *Appl. Environ. Microbiol.* **48**, 626–632.

Bayliss, C. E., and Houston, A. P. 1985. The effect of guar gum on microbial activity in the human colon. *Food Microbiol.* **2**, 53–62.

Belo, P. S., and de Lumen, B. O. 1981. Pectic substance content of detergent-extracted dietary fibers. *J. Agric. Food Chem.* **29**, 370–373.

Berghouse, L., Hori, S., Hill, M., Hudson, M., Lennard-Jones, S. F., and Rogers, E. 1984. Comparison between the bacterial and oligosaccharide content of ileostomy effluent in subjects taking diets rich in refined or unrefined carbohydrate. *Gut* **25**, 1071–1077.

Bertrand, D., Brillouet, J.-M., Rasper, V. F., Bouchet, B., and Mercier, C. 1981. Effects of rat digestion upon native, enzymatically or chemically modified wheat brans and native oat bran. *Cereal Chem.* **58**, 375–380.

Betian, H. G., Linehan, B. A., Bryant, M. P., and Holdeman, L. V. 1977. Isolation of a cellulolytic *Bacteroides* sp. from human feces. *Appl. Environ. Microbiol.* **33**, 1009–1010.

Bingham, S., Cummings, J. H., and McNeil, N. I. 1979. Intakes and sources of dietary fibre in the British population. *Am. J. Clin. Nutr.* **32**, 1313–1319.

Bittner, A. S., Burritt, E. A., Moser, J., and Street, J. C. 1982. Composition of dietary fiber: Neutral and acidic sugar composition of the alcohol insoluble residue from human foods. *J. Food Sci.* **47**, 1469–1477.

Björck, I., Nyman, M., Pedersen, B., Siljeström, N., Asp, N.-G., and Eggum, B. O. 1986. On the digestibility of starch in wheat bread—Studies *in vitro* and *in vivo*. *J. Cereal Sci.* **4**, 1–11.

Blackburn, N. A. 1984. The effects of a viscous unavailable polysaccharide on intestinal absorption. Ph.D. thesis, University of East Anglia.

Blackburn, N. A., and Johnson, I. T. 1981. The effect of guar gum on the viscosity of the gastrointestinal contents and on glucose uptake from the perfused jejunum in the rat. *Br. J. Nutr.* **46**, 239–246.

Blackburn, N. A., Holgate, A. M., and Read, N. W. 1984a. Does guar gum improve post-prandial hyperglycaemia in humans by reducing small intestinal contact area? *Br. J. Nutr.* **52**, 197–204.

Blackburn, N. A., Redfern, J. S., Jaryis, H., Holgate, A. M., Hanning, I., Scarpello, J. H. B., Johnson, I. T., and Read, N. W. 1984b. The mechanism of action of guar gum in improving glucose tolerance in man. *Clin. Sci.* **66**, 329–336.

Bouveng, H. O., and Lindberg, B. 1960. Methods in structural polysaccharide chemistry. *Adv. Carbohydr. Chem.* **15**, 53–89.

Bradbury, D., MacMasters, M. M., and Call, M. I. M. 1956. Structure of the mature wheat kernel II. Microscopic structure of pericarp, seed coat, and other coverings of the endosperm and germ of hard red winter wheat. *Cereal Chem.* **33**, 342–360.

Brice, R. E., and Morrison, I. M. 1982. The degradation of isolated hemicelluloses and lignin–hemicellulose complexes by cell-free rumen hemicellulases. *Carbohydr. Res.* **101**, 93–100.

Brillouet, J. M. 1982. Nonstarchy polysaccharides of legume seeds from the papilionoideae subfamily. *Sci. Aliment.* **2**, 135–162.

Brillouet, J. M., and Carré, B. 1983. Composition of cell walls from cotyledons of *Pisum sativum, Vicia faba* and *Glycine max*. *Phytochemistry* **22**, 841–847.

Brown, J. P. 1977. Role of gut bacterial flora in nutrition and health: A review of recent advances in bacteriological techniques, metabolism, and factors affecting flora composition. *CRC Crit. Rev. Food Sci. Nutr.* **8**, 229–336.

Browning, B. L. 1967. *Methods Wood Chem.* **11**, 785.

Bryant, M. P. 1974. Nutritional features and ecology of predominant anaerobic bacteria of the intestinal tract. *Am. J. Clin. Nutr.* **27**, 1313–1319.

Bryant, M. P. 1978. Cellulose digesting bacteria from human feces. *Am. J. Clin. Nutr.* **31,** S113–S115.

Burkitt, D. P. 1973a. Some diseases characteristic of modern western civilization. *Br. Med. J.* **1,** 274–8.

Burkitt, D. P. 1973b. Epidemiology of large bowel disease: The role of fibre. *Proc. Nutr. Soc.* **32,** 145–149.

Burkitt, D. P., and Trowell, H. C., eds. 1975. "Refined Carbohydrate Foods and Disease. Some Implications of Dietary Fibre." Academic Press, London.

Calvert, G. D., and Yeates, R. A. 1982. Adsorption of bile salts by soya-bean flour, wheat bran, lucerne (*Medicago sativa*), sawdust and lignin; the effect of saponins and other plant constituents. *Br. J. Nutr.* **47,** 45–52.

Carryer, P. W., Brown, M. L., Malagelada, J. R., Carlson, G. L., and McCall, J. T. 1982. Quantification of the fate of dietary fiber in humans by a newly developed radiolabelled fiber marker. *Gastroenterology* **82,** 1389–1394.

Chen, W. L., and Anderson, J. W. 1981. Soluble and insoluble plant fiber in selected cereals and vegetables. *Am. J. Clin. Nutr.* **34,** 1077–1082.

Chesson, A. 1983. A holistic approach to plant cell wall structure and degradation. *In* "Fibre in Human and Animal Nutrition" (G. Wallace and L. Bell, eds.), pp. 85–90. Royal Society of New Zealand, Wellington.

Chesson, A., and Monro, J. A. 1982. Legume pectic substances and their degradation in the ovine rumen. *J. Sci. Food Agric.* **33,** 852–859.

Chesson, A., Stewart, C. S., and Wallace, R. J. 1982. Influence of plant phenolic acids on growth and cellulolytic activity of rumen bacteria. *Appl. Environ. Microbiol.* **44,** 597–603.

Chesson, A., Gordon, A. H., and Lomax, J. A. 1983. Substituent groups linked by alkali-labile bonds to arabinose and xylose residues of legume, grass and cereal straw cell walls and their fate during digestion by rumen microorganisms. *J. Sci. Food Agric.* **34,** 1330–1340.

Cleave, T. L., Campbell, G. D., and Painter, N. S. 1969. "Diabetes, Coronary Thrombosis, and Saccharine Disease," 2nd Ed. Wright, Bristol.

Committee on Diet, Nutrition and Cancer. 1982. "Diet, Nutrition and Cancer." Natl. Academy Press, Washington, D.C.

Crampton, E. W., and Maynard, L. A. 1938. The relation of cellulose and lignin content to the nutritive value of animal feeds *J. Nutr.* **15,** 383–395.

Cummings, J. H. 1978a. Physiological aspects. *Top. Gastroenterol.* **6,** 49–62.

Cummings, J. H. 1978b. Nutritional implications of dietary fiber. *Am. J. Clin. Nutr.* **31,** S21–29.

Cummings, J. H. 1984a. Microbial digestion of complex carbohydrates in man. *Proc. Nutr. Soc.* **43,** 35–44.

Cummings, J. H. 1984b. Cellulose and the human gut. *Gut* **25,** 805–810.

Cummings, J. H., Hill, M. J., Jenkins, D. J. A., Pearson, J. R., and Wiggins, H. S. 1976. Changes in fecal composition and colonic function due to cereal fiber. *Am. J. Clin. Nutr.* **29,** 1468–1473.

Cummings, J. H., Southgate, D. A. T., Branch, W., Houston, H., Jenkins, D. J. A., and James, W. P. T. 1978. Colonic response to dietary fibre from carrot, cabbage, apple, bran and guar gum. *Lancet* **1,** 5–9.

Cummings, J. H., Southgate, D. A. T., Branch, W. J., Wiggins, H. S., Houston, H., Jenkins, D. J. A., Jivraj, T., and Hill, M. J. 1979. The digestion of pectin in the human gut and its effect on calcium absorption and large bowel function. *Br. J. Nutr.* **41,** 477–485.

Cummings, J. H., Stephen, A. M., and Branch, W. J. 1981. Implications of dietary fiber breakdown in the human colon. *In* Banbury Report 7. "Gastrointestinal Cancer: Endogenous Factors" (W. R. Bruce, P. Correa, M. Lyskin, S. R. Tannenbaum, and T. D. Wilkins, eds.), p. 71. Cold Spring Harbor Laboratory, Cold Spring Harbor, New York.

Darvill, A. G., McNeil, M., and Albersheim, P. 1978. Structure of plant cell walls. VIII. A new pectic polysaccharide. *Plant Physiol.* **62,** 418–422.

Darvill, A. G., McNeil, M., Albersheim, P., and Delmer, D. P. 1980. The primary cell walls of flowering plants. *In* "The Biochemistry of Plants" (N. E. Tolbert, ed.), Vol. 1, pp. 91–162. Academic Press, New York.

Darvill, A. G., Albersheim, P., McNeil, M., Lau, J. M., York, W. S., Stevenson, T. T., Thomas, J., Doares, S., Gollin, D. J., Chelf, P., and Davis, K. 1985. Structure and function of plant cell wall polysaccharides. *In* "The Cell Surface in Plant Growth and Development" (K. Roberts, A. W. B. Johnston, C. W. Lloyd, P. Shaw, and H. W. Woolhouse, eds.). *J. Cell Sci. Suppl.* **2,** 203–217.

Dehority, B. A. 1965. Degradation and utilization of isolated hemicellulose by pure cultures of cellulolytic rumen bacteria. *J. Bacteriol.* **89,** 1515–1520.

Dehority, B. A. 1967. Rate of isolated hemicellulose degradation and utilization by pure cultures of rumen bacteria. *Appl. Microbiol.* **15,** 987–993.

Dekker, J., and Palmer, J. K. 1981. Enzymatic degradation of the plant cell wall by a *Bacteroides* of human fecal origin. *J. Agric. Food Chem.* **29,** 480–484.

Dekker, R. F. H., and Richards, G. N. 1976. Hemicellulases: Their occurrence, purification, properties, and mode of action. *Adv. Carbohydr. Chem. Biochem.* **32,** 277–352.

de Vries, J. A., Rombouts, F. M., Voragen, G. A. G. J., and Pilnik, W. 1982. Enzymic degradation of apple pectins. *Carbohydr. Polymers* **2,** 25–33.

de Vries, J. A., den Uijl, C. H., Voragen, A. G. J., Rombouts, F. M., and Pilnik, W. 1983. Structural features of the neutral sugar side chains of apple pectic substances. *Carbohydr. Polymers* **3,** 193–205.

de Vries, W., Gerbrandy, S. J., and Stouthamer, A. H. 1967. Carbohydrate metabolism in *Bifidobacterium bifidum. Biochim. Biophys. Acta* **136,** 415–425.

Dinsdale, D., Morris, E. J., and Bacon, J. S. D. 1978. Electron microscopy of the microbial populations present and their modes of attack on various cellulosic substrates undergoing digestion in the sheep rumen. *Appl. Environ. Microbiol.* **36,** 160–168.

Dintzis, F. R., Legge, L. M., Deatherage, W. L., Baker, F. L., Inglett, G. E., Jacobs, R. A., Reck, S. J., Munoz, J. M., Klevay, L. M., Sandstead, H. H., and Shuey, W. C. 1979a. Human gastrointestinal action on wheat, corn, and soy hull bean—Preliminary findings. *Cereal Chem.* **56,** 123–127.

Dintzis, R., McBrien, J. B., Baker, F. L., Inglett, G. E., Jacob, R. A., Munoz, J. M., Klevay, L. M., Sandstead, H. H., and Shuey, W. C. 1979b. Some effects of baking and human gastrointestinal action upon a hard red wheat bran. *In* "Dietary Fibers: Chemistry and Nutrition" (G. E. Inglett and S. I. Falkehag, eds.), pp. 193–201. Academic Press, New York.

Dintzis, F. R., Watson, P. R., and Sandstead, H. H. 1985. Mineral contents of brans passed through the human GI tract. *Am. J. Clin. Nutr.* **41,** 901–908.

Drasar, B. S., and Hill, M. J. 1974. "Human Intestinal Flora." Academic Press, New York.

Dunaif, G., and Schneeman, B. O. 1981. The effect of dietary fiber on human pancreatic enzyme activity *in vitro. Am. J. Clin. Nutr.* **34,** 1034–1035.

Du Pont, M. S., and Selvendran, R. R. 1987. Hemicellulosic polymers from the cell walls of beeswing wheat bran. Part I: Polymers solubilised by alkali at 2°. *Carbohydr. Res.* **163,** 99–113.

Eastwood, M. A. 1978. Physical properties. *Top Gastroenterol.* **6,** 39–47.

Eastwood, M. A. 1983. Physical properties of fibre towards bile acids, water and minerals. *In* "Dietary Fibre" (G. G. Birch and K. J. Parker, eds.), pp. 149–163. Applied Science Publ., London.

Eastwood, M. A., and Hamilton, D. 1968. Studies on the adsorption of bile salts to non-absorbed components of diet. *Biochim. Biophys. Acta* **152,** 165–173.

Eastwood, M. A., and Kay, R. M. 1979. An hypothesis for the action of dietary fibre along the gastrointestinal tract. *Am. J. Clin. Nutr.* **32**, 364–367.

Eastwood, M. A., and Mitchell, W. D. 1976. Physical properties of fiber: A biological evaluation. *In* "Fiber in Human Nutrition" (G. A. Spiller and R. J. Amen, eds.), pp. 109–129. Plenum, New York.

Eastwood, M. A., Anderson, R., Mitchell, W. D., Robertson, J., and Pocock, S. 1976. A method to measure the adsorption of bile salts to vegetable fibre of differing water holding capacity. *J. Nutr.* **106**, 1429–1432.

Ebihara, K., Masuhara, R., and Kiriyama, S. 1981. Major determinants of plasma glucose-flattening activity of a water-soluble dietary fiber: Effects of Konjac Mannan on gastric emptying and intraluminal glucose diffusion. *Nutr. Rep. Int.* **23**, 1145–1156.

Ehle, F. R., Robertson, J. B., and Van Soest, P. J. 1982. Influence of dietary fibers on fermentation in the human large intestine. *J. Nutr.* **112**, 158–166.

Elsenhans, B., Sufke, U., Blume, R., and Caspary, W. F. 1980a. The influence of carbohydrate gelling agents on rat intestinal transport of monosaccharides and neutral amino acids *in vitro*. *Clin. Sci.* **59**, 373–380.

Elsenhans, B., Sufke, U., Zenker, D., Blume, R., and Caspary. W. F. 1980b. Direct and adaptive effects of dietary fiber on rat intestinal function and parameters. *Proc. Int. Congr. Gastroenterol., 11th, Hamburg* **E44**, 6.

Englyst, H. N. 1981. Determination of carbohydrate and its composition in plant materials. *In* "The Analysis of Dietary Fiber in Foods" (W. P. T. James and O. Theander, eds.), p. 71. Dekker, New York.

Englyst, H. N., and Cummings, J. H. 1984. Simplified method for the measurement of total non-starch polysaccharides by gas–liquid chromatography of constituent sugars as alditol acetates. *Analyst* **109**, 937–942.

Englyst, H. N., and Cummings, J. H. 1985. Digestion of the polysaccharides of some cereal foods in the human small intestine. *Am. J. Clin. Nutr.* **42**, 778–787.

Englyst, H. N., and Cummings, J. H. 1986a. Measurement of dietary fiber as nonstarch polysaccharides. *In* "Dietary Fiber: Basic and Clinical Aspects" (G. V. Vahouny and D. Kritchevsky, eds.), pp. 17–34. Plenum, New York.

Englyst, H. N., and Cummings, J. H. 1986b. Digestion of the carbohydrates of banana (*Musa paradisiaca sapientum*) in the human small intestine. *Am. J. Clin. Nutr.* **44**, 42–50.

Englyst, H., Wiggins, H. S., and Cummings, J. H. 1982. Determination of the non-starch polysaccharides in plant foods by gas–liquid chromatography of constituent sugars as alditol acetates. *Analyst* **107**, 307–318.

Fahey, G. C., Jr. 1979. The nutritional significance of chemically defined dietary fibers. *In* "Dietary Fibers: Chemistry and Nutrition" (G. E. Inglett and S. I. Falkehag, eds.), p. 117. Academic Press, New York.

Farness, P. L., and Schneeman, B. O. 1982. Effects of dietary cellulose, pectin and oat bran on the small intestine in the rat. *J. Nutr.* **112**, 1315–1319.

Faulks, R. M., and Timms, S. B. 1985. A rapid method for determining the carbohydrate component of dietary fibre. *Food Chem.* **17**, 273–287.

Figdor, S. K., and Bianchine, J. R. 1983. Calorie utilization and disposition of [^{14}C]polydextrose in man. *J. Agric. Food Chem.* **31**, 389–393.

Fincher, G. B. 1975. Morphology and chemical composition of barley endosperm cell walls. *J. Inst. Brew.* **81**, 116–122.

Finegold, S. M., and Sutter, V. L. 1978. Fecal flora in different populations, with special reference to diet. *Am. J. Clin. Nutr.* **31**, 5116–5122.

Finegold, S. M., Sutter, V. L., and Mathisen, G. E. 1983. Normal indigeneous intestinal flora. *In*

"Human Intestinal Microflora in Health and Disease" (D. J. Hentges, ed.), pp. 3–31. Academic Press, New York.

Fleming, S. E., and Rodriguez, M. A. 1983. Influence of dietaryfiber on fecal excretion of volatile fatty acids by human adults. *J. Nutr.* **113,** 1613–1625.

Fleming, S. E., and Vose, J. R. 1979. Digestibility of raw and cooked starches from legume seeds using the laboratory rat. *J. Nutr.* **109,** 2067–2075.

Fleming, S. E., Marthinsen, D., and Kuhnlein, H. 1983. Colonic function and fermentation in men consuming high fiber diets. *J. Nutr.* **113,** 2535–2544.

Ford, C. W. 1986. Comparative structural studies of lignin–carbohydrate complexes from *Digitaria decumbers'* (pangola grass) before and after chlorite delignification. *Carbohydr. Res.* **147,** 101–117.

Forrest, I. S., and Wainwright, T. 1977. The mode of binding of β-glucans and pentosans in barley endosperm cell walls. *J. Inst. Brew.* **83,** 279–286.

Freudenberg, K. 1968. The constitution and biosynthesis of lignin. *In* "Molecular Biology, Biochemistry and Biophysics" (A. Kleinzeller, G. F. Springer, and H. G. Wittmann, eds.), Vol. 2, pp. 45–122. Springer-Verlag, New York.

Fry, S. C. 1982a. Phenolic components of the primary cell wall. Feruloylated disaccharides of D-galactose and L-arabinose from spinach polysaccharide. *Biochem. J.* **203,** 493–504.

Fry, S. C. 1982b. Isoditryrosine, a new cross-linking amino acid from plant cell wall glycoprotein. *Biochem. J.* **204,** 449–455.

Fry, S. C. 1983. Feruloylated pectins from the primary cell wall: Their structure and possible functions. *Planta* **157,** 111–127.

Fuchs, H.-M., Dorfman, S., and Floch, M. H. 1976. The effect of dietary fiber supplementation in man. II. Alteration in fecal physiology and bacterial flora. *Am. J. Clin. Nutr.* **29,** 1443–1447.

Fulcher, R. G. 1982. Fluorescence microscopy of cereals. *Food Microstruct.* **1,** 167–175.

Gaillard, B. D. E., and Richards, G. N. 1975. Presence of soluble lignin–carbohydrate complexes in the bovine rumen. *Carbohydr. Res.* **42,** 135–145.

Gee, J. M., and Johnson, I. T. 1985. Rates of starch hydrolysis and changes in viscosity in a range of common foods subjected to simulated digestion *in vitro*. *J. Sci. Food Agric.* **36,** 614–620.

Gee, J. M., Blackburn, N. A., and Johnson, I. T. 1983. The influence of guar gum on intestinal cholesterol transport in the rat. *Br. J. Nutr.* **50,** 215–224.

Gheradini, F., and Salyers, A. A. 1982. Membrane-associated galactomannanase activity in *Bacteroides ovatus*. *Abstr. Annu. Meet. Am. Soc. Microbiol.*, p. 147, K64.

Glicksman, M. 1962. Utilization of natural polysaccharide gums in the food industry. *Adv. Food Res.* **11,** 109–200.

Godding, E. W. 1972. Therapeutic agents. *In* "Management of Constipation" (A. V. Jones and E. W. Godding, eds.), pp. 38–76. Blackwell, London.

Goldstein, A. M., Alter, E. M., and Saeman, J. F. 1973. Guar gum. *In* "Industrial Gums" (R. L. Whistler and J. N. BeMiller, eds.), pp. 303–321. Academic Press, New York.

Gorbach, S. L., Nahas, L., Weinstein, L., Levitan, R., and Patterson, J. F. 1967. Studies of intestinal microflora IV. The microflora of ileostomy effluent: a unique microbial ecology. *Gastroenterology* **53,** 874–880.

Gordon, A. H., Lomax, J. A., and Chesson, A. 1983. Glycosidic linkages of legume, grass and cereal straw cell walls before and after extensive degradation by rumen microorganisms. *J. Sci. Food Agric.* **34,** 1341–1350.

Gramstorff Fetzer, S., Kies, C., and Fox, H. M. 1979. Gastric disappearance of dietary fiber by adolescent boys. *Cereal Chem.* **56,** 34–37.

Grant, G. T., Morris, E. R., Rees, D. A., Smith, P. J. C., and Thorn, D. 1973. Biological interactions between polysaccharides and divalent cations: The egg-box model. *FEBS Lett.* **32,** 195–198.

Groleau, D., and Forsberg, C. W. 1981. Cellulolytic activity of the rumen bacterium *Bacteroides succinogenes*. *Can. J. Microbiol.* **27**, 517–530.

Groleau, D., and Forsberg, C. W. 1983. Partial characterization of the extracellular carboxymethyl cellulase activity produced by the rumen bacterium *Bacteroides succinogenes*. *Can. J. Microbiol.* **29**, 504–517.

Gubler, F., Ashford, A. E., Bacic, A., Blakeney, A. B., and Stone, B. A. 1985. Release of ferulic acid esters from barley aleurone. II. Characterisation of the feruloyl compounds released in response to GA_3. *Aust. J. Plant Physiol.* **12**, 307–317.

Haber, G. B., Heaton, K. W., and Murphy, D. 1977. Depletion and disruption of dietary fibre. Effects of satiety, plasma glucose, and serum insulin. *Lancet 1*, 679–682.

Hartley, R. D. 1978. The lignin fraction of plant cell walls. *Am. J. Clin. Nutr.* **31**, S90–S93.

Hartley, R. D. 1983. Non-carbohydrate constituents and properties of the plant cell wall in relation to its digestion. *In* "Fibre in Human and Animal Nutrition" (G. Wallace and L. Bell, eds.), pp. 81–84. Royal Society of New Zealand, Wellington.

Heath, M. F., and Northcote, D. H. 1971. Glycoprotein of the wall of sycamore tissue-culture cells. *Biochem. J.* **125**, 953–961.

Heller, S. N., Hackler, L. R., Rivers, J. M., Van Soest, P. J., Roe, D. A., Lewis, B. A., and Robertson, J. 1980. Dietary fiber: The effect of particle size of wheat bran on colonic function in young adult men. *Am. J. Clin. Nutr.* **33**, 1734–1744.

Hentges, D. J. 1978. Fecal flora of volunteers on controlled diets. *Am. J. Clin. Nutr.* **31**, S123–S124.

Hill, M. J. 1982. Influence of nutrition on the intestinal flora. *In* "Colon and Nutrition" (H. Kasper and H. Goebell, eds.), Falk Symposium 32, pp. 37–44. MTP Press, Lancaster.

Holloway, W. D., Tasman-Jones, C., and Lee, S. P. 1978. Digestion of certain fractions of dietary fiber in humans. *Am. J. Clin. Nutr.* **31**, 927–930.

Holm, J., Björck, I., Ostrowska, S., Eliasson, A.-C., Asp, N.-G., Larsson, K., and Lundquist, I. 1983. Digestibility of amylose–lipid complexes *in vitro* and *in vivo*. *Stärke* **35**, 294–297.

Holt, S., Heading, R. C., Carter, D. C., Prescott, L. F., and Tothill, P. 1979. Effect of gel fibre on gastric emptying and absorption of glucose and paracetamol. *Lancet 1*, 636–639.

Isaksson, G., Lundquist, I., and Ihse, I. 1982. Effect of dietary fiber on pancreatic amylase activity *in vitro*. *Hepato-Gastroenterology* **29**, 157–160.

James, W. P. T. 1980. Dietary fiber and mineral absorption. *In* "Medical Aspects of Dietary Fiber" (G. A. Spiller and R. K. McPherson, eds.), pp. 239–259. Academic Press, New York.

James, W. P. T., Branch, W. J., and Southgate, D. A. T. 1978. Calcium binding by dietary fibre. *Lancet 1*, 638–639.

Jenkins, D. J. A., Leeds, A. R., Newton, C., and Cummings, J. H. 1975. Effect of pectin, guar gum and wheat fibre on serum cholesterol. *Lancet 1*, 1116.

Jenkins, D. J. A., Goff, D., Leeds, A. R., Alberti, K. G. M. M., Wolever, T. M. S., Gassul, M. A., and Hockaday, T. D. R. 1976. Unabsorbable carbohydrates and diabetes: Decreased post-prandial hyperglycaemia. *Lancet 2*, 172–174.

Jenkins, D. J. A., Leeds, A. R., Gassull, M. A., Cochet, B., and Alberti, K. G. M. M. 1977. Decrease in post-prandial insulin and glucose concentrations by guar. *Ann. Intern. Med.* **86**, 83–132.

Jenkins, D. J. A., Wolever, T. M. S., Leeds, A. R., Gassull, M. A., Haisman, P., Dilawani, J., Goff, D. V., Metz, G. L., and Alberti, K. G. M. M. 1978. Dietary fibres, fibre analogues, and glucose tolerance. Importance of viscosity. *Br. Med. J.* **1**, 1392–1394.

Jenkins, D. J. A., Reynolds, D., Slavin, B., Leeds, A. R., Jenkins, A. L., and Jepson, E. M. 1980a. Dietary fiber and blood lipids: Treatment of hypercholesterolemia with guar crispbread. *Am. J. Clin. Nutr.* **33**, 575–581.

Jenkins, D. J. A., Wolever, T. M. S., Taylor, R. H., Barker, H. M., and Fielden, H. 1980b.

Exceptionally low glucose response to dried beans: Comparison with other carbohydrate foods. *Br. Med. J.* **281**, 578–580.

Jenkins, D. J. A., Wolever, T. M. S., Taylor, R. H., Barker, H. M., Fielden, H., and Jenkins, A. L. 1980c. Effect of guar crispbread with cereal products and leguminous seeds on blood glucose concentrations of diabetics. *Br. Med. J.* **281**, 1248–1250.

Jenkins, D. J. A., Wolever, T. M. S., Jenkins, A. L., Josse, R. G., and Wong, G. S. 1984. The glycaemic response to carbohydrate foods. *Lancet 2*, 388–391.

Jeraci, J. L. 1981. Interactions between rumen or human fecal inocula and fiber substrates. M.Sc. thesis, Cornell University Library, Ithaca, New York.

Jermyn, M. A., and Isherwood, F. A. 1956. Changes in the cell wall of the pear during ripening. *Biochem. J.* **64**, 123–132.

Jones, D. M. 1964. Structure and some reactions of cellulose. *Adv. Carbohydr. Chem.* **19**, 219–246.

Jones, L. H. P. 1978. Mineral components of plant cell walls. *Am. J. Clin. Nutr.* **31**, S94-98.

Johnson, D. B., Moore, W. E., and Zank, C. 1961. *TAPPI* **44**, 793.

Johnson, I. T. 1984. Fibre—How and why it works. *In* "Dietary Fibre in the Management of the Diabetic" (T. D. R. Hockaday and H. Keen, eds.), pp. 21–25. Medical Education Services, Oxford.

Johnson, I. T., and Gee, J. M. 1981. Effect of gel-forming gums on the intestinal unstirred layer and sugar transport *in vitro. Gut* **22**, 398–403.

Johnson, I. T., and Gee, J. M. 1982. Influence of viscous incubation media on the resistance to diffusion of the intestinal unstirred water layer *in vitro. Pflügers Arch.* **393**, 139–143.

Johnson, I. T., and Gee, J. M. 1986. Gastrointestinal adaptation in response to soluble non-available polysaccharides in the rat. *Br. J. Nutr.* **55**, 497–505.

Johnson, I. T., Gee, J. M., and Mahouney, R. R. 1984. Effect of dietary supplements of guar gum and cellulose on intestinal cell proliferation, enzyme levels, and sugar transport in the rat. *Br. J. Nutr.* **52**, 477–487.

Judd, P. A., and Truswell, S. 1981. The effect of rolled oats on blood lipids and fecal steroid excretion in man. *Am. J. Clin. Nutr.* **34**, 2061–2067.

Judd, P. A., and Truswell, A. S. 1982. Comparison of the effects of high- and low-methoxyl pectins on blood and faecal lipids in man. *Br. J. Nutr.* **48**, 451–458.

Judd, P. A., and Truswell, A. S. 1985. The hypocholesterolaemic effects of pectins in rats. *Br. J. Nutr.* **53**, 409–425.

Jung, H.-J. G. 1985. Inhibition of structural carbohydrate fermentation by forage phenolics. *J. Sci. Food Agric.* **36**, 74–80.

Kato, Y., and Nevins, D.-J. 1985. Isolation and identification of O-(5-O-feruloyl-α-L-arabinofuranosyl)-(1→3)-O-β-D-xylopyranosyl-(1→4)-D-xylopyranose as a component of *Zea* shoot cell walls. *Carbohydr. Res.* **137**, 139–150.

Kay, R. M., and Truswell, A. S. 1977. Effect of citrus pectin on blood lipids and fecal steroid excretion in man. *Am. J. Clin. Nutr.* **30**, 171–175.

Kay, R. M., and Truswell, A. S. 1980. Medical aspects of dietary fiber. *In* "Dietary Fiber: Effects on Plasma and Biliary Lipids in Man" (G. A. Spiller and R. M. Kay, eds.), pp. 153–173. Plenum, New York.

Kelleher, J., Walters, M. P., Srinivasan, T. R., Hart, G., Findlay, J. M., and Losewsky, M. S. 1984. Degradation of cellulose within the gastrointestinal tract in man. *Gut* **25**, 811–815.

Kelsay, J. L. 1978. A review of research on effects of fibre intake on man. *Am. J. Clin. Nutr.* **31**, 142–159.

Kelsay, J. L. 1981. Effect of diet fiber level on bowel function and trace mineral balances of human subjects. *Cereal Chem.* **58**, 2–5.

Kennedy, J. F., Sandhu, J. S., and Southgate, D. A. T. 1979. Structural data for the carbohydrate of Ispaghula husk ex *Plantago ovata* Forsk. *Carbohyd. Res.* **75**, 265–274.

Khan, A. R., Ghazala, Y. K., Mitchel, A., and Qadeer, M. A. 1981. Effect of guar gum on blood lipids. *Am. J. Clin. Nutr.* **34**, 2446–2449.

Kies, C., Sanchez, V. E., and Fox, H. M. 1984. Cellulose supplementation of a nutritionally complete liquid formula diet: Effects on gastrointestinal tract function of humans and fecal fiber recovery. *J. Food Sci.* **49**, 815–816, 837.

Kirkby, R. W., Anderson, J. W., Sieling, B., Rees, E. D., Lin Chen, W.-J., Miller, R. E., and Kay, R. M. 1981. Oat-bran intake selectively lowers serum low-density lipoprotein cholesterol concentrations of hypercholesterolemic men. *Am. J. Clin. Nutr.* **34**, 824–829.

Klose, R. E., and Glicksman, M. 1972. Gums. *In* "Handbook of Food Additives" (T. E. Furia, ed.), 2nd Ed., pp. 295–359. CRC Press, Cleveland, Ohio.

Kolattukudy, P. E. 1980. Cutin, Suberin and waxes. *Biochem. Plants* **4**, 571–645.

Kritchevsky, D., and Story, W. A. 1974. Binding of bile salts *in vitro* by non-nutritive fibre. *J. Nutr.* **104**, 458–462.

Kuksis, A. 1971. *In* "Bile Acids" (P. P. Nair and D. Kritchevsky, eds.), p. 204. Plenum, New York.

Laidlaw, R. A., and Percival, E. G. V. 1950. Studies of seed mucilages. Part V. Examination of a polysaccharide extracted from the seeds of *Plantago ovata* Forsk. by hot water. *J. Chem. Soc.* 528–534.

Lamport, D. T. A. 1965. The protein component of primary cell walls. *Adv. Bot. Res.* **2**, 151–218.

Lamport, D. T. A., and Catt, J. W. 1981. Glycoproteins and enzymes of the cell wall. *Encycl. Plant Physiol. New Ser.* **13B**, 133–165.

Latham, M. J., Brooker, B. E., Pettipher, G. L., and Harris, P. J. 1978a. *Ruminococcus flavefaciens* cell coat and adhesion to cotton cellulose and to cell walls in leaves of perennial ryegrass (*Lolium perenne*). *Appl. Environ. Microbiol.* **35**, 156–165.

Latham, M. J., Brooker, B. E., Pettipher, G. L., and Harris, P. J. 1978b. Adhesion of *Bacteroides succinogenes* in pure culture and in the presence of *Ruminococcus flavefaciens* to cell walls in leaves of perennial ryegrass (*Lolium perenne*). *Appl. Environ. Microbiol.* **35**, 1165–1173.

Leeds, A. R. 1979. Gastric emptying, fibre and absorption. *Lancet 1*, 872–873.

Lin, K. W., Patterson, J. A., and Ladisch, M. R. 1985. Anaerobic fermentation: Microbes from ruminants. *Enzyme Microb. Technol.* **7**, 98–107.

Lin, T. M., Kim, K. S., Karvinen, E., and Ivy, A. C. 1957. Effect of dietary pectin, "Protopectin" and gum arabic on cholesterol excretion in rats. *Am. J. Physiol.* **188**, 66–70.

Lindberg, J. E., Temrad, I. E., and Theander, O. 1984. Degradation rate and chemical composition of different types of alkali-treated straws during rumen digestion. *J. Sci. Food Agric.* **35**, 500–506.

Luria, S. E. 1960. The bacterial protoplasm: Composition and organization. *In* "The Bacteria" (I. C. Gunsalus and R. Y. Stanier, eds.), Vol. 1, pp. 1–34. Academic Press, New York.

McCleary, B. V., Matheson, N. K., and Small, D. M. 1976. Galactomannans and a galactoglucomannan in legume seed endosperms: Structural requirements for a β-mannanase hydrolysis. *Phytochemistry* **15**, 1111–1117.

McConnell, A. A., Eastwood, M. A., and Mitchell, W. D. 1974. Physical characteristics of vegetable foodstuffs that could influence bowel function. *J. Sci. Food Agric.* **25**, 1457–1464.

McCready, R. M., and McComb, E. A. 1954. Pectic constituents in ripe and unripe fruit. *Food Res.* **19**, 530–535.

McNeil, M., Darvill, A. G., Aman, P., Franzen, L.-E., and Albersheim, P. 1982. Structural analysis of complex carbohydrates using high-performance liquid chromatography, gas chromatography and mass spectrometry. *In* "Methods in Enzymology" (V. Ginsberg, ed.), Vol. 83, pp. 3–45. Academic Press, New York.

McNeil, M., Darvill, A. G., Fry, S. C., and Albersheim, P. 1984. Structure and function of the primary cell walls of plants. *Annu. Rev. Biochem.* **54**, 625–663.

McQueen, R. E., and Nicolson, J. W. G. 1979. Modification of the neutral detergent fiber procedure for cereals and vegetables by using α-amylase. *J. Assoc. Off. Anal. Chem.* **62,** 676–680.

Mares, D. J., and Stone, B. A. 1973a. Studies on wheat endosperm. I. Chemical composition and ultrastructure of the cell walls. *Aust. J. Biol. Sci.* **26,** 793–812.

Mares, D. J., and Stone, B. A. 1973b. Studies on wheat endosperm. II. Properties of the wall components and studies of their organisation in the wall. *Aust. J. Biol. Sci.* **26,** 813–830.

Markwalder, H. U., and Neukom, H. 1976. Diferulic acid as a possible crosslink in hemicelluloses from wheat germ. *Phytochemistry* **15,** 836–837.

Martin, J. T., and Juniper, B. E. 1970. *In* The Cuticles of Plants,'' pp. 54–70. Edward Arnold, London.

Meier, H., and Reid, J. S. G. 1982. Reserve polysaccharides other than starch in higher plants. *Encycl. Plant Physiol. New Ser.* **13A,** 418–471.

Mercier, C. 1980. Structure and digestibility alterations of cereal starches by twin-screw extrusion cooking. *In* "Food Process Engineering" (P. Linko, Y. Malkki, J. Olkku, and J. Larinkari, eds.), pp. 795–807. Applied Science Publ., London.

Mercier, C., Charbonniere, R., Grebaut, J., and de la Gueriviere, J. F. 1980. Formation of amylose–lipid complexes by twin-screw extrusion cooking of manoic starch. *Cereal Chem.* **57,** 4–7.

Michel, F., Thibault, J.-F., Mercier, C., Heitz, F., and Pauillade, F. 1985. Extraction and characterization of pectins from sugar beet pulp. *J. Food Sci.* **50,** 1499–1500, 1502.

Miller, T. L., and Wolin, M. J. 1981. Fermentation by the human large intestine microbial community in an *in vitro* semicontinuous culture system. *Appl. Environ. Microbiol.* **42,** 400–407.

Moore, W. E. C., and Holdeman, L. V. 1974. Human fecal flora: The normal flora of 20 Japanese–Hawaiians. *Appl. Microbiol.* **27,** 961–979.

Moore, W. E. C., Cato, E. P., Good, I. J., and Holdeman, L. V. 1981. The effect of diet on the human fecal flora. *In* Banbury Report 7. "Gastrointestinal Cancer: Endogenous Factors" (W. R. Bruce, P. Correa, M. Lyskin, S. R. Tannenbaum, and T. D. Wilkins, eds.), pp. 11–24. Cold Spring Harbor Laboratory, Cold Spring Harbor, New York.

Morgan, B., Heald, M., Atkin, S. D., Green, J., and Chain, E. B. 1974. Dietary fibre and sterol metabolism in the rat. *Br. J. Nutr.* **32,** 447–455.

Morris, E. J., and Bacon, J. S. D. 1976. Digestion of acetyl groups and cell-wall polysaccharides of grasses in the rumen. *Proc. Nutr. Soc.* **35,** 94A-95A.

Morris, E. J., and Bacon, J. S. D. 1977. The fate of acetyl groups and sugar components during the digestion of grass cell walls in sheep. *J. Agric. Sci.* **89,** 327–340.

Morris, V. J. 1986. Gelation of polysaccharides. *In* "Functional Properties of Food Macromolecules" (J. R. Mitchell and D. A. Ledward, eds.), pp. 121–170. Elsevier, London.

Morris, V. J., and Chilvers, G. R. 1983. Rheological studies of specific cation forms of Kappa carrageenan gels. *Carbohydr. Polymers* **3,** 129–141.

Morrison, I. M. 1972a. A semi-micro method for the determination of lignin and its use in predicting the digestibility of forage crops. *J. Sci. Food Agric.* **23,** 455–463.

Morrison, I. M. 1972b. Improvements in the acetyl bromide technique to determine lignin and digestibility and its application to legumes. *J. Sci. Food Agric.* **23,** 1463–1469.

Morrison, I. M. 1980. Hemicellulosic contamination of acid detergent residues and their replacement by cellulosic residues in cell wall analysis. *J. Sci. Food Agric.* **31,** 639–645.

Neilson, M. J., and Richards, G. N. 1982. Chemical structures in a lignin-carbohydrate complex isolated from the bovine rumen. *Carbohydr. Res.* **104,** 121–138.

Neukom, H., Providoli, L., Gremli, H., and Hui, P. A. 1964. Recent investigations on wheat flour pentosans. *Cereal Chem.* **44,** 238–244.

Nilsson, G., Lindberg, A. A., Lundblad, A., and Suensson, S. 1984. Plant arabinogalactans inhibiting bacterial adhesion. *Abstr. Int. Carbohydr. Symp., 13th, Utrecht,* C4.8.

Northcote, D. H. 1963. Changes in the cell walls of plants during differentiation. *Symp. Soc. Exp. Biol.* **17**, 157–174.

Northcote, D. H. 1969. Synthesis and metabolic control of polysaccharides and lignin during the differentiation of plant cells. *Essays Biochem.* **5**, 89–137.

Northcote, D. H. 1972. Chemistry of the plant cell wall. *Annu. Rev. Plant Physiol.* **23**, 113–132.

Oakenfull, D. G., and Fenwick, D. E. 1978. Adsorption of bile salts from aqueous solution by plant fibre and cholestyramine. *Br. J. Nutr.* **40**, 299–309.

O'Dea, K., Nestel, P. J., and Antonoff, L. 1980. Physical factors influencing postprandial glucose and insulin responses to starch. *Am. J. Clin. Nutr.* **33**, 760–765.

Olson, A. C., Gray, G. M., Chiu, M.-C., and Fleming, S. E. 1983. Cellulose, xylan, corn bran, and pectin in the human digestive process. *In* "Unconventional Sources of Dietary Fiber—Physiological and *In Vitro* Functional Properties" (I. Furda, ed.). *A.C.S. Symp. Ser.* **214**.

O'Neill, M. A., and Selvendran, R. R. 1980a. Glycoproteins from the cell wall of *Phaseolus coccineus. Biochem. J.* **187**, 53–63.

O'Neill, M. A., and Selvendran, R. R.1980b. Methylation analysis of cell wall material from *Phaseolus vulgaris* and *Phaseolus coccineus. Carbohydr. Res.* **79**, 115–124.

O'Neill, M. A., and Selvendran, R. R. 1983. Isolation and partial characterisation of a xyloglucan from the cell walls of *Phaseolus coccineus. Carbohydr. Res.* **111**, 239–255.

O'Neill, M. A., and Selvendran, R. R. 1985a. Hemicellulosic complexes from the cell walls of runner bean (*Phaseolus coccineus*). *Biochem. J.* **227**, 475–481.

O'Neill, M. A., and Selvendran, R. R. 1985b. Structural analysis of the xyloglucan from the cell walls of *Phaseolus coccineus* using cellulase derived oligosaccharides. *Carbohydr. Res.* **145**, 45–58.

Palmer, C. H. 1972. Morphology of starch granules in cereal grains and malts. *J. Inst. Brew.* **78**, 326–332.

Pearl, I. A. 1967. *In* "The Chemistry of Lignin," p. 37. Edward Arnold, London; Dekker, New York.

Pettipher, G. L., and Latham, M. J. 1979a. Characteristics of enzymes produced by *Ruminococcus flavefaciens* which degrade plant cell walls. *J. Gen. Microbiol.* **110**, 21–27.

Pettipher, G. L., and Latham, M. J. 1979b. Production of enzymes degrading plant cell walls and fermentation of cellobiose by *Ruminococcus flavefaciens* in batch and continuous culture. *J. Gen. Microbiol.* **110**, 29–38.

Pilnik, W., and Rombouts, F. M. 1985. Polysaccharides and food processing. *Carbohydr. Res.* **142**, 93–105.

Pippen, E. L., McCready, R. M., and Owens, H. S. 1950. Gelation properties of partially acetylated pectins. *J. Am. Chem. Soc.* **72**, 813–816.

Powell, D. A., Morris, E. R., Gidley, M. J., and Rees, D. A. 1982. Conformations and interactions of pectins. II. Influence of residue sequence on chain association in calcium pectate gels. *J. Mol. Biol.* **155**, 517–531.

Prins, R. A. 1977. Biochemical activities of gut microorganisms. *In* "Microbial Ecology of the Gut" (R. T. J. Clarke and T. Bauchop, eds.), pp. 73–183. Academic Press, New York.

Rainbird, A. L., Low, A. G., and Sambrook, I. E. 1982a. Lack of effect of guar gum on gastric emptying in pigs. *Proc. Nutr. Soc.* **42**, 24A.

Rainbird, A. L., Low, A. G., and Zebroska, T. 1982b. Effect of guar gum on glucose absorption from isolated loops of jejunum in conscious growing pigs. *Proc. Nutr. Soc.* **41**. 48A.

Reddy, N. R., Palmer, J. K., Pierson, M. D., and Bothast, R. J. 1983. Wheat straw hemicelluloses: Composition and fermentation by human colon *Bacteroides. J. Agric. Food Chem.* **31**, 1308–1313.

Reddy, N. R., Palmer, J. K., and Pierson, M. D. 1984. Hydrolysis of wheat straw hemicelluloses and heteroxylan (larchwood) by human colon *Bacteriodes ovatus* B4-11 enzymes. *J. Agric. Food Chem.* **32,** 840–844.

Redgwell, R., and Selvendran, R. R. 1986. Structural features of cell-wall polysaccharides of onion *Allium cepa. Carbohydr. Res.* **157,** 183–199.

Rees, D. A. 1969. Structure, conformation, and mechanism in the formation of polysaccharide gels and networks. *Adv. Carbohydr. Chem. Biochem.* **24,** 267–332.

Rees, D. A. 1982. Polysaccharide conformation in solution and gels—Recent results on pectins. *Carbohyd. Polymers* **2,** 254–263.

Richards, G. N. 1976. Search for factors other than "lignin-shielding" in protection of cell-wall polysaccharides from digestion in the rumen. *In* "Carbohydrate Research in Plants and Animals," Misc. Papers 12, pp. 129–135. Landbauwhogeschool Wageningen. Veenman and Zonen, Wageningen.

Richards, G. N. 1984. Lignin-carbohydrate complexes. *Plenary Lect. Abstr. Int. Workshop Plant Polysaccharides, Struct. function, Nantes, 47–53.*

Riley, R. G., and Kolattukudy, P. E. 1975. Evidence for covalently attached *p*-coumaric acid and ferulic acid in cutins and suberins. *Plant Physiol.* **56,** 650–654.

Ring, S. G., and Selvendran, R. R. 1978. Purification and methylation analysis of cell wall material from *Solanum tuberosum. Phytochemistry* **17,** 745–752.

Ring. S. G., and Selvendran, R. R. 1980. Isolation and analysis of cell wall material from beeswing wheat bran. *Phytochemistry* **19,** 1723–1730.

Ring, S. G., and Selvendran, R. R. 1981. An arabinogalactoxyloglucan from the cell wall of *Solanum tuberosum. Phytochemistry* **20,** 2511–2519.

Robertson, J. A., and Eastwood, M. A. 1981a. A method to measure the water-holding properties of dietary fibre using suction pressure. *Br. J. Nutr.* **46,** 247–255.

Robertson, J. A., and Eastwood, M. A. 1981b. An examination of factors which may affect the water holding capacity of dietary fibre. *Br. J. Nutr.* **45,** 83–88.

Robertson, J. A., and Eastwood, M. A. 1981c. An investigation of the experimental conditions which could affect water-holding capacity of dietary fibre. *J. Sci. Food Agric.* **32,** 819–825.

Robertson, J. B., and Van Soest, P. J. 1977. Dietary fiber estimation in concentrate feed stuffs. *J. Anim. Sci. Suppl.* 254–255.

Robertson, J. B., and Van Soest, P. J. 1981. The detergent system of analysis and its application to human foods. *In* "The Analysis of Dietary Fiber in Foods" (W. P. T. James and O. Theander, eds.), pp. 123–158. Dekker, New York.

Roediger, W. E. W. 1986. Metabolic basis of starvation diarrhoea: Implications for treatment. *Lancet 1,* 1082–1084.

Rombouts, F. M., Thibault, J.-F., and Mercier, C. 1983. Procédé de modification des pectines de betterave, products obtenus et leurs applications. Brevet d'Invention Francais No. 8307208.

Roth, H. P., and Mehlman, M. A., eds. 1978. "Role of Dietary Fiber in Health" *Am. J. Clin. Nutr. Suppl.* **31**(10).

Ruperez, P., Selvendran, R. R., and Stevens, B. J. H. 1985. Investigations of the heterogeneity of xyloglucans from the cell walls of apple. *Carbohydr. Res.* **142,** 107–113.

Salyers, A. A. 1979. Energy sources of major intestinal fermentative anaerobes. *Am. J. Clin. Nutr.* **32,** 158–163.

Salyers, A. A., Vercellotti, J. R., West, S. E. H., and Wilkins, T. D. 1977a. Fermentation of mucin and plant polysaccharides by strains of *Bacteroides* from the human colon. *Appl. Environ. Microbiol.* **33,** 319–322.

Salyers, A. A., West, S. E. H., Vercellotti, J. R., and Wilkins, T. D. 1977b. Fermentation of mucins and plant polysaccharides by anaerobic bacteria from the human colon. *Appl. Environ. Microbiol.* **34,** 529–533.

Salyers, A. A., Harris, C. J., and Wilkins, T. D. 1978. Breakdown of psyllium hydrocolloid by strains of *Bacteroides ovatus* from the human intestinal tract. *Can. J. Microbiol.* **24,** 336–338.

Salyers, A. A., Arthur, R., and Kuritza, A. 1981a. Digestion of larch arabinogalactan by a strain of human colonic *Bacteroides* growing in continuous culture. *J. Agric. Food Chem.* **29,** 475–480.

Salyers, A. A., Gherardini, F., and O'Brien, M. 1981b. Utilization of xylan by two species of human colonic *Bacteroides*. *Appl. Environ. Microbiol.* **41,** 1065–1068.

Salyers, A. A. Balascio, J. R., and Palmer, J. K. 1982. Breakdown of xylan by enzymes from human colonic bacteria. *J. Food Biochem.* **6,** 39–55.

Salyers, A. A., O'Brien, M., and Schmetter, B. 1983. Catabolism of mucopolysaccharides, plant gums, and Maillard products by human colonic *Bacteroides*. *In* "Unconventional Sources of Dietary Fiber—Physiological and *In Vitro* Functional Properties" (I. Furda, ed.). *A.C.S. Symp. Ser.* **214.**

Sandberg, A.-S., Andersson, H., Hallgren, B., Hassleblad, K., Isaksson, B., and Hulten, L. 1981. Experimental model for in vivo determination of dietary fibre and its effect on the absorption of nutrients in the small intestine. *Br. J. Nutr.* **45,** 283–294.

Sandberg, A.-S., Ahderinne, R., Andersson, H., Hallgren, B., and Hulten, L. 1983. The effect of citrus pectin on the absorption of nutrients in the small intestine. *Hum. Nutr. Clin. Nutr.* **37C,** 171–183.

Sandhu, J. S., Hudson, G. J., and Kennedy, J. F. 1981. The gel nature and structure of the carbohydrate of Ispaghula husk ex *Plantago ovata* Forsk. *Carbohyd. Res.* **93,** 247–259.

Sarkanen, K. V., and Hergert, H. L. 1971. Classification and distribution of lignins. *In* "Lignins" (K. V. Sarkanen and C. H. Ludwig, eds.), pp. 43–94. Wiley (Interscience), New York.

Schaller, D. 1978. Fiber content and structure in foods. *Am. J. Clin. Nutr.* **31,** S99–S102.

Schaller, D. 1981. Collaborative study of an analytical method for insoluble dietary fiber in cereals. *Cereal Foods World* **26,** 295–297.

Schel, J. H. N., Stasse-Wolthuis, M. Katan, M. B., and Willemse, M. T. M. 1980. Structural changes of wheat bran after human digestion, pp. 1–9. Mededelingen Landbauwhogeschool Wageningen.

Schneeman, B. O. 1978. Effect of plant fiber on lipase, trypsin, and chymotrypsin activity. *J. Food Sci.* **43,** 634–635.

Schneeman, B. O., and Gallaher, D. 1985. Effects of dietary fiber on digestive enzyme activity and bile acids in the small intestine. *Proc. Soc. Exp. Biol. Med.* **180,** 409–414.

Schweizer, T. F., and Wursch, P. 1979. Analysis of dietary fibre. *J. Sci. Food Agric.* **30,** 613–619.

Selvendran, R. R. 1975a. Cell wall glycoproteins and polysaccharides of parenchyma of *Phaseolus coccineus*. *Phytochemistry* **14,** 2175–2180.

Selvendran, R. R. 1975b. Analysis of cell wall material from plant tissues: Extraction and purification. *Phytochemistry* **14,** 1011–1017.

Selvendran, R. R. 1978. Bile salt binding sites in vegetable fibre. *Chem. Ind.* 428–430.

Selvendran, R. R. 1979. The binding of bile salts by vegetable fibre. *Qual. Plant.* **29,** 109–133.

Selvendran, R. R. 1983. The chemistry of plant cell walls. *In* "Dietary Fibre" (G. G. Birch and K. J. Parker, eds.), pp. 95–147. Applied Science Publ., London.

Selvendran, R. R. 1984. The plant cell wall as a source of dietary fiber: Chemistry and structure. *Am. J. Clin. Nutr.* **39,** 320–337.

Selvendran, R. R. 1985. Developments in the chemistry and biochemistry of pectic and hemi-cellulosic polymers. *J. Cell Sci. Suppl.* **2,** 51–88.

Selvendran, R. R., and Du Pont, M. S. 1980a. Simplified methods for the preparation and analysis of dietary fibre. *J. Sci. Food Agric.* **31,** 1173–1182.

Selvendran, R. R., and Du Pont, M. S. 1980b. An alternative method for the isolation and analysis of cell wall material from cereals. *Cereal Chem.* **57,** 278–283.

Selvendran, R. R., and Du Pont, M. S. 1984. Problems associated with the analysis of dietary fibre and some recent developments. *Dev. Food Anal. Tech.* **3**, 1–68.

Selvendran, R. R., and O'Neill, M. A. 1982. Plant glycoproteins. *Encycl. Plant Physiol. New Ser.* **13A**, 515–583.

Selvendran, R. R., and O'Neill, M. A. 1987. Isolation and analysis of cell walls from plant material. *In* "Methods of Biochemical Analysis" (D. Glick, ed.), Vol. 32, pp. 25–153. Wiley (Tube & Science), New York.

Selvendran, R. R., and Stevens, B. J. H. 1986. Applications of mass spectrometry for the examination of pectic polysaccharides. *Mod. Methods Plant Anal. New Ser.* **3**, 23–46.

Selvendran, R. R., March, J. F., and Ring, S. G. 1979. Determination of aldoses and uronic acid content of vegetable fibre. *Anal. Biochem.* **96**, 282–292.

Selvendran, R. R., Stevens, B. J. H., and O'Neill, M. A. 1985. Developments in the isolation and analysis of cell walls from edible plants. *In* "Biochemistry of Plant Cell Walls" (C. T. Brett and J. R. Hillman, eds.), pp. 39–78. SEB Seminar 28, Cambridge Univ. Press, London.

Shainkin, R., and Birk, Y. 1970. α-Amylase inhibitors from wheat: Isolation and characterization. *Biochim. Biophys. Acta* **221**, 502–513.

Shibuya, N., and Iwasaki, T. 1978. Polysaccharides and glycoproteins in the rice endosperm cell wall. *Agric. Biol. Chem.* **42**, 2259–2266.

Shibuya, N., and Misaki, A. 1978. Structure of hemicellulose isolated from rice endosperm cell wall: Mode of linkages and sequences in xyloglucan, β-glucan and arabinoxylan. *Agric. Biol. Chem.* **42**. 2267–2274.

Siddiqui, I. R., and Wood, P. J. 1974. Structural investigation of oxalate-soluble rapeseed (*Brassica campestris*) polysaccharides. Part III. An arabinan. *Carbohydr. Res.* **36**, 35–44.

Simson, B. W., and Timell, T. E. 1978. Polysaccharides in cambial tissues of *Populus tremuloides* and *Tilia americana*. II. Isolation and structure of a xyloglucan. *Cell. Chem. Technol.* **12**, 51–62.

Slade, A. P., Wyatt, G. M., Bayliss, C., and Waites, W. M. 1987. Comparison of populations of human faecal bacteria before and after *in vitro* incubation with plant cell wall substrates. *J. Appl. Bacteriol.* **62**, 231–240.

Slavin, J. L., Brauer, P. M., and Marlett, J. A. 1981. Neutral detergent fiber, hemicellulose and cellulose digestibility in human subjects. *J. Nutr.* **111**, 287–297.

Smith, M. M., and Hartley, R. D. 1983. Occurrence and nature of ferulic acid substitution of cell wall polysaccharides in graminaceous plants. *Carbohydr. Res.* **118**, 65–80.

Snow, P., and O'Dea, K. 1981. Factors affecting the rate of hydrolysis of starch in food. *Am. J. Clin. Nutr.* **34**, 2721–2727.

Southgate, D. A. T. 1969. Determination of carbohydrates in foods. II. Unavailable carbohydrates. *J. Sci. Food Agric.* **20**, 331–335.

Southgate, D. A. T. 1976. The chemistry of dietary fibre. *In* "Fiber in Human Nutrition" (G. A. Spiller and R. J. Amen, eds.), pp. 31–72. Plenum, New York.

Southgate, D. A. T. 1978a. Dietary fiber: Analysis and food sources. *Am. J. Clin. Nutr.* **31**, S107–110.

Southgate, D. A. T. 1978b. Chemical aspects. *Top Gastroenterol.* **6**, 13–38.

Southgate, D. A. T. 1982. Definitions and terminology of dietary fibre. *In* "Dietary Fibre in Health and Disease" (G. V. Vahouney and D. Kritchevsky, eds.), pp. 1–7. Plenum, New York.

Southgate, D. A. T. 1986. The relation between composition and properties of dietary fiber and physiological effects. *In* "Dietary Fiber: Basic and Clinical Aspects" (G. V. Vahouny and D. Kritchevsky, eds.), pp. 35–48. Plenum, New York.

Southgate, D. A. T., and Englyst, H. 1985. Dietary fibre: Chemistry, physical properties and analysis. *In* "Dietary Fibre, Fibre-Depleted Foods and Disease" (H. Trowell, D. Burkitt, and K. Heaton, eds.), pp. 31–55. Academic Press, London.

Southgate, D. A. T., Bailey, B., Collinson, E., and Walker, A. F. 1976. A guide to calculating intakes of dietary fibre. *J. Hum. Nutr.* **30**, 303–313.

Southgate, D. A. T., Hudson, G. J., and Englyst, H. 1978. The analysis of dietary fibre—The choices for the analyst. *J. Sci. Food Agric.* **29**, 979–988.

Spellman, M. W., McNeil, M., Darvill, A. G., and Albersheim, P. 1983. Characterization of a structurally complex heptasaccharide isolated from the pectic polysaccharide rhamnogalacturonan. II. *Carbohydr. Res.* **122**, 131–153.

Spiller, G. A., and Amen, R. J. 1975. Dietary fiber in human nutrition. *CRC Crit. Rev. Food Sci. Nutr.* **7**, 39–70.

Spiller, G. A., and Amen, R. J. (eds.) 1976. "Fiber in Human Nutrition." Plenum, New York.

Stanley, M., Paul, D., Gacke, D., and Murphy, J. 1973. Effects of cholestyramine, metamucil, and cellulose on fecal bile salt excretion in man. *Gastroenterology* **65**, 889.

Stasse-Wolthuis, M. 1980. The effects of various sources of dietary fibre on cholesterol metabolism and colonic function in healthy subjects. Ph.D. thesis, Agricultural University, Wageningen.

Stasse-Wolthuis, M. 1981. Influence of dietary fibre on cholesterol metabolism and colonic function in healthy subjects. *World Rev. Nutr. Diet.* **36**, 100–140.

Stephen, A. M. 1983. Other plant polysaccharides. *In* "The Polysaccharides" (G. O. Aspinall, ed.), Vol. 2, pp. 98–193. Academic Press, New York.

Stephen, A. M., and Cummings, J. H. 1979. Water-holding by dietary fibre *in vitro* and its relationship to faecal output in man. *Gut* **20**, 722–729.

Stephen, A. M., and Cummings, J. H. 1980a. The microbial contribution to human faecal mass. *J. Med. Microbiol.* **13**, 45–56.

Stephen, A. M., and Cummings, J. H. 1980b. Mechanism of action of dietary fibre in the human colon. *Nature (London)* **284**, 283–284.

Stevens, B. J. H., and Selvendran, R. R. 1980. The isolation and analysis of cell wall material from the alcohol-insoluble residue of cabbage (*Brassica oleracea* var. *capitata*.) *J. Sci. Food Agric.* **31**, 1257–1267.

Stevens, B. J. H., and Selvendran, R. R. 1981. A comparison of the compositions of dietary fibre from some cereal and vegetable products in relation to observed effects in faecal weight. *Lebensm, Wiss. Technol.* **14**, 301–305.

Stevens, B. J. H., and Selvendran, R. R. 1984a. Pectic polysaccharides of cabbage (*Brassica oleracea*). *Phytochemistry* **23**, 107–115.

Stevens, B. J. H., and Selvendran, R. R. 1984b. Hemicellulosic polymers of cabbage leaves. *Phytochemistry* **23**, 339–347.

Stevens, B. J. H., and Selvendran, R. R. 1984c. Structural features of cell wall polysaccharides of the carrot (*Daucus carota*). *Carbohydr. Res.* **128**, 321–333.

Stevens, B. J. H., and Selvendran, R. R. 1984d. Structural features of cell wall polymers of the apple. *Carbohydr. Res.* **135**, 155–166.

Stevens, B. J. H., Selvendran, R. R., Bayliss, C. E., and Turner, R. 1987. The degradation of cell wall material of apple and wheat bran by human fecal bacteria *in vitro*. *J. Sci. Food Agric.* (in press).

Story, J. A., and Kritchevsky, D. 1976. Comparison of the binding of various bile acids and bile salts *in vitro* by several types of fiber. *J. Nutr.* **106**, 1292–1294.

Talmadge, K. W., Keegstra, K., Bauer, W. D., and Albersheim, P. 1973. The structure of plant cell walls I. The macromolecular components of the walls of suspension-culture sycamore cells with a detailed analysis of the pectic polysaccharides. *Plant Physiol.* **51**, 158–173.

Taylor, R. H. 1979. Gastric emptying, fibre and absorption. *Lancet 1*, 872.

Teng, J., and Whistler, R. L. 1973. *In* "Phytochemistry—The Process and Products of Photosynthesis" (L. P. Millar, ed.), Vol. 1, pp. 249–269. Van Nostrand-Reinhold, New York.

Theander, O., and Aman, P. 1979. Studies on dietary fibre. I. Analysis of water-soluble and water-insoluble dietary fibre. *Swed. J. Agric. Res.* **9**, 97–106.

Thomsen, L. L., Tasman-Jones, C., Lee, S. P., and Roberton, A. M. 1982. Dietary factors in the control of pH and volatile fatty acid production in the rat caecum. *In* "Colon and Nutrition" (H. Kasper and H. Goebell, eds.), Falk Symposium 32, pp. 47–51. MTP Press, Lancaster.

Thornber, J. P., and Northcote, D. H. 1962. Changes in the chemical composition of a cambial cell during its differentiation into xylem and phloem tissue in trees. 3. Xylan, glucomannan, and α-cellulose fractions. *Biochem. J.* **82**, 340–346.

Timell, T. E. 1964. Wood hemicelluloses: Part 1. *Adv. Carbohydr. Chem.* **19**, 247–302.

Torres, A., and Thomas, R. D.1981. Polydextrose and its applications in foods. *Food Technol.* **35**, 44–49.

Trowell, H. 1960. "Non-Infective Disease in Africa," pp. 119–129 and 217–222. Edward Arnold, London.

Trowell, H. 1972a. Ischemic heart disease and dietary fibre. *Am. J. Clin. Nutr.* **25**, 926–932.

Trowell, H. 1972b. Crude fibre, dietary fibre and atherosclerosis (letter). *Atherosclerosis* **16**, 138–140.

Trowell, H. 1974. Definitions of fibre. *Lancet 1*, 503.

Trowell, H. 1976. Definition of dietary fibre and hypotheses that it is a protective factor in certain diseases. *Am. J. Clin. Nutr.* **29**, 417–427.

Trowell, H. 1979. "Dietary Fibre in Human Nutrition: A Bibliography." John Libbey, London.

Trowell, H., Southgate, D. A. T., Wolever, T. M. S., Leeds, A. R., Gassull, M. A., and Jenkins, D. J. A. 1976. Dietary fibre redefined. *Lancet 1*, 967.

Tsai, A. C., Elias, J., Kelley, J. J., Lin, R. S. C., and Robson, J. R. K. 1976. Influence of certain dietary fibers on serum and tissue cholesterol levels in rats. *J. Nutr.* **106**, 118–123.

Vance, C. P., Kirk, T. K., and Sherwood, R. T. 1980. Lignification as a mechanism of disease resistance. *Annu. Rev. Phytopathol.* **18**, 259–288.

Van Dokkum, W., Pikaar, N. A., and Thissen, J. T. N. M. 1983. Physiological effects of fibre-rich types of bread. 2. Dietary fibre from bread: Digestibility by the intestinal microflora and water-holding capacity in the colon of human subjects. *Br. J. Nutr.* **50**, 61–74.

Van Soest, P. J. 1965. Use of detergents in the analysis of fibrous feeds. II. Study of effects of heating and drying on yield of fiber and lignin in forages. *J. Assoc. Off. Anal. Chem.* **48**, 785–790.

Van Soest, P. J. 1973. Collaborative study of acid detergent fibre and lignin. *J. Assoc. Off. Anal. Chem.* **56**, 781–784.

Van Soest, P. J. 1981. Some factors influencing the ecology of gut fermentation in man. *In* Banbury Report 7. "Gastrointestinal Cancer: Endogenous Factors" (W. R. Bruce, P. Correa, M. Lyskin, S. R. Tannenbaum, and T. D. Wilkins, eds.), pp. 61–69. Cold Spring Harbor Press, Cold Springs Harbor, New York.

Van Soest, P. J. 1984. Some physical characteristics of dietary fibres and their influence on the microbial ecology of the human colon. *Proc. Nutr. Soc.* **43**, 25–33.

Van Soest, P. J., and Wine, R. H. 1967. Use of detergents in the analysis of fibrous feeds. IV. Determination of cell wall constituents. *J. Assoc. Off. Anal. Chem.* **50**, 50–55.

Van Soest, P. J., and Wine, R. H. 1968. Determination of lignin and cellulose in acid-detergent fiber with permanganate. *J. Assoc. Off. Anal. Chem.* **51**, 780–785.

Van Soest, P. J., Horvath, P., McBarney, M., Jeraci, J., and Allen, M. 1983. Some *in vitro* and *in vivo* properties of dietary fibers from non-cereal sources. *In* "Unconventional Sources of Dietary Fiber—Physiological and *In Vitro* Functional Properties" (I. Furda, ed.). *A.C.S. Symp. Ser.,* **24**.

Werch, S. C., and Ivy, A. C. 1941. On the fate of ingested pectin. *Am. J. Dig. Dis.* **8**, 101–105.

Whistler, R. L., and BeMiller, J. N., eds. 1973. "Industrial Gums." Academic Press, New York.

Williams, A. E., Eastwood, M. A., and Cregeen, R. 1978. SEM and light microscope study of the matrix structure of human feces. *Scanning Electron Microsc.* **II,** 707–712.

Williams, R. D., and Olmsted, W. H. 1936. The effect of cellulose, hemicellulose and lignin on the weight of the stool: A contribution to the study of laxation in man. *J. Nutr.* **11,** 433–449.

Wolever, T. M. S., Chan, C., and Law, C. 1983. The *in vitro* and *in vivo* anti-amylase activity of starch blockers. *J. Plant Foods.* **5,** 23–30.

Wolin, M. J., and Miller, T. L. 1983. Carbohydrate fermentation. *In* "Human Intestinal Microflora in Health and Disease" (D. J. Hentges, ed.), pp. 147–165. Academic Press, New York.

Wood, P. J., and Fulcher, R. G. 1978. Interaction of some dyes with cereal β-glucans. *Cereal Chem.* **55,** 952–966.

Wood, T. M., Wilson, C. A., and Stewart, C.-S. 1982. Preparation of the cellulase from the cellulolytic anaerobic bacterium *Ruminococcus albus* and its release from the bacterial cell wall. *Biochem. J.* **205,** 129–137.

Wyatt, G. M., Bayliss, C. E., and Holcroft, J. D. 1986. A change in human faecal flora in response to inclusion of gum arabic in the diet. *Br. J. Nutr.* **55,** 261–266.

York, W. S., Darvill, A. G., and Albersheim, P. 1984. Inhibition of 2,4-dichlorophenoxyacetic acid-stimulated elongation of pea stem segments by a xyloglucan oligosaccharide. *Plant Physiol.* **75,** 295–297.

York, W. S., Darvill, A. G., McNeil, M., and Albersheim, P. 1985. 3-Deoxy-D-*manno*-2-octulosonic acid (KDO) is a component of rhamnogalacturonan II, a pectic polysaccharide in the primary cell walls of plants. *Carbohydr. Res.* **138,** 109–126.

CHOCOLATE

ROBERT A. MARTIN, JR.*

Hershey Foods Corporation
Technical Center
Hershey, Pennsylvania 17033

*The author would like to acknowledge the following Hershey Foods Corporation individuals for contributions to this chapter: C. Babb, G. Bigalli, L. Campbell, J. Carpenter, D. Lehrian, J. Mihalik, G. Patterson, J. Rita, and J. Robbins. Also appreciated is the contribution by T. Gilmore, Dairy and Food Industries Supply Association, Rockville, Maryland.

211

I. INTRODUCTION

The purpose of this article is to review the subject of chocolate, emphasizing recent developments of the last 10 years. Fundamentals of chocolate itself or its processing will be minimally addressed. Readers are encouraged to familiarize themselves with earlier texts such as Minifie (1980) to gain an acquaintance with the fundamentals of chocolate. To provide readers with some assistance with the traditional operations involved in chocolate manufacture, a process diagram has been included as Fig. 1 (Zoumas and Finnegan, 1979). To better acquaint the reader with the complexities of chocolate flavor, the article by Foster (1978) is recommended.

Various technologies used in chocolate processing are secret and undocumented in the literature. Hence, although the section on cocoa fermentation reviews a wide span of literature, the sections on chocolate crumb processing or cocoa alkalization are written from a paucity of literature information due to the propriety of the processes used in manufacture.

This article is organized to present first a review of raw materials, followed by the combination of raw materials in the processing steps leading to the finished chocolate product. It is hoped that this will provide the reader a logical sequence of recent information relating to the manufacture of chocolate.

This article has been assembled from individual contributions by many authors dealing with widely different subject areas relating to chocolate. As such, some diversity of style and approach is evident throughout the various sections. Proper acknowledgment of the individual Hershey Foods Corporation author contributions is hereby acknowledged and appreciated: D. W. Lehrian, Manager, Ingredients Research (Sections II and III); G. L. Bigalli, Manager, Process Research (Sections IV and X); J. G. Rita, Manager, Sensory Research (Section V); J. A. Mihalik, Manager, Product Engineering (Sections VI, VIII, XIII, and XIV); J. R. Carpenter, Staff Scientist, Ingredients Research (Section IX); J. C. Robbins,

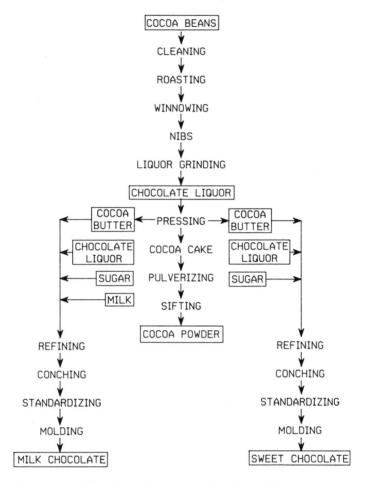

FIG. 1.   Flow diagram of chocolate and cocoa production. From *Kirk–Othmer: Encyclopedia of Chemical Technology*, Zoumas and Finnegan (1979); copyright © 1979, and reprinted by permission of John Wiley & Sons, Inc.

Group Leader, R&D Analytical Services (Sections XI and XV); L. B. Campbell, Manager, Product Development—Support Services (Section XII); C. W. Babb, Manager, Product Packaging (Section XVI); G. R. Patterson, Manager, Agricultural Research (Section XVII). Also appreciated is the contribution by T. M. Gilmore, Technical Director, Dairy and Food Industries Supply Association, Rockville, Maryland (Section VII).

II. ON FARM PROCESSING OF COCOA

A. OBJECTIVES

The purposes of on farm processing of cocoa are manifold. Processing usually consists of fermentation and drying. The fermentation is 2–8 days long depending on bean type, custom, and other factors. The fermentation process consists of a mixed external microbial fermentation that furnishes the acetic acid and heat that kill the cocoa bean and serve to activate the internal autolytic reactions in the cocoa bean. Collectively, the fermentation process removes the fruit pulp, kills the bean, thus preventing quality reduction by germination, and promotes the formation of flavor precursors by autolysis. The drying step stabilizes the product for long-term storage and improves the flavor by oxidizing and polymerizing polyphenols. Lehrian and Patterson (1983) give a detailed review of these processes, and this section will deal with research that has been done since the preparation of their review.

B. METHODS OF FERMENTATION

1. New Developments

Cocoa is fermented in various ways throughout the world depending on the scale of the operation and tradition. The principal formats include fermentation in piles on the drying floor, in heaps placed on banana leaves, in baskets, in wooden boxes, and in trays. Jacquet et al. (1981) have described and patented a method (Jacquet and Vincent, 1981) to ferment cocoa (2.5 kg) in an aqueous medium with agitation, aeration, pH adjustment, microbial inoculation, and temperature control (Fig. 2). The authors claim to produce a product with properties equal to traditionally fermented beans. The advantages claimed are an increase in the homogeneity of the product and a reduction in the time of processing. This is a radical change in processing which could encounter significant problems. Leaching of cocoa flavor precursors from the bean is perhaps the most likely and detrimental consequence. Reports on the operation of the process on an expanded scale have not been found in the literature.

2. Control of Acidity

Excessive acidity in cocoa beans is detrimental to the flavor and chocolate flavor impact of products manufactured from such beans. Studies directed toward prevention of the buildup of high levels of acids in beans have been

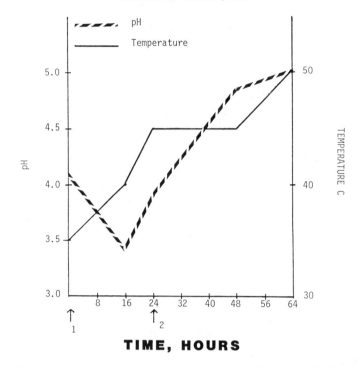

FIG. 2.   Change in temperature and pH during submerged fermentation. Arrow 1 indicates addition of 100 ml *Sacchromyces chevaliere* (1.2 × 10⁸ cells/ml). Arrow 2 indicates addition of 100 ml of *Acetobacter cylinum* (4.8 × 10⁸ cells/ml). After Jacquet and Vincent (1981).

conducted in many locations. Several of these were reviewed by Lehrian and Patterson (1983). Shepherd (1976) determined that noticeable variation in the propensity to build up acid exists in strata from the top to the bottom of a fermentation box. The upper level was most conducive to acidity buildup, the middle level was intermediate, and the bottom level was least likely to build up acidity. The increase in acidity tended to occur early in the fermentation period. By the fifth or sixth day, the net increase was small at all levels (Table I).

Schwartz *et al.* (1981) investigated factors which influence the effectiveness of a maturation or resting period after fermentation and before drying of cocoa beans. This concept was proposed by Liau (1976) and is based on the observation that acetic acid tends to be oxidized during the late stages of fermentation and early stages of drying. Liau (1976) has stated that this process is mediated by the enzyme (sic) co-enzyme A. A temperature between 40 and 50°C was recommended. Details on how these conclusions were drawn were not available.

One portion of the Schwartz *et al.* (1981) study determined the influence of turning frequency during the maturation period on dry bean pH. Turning the

TABLE I

CHANGES IN PULP AND COTYLEDON pH VALUES[a]

	Top	Middle	Bottom	Top	Middle	Bottom
Fermentary No. 1						
Day 1–2	−0.32	−0.19	+0.20	−1.13	−0.88	−0.57
Day 2–3	+0.21	+0.30	+0.43	−1.14	−0.66	−0.36
Day 3–4	−0.12	+0.08	+0.25	−0.52	−0.28	+0.05
Day 4–5	−0.09	+0.03	+0.20	−0.24	−0.08	+0.11
Day 5–6	+0.02	+0.06	+0.13	−0.11	−0.07	+0.01
Fermentary No. 2						
Day 1–2	−0.29	−0.20	+0.26	−1.41	−0.88	−0.69
Day 2–3	+0.23	+0.40	+0.43	−1.05	−0.70	−0.22
Day 3–4	−0.07	+0.03	+0.18	−0.38	−0.22	+0.15
Day 4–5	−0.08	+0.01	+0.15	−0.41	−0.19	+0.03
Day 5–6	−0.04	+0.02	+0.15	−0.13	−0.02	+0.10

[a] From Shepard (1976), with permission.

beans from box to box at 2.4-hr intervals during a 24-, 36-, or 48-hr maturation phase did not influence bean pH. Rotation of the entire fermentation box with a fork lift at similar intervals and maturation phase duration also had no influence on bean pH. A technique to spread cocoa beans in layers of less than five inches and stir them hourly for 24 hr after a 6-day fermentation was effective. Beans treated in this manner had pH values higher than typical Malaysian cocoa. The average pH obtained over 12 fermentations was 5.2 versus the usual value of 4.8. With this regime the temperature was less than 40°C. With mechanization this process could improve the quality of Malaysian cocoa beans which are generally considered to be too acidic. While the final bean pH and acidity level of the above-mentioned beans is definitely improved, it is not known what influence the lower pH condition during fermentation has on the enzymatic reactions which occur in the cotyledon giving rise to the cocoa flavor precursors. Such studies should be pursued.

C. MICROBIOLOGY OF FERMENTATION

1. Lactic Acid Bacteria

Recent research into the microbiology of cocoa fermentation has revealed a greater importance of lactic acid bacteria in this process than was once thought (Carr and Davis, 1980). This research has been extended by Passos et al. (1983) in Bahia, Brazil. They sampled typical Brazilian box fermentations on an 8-hr schedule for the 160 hr of the fermentation. Samples were collected at sites distant from the box walls and upper surface. Microorganisms were washed from the beans with sterile 0.1% peptone and sand and serially diluted. The diluted extract was plated on a medium consisting of 0.5% tryptone, 0.5% yeast extract, 0.1% glucose, 0.1% K_2HPO_4, 0.1% $CaCO_3$, 1.0% cocoa bean pulp, and 2.0% agar. Duplicate plates were incubated aerobically and anaerobically at the approximate temperature of the box sampling sites.

Bacterial isolates from these plates were characterized by the following criteria: ability to ferment various sugars, form gas from glucose, form ammonia from arginine, reduce nitrate, produce acid and form a clot on litmus milk, grow at 15 and 45°C, tolerance of 2% NaCl, and gamma hemolytic activity. This resulted in the identification of 10 species in the families Lactobacillaceae and Streptococcaceae. *Lactobacillus delbrueckii* was reported from a cocoa fermentation for the first time. Homolactic species were more common than heterolactic species (Table II).

Lactic acid bacteria were found to be more abundant than yeasts during the first 48 hr of fermentation. It is not clear if the method used has an equal chance of isolating various kinds of microorganisms. The lactic acid bacteria did follow at least a rough successional pattern with species of Lactobacillaceae more common early in the fermentation and Streptococcaceae species more common later in fermentation. The successional changes in bacterial species are probably related to changes in pH and temperature of the fermenting mass.

2. Filamentous Fungi

Filamentous fungi are common components in the microflora of commercial cocoa beans. Internal moldiness is a quality defect of cocoa and is associated with poor fat quality. Essentially nothing is known about the effect of external mold on cocoa quality. Ram (1976) reports a series of investigations on the

TABLE II

SPECIES OF LACTIC ACID BACTERIA ISOLATED[a]

Homolactic	Heterolactic
Lactobacillus casei	*Lactobacillus brevis*
L. *plantarum*	*Leuconostoc mesenteroides*
L. *delbrueckii*	
L. *lactis*	
L. *acidophilus*	
Pediococcus acidilactici	
P. *cerevisiae*	
Streptococcus lactis	

[a] Source: Carr and Davies (1980) and Passos *et al.* (1983).

TABLE III

FILAMENTOUS MOLDS OF COCOA[a]

Mold	Fermentation box, external	Barcaças, external	Warehouses External	Internal
Aspergillus flavus		X	X	X
A. niger		X	X	
A. glaucus			X	
Absidia sp.			X	
Geotricum sp.	X		X	
Botryodiplodia theobromae			X	
Penicillium sp.	X	X	X	X
Mucor		X	X	
Mortierella sp.	X	X	X	
Rhizopus sp.	X	X	X	
Syncephalastrum sp.		X	X	X
Paecilomyces sp.			X	
Fusarium sp.			X	

[a] After Ram (1976).

origin of infection in internally and externally moldy cocoa beans in Bahia, Brazil (Table III). Moldy beans were not found in fermentation boxes except when beans were not turned or when beans from *Phytophthora*- or other pathogen- and parasite-infected pods were fermented. Visible mold appeared in fermentation boxes only after the fifth day.

Molds were much more common on the sun driers (barcaças) but were not found on beans from artificially heated driers. This absolute cutoff is somewhat difficult to explain, but the much longer drying times associated with sun drying would definitely favor mold growth. Little mold was evident during the first 2 days of sun drying except when beans had been damaged prior to fermentation.

The same kinds of molds were found in farmers' and buyers' warehouses as on barcaças, indicating that mold infestation begins on the farm. Improper handling at any stage can result in moldy cocoa. Only cocoa from warehouses was checked for internal versus external mold.

D. STRUCTURAL CHANGES IN THE COCOA BEAN

The death of the cocoa bean by acetic acid poisoning and/or temperatures above 50°C results in a variety of subcellular structural changes that are important to subsequent production of flavor precursors and oxidative changes in cocoa components. Biehl *et al.* (1982a–c) and Biehl and Passern (1982), in a series of

TABLE IV

SUBCELLULAR CHANGES ASSOCIATED WITH UNIONIZED ACETIC ACID CONCENTRATION[a]

Buffer system	Unionized acetic acid	Liposome fusion time at 40°C	Relative protein swelling at 40°C	
			3 hr	15 hr
Acetic acid/NaOH, 150 mM, pH 3.0	147 mM	≤3 hr	None	None
Acetic acid/NaOH, 35 mM, pH 3.8	31 mM	15 hr	None	None
Acetic acid/NaOH, 35 mM, pH 5.5	5 mM	115 hr	Weak	Strong

[a] Source: Biehl et al. (1982a).

papers, describe structural changes in cells, water uptake, storage protein hydration, and protein hydrolysis in cocoa seeds and seed fragments in various buffers. These experiments describe the effect of a range of pHs, temperatures, osmotic environments, and other physical conditions on these processes. All of these experiments were carried out under nitrogen atmospheres. Biehl et al. (1977) have shown that long incubation times under anaerobic conditions result in some breakdown of compartmentation.

In these studies, seeds or seed pieces were killed by holding at 50°C and/or by treating with acetic acid buffers concentrated enough to contain a lethal amount of undissociated acetic acid, or seeds and seed pieces were incubated at 40°C in citrate buffers. Incubation at 40°C in citrate buffers at pH 5.5 resulted in the granulation and swelling of protein vacuoles. There is no effect on liposomes. Incubation in citrate buffer at 50°C for 15 hr resulted in death of the beans and agglomeration but not the fusion of liposomes. The protein vacuoles did not swell, and the membrane between the protein vacuoles and the ground plasm was destroyed. Effects of acetic acid buffers are strongly linked to nonionized acid contents as shown in Table IV.

Measurements of water uptake from pure water, various citric and acetic acid buffers, and citric acid buffer supplemented with 0.5, 1.0, or 1.5 M sucrose indicate that fresh mature cocoa seeds can take up as much as 27.5% water on a fresh weight basis at 30–40°C. Seeds did not take up water in 1 M sucrose. Seeds killed at 50°C in citric acid buffers took up less water than seeds incubated at 40°C. Water uptake was corrected for exudation of dissolved solids. In the heat killing experiments water uptake was slightly greater in acetic acid buffer than in citric acid buffer. This is probably explained by the greater separation of lipid and protein in the acetic acid buffers allowing more protein hydration. In both citric and acetic acid buffers at 50°C about equal amounts of tissue should be killed because the diffusivity of heat should be greater than the diffusivity of acetic acid and the cells should be heat killed.

It is not clear exactly what balance of forces drives water uptake in fresh cocoa beans, but the authors present evidence that about one-half of the water uptake is due to matrix forces. The loss of hydrophilic compartmentation also results in the loss of turgor potential which reduces the water potential near the protein vacuoles. This mechanism would result in less protein hydration. The extent of water uptake into cocoa beans over a 40-hr period at 40°C is of the same order as water uptake by germinating seeds in a comparable period. This may be the only evidence favoring the incipient germination theory which states that some flavor precursors are produced by germination-induced reactions.

E. CHEMICAL CHANGES DURING FERMENTATION

1. Introduction

Perhaps the most important result of fermentation is the autolytic process which occurs within the seed and generates the flavor precursors. Substantial changes occur in the proteins, sugars, polysaccharides, and polyphenolic compounds of the seed. In addition, metabolic by-products from the microorganisms present in the pulp surrounding the seeds traverse the testa and join the pool of flavor precursors and flavorants in the bean. The major metabolites known to traverse the testa are acetic and lactic acids and ethanol.

2. Recent Investigations

a. Polyphenolic Compounds. A method to extract and quantify (−)-epicatechin from cocoa beans was developed by Kim (1982). The method involves extraction of defatted beans, purification of the extract on a C_{18} medium, and quantification by HPLC. The level of (−)-epicatechin was determined in commercial samples of cocoa beans from a number of geographic locations. The experimental values ranged from 1.65 to 0.27% of the dry weight of defatted samples. Samples of beans which had been subjected to varying degrees of fermentation were analyzed. There was a clear decrease in the (−)-epicatechin content as fermentation proceeded.

The change in the content of other polyphenolic compounds during fermentation of one lot of Ivory Coast cocoa beans was studied by Cros *et al.* (1982a). They observed a 70% decrease in the level of total phenols over the course of an 8-day fermentation. Reductions in the content of both the tannin and nontannin fractions occurred. The reaction rate was fastest between day 2 and day 4 of fermentation. Many of the same components were present in 1-day fermented and 7-day fermented samples. Quantification of individual components was not attempted.

In a subsequent study (Cros *et al.,* 1982b), the level of red coloring material was determined in variably fermented samples of cocoa. The anthocyanin pigments decreased by 93% over the course of fermentation. The total extractable pigments were separated by adsorption chromatography on a mixture of adsorbants (Polyclar, Silica G, Silica 60; 2/1/7, w/w/w). The fractions which contained anthocyanins, red polymers, and yellow and brown polymers, respectively, were isolated. Spectrophotometric analysis (525 nm) of these fractions indicate a decrease in the anthocyanin fraction over fermentation and a concomitant increase in the yellow and brown polymer fraction. The red polymer fraction did not change dramatically over the course of the 8-day fermentation. From these studies it was possible to characterize three distinct stages of color change during fermentation. From 0 to 1 day there is little color change. From 2 to 4 days there is a decrease in anthocyanin content and an increase in yellow and brown polymer content. From 4 to 8 days there is little or no change in color. These data indicate that measurement of the pigment components of cocoa beans will not by itself be a satisfactory index of the degree of fermentation of samples of cocoa beans.

  b. Proteins. Biehl and Passern (1982) carried out a group of experiments comparing proteolysis in cocoa seeds and cocoa seed powders under a variety of incubation conditions. Acetone powders had a pH optimum between 4.5 and 5.5 and a temperature optimum of 55°C. Seed powders, in contrast to acetone powders, contain polyphenols and had a lower activity and a pH optimum of 3.5–4.0. With seed powders preincubations at a lower temperature (40°C) and the choice of buffer acid (acetic or citric) did not increase the proteolytic activity of the powder.

  Experiments using seeds or seed fragments incubated under anaerobic conditions differed from those using seed powders. More proteolytic activity was observed during the incubations if the first phase of the incubation took place at 40 rather than 50°C. This is in line with the electron microscope studies and the water uptake studies that indicate storage protein hydration is greater at 40°C and presumably more susceptible to proteolysis. This hydration effect was reduced if the incubation buffer contained large amounts of undissociated acetic acid.

  In a series of experiments using halved cotyledons incubated for 87 hr under the conditions listed in Table V, some rather strange results were obtained. These results indicate that within each buffer system proteolysis was at the same time limited by substrate availability and enzyme activity and that these limitations are additive. There is a small increase in proteolysis due to acetic acid which is consistent with its effect on subcellular structure. The acetic acid effect was doubled with a 40°C preincubation. Work by Biehl *et al.* (1982c) indicates that storage protein solubility is not appreciably different between pH 4.5 and 5.5.

  Using SDS–PAGE techniques with acetone powders of fresh, lyophilized unfermented cocoa strain ICS-1, Biehl *et al.* (1982c) were able to resolve 11 polypeptide bands in mature (160 days postpollination) seeds. The four major bands had molecular weights of 44,000, 26,000, 19,000, and 12,600. This

TABLE V

EFFECTS OF INCUBATION TEMPERATURE AND pH ON PROTEOLYSIS IN TWO BUFFER
SYSTEMS[a]

Buffer conditions	Preincubation	Relative proteolysis	Increase	Remarks
Citric acid/NaOH, 150 mM, pH 5.5	50°C	6	—	—
	40°C	8	33%	Presumed hydration effect
	50°C	15	150%	pH effect on enzyme
	40°C	17	183%	pH plus hydration
Acetic acid/NaOH, 200 mM, pH 5.5	50°C	9	—	—
	40°C	15	67%	Presumed hydration effect
	50°C	19	111%	Presumed pH effect on enzyme
	40°C	25	178%	pH plus hydration

[a] Preincubation for 15 hr followed by a 72-hr incubation at 50°C. Source: Biehl and Passern (1982) and Biehl et al. (1982b).

agrees only in part with Wright et al. (1982), who found four major polypeptide bands in fresh, mature, lyophilized seeds of CC67 with molecular weights of 43,000, 34,000, 22,000 and 14,000.

Comparison of extracts of sound mature seeds and germinating seeds revealed that the 43,000- and 34,000-molecular weight proteins are preferentially degraded during germination. This is presumptive evidence for storage protein status for these proteins. The 19,000-molecular weight protein did not appear in the germinating seed, and a similar band was found in leaves and stems of seedlings. Small fragments released by endopeptidase activity prevented following changes in the 12,600-molecular weight fraction. Degradation of storage proteins occurred during fermentation-like incubations. Proteolysis was more complete if the protein was allowed to hydrate at 40°C prior to increasing the digestion temperature to 50°C. Incubation in acetic acid buffers during the digestion period resulted in digestion of all protein bands.

The major portion of the increase in α-amino nitrogen was due to the creation of peptides rather than free amino acids. There was some leakage of the 19,000-molecular weight polypeptide. It is not clear how much can be deduced about the size of molecules free to move from cell to cell in fermenting beans, but this may be near the physical limit. From a practical point of view the process is probably so slow as to be of little importance.

Barel et al. (1983) prepared acetone powders from seed of a Trintario hybrid that had been box fermented for 0, 1, 2, 3, 4, 5, or 6 days. All samples were sun

TABLE VI

COCOA PROTEIN FRACTIONS ISOLATED FROM ION-
EXCHANGE SEPHADEX AT VARIOUS ELUENT pH VALUES:
MOLECULAR WEIGHT OF MAJOR COMPONENTS IN EACH
FRACTION[a]

Fraction	Eluent pH	Molecular weights of major constituents
A	3.10	9,000 16,000 32,000
B	3.50	Rare, not sized
D	4.50	22,000
E	5.00	22,000
F	7.00	15,000
G	13.00	Not sized

[a] After Barel *et al.* (1983).

dried for 12 days. Acetone powders were prepared, and the protein was extracted by the method of Timbie and Keeney (1977). The protein was additionally purified by gel filtration and fractionated on ion-exchange Sephadex. Five fractions were eluted at increasing pH, and, where possible, molecular weight estimates were made on a Sephacryl column. At least 15 polypeptides were evident in the ion-exchange eluent, but only six peptides could be assigned molecular weights (Table VI).

The total extractable protein increases slightly from day 0 to day 1. This might be due to a decrease in molecular size caused by endopeptidase activity. From days 1 to 5 extractable protein declines linearly. On day 6 there was a slight increase interpreted by Barel *et al.* (1983) as the salting out of protein from protein–polyphenol complexes. These slight variations may be immaterial as the coefficient of linear regression was 0.89 from 0 to 6 days.

During the first day the 32,000-molecular weight protein of fraction A was degraded, and at least part of the degradation products seem to accumulate in fraction E. Between the first and second days fraction E declines drastically while fraction F increases. After the third day little change occurs.

The gain or loss of nine amino acids from fractions A, E, and F were determined after 2 days of fermentation. The amino acids were alanine, valine, leucine, isoleucine, aspartic acid, glutamic acid, lysine, proline, and phenylalanine. All amino acids were lost from fractions A and E. Barel *et al.* (1983) considers this a liberation of amino acids, but because fraction F (see Table VI) gained these amino acids at least part of it is due to endopeptidase activity. Totalled over the three fractions, most amino acids had declined, but there was a gain for glutamic acid and no overall change for lysine. By day 6 only glutamic acid was gained in fraction F. Amino acid changes were slight after day 4 of fermentation.

Differences in sample preparation, protein extraction and fractionation procedures, genetic stocks used in the experiments, and the purpose of each experiment prevent detailed comparison of the work of various groups. Judging the work as a whole, however, no contradictions between the work of Biehl's group or Barel *et al.* (1983) seem to exist. The results described above show that now is the time for solving many of the problems of protein chemistry in cocoa fermentation and in the further processing of cocoa.

III. COCOA BEAN CHEMISTRY

A. BEAN QUALITY AND ITS ESTIMATION

1. Definition

The overall degree of excellence (quality) of commercial quantities of cocoa beans is determined by four fundamental factors: (1) purity, (2) yield, (3) uniformity, and (4) flavor and functional potential. The highest quality beans will be uniform throughout the lot, possess the desired flavor and functional potential for the intended use, have a high level of purity, and provide a yield superior for the particular grade.

2. Regulations

In the United States, the regulations concerning the acceptable quality of cocoa beans are promulgated in the *Code of Federal Regulations* (40 CFR 180, 402). Other guidelines followed by the Food and Drug Administration (FDA) in inspection of incoming cocoa beans are set forth in *Action Levels for Poisonous or Deleterious Substances in Human Food and Animal Feed* (FDA, 1980a) and *Food Defect Action Levels* published by the FDA (1980b). These regulations and guidelines define the allowable levels of moldy or insect-infested beans, the levels of pesticide residues, and specifications for the general condition of the product. These are summarized in Table VII.

Minifie (1980) summarizes the International Cocoa Standards for the assessment of cocoa bean quality. Also included in this review is the "Code of Practice" which has been internationally established and covers grade standards, inspection, sampling, testing, bagging, storage, and infestation of cocoa beans. The worldwide standard for cocoa products and chocolate is contained in Volume 7 of the *Codex Alimentarius* (Codex Alimentaris Commission, 1982). Regulations relating to cocoa butter are covered under Codex Standard 86-1981. Those relating to chocolate are contained in Codex Standard 87-1981, and those related to cocoa powders and cocoa sugar mixtures under Codex Standard 105-1981.

TABLE VII

PESTICIDE AND DEFECT ACTION LEVELS FOR COCOA BEANS

Action levels for pesticides[a]	
Benzene hexachloride (BHC)	0.5 ppm
DDT, DDE, and TDE	2.0 ppm
Lindane	0.5 ppm
Food defect action levels[b]	
More than 4% by count are moldy or insect infested including insect damages	
or	
Total of moldy cocoa beans plus insect-infested beans exceeds 6%	
or	
Animal excreta exceeds 10 mg/lb	

[a] Food and Drug Administration (1980a).
[b] Food and Drug Administration (1980b).

3. Characteristics Used as Quality Discriminators

Chocolate manufacturers measure a number of cocoa bean physical properties to judge the overall quality of an incoming lot. A number of these are summarized in Table VIII. These measurements are primarily used to assess the economic value of beans offered for sale. A description of the specific requirements associated with many of these parameters may be found in Minifie (1980).

The flavor of chocolate is a reaction flavor as will be described in more detail below. As such, it is reasonably well known that peptides and amino acids, sugars, and perhaps polyphenols are important precursors of chocolate flavors, which on roasting produce the characteristic chocolate flavor. Certain other organic compounds generated during the fermentation process probably contribute to the precursor pool or act as direct flavorants. The estimation of the levels of various flavor precursors has been reported by several authors (see Lehrian and Patterson, 1983, for details). Table IX shows several of the "chemical indicators" of cocoa bean quality and flavor potential which have been proposed (Lehrian et al., 1978; Rohan, 1969a–d; Rostagno, 1979). Few, if any, of these have achieved widespread application. However, research continues to clarify the utility of these measurements.

At present the best method to judge flavor and functional potential is to roast the beans, grind them into liquor, and taste this or a dark chocolate made from it. Flavor profiling is considered to be the best sensory evaluation procedure for this purpose. In this procedure, intricate flavors are described in terms of a set of simple, well-known flavors known as descriptors. In an effort to minimize the ambiguity which sometimes exists among tasters or between panels over the

TABLE VIII

PHYSICAL AND SENSORY PARAMETERS WHICH INFLUENCE THE
QUALITY OF COCOA BEANS AS JUDGED BY CHOCOLATE
MANUFACTURERS[a]

Average weight of a bean and uniformity of bean weight
Shell content and relative adherence
Fat content of beans
Foreign matter content
Presence of foreign flavors or odors
Mold contamination of beans
Color and structure of cotyledons (cut test)
Presence of insect-damaged, germinated, flat, shriveled or immature beans
Moisture content of bean
Taste of liquor for acceptable chocolate flavor

[a] After Minifie (1980), Powell (1981), and Vincent (1983).

interpretation of the descriptors used, Lopez and McDonald (1981) have published a list of common descriptors. In the explanation of the descriptors, they have attempted to give a likely chemical or physical reason for the generation of the flavor being described. Further efforts such as this one are needed in the field of cocoa flavor evaluation. Table X presents a list of flavor descriptors used to denote positive and negative contributors to chocolate flavor.

Lopez and McDonald have also described the limitations associated with the cut test with respect to prediction of chocolate flavor potential. They correctly point out that the test is an indication of degree of fermentation and affords only a vague indication of the intrinsic flavor potential of the beans.

TABLE IX

CHEMICAL MEASUREMENTS WHICH HAVE BEEN PROPOSED TO JUDGE OR
INDICATE COCOA BEAN QUALITY OR FLAVOR AND FUNCTIONAL POTENTIAL[a]

Melting characteristics of the cocoa butter
pH and/or titratable acidity
Reducing sugar, non-reducing sugar content, and ratio of same
Content of polyphenolic components and ratio of catechins to noncatechin tannins
Aroma index [UV absorbance (278 nm) of steam distillate of nibs]
Pigments content
Soluble nitrogen content, total nitrogen content, and ratio of soluble to total nitrogen
Amino acid analysis
Ammonia content
Ash content
Determination of smoke contamination

[a] After Lehrian et al. (1978), Rohan (1969a–d), and Rostagno (1979).

TABLE X

SOME DESCRIPTIONS USED IN THE CHARACTERIZATION OF CHOCOLATE FLAVOR QUALITY[a]

Components of basic chocolate flavor	Auxiliary flavors which complement chocolate when at low levels	Off flavors detrimental to chocolate flavor if at high levels
Cacao	Honey	Astringency
Acrid	Malt	Bitterness
Astringency	Fudge	Sourness
Bitterness	Toffee	Raisin
Fermented	Caramel	Fruity
Nutty	Nutty	Burnt
	Acid	Beany
	Raisin/juicy	Tobacco
	Fruity	Herbal
	Floral	Spicy
	Sweet	Phenolic
		Bready
		Earthy
		Moldy
		Alkaline
		Fishy
		Medicinal
		Oily
		Ham/smoke
		Putrefaction

[a] After Lopez and McDonald (1981).

Work by other researchers has shown a lack of reproducibility in the evaluation of color in the performance of the cut test (d'Ornano et al., 1968). A collaborative study involving seven laboratories studied the correlation between the cut test and pigment optical density. Each lab performed the cut test on a subsample of a lot of beans. They submitted their individual portions of slaty (unfermented), purple (under-fermented), semi-purple, and brown beans (properly fermented) separated from the sample to the coordinating lab. Subsequently the portions were tested by the Office International du Cacao et du Chocolat (OICC) method for colored pigments. In the cut test, the numbers of beans assigned to each class varied distinctly between laboratories. There were clearly differences in the definition of the four coloration categories among laboratories. This was further emphasized by the colorimetric analysis of the separated bean portions. These data indicate the need for an alternate test to determine the degree of fermentation of a sample of cocoa beans.

A Russian patent for such a test was issued to Gur'eva and Tserevitinova (1979). The test methodology includes grinding nibs to pass through a sieve with mesh size of 0.25 mm (No. 60). A weighed sample of 0.5 g is mixed with 50 ml of a 97 : 3 mixture of methanol and hydrochloric acid. This mixture is left at 5–10°C for 24 hr. The extract is recovered by vacuum filtration and analyzed spectrophotometrically at 460 and 530 nm. The ratio of the absorbances at these two wavelengths is calculated (A_{460}/A_{530}). A ratio greater than 1 is reported to indicate complete fermentation.

A study by Cros *et al.* (1982b) investigated the change in anthocyanins, red polymers, and yellow/brown polymers extracted from cocoa beans, over the course of two 8-day fermentations. The chemical composition of these fractions was not described. They also performed the above-described method to judge the degree of fermentation. They found that the anthocyanin, red polymer, and yellow/brown polymer fractions changed quantitatively during the first 3 days of fermentation and subsequently changed very little. Similar trends were measured by the absorbances at 460 and 530 nm. The ratio of A_{460}/A_{525} changed very little prior to day 3 after which it increased steadily. There is a lack of complete understanding of the changes in the polyphenol fraction during fermentation. Therefore, it is not possible to explain the small changes in the concentration of components which absorb at 460 and 525 nm resulting in the change in the ratio. There have not been studies reported which correlate the degree of fermentation measurement to organoleptic analysis; therefore, it is not yet possible to use the ratio of absorbance values as a cocoa bean quality measure.

Cocoa butter is an important and expensive raw material used in the manufacture of chocolate. The content and physical properties of this fat in chocolate directly influence its snap, gloss, mold release, and hardening time. Total fat in cocoa beans is routinely determined by Soxhlet extraction according to the OICC procedure Ba3-38/1954 (Glattli, 1962). Alternative procedures include refractive index, wide band NMR, and reflectance infrared spectroscopy. The U.S. standards of identity require certain levels of chocolate in certain products. Additional cocoa butter is used to adjust the viscosity of finished chocolate to meet the manufacturing requirements of its intended use. Minimizing the amount of added cocoa butter obviously reduces the costs of manufacturing. A number of manufacturing steps influence the requirement for added cocoa butter, and these will be discussed elsewhere. As stated above, the physical properties of cocoa butter, as dictated by its composition, influence its performance in chocolate.

Shukla *et al.* (1983) have described a method to analyze the triglyceride composition of cocoa butters using HPLC and UV detection at 220 nm. The method is simple and direct. The results show satisfactory accuracy and precision. A comparison of two methods to determine the triglyceride composition of five samples of cocoa butter showed good agreement. The composition determined by the HPLC method was very similar to that determined by an argentation TLC–GC method. These data were in good agreement with published data. The HPLC method is reported to separate 13 triglycerides in 90 min. Values

TABLE XI

COMPARISON OF PHYSICAL PROPERTIES AND TRIGLYCERIDE COMPOSITION OF COCOA BUTTERS FROM SEVERAL GEOGRAPHIC LOCATIONS[a]

Iodine value	Melting point (°C)	Solid fat index (dilatometry)					Monounsaturated triglycerides (%)	Diunsaturated triglycerides (%)
			20°C	25°C	30°C	35°C		
Brazilian (39.8)	Brazilian (34.5)	Malaysian	89.6	86.3	65.2	2.8	Malaysian (84.8)	Brazilian (15.5)
Sample A (37.4)	Nigerian (33.7)	Nigerian	85.9	81.7	56.6	0.8	Nigerian (83.0)	Sample A (11.2)
Nigerian (36.1)	Sample A (33.3)	Sample B	83.2	77.8	49.4	0.7	Sample B (82.2)	Sample B (8.2)
Sample B (36.0)	Sample B (32.8)	Sample A	79.5	76.4	49.9	0.7	Sample A (75.1)	Nigerian (6.2)
Malaysian (34.3)	Malaysian (32.5)	Brazilian	72.6	67.0	40.4	0.4	Brazilian (71.5)	Malaysian (4.8)

[a] After Shukla et al. (1983).

obtained for solid fat index (SFI), iodine value, melting point, and triglyceride composition for five samples of cocoa butter are shown in Table XI. Comparison of triglyceride composition and SFI shows good rank correlation between SFI and content of monounsaturated triglycerides (POP + POS + SOS, where P is palmitate, O oleate, and S stearate) and inverse rank correlation between SFI and content of diunsaturated triglycerides (POO + SOO). The value reported for the melting point of the Brazilian sample does not correlate with the SFI, iodine value, and triglyceride composition reported for the Bahia sample. Based on these data, a lower melting point would be predicted. Nevertheless, this rapid quantitative analysis of triglycerides holds promise as a qualitative descriptor of cocoa butters.

B. CHOCOLATE FLAVOR PRECURSORS

1. Amino Acids

Rohan (1963) reported the isolation of a methanol-soluble fraction from fermented cocoa beans which on roasting produced chocolate flavor. This fraction was shown to contain flavonoids, sugars, and amino acids. A qualitative separation of the amino acids in this fraction showed the presence of 22 amino acids. The conclusion was drawn that one specific amino acid was unlikely to be responsible for production of chocolate aroma. Rohan and Stewart (1967a) reported that the production of free amino acids during fermentation was rapid, reaching maximal amino acid concentration in the bean after about 4 days. Maravalhas (1972) confirmed the increase in free amino acid content of cocoa beans during fermentation. Table XII shows the absolute and relative content of individual free amino acids in Bahia beans before and after fermentation. These data show a relative increase in the level of arginine, leucine, lysine, phenylalanine, threonine, and valine during fermentation.

Rohan and Stewart (1969) showed that alanine, leucine, and valine produced chocolate flavor when heated with glucose and ($-$)-epicatichin. During roasting, the content of free amino acids was reduced to about 50% of the initial level. This was accompanied by a 90% reduction in the level of reducing sugars. During roasting, the rate and extent of degradation of eight groups of amino acids were determined by Rohan and Stewart (1969); however, specific conclusions relative to the importance of individual amino acids to chocolate flavor cannot be drawn from these data.

2. Reducing Sugars

Rohan and Stewart suggested in a number of papers that reducing sugars are important precursors of chocolate flavor. This theory was based on the observa-

TABLE XII

FREE AMINO ACID CONTENT AND COMPOSITION OF UNFERMENTED AND FERMENTED

BAHIA BEANS[a]

Amino acid	Unfermented		Fermented	
	mg/g	% of total	mg/g	% of total
Lysine	0.27	4.07	2.04	9.27
Histidine	0.34	5.12	0.26	1.18
Arginine	0.24	3.61	1.34	6.09
Aspartic acid	1.89	28.46	3.25	14.77
Threonine	0.09	1.36	0.74	3.36
Serine	0.35	5.27	1.01	4.59
Glutamic acid	1.22	18.37	1.90	8.63
Proline	0.45	6.78	0.92	4.18
Glycine	0.32	4.82	0.74	3.36
Alanine	0.42	6.33	1.54	7.00
Valine	0.08	1.20	0.83	3.77
Methionine	0.12	1.81	0.26	1.18
Isoleucine	0.18	2.71	0.67	3.04
Leucine	0.18	2.71	3.07	13.95
Tyrosine	0.25	3.77	1.16	5.27
Phenylalanine	0.24	3.61	2.28	10.36

[a] After Maravalhas (1972).

tion that reducing sugars were present in fermented cocoa beans which produced chocolate flavor when roasted but absent in unfermented cocoa beans which did not produce chocolate flavor when roasted (Rohan, 1963). Subsequent studies showed that fermented beans contained mainly glucose and fructose while unfermented beans contained mainly sucrose. The time course of sucrose inversion was determined in trial fermentations and was found to be complete in 4 days, well within the time cocoa is normally fermented. The increase in reducing sugars during fermentation was confirmed by Reineccius et al. (1972a) and Berbert (1979).

Reineccius et al. (1972a) quantified the various sugars in cocoa beans from several geographical locations. Their data show the same sugars are present but at different relative proportions in the samples tested. Of particular interest are the differences observed in the content of glucose and fructose among the samples. The ratio of fructose to glucose varied from 16 : 1 in Bahia beans to 1 : 1 in Sanchez beans. This is significant in light of the fact that ketoses have been reported to be three times more reactive than aldoses in forming volatiles (Kato et al., 1969). In further studies, Reineccius et al. (1972b) found that two to three times the quantity of alkylpyrazines were formed in Ghana beans in which fructose was the predominant sugar than formed in Sanchez beans in which sucrose was the predominant sugar. It is currently accepted that reducing sugars and amino acids in cocoa beans react via the Maillard reaction and Strecker degradation to form many of the components found in chocolate flavor.

3. Polyphenols

The third component found by Rohan (1963) in the chocolate aroma-producing methanolic extract of cocoa beans was a mixture of polyphenolic compounds. Forsyth (1955) showed the presence of four catechins and three leucocyanidins in cocoa beans. Rohan and Connell (1964) found these components and two flavanols (quercetin and quercetrin) and three phenolic acids (*p*-coumaric, caffeic, and chlorogenic) in the chocolate aroma precursor fraction.

Stewart (1970) reported on experiments in which the polyphenolics of cocoa beans were added to or excluded from several model systems which produced chocolate flavor on roasting. The conclusion drawn from these experiments was that the polyphenolic compounds enhanced the chocolate aroma production. The composition of the fraction added could not be characterized. Pure (−)-epicatechin was added to a model system containing a mixture of amino acids and glucose. On roasting, chocolate aroma was produced. The author did comment that the aroma was only chocolate-like and did not resemble a completely rounded chocolate aroma. No information on the flavor potential of the other polyphenolic components was provided.

4. Flavorants

In addition to the precursors of chocolate flavor present in fermented cocoa beans, there are a number of organic compounds which contribute to chocolate flavor as direct flavorants. Acetic acid and, to a lesser extent, a range of volatile and nonvolatile organic acids contribute to the final chocolate flavor. The levels of these acids and their changes during fermentation have been reported by several authors (Weissberger *et al.,* 1971; Lopez and Quesnel, 1973; Lopez, 1983). At low levels, acetic acid contributes to chocolate flavor; however, at high levels, it tends to mask the flavor. The effect of other organic compounds formed as microbial by-products during the fermentation process are poorly known but suspected to be significant. The most notable examples are those related to flavor defects in improperly fermented or dried cocoa. One example is the mold-induced flavor in very slowly dried cocoa. Much additional research is required to determine the full contribution of microbial by-products to the flavor of chocolate.

C. CHOCOLATE FLAVOR

1. Compounds Identified in Chocolate Flavor

The elucidation of the compounds which contribute to the prized flavor and aroma of chocolate has been built on the efforts of many individual contributors. The first published attempt to isolate and identify the components of chocolate aroma was that of Bainbridge and Davies (1912). Studying Arriba cocoa, they isolated an oil which contained 50% linalool as well as esters and fatty acids. Schmalfuss and Bartmeyer (1932), Steinman (1935), Mohr (1958), van Elzakker and van Zutphen (1961), and Dietrich et al. (1964) used classical analytical techniques to make notable contribution to this field of research.

Weurman and DeRooij (1961) identified volatile amines in the flavor of cocoa. A total of 16 compounds was identified by Bailey et al. (1962) in the headspace volatiles of ground cocoa beans. Quantitative differences among varieties were noted. These authors were the first to suggest and provide evidence that Strecker degradation was an important result of roasting, producing isobutyraldehyde and isovaleraldehyde.

Rohan and Stewart (1964) determined the levels of volatile and nonvolatile acids in cocoa beans from several geographic locations. These and other microbial by-products which enter the bean during the fermentation process act as bean flavorants. The importance of the other flavorants has not been well studied.

The "honeylike" or balsamic odor which is considered an important element in chocolate flavor was studied by Quesnel (1965). An extract of aromatic acids was obtained and separated. Eleven aromatic acids were identified in fermented cocoa, six of which were produced during fermentation. Phenylacetic and vanillic acids were the principal odoriferous compounds identified; however, a mixture of these does not typify the aroma of the extract. The author suggested that carbonyl compounds and other aromatic acids contribute to the odor of the extract.

The levels of monocarbonyls in fermented cocoa beans were determined by Boyd et al. (1965). They found approximately equal levels of methyl ketones and saturated aldehydes and 10-fold lower levels of 2-enals and 2,4-dienals. On roasting, the levels of methyl ketones decreased slightly, aldehydes tripled, and 2-enals and 2,4-dienals doubled. Variations in the levels of each component were observed among samples from various geographic regions. Other compounds found to increase during roasting were acetaldehyde, methanol, diacetyl, propionaldehyde, isobutyraldehyde, and isovaleraldehyde. The last two compounds were greatly increased during roasting (Pinto and Chichester, 1966). Analysis of the change in amino acids and sugars during roasting showed linear decreases with increasing duration of roast. Ammonia liberated during roasting can react with reducing sugars or other compounds to produce compounds important to the flavor of chocolate.

A number of intensive efforts were mounted in the late 1960s which resulted in a rapid expansion in the number of compounds identified in cocoa flavor. Marion *et al.* (1967) identified 57 compounds in the steam distillate of cocoa nibs. Flament *et al.* (1967) identified 62 compounds in fractions isolated by codistillation of cocoa nibs with propylene glycol. Muggler-Chavin and Reymond (1967) identified 56 compounds in the aroma fraction of cocoa beans from different regions using a headspace gas flushing technique. A codistillate of ethanol and cocoa powder was separated by Van der Wal *et al.* (1968, 1971), and 181 compounds were identified. An attempt to quantitatively combine the compounds identified produced a mixture only reminiscent of cocoa.

Fifty-six compounds in the steam-volatile fraction of roasted cocoa beans were identified by van Praag *et al.* (1968). Aldehydes, pyrazines, acetic acid, and isopentylacetate were found to contribute to cocoa aroma. Two chromatographic peaks were associated with a distinct cocoalike aroma. One was a mixture of isovaleraldehyde and methyl disulfide, and the other was identified as 5-methyl-2-phenyl-2-hexenal. This compound is reported to have a deep bitter persistent cocoa note and is the only compound thus far identified which alone approximates chocolate flavor. It was suggested that this compound is formed by a "dehydrated aldol condensation" product between phenylacetaldehyde, from phenylalanine, and isovaleraldehyde, from leucine. These two amino acids are the most abundant free amino acids in cocoa beans.

Lopez and Quesnel (1971) investigated the contribution of 67 compounds to the flavor and aroma of chocolate. They confirmed the importance of aldehydes, in particular isovaleraldehyde, isobutyraldehyde, and 5-methyl-2-phenyl-2-hexenal. They did not obtain chocolate flavor from heated mixtures of amino acids and sugars with or without $(-)$-epicatechin. Dimethyl disulfide, guaiacol, and acetophenone were also observed to be important to chocolate flavor as were maltol, pyrrole, the pyrazines, and pyruvic acid. A mixture of compounds in a synthesized pyrazine base solution produced acceptable chocolate flavor. The contribution of microbial metabolic by-products to the total chocolate flavor was stressed.

In a subsequent study, Lopez and Quesnel (1973) examined the production of C_3–C_5 volatile fatty acids during fermentations in wet and dry seasons. Increased production of these fatty acids was observed during the dry season and resulted in inferior chocolate flavors described as "weak," "dull," "raw," "woody," "flat," and having an "unpleasant sweetness."

Eleven sulfur compounds were found to give chocolate-like odors in mixtures with aldehydes at various proportions. None of these was reported to possess a complete chocolate odor (Lopez and Quesnel, 1974). Methyl-*S*-methionine was shown to be present in fermented and dried cocoa. This compound is extremely labile and decomposes to dimethyl sulfide which contributes to chocolate aroma (Lopez and Quesnel, 1976).

Landschreiber and Mohr (1974) reviewed the literature on cocoa aroma and listed 310 compounds thus far identified. The importance of pyrazines is stressed as are the effects of individual components, chocolate-like flavors, and flavor reinforcers. Specific components responsible for the characteristic cocoa aroma have not been identified, and sensory evaluation remains the method of choice for practical purposes.

Vitzthum et al. (1975) extracted the lipophilic fractions from cocoa liquor using supercritical CO_2, followed by steam distillation. The basic fraction of the resulting extract was shown to contain 57 pyrazines (34 newly identified), 4 oxazoles, 9 cycloalkapyrazines, 7 pyridines, 3 quinoxalines, and quinoline. Van Straten (1977) reviewed the volatile compounds identified in foods and compiled a list of 387 compounds which have been identified in cocoa.

Danehy (1983) has reviewed the chemistry of Maillard reaction and its contribution to food flavor and color. A large number of "standard" patents have been issued which are based on the Maillard reaction. In these, amino acids and carbonyl compounds are reacted to yield various flavors. In his opinion, these patents do not offer satisfactory descriptions of the reaction conditions to be of value to the patent holder or those who study the patents. Danehy points out that, while the precursors required for the Maillard reaction are present in fermented cocoa beans and the expected reaction products are present in the aroma and flavor fractions of cocoa liquor, it is still not known how they combine in intensity and specificity to produce chocolate flavor. Much additional work will be required to determine the specific precursor blend which leads to chocolate flavor.

2. Artificial Chocolate Flavors and Cocoa Extenders

In addition to the "standard" patents which employ the Maillard reaction referred to above, a number of patents have been issued for the use of specific compounds in chocolate flavorings. The compounds specified and patent references are compiled in Table XIII. The use of natural and artificial chocolate flavors varies in relation to the price of cocoa beans. The same is true for the impetus to introduce cocoa extenders. A number of bulking agents such as soybean flour, modified food starch, or dextrins with added flavor and color are offered as partial replacers for cocoa. Other cocoa substitutes which utilize Maillard technology in their production are available. These include carob, a toasted wheat germ product (Viobin Cocoa Replacer, Viobin, Corp., Monticello, IL), and a processed brewers yeast (Cocomost, Coors Food Products Co., Golden, CO). None of these have achieved a true cocoa flavor or aroma. The potential

TABLE XIII

COMPOUNDS CLAIMED IN PATENTS TO IMPART OR ENHANCE CHOCOLATE
FLAVOR IN FLAVORING MIXTURES

Compound	Reference
Tetramethylpyrazine	Moroe *et al.* (1969)
Alkyltrisulfides	Nakel and Hiler (1971)
2-Ethyl-3,5,6-trimethylpyrazine	Marion (1972)
2-Methyl-5,7-dehydrothieno[3,4-*d*]pyrimidine	Katz *et al.* (1973)
2,4-Diphenylcrotonaldehyde	Givaudan and Cie (1973)
2-[(Methylthio)methyl]-3-phenyl-2-propenal	Withycombe *et al.* (1979)
2,4,6-Triisobutyl-1.3.5-trioxane	Withycombe *et al.* (1980)
Ethyl methyl-2-isobutyl-3-oxazolines	Withycombe *et al.* (1980)

exists for the development of a true cocoa replacer based on an alternative plant source; however, much additional research will be required before this can be realized.

IV. CACAO BEAN PROCESSING (PRODUCTION OF CACAO LIQUOR)

A. INTRODUCTION AND PRINCIPLES OF ROASTING

Chocolate flavor does not exist naturally in the bean, rather it is a "reaction flavor" produced by a series of procedures that begins with the postharvest treatment of the bean and continuing through later processing in chocolate manufacture. The quality of the product is influenced by each one of the steps in the process: thus each deviation in an earlier stage would have some influence on the product at later stages.

In the past, most of the new developments in chocolate processing were contributions from chocolate equipment manufacturers. Despite a lack of fundamental scientific information, an excellent quality chocolate was obtained on the equipment available. Most research work has concentrated on the understanding of existing processing procedures rather than development of new ones. In recent years, a substantial effort has been made to achieve progress combining scientific information with equipment manufacturing experience.

The first material in the production line that contains the basic components of chocolate flavor is chocolate liquor, also called cacao liquor and cocoa mass. It is traditionally prepared by finely grinding pieces of the cotyledons of cacao beans (called nibs) which have been roasted and separated from the shell and germ. The

FIG. 3.   Production of cacao liquor by the roasting of whole cacao beans (traditional).

most common way to produce cacao liquor is shown in Fig. 3. Good descriptions of the process steps are found in articles by Minifie (1980), Kleinert (1972), and Boller (1983).

In order to obtain a good liquor, cacao beans must be cleaned from all foreign material. In practice, the operation is done in two separate steps: cleaning and destoning; it is not advisable to combine these two steps in a single machine. The operation consists of a series of screens, brushes, air separators, and magnetic separators. Poor operating practices at this stage could lead to poor flavor, unsanitary product, rheological problems, grittiness, and excessive wear of the processing equipment. Although the basic principles for cleaning are the same, there has been substantial improvement in the quality and efficiency of the operation, due mostly to better systems for the control of air processing operations.

The most important step in the development of chocolate flavor is in the roasting step since basic reactions of chocolate aroma occur in this process. The study of the formation of this flavor has been the object of research for many years. Rohan and Stewart (1966a,b) studied the changes of amino acids and sugars during roasting. Their work showed that most sugars and some of the amino acids are transformed and consumed during roasting. Their work was complemented with a study of chocolate aroma precursors produced during fermentation (1967a,b) followed by an overall review of roasting reactions by Rohan (1969a–e).

There are several methods to roast cocoa beans. The original and still the most common method starts by roasting previously cleaned beans. Kleinert (1966) reviewed some aspects of cocoa bean roasting and indicated that the roasting process can be divided into four phases. The initial phase consists of an evaporation of the superficial water. There are limits to the air temperature which can be used in this phase. There are also correlations between the relative humidity of the drying air, the air velocity, and the drying speed. The second phase occurs after the surface is no longer saturated with water and the moisture transported from the capillaries of the cacao bean to the surface is no longer sufficient to replace the moisture evaporating from the surface. The speed of drying, therefore, decreases. During the next phase, the drying progresses toward the inside of the product, the resistance to diffusion increases, and the speed of drying again decreases. In the fourth and last phase, the speed of drying decreases further while the hygroscopicity of the product increases. As a result, the air must be low in relative humidity to continue drying at this stage.

If the temperature of the roaster is too high, the outside of the bean will immediately be hardened during the early stages, making it more difficult for water to be transported through the capillaries to the surface. The consequences of this "case hardening" are uneven roasting, scorching of the outside of the bean, and low efficiency on the usage of flavor precursors available from the center of the bean. Following the previous line of thinking, a gradual increase in roasting temperature would provide for a most even reaction and most efficient utilization of the flavor precursors. The initiation of the roasting should be at a moderate temperature for the elimination of the excess of water and the equalization of the moisture in the beans; then the roasting could continue in air temperatures between 110 and 175°C.

Even if the above generalities are accepted by many, each manufacturer has his own criteria for roasting conditions, may even purposely favor "case hardening," and go to an even further spread of air temperatures ranging from 99 to more than 200°C. Beans used for production of cocoa powder are usually roasted at a higher temperature than those to be used for chocolate; however, for some "red" cocoas, lower temperatures are used.

Despite the wide use of chocolate, there is an insufficient understanding of the development of the flavor during roasting. Most manufacturers rely almost exclusively on experience. Danehy (1983) summarized the complexity of the reactions, giving reasons for the lack of information and the reliance on established techniques.

B. BATCH AND CONTINUOUS ROASTERS

The original cocoa bean roasters were batch roasters and, due to the larger number of parameters that affect the reaction, each roaster operator made special judgments on how much time and particular temperatures were needed. Controversy regarding the use of batch roasters over continuous roasters has been discussed by Kleinert (1966). He showed that, for all practical purposes, both types of roasters could give comparable results, although the operational parameters are not the same and the economics favors the continuous roasters. Despite the trend toward continuous roasters, there are some manufacturers that still prefer batch roasters because they are considered more versatile.

Batch roasters are drums in which beans are heated by direct fire, by conduction of heat through the walls of the cylinder, or by passage of hot air through the beans (which reduces the possibilities of burning). Batch roasters gained the confidence of the industry a long time ago due to their reliability.

The difficulty with continuous roasting is in part due to nonuniformity of the beans and an insufficient understanding of the interrelation of different bean parameters that influence cacao flavor reactions. Older models were often heated by direct fire; however, this practice is being replaced by modern systems in which air is heated in a separate environment and then drawn into the roaster. This tendency is common to all types of continuous roasters. One of the oldest continuous roasters is an elongated drum where beans are continuously charged, tumble inside of the drum and slowly travel to the exit. Drum roasters can, however, be heated by either direct fire or by hot air heated externally.

C. ROASTER CONFIGURATIONS

Fluid bed roasters are a product of the early 1960s. The air supply is heated in an upper box called a "Plenum" and is blasted by special tubes or jets over a flat shaker-bed where the beans are moving horizontally. The principle of heating is high air velocity, short time, and high temperature. The objective of using this system is the principle of fast heat penetration by maximizing the air volume. This principle is opposite to the ideas expressed by Kleinert (1966) which are generally accepted in the industry.

There is a more recent version of a roaster that combines the principles of the continuous drum with the fluid bed (jet roaster). The drum is divided into several compartments in which separate control of humidity and temperature is possible. The roaster is divided into six zones where parameters can be controlled to specific conditions. Roasting occurs by conventional heat transmission and by air "jet" action into the mass of the beans. It has the capability of adding steam in the second and third zones which promotes sterilization and uniform distribution of heat. This roaster is more versatile than batch or continuous ones.

The majority of modern roasters have a vertical configuration with several types of designs. One of the most common is the cascade type in which beans fall through a series of compartments. There are also straight vertical roasters where the beans stand in a column. Beans are pre-warmed, roasted, and cooled entirely by convection in a tangential direction to the fall of the beans; the speed of the flow is controlled by a regulating mechanism at the bottom of the machine. There are also vertical roasters in which the "fall" of the bean is controlled by a series of roasting shelves having special perforated slots which open automatically after a predetermined period. The product falls to the shelf below and in so doing is turned and mixed simultaneously.

In general, most recent models of roasters take into consideration the principles of different roasting zones for better functionality of the process. Although the mechanisms change among manufacturers, the basic principles are the same.

As indicated previously, the driving force in the process of roasting beans is the elimination of water, and each profile temperature gives different flavor results. Since the moisture content of beans changes from lot to lot and also within the lot, it is understandable why some manufacturers, working with small batches of beans, remain skeptical about continuous roasting. Also some manufacturers use different quality beans for different purposes, and thus feel more comfortable with the batch system. However, both types of roasters can give a good product if all conditions are adjusted properly.

D.   WINNOWING AND GRINDING

The most valuable part of the cacao bean is the nib which has to be separated from the shell and germ to obtain a good quality cacao liquor. The nib is obtained from roasted cacao beans in winnowing machines. The principle of these machines is to break the cacao beans, separate the nibs by screening into specific sizes, and use the difference in density of nib and shell for a second separation by air elutriation. It is very important to use the proper calibration of the machines to balance on one side the quality of the product and on the other the loss of good nibs in the shell. Most of the work in this field is done by the equipment manufacturers, and a general review is presented by Minifie (1980).

Nib grinding reduces the cacao nib to liquor; although it is a part of the process that seems very simple, however, it deserves considerable attention. The manner in which the different components of the chocolate mass are ground substantially influences the finished chocolate. Kleinert (1970) explained the interrelation of the physical properties of the chocolate and particle size. Niediek (1973) reviewed the basic information for the systematic steps for grinding cocoa nibs and also explained the influence of grinding on the behavior of liquor. Boller (1978, 1980) again emphasized these fundamental principles and their relation to practical work in the manufacture of chocolate and in regard to equipment requirements.

One of the most desirable features of a good grinding procedure is the ability to produce a well-defined maximum particle size and a narrow particle distribution range. The well-defined maximum size is to avoid grittiness and to liberate all the fat in the cells. The narrow distribution avoids problems during pressing (for cocoa powder production) or rheological problems in the chocolate mass. The desirable particle size of liquor is 5 μm less than the desirable particle size of the chocolate paste and 1–5 μm less than the final particle size of the cocoa powder. The best way to obtain these results is to grind the nibs in several successive increments rather than attempting the whole size reduction in one processing step.

Classically cacao liquor was produced by using stone mills. They were made of two horizontal disks and were in sets of three progressive size reduction steps. They were very good for fineness quality although low in output. Better outputs are obtained with modern grinder types. These consist of a pregrinder or coarse grinder, followed by one or two refiners or liquor grinders. The pregrinder can be a disk mill, a hammer mill, a pin mill, or an extruder mill. They produce a coarse paste that is then refined by some type of roll mill in which the maximum gap is adjustable. Another type of liquor refiner is based on the principle of high speed vertical ball milling.

The choice of the pregrinder should be based on the economics and output of the machine. The quality features are related to the capability of producing liquor with a minimum temperature increase; otherwise flavor changes introduced in the cocoa mass are additive to those produced earlier in the roaster. Another property to consider in the choice of pregrinder is the fluidity of the mass, which is also determined by the moisture in the nibs and the previous type of roast. The fluidity determines the efficiency of any successive liquor grinding operation. To avoid problems with fluidity, some manufacturers use two pregrinders in series or one pregrinder followed by an agitator to reduce the viscosity of the mass.

Well-refined cacao liquor facilitates the formulation of chocolate for optimum functionality of the mass. The cacao solids contain most of the flavor, and its flavoring power is maximized when it is finally divided.

The grittiness of chocolate is produced by particles above a certain size range. Most manufacturers consider a maximum of 35 μm ideal. Grittiness due to the cacao particle is perceived more easily than that due to sugar at the same particle size, because sugar is soluble in the mouth and is immediately rounded and reduced in size by solubilization. It is generally acceptable to have sugar particles up to 5 μm larger than the cacao liquor particles.

It is good manufacturing practice and good economical procedure to refine the liquor to a particle size smaller than the final product, because the liquor is less than one-fifth of the total mass (for milk chocolate). If all components of sweet or milk chocolate are ground finer, just to reduce the liquor particle size, there is an unnecessary consumption of energy. However, there is little effect on the final eating chocolate viscosity by fine grinding of the liquor, since the sugar particle size has the major influence on chocolate viscosity.

In summary, modern grinding technology, although more efficient and fast, must be done with specific understanding of the functionality of the final product that is produced.

E.   ALTERNATE METHODS OF LIQUOR PREPARATION

1.   Nib Roasting

Although the traditional way to make liquor starts with roasting clean beans, there are two other ways to accomplish this work: roasting shell-free cacao nibs and roasting raw ground cacao mass. The procedure to produce cacao liquor through roasting cacao nibs has the steps shown in Fig. 4. As with any other procedure, this modality has some advantages and some disadvantages. The

FIG. 4.   Production of cacao liquor by the roasting of raw cacao nibs.

decision depends on the product to be made, the size of the operation and the type of existing equipment and procedures.

The major difficulty in working with raw beans is efficiently separating the shell. In order to overcome this problem, a preparation step is introduced to loosen the shell. There are at least three types of preparation: conventional superficial drying, steam or moisture addition followed by conventional drying, or infrared treatment. In all cases, the purpose is to loosen the shell and decrease bacteria count and major contaminants originating from the shell. There are specific pieces of equipment for each one of the above choices.

The specially treated raw beans are then winnowed. Modern winnowing machines designed specifically for raw cacao beans have two "breaking" steps. The initial action achieved between two sliding rotating surfaces is followed by the conventional cracking effect and air classification. A disadvantage of this procedure is the possibility of higher bacteria count and dust originating from the shell. This potential problem is decreased substantially during pretreatment.

Among the advantages of roasting nibs is an increase of output for the same amount of energy input because the weight of the shell, which is about one-fifth of the total cocoa bean weight, does not have to be heated and does not consume energy. The phase of moisture evaporation is faster from the nib alone than from the whole bean and can be done more gently. A more uniform heat distribution occurs throughout. There are conflicting opinions on the disadvantages of roasting nib with relation to the migration of fat to the surface but, in general, "nib roasting" is preferred for low roast and "whole bean roasting" for high roast situations.

One advantage of nib roasting is that it can be used for a blend of bean varieties. While roasting blends of beans induces a loss of many desirable characteristics of some varieties, due to overroasting or underroasting, the blend of nibs has a more uniform size and moisture (adjusted during pretreatment). This permits better operation and control of the degree of roast of the total mass.

Although nib roasting can be done in most conventional roasters described previously, vertical types are most often used. One alternative available in the market is a batch roaster that does the work in a humid atmosphere (Mayer-Potschak, 1983). A small amount of water is added to the nibs at the beginning of the roasting cycle. This water and the water from the nibs favors three developments: a strong antimicrobial action by the steam produced, a volatilization of the undesirable incidental volatiles produced during fermentation (and some of those produced during roasting), and an even distribution of moisture and some water-soluble components throughout the whole mass of the nibs. This results in low bacteria counts, even roast, and elimination of extremely acidic compounds. It has some limitations on how well the degree of roasting and the Maillard reaction can be controlled, but certainly it is an advancement in roasting technology. The subsequent grinding of nibs is little changed from traditional bean roasting procedures as long as the final moisture content is the same.

2. *Liquor Roasting*

In the last few years there has been a new alternative for the production of cacao liquor which is based on the principle of roasting cacao mass. The equipment that is used for roasting raw mass was originally designed for liquor treatment and deacidification. This third method of producing cacao liquor is shown in Fig. 5.

The procedure is the same as that for nibs, except that the nibs are ground in a conventional pin mill. Due to the natural amount of water that exists in the raw nib, the mass is more viscous and the output of the mill decreases to 60% of the original capacity. The mass needs good agitation to decrease viscosity, but the best results are achieved by passing the mass twice thru the pin mill. The paste can then be roasted in this form.

In theory, roasting cacao mass favors the uniformity of the roast, because the moisture and flavor precursors are distributed uniformly, and the differences

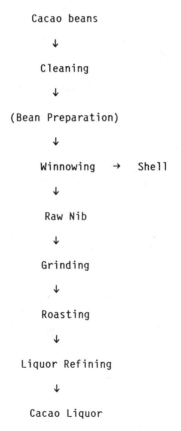

FIG. 5.   Production of cacao liquor by the roasting of raw cacao mass.

within the bean or the bean lot are reduced. The heat transfer is also optimized, and the rate of the reaction can be controlled. Another theoretical advantage is the possibility of eliminating undesirable volatile components formed during fermentation and storage. More ideally, if the mass roasting is to be performed properly, the elimination of undesirable volatiles should be done before roasting; in that case, the flavor of the product is "cleaner." This is particularly important for beans that have a high acidity or have smoke or ham type flavors.

There are two types of mass roasters: continuous or batch. In the continuous roasters, the cocoa mass is fed into a reactor in which a thin film of the liquor material is developed. The film moves between a heating jacket and a central rotating cylinder–cone assembly. There is the capability to inject steam at a midpoint of the cylinder; this steam injection favors the elimination of acids and also has the advantage of reducing the bacteria count of the liquor. The dwell time in the machine, however, is relatively short, 50–100 sec, and accurate control of this parameter is difficult.

The batch system has all the advantages previously mentioned for a discontinuous system, is more controllable, and consists of a reaction vessel in which the surface for heat transfer and dispersion capabilities has been maximized. It also has capabilities for injection of hot air, nitrogen, or for applying a vacuum. The raw liquor can be pasteurized and treated with vacuum for the elimination of water and undesirable volatiles. Then the mass can be heated and hot air can be introduced to favor the roasting process. This system is more conductive to better control and to the application of specific chemical principles in the optimization of flavor development.

V. ALKALIZATION (DUTCHING)

The alkalization of cacao products originated in the early 1800s and has been a common production process ever since. Documentation on variations of the process is evident in the literature wherein the process varied, the starting cacao material varied, and the alkalizing agent varied. The permutations involving all three variables have been tried and reported so that there would appear to be nothing new in alkalization. To a great extent this is true, but with advancing technology, some of the variations are being retried or modified with success.

The regulatory constraint on alkalizing, as covered in the *Code of Federal Regulations* (CFR 21, Food and Durgs, Part 163.110, 1980), somewhat limits the process and definitely limits alkalizing agents to the bicarbonates, carbonates, or hydroxides of sodium, ammonium, or potassium; or the carbonate or oxide of magnesium. The alkali or combination of alkalies cannot be greater in neutralizing value than the neutralizing value of 3 parts by weight of anhydrous potassium carbonate to 100 parts by weight of cacao bean shelled or unshelled. The regulation does not reference the cation effect, only the neutralizing effect.

The addition of a dry alkali or solution of alkali can be applied to unshelled beans, shelled beans (nibs), ground beans (liquor), or partially defatted liquor (cocoa powder) to produce the effects of alkalizing. The major effects or observable reactions as outlined by Clarke (1949) are listed below.

1. Absorption of water and swelling (hydration) of the cell walls, proteins, starch, and fiber; physical opening up of the cacao nib or particle.
2. Neutralization of plant acids (acetic, citric, tartaric, tannic, and others).
3. Hydrolysis of starches, natural glycosides, and resins; formation of simpler compounds, some of which are acid or amphoteric in character.
4. Neutralization of secondary compounds and formation of salts.
5. Reduction of tannins to less astringent substances, some of which act as polyhydroxybenzene compounds, absorbing oxygen from air.
6. Hydrolysis of esters to enable interaction among flavor compounds.
7. Formation of basic salts with theobromine, for example, sodium theobrominate.
8. Denaturation or decomposition of proteins, formation of globulin, and probably other protein reactions.
9. Carbon dioxide release from carbonate-bearing agents used in the process.
10. Browning reactions (Maillard reactions) probably among some of the reducing sugars and proteins, giving rise to color and flavor reactions.
11. Reaction of carbohydrates with alkaline agents to produce such weak acids as mucic, and possibly humic acid, with which they form salts.
12. Cellulosic degeneration, for which there is some evidence, to substances that suggest vanillin flavors and to substances such as caramel with red–brown colors and caramel flavors.
13. Neutralization of free fatty acids to form alkaline soaps; probably hydrolysis, decomposition, or partial destruction of naturally occurring lecithin.

Necessary beyond the substrate and alkali are temperature, oxygen, and naturally occurring water or added water. From a user's point of view, color appears to be the single most important specification for the purchase of an alkalized powder. Color can vary from a light brown to a reddish-brown through to a charred black depending on bean variety, alkalizing agent, amount of alkalizing agent, air flow, roasting and drying temperatures, and processing equipment utilized. Alkalization in the presence of oxygen changes the natural chocolate hue from yellow to red that provides a deeper brown color and is preferred. The red color development cannot be attained without sufficient air flow during the process.

Flavor is the next important criterion for alkalized powder selection. The flavor dramatically changes as a result of the treatment. The natural chocolate bouquet is reduced in light aromatics and takes on heavier roasted nutty and woody notes. A metallic flavor becomes evident and, if sufficient alkalizing occurs, soapiness may be detectable. In the undiluted stage, the powder is unpalatable. Third on the list of priorities for specifications is pH, which is a function of the starting cacao material and the type and quantity of alkalizing agent.

The amount and form of each ingredient and methods of processing are specific to each manufacturer and are either classified as trade secrets or protected by patent. Regardless, the chemistry as outlined can be translated from the most recent literature, mostly patents, into the practical aspects of color, flavor, and pH changes to determine what is new.

Recently the literature refers to the alkalization of cocoa powders rather than nibs. A British patent application (Chalin, 1977) from a U.S. patent application (Chalin, 1976) highlights the treatment of a powder rather than a liquor, nib, or bean. The advantages of alkalizing a powder are obvious. None of the prime cocoa butter that is pressed out prior to alkalizing is subjected to possible saponification. Surface area is increased together with minimum fat hindrance to speed a more complete reaction. In the past, the problem with this approach had been the large amounts of water necessary to hydrate the powder which later had to be removed. The above U.S. patent addresses the problem with the fairly new technology of high pressure extrusions that requires minimal water addition (20–35%) and minimal reaction time, 2.5–5.0 min at pressures between 500 and 1300 psi. The patent does not account for air addition to support color development.

The NARS (nibs alkalizing, roasting, and sterilizing) process (Anonymous, 1979) outlined in the literature reverts to the more conventional method of alkalizing nibs. The process highlights ten features and advantages, two of which refer to alkalization controlled variation of color, and exact pH control, but neither claim is new.

A recent U.S. patent on alkalization was issued (Bandi et al., 1982) for the claim of solubility. The patent stresses the equipment design used to alkalize a liquor. The claims made do not limit the process to liquor, but the diagramed process needs a pumpable mass. The mass is exposed to an injected steam/alkali solution stream under pressure. The mass is thoroughly mixed, under pressure at >120°C for 30–80 sec, after which the mass is subjected to a sudden expansion. The mass or liquor is then dried while constantly mixing. No claim is made for color or pH. The patent claims to produce a "solubilized liquor."

More recently, a U.S. patent was issued (Eggen, 1982) for alkalization of an enzymatically treated low fat cocoa powder. Here again the main claim is solubility, but mention is made regarding color development. The powder is made into a slurry that is treated with amylase to act on the starches. After enzyme activity, the slurry is alkalized and is prepared as a syrup by adding sugars or dried into a powder.

Another patent on alkalization is a Japanese patent (Shimatani, 1977) that utilizes pressure to develop pigmentation in a cocoa powder. Cocoa powder is reacted with alkali solution at 110–135°C. for 5–36 hr under a pressure of 1.3 kg/cm² air. The main claim of this process is to develop an edible red color, not to develop an alkalized cocoa.

Not in the literature, but in industrial consideration, is the custom blending of cocoa powder with a suitable alkalizing agent and oxidizing agent to develop the reaction in the end product. All of the previously defined alkalizing processes require the addition and later removal of water to complete the reaction. Since the major use of alkalized powders is in the baking industry, which adds water and heat to make their end product, the alkalizing of the powder could be completed within the product, thereby reducing processing steps, saving energy, and reducing cost.

In summary, many combinations in the alkalization process have been tried and documented. The recent developments cited deal with new technologies developed over the last several years. Three examples deal with the use of high pressure to complete the reaction. The pressures are attained with the use of high pressure vessels or high pressure extruders. Custom blending, although not an accepted practice as of yet, can be adapted to baking applications. The introduction of enzyme treatment could lead to new developments in the alkalization process if given regulatory clearance.

The future outlook does not include a change in the need for an alkalized powder. The deep color and unique flavor will remain desirable within a wide range of products. The means by which that powder is produced, however, will change. The emergence of genetic engineering within the last decade would imply that enzymatic treatment would be the way of the future. On the other hand, enzymatic treatment appears to be technological overkill for a fairly simple reaction. The future holds (1) better control, and understanding, of the raw materials used in the reaction; (2) concentration on processes to react cocoa powder as opposed to beans, nibs, or liquor; and (3) development of the latest high pressure processes to shorten reaction time, to minimize water incorporation, and to reduce energy requirements, thereby reducing overall cost.

VI. COCOA BUTTER

A. INTRODUCTION

Cocoa butter is derived from cocoa beans primarily by mechanical pressing of the milled roasted bean. There is no exact internationally agreed upon definition of cocoa butter in respect to the specifics of pressing or bean processing (Minifie, 1980). Cocoa butter obtained in other ways such as mechanical "expressing" of beans and shells or solvent extraction is not considered "prime" butter. Sometimes a "pure" butter is blended with cocoa butter expressed from alkalized liquor. Usually the latter butter will be deodorized before blending.

Specific properties of cocoa butter will vary depending on the geographical source, the crop conditions, the conditions of roasting and pressing, etc. (Chatt, 1953). For instance, the Bahia bean from Brazil yields a softer (lower melting point) butter than a West African bean. The melting characteristics of a cocoa butter have been correlated with daily temperatures during the cropping season (Lehrian et al., 1980).

The melting characteristics of the cocoa butter largely affect the desirable melt-in-the-mouth quality of a chocolate product. Fortuitously cocoa butter is generally hard at room or storage temperature but becomes fluid at body temperature, melting at a rate so that the fat will not feel too hard or too soft from instant to instant. Both the melting characteristics and the flavor are to be considered when viewing the function of cocoa butter in chocolate. Depending on the size of the chocolate factory and the blend of cocoa beans that are used in a particular formula, some of the cocoa butter added to a formula may not correspond to the beans that were used for the chocolate liquor component of the final product. Variations in flavor due to the source of cocoa butter can occur, and there is a tendency to deodorize cocoa butter to a standard flavor (Cook and Meursing, 1982). Cocoa butters both in Europe and the United States range from "refined" or "deodorized" to a fairly strong flavor. The deodorized cocoa butters can be bland enough to have no flavor. This bland butter is usually preferred for milk chocolates.

B. COCOA BUTTER COMPOSITION

Cocoa butter, like most natural fats, is largely a triglyceride. The basic glycerine structure possesses three extensions that contain fatty acids, primarily oleic, stearic, and palmitic. On any glycerine base, various combinations of the three acid types exist resulting in a complex combination of melting characteristics. The melting point of cocoa butter covers a range for complete fusion of 32–34°C and an incipient fusion range of 31.2–32.7°C (Minifie, 1980). The amounts and positions of the three fatty acids affect the melting characteristics. At any temperature the solid fat concentration is affected by the ratio of saturated to unsaturated fatty acids. The approximate total concentration of the fatty acids in cocoa butter are oleic 38.1%, stearic 35.4%, and palmitic 24.4%. Some linoleic acid is present at about 2% (Chatt, 1953).

Cocoa butter is composed largely of triglycerides (~94%) with small amounts of diglycerides (~4%) and monoglycerides (<0.5%). Some free fatty acids (~1.3%) are also present. In the triglycerides of cocoa butter, the fatty acids are arranged so that approximately 37% is in the oleopalmitostearic (POS) configuration; the SOS configuration occurs in about 25% of the cases and the POP is approximately 20%. Exact amounts depend on the specific cocoa bean variety. Existence of SOO and POO type triglycerides cause adverse crystallinity effects, and are a less desirable constituent in cocoa butter.

The presence of the various fatty acid combinations creates a considerable challenge to researchers who are pursuing the understanding of crystalline phenomena that occur within chocolate over time. Each of the triglycerides has polymorphic crystalline forms, each form being most stable at particular temperature ranges. Over time there is a tendency toward formation of the most stable form. One result is the concentration of SOS triglycerides in the solid phase of the cocoa butter thus affecting a change in the overall properties of the cocoa butter (Manning, 1984).

At temperatures below 93°F the degree of solidification of cocoa butter is often characterized by solids–fat ratio data. For example, at 80°F about 67% of the cocoa butter is in the solid phase while at 50°F approximately 83% is solid.

C. DEODORIZATION

1. Purpose

In many chocolate processes, particularly for milk chocolate, it is important to achieve flavor consistency by using a bland cocoa butter. The cocoa butter can be deodorized by vacuum steam distillation. The deodorization process is common in the production of other vegetable fats, as part of a total fat "refining" process. For cocoa butter, usually only the steam deodorization step is used. In a deodorization process the cocoa butter is subjected to steam stripping at high temperature and high vacuum. Oxygen must be absent to avoid adverse effects on the subsequent fat stability (Bailey, 1949).

Experiments have shown that adverse conditions during deodorization have caused a softening of the cocoa butter and an increase in the saturated fats at the number two position (Meara et al., 1974). Small amounts of flavor and aroma compounds are lost during deodorization, including esters, aromatics, pyrazines, pyrroles, carbonyls, aldehydes, and ketones (Rostagno et al., 1970). There is some loss of tocopherol, a natural antioxidant in vegetable fats. Trace amounts of light free fatty acids are also lost. Typically free fatty acids are reduced from ~0.5 to ~0.1%. Final reductions to about 0.03% are possible. Although the reduction of free fatty acids generally parallels the elimination of undesirable flavors and is used as an indication of deodorization effectiveness, the change in free fatty acid content may contribute only slightly to flavor change (Gavin, 1978; Rostagno et al., 1970). The loss of free fatty acids would theoretically correlate with improved stability, but there is often a reduction in stability of the oil during deodorization as evidenced by an increase of the peroxide value; major factors are presence of oxygen and temperature. By operating below 238°C various undesirable reactions can be avoided such as cis–trans isomerization, interesterification, decomposition, and polymerization (Davies *et al.*, 1979).

With a particular deodorization process, Rostagno *et al.* (1970) report a loss of approximately 20% of tocopherols, but the deodorization process did not alter in any significant manner the composition of the cocoa butter and its stability to oxygen. There are four types of tocopherols that can be involved, with different oxidative stabilities, but ordinary analytical methods usually measure just the total tocopherol content (Carpenter, 1979).

2. Methods

Deodorization can be carried out as a batch, semicontinuous, or continuous process.

a. Batch Process. In the batch process an evacuated vessel contains a coil for heating with steam or heat transfer liquid. Direct steam is also sparged into the bottom of the vessel, which typically might contain 10,000 kg of cocoa butter. The ordinary steam requirement for sparging or stripping is of the order of 1–3 lb/100 lb of cocoa butter, but this depends on the extent of deodorization that is desired and can be correlated with the amount of fatty acid removed (Dudrow, 1983). Likewise, steam usage as high as 50–100 pounds of oil can occur. Temperature and vacuum vary and interrelate with the amount of stripping steam and processing times. Generally oils are heated to temperatures above 210°C for 1–4 hr under reduced pressure corresponding to 1–6 mm Hg absolute. Finally the cocoa butter is cooled below 65°C before it is removed from the vessel. It is important that this step be done in the same vessel or under vacuum conditions and possibly with stripping steam to avoid high temperature exposure to air. The material of construction is important; metals or alloys should be chosen that contribute minimal prooxidative effects. For this, the better grades of stainless steel are preferred.

b. Semicontinuous Process. Semicontinuous deodorization processes involve a tower in which a series of tanks sequentially treat the oil in separate batches. Each batch receives a specific treatment before moving by gravity to the next treatment step. The steps involve deaerating, heating, steam-stripping, and cooling. The entire tower is held under the same vacuum.

c. Continuous Process. As one progresses from batch deodorization toward continuous deodorization, there is an improvement in stripping efficiency, a reduction of losses due to entrainment and hydrolysis, and a reduction in utility costs. The latter savings occur through lower peak utility charges and better heat recovery with smaller heating and cooling auxiliaries. Each fat or oil receives identical treatment throughout the deodorization with minimal intermixing (Gavin, 1978).

Modern continuous deodorizers can process fats and oils at up to 60,000 lb/hr. In one type a tower contains shallow trays with bubble caps. The cocoa butter moves downward counter to the rising flow of steam. In another type, the fat is preheated by interchange with the exit stream and then atomized into a flow of steam where a two-phase flow pattern develops. The two-phase mixture passes through a special mixer/contactor with closely spaced contacting surfaces for further development of a flow pattern. Then the stream flows to a vapor/liquid separator. The vapor goes on to the condenser and vacuum system that operates at 3–5 torr.

One patent application (Thuren, 1979) calls for the homogenization of the cocoa butter with water at 10% weight and then treatment by steam distillation in a thin-layer evaporation unit operating at 10–30 mm Hg. The steam pressure is approximately 2–3 atm. The short time treatment is claimed to reduce deterioration in terms of peroxide value and achieve a relatively low loss of tocopherols.

VII. MILK AND MILK-DERIVED PRODUCTS AS COMPONENTS OF CHOCOLATE

A. TRADITIONAL FORMS OF MILK

Milk in its various forms has been used as an ingredient in milk chocolate since its introduction by Daniel Peters in 1876. Its contributions to the flavor, color, and texture are expected characteristics of milk chocolate. Both the nonfat milk solids and the lipid fraction contribute to the flavor and color development during the crumb and conching stage in chocolate manufacture. The end product has a distinct creamy, partly caramelized, and/or lipolyzed flavor.

1. General Composition

The specific composition of bovine milk is a dynamic parameter depending on the specific breed, stage of lactation, season, herd management, individual cow, and its health and nutritional level. Therefore, any discussion on milk composition can only be on averages. Milk contains water, fat, proteins, lactose, and minerals. An average gross composition of bovine milk would be as follows (Wah and Merril, 1963): water, 87%; fat, 3.5–3.7%; lactose, 4.8%; protein, 3.5%; and minerals, 0.7%. In 60 specific Federal marketing orders, the average fat content of 90,000 samples was 3.47%, ranging between 3.22 and 3.84% (Anonymous, 1971).

2. Composition of Bovine Milk Fat

Milk fat is a complex misture of triglycerides composed of over 170 fatty acids (Kinsella, 1970) of varying carbon number, degree and position of unsaturation, and/or branching. Table XIV lists the most common fatty acids in bovine milk fat (Kurtz, 1974). The predominate fatty acids are oleic and palmitic followed by myristic and stearic. Milk fat is unusual in that it contains a large amount of low carbon number fatty acids and unique in that it contains butanoic acid.

3. Bovine Milk Proteins

Generally the proteins can be apportioned in two main groups, caseins and whey proteins. The caseins may be further divided into four major fractions, i.e., α_1-, α_2-, β-, and κ-caseins all of which may contain subfractions or genetic polymorphs (Table XV). Genetic polymorphs possess unique primary structures. A complete discussion of the bovine milk protein nomenclature is given by Eigel et al. (1984). Casein subunits assemble in vivo to form highly structured aggre-

TABLE XIV

MOST COMMON FATTY ACIDS IN BOVINE MILK FAT[a]

Common name	Carbons : double bonds	Content (%)
Saturated		
Butyric acid	4 : 0	3.5
Caproic acid	6 : 0	2.2
Caprylic acid	8 : 0	1.0
Capric acid	10 : 0	1.8
Lauric acid	12 : 0	3.0
Myristic acid	14 : 0	11.2
Palmitic acid	16 : 0	25.5
Stearic acid	18 : 0	12.0
Monounsaturated		
Myristolic acid	14 : 1	0.7
Palmitoleic acid	16 : 1	2.2
Oleic acid	18 : 1	29.8
Diunsaturated		
Linoleic acid	18 : 2	2.8
Polyunsaturated		
Linolenic	18 : 3	0.6
Branched chain acids	—	2.2
Hydroxy acids	—	0.2
Keto acids	—	0.3
Remainder	—	1.0

[a] Adapted from Webb et al. (1974).

TABLE XV

COMPOSITION AND SELECTED PROPERTIES OF MAJOR BOVINE MILK PROTEINS AND THEIR
COMPONENTS[a]

Protein	Composition in skim milk (g/liter)	Number of components[b]	Number of genetic variants	Approximate molecular weights	Approximate isoelectric points
Casein fraction					
α_{s1}-Caseins	12–15	2	5	23,600	4.5
α_{s2}-Caseins	3–4	4	4	25,200	—
β-Caseins	9–11	9	7	24,000	4.9
κ-Caseins	2–4	7	2	19,000	5.5
Whey proteins					
β-Lactoglobulins	2–4	1	8	18,300	5.13
α-Lactalbumins	0.6–1.7	7	2	14,200	4.2–4.5
Serum albumin	0.4	1	—	66,300	4.7–4.9
Immunoglobulins[c]	0.45–1.05	5	—	150,000–1,000,000	5.5–8.3
Secretory component	0.02–0.1	1	—	79,000	—

[a] Adapted from Eigel et al. (1984).

[b] In homozygote cow's milk there would be one genetic variant for each protein family, but each may contain more than one component. The number of minor components of κ-casein and α-lactalbumin are uncertain.

[c] Immunoglobulins are class differences.

gates called micelles. Micellular casein structure has been reviewed by Farrell and Thompson (1974).

The whey proteins are water soluble in milk at all pHs. They consist of β-lactoglobulin, α-lactalbumin, serum albumin, the immunoglobulins, and the secretory component fraction (Table XV). α-Lactalbumin and β-lactoglobulin are the two of commercial interest and make up 80% of the whey protein content. Both major protein fractions have emulsification properties which aid in blending ingredients, and they absorb at fat surfaces to improve emulsion stability. Caseins are able to bind twice their weight in water, producing a drying effect.

4. Lactose

Lactose is the least variable of the milk components with an average composition of 4.8%. Lactose, which is unique to milk, can have an important effect on the flavor, color, and texture of milk chocolate. Lactose is a reducing sugar and can undergo Maillard browning and caramelization both of which will affect the flavor of the final product.

Lactose can also affect the texture of the milk chocolate. Lactose is less soluble (16% at room temperature) than sucrose or glucose. The crystalline form of lactose is an important textural factor. Above 93.5°C, β-anhydride crystals form. This is an unstable form which reverts to α-anhydride on cooling (Neilson, 1963). α-Anhydride crystals are less soluble and may produce a sandy texture. Supersaturated solutions of lactose may form amorphous lactose. Amorphous lactose is hygroscopic and will absorb available environmental water. Dry milk products containing lactose glass therefore tend to become lumpy or cake together during storage unless protected from moisture absorption.

5. Condensed and Sweetened Milk

Fluid milk is rarely if ever used in the manufacture of milk chocolate. The chief forms of milk used in chocolate manufacture are concentrated forms such as evaporated milk, sweetened condensed milk, and dry milk powder.

a. Processing.   The process for manufacturing concentrated milks begins with full cream, partially, or wholly skimmed milk which is preheated to 71–88°C for 10–30 minutes. For special purposes HTST (high temperature, short time) forewarming up to 138°C for a few seconds may be used. The heat treatment should be severe enough to destroy pathogens, yeasts and molds, inactivate enzymes, and generally reduce the spoilage bacteria count.

If sweetened condensed whole milk is the final product, sucrose is added to the hot milk, and the mixture is evaporated under vacuum. A common formula for sweetened condensed milk is 30% skim milk solids, which include 2.5% ash, and 16% lactose together with 42% sucrose and 28% water. This results in a sucrose in water percentage of 60% which is considered minimum for commercial use. A sugar in water percentage of 62.5% insures greater safety and superior keeping qualities. In the sweetened condensed milk products, 75% of the water is removed. The sugar in sweetened condensed milks acts as a preservative, and reasonable storage periods can be expected without sterile packing.

Unsweetened concentrated milks are prepared much in the same manner as sweetened condensed milks except without the added sucrose but with homogenization. Unsweetened concentrated milks must be sterilized in sealed containers unless it is used within 24 hours. If cooled to maximum of 7°C it can be held for a longer time.

b. Composition.   Typical compositions of condensed milks are given in Table XVI for comparative purposes. For manufacturing processes calculations, one must check the actual milk supply by analytical analysis for exact concentrations of components.

Block or "solidified" milk is a highly concentrated form of sweetened condensed milk produced by further removal of water to a resulting solids content of 90–93%. It is mainly a product produced in Holland and Denmark. A typical composition is milk solids nonfat 26.5%, milk fat 18.5%, moisture 9.0%, and sugar 46.0%.

TABLE XVI

TYPICAL COMPOSITION OF CONCENTRATED MILKS[a]

Component (%)	Evaporated milk	Sweetened condensed whole milk	Condensed skim	Sweetened condensed skim
Fat	7.9	8.7	0.3	0.3
Protein	7.0	8.1	10.0	10.0
Moisture	73.8	27.1	73.0	28.4
Lactose	9.7	11.4	14.7	16.3
Sucrose	0	44.3	0	42.0
Ash	1.6	1.8	2.3	2.3
Calcium	0.252	0.262	0.250	0.300
Phosphorus	0.205	0.206	0.200	0.230
Lactic acid	0	0	0	0

[a] Adapted from Webb *et al.* (1974).

c. Milk Ingredients. Milk-derived ingredients are important to the flavor, texture, and appearance of chocolate. Fat bloom, a major problem in chocolates, may be delayed or prevented if proper attention is paid to conching, if the milk fat to cocoa butter ratio is 1 : 10, and proper tempering and cooling take place (Hugunin and Nishikawa, 1978). There are also cost and regulatory advantages to using milk-derived ingredients. Milk solids nonfat (MSNF) are important to the flavor of milk chocolate, and U.S. Standards of Identity require 3.66% milk fat and 12% milk solids. On heating, the MSNF become caramelized and undergo Maillard reactions which improve the rich, creamy, partly caramelized flavor of milk chocolate (Hugunin and Nishikawa, 1978).

The heat stability of milk proteins is important in milk processing. Non-casein milk proteins are relatively heat labile, undergoing complete denaturation at 90°C in 10 min while the caseins are rather heat stable. An additional reaction that accompanies whey protein denaturation is protein aggregation. Whey proteins aggregate in the presence of calcium ions to form precipitates that are sedimentable at 1,000 g (Lim, 1980).

Heating skim milk causes a disulfide interaction between β-lactoglobulin and κ-casein. Kinsella (1976) and Pour-El (1976) have summarized the literature on functional properties of proteins. The main points expressed by Kinsella are as follows: (1) functional properties are influenced by and may vary according to the source, composition, and structure, method of preparation, thermal processing, and other environmental conditions such as pH, temperature, and ionic strength; (2) using new protein forms in development is a trial and error approach and thus may be labor intensive and expensive; (3) there is a need for standard methodologies for testing functionality and evaluating characteristics and potential applications; (4) model systems may be useful in objectively evaluating a protein's behavior; (5) however, extrapolating data from model systems to more complex systems is not always possible.

6. Dried Milk

The use of dried whole milk is often the most economical means of manufacturing milk chocolate. Other advantages include a microbiologically stable product which is ready to mix with chocolate liquor, sugar, and cocoa butter without having considerable investment in dehydrating equipment and additional manpower. Chocolates prepared with milk powder have been criticized because they lack some of the flavor attributes associated with the liquid process (Koch, 1961); this defect can be overcome (Minifie, 1974).

a. Drying. The most common method used to produce dried milk is spray drying, although drum or roller dryer is still used, especially in the United Kingdom. Drum drying requires less capital outlay than spray drying but usually produces a poorer quality product. The drum process dehydrates homogenized milk concentrated to 23% solids by feeding the product onto internally steam heated drums. The moisture is removed from the milk film in one revolution or less, with the dried product being scraped and sized.

In spray drying the concentrated milk at 40–45% solids is atomized through a pressure chamber or centrifugal plate into a tower in which hot turbulent air is flowing at 150–200°C. The milk dehydrates quickly as it falls to the bottom of the chamber. Fluidizing may be used in an instantizing process. The particles are separated in a cyclone separator. Foam spray dried whole milk using nitrogen gas has been researched extensively by the U.S. Department of Agriculture and found to produce a superior product (Sills, 1970; Hanrahah *et al.,* 1962; Tamsma *et al.,* 1973; Kurtz *et al.,* 1971). The general methods and equipment used for the traditional manufacture of milk powders have been reviewed by numerous authors (Pallansch, 1970; Hall and Hedrich, 1971).

A novel process is offered by the Damrow Company (Fond du Lac, WI), a Division of DEC International, that allows for the drying of heretofore difficult materials, e.g., those with high total solids, sucrose or other sugars, or high fat. The system, termed the Filtermat Dryer, has a low-profile spray tower in which most of the drying takes place. The product then falls onto a continuous porous belt for final drying, cooling, and instantizing. The manufacturer claims much versatility, short exposure time to critical moisture levels, and gentle final drying resulting in high quality powders.

b. Composition. Typical compositions of whole and skim milk powder are given in Table XVII. Milk powder has a moisture level of about 3% and never above 5% by U.S. Standards of Identity. Nonfat dry milk has a maximum of 1.5% milk fat by U.S. Standards of Identity. The American Dry Milk Institute (1971) has established specifications for three classes of skim milk powder according to its heat treatment. The criteria are based on the amount of soluble or undenatured whey protein per gram of powder (Table XVIII).

TABLE XVII

TYPICAL COMPOSITION OF DRIED MILK POWDER[a]

Component (%)	Whole milk powder	Skim milk powder (conventional)	Skim milk powder (instant)
Protein	26.4	35.9	35.8
Fat	27.5	0.8	0.7
Moisture	2.0	3.0	4.0
Lactose	38.2	52.3	51.6
Ash	5.9	8.0	7.9
Calcium	0.909	1.308	1.293
Phosphorus	0.708	1.016	1.005

[a] Adapted from Webb et al. (1974).

c. *Solubility.* Spray dried milk is more soluble than roller process powders. The degree of solubility is a function of the amount of denatured protein. Under properly controlled spray drying conditions, little change occurs in milk protein structure and solubility. Changes in serum proteins are especially slight for low heat powders (Harland et al., 1952).

A high solubility index refers to increases in the amount of insoluble matter in dried milks. As the casein undergoes denaturation, it will not form a stable dispersion when recombined with water, and settling occurs. The following factors adversely affect the solubility index of spray dried milks: high accumulative heat treatment; poor quality milk; and drying conditions inappropriate for the dryer design. Preheating milk to insure optimum stability decreases protein denaturation during drying. Slow drying at high total solids causes rapid casein denaturation. Large droplets requiring more time to dry increase the solubility index. Increased pH or salt content will increase denaturation with a given heat treatment. Severe heating of the milk film, such as in drum drying, denatures substantial amounts of milk protein.

The stability of dry milk will be affected adversely if stored under high moisture and temperature conditions. High moisture promotes insolubility as a

TABLE XVIII

CLASSIFICATION OF DRY MILK ACCORDING TO HEAT TREATMENT[a]

Classification	Soluble protein (N, mg/g of powder)
Low heat	>6.0
Medium heat	>1.5, <6.0
High heat	<1.5

[a] American Dry Milk Institute (1971).

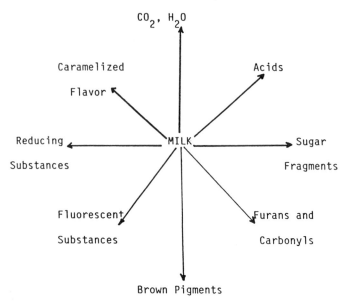

FIG. 6.   Potential lactose and lactose–protein heat-induced changes in dried dairy products. From Patton (1955).

function of both moisture and temperature (Henry *et al.*, 1948, 1949). Below 4% moisture and, if stored at low relative humidity (RH) and temperatures, solubility changes are relatively insignificant in milk powders. The other factor affecting the keeping properties of milk powder is oxygen access. The shelf life of full cream powder can be greatly extended if the product is vacuum packed with an inert gas.

d.   Flavor Changes.   All products prepared from milk will have flavors arising from several factors. Excessive heating will change the flavor of milk; this is well documented. These flavors are transmitted to milk powders and are generally detrimental. Milk powders prepared with mild heat treatment have a mild flavor and little flavor is imparted to the milk chocolate. The most important heat-induced changes in dried dairy products are these involving lactose alone or those involving lactose–protein interaction. Patton (1955) has summarized these reactions (Fig. 6).

The Maillard reaction and the Amadori rearrangement leads to many of the components shown in Fig. 6. These reactions have low energy requirements and are autocatalytic. The Maillard products in low concentration can enhance milk chocolate flavor; however, in significant amounts they are disagreeable. Direct caramelization has a high activation requirement and is generally of lesser importance. Nevertheless, intermediate breakdown products can have an effect on milk chocolate flavor. As many as 80 browning compounds have been identified in model systems, and their interaction is undoubtedly complex and not well understood.

B. MILK-DERIVED INGREDIENTS

1. Whey and Whey-Based Products

Whey or whey components are not allowed for use in milk chocolate under the U.S. Standard of Identity for milk chocolate. Whey and whey solids have been considered largely a waste by-product of cheesemaking operations. Whey contains most of the water-soluble proteins, β-lactoglobulin, α-lactalbumin, the immunoglobulins, and the secretory component. These proteins are very high quality with protein efficiency ratios of 3.2–3.4. However, the protein content of dried whey is generally low (Table XIX), with lactose being the predominating component of the whey.

Whey production for 1981 was 2,400,000,000 lb on a solids basis of which 1,066,000,000 lb or 44.4% was unutilized as waste. The remaining whey, about 56%, enters the whey processing industry. Of the 1,334,000,000 lb processed, approximately 30% is underutilized from an economic point of view, as animal feed (Teixeira et al., 1983). The largest single use of whey solids, about 75%, is in the form of whole dried whey. The least utilized form of whey is demineralized whey, accounting for about 2% of the total production in 1981. The outlook for the future availability of whey solids at attractive prices is good because of the large amounts that go unutilized or underutilized. Heretofore, the confectionery industry has not taken advantage of this potential by using only about 0.5% in 1975 (Clark, 1977).

The highest quality dried whey is produced from sweet whey, especially that

TABLE XIX

TYPICAL COMPOSITION OF DRIED WHEY[a]

Component (%)	Sweet whey	Acid whey
Protein	12.9	13.0
Fat	0.9	0
Moisture	4.5	3.2
Lactose	73.5	66.5
Ash	8.0	10.2
Calcium	0.646	1.44
Phosphorus	0.589	1.17
Lactic acid	2.3	8.6

[a] Adapted from Webb et al. (1974).

produced from Swiss or Parmesan cheese operations. The highest U.S. government standard is extra grade standard. Sweet whey can be converted into a stable nonhygroscopic free-flowing powder by concentrating and drying. Drying acid whey is more problematic and is not as well accepted by food processors.

If the product cannot withstand high mineral content, there are demineralization techniques being used. These are ion exchange and electrodialysis, and both are being used to remove mineral salts from whey prior to dehydrating. Lactose may be crystallized in a pretreatment step. These demineralized and/or delactosed whey powders can be used at higher levels as a replacement for nonfat milk or condensed milk. Whey processors offer a variety of specialty whey products for individualized applications. The few examples given here are by no means exhaustive nor are they necessarily endorsed by the authors but are rather to serve as examples.

A relatively new whey-based product is a compound coating; a whey blend to replace milk solids in coatings used by ice cream novelty makers, candy makers, and bakers (Saal, 1976). The coatings must be called compound coatings to distinguish them from true chocolate coatings which have a Standard of Identity. Most compound coatings are made with cocoa powder, and whey-based solids rather than liquid whey are used to modify the flavor of the cocoa. These compound coatings give the same flavor that nonfat milk contributes. The whey solids main function is to reduce cocoa harshness, and a secondary function is lightening the color to that of milk chocolate.

Other examples of skim milk replacers are based on whey/caseinate blends. These blends are generally formulated to have comparable or superior functional and nutritional properties to skim milk powder. Some of the blends may incorporate buttermilk powder which imparts a rich, buttery flavor to products. The results of an extensive evaluation by Mohler et al. (1981) using sweet whey, whey/calcium caseinate blends, and partially demineralized whey/calcium caseinate blends, showed that a light, chocolate-flavored compound coating with consumer acceptance equivalent to that of nonfat dry milk-based coating can be formulated.

There are also cocoa substitutes available that are whey based. These are blends of specially processed whey solids and natural or artificial components. They replace cocoa on a pound for pound basis at high levels (May and Fernandez, 1978). They provide the necessary aromatic qualities and the nonvolatile dark chocolate bitter notes.

The obvious advantage of whey and whey blends is that they are more cost effective (Campbell, 1975), but what about their functional properties? Whey or whey-based blends are no longer just cheap substitutes for nonfat dried milk (NDM) solids. Some characteristics of whey solids favor its use in place of NDM solids. An example is its ability to accentuate flavor. O'Connell (1974) reported whey substitution of 13% for NDM allowed for 20% less chocolate liquor. A taste test of the candy bars showed that 80% preferred the whey-based candy.

Other functional properties of whey solids include moderate to high protein concentrations of superior nutritional qualities. Whey protein contains nearly 63% essential amino acids while egg albumin and casein contain 51 and 49.5%, respectively. Whey proteins have excellent foaming abilities and stability and, in the undenatured form, they are soluble, free flowing and nonhygroscopic. If the Maillard reaction is desired, whey solids are prime substrates. In short there is a whey-based product that has virtually any application in which a replacement for casein or NDM is desired.

2. Lactose

Cocoa mass, cocoa butter, milk solids, and sugar are the essential components of cocoa and milk chocolate products. The only added sugars under U.S. Standards of Identity for milk chocolate are sucrose and certain mixtures of two or more of dextrose, dried corn syrup, dried glucose syrup, and sucrose wholly or partly refined.

In 1975, directives from the Council of the European Economic Community modified the standards for cocoa and chocolate products to allow up to 50% of the total weight of a product to be lactose without carrying a label declaration (Kube and Pritzwald-Stegman, 1976). If a cocoa or chocolate product contained 50% sucrose, 10% of the sucrose may be replaced by lactose. The use of lactose in the formulation requires no changes in the existing process. Lactose can be used as sucrose and may be used in conventional and modern processes without causing any problems (Kube and Pritzwald-Stegman, 1976). In standard recipes where only 5% of the sucrose was replaced by lactose, no taste differences were detected. In nonstandard formulas where 20% lactose replacement was used, decreased sweetness and increased bitterness occurred, but increases in flavor, snap and homogeneity were noted (Kube and Pritzwald-Stegman, 1976).

The hydrolysis of lactose into glucose and galactose by means of β-galactosidase yields a product which is sweeter and more soluble than lactose. Lactose has a maximum solubility of 18% at 25°C while the solubility of glucose and galactose is 50 and 43%, respectively, at 25°C. The blend of monosaccharides are two to three times sweeter than lactose. Therefore, if the lactose is converted to the monosaccharides either in milk, whey or in a whey permeate before the production of milk chocolate, a substantial amount of sucrose could be saved. The monosaccharides will readily enter into the Maillard reaction, and, where this is desirable, another advantage is realized.

3. Milk Fat

Milk fat is well documented as an important component in milk chocolate and will not be reviewed here. However, lipase-modified milk fat or whole milk changes the flavor of whole milk solids. Lipases hydrolyze the ester bonds of triglycerides, releasing mono and diglycerides and free fatty acids. It is the free fatty acids that provide aroma and flavor enhancing properties to milk solids.

When the lipolyzed dairy products are used in milk chocolate a rich, distinctive flavor is imparted to the product. Lipase-modified dairy products are not added to milk chocolate solely to create a strong milk flavor note. At low levels they round off or enrich the flavor, and at intermediate to high levels they yield a buttery or cheeselike flavor. In each case, products containing the lipase-modified milk solids do not carry the actual flavor of the fatty acid profile, but, instead, the profile modifies or enhances the total flavor (Ziemba, 1969).

VIII. SUGAR

Sucrose is a major raw material in chocolate. It is used in the crystalline form and represents about one-half of the formula weight. For chocolate, FDA standards permit sucrose (cane or beet), anhydrous dextrose (from hydrated starch), and dried corn sweeteners (Cook and Meursing, 1982). The primary source of sucrose in the United States is the raw sugar that is derived both from beet and sugar cane. In the United States more raw sugar is grown than is imported, and over half of the raw sugar is derived from beets. Highly refined sugar is used for chocolate manufacture, and, with this extent of refining, the source of either beet or cane sugar is hardly distinguishable (Minifie, 1980).

After the raw sugar is processed, the type that is destined for chocolate manufacture is graded according to particle size. Although other characteristics are of concern, such as color, sediment, ash, and moisture, the particle size indicates the grade. A finer sugar can be called "extra-fine granulated," and a more coarse sugar called "medium." There are no fixed size grades in the United States, and each sugar refinery may have its own standards (Pancoast and Junk, 1980). An example of an extra-fine granulated sugar is one with 95% of the particles passing through a 20 mesh (840 μm) screen and 3% through a 100 mesh (149 μm) screen. The sugar must be dry and contain no invert sugar or yellowish coloration that is evident in the "weak" sugars from the lesser developed processes (Lees, 1980).

At relative humidities below 60%, the equilibrium moisture content of sugar is low (<0.02%) compared to the other ingredients in chocolate. As the relative humidity rises above 60%, the moisture content of the sugar increases, approaching 0.1% water at 80% RH. In the storage of sugar, moisture is a serious concern (Pancoast and Junk, 1980). Humidity change causing a large moisture increase results in an eventual fusion at points of contact of the sugar crystals, which results in sugar lumping. Also temperature changes between the inside and outside of the silo can cause moisture migration from warm sugar to cold sugar causing lumping to occur either at the center of the silo or near the wall depending on whether the outside condition was warmer or colder, respectively.

While sugar is being processed into chocolate, the crystalline character can be affected such that an amorphous aspect develops to various degrees, mostly on the surface of the particles. If the sugar is dissolved in water or if it is initially in the form of liquid sugar, as the water is removed during the process the sugar can take on an amorphous form. When size reduction takes place during refining, there is some evidence that the energy needed to fracture the sugar causes a short-term surface temperature exceeding 1000°C (Niedick, 1975). It is suspected that the resulting surface is in the amorphous state. The sugar in this state tends to absorb a relatively large amount of water at any given humidity (Niedick, 1975). One test showed amorphous sucrose reaching a moisture content of over 5% at 40% RH. A "honey type" sugar resulted. The existence or absence of this surface phenomenon during processing can greatly affect the final properties of the chocolate (Niedick and Babernics, 1981). Further attention is given to this subject in Section XIII.

For certain processes liquid sugars may be desirable when it offers economic advantages. Liquid sugar is a syrup of a highly concentrated water solution of sucrose. Concentrations up to 67% are possible. Variations of liquid sugar in the confectionery industry could contain some invert sugar, but for the chocolate industry only sucrose is used.

IX. SWEETENERS AND BULK FILLERS

A. INTRODUCTION

Chocolate manufacturing is very dependent on sucrose (sugar). Since a dry sweetener is required, the advances in high fructose corn syrup technology that have revolutionized the manner in which many other foods are sweetened has not affected the chocolate industry. In fact, chocolate and confectionery may have become less cost competitive in the marketplace against other foods such as jams and jellies, bakery products, and carbonated sodas which benefit from sweetener flexibility.

There are other reasons for examining alternative sweeteners and bulking agents for chocolate, namely, health-related objectives (prevention of tooth decay, weight control, suitability for diabetics) and advertising claims ("sugar free"). A wide range of sweeteners and bulking agents will be examined briefly to understand how the properties of each relate to chocolate manufacturing, the health objectives, and, ultimately, to consumer acceptance.

B. NUTRITIVE BULK SWEETENERS

1. Sugars

a. Corn Syrup Solids. Corn syrup solids typically will contain 3–4% moisture. Since they have an amorphous noncrystalline character, they tend to be very hygroscopic. At 60% RH, a 42 D.E. (dextrose equivalent) corn syrup solid will absorb 10% moisture from the atmosphere in 24 hr (Pancoast and Junk, 1980).

Corn syrup solids have not been used extensively in chocolate for two reasons: (1) Moisture added to chocolate, either by ingredients or through absorption from the atmosphere, is difficult to remove. Higher chocolate viscosities require additional cocoa butter to maintain fluidity, thereby negating any cost savings achieved through partial substitution of corn syrup solids for sucrose. (2) Corn syrup solids with low D.E. values lack sweetness relative to sucrose. The Standards of Identity for sweet chocolate and milk chocolate in the United States allow dried corn syrup (with 40 D.E. minimum) as a partial sucrose replacement, up to one-fourth of the total saccharide content.

O'Rourke (1959) patented a process for a heat-resistant chocolate containing corn syrup solids as the preferential humectant. Mixing and refining steps were carried out under a controlled atmosphere (45% RH maximum). After molding, the chocolate was placed under appropriate conditions (such as 84°F and 88% RH) to allow water absorption, forming a heat-resistant structure.

b. Dextrose. Dextrose is commonly substituted for sucrose in many foods, but it has not been widely accepted by the chocolate industry. The phase diagram for dextrose indicates that there are three distinct crystalline types possible: α-monohydrate, α-anhydrous, and β-anhydrous. Dextrose hydrate is not satisfactory for addition to chocolate since it contains about 8.5% water and tends to release that moisture during refining or as the temperature approaches 50°C. The α type is the more common form of anhydrous crystalline dextrose. The method chosen for producing a crystalline product should preclude the formation of any glassy or amorphous dextrose which is extremely hygroscopic compared to the crystalline state. Spray drying, for instance, is particularly unsuitable for dextrose since a mixture of crystalline and amorphous types result. Over the years, numerous patents have been granted for manufacturing anhydrous dextrose, and it is commercially available.

The tendency for moisture absorption is an important characteristic that can interfere with normal chocolate manufacturing procedures. The critical environmental factors which can affect the moisture uptake are relative humidity of the surrounding air, temperature, and time of exposure. Dextrose is more hygroscopic than sucrose or lactose, but less than crystalline fructose (Pancoast and Junk, 1980, from data developed by Sokolovsky, 1937). The moisture content of anhydrous dextrose as received should not exceed 0.2%.

Flavor development by browning or Maillard reactions are much more likely to occur than with sucrose due to the reactivity of the free aldehyde group. Although dextrose is often reported to be only 0.6–0.8 times as sweet as sugar, it is possible to substitute up to 20% dextrose in many foods without noticing any sweetness loss due to the synergism between sucrose/dextrose mixtures.

Anhydrous dextrose has a cooling effect when it dissolves in the mouth, due to the negative heat of hydration (-14.5 cal./g.).

Unlike dextrose hydrate, the anhydrous form does not have a significant price advantage over sucrose under current market conditions. Anhydrous dextrose can be added to sweet chocolate and milk chocolate in the United States provided the level does not exceed one-third of the total saccharide content.

    c. Crystalline Fructose.   Fructose crystallizes only in the anhydrous form of β-D-fructopyranose, which is the sweetest of several anomers found in fructose solutions. Crystalline fructose is 1.7 times as sweet as sugar, whereas solutions have variable sweetness with lower potency, i.e., 1.0–1.5 times. Crystalline fructose has been used in chocolate and carob coatings, but the price has discouraged widespread use. It is very hygroscopic, similar to sorbitol, and requires humidity control (60% maximum) especially at the refining and conching stages.

Zimmerman (1974) has discussed chocolate processing requirements with fructose. More energy is required to grind fructose crystals, but if refined too far, the mass will thicken due to excessive surface area. Moisture uptake from the atmosphere or from ingredients, especially milk powders, must be avoided to prevent fructose agglomeration. Although the *Codex* standards allow up to 0.5% moisture in fructose, chocolate processors require 0.1% maximum as received in sealed containers. Chocolate containing fructose should be processed quickly with temperatures not exceeding 105°F.

Since fructose is a very reactive keto-sugar, flavor interactions occur much faster at lower temperatures than with sucrose. Formulas with 35% fructose are equally as sweet as 42–44% sucrose. This is helpful when using dry milk powders to achieve a richer milk flavor. Calories could be cut slightly (5–10%) in milk chocolate if a suitable bulking agent were available to substitute for sucrose. Fructose contains 4 calories/g and is absorbed at a moderate rate by facilitated diffusion. It may be helpful for some diabetics since blood glucose rises less than after ingesting sucrose and the initial liver metabolism is not insulin dependent.

    d. Sorbose.   L-Sorbose is about 80% as sweet as sugar and has a clean taste free of any off flavors. It crystallizes easily from solution and is not hygroscopic. As a keto-sugar, the chemical reactivity will be similar to fructose. Although known during the 1800s to exist in sorb apples and mountain ash berries, it is not a product of plant growth but rather is formed by bacterial fermentation in overripe fruit. Sorbose has been detected in fermented cocoa beans prior to roasting (Reineccius *et al.,* 1972a).

Ogunmoyela and Birch (1984a,b) reported that dark chocolate sweetened with L-sorbose compares favorably with the taste of traditional sugar-sweetened dark chocolate, can be produced without any major modifications to the chocolate process, has humectant properties similar to sucrose, and is unusually resistant to mold growth. L-Sorbose can be produced by the biochemical fermentation of sorbitol with bacteria such as *Acetobacter suboxydans* and is an intermediate in the commercial synthesis of Vitamin C.

e. Others

Type of sugar	Reference
β-Lactose	—
Isomaltulose	Bucke and Cheetham (1979)
Maltose hydrate	—
Fructose terminal oligosaccharides (coupling sugars)	Okada *et al.* (1972)

2. Polyhydric Alcohols

a. Sorbitol.   Sorbitol is widely used in diabetic chocolates as a sugar replacement. Since sorbitol is only 60% as sweet as sugar, these products are generally not considered sweet enough. Crystalline sorbitol has a cooling effect in the mouth when consumed. Formulas for diabetic chocolates tend to use less sorbitol or mannitol than standard chocolates containing sucrose, to minimize the laxative action of the sugar alcohols. Chocolate formulations containing sorbitol have been published by Riesen (1977) and by Griffin and Lynch (1968) from Lensack (1965).

Sorbitol is very hygroscopic and requires humidity control (50% RH maximum) especially at the refining and conching steps where moisture pickup is most likely to occur. The moisture level in the starting ingredients should be kept to a minimum as well. Minifie (1980) recommends 115°F maximum processing temperature to avoid undesirable thickening and warns against letting the chocolate sit undisturbed for any period of time as it tends to ''congeal'' or partially set. Moisture-proof packaging should be considered for diabetic chocolates with sorbitol.

b. Mannitol.   Mannitol is being used by some manufacturers in diabetic chocolates. The following comparison summarizes its relative merits versus sorbitol.

Advantages
1. Nonhygroscopic:Mannitol does not require humidity control in production areas.
2. Lower calorie content: Mannitol contributes only about 2.0 calories/g which is beneficial to diabetics.

Disadvantages
1. Higher Cost: Mannitol is more expensive than sorbitol since it can be

produced only in low yields by the reduction of fructose, invert sugar, or dextrose.

2. Poor tolerance: Mannitol is slowly absorbed and only partially metabolized (Nasrallah and Iber, 1969), leading to a laxative effect.

Mannitol is 60% as sweet as sugar and has a cooling effect.

c. Xylitol. Several xylitol reviews have appeared in *Advances in Food Research* and are listed for reference: Hyvönen *et al.* (1982), "Food Technological Evaluation of Xylitol"; Ylikahri (1979), "Metabolic and Nutritional Aspects of Xylitol"; Mäkinen (1979), "Xylitol and Oral Health."

Xylitol is a crystalline substance with sweetness equal to sucrose. Its cooling effect is the largest of any commercially available polyol. Xylitol is extremely promising as a sugar replacement for the prevention of tooth decay. It is also used for diabetics in Europe and has 4 calories/g. After adaptation, the laxative effects are very mild in comparison to other polyols. The major factor discouraging its use is the price. Production involves the hydrolysis of xylan from wood or corncobs to xylose followed by a reduction step.

Chocolates were prepared with xylitol for the Turku studies on dental health (Scheinin and Mäkinen, 1975). Sucrose can be replaced in a direct 1 : 1 relationship with no major problems. Chocolate containing xylitol was reported to have a lower viscosity. According to Dodson and Wright (1982), temperatures should not exceed 130°F during processing. The hygroscopicity of xylitol is low, and it can tolerate up to 80% RH conditions without significant moisture uptake.

d. Others

Type	Reference
Lactitol	Van Velthuijsen (1979)
Maltitol	Celia (1985)
Isomalt	Schiweck *et al.* (1975, 1980)

3. Amino Acids

Glycine is the only amino acid to be studied as nutritive bulk sweetener (Anonymous, 1983).

C. HIGH INTENSITY SWEETENERS

1. Artificial

a. Saccharin. Saccharin was discovered in 1879 and has been used for over 80 years as a sugar substitute, primarily in carbonated beverages and as a tabletop sweetener. It is 300 times as sweet as sugar but has a bitter, metallic aftertaste which some find objectionable.

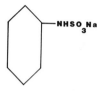

FIG. 7.   Structure of sodium cyclamate.

b. Cyclamate. The cyclamates were discovered in 1937 at the University of Illinois by Michael Sveda. The sodium and calcium salts of cyclamic acid are only 30 times as sweet as sugar, but the sweetness quality is considered quite good. In addition, they are heat stable, nonreactive, and dissolve easily in water (Fig. 7).

c. Aspartame. The intense sweetness of aspartame (Fig. 8) was discovered in 1965 by chemist James Schlatter at G. D. Searle. Subsequently, a patent was assigned to Searle covering use as a sweetener (Schlatter, 1970). Aspartame is 180 times as sweet as sugar and is virtually free of any off tastes. The sweetness character is outstanding and comes closest of any high intensity sweetener to matching sucrose. It is synergistic with many sugars and other intense sweeteners.

Production and purification patents granted to Ariyoshi *et al.* (1974) describe a method for linking the anhydride of L-aspartic acid with the methyl ester of L-phenylalanine in the α configuration. Aspartame can be degraded by three mechanisms into nonsweet compounds: deesterification of the methyl ester group, hydrolysis of the peptide linkage, and internal cyclization to form diketopiperazine. Whereas aspartame sweetness is readily lost in solution when heat is applied or the pH is unfavorable, it is quite stable in the dry state. Since chocolate is a fat system, aspartame is not likely to dissolve. Instead, it will be milled

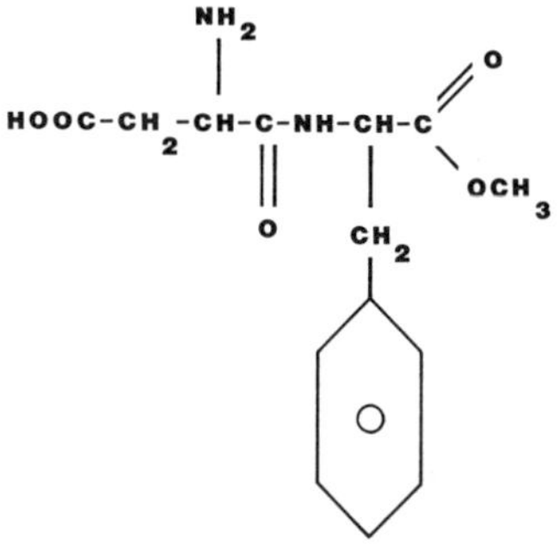

FIG. 8.   The structure of aspartame, α-L-aspartyl-L-phenylalanine methyl ester (APM).

into extremely fine particles uniformly distributed throughout the chocolate until it dissolves on the tongue, releasing sweetness. Aspartame has flavor-enhancing properties which could accentuate certain flavor notes in chocolate. In combination with a sugar or polyhydric alcohol, aspartame could provide a significant portion of the sweetness.

d. Sucralose. A new class of intensely sweet chlorosucrose derivatives was discovered by Tate and Lyle researchers in 1975. Hough *et al.* (1979) disclosed the structures and relative sweetness for several compounds. Attention has focused on 4,1′,6′-trichloro-4,1′,6′-trideoxygalactosucrose (referred to as sucralose), which is 600 times as sweet as sucrose. The manufacturer claims that sucralose has a good quality taste perception similar to sucrose, without any sweetness delay or unpleasant aftertaste. Several methods for synthesizing sucralose have been disclosed, but it is uncertain if a practical economic means of production has been identified. Long-term toxicity tests should be completed in 1985.

e. Acesulfame-K. Acesulfame-K is a high intensity sweetener patented by Hoechst in West Germany. Clauss and Jensen (1973) described synthesis techniques for oxathiazinone dioxides and pointed to the potassium salt of the 6-methyl derivative as a preferred sweetener. The name acetosulfam for this compound was later changed in favor of acesulfame-K. Sweetness is about 130 times sucrose and is perceived quickly, followed by a metallic taste. Clauss *et al.* (1976) reported on the chemical and physical properties and stability of acesulfame-K. It has excellent solubility in water and is very stable to heat and pH extremes typically encountered in foods. Acesulfame-K is expected to have a significant cost advantage over aspartame, suggesting its use as an extender.

2. Natural

a. Glycyrrhizin. Glycyrrhizin, extracted from the licorice root (*Glycyrrhiza glabra* L.), is the most familiar high intensity sweetener of natural origin. The ammonium salt (AG) is 50 times as sweet as sugar and has a delayed onset with licorice-like aftertaste. The flavor properties of ammoniated glycyrrhizin prevent widespread use as a sucrose replacement. It has been recommended as a flavor potentiator in many foods, including those which contain cocoa or chocolate. Morris (1967) demonstrated that cocoa levels could be reduced by 8–10% through the potentiation effect of ammoniated glycyrrhizin.

b. Thaumatin. Talin is Tate and Lyle's trademark for a protein sweetener extracted and purified from the fruit of a West African perennial plant *Thaumatococcus danielli.* Talin is an extremely powerful sweetener (roughly

2500 times sucrose) characterized by slow onset and lingering sweetness. Higginbotham *et al.* (1981) have studied the flavor enhancement properties of Talin and found that it lowers the threshold levels of many flavors (such as chocolate by a factor of two).

c. Stevia. Stevia rebaudiana Bertoni is a small perennial shrub native to Paraguay and Brazil that contains several related sweeteners in its leaves. Stevioside, the major component, is 200 times as sweet as sugar but has a bitter aftertaste and a slight sweetness delay. Rebaudioside A is a higher quality sweetener free of bitterness and with a potency of 350 times sugar (Morita *et al.*, 1978).

D. BULKING AGENTS

1. Sugar Replacement

a. Polydextrose. Polydextrose is a highly branched glucose polymer formed by the condensation of glucose and sorbitol with a citric acid catalyst (Rennhard, 1973). It was commercially introduced in 1981 by Pfizer as a nonsweet low calorie bulking agent suitable for replacing sucrose and a portion of the fat in many foods. There are two types, a dry, noncrystalline powder with some residual unreacted citric acid and a 70% liquid solution partially neutralized to pH 5–6 with potassium hydroxide. Since polydextrose is an amorphous substance, the powder is quite hygroscopic and should be stored at low relative humidity in a closed container to avoid moisture uptake. According to Torres and Thomas (1981), polydextrose will reach equilibrium at 10% moisture content when held at 52% RH and 25°C.

b. L-Sugars. Although D-sugars predominate in nature, some L-sugars can be found in small quantities; these include sorbose, arabinose, galactose, rhamnose, and fucose. A patent was granted covering the use of ten L-hexose sugars in foods (Levin, 1981). One of the biggest obstacles facing L-sugars is the development of a practical inexpensive synthesis. Some examples are given below to illustrate how L-sugars can be formed.

Sugars	References
L-Gulose	Hearon and Witte (1982) (L-gulono-γ-lactone can be chemically reduced to L-gulose)
L-Sucrose	Queens University, Kingston, Ontario (1979)
L-fructose	Mayo and Anderson (1968)

There has been little evidence generated to support the contention that L-sugars are nonnutritive, will retard spoilage, and do not promote tooth decay. Since D- and L-sugars are optical isomers, their physical properties are identical except for rotation of polarized light (Fig. 9). The chemical properties are identical except toward optically active reagents which are common in living organisms.

c. *Hydrocolloids.* Many hydrocolloids cannot be digested and are considered nonnutritive. However, they are not acceptable for replacing sugar in chocolate at levels above 5%. Whereas sugar readily dissolves in the mouth, many hydrocolloids thicken considerably as hydration commences. This imparts an unpleasant, sticky sensation in the mouth or throat and prevents a clean release.

d. *Others.* Several other types of potentially low or noncaloric bulking agents have been considered as sugar replacements: glucosylsorbitol (Layton and Vlazny, 1978), polysugar (Usmani and Salyer, 1979), and D-arabitol (Beereboom, 1979)

2. Fat Replacement

a. *Potential for Calorie Reduction.* In a typical milk chocolate formulation containing 32% total fat and 42% sugar, the major source of calories is the fat

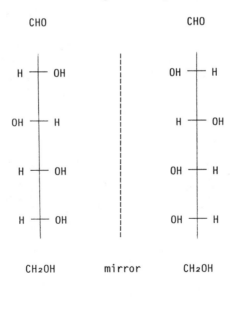

FIG. 9. Structure of glucose isomers.

(50%) followed by sugar (30%) and other ingredients (20% of total calories). Additional ways to reduce calories are (1) use less fat or (2) Find a noncalorie fat substitute.

b. Sucrose Polyester.   A patent on food applications of sucrose polyester (SPE) was issued to Mattson and Volpenhein (1971). SPE consists of a synthetic mixture of hexa-, hepta-, and octa- long chain fatty acid esters of sucrose and has taste, texture, and physical properties resembling conventional fats. There is no calorie contribution since intestinal enzymes are unable to utilize SPE. Thus, it is nonabsorbable. A concern with SPE is the possible loss of fat-soluble vitamins, especially vitamins A and E.

E. OUTLOOK

During the last 15 years, significant advances have occurred in both bulk-type and high intensity sweeteners. The introduction of high fructose corn syrup during the 1970s and aspartame in the 1980s represents a serious challenge to the established sugar market in a broad range of foods and drinks. The status of numerous other potential sugar replacements has been presented in this article. It remains to be seen which alternative sweeteners, if any, can have a measurable impact on the chocolate industry which has for years been closely associated with crystalline sucrose. Small amounts of crystalline fructose, anhydrous dextrose, sorbitol, mannitol, xylitol, maltitol, and β-lactose have been used around the world in specialized chocolate applications. Other potential bulk replacements such as L-sorbose, isomaltulose, lactitol, and isomalt, are nearing market introduction and could be considered for use in chocolate. The new high intensity sweeteners cannot be added to chocolate without first identifying a suitable bulking agent.

F. RESEARCH NEEDS

Additional research and development by sweetener manufacturers will be required to deal with many unsolved problems. Listed below are some examples where further efforts are likely to be focused.

1. Production of an essentially dry crystalline high fructose corn syrup which is not so hygroscopic as to be unsuitable for chocolate. The cost should be more similar to high fructose corn syrup than pure crystalline fructose.
2. Improved methods of aspartame production to reduce cost and increase supplies. New enzyme coupling methods and genetic engineering are among the approaches being studied.
3. Development of nonmetabolizable L-sugars.

4. Identification of a low or noncaloric bulking agent with little or no laxative effect.
5. An efficient technique for synthesizing sucrose from the components of high fructose corn syrup.
6. Clarification of the safety issues surrounding xylitol resulting from clinical studies.
7. Improvement in aspartame stability through new structures that may share features in common with other protein sweeteners.
8. Application of theories that explain why molecules are sweet such as the AH, β-γ hypothesis (Shallenberger and Lindley, 1977) which may lead to construction of entirely new sweeteners with computer assistance.
9. More interest in noncaloric cocoa butter substitutes.
10. Revision of legal standards for chocolate in each country to reflect availability of new sweeteners.

X. COCOA BUTTER AND CONFECTIONERY FATS

A. COCOA BUTTER

Cocoa butter is the fat obtained from the cacao bean or chocolate liquor. It can be produced by hydraulically pressing cacao liquor and is called "Prime Pressed." It can also be mechanically obtained by an expeller or a screw press, or it can be extracted with a solvent. Most commercial dark and milk chocolates contain between 30 and 38% total fat, most of which is cocoa butter, although in milk chocolate approximately 3.66–6% is milk fat.

Of all the fats used in the confectionery industry, cocoa butter is historically the most important, not only because it is the natural constituent of chocolates, but because it has been the standard to be imitated for many years. The main reason for its desirability is its unique melting characteristics. At normal room temperatures, below 26°C, it is hard and brittle, yet it melts rapidly and completely at the temperature of the mouth. The plastic range is also very short in comparison with other fats. This melting property is associated with the public perception of quality in chocolates.

The unique melting characteristic is due to a very simple fatty acid and triglyceride composition. The variability of the percentages in Table XX is due mostly to the climatic conditions at the time of the seed development, the growing location, and the bean variety. Palmitic (P), oleic (O), and stearic (S) account for more than 90% of the fatty acids in cocoa butter. They have the tendency to form specifically symmetrical triglycerides with oleic acid in the second position: POP, POS, and SOS.

The triglyceride composition of cocoa butter was originally reported by Hil-

TABLE XX

FATTY ACID COMPOSITION OF COCOA BUTTER

Fatty Acid	Carbon No.	Percentage
Lauric	C_{12}	0 – 0.1%
Myristic	C_{14}	0.1 – 0.2%
Palmitic	C_{16}	24.5 – 27.8%
Palmitoleic	$C_{16:1}$	0.2 – 0.4%
Stearic	C_{18}	32.1 – 35.6%
Oleic	$C_{18:1}$	32.2 – 38.6%
Linoleic	$C_{18:2}$	2.6 – 4.0%
Linolenic	$C_{18:3}$	0.1 – 0.2%
Arachidic	C_{20}	0.5 – 1.1%

ditch and Stainsby (1936) and later by Meara (1949). The main glycerides were believed to be 2-palmitooleostearin (52–57%) and 2-oleodistearin (18–22%). Lutton (1957) demonstrated later that the main triglyceride was 2-oleopalmitostearin or POS. Similar findings were also reported independently by Chapman et al. (1957). The more recent literature reports slightly different trygliceride values mainly due to the development of new chromatographic techniques; these values are usually expressed as a function of the symmetrical triglyceride fraction. Kattenberg (1981) reported a fraction of monosaturated symmetrical triglycerides ranging from 63.7 (Brazil) to 77.2% (Ivory Coast) with the following distribution: POP (16.5–16.3%), POS (46.2–46.4%), SOS (32.5–33.2%), others (4.4–4.8%). This system of reporting has been used by several researchers in the 1970s and 1980s as will be mentioned later. For simpler explanations, it is also reported directly: Jewell and Bradford (1981) reported POP, 14%; POS, 37%; SOS, 25%; others; 4%, which adds to 80%: Faulkner (1981) reported POP, 16%; SOS, 26%; "total Symmetrical," 82%.

Considerable research has been done on the crystallization properties of cocoa butter. Vaeck (1951a,b, 1960) reported an abstract of early works and his own efforts with four polymorphic forms of cocoa butter. Since then, Duck (1964), Willie and Lutton (1966), Chapman (1971), Lovegren et al. (1976), and Lovegren and Feuge (1965) have studied and identified six polymorphic forms; however, each one used a slightly different nomenclature for their identification. A comparison of these nomenclatures was done by Chapman (1971) and reviewed more recently by Manning and Dimick (1981) and Jewell (1981).

Lutton (1972) and Jewell (1981) have presented good explanations for the relation between the crystalline structure and the configuration of the fat molecule. When the POP, POS and SOS triglycerides are in a pure state, they will organize by superpositioning the oleic acid in the second position creating a stable crystal. If the amount of oleic acid was increased as little as 1%, the excess would have to occupy another position in the triglyceride, thus altering the crystalline structure and decreasing the melting profile of the butter. This is one of the causes for the so-called soft cocoa butters. This phenomenon would occur to some extent in the same growing location and in the same variety at different months of cacao production, as reported by Berbert and Alvin (1972), Lehrian *et al.* (1980), and Jewell (1981).

The melting characteristic of cocoa butter makes this fat ideal for confectionery, but it presents some difficulties during chocolate manufacture. The trade name for the proper crystallization of the fat in the chocolate is "tempering," and the lack of crystallization would result in softening of the product and a discoloration of the surface called "bloom." Tempering and bloom are further discussed in Section XV.

One important factor relating to cocoa butter technology has been the increasing knowledge of its composition. The availability of better analytical methods has facilitated this work, especially the analysis of triglycerides (Litchfield, 1972) and fatty acid distributions, which methodology has been officially accepted and revised by the American Oil Chemists Society (AOCS) (1969, 1981), the OICC (1973), and the International Union of Pure and Applied Chemisty (IUPAC) (1979). These methods have been evaluated by Herb (1968), Herb and Martin (1970), and Firestone and Horwitz (1979). Special methodology and discussion on applications for confectionery fats were presented by Bigalli (1981). Another major factor has been the growing awareness of scientists and technologists of the interplay of the structure of the symmetrical triglycerides, their physical behavior, and their functionality in the practical aspects of chocolate processing. Indeed, the understanding of cocoa butter structure and behavior is parallel to that of all other confectionery fats because the basic principle and applications are interrelated.

B. CONFECTIONERY FATS

Since the 1930s, there has been interest in using fats other than cocoa butter in confections; however, when a fat of different composition is added to cocoa butter, the crystalline form of the resulting fat is generally altered, producing a change in the melting profile of the fat. This change is called "incompatibility" and often is observed by softening or bloom in the product. The degree of "compatibility" is related to the proportion of the confectionery fat that can be added to cocoa butter (or vice versa), without producing the softening effect.

These fats other than cocoa butter were originally called "hard butters," but there is some confusion in the classification of confectionery fats. One very good compatibility chart was presented by J. A. Wolfe (1977). Depending on how hard butters are used, they can be *extenders,* when the fat is added to cocoa butter generally in proportions up to 15% (occasionally up to 50%); or they can be *replacers* when the hard butter is the majority of the fat and the cocoa butter originates from the cocoa powder. Hard butters are found in both types of formulations and the most compatible fats can work well in both types of applications. Minifie (1980) and Faulkner (1981), among others, divide these fats into *substitutes* when they do not have the symmetrical triglyceride configuration and *equivalents,* also called CBEs or cocoa butter equivalents, when the fats are composed of fractions of fats containing these symmetrical triglycerides.

1. Lauric Fats

Lauric fats for the confectionery industry are made from palm kernel oil, coconut oil, babassu oil, and several others. They contain between 40 and 54% lauric acid. A summary of the principles for the use of these fats was presented by Laning (1981). They were originally made to replace cocoa butter; however, with time they have been used in a number of applications based on their own merits. The manufacturers of these fats have created a wide variety of melting characteristics or solid fat contents by processing methods such as partial hydrogenation, interesterification, and fractionation. Lauric fats are not compatible with cocoa butter. Used as a cocoa butter extender or substitute, only very small amounts of this fat can be added without producing a eutectic effect which causes soft chocolates. This incompatibility has discouraged the addition of lauric fats to chocolate. However, they have grown in their own right as confectionery fats. As a replacer, fractionated lauric fats can be the main fat to be formulated with cocoa powder as long as the cocoa butter from the powder is no more than 6% of the total fat in the system. Other applications of these fats take advantage of the softening effect of the eutectic fat mixture for centers and creams, but most often they are used in nonchocolate flavor coatings. The detection of lauric fats in chocolate products is easily determined by the fatty acids distribution using lauric acid as the indicator.

2. Nonlauric Substitutes

Paulicka (1981) described nonlauric substitute (extender) and replacer fats as those made from oils like soybean, cottonseed, and peanut in the United States, and palm, oleic, or rapeseed oil in Europe. Corn, sunflower, and safflower oils could also be used. The desired physical characteristics are achieved by increasing the amounts of trans fatty acids. Indeed, most of the C_{18} acid in these fats is elaidic and not oleic acid. These fats are made by hydrogenation followed by solvent fractionation. The degree and type of process determines the quality, application, and cost of the fat. They can be made in a range of quality and compatibility to be used as extenders in small quantities, but they are most often used as replacers. They are detectable by their fatty acid distribution, especially the determination of trans acids or the elaidic to oleic ratio.

3. Cocoa Butter Equivalents

Fats made from symmetrical triglycerides that come from fats and oils other than cacao beans have received the name of cocoa butter equivalents or CBEs. They were developed by fractionation of palm oil from acetone solution. The manufacture was disclosed in British Patents No. 827,172 and 924,805. At present, they are produced from palm oil with or without addition of fats from other sources. Palm oil (from *Elacis guineensis*) can provide the POP and some POS but very little SOS, as was observed by Tan *et al.* (1981).

The main triglycerides of Illipe butter (*Shorea stenoptera* L.) are POS and SOS, and the minor constituent is POP. For this reason, it is considered the closest in composition to cocoa butter. A thorough study of this fat was presented by Bracco *et al.* (1970); however, the production of Illipe butter is very limited. Shea butter (*Butryospermum parkii*) contains SOS at 74% of the symmetrical triglycerides.

There are several plants that produce the above triglycerides in significant quantities. Bracco (1973) presented information about 14 of these fats. Each one of the three more abundant fats used in making CBEs has one dominant triglyceride: palm, POP; Shea, SOS; Illipe, POS. In all commercial CBEs, however, the final proportion of these triglycerides is neither equal to cocoa butter nor are they equal among themselves; for this reason, there are several levels of quality and compatibility. Manufacturers of CBEs provide fats that have quite different triglyceride composition. As an extension of Faulkner's report (1981), his company has published a summary of cocoa butter equivalents in which a comparison between the percentage of symmetrical triglycerides of two CBE butters is made with those of West African cocoa butter (Table XXI). This is a very good example of the possibilities that can be found commercially.

Since CBEs are produced from blends of fats from different sources, and because they are crystallized under each manufacturer's own expertise, they have several levels of quality, compatibility, and application. A more recent approach for the production of a cocoa butter equivalent has been by synthesis. In this method, the fat is produced starting with less expensive oils; the triglycerides are partially hydrolyzed and selectively reesterified with the unsaturated fatty acid in the second position. This technology has been disclosed by U.S. Patents

TABLE XXI

COMPARISON OF COMMERCIAL CBEs WITH COCOA BUTTER

	POP (%)	POS (%)	SOS (%)
West African cocoa butter	16	40	27
CBE No. 1	34	15	35
CBE No. 2	42	12	22

3,410,881; 3,808,245; 3,809,712; 3,809,711; 3,882,155; and French Patent 74 36995. Although laboratory samples have been made with promising results, production has not been brought to commercial realization.

Extender and replacer confectionery fats can be used legally in most countries, but product labeling differs from one country to the other. In the United States, only cocoa butter or milk fat can be added to dark or milk chocolate if the manufacturer wants to maintain the standard of identity for dark or milk chocolate; however, other fats can be added in any proportion if the product is not identified as dark or milk chocolate.

In the United Kingdom, it is possible to add a true CBE containing mostly symmetrical triglycerides in a proportion up to 5% of the total weight of fat and still retain the label chocolate. This situation generated controversy within the countries of the European Common Market, most of which have traditionally maintained a situation almost identical to that in the United States. The technical factors related with chocolate making are no longer a major issue. CBE triglycerides can be obtained from a series of natural sources and the fractionation technology is well developed. In practice, CBEs are only modestly cheaper than cocoa butter. The economic advantages might be more evident during years of poor cacao crops and uneven cocoa quality.

The potential advantage for the use of CBEs favors the application as cocoa butter improvers (CBI) in which the manufacturer would use these high quality, highly compatible symmetrical fats for the adjustment of the melting characteristic of the chocolate. This could have usage in enrobed products, in the correction of naturally low melting cocoa butters, and in products to be made for summertime distribution. Although these applications have general appeal, it cannot legally be done in chocolate with the present standard of identity in many countries.

One of the difficulties often mentioned with the use of CBEs has been their detection and quantitation; regulatory agencies in some countries have objected to the addition of fat that cannot be detected. In some instances, the differences between CBEs and cocoa butter are very small and there is no easy way to determine the proportion of added CBE with accuracy.

The determination of CBEs in chocolate became possible through the work of Padley and Timms (1979, 1980) and Fincke (1979, 1980). These methods were based on the analyses of intact triglycerides following the observations reported previously by Bracco et al. (1970). In a mixture of cocoa and Illipe butter, the ratio of C_{50} (carbon number of the triglyceride POP) to C_{54} (SOS) could be used as an index for characterization of the mixture. The method requires an elaborate calculation and a different correction value for each CBE; however, it can provide information of several levels of confidence (depending on the fat) at 5% CBE addition in the chocolate, although the results are less reliable at lower percentages. The new analytical methodology has been part of the considerations for the inclusion of CBEs in the standard of identity for chocolates in several countries, but no decision has been reached at the present time.

XI. EMULSIFIERS

A. INTRODUCTION

Emulsifiers or surface active agents can reduce chocolate viscosity by allowing the polar sucrose particles to exist within the nonpolar fat phase at a lower system energy than would normally exist without an emulsifier. Very much simplified, the polar moiety of the emulsifier is associated with the polar sucrose particles while the lipophilic moiety of the emulsifier interacts with the continuous lipid phase. In this manner, abrupt polar–nonpolar phase boundaries in the chocolate suspension are avoided by use of an emulsifier as a polarity buffering agent. With some emulsifiers such as lecithin which have electronic charges, electrostatic potentials between phases of different polarity are also reduced, leading to a lower overall system energy. As a result, the lubricity or slip of the sugar system is increased and the overall viscosity is lowered (Ziegelitz, 1982).

Emulsifiers typically have optimum concentrations in actual use; if the content of the emulsifier is increased beyond the optimum needed for viscosity reduction, the viscosity may begin to increase. In the case of lecithin, the reasoning visualizes the lipophilic ends extending into the fat phase becoming so numerous as to hinder the free movement of sucrose molecules in the fluid fat phase.

B. LECITHIN AND RELATED EMULSIFIERS

Commercial lecithin is almost entirely of soy origin and is extracted from the soybean by a succession of solvent extraction and precipitation steps (Szuhaj, 1983). It contains approximately 62–70% of acetone-insoluble phosphatides. The remaining 29–37% is primarily soybean oil or acetone-soluble constituents plus 1% moisture. Chocolates usually contain around 31% fat in combination with about 0.3% soy lecithin, a blend which gives about the same fluidity as a 36 or 37% fat content chocolate which contains no lecithin, thus saving 5–6% cocoa butter. The optimum amount of lecithin will vary with the initial fat and moisture content of the mass at the time of addition. The solids are sugar and ground cocoa in the case of dark chocolate, in addition to which in milk chocolate milk solids and perhaps milk fat are present.

Due to the presence of these irregular shaped particles, solid chocolate does not flow as a Newtonian liquid but rather exhibits non-Newtonian flow resistance properties having both an initial yield value and a plastic viscosity. Chocolate flow is greatly dependent on the ease with which the solid particles are able to move over and around one another within the liquid fat portion (Stisrup, 1970). Thus it becomes obvious that the incorporation of a surface active lubricating or "slip" agent such as lecithin will have a considerable effect on the fluidity of the mass. Chocolate with a tempered working viscosity suitable for molding or enrobing can thus be manufactured with a much lower cocoa butter percentage if lecithin is used.

The recognized optimum usage amount of 0.3% lecithin is not constant under all conditions. The moisture content of the chocolate has a considerable effect as well as the degree of particle/solids refinement. Generally, the higher the moisture content and the greater the amount of solids refinement, the greater is the need for lecithin. With soy lecithin, viscosity reduction in dark or milk chocolates ceases near the 0.5% addition level and further addition increases the overall viscosity. A level of about 0.2–0.3% is usually optimum for chocolate depending on formulation.

Chocolate has two separate rheological flow properties, both of which are required to describe its flow behavior. Yield value as expressed in dynes/cm^2 is that force which must be overcome in order to initiate flow. Plastic viscosity expressed in poise is that additional force required to sustain flow after the yield value has been surpassed. The equations derived by Casson (1957) and described by Steiner (1958) closely approximate the flow properties of chocolate, and Casson yield value and Casson plastic viscosity are typically cited to describe the flow properties of chocolate.

The effect of lecithin on each viscosity parameter has been previously described (Chevalley, 1975). Whenever high amounts of lecithin are used a thickening of the chocolate will occur where the yield value will increase with subsequent lecithin additions after having previously reached a minimum between 0.3 and 0.5% level of lecithin addition. Generally the plastic viscosity will decrease rapidly at low levels of lecithin addition, after which additional lecithin addition has markedly less effect (Minifie, 1980).

The manner in which lecithin is added to chocolate is quite important; generally the bulk of it is added during the late stages of the manufacturing process since intense shear and prolonged mechanical working may adversely affect the functionality especially when coupled with high heat. Normally as a mechanical processing aid, usually about one-quarter to one-third of the total amount of lecithin is added at the first ingrediation/mixing step; however the full functionality of this portion may be somewhat impaired due to subsequent process degradation. The remainder of the lecithin is added an hour or two before the end of conching which allows adequate time for its complete dispersion. Final viscosity adjustment should be completed with the addition of cocoa butter. Too early an addition of lecithin, as at the beginning of the conching process, may be detrimental because it suppresses the desired evolution of light acids and moisture which takes place during the early stages of conching.

Another emulsifier (Chevalley, 1975) which is classified as being highly efficient is YN synthetic phospholipid (British Patent 1,032,465) (Cadbury, 1966) which is being used extensively in Europe. The active portion of YN synthetic phospholipid is primarily a mixture of various phosphatidic acids in the form of their ammonium salts. YN does not have any adverse flavor effect in milk chocolate as does soy lecithin and has slightly better viscosity reducing powers; YN is also more constant in composition from batch to batch than is soy lecithin (Chevalley, 1975).

The viscosity reducing power of YN continues to the 0.8% addition level. YN also shows a greater viscosity reduction in the lower range of 0.1–0.5% addition compared to lecithin. Reportedly YN has a viscosity reducing ability about five-thirds that of soy lecithin (Minifie, 1980). Although YN has been used in Europe since 1962 and all evidence thus far has confirmed its freedom from any toxicity concerns, it is not yet approved for use in the United States as a lecithin substitute. A number of European chocolate manufacturers have changed from using lecithin to either straight YN phospholipid or a combination of YN and polyglycerol polyricinoleate; this combination surpasses the rheological advantages of lecithin alone without incurring the "off flavors" typical of high levels of lecithin.

C. POLYGLYCEROL POLYRICINOLEATE

Polyglycerol polyricinoleate (PGPR) was patented by Unilever (1955) (British Patent 723,244) (Chevalley, 1975) and has seen considerable use as an emulsifier for chocolates in Europe (Banford et al., 1970). PGPR has the ability of significantly reducing the yield value of chocolate. At the same time, however, PGPR minimally affects the plastic viscosity. If PGPR is used together with lecithin or synthetic YN phospholipid, it then becomes possible to manipulate both the chocolate yield value or plastic viscosity in a chocolate of constant fat content to obtain the best possible flow properties for a particular use.

PGPR appears to act or perform synergystically with lecithin. Usually the greatest reduction in yield value is produced not by either of these two emulsifiers alone but a mixture of the two which is dependent on the particular chocolate formula and process used. Usually a ratio 2–2.5 parts lecithin to 1 part PGPR is found to be optimum at a combined use level of 0.3 to 0.5%. The specific mechanism by which PGPR causes a reduction in the yield value of chocolate has not been sufficiently explained at this time.

D. OTHER EMULSIFIERS

Following is a listing and brief description of the other interesting emulsifiers evaluated by the chocolate industry:

1. Calcium—steroyl lactoyl lactate has a viscosity reducing effect similar to lecithin with little effect on the yield value (Stisrup, 1970).
2. Sodium dipalmitate when added to chocolate produces a high yield value and increases sag resistance for free form chocolates and for decorating chocolates (Chevalley, 1975).
3. Various hydrogenated fats have been tried specifically to manipulate the consistency/viscosity of chocolate coatings.
4. Sorbitan monostearate and Polysorbate 60 combinations have been used both as emulsifiers and for retarding the formation of fat bloom in chocolate.
5. Chovis compounds which bear a close resemblance to YN synthetic phospholipids were used for a short time in chocolate coatings (Minifie, 1980).
6. Other emulsifiers such as glyceryl (ol) monostearates are often added with lecithin to improve dispersion in confectionary products such as caramels and fudges as well as chocolate.
7. Another efficient chocolate emulsifier is diacetylated tartaric acid ester which affects primarily the yield value (Musser, 1980).

XII. MILK CRUMB

A. GENERAL

There is no government standard for milk crumb in the United States, but it can generally be described as "the product produced by the drying of an aqueous mixture of milk or milk product, sucrose or combination of sucrose with other sweeteners, and chocolate liquor, and/or other cocoa derivatives." Most commonly used chocolate crumb consists simply of whole milk, sucrose, chocolate liquor, and cocoa butter.

The use of milk crumb usually results in a rich, delicately flavored milk chocolate that is difficult to achieve by any other means. Various flavors can be developed, such as the caramelized European or English crumbs or the stronger buttery flavored American crumb; these are difficult to develop with the use of unreconstituted powdered milks. The flavor, stability, physical properties, and manufacture of milk crumb have been studied over the years, and many patents, processes, and uses have been proposed or developed. It is the purpose of this section to review the more recent developments in milk crumb manufacture and use. This section also should be prefaced by reminding the reader that milk crumb processing is normally the most proprietary operation of the overall milk chocolate manufacturing process. Therefore, a very limited amount of information is available through normal published sources.

B. FORMULATION VARIABLES

Common variables in crumb formulation include milk fat content, milk solids nonfat content, the milk form, cacao fat content, cacao solids nonfat content, the form of cacao product used, the sweetener content, and form of sweetener used. The milk fat content in milk crumb may vary from a very low level of less than 1% to a high level of over 12%. This is determined by the type and quantity of milk product used. British Patent 1,430,017 (Caverly, 1976) describes a crumb composition whereby skim milk is used in place of whole milk to produce a milk fat-free crumb to which a vegetable fat or additional cocoa butter is added in place of the milk fat. The milk fat content directly affects the melting characteristics and firmness of the resultant milk chocolate. By replacing the milk fat with a higher melting fat, a more resistant product can be produced which is better suited for hot, tropical climates. Conversely, a higher milk fat content produces a milk chocolate with better eating qualities for a colder climate.

The nonfat milk solids content in milk crumb may also be varied to range from a low of less than 20% to as high as 50%. Higher nonfat milk solids concentrations produce a lighter colored, milkier tasting product while low milk solids are used in darker color milk chocolates. In the United States and in Canada both the milk fat and nonfat milk solids contents in milk chocolate must be within a specified standard range to be legally labeled milk chocolate. All milk chocolate standards in the United States require at least 12% milk solids (*Code of Federal Regulations*, 1980). In regular milk chocolate at least 3.66% milk fat (by weight of chocolate) must be present, and the ratio of nonfat milk solids to milk fat must not exceed 2.43 : 1. In skim milk chocolate the milk solids can be made up entirely of nonfat milk solids. Since most or all of the milk solids would be supplied in the crumb, the crumb composition will vary accordingly.

The milk source in crumb manufacturing is usually in a concentrated form, either evaporated or reconstituted milk powder. Concentrating by condensing or evaporation, either with or without sugar, is the common practice in the United States, while reconstituting spray-dried milk to a concentrated form and mixing with liquid sucrose prior to processing is a common practice in the United Kingdom. This will be covered more thoroughly in Section XII,C. The source of cacao product used in crumb can also vary although chocolate liquor is most common. Cocoa powder and cocoa butter are also used in certain situations to achieve specific fat to cocoa solids ratios.

One of the major flavor reactions during many crumb processes is the Maillard reaction. This will be discussed in more detail in Section XII,D but is mentioned here because of two related patents which also affect formulation. The Maillard Reaction is a reaction of the carbonyl groups from a reducing sugar and free amino groups from the protein to form flavors ranging from a slight "cooked" or "toasted" note to a caramel-type flavor. A darker color also results in the crumb. Both British Patent 1,434,748 (Turos, 1976) and U.S. Patent 3,900,578 (Turos, 1975) cover a process whereby an amino acid such as lysine and reducing sugar such as dextrose are added to the liquid concentrate prior to processing. The resultant increase in Maillard reaction reportedly causes a more intense flavor in the milk crumb. However, the direct addition of an amino acid is not permitted under the U.S. Standards of Identity for milk chocolate. In addition to sucrose and dextrose, other sugars permitted in milk chocolate (and milk crumb) include lactose and fructose, as well as powdered corn sweetener.

C. PROCESSING VARIATIONS

The processing of milk crumb is the more important aspect of crumb manufacturing. The specific process type and conditions usually provide the uniqueness of various types of milk chocolates and, in fact, provides most of the advantages chocolate crumb milk chocolate has over other types of milk chocolate. It is the "process" rather than the formula that produces the significant differences in flavor between European, English (or Irish), and American milk chocolates.

1. Conventional Processes

Conventional methods of milk crumb processing include (1) drum drying, (2) melange, (3) vacuum drying, and (4) oven drying. These processing methods have existed for many years and account for a large percentage of the milk crumb manufactured around the world.

All methods of crumb processing begin with condensed or evaporated milk in a concentrated form. Many chocolate crumb manufacturers purchase fresh fluid milk direct from the farmer/producer or from a farmer-owned cooperative. This milk usually undergoes the traditional fluid milk processing used by the fluid milk industry. This includes cooling, clarification, pasteurization, and standardization to a given fat and total solids ratio. The milk is then evaporated either with or without sucrose to a concentration similar to commercial condensed milks. In the United States the usual solids are 71–75% for sweetened condensed milks and 26–30% for unsweetened condensed milks. Up to this point processing usually takes place in state-of-the-art dairy equipment including continuous multiple effect evaporators. However, it is at this point that most processes differ to produce the uniquely different types of milk crumb.

At this point in the process the sugar is usually added if it has not been added to the fluid milk prior to condensing. The sweetened condensed milk is then further condensed to approximately 90% solids in either a continuous high density evaporator or in a batch-type evaporator. The chocolate liquor is usually mixed with the condensed milk to form a heavy paste. This is accomplished in a number of ways but traditionally was accomplished in a melange.

The traditional melange method of crumb manufacturing involves continued mixing and working of the paste while heat is applied. As moisture is driven off the paste gradually changes from an oil-in-water paste to a water-in-oil crumb. As melanging continues the crumb becomes dryer until it approaches the dusty stage. At this point it may pass through a higher temperature dryer to reduce the final moisture to approximately 1% or less. The crumb may then be ground into a fine powder or refined into flakes and stored until needed for milk chocolate manufacturing.

The oven drying method is another traditional method used primarily in Western Europe and the United Kingdom. The paste may be placed in shallow pans and dried in a vacuum oven or it may be placed on a continuous band and dried in a continuous vacuum oven. One such method involves baking in trays at 220–225°F for 7.5 hr (Hynd, 1970). In both processes the moisture is reduced to less than 1%, and the bricks or lumps must be broken or ground into a powder. Obviously the flavor of the crumb is affected by the temperature and time of the drying process and varies by manufacturer according to the flavor desired in the individual type of milk chocolate.

The paste may also be dried on a rotary, continuous drum dryer. In this processing method a much less viscous milk concentrate is required. Usually the final condensing state is eliminated and the 75% solids concentrate is pumped directly into a trough feeding the dryer. A thin, even layer of condensed milk is spread over the hot, rotating drum. Usually after one-half revolution the film is dried to less than 1% moisture and is scraped off the drum surface by a stationary knife blade.

A variation of the rotary drum drying process involves the use of reconstituted milk powder (Lench, 1973). Granulated sugar is dissolved in water to form a syrup which is then mixed with milk powder and butterfat in a high speed mixer. The mixture is then cooked in a vaccum cooker to reduce the moisture content and develop the Maillard reaction to produce a slight caramelized flavor. Chocolate liquor is then added to form a paste which is dried on a specially designed double roller vacuum drum dryer. A rotary drum dryer is utilized to achieve the final moisture content of less than 1%.

2. Spray-Drying Processes

British Patent 1,306,356 (Veltman *et al.*, 1973) describes a unique spray-drying process for producing an improved milk crumb. Advantages of this process are claimed to be savings in time and energy and a resultant crumb with less flavor deterioration by caramelization and oxidation. (Note that some crumb processes utilize these reactions as flavor advantages.)

The process involves both a solid and liquid phase. The liquid phase comprises the total crumb ingredients in an aqueous solution that can be atomized through a spray-dryer nozzle. This atomized liquid is sprayed onto a solid phase which is carried past the atomizer nozzle in a current of heated gas. The solid phase is comprised of dried milk crumb which is partly recycled. Therefore a continuous operation results in steady-state conditions using a recycle product having the final crumb composition as the sole solid feed and using a liquid feed having the desired final crumb composition plus additional water. Both nozzle and centrifugal-type spray dryers can be used. The process is also covered in the United States by Patent 3,702,252 (Veltman *et al.*, 1972).

A second type of spray-dry crumb process exists in the United States by use of the Filtermat-type dryer (Damrow Company, Fond du Lac, WI). This dryer operates by spraying a solution of the final milk crumb composition plus water into a current of heated gas. The atomized particles are partially dried in the chamber, then fall to a moving, continuous belt filter where a foamlike mat is formed. Subsequent hot and cold air is forced through the mat of milk crumb particles to complete the drying process. The dried bed or mat of crumb is then mechanically removed from the filter and pulverized or ground to the desired size. Both of these spray-dried processes are of recent invention, and the author is unaware of any commercial installation utilizing either process at this time.

3.   Other Crumb Processes

A unique continuous crumb manufacturing process was developed and patented in the United States in the late 1970s. This process and equipment necessary to apply it are covered by U.S. Patent 4,086,371 (Minifie and Czyzewski, 1978) and 4,267,703 (Minifie and Czyzewski, 1981). This process is known as the Groen continuous milk chocolate crumb system and is now installed commercially in at least three countries.

This method is illustrated in Fig. 10 and involves a four-step process (Christianson, 1976). Step 1 is premixing and preheating the aqueous feed. Normally the aqueous feed consists of either sweetened condensed milk or reconstituted dry milk, sugar, water, and chocolate liquor standardized to 71% total solids and preheated to 160°F. Step 2 consists of pumping the premix into a dual jacketed, vertical scraped surface heat evaporator. The total solids increases from 71 to 94% during this step. Residence time in the evaporator is 3–6 min and, combined with a discharge temperature of 255–285°F, permits sufficient progression of Maillard reaction to produce a pleasant caramelized flavor. Step 3 is a vertical rotor/stator crystallizing unit that has intermeshing blades in a progressively narrowing annular gap. The volume of air space inside the crystallizer is large compared to the volume of product and results in cooling, sugar crystallization, and additional moisture removal to 1.5–3.0%. Step 4 is the final drying, and the type of dryer is dependent on the percent final moisture desired. The finished crumb can then be stored as is or pulverized to a specified particle size. This

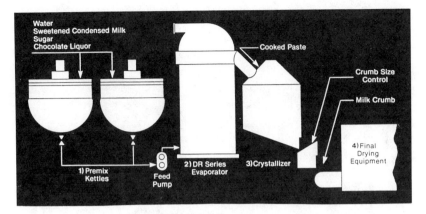

FIG. 10.   The Groen continuous milk chocolate crumb process.

method is one of the few commercially proven improvements in milk crumb manufacture during the last 10 years.

A second unique method of milk crumb manufacture is the Carver–Greenfield process which is described by U.S. Patent 3,076,715 (Greenfield, 1963). Although this process has not yet been proven commercially, it has been demonstrated on a pilot scale and appears to be very unique in relation to commerical crumb processes. It has been used commercially in other segments of the food industry.

A simplified explanation of the Carver–Greenfield Process for milk crumb manufacture is to fluidize 50–75% concentrated sweetened whole milk with liquid cocoa butter or a mixture of cocoa butter and milk fat similar to the ratio normally found in finished crumb. Chocolate liquor may also be mixed in if a final milk crumb formula is desired. This mixture is then pumped into an evaporator operating under a high vacuum where the moisture is removed. The mixture leaving the evaporator is a suspension of dry solids and oil. The essentially moisture-free fluid mixture is then centrifuged to remove the oil. The dry powder can be stored or immediately used in milk chocolate manufacturing. This system is illustrated in Fig. 11. The process is revolutionary and truly unique in that it (1) produces a crumb under low temperatures, (2) it allows almost total crystallization of the sugars, and (3) it produces a crumb that is basically non-hygroscopic. These three advantages are not generally true of spray-dry processes, but the product has similar properties to milk crumb produced by traditional processes.

A third type of unique "crumb" manufacturing process is described in U.S. Patent 3,622,342 (Rusoff, 1971). This process is simply a method of utilizing all dry ingredients and, therefore, differentiates from all other processes, in that minimal moisture removal occurs. The process comprises an initial dry blending

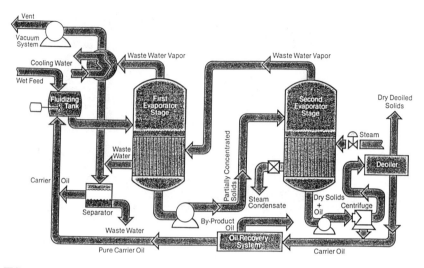

FIG. 11.   An illustration of the Carver–Greenfield process utilizing multiple effect evaporation.

of sucrose or other sweeteners, whole milk solids or nonfat milk solids, and chocolate liquor to form a dry mixture. This mixture is then passed through an extruder with the addition of a small prescribed amount of water. The extruder temperature is between 220 and 270°F, and the product residence time in the extruder is 1–3 sec. The extrudate is then cooled and comminuted to form the desired crumb compositions. This process obviously utilizes a minimum of equipment and space and eliminates the problems associated with liquid handling and processing of a perishable ingredient such as fluid milk.

D.   FLAVOR DEVELOPMENT

Very little work has been published on the flavor development of various crumb processes. However, it is generally understood that certain chemical reactions contribute to specific processes and types of crumb. The Maillard reaction is perhaps the most common flavor reaction in milk crumb although it is not prevalent in all crumb processes. It is very temperature dependent and usually is a major flavor contributor in the higher temperature processes. Therefore, it may or may not be a factor in a specific process, depending on the temperatures used in the drying phases of the process.

The Maillard reaction is a rather complex group of reactions that may occur under varying conditions. However, a very simplified definition is the sequence of reactions that initiates with a reaction between a free amino group (of an amino acid, peptide, or protein) and a glycosidic hydroxyl group (of a reducing sugar). The reaction terminates with the formation of brown melanoidins which are associated with a pleasant caramelized flavor. This reaction is most commonly associated with European and English-type milk chocolates produced by traditional crumb processes. Of the newer processes the Groen process utilizes this reaction as a major flavor source.

A second type of flavor reaction associated with specific processes is the lipid oxidation reaction. This is the classical breakdown of unsaturated bonds in fat by oxygen. The reaction results in a lard or cardboard-type flavor which by itself is offensive but when combined with other flavors produces a characterizing flavor in certain types of milk chocolates. This flavor is most usually associated with English or Irish-type chocolates and may be a result of the crumb process or crumb storage. Use of reconstituted whole dry milk powder to manufacture crumb can also result in this flavor.

A third type of flavor which is often associated with American and Canadian-type chocolates is produced by the lipolysis of the milk fat (Woo and Lindsay, 1980). This reaction is usually the result of action by a lipase enzyme on the milk fat triglycerides to cleave free fatty acids. This reaction usually results in a very milky, buttery, or cheesy flavor. This reaction is prevalent in American-type chocolate but is not common in European-type chocolates. Many other flavor reactions occur during milk crumb processing but these three are presented as examples of the most common characterizing flavor reactions.

E. ADVANTAGES OF MILK CRUMB

The advantages of milk crumb in milk chocolate manufacture can be summarized in four terms: (1) flavor, (2) storage potential, (3) economics, and (4) cocoa butter usage. The greatest advantage is obviously the flavor that is difficult to develop in a milk chocolate by any other commercial means. However, milk crumb can be stored for long periods of time with minimal deterioration relative to storing dried milk in other forms. This permits the manufacture of milk crumb during the flush milk season when prices are lower. It also permits milk crumb to be shipped virtually around the world as an export or import product. The economics of the crumb process can be claimed to be favorable or unfavorable depending on the process involved and the individual situation. Nonetheless, it is generally favorable when items such as cocoa butter usage and improved sales due to better flavor are considered. Finally, milk crumb usually requires less cocoa butter to produce a quality milk chocolate than spray-dried milk. This may be due to the crystalline form of sugar and the free fat content of milk crumb.

XIII. REFINING

A. PURPOSE

The primary purpose of the refining step is to accomplish a size reduction of the particles in the chocolate mass (Cook and Meursing, 1982). Refining is performed after the ingredients have been mixed together and usually precedes the conching step. After refining, some of the cocoa butter still remains to be added, and usually all of the lecithin is not yet present. The chocolate mass, sometimes referred to as "crumb," is in a rather dry or nonliquid state.

Presently refining is accomplished either by roll refiners or by employing ball mills. The former is the more commonly used method for refining chocolate, while many consider the ball mill to give a finer grind, and more suitable for cocoa liquor grinding. During the refining process some emulsification is accomplished. The result is a more thorough distribution of cocoa butter covering the solid particles. Some flavor effects occur. One aspect of flavor development involves the interchange of flavors primarily due to reactions with the surface of sugar particles. It is theorized that amorphous surfaces are created as the sugar particles fracture, and these surfaces are highly reactive to flavor interchange (Niedick, 1975).

During refining the chocolate is subject to the physical forces of shearing, crushing, abrasion, and attrition (Lees and Jackson, 1975). To produce the required smoothness and texture in the final product the particle sizing must be controlled to produce a certain particle size range, but in practice this is often stated as the percentage of particles below a certain micrometer size. For production control purposes a popular technique is to use a thickness micrometer to indicate the size of the larger particles below which 80–90% of all the particles may be represented.

In the United States, the micrometer reading of chocolate tends to be higher than elsewhere. In the United Kingdom the chocolates have micrometer values of 20–30 μm (0.02–0.03 mm), while on the Continent the values are 15–22 μm (Lees and Jackson, 1975). Too fine a particle size or micrometer reading, such as 15 μm causes a sticking to the palate. It is generally agreed that discreet particle sizes below 20–25 μm cannot be detected by the palate.

B.   OPERATION

1.   Ball Mills

Ball mills, sometimes called attritors in the chocolate industry, usually contain a vertical mixing shaft and are filled with metal balls that are up to 6 mm in diameter. As the mixer rotates, the balls impact against each other and crush any intervening particles. The liquor or chocolate that is being ground is circulated externally and recycled through the mill until the desired fineness is achieved. These mills are more often used to grind liquor rather than chocolate, due to the tendency to produce ultrafine particles.

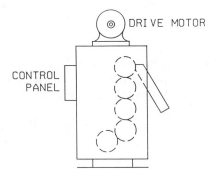

FIG. 12.   Five-roll refiner.

2.   Roll Refiners

Roll refiners usually contain five steel rolls although some three-roll refiners are being used in smaller operations. The rolls are mounted on a horizontal axis and each one is positioned in close proximity to the next roll to permit transfer of the chocolate from roll to roll. In Fig. 12 a side view is shown to illustrate the relative roll positioning. The rotational speed increases from roll to roll, and the final or top roll rotates at speeds approaching 500 rpm. The stepwise reduction of particle size is believed to effect a narrow size distribution. As the chocolate moves from roll to roll a shearing and crushing action takes place in the gap between roll pairs. In Fig. 13, the relative reduction in particle size at each stage is illustrated. The chocolate enters the bottom roll where it is fed into a dam and

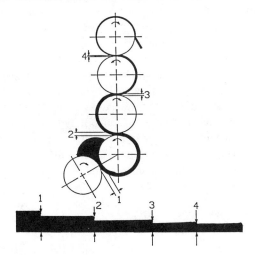

FIG. 13.   Stagewise grinding with five-roll refiner.

moves upward to finally discharge from the top roll with the aid of a scraping knife.

The first generation of five-roll refiners employed a mechanical force that was exerted between rolls to keep the rolls pressed tightly together. The adjustments were made with handwheels on the front of the machine. The latest generation of refiners uses hydraulic force to maintain roll pressure. Pressure settings for each side permit fixing of the pressure between any pair of rolls or on some models controlling the pressure on the top three rolls against the fixed second roll while another setting controls the pressure of the first against the second roll. The temperature of each roll is automatically controlled by water fed to the inside of the roll. Roll temperatures do not differ appreciably from the handling temperature of the chocolate. It is, however, important for product uniformity to hold the roll temperatures constant.

In order to effect a transfer of chocolate from roll to roll a speed increase must occur between each roll pair such that the first roll speed may be 30 rpm while the fifth roll speed would be 300 rpm (Fincke, 1965). The exact ratio of speeds between any two rolls depends on the viscosity characteristics of the chocolate and the amount of grinding that is desired. The first transfer point may have a roll speed ratio of 3 : 1 while the last transfer point might be 1.4 : 1. If the chocolate is relatively low in viscosity, offering little counterpressure within the roll gap, a lower ratio may be desirable at the first transfer point to avoid overgrinding and reduced refiner output.

In some cases improvements are possible by employing refiner rolls in a two-stage system. If there is a sugar pulverization step upstream, this can be omitted and a refiner used to do the initial size reduction. Thus the particle size can be brought down from around 400 to about 150 μm in this "prerefining" step. It is claimed that less fines (below 10 μm) are created and a higher output can be obtained from the following secondary refiners. Also, the prerefiner serves to accomplish some kneading, thus reducing the required mixing time upstream.

Ordinarily, the output of a refiner that is 1300 mm wide is over 700 kg/hr of a 25-μm paste. For a coarser grind such as 35 μm an output of over 900 kg/hr is possible. Lately the large refiners have widths of up to 2500 mm and correspondingly higher outputs. The usage of modern hydraulic refiners began in the 1950s, and they are manufactured by Bauermeister, Buhler, Carle & Montanari, Lehmann, and Thouet, all from Europe. A ball mill is employed in separate processes sold by Bauermeister, Lehmann, and Wiener, and includes a mixing and conching vessel.

3. Other Methods

In the McIntyre conche described in Section XIV, the particle size of the chocolate is reduced by the action of blades mounted on a central rotating shaft that impact against a peripheral stationary wall that is machined in a ratchet-like fashion. In this batch operation, ingredients are mixed, refined, and conched in the same vessel. In the Mosimann process (also described in Section XIV), an air jet pulverizer is used to reduce the particle size of the chocolate. High air movement causes particles to impact against each other and then fragment (Mosimann, 1963). These processes are not known to be used in large production situations.

Future processes have been visualized that use preground ingredients, thus obviating the need for refiners or ball mills (Timme, 1984). Yet, more manufacturers are featuring ball mills in processes aimed at smaller product volumes. Others visualize larger five-roll refiners having more sophisticated features that will eventually include particle size control by automatic roll pressure adjustment based on optical particle size measurement of the chocolate on the top roll.

C. PRODUCTION OF AMORPHOUS SUGAR

Reference to the production of amorphous sucrose (and amorphous lactose) during the chocolate refining process has been described by Niediek (1975, 1977a,b). Initially the existence of sucrose in the amorphous state in chocolate appeared derived solely by inference as supporting scientific evidence in the chocolate literature was marginal; later, however, Niediek referenced the 1956 work of Markower and Dye (Niediek and Barbernics, 1980), describing the existence of amorphous sugar itself and its hygroscopic properties.

It was claimed that on milling sucrose, amorphous sugar ($\sim$3%) was produced which absorbed available moisture and subsequently recrystallized, the excess moisture being desorbed in the recrystallization process. Of fundamental importance to the chocolate manufacturer was the suggestion (Niediek, 1977a) that aromatic flavor components absorbed onto the surface of the amorphous sugar and presumably remained during subsequent sugar recrystallization.

In a subsequent publication, Niediek (1977b) reported a 100-fold increase in the reducing sugars glucose and fructose as a result of grinding sucrose within a fat carrier. It is suggested that these reducing sugars can interact with the proteins of flavor components, presumably developing durther desirable flavor(s) in the chocolate. In this process of sucrose grinding, Niediek states that amorphous sugar can absorb 100 times as much moisture as would crystalline sugar. Reference is again made to the strong flavor absorption and retention properties of amorphous sugar wherein 2% by weight of vanillin can be absorbed.

Considerable skepticism concerning the actual production and existence of amorphous sucrose in chocolate processing exists, and is perhaps reinforced by frequent mention of the highly unstable, transitory amorphous state. The extreme hygroscopicity of amorphous sucrose with its ability to absorb water present in other chocolate ingredients or from a humid atmosphere leads to rapid sucrose recrystallization; hence it is difficult to actually measure the presence of the amorphous state during actual chocolate manufacture. However, in more recent publications by Niediek (1982; Niediek and Barbernics, 1980) considerable information is presented describing the properties of amorphous sucrose in great detail; this recent information has reduced some of the earlier skepticism concerning the existence of amorphous sucrose in chocolate processing, although, lacking a means of direct measurement for the amorphous sucrose, some claims remain highly inferential in nature.

Recently Chinachoti and Steinberg (1986) quantified the amorphous state of sucrose using X-ray diffraction of starch-sucrose mixtures which had been subjected to absorption and desorption of water. The hysteresis observed is due to the presence of amorphous sucrose. Of direct interest and applicability to the chocolate industry is the work of Mathlouthi *et al.* (1986), wherein the use of differential thermal analysis allows both qualitative and presumably quantitative assessment of amorphous and crystalline sucrose. One now has a potentially convenient and rapid tool to characterize the state of sucrose in the chocolate manufacturing process.

XIV.   CONCHING

The conching process traditionally has been carried out as a separate step, usually after refining, and can involve over 72 hr of treatment. The treatment is largely mechanical, in which the chocolate is subject to physical action of rollers, paddles, or a variety of rotational mechanisms. Flavor variations can be produced depending on the temperature, degree of agitation, and amount of exposure to air or other gases. The treatment has been predominately a batch operation in which from 2 to 50 tons of chocolate are processed. Numerous chemical and physical reactions take place, and the chocolate develops characteristics of increased smoothness and mellowing of flavor.

The process evolved from the ancient Mexican practice of hand grinding cocoa beans between a roller and curved plate. In the early 1800s the Bozelli grinding machine mechanized the process (M. G. Reade, personal communication). The more modern reciprocating conche dates back to 1879, and the design is attributed to Rudolph Lindt of Switzerland. A reciprocating roller worked the chocolate over a granite bed. The overall shape resembled a conche shell, thus the inception of the word "conche." Modifications of the original conche are still used and are called "longitudinal" conches.

A.   PHYSIOCHEMICAL REACTIONS

Research is presently being carried out throughout the world to gain a better understanding of the specific changes that take place during conching. At least 39 compounds have been identified that experience a change in concentration. Actually there are hundreds of compounds that have been identified in cocoa products (Cook and Meursing, 1982). From the physical standpoint there is a degree of deagglomeration that takes place along with some rounding off of rough particle edges of cocoa and sugar (Hoskin and Dimick, 1980).

Emulsification is enhanced as the individual particles of sugar and cocoa are more completely surrounded by cocoa butter, thus imparting a smoothness or favorable texture to the chocolate. Some of the more volatile components such as water and acetic acid are evaporated. Water concentration changes during conching have been seen to correlate with flavor development (Mohr et al., undated). Finally, the removal of water is necessary, not only from the flavor development standpoint, but in many cases to effect an improvement of the chocolate flow characteristics so that it can be more easily handled in the subsequent molding and enrobing steps.

Acetic acid, which may be present at concentrations as high as 0.15%, is a major acid in chocolate. It is evaporated during conching, but more is continually formed probably due to oxidation of aldehydes, ketones, and alcohols (Hoskin and Dimick, 1979). There has been a range of opinion as to the role of the acetic acid and other free fatty acids in respect to flavor contribution (Bartusch, 1960; Cook, 1976). Recent documentation showed little change in the volatile fatty acid concentration of chocolate throughout conching, though there is some loss reported at higher temperatures with intensive mixing (Dimick and Maniere, 1977). When the conche was covered, with reduced oxidation, the free fatty acid concentration was slightly lower. Loss of astringency during conching also has been attributed to the reduction of phenolic compounds as well as total volatiles (Lehrian et al., 1978). Volatile compounds that were found to diminish in the space above the chocolate mass during conching were pyrazines, esters, aldehydes, furans, alcohols, acids, and others.

During conching nonenzymatic temperature-dependent reactions are occurring involving amino acids, peptides, and glucose. Also other kinds of flavor reactions occur producing Strecker aldehydes, furans, pyrroles, pyrazines, etc., in the form of heterocylic compounds (D. Ley, personal communication).

The role of air or other gases is not clearly or universally established. Some experimenters have seen more favorable results with respect to flavor when the chocolate contacted air as opposed to nitrogen or vacuum (Aastad, 1941; M. G. Reade, personal communication). Undoubtedly more rapid moisture removal can be effected by increased contact with a gas or using a vacuum.

B. PROCESSING CONDITIONS

Variables that are involved in conching are time, temperature, aeration, and agitation. There are no exact conditions that are agreed upon as being best. Each chocolate manufacturer will develop a set of conditions which produce the particular flavor and texture that is desired in the product. Also the conditions required for conching are affected by the particular chocolate formula as well as the type of cocoa beans that are used and the manner in which the beans are roasted. The conditions will differ depending on whether the chocolate is dark chocolate or milk chocolate. In the latter case the processing will be different if milk powder is used as opposed to condensed milk (Cook, 1976). Also there are different requirements for whole milk powder versus nonfat dry milk. Conching requirements will vary depending on the degree of pretreatment that the milk and other ingredients receive.

Flavor development occurs to various degrees in crumb processes preceding the conching step. Thus, the following conche treatment may only contribute a minor benefit in respect to flavor although textural development is quite important. The requirements of a conche step can be minimal, as with some milk chocolates, or can be more exacting such as when a relatively strong-flavored dark chocolate is being processed. Some experts feel that, prior to conching, if a relatively high bean roasting temperature is used, there is not much which can be done in regard to flavor development during conching. Strong roasting produces limited free amino acids, reducing the possible extent of subsequent Maillard reactions (D. Ley, personal communication).

The time requirement for conching will depend on the extent of ingredient pretreatment and on the final flavor and quality of the chocolate; thus conching can vary between minutes and days. Generally the conventional longitudinal conches process chocolate from 1 to to 4 days. The more modern rotary conche processes run from 8 to 24 hr. Many manufacturers, particularly in Europe, operate conching in stages; there is an initial dry stage, at a fat content of ~24%, an intermediate plastification, and a final liquefaction stage, where the final fat addition is made. The purpose of the dry stage is to permit mechanical friction to assist in reducing agglomerates, improve particle coating, enhance flavor interactions, and to promote volatization of unwanted components.

Operating temperatures as high as 80–100°C are used for dark chocolate, while milk chocolates are conched at lower temperatures, usually between 45 and 60°C. The upper limit for processing milk chocolate pastes is determined by the extent of caramel-type flavor that is desired. Also, above 60°C physical changes occur with the milk protein that can affect flavor and texture. In many cases the chocolate temperature is allowed to rise naturally due to the frictional heat of conching and then controlled after an optimum temperature is reached.

As mentioned above, the role of air in the conching process is elusive, although most experimenters feel that a certain amount of air contact is important and most of the presently-manufactured conches allow for a certain amount of chocolate to air surface exposure. Since there are stages during conching when different parameters become important, there is probably one period in the conche cycle when air contact is more important than in another period. A more rapid loss of moisture and other volatiles can take place if a relatively large amount of chocolate surface is exposed to air.

During conching a certain amount of motion is important since it aids in the smoothing process, enhances sorption phenomena and flavor reactions, and provides surface for volatization (Mohr *et al.*, undated; Bartusch, 1960). The agitation occurring in the longitudinal conche is relatively moderate in intensity although some manufacturers regard the "slapping" action after each stroke an important feature. Most modern conches employ a rather intensive physical working of the chocolate, which is believed to contribute to a shortening of the conching time requirement. There are practical limits to the benefits of increasing the shear stress on the chocolate; there are periods during conching when it is more beneficial, and other periods when it is less beneficial.

C. TYPES OF CONCHES

The longitudinal conche is still in considerable use throughout the world. With this conche there are compromises between the demands of mixing, kneading, and homogenizing. Even to this day many manufacturers feel that their best quality chocolate can be made only in a longitudinal conche. Certainly if one regards the conching process as a flavor "mellowing" and physical smoothing step, it is understandable how the longitudinal conche came to be regarded as the ultimate process for producing quality chocolate. However, this belief does not necessarily have a sound scientific basis, and more research is being done in industry and in academia to clarify the function of conching and to better understand the changes that are occurring.

Documented technical concerns about conching and the longitudinal conche date to 1941 when Aastad questioned the waste of power by the longitudinal conche. He spoke of other types of conches but knew of none that produced an improved flavor. Others have questioned the efficiency of the longitudinal conche, and researchers have more recently compared rotary conches with the longitudes; a quantitative comparison does not clearly favor one over the other (Minifie, 1980). The decision lies in the precise flavor and texture that is desired and the time and power that is required.

1. Longitudinal Conche

The capacity of the longitudinal conches has usually ranged from approximately 0.25 to 5 tons of chocolate). Some conches were known to have a capacity of almost 50 tons. Reciprocating arms move rollers back and forth across a bed at a rate of 20–30 strokes/min. The bed can be flat or grooved and usually contains chocolate mass to a depth of 30–45 cm (Cook, 1976). There are often two opposing conche compartments so that the central drive system between the two conche halves can operate in physical dynamic balance. The rollers are approximately 750 mm in length, and there can be one or several rollers across each compartment; then there can be several rollers in each line in the perpendicular direction. Both the rollers and the bed have been made of granite; in some cases one or the other has been metal.

The longitudinal conches generally do not have cooling jackets as do the modern rotary conches. Some chocolate manufacturers cover their conches; others do not. A factor which led to the acceptance of the rotary conches was that the longitudinal conches were not as amenable to operating in an initial dry stage mode. The better designed, higher powered drive systems of the rotary conches handled the dry conching step with ease.

2. Rotary Conches

The rotary conches now available possess features that promote a more rapid conching process. Energy or shear can be applied to the chocolate at much faster rates. The conching times vary from as low as 15 min to about 24 hr. Usually the process takes 8–24 hr. Beside the generally more intensive shearing of the chocolate, some conches provide aeration, kneading, and rolling. Capacities of the batch conches range from about 1 to 12 tons.

The major feature of the rotary conches is one or more mixing blades or plows that are mounted either on a horizontal or vertical drive shaft. The mixing speeds range from about 10 to 50 rpm for the batch conches and up to several hundred rpm for continuous conches. The revolution rate usually is controlled at a slower rate in the early stage of the conche cycle, and the speed is increased as the chocolate becomes less viscous. Finally, when lecithin is added to aid in viscosity reduction and a final addition of cocoa butter is made, the speed is generally at a maximum. Following is a description of current rotary conches.

a. Babcock Gardner (Formerly Tourell Gardners Ltd.).   Originally manufactured by the Tourell Company in collaboration with Cadbury, the Babcock Gardner conche is a continuous process that conches chocolate in less than 3 hr. These conches are primarily noted for use in chocolate crumb processes, such as the Cadbury process in England (Powell, 1970). There are three, four, and, recently, five stages of horizontal mixing and in some cases, depending on the chocolate produced, one or two vertical mixing stages. The first two stages contain two mixing shafts on a horizontal line with each other, and the next stage(s) contains two mixing shafts on a vertical line with each other. Mixing speeds can be as high as several hundred revolutions per minute. The chocolate flows by gravity from stage to stage until the third stage, after which it is pumped to succeeding stages. In Fig. 14, a system is shown with four horizontal stages.

The beginning stages are operated in a dry state where the cocoa butter content may be 24–27%. In the later stages, possibly in a final vertical stage, the chocolate is thinned by the addition of lecithin and cocoa butter. The current trend is away from using the vertical stages.

FIG. 14. Babcock Gardner (Tourell) continuous conche. Courtesy of Babcock Gardner, Saint Blazey—PAR, Cornwall, England.

b. Carle and Montanari. The Clover 60 handles 6 tons of chocolate in the dry state where the fat content is below 27%. After the chocolate is liquefied by the final cocoa butter addition there is a corresponding increase in the final weight of the batch. There are four interconnecting compartments with a corresponding vertical mixer. The mixer has a low speed of 14 rpm and a high speed of 28 rpm. On top of the conche is a conical granite bowl within which three conical granite rollers rotate, to provide a smoothing or delumping of the chocolate. This action is referred to as a ''longitudinal effect'' since it is regarded as a circular version of the longitudinal conche. The chocolate is continuously circulated up through the rollers, recycling the complete conche in about every 30 min. The conche is depicted in Fig. 15.

c. Frisse. The largest standard Frisse conche, the DUC-6, has a dry capacity of over 13,000 pounds. Three horizontal mixing blades are arranged in separate but interconnecting cylindrical troughs, the outer two having a smaller diameter than that of the center trough and rotating faster than the center blade.

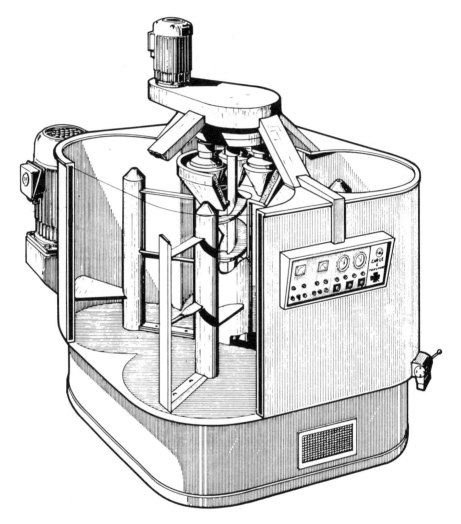

FIG. 15.   Carle and Montanari Clover conche. Courtesy of Carle & Montanari, Hackensack, New Jersey.

The conche action is called "double overbeating." The mixing action is reversed and speeded up after the dry and plastification stages are completed so that the front end of the mixing blade makes a more blunt angle with the liquid chocolate while initially the blade face contacted the more dry crumb at a sharper angle (see Fig. 16).

Frisse recommends a three-stage operation starting with "dry" conching at 24–27% fat. In this stage the temperature and power use rise until, after 2–6 hr,

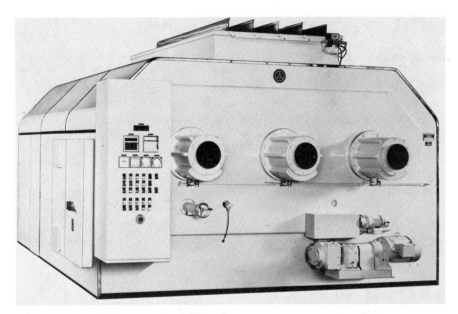

FIG. 16. Frisse DUC conche. Courtesy of Richard Frisse, Maschinenfabrik, Herford, West Germany.

the power peaks and the moisture drop becomes significant. The second, plastification stage sees the temperature reach a maximum. Finally the mixing speed is increased, then lecithin and cocoa butter are added as the chocolate temperature is lowered. At the top of the conche there are dampers which can control the amount of natural exhaustion or air circulation in the head space.

d. Konti Conche. A continuous conching process was developed at the Dresden University in combination with the VEB machine factory at Heidenau and called the HSG or high shear gauge process. The particular equipment, called a Konti Conche Type 420, was designed for high shear treatment. The process is comprised basically of two stages, represented by vertical columns containing mixer blades in a rotor–stator arrangement. A low-fat chocolate is fed to the bottom of two parallel columns along with conditioned air. High shearing forces are transmitted to the chocolate. Lecithin is added near the top of the column. There are intermediate sections for air disengagement and fat addition before a final homogenization step. The nominal output of the conche is 1000 kg/hr. The treatment time is approximately 15 min.

e. McIntyre Conche. Several companies are selling a conche that at one point was referred to as the McIntyre conche, produced originally by Low &

Duff Ltd. The batch size is relatively smaller than for other conches. A combination of grinding and conching occurs, as a mechanism on a horizontal shaft, which contains flexible plates, rotates against a peripheral serrated surface.

f. Lloveras. The MOLA 4000 roughly resembles the Carle and Montanari conche, but has three vertical mixing chambers and upper stone cylinders through which the chocolate is recirculated. It has a dry capacity of 12,000 kg. Another conche marketed by Lloveras is called the Mura conche. It is designed for semiliquid conching and medium outputs. In a double-jacketed cylinder, a horizontal axle is mounted, containing shovels that are inclined to suspend the mass while it is swept by a large air flow. The largest capacity is the 6-ton Mura 6000.

g. Petzholdt. The PVS 5000 Super Conche has a capacity of 5000 kg of crumb charge. It features a vertical rotor along with a centrifugal spraying disk. The rotor comprises a wall and bottom scraper and an inclined-face stirrer that produces a three-dimensional stirring action. A "dry" conche stage is recommended at the beginning, and a lower speed can be used. Later, after plastification, the flavor and texture refining are carried out by circulating the chocolate through a central uptake pipe through the spraying system. The spray disk traveling at a peripheral speed of approximately 12 m/sec creates an average droplet diameter of about 1 mm, thus effecting a surface area generation of around 5000 m^2 as the entire content of the conche is circulated five to seven times per hour.

Petzholdt recommends the above conche for traditional chocolate processing but also promotes an alternate process called the Luwa–Petzholdt process. This process employs a thin film roasting and treatment of liquor followed by an intensive mixing process where other ingredients are added. This step contains dual vertical mixing units that feature a pair of intermeshing worm screws and an inclined mixing plow (Fig. 17). The homogenization and texture development occur in this step while much of the flavor development can be carried out in the previous step, where milk powder can be treated along with the cocoa liquor. The entire process employs another thin film treatment step and final flavor refinement with a second intensive mixer.

h. Thouet. The Thouet conche contains two large horizontal mixing compartments with a smaller lower interconnecting compartment. In some respects it resembles the Frisse conche. Three stages of operation are recommended: dry working, plasticizing, and liquefying. The largest standard size is the DRC-12 which has a dry capacity of 12,000 kg.

i. Wiener. The Wiener chocolate process combines mixing, grinding, and conching in one compact plant. Chocolate ingredients are charged to the conche

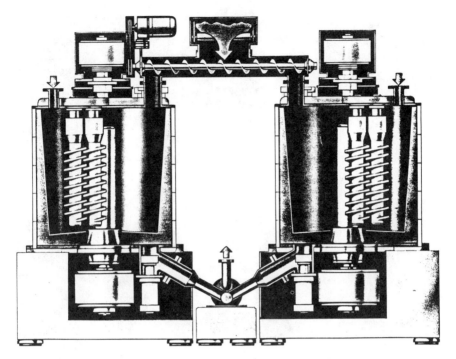

FIG. 17.   Petzholdt intensive "Veredler." Courtesy of Petzholdt, Frankfurt, West Germany.

unit for mixing, and then the mass is circulated through an attritor (ball mill) and back to the conche. After the desired particle size is reached the circulation is discontinued, and the conching process operates similar to other batch processes. The conche contains a spinning disk at the top that is called a "taste changer." The process requires 8–24 hr and can produce up to 24 tons in 24 hr. The Wiener plant is depicted in Fig. 18.

j.   Bauermeister.   The Bauermeister conche has a tilted configuration. The latest model has two intersecting compartments with separate mixing systems. Each mixing system contains a blade that rotates to wipe the wall, while a more robust paddle contributes a strong mixing action. The drive system is positioned so that the shaft enters the bottom of the conche. Presently, Bauermeister manufacturers a system called the Production Plant SHA 5000, with a throughput of up to 5000 kg in 8–16 hr. The system contains a ball mill in a circulation system with a horizontal conche tank. A two-roller mill is mounted on the top of the conche through which premixed ingredients are fed. The latter mill serves to reduce circulation requirements through the ball mill. In the top of the conche there is a centrifugal disk to spread the paste into a thin layer providing shear

FIG. 18.   Wiener process. Courtesy of Wiener & Co., Apparatenbouw b.v., Amsterdam.

stress and contacting with preheated air. Lecithin is automatically added, based on circulating pump pressure.

k. Lehmann. As in the case of the Wiener and Bauermeister systems, the Lehmann plant also uses a ball mill in a circulation system with a conching device and mixing tank. The "conche" is a jacketed, thin-film reactor with a vertical shaft by which intense agitation is applied as the paste circulates through the unit. Deaeration is accomplished by evacuation from the top of the thin-film unit. The largest unit, an EMA 40, will process 4000 kg in 8–12 hr.

l. McCarter. The only manufacturer in the United States that produces a machine that is marketed as a conche is McCarter. The machine is called a Pugmill Conche; the twin horizontal shafts operate at two speeds, 16 or 37 rpm, and batches up to 12,000 lbs can be processed.

D.   OTHER CONCHE SYSTEMS AND PROCESSES

1.   Conches

In addition to the conches listed above which are actively being marketed, there are others which in some cases represent the early generations of rotary conches, but which are still useful and part of existing chocolate processes in various parts of the world. Two examples that are used for partial or total conching are (1) the Suchard conche: this is a relatively small volume conche, usually with an open top and with a vertical shaft that plows the chocolate in a rotary movement; and (2) the Mikrovaerk conche: this is also a relatively small volume, closed conche with warm air blown into the bottom. Two vertical shafts mix the chocolate. Residence time is relatively short.

2. Processes and Treatments

Various processes or treatments have been patented or proposed that affect the cocoa bean and other ingredients such that a conching step as such is not needed. The following processes are not known to be in widespread use.

a. The Mosimann Process (Mosimann, 1963; Anonymous, 1965). In the Mosimann process, as proposed, toasted cocoa nibs are first pulverized; then, along with sugar, milk powder, and cocoa, the mixture is continuously and automatically dosed to a jet mill. Here further pulverization and refining take place. Next the cocoa mass is classified in a cylone. A plastification step then uses a Buss Ko-Kneader. Prior to the final refining, homogenization is performed in a horizontal cylinder with revolving blades. Next an ''aeration'' step is carried out in several stacked cylinders into which the mass is sprayed, and a vacuum removes undesirable gases. Finally an ''ultrason'' treatment uses high-frequency oscillations to accomplish a ''refining'' that reduces or eliminates the need for conching.

b. The B.F.M.I.R.A. Continuous Chocolate Manufacturing Process (Elson, 1971; van Veen, 1971). The B.F.M.I.R.A. process is a continuous process for plain (dark) chocolate and claims to eliminate the need for conching. The process emphasizes the importance of roasting for flavor development. Chocolate liquor is roasted either in a batch or a continuous process. The latter process employs a scraped surface heat exchanger to heat the liquor before spraying into a chamber to achieve moisture removal. Then a tubular heating unit is used to roast the liquor to approximately 140°C for 9 min. The liquor is then sprayed into a tower where undesirable flavors are volatilized. Next sugar and fat are added in a continuous mixer. There is a refining step, and the final ingredients (lecithin, flavoring) are added prior to a treatment with a high shear rate mixer.

c. LSCP Process. The patented LSCP process was developed during the 1960s by Lindt and Sprungli in collaboration with Gebrüder Buhler A.G. Experiments showed that both dark and milk chocolates can be made, without conching, with resulting flavors which are hardly distinguishable from that with standard processing (Kleinert, 1971). The cocoa nibs are treated by the LBCT cocoa alkalinizing method with the intention of removing unpleasant constituents in the early processing stages, and at this time to carry out the necessary flavor-producing reactions. The other ingredients are also treated in a reactor such to effect the desired flavor results. The entire mixture is then roller refined and given an intensive mix in a "plasticizer."

   d. Ultrasonic Conching.   An early conche system developed by Nordenskjold and Holmquist employed an ultrasonic treatment.

3. Other Manufacturers

Nearly all of the conching processes used today originated in Europe or England. Some other of the early manufacturers of equipment or those who developed processes are Aastad, Beetz, Droste, Heuze, Malevez and Simon Reunis, Hildebrand, and Lauenstein.

XV. TEMPERING

A. RATIONALE

The process by which cocoa butter is solidified from the molten fluid state is commonly referred to by the term "tempering." Fat "tempering" means "to develop seed crystal or nucleate with temperature control while mixing to uniformity" (Reade, 1980). The aim of this preliminary nucleation is to set the fat phase of the product as homogeneously as possible and with the smallest fat crystals so that the finished product has a good gloss, hard snap, slow finger meltdown, and no tendency to bloom. The only material which tempers or changes its structure in the chocolate mixture or coating is the cocoa butter and/or total fat phase (Kleinert, 1969). Different fats have different mixtures of glycerides which result in varied solidification and melting characteristics. Cocoa butter is normally completely solid below $-10°C$ (14°F) and completely melted and free from residual crystals at 42°C (107.6 °F) or above (Kleinert, 1969).

   If the cocoa butter portion of a chocolate has solidified evenly and homogeneously with small crystals of the β' or stable β polymorphic form, which has the lowest remaining energy level, this will result in a fairly stable chocolate which will undergo a minimum amount of latent crystal heat change after initial solidification. If certain principles are not followed, the final chocolate will solidify in a crystal matrix which will undergo further dynamic change in terms of latent heat release, resulting in a shortened and unsatisfactory product shelf life (Kleinert, 1969). Thus, polymorphic transitions of fats occur from a less stable to a more stable form.

   A well-tempered fat or chocolate of primarily β' and stable β crystal form normally has set up with small crystals less than 1.0 μm in size (Cruickshank and Jewell, 1977), usually between 0.5 and 1.0 μm; whereas poorly tempered chocolate consisting of major portions of unstable, γ, α, and β″ crystal forms contains larger crystals from 1.0 to 2.0 μm. Such chocolate has a coarse, streaky, and inhomogeneous structure, has a softer texture, less heat resistance, plus it exhibits a high tendency for fat bloom.

From a physical or structural viewpoint, the initial crystallization is seen as developing in a three-dimensional network which solidifies the mass and provides a large internal surface area on which the remaining liquid is able to crystallize. The finer the network of crystallized fat, the quicker the chocolate will be fully crystallized and the smaller will be any pockets of liquid which remain. This is a benefit as it limits the availability of the remaining liquid fat for growth of large unstable crystals. Physically it is quite apparent that larger crystals will result in a more coarse, unstable, and dispersed crystal network which will have adverse latent properties (Duck, 1970).

It is commonly thought that the solidified crystal network is completed by the time the solidified product exits from the cooling tunnel. However, in actuality further crystal addition (normally from 1.0 to 5.0%) to the initial solidified framework takes place for the next 3 or 4 days before the chocolate stabilizes. In summary, tempering serves to transform the fat phase in melted, fluid chocolates and coatings into a solid form of low latent heat content consisting of small dense crystals which yield products with good gloss, good snap, a certain amount of plasticity, and most of all good shelf life and flavor retention.

B. THEORY OF TEMPERING

In 1951, Vaeck, using a capillary melting point tube technique, first characterized the various solid crystal polymorphic forms of cocoa butter, naming them with Greek letter names given similar pure fat compounds by earlier workers (Duck, 1964). Vaeck (1960) showed that the most unstable form was the γ form which melts at 17.8°C (64.0°F). This form has a lifetime of 1 min or less after which it spontaneously changes to the next most unstable or α form. The α form melts at 23.6°C (74.5°F). If this form is held for about 1 hr at just under its melting temperature a third spontaneous form which Vaeck called the β″ appears. The β″ form melts at 28.1°C (82.5°F) and appears to have a lifetime of about 1 month, changing to the β′ form. The β′ form melts at 33.1°C (91.5°F) and is the highest form of unstable crystal. However, it has the same physical size as the stable β form, 1.0 μm or less. The existence of this β′ form was implied by Vaeck; however, he was unable to prove the existence of this form with his melting point technique. However, between 1961 and 1964, the existence of the β′ form was confirmed (Duck, 1964) from viscosity determinations of the solid fat in partially solidified chocolate and from dilatometry studies.

Work by Steiner (1963) with mixtures of two pure cocoa butter triglycerides

TABLE XXII

COCOA BUTTER CRYSTAL TEMPERATURE RANGES

Crystal type	Existing temperature range	Melting point
γ	<17.8°C	17.8°C (64.0°F)
α	17.9–23.6°C	23.6°C (74.5°F)
β″	23.7–28.1°C	28.1°C (82.5°F)
β′	28.2–33.1°C	33.1°C (91.5°F)
Stable β	33.2–34.4°C	34.4°C (94.0°F)

showed that the polymorphic forms described by Vaeck for cocoa butter are the result of both polymorphic behavior of the triglyceride components and the phase (packing) relations of the triglycerides present in cocoa butter. It was concluded that the β′ form was a fifth polymorphic form with a 33.1°C (91.5°F) melting point. A temperature of 30.1°C (86.2°F) is the temperature at which both β and β′ crystals grow at the same rate during seeding.

Thus, from the original work done by Vaeck plus that of W. Duck, there are five practical polymorphic forms of cocoa butter which actually exist within overlapping temperature ranges with each having generally recognized melting or fusion points as shown in Table XXII. These crystal forms can easily be identified from differential scanning calorimetry (DSC) thermograms. Over the years several researchers have stated that six polymorphic forms of cocoa butter actually exist; however, this claim is still subject to question. Although these reported six forms are interesting, for practical in-plant evaluation of "real world" fast moving tempering conditions, the five forms suspected by Vaeck and recognized by Duck (1964) and Duross and Knightly (1970) have repeatedly proven useful and valid.

C. AUTOMATIC CHOCOLATE TEMPERING

Of the various methods of tempering which have been developed, the three-stage continuous process has proven to be a practical significant advance throughout the chocolate industry for commercial tempering operations. In the three-stage (or zone) process, completely melted fluid chocolate is preconditioned from about 41°C (105.8°F) to about 32°C (89.6°F) in the first stage, and lowered to about 27–27.5°C (80.6–81.5°F) in the second seeding stage, while being mixed continuously. In the final reheating or third stage, the chocolate is carefully warmed beyond 28.1°C (82.5°F) to a delivery or depositing temperature which varies between 29 and 31°C (84.2–87.8°F) depending on the type of chocolate (milk chocolate or dark chocolate). At temperatures above 28.1°C

(82.5°F) in the third stage, the crystals of the unwanted unstable γ, α, and β crystals have been melted so that the remaining cocoa butter contains a majority of β' crystal with a small amount of stable β crystal present.

D. NON-COCOA BUTTER FATS

Today there are a number of commercial cocoa butter equivalent or cocoa butter substitute fats available to the confectioner of both the lauric and nonlauric type. These vegetable fats do not exhibit the classic polymorphism of cocoa butter with its five or six forms of crystal. A variety of fractionated and hydrogenated fats can be and are derived from a basic oil stock such as palm kernel oil. In a refined commercial form these vegetable fats crystallize into a single crystal β' equivalent fat structure without the formal tempering required for cocoa butter-based chocolate. The final melting points of the solidified crystal obtained from these type fats normally falls in the β' temperature range of 28.2–33.1°C.

E. EFFECTS OF BUTTERFAT, LECITHIN, AND OTHER EMULSIFIERS ON TEMPER

Fats other than cocoa butter are occasionally added to chocolate. Although of animal origin, one fairly compatible fat that is widely used is butterfat, which does impart a degree of bloom resistance to the milk chocolate (Korfhage, 1967). It is added in varying amounts and does not change the polymorphism of the cocoa butter. However, free butterfat does affect the rate of cocoa butter crystallization slightly and softens the final set or hardness of temper.

Whenever increasing levels of milk fat are added to cocoa butter, one of the most marked effects is a reduction in the amount of total fat which will solidify. Milk fat is relatively soft with a melting point of about 90°F. During the tempering and subsequent solidification of finished paste into hardened milk chocolate the milk fat sets up in its own crystal network interdispersed within the network or framework of the cocoa butter crystal. Lecithin and various types of other emulsifiers also produce an inhibiting effect upon crystal set and/or hardness.

When free butterfat or lecithin is present, the tempering of milk chocolate requires a slight overall lowering of controlling temperatures (about 1–2°F). Milk chocolate formulas employing spray-dried milk, wherein the butterfat is not free, will temper almost like a dark chocolate, and the final "hardness of set" will approximate that of nonmilk chocolate. A considerable lowering of the melting point will occur whenever 30% or more total milk content with free butterfat is introduced into a particular chocolate formula (Jewell and Bradford, 1981).

F. FAT BLOOM AND ANTIBLOOM AGENTS

Chocolate bloom is an abnormal growth form of the stable β fat crystal which forms as a result of latent crystal heat changes, partial melting, and/or the dissolving and transport action of liquid oils moving to the chocolate surface which penetrate the solid cocoa butter matrix. If conditions are such that a fairly slow rate of crystal growth then occurs, a majority of the cocoa butter will recrystallize in stable β form. The slow change from β' to stable β form allows abnormally long needlelike β crystals to grow and protrude from the surface in an erratic manner. Abnormal stable β crystals developed via transport and slow bloom growth exhibit typical crystal sizes of about 4–5 μm which diffuse incident light, giving the bloom a white appearance on the chocolate. Bloom then is a product of slow crystal growth emanating from untempered or detempered fat which allows the freed liquid cocoa butter to migrate toward areas of growing crystals whereby fat-rich and fat-deficient zones develop within the mass and on the surface. Normally developed stable β crystals for which a proper tempering procedure has been employed usually have a small crystal size of less than 1 μm. Milk fat and lecithin are known for their bloom-moderating effects in chocolate. In addition a variety of surfactants can be and are used in chocolate to prevent fat bloom. The most common are sorbitan tristearate, sorbitan monostearate, and polyoxyethylene sorbitan monostearate.

Sorbitan monostearate inhibits the ability of the liquid fat fractions to migrate to the chocolate surface as they undergo monotropic transformation from less stable to the most stable β form of crystal. As the crystals transform from one polymorphic form to the next most stable, they temporarily liquify due to the released heat of fusion and migrate to the surface by capillary action via the cocoa solids, sugar, powdered milk solids, etc. Sorbitan monostearate has the ability to form a monolayer on the cocoa solids, sugar, etc., which impedes the mobility of the migratory cocoa fat by reducing its ability to creep by capillary action across the milled and shredded fibrous solid material of chocolate. In studies cited throughout the literature, a 1.0% surfactant level of a 60/40 blend of sorbitan monostearate and Polysorbate 60 is most commonly given as the optimum level to prevent bloom. The Polysorbate 60 improves the dispersibility of the sorbitan monostearate throughout the chocolate.

However, one major drawback occurs with the use of these types of surfactants. It is also known that chocolates containing 1.0% of the 60/40 surfactant blend do not temper or crystallize in the normal time when the usual tempering conditions established for same chocolate containing no surfactant are used. Although these surfactants do add bloom resistance they significantly inhibit the crystallization of the total cocoa butter fat phase and soften the final set. The tempering or crystallization temperatures have to be lowered to 27°C (80.6°F) or below before normal crystallization rates can be obtained; even at this low temperature the crystallization rates are reduced. Temperatures lower than 27°C are undesirable as larger amounts of unstable type crystals will develop during seeding.

G.   EVALUATION OF TEMPER WITH DSC

Differential Scanning Calorimetry (DSC) is now a widely used technique for the performance study of cocoa butters and other fat systems by chocolate manufacturers both in the research laboratories and, more recently, as a quality control tool in the plants (Burroughs, undated). A DSC test can reveal the following performance parameters of chocolate:

1. The original state of temper in the various polymorphic forms
2. Solidification difficulty from the molten state
3. Formation of an undesired fat mixture
4. Major solidification differences between individual batches or types of fat
5. Degree of hardness relative to a standard

H.   NEW TEMPERING METHODS/PROCESSES

There are several patented systems that are quite different from the traditional approach to chocolate tempering (Von Drachenfelds *et al.*, 1962; Cruickshank and Jewell, 1977). Fuege *et al.* (1963) used the principle of intensive agitation under increased pressure during cooling and claimed production of finer fat crystals. Kleinert (1972) used cyclothermic tempering, a form of double tempering, which he claimed gave increased heat resistance to chocolate. Finally, the 1969 Kreuter patent was a refinement of this process and is a conventional tempering cycle which is carried out very slowly (Cruickshank and Jewell, 1977). The Kreuter process claims additional benefits of better heat stability after solidification.

XVI.   CONFECTIONERY PACKAGING

A.   INTRODUCTION

The packaging requirements of chocolate confectionery products are similar to those of other products and fall into three areas: protection, function, and sales appeal.

1.   Protection

The product should be protected by the package from all hazards from the time of manufacture until consumption is completed. Desirable attributes such as flavors need to be kept inside the package to prolong shelf life while undesirable environmental odors need to be excluded. The product must also be protected from shock, vibration, and compression during distribution.

2. Function

The package should be functional and facilitate the manufacture, shipping, storage, display, and use of the product. Increasingly, the recyclability and disposability of materials chosen should be considered for their impact on the solid waste stream.

3. Sales Appeal

The package should promote the product. The package must attract the shopper, appeal to emotions, inform, and trigger the sale.

These three requirements are best achieved by using a thorough package development cycle which includes input from many sources. During the package development cycle, product needs and wants are quantified, packaging machinery considered, regulatory requirements reviewed, tamper evidence acknowledged, package systems and materials selected, and all package attributes thoroughly tested.

B. PRODUCT REQUIREMENTS

In order to develop suitable packaging, the protection needs of the product should first be quantified. Generally, this consists of preserving product quality as measured by flavor, texture, nutrition, appearance, and safety throughout the desired time period and distribution system. Product quality can often be affected by the following:

1. Oxygen, which will react with some product ingredients (e.g., fats and oils) to produce undesired flavor or color changes
2. Water vapor gain or loss, which will induce undesired texture changes in some products (such as wafers, toffees, nougats, and licorice) and which may be a catalyst to oxidation
3. Light and heat which may degrade vitamins and fade colors
4. Microorganisms

The literature contains studies concerning the protection needs of many foods including chocolate and confectionery products; these can assist in product packaging design.

Milprint (a supplier of converted flexible materials) has compiled a qualitative

TABLE XXIII

PERMEABILITY REQUIREMENTS BY CHOCOLATE BAR TYPES[a]

| | | | Chocolate coated | | | | | | | |
| | | | | Chocolate-covered marshmallow | | | | | | |
	Nougat center	Nougat with nuts	Chocolate with or without nuts	Thick coat	Thin coat	Wafer cookie	Wafer cookie with nuts	Nuts salted	Nuts in sugar-syrup matrix	Nutritional bar
Water vapor transmission rate										
High	×	×	×	×						
Medium					×			×	×	
Low						×	×			×
Oxygen transmission rate										
High	×	×	×	×						
Medium					×	×		×		×
Low							×		×	
Light filter										
None	×	×	×	×	×	×				
Some							×	×	×	×

[a] Source: Milprint, Inc.

TABLE XXIV

DEGREE OF PERMEATION PROTECTION REQUIRED BY VARIOUS FOODS FOR A 1-YEAR
SHELF LIFE AT $25°C$[a]

Food or beverage	Maximum estimated acceptable O_2 gain (ppm)	Maximum acceptable H_2O gain or loss (%)
Canned milk, Canned meats, Canned fish, poultry	1–5	3 loss
Canned vegetables, soups, spaghetti, catsup, sauces	1–5	3 loss
Canned fruits	5–15	3 loss
Nuts, snacks	5–15	5 gain
Dried foods	5–15	1 gain
Fruit juices, drinks	10–40	3 loss
Oils, shortenings	50–200	10 gain
Salad dressings	50–200	10 gain
Jams, jellies, syrups, pickles, olives, vinegars	50–200	3 loss
Peanut butter	50–200	10 gain

[a] Source: Marcus (1982).

table which lists generic types of chocolate and confectionery products and their permeability requirements for oxygen, water vapor, and light (Table XXIII). Marcus (1982) summarized the degree of permeation protection required by various plastics (Tables XXV and XXVI), and provided Eqs. (1) and (2) for calculating how they are related. The article describes rigid containers but should be considered applicable for flexible packages.

TABLE XXV

REPRESENTATIVE WATER VAPOR TRANSMISSION RATES[a]

Resin	Water vapor transmission rate (g/ml/100 in.^{2}/24 hr at 100 °F and 90% RH)
High barrier Saran resins	0.1–0.15
Polypropylene	0.25
High density polyethylene	0.3–0.4
Low density polyethylene	1.0÷1.5
Polyester	1.0–1.3
Rigid polyvinyl chloride	0.9–5.1
Nitrile barrier resin	5.0
Polystyrene	7.0–10.0
Hydrolyzed ethylene–vinyl acetate	13.9
Nylon	16–22

[a] Source: Marcus (1982).

TABLE XXVI

REPRESENTATIVE OXYGEN TRANSMISSION RATES[a]

Resin	Permeability (cm³/ml/100 in.²/day/atm at 23°C)
Hydrolyzed ethylene–vinyl acetate	0.02 (dry only)
High barrier Saran resins	0.05–0.15
Nitrile barrier resin	0.8
Nylon 6	2.6
Polyester	3–4
Rigid polyvinyl chloride	5–20
Polypropylene	150.0
High density polyethylene	150.0
Polystyrene	350.0
Low density polyethylene	420.0

[a] Source: Marcus (1982).

$$\% \text{ water vapor per year} = \frac{12.9(A)(P_w)}{t(W)} \tag{1}$$

$$\text{ppm } O_2 \text{ per year} = \frac{10,500 \ (A)(P_{O_2})}{(273 + T)(t)(W)} \tag{2}$$

Where A is the plastic area of container in square inches, t the barrier layer thickness in mils, P_{O_2} the oxygen permeability constant of the barrier in cubic centimeters per mil per 24 hr per atmosphere, P_w the water vapor permeability in grams per mil per 100 in.² per 24 hr at 38°C and 90% RH, T the temperature in degrees Celsius, and W the weight of container contents in avoirdupois ounces.[1] DeMan (1976) describes the phenomenon of sorption isotherms where a product gains or loses moisture (percent product moisture) depending on the relative humidity [equilibrium relative humidity or water activity (Aw)] in which it is stored.

Michigan State University School of Packaging has developed Eq. (3), based on work done by Clifford *et al.* (1977), which combines product, package, and storage environment information to predict product shelf life for moisture sensitive products[1]:

$$t = \frac{-2.3lw}{\bar{P}AP_s b} \log_{10} \frac{(\text{RH}_{ext} - \text{RH}_{int}) \text{ at time } t}{(\text{RH}_{ext} - \text{RH}_{int}) \text{ at time } 0} \tag{3}$$

Where t is the time for the relative humidity inside the package to reach the value RH_{int} at time t in hours, days, months, etc., l the material thickness in meters, $\bar{P}$

[1] Source for Eqs. (1)–(3): Marcus, Stanley A., Multi-layer plastic food containers: An idea whose time has come. *Food and Drug Packaging*, August, 1982.

the permeability constant of packaging material in grams of water per mil per square meter per day per millimeter Hg at temperature of test, A the surface area of package in square meters, P_s the saturation vapor pressure of water at temperature of test, b the slope of the linear region of the sorption isotherm of product, at temperature of test, when x axis is moisture content y axis is percent relative humidity, w the dry weight of product packaged, RH_{ext} the relative humidity external from package, and RH_{int} the internal relative humidity of package.

Salame (1974) describes the permeability aspects of several polymers and their suitability for use with various food products. He cautions that other parameters beside permeability can be equally important in selecting plastics; these include adsorption, extraction, formability, cost, and other factors. Needs should be quantified on an individual product basis using similar product information only as a directional indicator to be verified by later product/package testing. The means of satisfying the product, process, and distribution system requirements are provided by the packaging materials chosen. Thus, having gathered relevant information on the product needs, attention is focused on the particular packaging materials which provide the necessary product protection qualities identified above.

C. PACKAGING MATERIALS

Minifie (1970) described the polymerization, properties, and uses of many plastic films and flexible materials. These include cellulose film (Cello), low density polyethylene (LDPE), high density polyethylene (HDPE), polypropylene (PP), polyvinyl chloride (PVC), polyvinylidene chloride (PVDC), polyamide–nylon, polyethylene terephthalate–polyester (PET), aluminum foil, and papers. Several newer materials suitable for chocolate and confectionery packaging have also appeared in use:

1. Linear low density polyethylene (LLDPE) has greater water vapor barrier characteristics than LDPE. It also has greater stiffness than LDPE, which allows stronger film products at equivalent gauge or downgauged film with equivalent strength when compared to LDPE films.

2. Acrylonitrile provides good chemical resistance and oxygen and odor barrier, but a relatively poor water vapor barrier. Regulatory concern over migration of the monomer into foods has limited its use to nonfood contact applications within a co-extruded film, lamination, or container.

3. Ethylene vinyl alcohol (EVAL) has a very low oxygen transmission rate, but this increases significantly when exposed to relative humidities of 90% or greater. The oxygen barrier will return to its original level after the moisture in the material returns to previous levels.

Lamination technology using multiple films is often applied wherein packaging materials having different properties (e.g., one layer is a good oxygen barrier, the other a good moisture barrier) can complement each other to provide more complete protection for a sensitive product. The development of the coextrusion process (which takes resin fed from several extruders, combines them with tie layers in the feed block, and extrudes them as one single layer) has permitted thinner gauges of material combinations not possible with laminations. Thus the desired protective properties can be engineered into a final film or rigid container by selecting the polymers and thicknesses desired and combining them into one process.

In the final phase of the packaging design process, transmission rate testing of packages and shelf life testing of packaged product, can confirm the adequacy of the chosen package system for the intended product, expected storage conditions, and desired shelf life.

D. PACKAGE EVALUATION

There are a number of tests that can be used to evaluate the primary package and its component materials. Qualitative identification of materials provides confirmation with specifications. With polymers infrared spectroscopy yields the chemical fingerprint, and gel permeation chromatography produces the molecular weight distribution. Polymer thermal properties can be determined using DSC and its mechanical and gravimetric analogs.

Organic and inorganic gases and vapors pass through different plastics at different rates. Transmission occurs by the permeant being dissolved on the polymer surface, migrating through "openings" between the polymer chains toward the side with lower permeant concentration, and desorbing from the polymer's other surface. These vapors or gases may be the flavors of the product escaping or the intrusion of unwanted odors from the environment. Properly designed experiments utilizing gas chromatography can be performed to optimize packaging which retains the desirable flavors within the product and rejects objectionable external contaminants. In chocolate and confectionery products the former may be mint or fruit flavors, while the latter may be tobacco or chemical odors. Accomplishment of these two tasks is particularly difficult with chocolate and confectionery products due to their high fat contents which make them highly susceptible to the absorption of various flavors and odors.

Protection from the effects of ultraviolet (UV) and visible light (vis) on the product can be evaluated by employing transmission UV–vis spectroscopy to analyze the packaging material properties. Another area of concern is migration of components from the material into the food product. A 5-year study comparing food-simulating solvents to actual food products for extraction of plastic constituents was recently completed by Arthur D. Little for the FDA. Spectrographic, chromatographic, and isotopic labeling methods were compared. Preliminary results reported low correlation between these and established methods.

High levels of retained printing solvents can induce off odors and flavors in products. Residual printing solvents can be tentatively identified and quantified by heating the material in a septum-fitted jar and injecting a sample of the headspace into a gas chromatograph to compare the peak retention times with known compounds (ASTM Method F-151). A qualitative method may use fresh chocolate or other confectionery product (not wrapped) stored inside a closed jar with the wrapping material in question for 24 hr followed by an organoleptic comparison to control product.

E. SUMMARY

Since 1970, the use of flexible packaging materials has continued to grow, but the mix has changed; the use of traditional cellulose film has decreased tremendously, being replaced by materials such as polyester and polypropylene. These and newer materials and processes will provide ever increasing protection to chocolate and confectionery products.

XVII. *Theobroma cacao* L. CELL AND TISSUE CULTURE

A. INTRODUCTION

Since the first report of establishment of a cocoa tissue culture (Archibald, 1954), tissue and cell cultures of *Theobroma cacao* L. have been established from explants of stem (Archibald, 1954; Townsley, 1974; Hall and Collin, 1975; Evans, 1980), petioles (Townsley, 1974), leaves (Pence *et al.,* 1979; Searles *et al.,* 1976), hypocotyl (Hall and Collin, 1975), roots (Hall and Collin, 1975), fruit (Pence *et al.,* 1979; Searles *et al.,* 1976; Evans, 1980), embryos (Ibanez, 1964; Esan, 1977; Pence *et al.,* 1979; Tsai and Kinsella, 1981a; Hall and Collin, 1975; Prior, 1977; Evans, 1980), and anther filaments (Prior, 1977; Evans, 1980). Tissue and cell cultures have been used to investigate problems in plant pathology (Prior, 1977; Evans, 1980), lipid metabolism (Tsai and Kinsella, 1981a,b, 1982a,b; Tsai *et al.,* 1982), somatic embryo development (Esan, 1977; Pence *et al.,* 1979, 1980, 1981a,b; Janick *et al.,* 1982; Wright *et al.,* 1982), flushing (Orchard *et al.,* 1979), production of cocoa aroma (Townsley, 1974), and other problems. Only one successful attempt at shoot organogenesis has been reported (Esan, 1982). Callus cultures may produce roots in an unpredictable fashion (Pence *et al.,* 1979), and no plants have been produced via somatic embryogenesis.

TABLE XXVII

HORMONES AND GROWTH STIMULANTS GIVING OPTIMAL GROWTH OF CALLUS AND SUSPENSION CULTURE

Authority	Auxin[a]	Cytokinin	Other	Base medium	Remarks
Archibald (1954)	—	—	Pure coconut water	Whites	Callus
Hall and Collin (1975)	2 mg/liter IAA + 2 mg/liter IBA	0.1 mg/liter kinetin	10% v/v coconut water	Murashige and Skoog	Callus
	2 mg/liter IAA + 2 mg/liter IBA	0.5 mg/liter kinetin	10% v/v coconut water	Murashige and Skoog	Cell suspension
Searles et al. (1976)	No auxin	2–6 mg/liter kinetin	—	Murashige and Skoog	Callus
	0–0.5 mg/liter IAA	0.25–1 mg/liter zeatin	—	Murashige and Skoog	Callus
Tsai and Kinsella (1981a)	0.5 mg/liter 2,4-D	0.1 mg/liter kinetin	—	Murashige and Skoog	Suspensions
Jalal and Collin (1979)	1.0 mg/liter 2,4-D	—	10% v/v coconut water	Murashige and Skoog	Callus
	1 mg/liter IBA	0.05 mg/liter kinetin	—	Hall and Collin (1975)	Callus
	10 mg/liter IBA	0.5 mg/liter kinetin	—	Hall and Collin (1975)	Suspension

[a] IAA, Indoleacetic acid; IBA, indolebutyric acid; 2,4-D, 2,4-dichlorophenoxyacetic acid.

Cacao calli and cell suspensions grow on a fairly wide variety of liquid and solid media, including White's medium (Archibald, 1954), PRL-4 medium (Townsley, 1974), Murashige and Skoog medium (Pence *et al.*, 1979; Prior, 1977; Hall and Collin, 1975), coconut water (Archibald, 1954), Wood and Braun medium (Hall and Collin, 1975), and Heller's medium (Hall and Collin, 1975), either with or without various modifications. Growth is usually more rapid with the more complex media. Coconut water, the most complex of all, supports very rapid callus growth. Buds have been cultured in Linsmaier and Skoog medium (Orchard *et al.*, 1979).

There are no unusual hormone requirements for establishment of callus or suspension cultures as indicated by Table XXVII. The auxins indoleacetic acid (IAA), indolebutyric acid (IBA), 2,4-dichlorophenoxyacetic acid (2,4-D), and naphthaleneacetic acid (NAA) are all biologically active as are the cytokinins kinetin and zeatin. Optimum hormone requirements for callus and suspension cultures vary, but no pattern is discernable.

Callus and cell cultures are capable of growing in both light and dark on various photoperiods and intensities of 1,000–2,000 lux and over a fairly wide range of temperatures, but growth is best around 25–30°C (Hall and Collin, 1975; Tsai and Kinsella, 1981a). Patents on cocoa tissue culture processes have been issued for production of cotyledons in culture (Janick and Pence, 1980, 1981; Janick *et al.*, 1981) and production of lipids in cell suspensions (Kinsella and Tsai, 1981).

B. SHOOT ORGANOGENESIS

Esan (1982) cultured embryo axis explants from green mature fruit at 26 ± 2°C under 150–250 lux fluorescent light for 14 hr/day on the modified Murashige and Skoog medium in Table XXVIII. Axes were cultured at several levels of NAA, with the best results between 2 and 5 mg/liter.

Calli were derived from the radicle, hypocotyl, and plumule. These were subcultured at 50, 60, 70, 80, and 90 days after induction on shoot regeneration medium. There was considerable variation between and within treatments. Organogenesis did not occur in all ages of the radicle and hypocotyl calli. The adventitious buds did not always fully develop, often appearing to be vestigial. The most leaf development appeared in the 70-day treatment. All plumule subcultures except the 90-day treatment produced shoots. None of the calli produced roots nor did any of the shoots.

C. SOMATIC EMBRYOGENESIS

Esan (1977) reported the first *in vitro* somatic embryogenesis in cocoa on cultured immature embryos on a medium containing low levels of NAA. The

TABLE XXVIII

MEDIA USED FOR CALLUS FORMATION AND SHOOT REGENERATION: MS
SALTS MODIFIED TO CONTAIN CALCIUM NITRATE[a] AND ORGANIC
FRACTION MADE TO CONTAIN BACTERIOLOGICAL PEPTONE[b]

Addenda to Murashige–Skoog salts formulation (ppm)	Callogenesis	Shoot regeneration
$Ca(NO_3)_2$[a]	300.00	300.00
Sucrose	50,000.00	20,000.00
Bacteriological peptone[a]	100.00	10.00
Naphthaleneacetic acid	2.0	0.01
Kinetin	0.01	1.0
Bacto agar	8,000.00	8,000.00
Inositol	100.00	400.00
Nicotinic acid	—	1.00
Glycine	—	2.00
Pyridoxine HCl	—	1.00
Thiamin HCl	—	4.00
pH (adjusted with 1 N NaOH)	6.1	6.1

[a] $Ca(NO_3)_2$ and bacteriological peptone were supplemented to MS formulation.
[b] From Esan (1982), with permission.

embryos grew from epidermal cells and on suspensorlike structures. These observations were substantiated by Pence et al. (1979). Somatic embryos were
produced on the surface of immature zygotic embryos, approximately 120 days
postpollination, on NAA-free medium. NAA promoted callus growth and root
organogenesis. Further work (Pence et al., 1980) revealed that, at 8–48 μM,
NAA plus 10% v/v coconut water promoted embryogenesis, but 8 μM 2,4-D and
80 μM IAA in the presence of 10% v/v coconut water were more active. Kinetin
inhibited in the presence of coconut water. Liquid medium allowed more embryogenesis and greater embryo growth rates than solid medium.

Histological examination (Pence et al., 1980) of the asexual embryos revealed
two processes called "budding" and "nonbudding." The budding process is
more common. Embryos arise directly from globular hairs on the axis, or ovoid
structures arise near the edge of the cotyledon or near cut edges. The ovoids
produce hairs or suspensor-like structures, and the embryos are produced at the
distal end of the hairs. In the nonbudding process, embryos are directly produced
from the ovoid structures. Embryogenic tissue remained embryogenic in culture
for 3 years (J. Janick personal communication), and asexual embryos could be
induced to undergo embryogenesis.

Studies of storage product accumulation in zygotic embryos (Wright et al.,
1982) indicate that storage lipids and proteins and the secondary products, anthocyanins and methylxanthines, are accumulated simultaneously. This adds sub-

stance to the discovery of the so-called sucrose effect reported by Pence *et al.* (1981b). Increasing sucrose concentrations up to 27% w/v resulted in increased lipid accumulation and an increase in the total fatty acid component of the lipids. The increased total fatty acid is interpreted as an increase in triglycerides. The sucrose effect also changes the fatty acid profile of the lipid fraction in a manner consistent with this interpretation. Stearic and oleic acid mole percentages increase, and linoleic and linolenic acid mole percentages decrease. These effects roughly parallel the events during normal seed maturation, but the linoleic acid did not decline to the levels found in mature seeds. This seems to be due to insufficient synthesis of oleic and stearic acids to dilute the linoleic sufficiently and possibly to incomplete inhibition of linoleic synthesis. Janick *et al.* (1982) demonstrated that cocoa butter-like substances were produced by asexual embryos in culture and that the yield of cocoa butter-like triglycerides increased with increasing sucrose concentration of the culture media.

D. LIPID METABOLISM IN SUSPENSIONS AND CALLUS CULTURES

Tsai and Kinsella have described a number of aspects of lipid metabolism in callus and cell suspension cultures of *T. cacao*. In contrast to the lipids of mature cocoa embryos, which are around 98% triglycerides, the lipids of rapidly growing callus and cell suspension cultures are only around 13% triglycerides (Tsai and Kinsella, 1981b). Indeed, neither callus lipid nor suspension lipid resembled embryo lipid even in embryos as young as 115 days postpollination. The lipid fraction of 5-week-old callus and 2-week-old cell suspension cultures contained around 9% sterols and over 70% polar lipids. The distribution of oleic, linoleic, and linolenic acids between the phospholipid and glycolipid fractions was quite different for calli and cell suspensions, showing net biochemical difference between the two systems. One way in which triglycerides from cocoa embryos, calli, and cell suspensions resemble each other is that the glycerol two position tends to be filled with an unsaturated fatty acid at greater than chance proportion while the glycerol one and three positions tend to be filled with saturated fatty acids in greater than chance proportions.

Tsai and Kinsella (1982b) conducted labeling experiments with suspension cultures using acetic, palmitic, stearic, oleic, and linoleic acids. Only acetate labeled all classes of lipids. Labeled palmitic, oleic, and linoleic were found mostly in phospholipids with lesser amounts in triglycerides and 2–3% in the free fatty acids. In contrast, labeled stearic acid was found to be 60% in free fatty acids, 25% in phospholipid, and 10% in triglyceride. Addition of 50 μ*M* stearic acid at the beginning of a 2-week subculturing of cell suspension doubled the triglyceride synthesis but had no effect on its fatty acid composition.

Increasing the sucrose content of the subculture medium from 3 to 5% increased triglyceride percentage of total lipid and decreased oleic acid and linoleic acid content (Tsai *et al.*, 1982). When the increased sucrose was companied by 10% v/v coconut water, the triglyceride percentage increased to around 21% and fatty acid composition more closely resembled cocoa butter; however, a considerable difference remains. The stearic acid content is less than 10% and the linolenic acid is greater than 10%. Linoleic acid is nearly 20% of the fatty acid composition. The effect of sucrose in these experiments resembles that reported by Pence *et al.* (1981b).

Radioactive labeling of the lipid classes with [^{14}C]acetate gives early labeling peaks of polar lipids and a steady buildup of triglycerides, showing that these lipid classes are associated with different subcellular compartments. The fatty acids labeled with acetate show radioactivity peaks at 2–4 hr after acetate addition for saturated and monoenoic fatty acids. Trienoic acids also peaked at about 4 hr with a secondary peak at 48 hr. Dienoic acids radioactivity peaked at 24 hr. Lauric acid ^{14}C-labeling studies show the following peaks:

Acids	Hours to peak
Trienoic	2
Monoenoic	more than 4, less than 24
Dienoic	2–48
Saturation	24

Tsai and Kinsella (1982a) interpret this as being consistent with two pathways for the synthesis of trienoic acids: one via desaturation of stearic acid and the other via desaturation of lauric acid and its elongation to linoleic acid.

Tsai and Kinsella (1982b) found that exogenous palmitic and stearic acids were not desaturated. Exogenous oleic acid was rapidly converted to linoleic acid and linolenic acid. Exogenous linoleic acid was slowly converted to linolenic acid. Cocoa suspension cultures seem to lack the ability to acylate the acyl carrier protein synthetase to acylate acyl carrier protein with palmitate or stearate but do have a thiokinase that acylates CoA with oleic acid and desaturases capable of acting on oleic and linoleic acids.

E. SECONDARY METABOLISM

Cocoa tissue cultures offer a tool for controlled biochemical and physiological experiments in secondary product metabolism. Polyphenols and methylxanthines are important secondary metabolites of cocoa beans and have a role in chocolate flavor and other properties of chocolate. Jalal and Collin (1977) compared the polyphenol production of various cocoa tissues including cotyledon-derived callus tissue. Callus tissue and mature cotyledon differ markedly in quantity and quality of polyphenols. Of the 17 cotyledon polyphenols and 11 callus polyphenols isolated as separate spots by two-dimensional thin-layer chromatography on cellulose, only 3 were common to both tissues. These were (−)-epicatechin

TABLE XXIX

EFFECT OF XANTHINE DERIVATIVES ON SYNTHESIS OF THEOBROMINE
BY SUSPENSION CULTURES

Xanthine derivative	Methionine	Effect
Hypoxanthine	−	Compound taken up, no methylated xanthines formed
Hypoxanthine	+	7-Methylhypoxanthine formed
Xanthine	−	Uptake, slight accumulation of 1- and 7-methylxanthine
Xanthosine monophosphate	−	No methylxanthines detected
7-Methylxanthosine	−	7-Methylxanthine formed
7-Methylxanthosine	−	Theobromine formed, no caffeine

and leucocyanidins 1 and 2. Suspension cultures (Jalal and Collin, 1979) have a still simpler spectrum of polyphenols, indicating that polyphenol synthesis is closely related to differentiation.

A further demonstration of the metabolic difference between cotyledons and callus was the apparent inability of callus culture to biosynthesize caffeine and theobromine (Jalal and Collin, 1979). Precursor feeding studies (Table XXIX) indicate that suspension and callus cultures lacked the ability to synthesize 7-methylxanthine, a precursor of theobromine.

Work utilizing cultures more differentiated than cell suspensions and calli has centered on the culture of immature zygotic embryos and asexual embryos resembling the immature stages of zygotic embryos. Esan (1977) noted that when immature embryos were cultured in media of increasing sucrose content (1–20%) the pigmentation of the embryos could be rated on a visual scale. No pigment was visible at 1% sucrose, and the apparent anthocyanin rating plateaus at 15–20% sucrose. No chemical analysis was done to verify the scale. The work of Pence et al. (1981a) demonstrated increased anthocyanin concentrations on a dry weight basis in asexual embryos with increasing sucrose concentration from 3 to 27%. In these experiments, coconut water and NAA were found to have no effect on anthocyanin accumulation. The anthocyanins of asexual embryos cochromatographed with those of zygotic embryos.

F. EMBRYONIC AXIS GROWTH AND STORAGE

Ibanez (1964) was the first to culture the embryonic axis of cocoa. He used mature seed of UF 613 for an explant source. The axis grew into a "seedling" on Rudolph and Cox medium modified by replacing sucrose with glucose. In his experiments, the axis would not "germinate" with glucose as the sole carbohydrate.

Hall and Collin (1975) found that the axis of mature embryos was a poor explant source for establishing callus cultures because a few weeks are required for callus induction. Their work was apparently done using Murashige and Skoog salts with twice the vitamins and amino acids and supplemented with 10% v/v coconut water, 2 mg/liter IAA plus 2 mg/liter IBA, and 0.1 mg/liter kinetin. Once growth was induced, axis callus grew rapidly.

In contrast to these authors, Esan (1977) used tissue cultures as an embryo banking technique. On Heller's agar medium, embryonic axis could be stored up to 12 months and germinated by transferring the axis to basal medium supplemented with 50 mg/liter of gibberellic acid (GA_3). Embryonic axis could not be stored on Murashige and Skoog salts with glucose or sucrose because of germination.

It seems that the great variation in the organic components of these media eliminate the likelihood of any organic component being responsible for growth inhibition or induction. The inorganic constituents are quite different between these media, and Heller's medium is the least complete and also contains aluminum chloride and nickel chloride hexahydrate that may inhibit germination.

G. PHYSIOLOGY OF FLUSHING

Orchard et al. (1979) used shoot tip cultures on Linsmaier and Skoog medium to investigate the flushing behavior of cocoa. Shoot tips were taken at the F-1, F-2, I-1, and I-2 stages (Greathouse et al., 1971) and cultured on both solid and liquid media. A viscous exudate from the explant inhibited growth on solid medium. Only buds in the I-2 stage showed any signs of growth when treated with GA_3 or kinetin. IAA, IBA, NAA, and zeatin had no effect on bud break (Table XXX).

TABLE XXX

BEHAVIOR OF EXCISED I-2 COCOA TERMINAL BUDS IN RESPONSE TO VARIOUS HORMONE TREATMENTS IN LIQUID LINSMAIER AND SKOOG MEDIUM[a]

Hormone	Concentration (mg/liter)	Bud response
Kinetin	5.0	45% bud break
Gibberellic acid	1.0	45% bud break; 25 days to bud break
Gibberellic acid	5.0	75% bud burst and leaf growth; 10–15 days to bud break
Gibberellic acid	10.0	75% bud burst and leaf growth; 7 days to bud break
Kinetin plus abscisic acid	5.0 + 5.0	No growth
Gibberellic acid plus abscisic acid	10.0 + 5.0	75% bud break; reduced leaf growth

[a]After Orchard et al. (1979).

H. PLANT PATHOLOGY APPLICATIONS

Archibald (1954) was the first to deliberately culture cocoa tissue from infected explants; however, technical limitations prevented assay of the callus for cocoa swollen shoot virus. Since that time, the application of cocoa tissue culture to disease problems has turned to the study of fungal pathogens. Use of plant tissue culture for the coculture of fungal pathogens with unknown and exacting nutritional requirements has become relatively common. Prior (1977) used this technique to culture *Oncobasidium theobromae* Talbot & Keane, the causative agent of vascular streak dieback, on cocoa callus. Good vegetative growth of the fungus was obtained, but sporulation did not occur. Monilioid hyphae were produced. The formation of the hyphae is probably the first event in spore formation, and, if this is true, Prior's data show that particular light and temperature regimes are unlikely to be necessary in the formation of monilioid hyphae.

Evans (1980) used coculture techniques to study certain aspects of the life cycle of *Crinipellis perniciosa* (Stahel) Singer (the causative agent of witches' broom) and their relationship to the disease process. This work substantiates the dual mycelium theory of the disease. Basidiospores germinating on active callus produce short apically swollen hyphae, chains of globose cells, some with thick walled terminal cells, or a swollen convoluted mycelium. These are similar to the hyphae found in green brooms and early stages of fruit infection. As the calli decline in vigor, a finer, vigorously growing mycelium quickly overran the callus. This mycelium is similar to that found in necrotic brooms.

I. SPECULATION

The application of tissue and cell culture technologies to the cocoa and chocolate industry center around their application to agricultural production and the advancement of cocoa biology. Some of these applications are listed in Table XXXI. The chief impediment to this work is the lack of basic information on *T. cacao* and its close relatives. In special cases, it may be possible to bypass

TABLE XXXI

SOME POSSIBLE APPLICATIONS OF CELL AND TISSUE CULTURE
TO COCOA AGRICULTURE AND BIOLOGY

Rapid propagation via organogenesis and somatic embryogenesis
Genetic transfers via cell fusion and vectors
Germplasm storage
Generation of genetic variability and selection of desirable variants
Biochemical and physiological studies
Virus and other pathogen research

agricultural production to produce precursors for the industrial production of chocolate flavors, and a more remote possibility is the commercialization of *in vitro* cocoa butter production. The disadvantages of these processes are economic rather than technical.

XVIII. RESEARCH NEEDS

One will notice that the sections covering the individual ingredients convey a high degree of information and involve a greater degree of literature citation than do the sections covering the processing of chocolate ingredients (refining, conching, etc.). Chocolate manufacturers regard the details of their unit operations as highly confidential. Equipment manufacturers often extoll the advantages of new processing machinery without exploring or releasing scientific documentation of organoleptic changes which occur in particular processing steps.

However, in due perspective, it must be remembered that the presently available flavors of marketed chocolate evolved using specific manufacturing equipment and ingredient manipulations, unique to a particular company. Additionally, prior to the early 1960s, adequate tools for the documentation of chocolate flavor (such as gas–liquid chromatography or sophisticated liquid chromatography) were in their early stages of development. The last two decades have thus seen a burgeoning of chocolate flavor research in both fermentation and processing areas. One's perspective must be tempered by the realization that chocolate contains hundreds of known compounds, and that even today no completely adequate synthetic chocolate flavor has been forthcoming.

If indeed a common thread prevails in chocolate research, it is an enhanced understanding of chocolate flavor and the components and processing which influence it. This research is evident primarily in three areas: (1) the study of cacao fermentation to discover and develop the proper flavor precursors in cocoa beans; (2) the study of the reaction flavors developed during cacao roasting; and (3) the study of the effects of each unit operation contributing to flavor changes. Area (3) actually receives considerable attention since once a manufacturer has a "winning" flavor profile combination he strives to consistently reproduce it. Should new, more efficient processing equipment be acquired, flavor changes will likely occur. The cacao flavor chemist will explore the changes and seek to modify the processing conditions to approach the previously desired flavor attributes.

Future research in chocolate (not previously mentioned in each section) is required in the following areas to gather a better understanding of this complex food:

1. Elucidation of the biochemical pathways leading to the production of favorable cacao flavor precursors.

2. Examination of the chemical changes occurring during the roasting process; delineation of the differences between flavor and filler cocoa bean categories.
3. Determination of the chemical flavor changes occurring in the alkalization process.
4. Obtaining of a better understanding of milk constituent changes in crumb flavor development.
5. Development of a viable bulk filler to replace sucrose for dietary confections.
6. Conducting of research specifically documenting the physicochemical properties and behavior of amorphous sucrose; documentation of the existence of amorphous sugars throughout the chocolate manufacturing process.
7. Description of the flavor reactions occurring in the refining process in the high pressure, high instantaneous heat microenvironment of the refining step; verification of the existence of the amorphous sucrose state and its potential for enhanced flavor retention in chocolate.
8. Clarification of to what extent the conching step performs a flavor changing step; that is, do reactions occur in conching, or does the process simply provide a "buffering action" to "mellow" off flavors produced by previous processing via exchange with the air environment?

ACKNOWLEDGMENTS

The author sincerely thanks Mildred Sholly and Eileen Deimler, who typed the manuscript, for their enduring patience.

REFERENCES

Aastad, K. 1941. Studien über Concheringsprocesse.

American Dry Milk Institute (ADMI). 1971. Classification of dry milks according to heat treatment. The American Dry Milk Institute, Chicago, Illinois.

American Oil Chemists Society (AOCS). 1969. Preparation of methyl esters of long-chain fatty acids. Official and Tentative Methods of the American Oil Chemists Society. Ce 2-66.

American Oil Chemists Society (AOCS). 1981. Fatty acid composition by gas chromatography. Official and Tenatative Methods of the American Oil Chemists Society. Ce 1-62.

Anonymous. 1965. New method of chocolate processing. *Food Process. Market.* June.

Anonymous. 1971. Statistical reporting service, fluid milk and cream, March 19. U.S. Department of Agriculture, Washington, D.C.

Anonymous. 1979. Cocoa preparation by Barth's newly developed NARS short dwell process. *Confect. Prod.* **45**, 546–548.

Anonymous. 1983. Sweet tasting amino acid, glycine, enhances flavor and provides functional properties. *Food Process.* **44**, 90.

Archibald, J. F. 1954. Culture *in vitro* of cambial tissue of cacao. *Nature (London)* **173**, 351–352.

Ariyoshi, Y., and Toi, K. 1974. Method of purifying α-L-aspartyl-L-phenylalanine lower alkyl esters of peptide impurities. U.S. Patent 3,833,554.

Ariyoshi, Y., Yamatani, T., Uchiyama, N., Yasuda, N., Toi, K., and Sato, N. 1974. Method of producing α-L-aspartyl-L-phenylalanine alkyl esters. U.S. Patent 3,833,553.

Bailey, A. E. 1949. The semicontinuous deodorization of fats. *J. Am. Oil Chem. Soc.* **26**, 166–170.

Bailey, S. D., Mitchell, D. G., Bazinet, M. L., and Weurman, C. 1962. Studies on the volatile components of different varieties of cocoa beans. *J. Food Sci.* **27**, 165.

Bainbridge, J. S., and Davies, S. H. 1912. The essential oil of cocoa. *J. Chem. Soc.* **101**, 2709.

Bandi, J. P., Jubicek, F., and Raboud, P. B. 1982. Process for solubilizing cocoa. U.S. Patent 4,349,579.

Banford, H. F., Gardner, K. J., Howat, G. R., and Thomson, A. F. 1970. The use of polyglycerol polyricinoleate in chocolate. *Confect. Prod.* **6**, 359–365.

Barel, M., Guyot, B., and Vincent, J. C. 1983. Cocoa protein fractions before and after roasting. Influence of fermentation. *Cafe Cacao The* **27**, 127–144.

Bartusch, W. 1960. Investigation on the chemical and physical changes of chocolate mass during conching. *Br. Food Manuf. Ind. Res. Assoc. Res. Tech. Circ.* 332.

Beereboom, J. 1979. Low calorie bulking agents. In *CRC Crit. Rev. Food Sci. Nutr.* **11**, 410.

Berbert, P. R. F. 1979. Contribucao para o conhecimento dos acucares componentes da amendoa e do mel de cacau. *Rev. Theobroma (Brasil)* **9**, 55–61.

Berbert, P. R., and Alvin, P. 1972. Fatores que afetam o indice de iodo da manteiga de cacau do Brasil. *Rev. Theobroma (Brasil)* **2**, 3.

Biehl, B., and Passern, D. 1982. Proteolysis during fermentation-like incubation of cocoa seeds. *J. Sci. Food Agric.* **33**, 1280–1290.

Biehl, B., Passern, U., and Passern, D. 1977. Subcellular structures in fermenting cocoa beans. Effect of aeration and temperature during seed and fragment incubation. *J. Sci. Food Agric.* **28**, 41–52.

Biehl, B., Passern, D., and Sagemann, W. 1982a. Effect of acetic acid on subcellular structures of cocoa bean cotyledons. *J. Sci. Food Agric.* **33**, 1101–1109.

Biehl, B., Quesnel, V. C., Passern, D., and Sagemann, W. 1982b. Water uptake by cocoa seeds during fermentation-like incubation. *J. Sci. Food Agric.* **33**, 1110–1116.

Biehl, B., Wewetzer, C., and Passern, D. 1982c. Vacuolar (storage) proteins of cocoa seeds and their degradation during germination and fermentation. *J. Sci. Food Agric.* **33**, 1291–1304.

Bigalli, G. 1981. Usefulness and limitations of fatty acids distribution determination in the confectionery industry. *Pa. Manuf. Confect. Assoc. Proc. Annu. Prod. Conf., 35th, Drexel Hill, Pennsylvania* pp. 82–86.

Boller, G. 1978. Designing a modern high efficiency mixing and refining plant. *Pa. Manuf. Confect. Assoc. Proc. Annu. Prod. Conf., 32nd, Drexel Hill, Pennsylvania*, pp. 88–93.

Boller, G. 1980. Aspects of liquor grinding. *Pa. Manuf. Confect. Assoc. Proc. Annu. Prod. Conf., 34th, Drexel Hill, Pennsylvania*, pp. 88–93.

Boller, G. 1983. Chocolate manufacturing problems and solutions. *Manuf. Confect.* **63**, 36–40.

Boyd, E. N., Keeney, P. G., and Patton, S. 1965. The measurement of monocarbonyl classes in cocoa beans and chocolate liquor with special reference to flavor. *J. Food Sci.* **30**, 854–859.

Bracco, U. 1973. Graisses pour confiserie: Aspects technologiques, analytiques et physiologiques. *Riv. Soc. Ital. Sci. Alim.* **2**, 145–152.

Bracco, U., Rostagno, W., and Egli, R. H. 1970. A study of cocoa butter–Illipe butter mixtures (*Shorea stenoptera* L.). *Rev. Int. Choc.* **25**, 44–48.

Bucke, C., and Cheetham, P. 1979. Preparation of products for human or animal consumption using a sucrose substitute. British Patent Application 2,066,639A.

Burroughs, P. Date unknown. Applications of DSC to the study of cocoa butters. DuPont (UK) Ltd.

Cadbury Bros. Ltd. 1966. Phosphorylated glyceride derivatives for use as emulsifying agents. British Patent 1,032,465.

Campbell, L. B. 1975. Dairy products and their alternatives in chocolate and confections. *Manuf. Confect.* **55**, 45–52.

Carpenter, A. P. 1979. Determination of tocopherols in vegetable oils. *J. Am. Oil Chem. Soc.* **56**, 668–670.

Carr, J. G., and Davis, P. A. 1980. Cocoa fermentation in Ghana and Malaysia—Further microbiological methods and results. University of Bristol, Bristol, UK.

Casson, N. 1957. A flow equation for pigment–oil suspensions of the printing ink type. *Bull. Br. Soc. Rheol.* **52**, 5.

Caverly, B. L. 1976. Chocolate compositions. British Patent 1,430,017.

Celia, G. 1985. Malbit®-maltitol: An alternative sweetener. *Confect. Manuf. Market.* **22**, 16–26.

Chalin 1976. Method of dutching cocoa. U.S. Patent 3,997,680.

Chalin 1977. Dutching of cocoa. British Patent 1,496,087.

Chapman, D., Crossley, A., and Davies, A. C. 1957. The structure of the major component glyceride of cocoa butter, and of the major oleodisaturated glyceride of lard. *J. Chem. Soc.* 1502–1509.

Chapman, G. M. 1971. Cocoa butter and confectionery fats. Studies using programmed temperature X-ray diffraction and differential scanning calorimetry. *J. Am. Oil Chem. Soc.* **48**, 824–830.

Chatt, E. M. 1953. "Cocoa: Cultivation, processing, Analysis." Wiley (Interscience), New York.

Chevalley, J. 1975. Rheology of chocolate. *J. Texture Stud.* **6**, 177–192.

Chinachoti, P., and Steinberg, M. P. 1986. Moisture hysteresis is due to amorphous sugar. *J. Food Sci.* **51**, 453–455.

Christianson, B. 1976. The continuous production of milk crumb. *Manuf. Confect.* **56**, 69–72.

Clark, W. S. 1977. Special qualities of whey add distinctive character to confection snacks. *Candy Snack Ind.* **142**, 38–40.

Clarke, W. T. 1949. Chocolate and cocoa. *In* "Kirk-Othmer: Encyclopedia of Chemical Technology," Vol. 3. Wiley, New York.

Clauss, K., and Jensen, H. 1973. Oxathiazinone dioxides—A new group of sweetening agents. *Angew. Chem. Int. Ed. Engl.* **12**, 869–876.

Clauss, K., Lück, E., and Von Rymon Lipinski, G. W. 1976. Acetosulfam, ein neuer Süsstoff. *Z. Lebensm. Unters. Forsch.* **162**, 37–40.

Clifford, W., Gyeszley, S., and Manathunya, V. 1977. Accelerated tests vs. calculations based on product/package properties. *Package Deve. Syst.* Sept./Oct., 29–32.

Code of Federal Regulations. 1980. Title 21, Part 163. Office of the Federal Register, National Archives and Record Service, General Services Administration, Washington, D.C.

Code of Federal Regulations. 1981. Title 40, Parts 180, 402. Office of the Federal Register, National Archives and Record Service, General Services Administration, Washington, D.C.

Codex Alimentarius Commission 1982. Codes Standards for Cocoa Products and Chocolate, Codex Ailmentarius, Vol. 7, first ed.

Cook, L. R. 1976. Conching, why, when and how. *Pa. Manuf. Confect. Assoc. Proc. Annu. Prod. Conf., 30th, Drexel Hill, Pennsylvania*, pp. 52–55.

Cook, L. R., and Meursing, E. H. 1982. "Chocolate Production and Use." Harcourt, Brace Jovanovich, Inc., New York.

Cros, E., Villeneuve, F., and Vincent, J. C. 1982a. Research on a cocoa fermentation index. I. Development of total tannins and phenols in cocoa beans. *Cafe Cacao The* **26**, 109–114.

Cros, E., Rouly, M., Villeneuve, F., and Vincent, J. C. 1982b. Research on a cocoa fermentation index. II. Estimation of the red coloring matter of cocoa beans. *Cafe Cacao The* **26**, 115–122.

Cruickshank, D. A., and Jewell, G. G. 1977. Structural studies on tempered cocoa butter. *Br. Food Manuf. Ind. Res. Assoc. Res. Rep.* 256.

Danehy, J. 1983. The ubiquitous Maillard reaction. *Chemtech* **13**, 412–418.

Davies, M. G., Jawad, I. M., and Weir, G. S. D. 1979. The effects of refining on the compositions of vegetable oils. *Br. Food Manuf. Ind. Res. Assoc. Sci. Technol. Surv.* **112**.

DeMan, J. M. 1976. Water. *In* "Principles of Food Chemistry," pp. 1–33. AVI Publishing, Westport, Connecticut.

Dietrich, P., Lederer, E., Winter, M., and Stoll, M. 1964. Flavors. 11. Cocoa flavor. *Helv. Chim. Acta* **47**, 1581.

Dimick, P. S., and Maniere, F. Y. 1977. Effect of conching on the flavor of dark semi-sweet chocolate. *Pa. Manuf. Confect. Assoc. Proc. Annu. Prod. Conf., 31st, Drexel Hill, Pennsylvania*, pp. 25–34.

Dodson, A., and Wright, S. 1982. The new sweeteners: A confectioner's viewpoint. *Food Flavour. Ingred. Process. Pack.*, **4**, 29–59.

d'Ornano, M., Wilbaux, R., Chassevent, F., and Hahn, D. 1968. Comparison between the cut test and the pigment optical density for estimating the degree of fermentation of cocoa beans. *Cafe Cacao The* **12**, 53–62.

Duck, W. N. 1964. The measurement of unstable fat in finished chocolate. *Manuf. Confect.* **44**, 67–72.

Duck, W. 1970. A method to measure the percent solid seed crystal in tempered chocolate. *In* "Twenty Years of Confectionery and Chocolate Progress," pp. 240–251. AVI Publishing, Westport, Connecticut.

Dudrow, F. A. 1983. Deodorization of edible oil. *J. Am. Oil Chem. Soc.* **60**, 224–225.

Duross, J., and Knightly, W. 1970. Relationship of sorbitan monostearate and Polysorbate 60 to bloom properly tempered chocolate. *In* "Twenty Years of Confectionery and Chocolate Progress," pp. 262–272. AVI Publishing, Westport, Connecticut.

Eggen, I. B. 1982. Cocoa product and process of preparation, U.S. Patent 4,343,818.

Eigel, W. N., Butler, J. E., Ernstrom, C. A., Farrell, H. M., Harwalkar, U. R., Jenness, R., and Whitney, R. McL. 1984. Nomenclature of the proteins of cow's milk: Fifth revision. *J. Dairy Sci.* **67**, 1599–1631.

Elson, C. R. 1971. Part II, The continuous process. *Br. Food Manuf. Ind. Res. Assoc. Res. Rep.* 170.

Esan, E. B. 1977. Tissue culture studies on cacao (*Theobroma cacao* L.)—A supplementation of current research. *Int. Cocoa Res. Conf. Proc., 5th, Sept. 1975, Ibadan, Nigeria*, pp. 116–125.

Esan, E. B. 1982. Shoot regeneration from callus derived from embryo axis cultures of *Theobroma cacao in vitro. Turrialba* **32**, 359–364.

Evans, H. C. 1980. Pleomorphism in *Crinipellis perniciosa*, causal agent of witches' broom disease of cocoa. *Trans. Br. Mycol. Soc.* **74**, 515–523.

Farrell, H. M., and Thompson, M. P. 1974. Physical equilibria: Proteins. *In* "Fundamentals of Dairy Chemistry," (B. H. Webb, A. H. Johnson, and J. A. Alford, eds.), 2nd Ed., pp. 442–473. AVI Publishing, Westport, Connecticut.

Faulkner, R. W. 1981. Cocoa butter equivalents are truly speciality vegetable fats. *Pa. Manuf. Confect. Assoc. Proc. Annu. Prod. Conf., 35th, Drexel Hill, Pennsylvania*, pp. 67–73.

Fincke, A. 1965. "Handbuch der Kakaoerzeugnisse," 2nd Ed., p. 219. Springer-Verlag, Berlin and New York.

Fincke, A. 1979. Untersuchungen zur Triglyceridstruktur der Kakaobutter un einiger Kakaobutter— Austauschfette. *Gordian* **5**, 112–116.

Fincke, A. 1980. Möglichkeiten und Grenzen einfacher gaschromatographischer Triglyceridanalysen zun Nachweis frender Fette in Kakaobutter und Schokoladenfetten. *Dsch. Lebensm. Rundschau* **76**, 162–167.

Firestone, D., and Horwitz, W. 1979. IUPAC gas chromatographic method for determination of fatty acid composition: Collaborative study. *J. Am. Oil Chem. Soc.* **62**, 709–721.

Flament, I., Willhalm, B., and Stoll, M. 1967. Research on aromas. 16. Cocoa aroma. *Helv. Chim. Acta* **50**, 2233.

Food and Drug Administration (FDA). 1980a. Action levels for poisonous or deleterious substances in human food or animal feed. Bureau of foods (HFF-326), Washington, D.C.

Food and Drug Administration (FDA). 1980b. The food defect action levels. Bureau of Foods (HFF-326), Washington, D.C.

Forsyth, W. G. C. 1955. Cacao polyphenolic substances. 3. Separation and estimation on paper chromatograms. *Biochem. J.* **60**, 108.

Foster, H. 1978. What is chocolate flavor? *Manuf. Confect.* **58**, 51–59.

Fuege, R. D., Lovegren, N. V., Mitchham, D., and Landmann, W. 1963. *Confect. Manuf.* **8**, 514.

Gavin, A. M. 1978. Edible oil deodorization. *J. Am. Oil Chem. Soc.* **55**, 783–791.

Givaudan, L., and Cie. 1973. Aromatizing agent. British Patent 1311055.

Glattli, V. M. 1962. "Methods of Analyses." Office International du Cacao et du Chocolat, Zurich.

Greathouse, D. C., Laetsch, W. M., and Phinney, B. O. 1971. The shoot growth rhythm of a tropical tree, *Theobroma cacao. Am. J. Bot.* **58**, 281–286.

Greenfield, C. 1963. Dehydration of fluid fatty mixtures above normal coagulation temperature. U.S. Patent 3,076,715.

Griffin, W., and Lynch, M. 1968. Polyhydric alcohols. *In* "Handbook of Food Additives" (T. Furia, ed.), pp. 459–460. Chemical Rubber Co., Cleveland, Ohio.

Gur'eva, K. B., and Tserevitinov, O. B. 1979. Method for evaluating the degree of fermentation of cacao beans. USSR Patent 2,516,658.

Hall, C. W., and Hedrich, T. I. 1971. "Drying of Milk and Milk Products," 2nd Ed. AVI Publishing, Westport, Connecticut.

Hall, T. R. H., and Collin, H. A. 1975. Initiation and growth of tissue cultures of *Theobroma cacao. Ann. Bot.* **39**, 555–570.

Hanrahah, F. P., Tamsma, A., Fox, T. K., and Pallansch, M. J. 1962. Production and properties of spray-dried whole milk foam. *J. Dairy Sci.* **45**, 27–31.

Harland, H. A., Coulter, S. T., and Jenness, R. J. 1952. The effect of the various steps in the manufacture on the extent of serum protein denaturation in nonfat dry milk solids. *J. Dairy Sci.* **35**, 363–368.

Hearon, W., and Witte, J. 1982. Process of making L-gulono-γ-lactone. U.S. Patent 4,337,202.

Henry, K. M., Kon, S. K., Lea, C. H., and White, J. C. D. 1948. Deterioration on storage of dried skim milk. *J. Dairy Res.* **15**, 292–368.

Henry, K. M., Kon, S. K., Lea, C. H., and White, J. C. D. 1949. Protein degradation in stored milk powder. *Int. Dairy Congr., 12th* **2**, 166–174.

Herb, S. F. 1968. Gas–liquid chromatography of lipids, carbohydrates and amino acids. *J. Am. Oil Chem. Soc.* **45**, 784.

Herb, S. F., and Martin, V. G. 1970. How good are analyses of oils by GLC? *J. Am. Oil Chem. Soc.* **47**, 415.

Higginbotham, J., Lindley, M., and Stephens, J. 1981. Flavor enhancing properties of Talin protein sweetener (Thaumatin). *In* "The Quality of Foods and Beverages" (G. Inglett and G. Charalambous, eds.), Vol. I, p. 91. Academic Press, New York.

Hilditch, T. P., and Stainsby, W. J. 1936. The component glycerides of cacao butter. *J. Soc. Chem. Ind.* **55**, 95T.

Hoskin, J. M., and Dimick, P. S. 1979. Volatile fatty acid changes during the conching of chocolate. *Pa. Manuf. Confect. Assoc. Proc. Annu. Prod. Conf., 33rd, Drexel Hill, Pennsylvania*, pp. 23–31.

Hoskin, J. M., and Dimick, P. S. 1980. Observations of chocolate during conching by scanning electron microscopy and viscometry. *J. Food Sci.* **45**, 1541–1545.

Hough, L., Phadnis, S., Khan, R., and Jenner, M. 1979. Sweeteners. British Patent 1,543,167.

Hugunin, A. C., and Nishikawa, R. K. 1978. Milk-derived ingredients lend flavor, texture, nutrition to confections. *Food Prod. Dev.* **12**, 46–48.

Hynd, J. 1970. Utilization of milk proteins. *J. Soc. Dairy Technol.* **23**, 97.

Hyvönen, L., Koivistoinen, P., and Voirol, F. 1982. Food technological evaluation of xylitol. *Adv. Food Res.* **28**, 373–403.

Ibañéz, M. L. 1964. The cultivation of cacao embryos in sterile culture. *Trop. Agric. Trinidad* **41**, 325–328.

International Union of Pure and Applied Chemistry (IUPAC)—Paquot, C. 1979. *In* "Standard Methods for the Analysis of Oils, Fats and Derivatives" (C. Paquot, ed.). Pergamon, Oxford.

Jacquet, M., and Vincent, J. C. 1981. Process for the fermentation of cocoa beans. Br. Patent 6B 2,059,243.

Jacquet, M., Vincent, J. C., Rios, G. M., and Gibert, H. 1981. Fermentation of cocoa beans in a triple phase fluidized bed. *Cafe Cacao The* **25**, 45–54.

Jalal, M. A. F., and Collin, H. A. 1977. Polyphenols of mature plant, seedling, and tissue cultures of *Theobroma cacao. Phytochemistry* **16**, 1377–1380.

Jalal, M. A. F., and Collin, H. A. 1979. Secondary metabolism in tissue cultures of *Theobroma cacao. New Phytol.* **83**, 343–349.

Janick, J., and Pence, V. C. 1980. Method of non-agricultural production of cotyledons. U.S. Patent 4,204,366.

Janick, J., and Pence, V. C. 1981. Plant tissue produced by non-agricultural proliferation of cacao embryos. U.S. Patent 4,301,619.

Janick, J., Hasegawa, P. M., and Pence, V. C. 1981. Method for production of mature asexual cacao embryos and production thereof. U.S. Patent 4,291,498.

Janick, J., Wright, D. C., and Hasegawa, P. M. 1982. *In vitro* production of cacao seed lipids. *J. Am. Soc. Hort. Sci.* **107**, 919–922.

Jewell, G. G. 1981. Factors influencing the crystallization of chocolate. *Pa. Manuf. Confect. Assoc. Proc. Annu. Prod. Conf., 35th, Drexel Hill, Pennsylvania*, pp. 63–66.

Jewell, G. G., and Bradford, L. 1981. Considerations in chocolate formulation. *Manuf. Confect.* **61**, 26–30.

Kato, H., Yamamoto, M., and Fujimaki, M. 1969. Mechanisms of browning degradation of D-fructose and special comparison with D-glucose–glycine reactions. *Agric. Biol. Chem.* **33**, 939.

Kattenberg, H. R. 1981. The quality of cocoa butter. *Manuf. Confect.* **61**, 32.

Katz, I., Wilson, R. A., Evers, W. J., Vock, M. H., and Verhoeve, G. W. 1973. Novel cyclic flavoring compositions and processes. U.S. Patent 3,726,692.

Kim, H. 1982. High performance liquid chromatographic determination of (−)–epicatechin in cocoa beans and the effects of varietal types, curing and roasting on its concentration. MS thesis, Pennsylvania State University.

Kinsella, J. E. 1970. Functional chemistry of milk products in candy and chocolate manufacture. *Manuf. Confect.* **50**, 45–54.

Kinsella, J. E. 1976. Functional properties of proteins in foods: A survey. *CRC Crit. Rev. Food Sci. Nutr.* **7**, 219–280.

Kinsella, J. E., and Tsai, C. H. 1981. Cocoa bean cell culture. U.S. Patent 4,306,022.

Kleinert, J. 1966. Some aspects of cocoa bean roasting. *Rev. Int. Choc.* **21**, 210–228.

Kleinert, J. 1969. Lecture at Solinger School: The correlation between tempering and structure. *Rev. Int. Choc.* **25**, 386–399 (1970).

Kleinert, J. 1970. Particle size investigation of cocoa mass, cocoa powder and chocolate. *Rev. Int. Choc.* **25**, 274, 329.

Kleinert, J. 1971. Chocolate manufacture by the LSCP process. *Rev. Int. Choc.* **26**, 113–119.

Kleinert, J. 1972. Chocolate technology in past, present and future. *Rev. Int. Choc.* **27**, 255–272.

Koch, J. 1961. Milk crumb, the modern milk chocolate ingredient. *Manuf. Confect.* **41**, 23–25.

Korfhage, R. 1967. Scientific reasons for tempering chocolate. Ambrosia Chocolate Company Paper to AACT Atlanta Section, Feb. 24.

Kube, I. J., and Pritzwald-Stegman, D. B. 1976. Lactose in cocoa and chocolate products. *CCB Rev. Choco. Confect. Bakers* **1,** 30–33.

Kurtz, F. 1974. The lipids of milk: Composition and properties. *In* "Fundamentals of Dairy Chemistry," (B. H. Webb, A. H. Johnson, and J. A. Alford, eds.), 2nd Ed., pp. 153–157. AVI Publishing, Westport, Connecticut.

Kurtz, F. E., Tamsma, A., and Pallansch, M. J. 1971. Organoleptic properties of foam spray-dried products made from deodorized milk fat and skim milk. *J. Dairy Sci.* **54,** 173–177.

Landschreiber, E., and Mohr, W., 1974. Composition of cocoa aroma. *Int. Congr. Cocoa Choc. Res., 1st,* pp. 124–134.

Laning, S. J. 1981. Lauric fats for the confectionery industry. *Pa. Manuf. Confect. Assoc. Proc. Annu. Prod. Conf., 35th, Drexel Hill, Pennsylvania,* pp. 79–81.

Layton, R., and Valzny, J. 1978. Glucosylsorbitol adds bulk without sweetness, calories. *Food Prod. Dev.* **12,** 53.

Lees, R. 1980. "A Basic Course in Confectionery." Specialized Publications, Surbiton, Surrey, U.K.

Lees, R., and Jackson, E. B. 1975. "Sugar, Confectionery and Chocolate Manufacture," 1st Ed. Chemical Publishing, New York.

Lehrian, D., and Patterson, G. 1983. Cocoa fermentation. *Biotechnology* **5,** 529–575.

Lehrian, D. W., Keeney, P. G., and Lopez, A. S. 1978. Method for the measurement of phenols associated with the smoky/hammy flavor defect of cocoa beans and chocolate liquor. *J. Food Sci.* **43,** 743–745.

Lehrian, D. W., Keeney, P. G., and Butler, D. R. 1980. Triglyceride characteristics of cocoa butter from cacao fruit matured in a microclimate of elevated temperature. *J. Am. Oil Chem. Soc.* **57,** 66–69.

Lench, M. 1973. Cadbury brings its chocolate know-how to the United States. *Candy Snack Ind.* **139,** 24–29.

Lensack, G. 1965. Talk presented to the Milwaukee chapter, American Association of Candy Technologists, April 21.

Levin, G. 1981. Sweetened edible formulations. U.S. Patent 4,262,032.

Ley, D. 1983. Comparison and judgement of conching systems. *Manuf. Confect.* **63,** 68–71.

Liau, H. T. L. 1976. Raw cocoa processing. Technical Bulletin No. 2, Department of Agriculture, Sabah, Malaysia.

Lim, D. M. 1980. Functional properties of milk proteins with particular reference to confectionery products. *Br. Manuf. Ind. Res. Assoc. Sci. Tech. Surv.* 120.

Litchfield, C. 1972. "Analysis of Triglycerides." Academic Press, New York.

Lopez, A. S. F. 1983. Factors associated with cacao bean acidity and the possibility of its reduction by improved fermentation. *Rev. Theobroma* **13,** 233.

Lopez, A., and Quesnel, V. C. 1971. An assessment of some claims relating to the production and composition of chocolate aroma. *Rev. Int. Choc.* **26,** 19.

Lopez, A., and Quesnel, V. C. 1973. Volatile fatty acid production in cacao fermentation and the effect on chocolate flavor. *J. Sci. Food Agric.* **24,** 319–326.

Lopez, A., and Quesnel, V. C. 1974. The contribution of sulphur compounds to chocolate aroma. *Int. Congr. Cocoa Choc. Res., 1st,* pp. 92–104.

Lopez, A., and Quesnel, V. C. 1976. Methyl-*S*-methionine sulphonium salt: A precursor of dimethyl sulphide in cacao. *J. Sci. Food Agric.* **27,** 85–88.

Lopez, A. S., and McDonald, C. R. 1981. A definition of descriptors to be used for the qualification of chocolate flavors in organoleptic training. *Rev. Theobroma* **11,** 209–217.

Lovegren, N. V., and Feuge, R. O. 1965. Solidification of cocoa butter. *J. Am. Oil Chem. Soc.* **42,** 308–312.

Lovegren, N. V., Gray, M. S., and Feuge, R. O. 1976. Effect of liquid fat on melting point and polymorphic behavior of cocoa butter and cocoa butter fraction. *J. Am. Oil Chem. Soc.* **53,** 108–112.

Lutton, E. S. 1957. On the configuration of cocoa butter. *J. Am. Oil Chem. Soc.* **34,** 521.

Lutton, E. S. 1972. Lipid structures. *J. Am. Oil Chem. Soc.* **49,** 1–9.

Mäkinen, K. 1979. Xylitol and oral health. *Adv. Food Res.* **25,** 137–158.

Manning, D. M. 1984. Thermal and compositional properties of cocoa butter during static and dynamic crystallization. Thesis in food science, Pennsylvania State University.

Manning, D. M., and Dimick, P. S. 1981. Cocoa butter crystallization studies. *Pa. Manuf. Confect. Assoc. Proc. Annu. Prod. Conf., 35th, Drexel Hill, Pennsylvania,* pp. 56–62.

Maravalhas, N. 1972. Amino acids in fermented and unfermented cocoa beans. *Rev. Int. Choc.* **27,** 22–23.

Marcus, S. A. 1982. Multi-layer plastic food containers: An idea whose time has come. *Food Drug Pack.* **46,** 22–36.

Marion, J. P. 1972. Process for manufacture of an aromatizing product. Swiss Patent 527,204.

Marion, J. P., Muggler-Chaven, F., Viani, R., Bricout, J., Reymond, D., and Egli, R. H. 1967. Composition of cocoa aroma. *Helv. Chim. Acta* **50,** 1509.

Markower and Dye. 1956. *J. Agric. Food Chem.* **4,** 72–81.

Mathlouthi, M., Cholli, A. L., and Koenig, J. L. 1986. Spectroscopic study of the structure of sucrose in the amorphous state and in aqueous solution. *Carbohydr. Res.* **147,** 1–9.

Mattson, F., and Volpenhein, R. 1971. Low calorie fat-containing food compositions. U.S. Patent 3,600,186.

May, W. A., and Fernandez, I. 1978. Marriage of cocoa and whey solids receives joint blessings of cheesemakers, chocolate producers. *Food Prod. Dev.* **12,** 38–42.

Mayer-Potschak, K. 1983. Roasting in humid atmosphere. *Manuf. Confect.* **63,** 193–197.

Mayo, J., and Anderson, R. 1968. Enzymic preparation of L-fructose. *Carbohydr. Res.* **8,** 344–347.

Meara, M. L. 1949. The configuration of naturally occurring mixed glycerides. Part V: The configuration of the major component glycerides of cacao butter. *J. Chem. Soc.* 2154–2157.

Meara, M. L., George, P. I., and Beecham, P. T. 1974. Studies of satisfactory and unsatisfactory cocoa butters. *Br. Food Manuf. Ind. Res. Assoc. Res. Rep.* **205.**

Minifie, B. W. 1970. "Chocolate, Cocoa and Confectionery, Science and Technology," 1st Ed., pp. 442–486. AVI Publishing, New York.

Minifie, B. W. 1974. The manufacture of crumb milk chocolate and other methods of incorporation of milk in chocolate. *Manuf. Confect.* **54,** 19–26.

Minifie, B. W. 1980. "Chocolate, Cocoa and Confectionery Science and Technology," 2nd Ed. AVI Publishing, Westport, Connecticut.

Minifie, B. W., and Czyzewski, T. S. 1978. Method for manufacturing crystalline confectionery food products. U.S. Patent 4,086,371.

Minifie, B. W., and Czyzewski, T. S. 1981. Method and apparatus for manufacturing crystalline food products. U.S. Patent 4,267,703.

Mohler, M. R., Hugunin, A. G., and Ebers, K. (1981). Whey-based nonfat milk replacers in light chocolate-flavored compound coatings. *Food Technol.* **35,** 79–81.

Mohr, W. 1958. Untersuchungen über das Kakao Aroma Unter besonderer Berüchsichtigung des Conchierens von Schokoladenmassen. *Fette Seifen Anstrichm.* **60,** 661.

Mohr, W., Ziegleder, G., and Lehnert. Undated. The principles of flavor refining in milk-free and milk-containing chocolate masses, part I. *Commun. Inst. Food Technol. Pack. (Munich).*

Mohr, W., Heiss, R., Ziegleder, G., and Biebl, F. Undated. The principles of flavor refining in milk-free and milk-containing chocolate masses, part II. *Commun. Inst. Food Technol. Pack. (Munich).*

Morita, T., Fujita, I., and Iwamura, J. 1978. Sweetening compound, method of recovery, and use thereof. U.S. Patent 4,082,858.

Moroe, T., Hattori, S., Saito, A., and Muraki, S. 1969. Method of improving the flavor of cocoa- and chocolate-flavored materials. U.S. Patent 3,459,556.

Morris, R. 1967. Potentiation of chocolate flavor with ammoniated glycyrrhizin. U.S. Patent 3,356,505.

Mosimann, G. 1963. Physical and chemical reactions to connection with Mosimann's process for automatic production. *Rev. Int. Choc.* **18**, 208–218.

Muggler-Chavin, F., and Reymond, D. 1967. Constituants aromatiques de cacaos de diverses provenances. *Mitt. Geb. Lebensmittelunters. Hug.* **58**, 466–472.

Musser, J. 1980. The use of monoglycerides in chocolate and confectionery coatings. *Manuf. Confect.* **60**, 69–80.

Nakel, G. M., and Hiler, G. D. 1971. Organic trisulfide-containing chocolate flavor compositions. U.S. Patent 3,619,210.

Nasrallah, S., and Iber, F. 1969. Mannitol absorption and metabolism in man. *Am. J. Med. Sci.* **258**, 80–88.

Neilson, A. 1963. Lactose in confections. *Manuf. Confect.* **43**, 25–27.

Niediek, E. A. 1973. Zerkline Runpseigenchaften der Kakaobohnen Masse. *Rev. Int. Choc.* **28**, 30–36, 72–77.

Niedick, E. A. 1975. Grinding and particle size analysis in food technology with particular reference to cocoa and sugar. *Eur. Symp. Eng. Food Qual., 6th, Sept., Cambridge, U.K.*

Niediek, E. A. 1977a. Potential future developments in chocolate making technology. *Süsswaren* **9/10**, 316–334.

Niediek, E. A. 1977b. Mixing and refining of chocolate. The Sarotti example. *Süsswaren* **21**, 652–654.

Niediek, E. A. 1982. Investigations into the influence of flavour adsorption of sugars on the flavour quality of different chocolates. *Rev. Choc. Confect. Bakery* **7** (1).

Niediek, E. A., and Barbernics, L. 1980. Generation of amorphous sugar in the course of fine refining of chocolate masses. *Gordian* **80**, 267–269.

Niediek, E. A., and Babernics, L. 1981. Problems of exchange reactions during conching. *Choc. Confect. Bakery* **6**, 25–26.

O'Connell, R. T. 1974. Whey in chocolate confections. *Proc. Whey Prod. Conf., Chicago* Publ. No. 3996, p. 116. ERRC, U.S. Department of Agriculture, Wyndmoor, Pennsylvania.

Ogunmoyela, O., and Birch, G. 1984a. Effect of sweetener type and lecithin on hygroscopicity and mold growth in dark chocolate. *J. Food Sci.* **49**, 1088.

Ogunmoyela, O., and Birch, G. 1984b. Sensory considerations in the replacement in dark chocolate of sucrose by other carbohydrate sweeteners. *J. Food Sci.* **49**, 1024.

Office International du Cacao du Chocolat (OICC). 1973. Methods of analysis. Preparation of methyl esters of fatty acids, 17a-E/1973. Analysis of methyl esters of cocoa butter fatty acids by gas–liquid chromatography, 17b-E/1973. Office International du Cacao et du Chocolat, Geneva.

Okada, S., Tsuyama, N., Kurimoto, M., and Sugimoto, K. 1972. Process for the production of starch syrups that have fructose on their molecular ends. U.S. Patent 3,703,440.

Orchard, J. E., Collin, H. A., and Hardwick, K. 1979. Culture of shoot apices of *Theobroma cacao*. *Physiol. Plant.* **47**, 207–210.

O'Rourke, J. 1959. Chocolate product and process. U.S. Patent 2,904,438.

Padley, F. B., and Timms, R. E. 1979. Determination of cocoa butter equivalents in chocolate. *Chem. Ind.* 918–919.

Padley, F. B., and Timms, R. E. 1980. Determination of cocoa butter equivalents in chocolate. *J. Am. Oil Chem. Soc.* **57**, 286–293.

Pallansch, M. J. 1970. Dried products. *In* "By-Products from Milk" (B. H. Webb and E. O. Whittier, eds.), 2nd Ed., pp. 124–182. AVI Publishing, Westport, Connecticut.

Pancoast, H. M., and Junk, W. R. 1980. "Handbook of Sugars," 2nd Ed. AVI Publishing, Westport, Connecticut.

Passos, F. M. L., Silva, D. O., Lopez, A., Ferreira, C. L. L. F., and Guimaraes, W. V. 1983. Characterization and percentual distribution of lactic acid bacteria in traditional cocoa bean fermentations in Bahia. *J. Food Sci.* **49**, 205–208.

Patton, S. 1955. Browning and associated changes in milk and its products: A review. *J. Dairy Sci.* **38**, 457–478.

Paulicka, F. R. 1981. Non-lauric substitute and replacer confectionery coating fats. *Pa. Manuf. Confect. Assoc. Proc. Annu. Prod. Conf., 35th, Drexel Hill, Pennsylvania,* pp. 74–78.

Pence, V. C., Hasegawa, P. M., and Janick, J. 1979. Asexual embryogenesis in *Theobroma cacao* L. *J. Am. Soc. Hort. Sci.* **104**, 145–148.

Pence, V. C., Hasegawa, P. M., and Janick, J. 1980. Initiation and development of asexual embryos of *Theobroma cacao* L. *in vitro. Z. Pflanzenphysiol* **98**, 1–14.

Pence, V. C., Hasegawa, P. M., and Janick, J. 1981a. *In vitro* cotyledonary development and anthocyanin synthesis in zygotic and asexual embryos of *Theobroma cacao. J. Am. Soc. Hort. Sci.* **106**, 381–385.

Pence, V. C., Hasegawa, P. M., and Janick, J. 1981b. Sucrose-mediated regulation of fatty acid composition in asexual embryos of *Theobroma cacao. Physiol. Plant.* **53**, 378–384.

Pinto, A. O., and Chichester, C. O. 1966. Changes in the content of free amino acids during the roasting of cocoa beans. *J. Food Sci.* **31**, 726.

Pour-El, A. 1976. Measurement of functional properties of soy proteins. *In* "World Soybean Research" (L. D. Hill, ed.), pp. 918–946. Interstate Printers and Publishers, New York.

Powell, B. P. 1970. New developments in chocolate and confectionery in Europe. *Pa. Manuf. Confect. Assoc. Proc. Annu. Prod. Conf., 24th, Drexel Hill, Pennsylvania,* pp. 70–80.

Powell, B. D. 1981. The quality of cocoa beans—The needs of the manufacturer. *Int. Cocoa Res. Conf., 8th, Columbia.*

Prior, C. 1977. Growth of *Oncobasidium theobromae* Talbot and Keane in dual culture with callus tissue of *Theobroma cacao* L. *J. Gen. Microbiol.* **99**, 219–22.

Queens University, Kingston, Ontario. 1979. L-Sucrose and process for producing same. Br. Patent 1,556,007.

Quesnel, V. C. 1965. Chloroform-extractable aromatic acids of cacao. *J. Sci. Food. Agric.* **16**, 596–599.

Ram, C. 1976. Moulds of commercial cocoa and their infection origin in farm processing cocoa in Bahia, Brazil. *Fitopatol. Brasil.* **1**, 77–89.

Reade, M. G. 1980. Tempering and temper testing. *Manuf. Confect.* **60**, 29–32, 51–54.

Reineccius, G. A., Anderson, D. A., Kavanagh, T. E., and Keeney, P. G. 1972a. Identification and quantification of the free sugars in cocoa beans. *J. Agric. Food Chem.* **20**, 199–202.

Reineccius, G. A., Keeney, P. G., and Weissberger, W. 1972b. Factors affecting the concentration of pyrazines in cocoa beans. *J. Agric. Food Chem.* **20**, 202–206.

Rennhard, H. 1973. Polysaccharides and their preparation. U.S. Patent 3,766,165.

Riesen, A. 1977. Dietetic chocolate composition. U.S. Patent 4,011,349.

Rohan, T. A. 1963. Studies on the precursors of chocolate aroma. *Br. Food Manuf. Ind. Res. Assoc. Tech. Circular* 228.

Rohan, T. A. 1969a. The flavor of chocolate, its precursors and a study of their reaction. *Gordian* **69**, 443.

Rohan, T. A. 1969b. The flavor of chocolate, its precursors and a study of their reaction. *Gordian* **69**, 500–501.

Rohan, T. A. 1969c. The flavor of chocolate, its precursors and a study of their reaction. *Gordian* **69**, 542–544.

Rohan, T. A. 1969d. The flavor of chocolate, its precursors and a study of their reaction. *Gordian* **69**, 587–590.

Rohan, T. A. 1969e. The flavour of chocolate. *Food Process. Market.* **38**, 12–17.

Rohan, T. A., and Connell, M. 1964. The precursors of chocolate aroma: A study of the flavanoids and phenolic acids. *J. Food Sci.* **29**, 460.

Rohan, T. A., and Stewart, T. 1964. The volatile and non-volatile acids of cocoa beans. *Rev. Int. Choc.* **19**, 502–506.

Rohan, T. A., and Stewart, T. 1966a. Precursors of chocolate aroma: Changes in free amino acids during roasting. *J. Food Sci.* **31**, 202–205.

Rohan, T. A., and Stewart, T. 1966b. Precursors of chocolate aroma: Changes in the sugars during the roasting of cocoa beans. *J. Food Sci.* **31**, 206–209.

Rohan, T. A., and Stewart, T. 1967a. The precursors of chocolate aroma: Production of free amino acids during fermentation of cocoa beans. *J. Food Sci.* **32**, 395–398.

Rohan, T. A., and Stewart, T. 1967b. The precursors of chocolate aroma: Production of reducing sugars during fermentation of cocoa beans. *J. Food Sci.* **32**, 399–402.

Rohan, T. A., and Stewart, T. F. 1969. The flavour precursors of chocolate. *Br. Food Manuf. Ind. Res. Assoc. Res. Rep.* 145.

Rostagno, W. 1979. Experiences using imported chocolate liquor *Proc. Annu. Prod. Conf. Pa. Manuf. Confect. Assoc., 33rd, Drexel Hill, Pennsylvania,* p. 64.

Rostagno, W., Reymond, D., and Viani, R. 1970. Characterization of deodorized cocoa butter. *Rev. Int. Choc.* **25**, 352–353.

Rusoff, I. I. 1971. Process for preparation of milk crumb compositions. U.S. Patent 3,622,342.

Saal, H. 1976. Kraft seeks to improve uses for whey and finds new applications. *Am. Dairy Rev.* **18**, 14–22.

Salame, M. 1974. The use of low permeation thermoplastics in food and beverage packaging. *Meet. Am. Chem. Soc. Div. Org. Coat. Plastics Chem., 167th* **34** (1).

Scheinin, A., and Mäkinen, K. 1975. Turku sugar studies. *Acta Odent, Scand.* **33** (Suppl.), 70.

Schiweck, H., Steinle, G., and Haberl, L. 1975. Low calorie sweetener and sweetener base. U.S. Patent 3,865,957.

Schiweck, H., Steinle, G., Müller, L., Gau, W., and Munir, M. 1980. Glucopyranosido-1,6-mannitol, a process for producing the same and its use as a sugar substitute. U.S. Patent 4,233,439.

Schlatter, J. 1970. Peptide sweetening agents. U.S. Patent 3,492,131.

Schmalfuss, H., and Barthmeyer, H. 1932. Detection of diacetyl and acetyl methyl carbinol in foodstuffs. *Z. Untersuch. Lebensmitt.* **63**, 283–288.

Schwartz, P. B., Wong, D. Y. C., and Bridger, R. 1981. Some notes on maturation of cocoa beans as a means to reduction of acidity. *Planter (Kuala Lumpur)* **57**, 548–587.

Searles, B. R., Alvim, P. de T., and Sharp, W. R. 1976. Hormonal control of cellular proliferation in cultured callus derived from *Theobroma cacao* L. *Rev. Theobroma* **6**, 77–81.

Shallenberger, R., and Lindley, M. 1977. A lipophilic–hydrophobic attribute and component in the stereochemistry of sweetness. *Food Chem.* (2), 145–153.

Shepherd, R. 1976. Large scale processing of cocoa beans temperature and acidity trends. *Planter (Kuala Lumpur)* **52**, 311–322.

Shimatani. 1977. Process for manufacturing edible pigment. Japanese Patent 48190.

Shukla, V. K. S., Schioty Nielsen, W., and Batsberg, W. 1983. A simple and direct procedure for the evaluation of triglyceride composition of cocoa butters by high performance liquid chromatography—A comparison with the existing TLC–GC method. *Fette Seifen Anstreichm.* **85**, 274.

Sills, M. W. 1970. Market test of dry whole milk: Nine supermarkets, Lansdale, PA area. ERS-433. U.S. Department of Agriculture, Economic Research Service, Washington, D.C.

Sokolovsky, A. 1937. Effect of humidity on hygroscopic properties of sugar and caramel. *Ind. Eng. Chem.* **29**, 1422–1423.

Steiner, E. H. 1958. A new rheological relationship to express the flow properties of melted chocolate. *Rev. Int. Choc.* **13**, 290.

Steiner, E. H. 1963. Some aspects of chocolate and confectionery research at B.F.M.I.R.A., Leatherhead. *Pa. Manuf. Confect. Assoc. Proc. Annu. Prod. Conf., 17th, Drexel Hill, Pennsylvania.*

Steinman, A. 1935. Presence of acetaldehyde in tropical fruit. *Z. Lebansm. Unters. Forsch.* **69**, 479–481.

Stewart, T. F. 1970. The precursors of chocolate aroma. *Br. Food Manuf. Ind. Res. Assoc. Res. Rep.* **157.**

Stisrup, K. 1970. Emulsifiers: Their influence on the production, micro-structure and quality of toffees, chocolate and coatings. *Manuf. Confect.* **50**, 35–39.

Szuhaj, B. F. 1983. Lecithin production and utilization. *J. Am. Oil Chem. Soc.* **60**, 258A–261A.

Tamsma, A., Kurtz, F. E., and Pallansch, M. J. 1973. Comparison of flavor and physical properties of foam spray-dried whole milks prepared from concentrates foam with air and nitrogen. *J. Dairy Sci.* **55**, 161–163.

Tan, B. K., Hamilton, R. J., and Berger, K. C. 1981. Glyceride analysis of palm oil after solvent fractionation. *J. Am. Oil Chem. Soc.* **58**, 1.

Teixeira, A. A., Johnson, D. E., and Zall, R. R. 1983. Outlook for whey as an ingredient. *Food Eng.* **55**, 106–108.

Thuren, K. E. P. 1979. Continuous deoderization of cocoa butter in thin layers. U.K. Patent Appl., Fazer, A.B., Sweden.

Timbie, D. J., and Keeney, P. B. 1977. Extraction, fractionation and amino acid composition of Brazilian common cocoa proteins. *J. Agric. Food Chem.* **25**, 424–426.

Timme, E. 1984. Interpack seminar. *Solingen Zentralfachschule Dtsch. Süsswarenwirtschaft* **19**, 5–17.

Torres, A., and Thomas, R. 1981. Polydextrose and its application in foods. *Food Technol.* **35**, 44–49.

Townsley, P. M., 1974. Chocolate aroma from plant cells. *J. Inst. Can. Sci. Technol. Aliment.* **7**, 76–78.

Tsai, C. H., and Kinsella, J. E. 1981a. Initiation and growth of callus and cell suspensions of *Theobroma cacao* L. *Ann. Bot.* **48**, 549–557.

Tsai, C. H., and Kinsella, J. E. 1981b. Tissue culture of cocoa bean (*Theobroma cacao* L.): Changes in lipids during maturation of beans and growth of cells and calli in culture. *Lipids* **16**, 577–582.

Tsai, C. H., and Kinsella, J. E. 1982a. Tissue culture of cocoa beans (*Theobroma cacao* L.): Incorporation of acetate and laurate into lipids of cultured cells. *Lipids* **17**, 367–371.

Tsai, C. H., and Kinsella, J. E. 1982b. Tissue culture of cocoa bean (*Theobroma cacao* L.): Incorporation of fatty acids into lipids of cultured cells. *Lipids* **17**, 848–852.

Tsai, C. H., Wen, M. C., and Kinsella, J. E. 1982. Cocoa bean tissue culture: Lipid composition and fatty acid metabolism. *J. Food Sci.* **47**, 768–773.

Turos, S. 1975. Process for preparing so-called crumb for the manufacture of milk chocolate. U.S. Patent 3,900,578.

Turos, S. 1976. Preparation of crumb for milk chocolate. Br. Patent 1,434,748.

Unilever Limited, 1955. Improvements in or relating to surface-active agents. Br. Patent 723,244.

Usmani, A., and Salyer, I. 1979. Poly-sugar: Modification of poly(vinyl alcohol). *J. Macromol. Sci. Chem.* **13**, 937–952.

Vaeck, S. V. 1951a. Recherches sur le polymorphisme de quelques graisses naturelles. I: Etude termique et microscopique du beurre de cacao. *Rev. Int. Choc.* **4**, 100–113.

Vaeck, S. V. 1951b. Recherches sur le polymorphisme de quelques graisses naturelles. II: Etude calorimetrique du beurre de cacao. *Rev. Int. Choc.* **12**, 350–361.

Vaeck, S. V. 1960. Cacao butter and fat bloom. *Manuf. Confect.* **40**, 35–46, 71–73.

van der Wal, B., Sipma, G., Kettenes, D. K., and Semper, A. Th. J. 1968. Some new constituents of roasted cocoa. *Recl. Trav. Chim. Pays-Bas* **87**, 238.

van der Wal, B., Kettenes, D. K., Stoffelsma, J., Sipma, G., and Semper, A. Th. J. 1971. New volatile components of roasted cocoa. *J. Agric. Food Chem.* **19**, 276–280.

van Elzakker, A. H. M., and van Zutphen, H. J. 1961. Analysis of cocoa aromas with the aid of GC. *Z. Lebensm. Unters. Forsch.* **115**, 222–226.

van Praag, M., Stein, H. S., and Tibbetts, M. S. 1968. Steam volatile aroma constituents of roasted cocoa beans. *J. Agric. Food Chem.* **16**, 1005–1008.

van Straten, S. 1977. Volatile compounds in food. Central Institute for Nutrition and Food, Zeist.

van Veen, P. 1971. Part I, The batch process. *Br. Food Manuf. Ind. Res. Assoc. Res. Rep.* No. 170.

Van Velthuijsen, J. 1979. Food additives derived from lactose: Lactitol and lactitol palmitate. *J. Agric. Food Chem.* **27**, 680–686.

Veltman, P. L., Brederode, H. V., and Verdouk, J. C. J. 1972. Spray-drying solid particles of sugar and recycled crumb product with liquid component of water, sugar, cocoa material, and milk solids to produce chocolate crumb. U.S. Patent 3,702,252.

Veltman, P. L., Brederode, H. V., and Verdouk, J. C. J. 1973. Chocolate crumb and process for making it. Br. Patent 1,306,356.

Vincent, J. C. 1983. Cocoa quality expectations. *Raw Cocoa Prod. Symp. Proc. Solingen.*

Vitzthum, O. G., Werkhoff, P., and Hubert, P. 1975. Volatile components of roasted cocoa: Basic fraction. *J. Food Sci.* **40**, 911–916.

Von Drachenfelds, H. J., Kleinert, J., and Hanssen, E. 1962. *Rev. Int. Choc.* **17**, 409.

Wah, B. K., and Merril, A. L. 1963. Agricultural Handbook No. 8, 189. U.S. Department of Agriculture, Washington, D.C.

Webb, B. H., Johnson, A. H., and Alford, J. A. 1974. "Fundamentals of Dairy Chemistry," 2nd Ed., p. 71. AVI Publishing, Westport, Connecticut.

Weissberger, W., Kavanagh, T. E., and Keeney, P. G. 1971. Identification and quantification of several nonvolatile organic acids of cocoa beans. *J. Food Sci.* **36**, 877–879.

Weurman and DeRooij, C. 1961. Volatile amines in the odors of food. *J. Food Sci.* **26**, 239.

Willie, R. L., and Lutton, E. S. 1966. Polymorphism of cocoa butter. *J. Am. Oil Chem. Soc.* **43**, 491–496.

Withycombe, D. A., Hruza, A., Vock, M. H., Giacino, C., Mookherjee, B. D., Pittet, A. O., and Schreiber, W. L. 1979. α-Substituted alkylidene methionals and uses thereof in foodstuffs and flavors for foodstuffs. U.S. Patent 4,156,029.

Withycombe, D. A., Mookherjee, B. D., Vock, M. H., and Vinals, J. F. 1980. Flavoring with mixtures of 2,4,6-triisobutyl-1.3.5-trioxane and 2-isobutyldialkyl oxazolines. U.S. Patent 4,191,785.

Wolfe, J. A. 1977. CBE's and Codex. *Manuf. Confect.* **57**, 53.

Woo, A. H., and Lindsay, R. C. 1980. Free fatty acid analysis for flavor control in milk chocolate. *Manuf. Confect.* **60**, 43–47.

Wright, D. C., Park, W. D., Leopold, N. R., Hasegawa, P. M., and Janick, J. 1982. Accumulation of lipids, proteins, alkaloids, and anthocyanins during embryo development *in vivo* of *Theobroma cacao* L. *J. Am. Oil Chem. Soc.* **59**, 475–479.

Ylikahri, R. 1979. Metabolic and nutritional aspects of xylitol. *Adv. Food Res.* **25**, 159–180.

Ziegelitz, R. 1982. Lecithin. *Confect. Prod.* **48**, 284–290.

Ziemba, J. 1969. Enzymes enhance the flavor of milk solids. *Food Eng.* **41**, 105–110.

Zimmerman, M. 1974. Fructose in the manufacture of dietetic chocolate. *Manuf. Confect.* **54**, 39–48.

Zoumas, B. L., and Finnegan, E. J. 1979. Chocolate and cocoa. *In* "Kirk–Othmer: Encyclopedia of Chemical Technology" (R. E. Kirk and D. F. Othmer, eds.), pp. 1–19. Wiley, New York.

ENDOGENOUS PROTEOLYTIC ENZYMES IN SKELETAL MUSCLE: THEIR SIGNIFICANCE IN MUSCLE PHYSIOLOGY AND DURING POSTMORTEM AGING EVENTS IN CARCASSES

A. ASGHAR*

Department of Food Science
University of Alberta
Edmonton, Alberta
Canada T6G 2P5

A. R. BHATTI

Preventive Medicine Section
Defence Research Establishment, Suffield
Ralston, Alberta
Canada T0J 2N0

*Present address: Department of Food Science, Michigan State University, E. Lansing, MI. 48824, U.S.A.

343

I. INTRODUCTION

The enzymes with the ability of hydrolyzing peptide bonds are called proteases or proteinases. The former term had more commonly been used in the old literature, whereas the latter was adopted by the Enzyme Commission in 1972 for enzyme nomenclature. Proteinases in fact can catalyze five types of reactions (Mihalyi, 1972; Kullmann, 1985), namely, (1) cleaving of peptide bond, (2) cleaving of amide bond, (3) synthesis of peptide bond and transpeptidation, (4) cleaving of ester bond of amino acids, and (5) exchange of oxygen between water and carbonyl group of amino acids. The first three reactions involve a C—N bond, while the last two are concerned with a C—O linkage. However,

$$\text{cleavage of peptide bond } (-\overset{\displaystyle \overset{O}{\|}}{C}\overset{\downarrow}{-}\underset{\displaystyle \underset{|}{H}}{N}-), \text{ having } 65.9 \text{ kcal energy (Pauling,}$$

1960), is the characteristic function of proteinases, and the equilibrium of reaction lies on the side of hydrolyzed products. The reverse reaction appears only under unphysiological conditions, or occurs on accumulation of large excess of the products. The overall process involves splitting of not only C—N bonds but also O—H bonds of water, beside the formation of two new C—OH and N—H bonds. The net energy for the complete reaction is +3.7 kcal (Pauling, 1960).

Although the proteolytic changes in the stomach during food digestion were realized by Reaumur as early as 1752, it was Salkowaski who, in 1890, reported the degradation of mammalian tissues brought about by some endogenous proteases. Jacoby (1900) used the term "autolysis" to describe this phenomenon. These early studies provided initiative for other investigators to unravel the chemical nature of the changes produced by endogenous proteolytic enzymes (Hedin, 1904; Fischer and Abderhalden, 1905; Vernon, 1908; Dernby, 1918; Willstatter and Bamann, 1929). As only a few proteolytic enzymes were known in the beginning, they were classified on the basis of their origin such as trypsin and chymotrypsin from pancreas, pepsin and renin from stomach, papain from papaya. Sometimes they were classified into acid, alkaline, and neutral proteases, depending on their pH requirement, or into proteases and peptidases, depending on substrate requirements.

However, the later developments in the use of synthetic substrates for the study of proteolytic enzymes (Bergmann and Fruton, 1941) dramatically increased the dimensions of proteases. These advances led to the classification of these enzymes into two main groups: the exopeptidases and endopeptidases. The former need the presence of either a free α-NH_2 or α-COOH group adjacent to scissible bond, whereas the latter cleaves peptide bonds of the polypeptide chain distant to the termini. The use of synthetic substrates also helped in elucidating the structure–function relation of exopeptidases which have been further classified into aminopeptidases, carboxypeptidase, dipeptidases, and dipeptidylpeptidases. Similarly, the endopeptidases have been subdivided into four groups, namely, the serine, cysteine (thiol), aspartate, and metalloproteases, depending on the nature of the active site which is determined by using specific protease inhibitors (Hartley, 1960; Barrett, 1980; Barrett and McDonald, 1980; Bird and Carter, 1980). We have maintained this latest trend of the classification of proteinases in presenting the proteolytic enzymes of skeletal muscle.

A vast number of proteases seem to have been discovered in mammalian tissues. The directory compiled by Barrett and McDonald in 1980 suggests the presence of at least 144 proteolytic enzymes in mammalian tissues, out of which 41 are exopeptidases and 103 are endopeptidases. Among exopeptidases, 9 each are amino- and carboxypeptidases, whereas the remaining are peptidases (di-, tri-, ω, etc.). On the other hand, among endopeptidases, 59, 15, 12 and 11, respectively are serine, thiol, aspartate, and metallopeptidases. The catalytic mechanism of the remaining 6 endopeptidases was not clear at that time.

Although certain organs such as liver, spleen, and kidney of different species are the richest sources of most of the proteolytic enzymes, skeletal muscles also seem to contain a wide spectrum of proteases. Despite the fact that their activity in muscle is much lower than in other tissues, they play important roles in protein turnover during growth and development of animals and in pathological conditions of muscle. Some endogenous proteases also contribute to tenderness of meat during the postmortem aging process. It should be emphasized that the origin and distribution of some proteolytic enzymes in the cellular structure of muscle are not yet precisely known. Uncertainty also prevails about some muscle proteinases as to whether they originate from muscle cells per se, or they reside in other cells associated with skeletal muscles. Available information on all these aspects of skeletal muscle proteinases, with particular reference to meat animals, has been integrated in this article. In addition, we have also discussed at length their contribution in improving meat tenderness and in the formation of flavor precursors during the postmortem aging process.

II. EXOPEPTIDASES IN SKELETAL MUSCLES

Those proteolytic enzymes which hydrolyze peptide bonds from the N or C terminus are called exopeptidases. Sometimes they are classified into two groups: the oligopeptidases and polypeptidases. The former require a specific distance (2, 3, or 4 residues) from the N or C terminus to cleave the bond, whereas the latter only need a free residue at one of the termini (McDonald and Schwabe, 1977). However, different modes of action of expopeptidases on synthetic substrates led their further classification into four main groups that is, the aminopeptidases, carboxypeptidases, dipeptidases, and dipeptidylpeptidases (Barrett and McDonald, 1980; Bird and Carter, 1980).

A. AMINOPEPTIDASES (EC 3.4.11)

Those exopeptidases which require the presence of a free α-amino (α-NH$_2$) or α-imino (α-NH) group to initiate cleaving the peptide bond from the N terminus, and which release free amino or imino acids from polypeptide chains, are classified as amino- or iminopeptidases (as appropriate). They are also called α-aminoacylpeptide hydrolases. The presence of two forms of aminopeptidases in skeletal muscle has been reported. They are leucine aminopeptidase and arylamidases.

1. Leucine Aminopeptidase

The leucine aminopeptidase cleaves the N-terminal peptide bond of those unsubstituted amides and peptides in which a leucine residue is present at the N terminus and is in the L configuration. Leucine amide is the usual synthetic substrate used to assay the activity of leucine aminopeptidase (Bird and Carter, 1980). This aminopeptidase shows V_{max} at pH 7.8–8.0 and is activated by Mg^{2+} and Mn^{2+} cations (DeLange and Smith, 1971). In rabbit and rat skeletal muscles, Smith (1948a) identified the activity of this enzyme using Leu-Gly and

Leu-Gly-Gly as the substrates. Joseph and Sanders (1966) further characterized it from porcine muscle. Its molecular weight was reported to be 150,000, and the enzyme rapidly lost activity below 7.0. The presence of leucine aminopeptidase activity was also noted in human skeletal muscle (Bury and Pennington, 1973).

2. Arylamidases or Cathepsin III

Those aminopeptidases which hydrolyze such chromogenic substrates as aminoacyl p-nitroanilides and 2-naphthylamides have been called arylamidases to distinguish them from leucine aminopeptidase (Patterson et al., 1963; Bird and Carter, 1980). They are thiol enzymes and are inhibited by puromycin (Ellis and Perry, 1966). In skeletal muscle the activity of acid (pH 6.0), basic (pH 7.8), and neutral (pH 7.0) arylamidases has been identified by using lysyl-, arginyl-, and leucyl-2-naphthylamide, respectively, as substrate (Bury and Pennington, 1973; Kar and Pearson, 1976a,b). The molecular weight of neutral arylamidase was estimated to be 257,000 and the basic was 105,000 (Bury et al., 1977). About 60–90% of the activity of these aminopeptidases was observed in soluble fraction of the sarcoplasm (Hardy et al., 1975; Parsons and Pennington, 1976; Bury et al., 1977), suggesting that arylamidases are present in free form. In contrast, differential centrifugation study by Goodall (1965) had indicated the association of arylamidase activity with lysosomes and heavy mitochondrial fractions. The arylamidase activity in human skeletal muscle was shown to be stimulated by 1 mM of such divalent cations as Ca^{2+}, Zn^{2+}, Mg^{2+}, and Mn^{2+} (Bury and Pennington, 1973).

B. CARBOXYPEPTIDASES (EC 3.4.12)

The exopeptidases which require the presence of an unsubstituted amino acid residue, that is, a free α-carboxyl group (α-COOH), to initiate hydrolyzing of a peptide bond from the C terminus, and produce free amino acids, were formerly named carboxypeptidases. Now they have been classified as peptidylamino-acid hydrolases (McDonald and Schwabe, 1977). The activity of two peptidylamino-acid hydrolases has been observed in skeletal muscle. They are lysosomal carboxypeptidase A and lysosomal carboxypeptidase B.

1. Lyosomal Carboxypeptidase A (or Cathepsin A)

Lyosomal carboxypeptidase A (McDonald and Schwabe, 1977) which is commonly known as cathepsin A, hydrolyzes C-terminal peptide bonds provided any one of hydrophobic amino acids (preferably) or other residues, but not one of the basic amino acids, constitutes the penultimate residue of the concerned peptide bond (Tallan et al., 1952). Possibly the same enzyme earlier was named cathepsin I by Fruton et al. (1941). Since the properties of this carboxypeptidase do not qualify it to be classified as cathepsin, McDonald and Schwabe (1977) suggested that this enzyme be better named lysosomal carboxypeptidase A (lysosomal CP-A), because it was found in association with lysosome-like particles (Iodice *et al.*, 1972). The characteristics of this enzyme from other tissues indicate it to be a serine proteinase (Bird and Carter, 1980). A study by Logunov and Orekhovich (1972) revealed that lysosomal CP-A also has some endopeptidase ability at hydrophobic sites on oligopeptides as shown by cleaving Z-Glu-Tyr-OEt, which is a substrate for pepsin. This suggests that cathepsin A is a relatively nonspecific exopeptidase.

Bodwell and Pearson (1964) reported the presence of cathepsin A activity in bovine skeletal muscle. Low activity of this enzyme was also observed in porcine (Parrish and Bailey, 1966), rabbit, and chicken muscles (Iodice *et al.*, 1966). However, Caldwell and Grosjean (1971) observed 100 times higher activity of cathepsin A than that of cathepsin B in chicken breast muscle. Cathepsin A showed V_{max} at pH 5.5.

2. *Lysosomal Carboxypeptidase B (Cathepsin B2)*

Cathepsin B2-like activity has been observed in many mammalian tissues and was described in literature under different names such as cathepsin IV (Fruton *et al.*, 1941), catheptic carboxypeptidase B (Greenbaum and Sherman, 1962), and catheptic carboxypeptidase G (Taylor and Tappel, 1974). McDonald and Schwabe (1977) proposed lysosomal carboxypeptidase B as the name for cathepsin B2-like activity in tissues. Cathepsin B2 is a thiol proteinase with molecular weight of 47,000–52,000 (Otto and Bhaki, 1969; Barrett, 1972) and hydrolyzes Bz-Gly-Arg as a substrate from the C terminus at pH 5.5–6.0. However, this enzyme is nonspecific as it can set free all amino acids, but proline, from N-blocked dipeptides at a reasonable rate (Ninjoor *et al.*, 1974; McDonald and Ellis, 1975). Cathepsin B2 also showed amidase activity on an amide (Bz-Agr-NH$_2$) substrate at pH 5.6 (Otto, 1971).

Cathepsin B2 was isolated from skeletal muscle by Distelmaier *et al.* (1972) and Hardy *et al.* (1975), and they reported its molecular weight, respectively, as 53,500 and 45,000. Many researchers have substantiated the fact that cathepsin B2 acts like a carboxydipeptidase on appropriate substrates (Aronson and Barrett, 1978; Nakai *et al.*, 1978; Bond and Barrett, 1980; Hannappel *et al.*, 1982; Katunuma *et al.*, 1983; Towatari and Kutunuma, 1983; Hirao *et al.*, 1984).

C. DIPEPTIDASES (EC 3.4.13)

Those enzymes which hydrolyze the peptide bond of dipeptides and require both α-NH$_2$ and α-COOH groups in free (unsubstituted) form, respectively, at the N and C termini of the dipeptides have been classified as dipeptidases (Bird and Carter, 1980). On the basis of the specificity for a particular amino acid involved in the dipeptide, they were named accordingly. For example, the activities of prolinase, prolidase, glycyl-leucine dipeptidase, and glycyl-glycine dipeptidase have been reported in several mammalian tissues including skeletal muscle.

1. Prolinase (EC 3.4.13.8)

The dipeptidase which hydrolyzes dipeptides containing N-terminal proline or hydroxyproline (such as Pro-Gly) has been named prolinase or prolyl dipeptidase (Bird and Carter, 1980). A study by Smith (1948c) suggested the presence of prolinase activity in skeletal muscles of rabbits and rats. Prolinase exhibited maximum activity at pH 8.0. It was activated by manganese ions and inhibited by citrate, phosphate, and pyrophosphate ions.

2. Prolidase (EC 3.4.13.9)

The dipeptidase which cleaves only those dipeptides in which the peptide bond lacks hydrogen atom has been designated prolidase (Smith, 1948c). Prolidase activity was also observed by Smith (1948c) in skeletal muscle of different species. It showed V_{max} at pH 7.5 and 8.2 in the presence of Mn^{2+}.

3. Glycyl-Leucine Dipeptidase (EC 3.4.13.11)

The activity of glycyl-leucine dipeptidase was detected by Smith (1948b) in rabbit and rat skeletal muscle. Weinstock et al. (1956) also reported its activity in skeletal muscle. Although Smith (1948b) observed the activation of glycyl-leucine dipeptidase by Zn^{2+} in the presence of PO_4^{3-} at pH 8.0, Weinstock et al. (1956) found an inhibitory effect of these ions on the activity. However, Mn^{2+} had no effect on the activity of this enzyme (Krzysik and Adibi, 1977).

4. Glycyl-Glycine Dipeptidase (EC 3.4.13.11)

The rabbit and rat skeletal muscles also contain the activity of glycyl-glycine dipeptidase (Smith, 1948b). This enzyme was shown to be activated by Co^{2+} at pH 7.0–7.6 (Smith, 1948b; Krzysik and Adibi, 1977). Two activities of dipeptidases were also reported by Bodwell and Pearson (1964) in bovine skeletal muscle extract. These dipeptidases hydrolyzed Gly-Tyr and Leu-Tyr dipeptides.

D. DIPEPTIDYLPEPTIDASES (EC 3.4.14)

The proteolytic enzymes which catalyze the consecutive release of intact dipeptides from the unsubstituted N terminus of polypeptides have been classified as peptidyldipeptide hydrolases (McDonald and Schwabe, 1977) or dipeptidylpeptidases (Bird and Carter, 1980). Formerly, they were categorized peptidyl dipeptidases. On the basis of dipeptide 2-naphthylamide substrate specificity, the activities of four peptidyldipeptide hydrolases have been detected in skeletal muscle (McDonald et al., 1971; Bury and Pennington, 1975) as described below.

1. Dipeptidyl Aminopeptidase I or Cathepsin C (EC 3.4.14.1)

Dipeptidyl aminopeptidase I which is commonly known as cathepsin C, has also been reported in the literature under other names such as dipeptidyl peptidase I, dipeptidyl arylamidase I, dipeptidyl transferase, and glucagon-degrading enzyme (McDonald and Schwabe, 1977). The synthetic substrates used to identify the activity of cathepsin C are Gly-Arg- and Gly-Phe-2-naphthylamide at pH 5.6. Cathepsin C prefers that the penultimate amino acid residue should be in the L configuration and possibly contain a hydrophobic side chain, although the latter condition is not a strict prerequisite (Planta et al., 1964). Generally speaking cathepsin C cleaves amide, ester, arylamide, and peptide substrates with the following sequence: $X—Y\overset{\downarrow}{—}Z$, provided X is not arginine or lysine, and Y or Z is not proline.

A thiol group constitutes the active site of cathepsin C (Fruton and Mycek, 1956). It has a molecular weight about 200,000 and is composed of 8 subunits (6 identical, 2 different) which can disassociate in denaturing reagents such as urea at pHs below 3.0 (Metrione et al., 1970). Chloride ions are required for its activation at pH 5–6 (McDonald et al., 1966, 1974). Several workers purified cathepsin C from skeletal muscles (Bury and Pennington, 1975; Hardy et al., 1977); however, its activity was found to be relatively lower in muscle (Bouma and Gruber, 1964; Lutalo-Bosa and MacRae, 1969) than in other tissues (Gutmann and Fruton, 1948). A study by Iodice et al. (1972) on chicken breast muscle assigned the location of cathepsin C in the lysosome-like particles, where it appears to be bound to the membrane (Hardy et al., 1975). Fluorescence histochemical study by Stauber and Ong (1982b) has shown the presence of cathepsin C in lysosomal particles of various muscle. Its activity was the highest in soleus, and least in cardiac and extensor digitorum longus muscles.

2. Dipeptidyl Aminopeptidase II (EC 3.4.14.2)

The other terms used in the literature for defining dipeptidyl aminopeptidase II (DAP II) are dipeptidyl arylamidase II and carboxytripeptidase (Bird and Carter, 1980). The molecular weight of DAP II has been reported to be 130,000, and its activity is evaluated on Lys-Ala-2-naphthylamide at pH 4.5–5.5 (McDonald et al., 1968). It cleaves the dipeptide from the N terminus of the peptide $X—Y\overset{\downarrow}{—}Z$, especially when X is lysine or arginine, and Y may be proline. In contrast to cathepsin C, its active site is not a thiol group nor does it need Cl⁻ for activation (Kar and Pearson, 1978; Parsons *et al.*, 1978). DAP II also displays carboxytripeptidase activity at pH 4.5 (McDonald and Schwabe, 1977).

DAP II activity has been detected in human and rat skeletal muscles (McDonald *et al.*, 1971; Bury and Pennington, 1975; Parsons and Pennington, 1976; Kar and Pearson, 1978) and in cardiac muscle (Vanha-Perttula and Kalliomäki, 1973). The enzyme was found mainly in the lysosomal fraction of muscle (Hardy *et al.*, 1977; Pennington, 1977), although the activity was relatively lower than in other tissues.

3. Dipeptidyl Aminopeptidase III (EC 3.4.14.4)

The dipeptidyl aminopeptidase III (DAP III) cleaves dipeptides sequentially from the unsubstituted N terminus of polypeptides at pH 7–8 (McDonald *et al.*, 1971). Generally Arg-Arg-2-naphthylamide, which is not affected by DAP II and DAP IV, is used as a substrate to identify its activity at pH 8.5 in the presence of 1 mM puromycin to inhibit the activity of arylamidase (Kar and Pearson, 1978). DAP III activity has been reported in rat (McDonald *et al.*,

TABLE I

SOME CHARACTERISTICS OF THE EXOPEPTIDASES OF SKELETAL MUSCLE

Exopeptidase[a]	Molecular weight	pH range for activity	Cellular distribution
Aminopeptidases			
Leucine aminopeptidases	150,000	7.8–8.0	Cytosolic
Arylamidases (cathepsin III)			
Neutral	257,000	~7.0	Cytosolic
Basic	105,000	~8.0	Cytosolic
Acidic	—	~6.0	—
Carboxypeptidases			
Cathepsin A	100,000	~5.5	Lysosomal
Cathepsin B2	52,000	5.5–6.0	Lysosomal
Dipeptidases			
Prolinase	300,000	8.0–8.8	Cytosolic
Prolidase	108,000	7.5–8.2	Cytosolic
Glycyl-leucine dipeptidase	—	7.8–8.0	Cytosolic
Glycyl-glycine dipeptidase	—	7.0–7.5	Cytosolic
Dipeptidylpeptidases			
Dipeptidyl aminopeptidase I (cathepsin C)	200,000	5–6	Lysosomal
Dipeptidyl aminopeptidase II	130,000	4.5–5.5	Lysosomal
Dipeptidyl aminopeptidase III	80,000	7.0–8.5	Cytosolic
Dipeptidyl aminopeptidase IV	250,000	~7.5	Microsomal

[a] Derived from Bird and Carter (1980).

1971) and human skeletal muscles (Parsons and Pennington, 1976). In contrast to DAP II, DAP III was shown to be cytosolic in origin, and its activity was inhibited by 1 mM EDTA and benzethonium chloride. It is possibly a serine peptidase, with molecular weight of 80,000, although it showed some thiol activation.

4. Dipeptidyl Aminopeptidase IV (EC 3.4.14.5)

Dipeptidyl aminopeptidase IV (DAP IV) hydrolyzes the peptide bond from the unsubstituted N terminus of polypeptides with a sequence X—Y$\overset{\downarrow}{—}$Z, in which Y is a proline residue, and it produces dipeptide at pH 7.5. Usually a Gly-Pro-2-naphthylamide substrate, which is not affected by DAP I, II, and III (McDonald and Schwabe, 1977) nor by arylamidase (Kar and Pearson, 1978), is used for DAP IV assay. Kar and Pearson (1978) have detected the activity of DAP IV in human skeletal muscle. They located this enzyme in the microsomal fraction of muscle.

In Table I are recorded some of the physical properties of aminopeptidases, carboxypeptidases, dipeptidases, and dipeptidylpeptidases which have been discovered in skeletal muscle from different species.

III. ENDOPEPTIDASES IN SKELETAL MUSCLES

By definition, endopeptidases cleave peptide bonds of a polypeptide chain distant to the termini, which have no charged group on the α carbon atom flanking the scissible bond. However, they do not have absolute specificity for the topography of the susceptible bonds as they can hydrolyze terminal bonds also, though at a slow rate, provided their other specificity requirements are satisfied (Mihalyi, 1972). As the substrate specificities of endopeptidases are not known, they have been classified into four groups on the basis of catalytic mechanism (Bird and Carter, 1980), which is determined by their sensitivity to specific inhibitors. These groups are serine proteinases, thiol proteinases, carboxyl proteinases, and metalloproteinases.

A. SERINE PROTEINASES (EC 3.4.21)

Those endopeptidases which have a unique reactive serine residue in the active center have been classified as serine proteinases. In fact, the nucleophilic character of the serial OH group in these enzymes is enhanced by the transfer of electronic charge from the COOH group of a buried aspartic acid residue through an intermediate amidazole group of histidine (Blow et al., 1969; Blow and Steitz, 1970). Since these enzymes show maximum activity at a high pH value

(8.0), they are also called alkaline proteinases (Bird et al., 1980). Serine proteases are inhibited by acylation of the serial OH group with diisopropyl fluorophosphate (DFP) (Jansen et al., 1949) or sulfonyl fluoride (Fahrney and Gold, 1963) or by alkylation of histidine's imidazole group by α-halogenylcarbonyl compounds (Shaw et al., 1965; Beeley and Neurath, 1968).

Although Hedin, in 1904, had reported the presence of an alkaline proteinase called leino-α-protease in the spleen, no alkaline endopeptidase was detected in skeletal muscle by Smith during his studies in 1948. However, later on many investigators succeeded in identifying the chymotrypsin-like activity in skeletal muscles of different species (Koszalka and Miller, 1960; Makinodan et al., 1982). These findings are summarized below.

1. Myofibrillar Serine Proteinase

Noguchi and Kandatsu (1971) identified an alkaline proteinase activity (pH 9.0) in the supernatant and pellet, obtained by centrifuging the rat skeletal muscle homogenate at 10,000 g. Since the activity in the pellet was 9 times higher than in the supernatant, the enzyme was thought to be associated with myofibrils. A similar proteinase activity was also reported by Holmes et al. (1971) in myofibrils from rat skeletal muscle, and it showed V_{max} at pH 8.3. Their findings suggested that a hydroxyl group was responsible for the enzymatic activity.

This proteinase (MW 25,000) was purified only from rat skeletal muscle (Noguchi and Kandatsu, 1971), and it was not detected in rabbit, chicken, and guinea pig skeletal muscle (Noguchi and Kandatsu, 1969, 1970). The peptide bonds labile to this enzyme are those which are formed by Try-Leu and Phe-Phe residues (Noguchi and Kandatsu, 1976). Another group of researchers (Mayer et al., 1974a) also described the alkaline proteinase activity associated with myofibrils of rat skeletal muscle. However, a study by Noguchi and Kandatsu (1976) suggested that the proteinase which they had isolated earlier and that of Mayer et al. (1974a) may be the same enzyme. A similar proteinase (MW 26,000), called myosin-cleaving protease, was purified by Murakami and Uchida (1978) from rat cardiac myofibrils. It showed the properties of serine proteinase (alkaline pH), and did not require Ca^{2+} for activation (Murakami and Uchida, 1979, 1980).

2. Group Specific Proteinase

Katunuma et al. (1975) and Sanada et al (1978a) isolated a serine proteinase (MW 22,000–24,000) from rat skeletal muscle and other tissue powder (acetone treated) by extracting with 0.5 M potassium phosphate buffer (pH 8.5). It showed maximum activity at pH 8.0. Because of its action on specific proteins,

Katunuma and Kominami (1977) later named it "group specific proteinase." This enzyme was also chymotrypsin-like as it could hydrolyze synthetic substrates for chmyotrypsin (e.g., Ac-Tyr-OEt, Ac-Phe-OEt, Ac-Try-OEt), but it had little effect on trypsin substrates (e.g., Tos-Arg-OME, Bz-Arg-OEt).

Another study by Katunuma and associates (Kobayashi *et al.*, 1978) showed that this proteinase preferably cleaved peptide bonds between Phe-Thr, Tyr-Ser, Tyr-Leu, Try-Leu, and Tyr-Ile residues, suggesting its preference for those peptide bonds which have aromatic amino acid residues on the carboxyl side. Many properties of this proteinase seem to be identical to that of myofibrillar proteinase. However, the former was shown to be inhibited by Ca^{2+} (Katunuma *et al.*, 1975) whereas the latter was not affected at all by these cations (Mayer *et al.*, 1974a; Murakami and Uchida, 1978, 1979).

3. Cytosolic and Myofibrillar Proteinases

Reinauer and co-workers (Dahlmann and Reinauer, 1978; Reinauer and Dahlmann, 1979; Dahlmann *et al.*, 1979) have observed in rat skeletal muscle homogenate the activity of two proteinases at alkaline pH. One enzyme, with a molecular weight of 25,000, was isolated from cytoplasmic fraction, and hence was called cytosolic protease. It showed chymotrypsin-like properties. The other proteinase (MW 30,800) was isolated from myofibrillar fraction and thus named myofibrillar protease. This enzyme with trypsin-like activities was resolved into several isozymic forms by isoelectric focusing. Each one showed detectable activity in the pH range 7–5.

4. ATP-Activated Alkaline Proteinase

Etlinger and Goldberg (1977) have described the presence of an ATP-stimulated protease in reticulocytes, which exhibited maximum activity at pH 7.8. This enzyme (MW 550,000) was partially purified from rat liver (DeMartino and Goldberg, 1979). Most of the proteinase inhibitors, except DFP and *o*-phenanthroline, had no effect on its activity. Among nucleotides, ADP, AMP, and cAMP did not influence the activity, whereas GTP, CTP, and UTP all activated the enzyme but to a lesser extent than did ATP. Although Goldberg and co-workers (Libby and Goldberg, 1978, 1980a,b; Libby *et al.*, 1979) strongly believe that a similar proteinase is involved in the degradation of muscle proteins, the enzyme has not been characterized in the skeletal muscular system. Lately, it has been identified in rat cardiac muscle (DeMartino, 1983).

Regarding the function of ATP in the proteolysis, two propositions have been made. According to one, ATP may be needed to unfold the helix of protein before the chain could be hydrolyzed (Nobrega *et al.*, 1972; Abdel-Monem and Hoffman-Berling, 1976). If unfolding of the helix is a prerequisite for proteolysis, then all endopeptidases would require the presence of ATP which, in fact, is contrary to general observations. The second proposition assigns a role for ATP in modifying the ATP-dependent protease or in inactivating the endogenous inhibitor (Goldberg et al., 1979).

B. THIOL PROTEINASES (EC 3.4.22)

In the case of thiol proteinases one or more SH groups constitute the active centers which catalyze the reaction. They are inhibited by oxidizing and alkylating agents and by heavy metal ions which bind the SH group (Mihalyi, 1972). Dipyridyl disulfides and 5,5'-dithiobis(2-nitrobenzoic acid) are considered specific inhibitors for thiol proteases by some researchers (Wharton et al., 1968; Brocklehurst and Little, 1972) as they react only with the SH group to form a disulfide linkage. Several thiol proteases have been reported in skeletal muscle. They are cathepsins B1, H, L, and Ca^{2+}-activated neutral proteinases.

1. Cathepsin B1 (EC 3.4.22.1)

Originally cathepsin B was isolated from liver lysosome (Greenbaum and Fruton, 1957) and was called cathepsin II. It was identical to trypsin as it deamidated the trypsin's substrate (Bz-Arg-NH_2) under reducing conditions. Later, it was revealed that the original cathepsin B was composed of two molecular species (Otto and Bhaki, 1969). The low molecular weight (25,000) component was designated B' (now called simply cathepsin B), and the high molecular weight (52,000) component was given the name of cathepsin B2. In fact the molecular weight of cathepsin B1 varies from 24,000 to 28,000 in various tissues, and isoelectric focusing results indicate the presence of multiple forms with pI values varying from 4.7 to 5.6 (Franklin and Metrione, 1972; Keilová and Tomäsek, 1973; Otto and Riesenkönig, 1975; Barrett, 1973; Etherington, 1974; Takahashi et al., 1979; Locnikar et al., 1981). This possibly explains why the optimum pH requirements for cathepsin B1 varied widely (3.5–6.0). The optimum pH value also varied depending on the nature of substrates (e.g., 4–3 for native protein, 6.0 for azoprotein); however, the V_{max} has generally been found at pH 6.0 (Barrett, 1972, 1973). The activity of cathepsin B1 depends on the SH group (Keilová and Turková, 1970; Snellman, 1971; Husain and Baqai, 1976), and the enzyme is unstable above pH 7.0.

Among the catheptic thiol proteases, only cathepsin B1 from rat liver has been sequenced (Katunuma and Kominami, 1983). It is a glycoprotein, composed of 252 amino acid residues, and the asparigine residue at position 111 is glycosylated. The cysteine and histidine residues, respectively, at positions 2, 9, and 197 constitute the active sites. There appear to be many similarities between cathepsin B1 and papain (Mitchel et al., 1970) with respect to their sequence.

A detectable but relatively low activity of cathepsin B1 has been reported in skeletal muscles from different species (Bouma and Gruber, 1964; Randall and MacRae, 1967; Lutalo-Bosa and MacRae, 1969; Pluskal and Pennington, 1973a). This enzyme was located in the lysosomal fraction of muscle (Kar and Pearson, 1977; Bird *et al.*, 1978; Hardy and Pennington, 1979) and of other tissues (Otto, 1971; Nakashima and Ogino, 1974; Davidson and Poole, 1975). The molecular weight of cathepsin B1 from skeletal muscle was shown to be 25,500 (Hardy *et al.*, 1975) and 27,000 (Bird *et al.*, 1977). Earlier, Distelmaier *et al.* (1972) had recorded its molecular weight as 37,000, which on autolysis during storage reduced to 26,000. In view of this, whether the isozymes of B1 really exist *in situ* or perhaps originate from autolysis of the native form during preparatory steps needs consideration.

Earlier studies, as reviewed by Keilová (1971) and Otto (1971) indicated that cathepsin B1 can cleave a number of peptide bonds. This occurred perhaps due mostly to the contamination of enzyme with other peptide hydrolases, because the pure preparation of cathepsin B1 could catabolize only a few specific peptide bonds (MacGregor *et al.*, 1979; Kirschke *et al.*, 1980). The most specific synthetic substrates now employed to identify cathepsin B1 activity are Bz-DL-Arg-4-nitroamide, Bz-DL-Arg-2-naphthylamide (Otto, 1971) and Bz-Arg-Arg-2-naphthylamide (McDonald and Ellis, 1975).

2.　Cathepsin H

Kirschke *et al.* (1976, 1977b) isolated a thiol endopeptidase with a molecular weight of 28,000 from rat liver lysosomes and named it cathepsin H. According to Barrett and McDonald (1980), several proteases with properties similar to that of cathepsin H have been reported in the past with different names such as L20C21 (Bohley *et al.*, 1971), cathepsin B3 (Kirschke *et al.*, 1973), cathepsin B1a (Husain and Baqai, 1976), and BANA-hydrolase (Singh *et al.*, 1978). Cathepsin H shows both amino- and endopeptidase activities (Kirschke *et al.*, 1977b), and it exists in two multiple forms with pI 7.1 and 7.3, which exhibit activity at pH above 7 (Locnikar *et al.*, 1981). However, the V_{max} is generally observed at pH 6.0 (Schwartz and Barrett, 1980; Katunuma and Kominami, 1983). The activity of cathepsin H was detected in skeletal muscle cell culture by many investigators (Bird *et al.*, 1981; St. John *et al.*, 1981; Stauber and Ong, 1982a; Kirschke *et al.*, 1983). Cathepsin H also possesses aminopeptidase activity, and Barrett (1980) considered that cathepsin H and leucine aminopeptidase may be one and the same enzyme.

3.　Cathepsin L

Bohley *et al.* (1971) isolated an endopeptidase, called L20C5, from liver lysosomes. It was renamed by them as cathepsin L (Kirschke *et al.*, 1973).

Cathepsin L (MW 24,000) has many physicochemical similarities with cathepsin H, but it showed maximum activity at pH 5.0 (Kirschke *et al.*, 1977a,c; Towatari *et al.*, 1978). It exists in several multiple forms (p*I* 5.8–6.1) which show activity at a wide pH range (5.0–6.0). Cathepsin L is shown to be activated by ATP which possibly is required in a step before the first proteolytic cleavage commences (Olden and Goldberg, 1978). Okitani *et al.* (1980) have identified the cathepsin L activity in rabbit skeletal muscle. Its activity in muscle cell culture has been identified by several researchers (Bird *et al.*, 1981; Kirschke *et al.*, 1983). The studies by Kärgel *et al.* (1980) and Katunuma *et al.* (1983) demonstrated that cathepsin L has specificity for cleaving those peptide bonds which involve nonpolar amino acid residues (e.g., Leu, Val, Try, Tyr) in position P2.

4. Cytosol Insulin–Glucagon Proteinase

Cytosol insulin–glucagon proteinase (also called insulinase or insulin-specific protease) has been found in several tissues including skeletal muscle of rat (Brush, 1971; Duckworth *et al.*, 1972). It is a thiol endopeptidase with molecular weight of 80,000 (Burghen *et al.*, 1972) and cleaves the peptide bond of the β chain of insulin at Tyr^{16}-Leu^{17} (Duckworth *et al.*, 1979). It can also degrade glucagon (Baskin *et al.*, 1975). The optimum pH for its activity is 7.5. It is inhibited by some endogenous inhibitor present in the serum (Brush, 1973) and also by EDTA.

5. Ca^{2+}-Activated Neutral Proteinase

Calcium-activated neutral proteinase (CANP) seems to be widely distributed in the cytoplasm of both vertebrate and invertebrate tissues. In the literature, it has been reported under different names, such as neutral, Ca^{2+}-activated protease from rat brain (Guroff, 1964), kinase activating factor from skeletal muscle (Huston and Krebs, 1968), calcium-activated factor (CAF) from pig muscle (Busch *et al.*, 1972), calcium-activated sarcoplasmic factor (CASF) from rabbit muscle (Suzuki and Goll, 1974), calcium-activated neutral protease (Okitani *et al.*, 1974; Reddy *et al.*, 1975), or simply calcium-activated protease (Dayton *et al.*, 1975). Some Japanese enzymologists (Murachi *et al.*, 1981a,b) preferred to call it calpain on the basis of generic nomenclature (cal stands for calcium, and pain for thiol proteases, such as papain).

As the name suggests, calcium-activated neutral protease (CANP) shows maximal activity at neutral pH (7.5) for degrading protein and requires 1–5 m*M* Ca^{2+} for activation under reducing conditions. A thiol group is believed to constitute the active site of the enzyme (Waxman, 1981; Murachi *et al.*, 1981; Murachi, 1985). As for other cysteine proteinases, Cys^5 is shown to be active site in CANP (Suzuki *et al.*, 1983). Most of the studies reported the molecular weight of CANP as 110,000. However, disparity exists among the different findings regarding its subunit components. While CANP from chicken breast (Ishiura *et al.*, 1978; Kubota *et al.*, 1981; Suzuki *et al.*, 1981), bovine cardiac (Toyo-Oka and Masaki, 1979), and rabbit skeletal (Azanza *et al.*, 1979) muscles is shown to be comprised of only one polypeptide chain, others found the presence of two nonidentical subunits of MW 80,000 and 30,000 in a molecule of CANP isolated from porcine (Dayton *et al.*, 1976), human (Suzuki *et al.*, 1979), bovine cardiac (Waxman and Krebs, 1978; Szpacenko *et al.*, 1981) skeletal myoblasts (Kaur and Sanwal, 1981), and chicken breast muscle (Nagainis *et al.*, 1983; Kawashima *et al.*, 1984).

Contrary to the general consensus of opinion, although Azanza *et al.* (1979) noticed the presence of a 30,000 component in their preparation, it was regarded as a contaminant, because they found that its presence was not essential for CANP activity. In view of this, the role of two subunits of CANP is yet to be seen. However, it would be proper here to mention the interesting discovery that Gardell and Tate (1979) made about the two subunits (MW 22,000 and 46,000) of γ-glutamyl transpeptidase from rat kidney. In this case, the transpeptidase activity was found to reside only in the heavy subunit, whereas the light subunit contained the protease activity. It is likely that two subunits in CANP may be responsible for different activities in tissues.

The discrepancy in subunit composition of CANP may be ascribed to variation in the composition of the extracting buffer system. For instance, some investigators used 5 mM EDTA as a buffer system for the extraction of CANP from muscle (Hathaway *et al.*, 1982; Mellgren *et al.*, 1982; Nagainis *et al.*, 1984) to keep the endogenous free Ca^{2+} concentration low to avoid autolytic degradation of the 30,000 subunit. On the other hand, Ishiura *et al.* (1978) have relied on merely 1 mM EDTA which may not be sufficient to reduce the free Ca^{2+} below critical level at which autolysis of the 30,000 subunit occurs. An ionic strength of the buffer system greater than 0.3 (Nagainis *et al.*, 1984) and use of organomercury compounds such as hydroxymercuribenzoate (Mellgren *et al.*, 1982) also seem to contribute in the separation of the 80,000 and 30,000 subunits during purification, and hence may cause the loss of the 30,000 subunit. Besides, Nagainis *et al.* (1984) remarked that fairly heavy loading of SDS–PAGE with sample is generally required to detect the presence of those polypeptides whose concentration is very low in the sample.

Until 1980, only one form of CANP was known which required millimolar (1– 5 mM) Ca^{2+} for activation. Mellgren (1980) then isolated from cardiac muscle another form of CANP which displayed a high affinity for Ca^{2+} and which was activated by merely micromolar (50–70μM) Ca^{2+} concentrations. It has a lower negative charge than the original form. Mellgren's findings were substantiated later by several other researchers (Dayton *et al.*, 1981; Szpacenko *et al.*, 1981; Inomata *et al.*, 1983). Like the original one, this form also consists of two subunits with molecular weights of 79,000–80,000 and 28,000–30,000, suggesting the existence of different isozymes of CANP in muscles. The two forms of CANP have been designated by different names in the literature. For example, the second form of CANP, sometimes referred to as "low calcium activated factor" or "μM-CAF," has also been named calcium-dependent protease I (Barrett and McDonald, 1980), because it is eluted from a DEAE–cellulose column before the original form. For that matter, the original form has been designated as calcium-dependent protease II. It is also called "high-calcium activated factor," "mM-CAF," or "mM-CANP."

In contrast to the general observations, Hara et al. (1983) isolated from monkey cardiac muscle the two forms of CANP which required millimolar Ca^{2+} for activation. The less acidic one (called form I CANP) consisted of two subunits with molecular weights of 74,000 and 28,000, and the more acidic one (called form II CANP) had subunits' molecular weights of 74,000 and 26,000. Recently Zimmerman and Schlaepfer (1984a) reported the presence of three forms of CANP in rat skeletal muscle and brain. Two forms with molecular weights of 154,000 and 96,000 had high affinity for Ca^{2+} (μM-CANP), and the third one (MW 76,000) had low affinity for Ca^{2+} (mM-CANP). They believe that a Ca^{2+}-induced unidirectional process may be generating the low molecular weight form which has low affinity for Ca^{2+} but has 3–6 times higher specific activity than the other forms. On the other hand, Dayton et al. (1981) thought that in vivo posttranslational dephosphorylation of mM-CANP might be giving rise to μM-CANP. This would change the molecular weight insignificantly but would markedly increase the charge on the molecule. However, Zimmerman and Schlaepfer (1984b) believe that the both forms are phosphorylated by CANP-associated kinase for modulating their activity.

Another mechanism by which μM-CANP may be formed in muscle is the autolysis of the mM-CANP form. Many researchers have shown that a limited autolysis of the high CANP form in vitro significantly reduced its Ca^{2+} requirement for activation, and hence mM-CANP was converted to μM-CANP (Kubota et al., 1981; Suzuki et al., 1981; Dayton, 1982; Hathaway et al., 1982; Nagainis et al., 1984). A study by Suzuki et al. (1981) indicated that the heavy subunit (82,000) of CANP reduced to 79,000 during autolysis and the resulting enzyme needed 150 μM Ca^{2+} for half maximal activity. However, Nagainis et al. (1984) have shown that both heavy (80,000) and light (30,000) subunits of CANP were reduced to 77,000 and 18,000, respectively, during autolysis, which was performed in the presence of 1 mM Ca^{2+} at 0°C for 1–5 min. The autolyzed enzyme required merely 10–40 μM Ca^{2+} for activation.

These studies suggest that the low Ca^{2+}-requiring form may be originating from the autolytic digestion of the high Ca^{2+}-requiring form. Many examples are known in enzymology where some enzymes undergo autoactivation by removal of an inhibitory polypeptide from the zymogen (Young, 1979). However, the possibility of μM-CANP form originating from mM-CANP by autolysis in *vivo* is not convincing on the grounds that in some species the molecular weight of low Ca^{2+}-requiring form was found to be higher than that of high Ca^{2+}-requiring form (Inomata *et al.*, 1983; Zimmerman and Schlaepfer, 1984a), although the former quantitatively constitutes only about 5–30% of the latter (Dayton *et al.*, 1981; Szpacenko *et al.*, 1981). The CANP content seems to vary considerably between species. For example, 2.8–4.6 mg was obtained from 1 kg chicken breast muscle (Ishiura *et al.*, 1978; Nagainis *et al.*, 1984) whereas only 0.3–0.4 mg was recovered from 1 kg porcine (Dayton *et al.*, 1976) or rabbit skeletal muscle (Mellgren *et al.*, 1982). However, Inomata *et al.* (1983) isolated 0.54 mg of μM-CANP from 1 kg of rabbit muscle.

Controversy also exists about whether or not the two forms of CANP are immunologically identical. Some researchers have shown that the two forms cross-reacted with antibody prepared against the 80,000 MW subunit of the high Ca^{2+}-requiring form (Dayton *et al.*, 1981; Szpacenko *et al.*, 1981). Even the three forms of CANP which were isolated by Zimmerman and Schlaepfer (1984a) cross-reacted immunologically. In contrast, an immunoautographic and peptide mapping study by Wheelock (1982) revealed immunological identity only in the 30,000 subunit, whereas the 80,000 subunit of μM- and mM-CANP substantially differed from each other. This suggests that the 80,000 subunit possibly exists in multiple forms (Sasaki *et al.*, 1983).

CANP seems unique among proteinases in that it has no effect on small peptide substrates (Ishiura *et al.*, 1979) and requires fairly long polypeptides to express its activity. It hydrolyzed the oxidized insulin β chain between His^5-Leu^6, Gly^8-Ser^9, Glu^{13}-Ala^{14}, Tyr^{16}-Leu^{17}, and Tyr^{26}-Thr^{27}. The major peptides formed were Leu^{17}-Ala^{30} (78%), Ala^{14}–Tyr^{16} (47%), Phe^1–Gly^8 (28%), Thr^{27}–Ala^{30} (23%), and Leu^6–Tyr^{26} (11%). This suggests that CANP does not require any specific sequence of amino acids for cleaving the peptide bond. However, Hirao *et al.* (1983) reported that CANP from cardiac muscle has the tendency to cleave the bonds around the paired basic amino acid residues in a neuropeptide substrate.

C. ASPARTATE PROTEINASES (EC 3.4.23)

Those proteinases in which the COOH group of an aspartic acid residue constitutes the active site are classified as aspartate (or aspartic) proteinases. Pepsin and rennin belong to this class. Acid proteinases require low pH (2–4) for activation. They are inhibited by esterifying reagents such as diazo-acetylnorleucine methyl ester in the presence of Cu^{2+} (Lundblad and Stein, 1969; Takahashi *et al.*, 1974), *p*-bromophenacyl bromide, trimethyloxonium fluoroborate (Paterson and Knowles, 1972), or pepstatin (Umezawa and Aoyagi, 1977). Only two endopeptidases with a COOH group as the active site have been reported in skeletal muscle: cathepsins D and E.

1. Cathepsin D (EC 3.4.23.5)

Among catheptic enzymes, cathepsin D was discovered first, and it appeared in the literature under different names such as leino-β-protease (Hedin, 1904), β-protease (Vernon, 1908), kathepsin (Willstäter and Bamann, 1929), or cathepsin (Pozzi, 1935; Anson, 1940). With the discovery of several more catheptic proteases, this enzyme was named cathepsin D (Press *et al.*, 1960). It is an endopeptidase which requires at least five residues in the substrate to express its activity at pH 3–5. Its molecular weight is reported in the range of 42,000–60,000 depending on the tissue or species (Turk *et al.*, 1957, 1980; Barrett, 1970; Erickson *et al.*, 1981). Some researchers claimed that cathepsin D is composed of a single chain polypeptide, others found two dissimilar chains linked by a noncovalent bond (Ogunro *et al.*, 1982). Evidence also suggests its existence in multiple forms (Sapolasky and Woessner, 1972; Huang *et al.*, 1979; Yamamoto *et al.*, 1979a) whose pH requirement for V_{max} varied from 2.8 to 5.0. Pulse–chase experiments by Samarel *et al.*, (1984) have shown that the multiple forms of cathepsin D originated from a common high molecular weight precursor which was synthesized in a nonlysosomal intracellular component.

Cathepsin D is an acid proteinase (Kazakova and Orekhovich, 1972; Woessner, 1977a; Fruton, 1980; Huang *et al.*, 1980) in which the carboxyl groups of the Asp^{32} and Asp^{215} residues constitute the active site. Keilová *et al.* (1968) have shown that cathepsin D promptly hydrolyzed the peptide bonds between Phe-Phe, Phe-Tyr, and Leu-Tyr and less willingly those between Glu-Ala and Tyr-Leu in a polypeptide. Somewhat similar results were obtained by Suzuki *et al.* (1969) by using the β-chain of insulin. On the other hand, Lin and William (1979) found the bonds between Phe-Phe, Phe-Try, Phe-Val, Leu-Phe, Ala-Ala, and Ala-Tyr all susceptible to cathepsin D, suggesting that it prefers to hydrolyze those peptide bonds which involve hydrophobic amino acid residues, at least one of which is aromatic.

As far as skeletal muscle is concerned, cathepsin D activity was first identified by Balls (1938) in beef. Later, many investigators reported its activity in skeletal muscles of rabbit (Snoke and Neurath, 1950; Atsushi and Masao, 1968; Suzuki *et al.*, 1969), bovine (Sliwinski *et al.*, 1959; Bodwell and Pearson, 1964; Valin, 1967), chicken (Iodice *et al.*, 1966), porcine (Parrish and Bailey, 1966), and rat (Bird *et al.*, 1977; Schwartz and Bird, 1977). Cathepsin D is localized in the lysosomal fraction of cells (Poole *et al.*, 1972; Bird *et al.*, 1978). It is shown to be activated by ATP (Watabe *et al.*, 1976).

2. Cathepsin E (EC 3.4.23.7)

Along with cathepsin D, Lapresle and Webb (1962) isolated another enzyme from rabbit spleen which showed activity at a much lower pH (2.5) than required by cathepsin D. This enzyme, with a molecular weight of 100,000, was named cathepsin E (Lapresle, 1971). On the other hand, the cathepsin E identified by Turk *et al.* (1968) in bovine spleen had a molecular weight of 305,000. They also demonstrated the conversion of cathepsin E to D by autolysis during storage at 25°C (Turk *et al.*, 1969). However, a study by Barrett and Dingle (1972) disproved the notion that cathepsin E is a precursor of cathepsin D.

Like cathepsin D, cathepsin E is also a COOH-group-dependent endopeptidase and requires low pH (2–3.5) for activation. It degrades serum albumin, hemoglobin (Jasani *et al.*, 1978), and immunoglobin G (Ghetie and Mihaescu, 1973) but has no effect on synthetic substrates. Cathepsin E has been found mostly in polymorphonuclear leukocytes and macrophages of bone marrow, and in the spleen (Turk *et al.*, 1980). It was never reported in skeletal muscle until 1978, when Venugopal and Bailey indicated its activity in bovine and porcine diaphragm muscle. Soon after Guba and co-workers (Sohar *et al.*, 1981) also identified cathepsin E activity in soleus (red) muscle in addition to that of cathepsins B and D. Uncertainty yet exists about the actual origin of cathepsin E activity in muscle. Whether polymorphonuclear leukocytes of blood residue and macrophages in muscle are the actual sources of cathepsin E or it is present in muscle cells per se still needs to be established.

D. METALLOPROTEINASES

The activity of metalloproteinases depends on the presence of a metal cation (e.g., Ca^{2+}, Zn^{2+}), which may be strongly or loosely bound with the protein moiety. The cation always maintains a stoichiometric relationship with the protein molecule (Vallee, 1955). Metalloenzymes are inhibited by cyanides. Collagenases, carboxypeptidase A, and some aminopeptidases are examples of metalloproteases (Matsubara and Feder, 1971). However, some of the collagenases from fungi and arthropods are serine proteinases, and some from aerobic and anaerobic bacteria are Zn-metalloproteinases (Keil, 1980).

Collagenases

Collagenases hydrolyze specific peptide bonds located in the triple helix of collagen in its native conformation (pH 7.5). They are stimulated by Ca^{2+} and thiol reagents. The molecular weights of collagenases vary from 32,000–33,000 (Woolley *et al.*, 1975b) to 158,000 (Hook *et al.*, 1972) in different sources. They have been located in different mammalian connective tissues, fibroblasts, leucocytes, platelets, and epithelial tissues (Reddick *et al.*, 1974; Harris and Krane, 1974; Harris and Cartwright, 1977). Woessner (1977b) have indicated that collagenase may be present in two forms in mammalian tissue: one form with molecular weight of 77,000 is latent, and the other (MW 60,000) is active. However, collagenases from different sources have been shown to degrade collagen type II, $[\alpha 1(II)]_3$, at a rate 5–6 times slower than they cleave collagen type

I, [α1(I)$_2$α2(I)], (Harris and Krane, 1974; Nagai, 1973; Woolley *et al.*, 1973, 1975a,b; Harris *et al.*, 1980). Collagen type III, [α1(III)]$_3$, is degraded at the same rate as is type I (Harris *et al.*, 1980). Relatively high levels of glycosylation and hydroxylation (Miller and Gay, 1982) in collagen type II may account for its high resistance to collagenases.

Collagenase has not so far been isolated from skeletal muscle, except that Venugopal and Bailey (1978) reported the presence of true collagenase activity in homogenate of bovine and pork diaphragm muscle. The activity, though very weak, was especially present in 3500 *g* sediment of muscle homogenate. Earlier, Laakkonen *et al.* (1970) also indicated the presence of collagenase activity in bovine muscle. However, they had used a synthetic substrate, Bz-Pro-Leu-Gly-Pro-D-Arg, which other researchers (Seifter and Harper, 1971) did not consider to be specific for mammalian collagenases.

The salient features of different endopeptidases (serine, thiol, aspartate, and metalloproteinases) which have been discovered in skeletal muscles are summarized in Table II.

TABLE II

SOME CHARACTERISTICS OF THE ENDOPEPTIDASES OF SKELETAL MUSCLE

Endopeptidase[a]	Molecular weight	pH range for activity	Cellular distribution
Serine proteinases			
Myofibrillar serine protease	25,000	8.3–9.0	Cytosolic
Myosin cleaving protease	26,000	7.5–9.5	Cytosolic
Group specific protease	24,000	9–10.5	Cytosolic
Cytosolic protease	25,000	9.5	Cytosolic
Myofibrillar protease	30,800	9.5	Cytosolic
ATP-activated alkaline protease[b]	550,000	7.8	Cytosolic
Thiol proteinases			
Cathepsin B1	25,000	4–6.5	Lysosomal
Cathepsin H	28,000	5.5–6.5	Lysosomal
Cathepsin L	24,000	3–6.5	Lysosomal
Cytosol insulin–glucagon protease	80,000	7.5	Cytosolic
mM- and μM-CANP	110,000	7.5	Cytosolic
Aspartate proteinases			
Cathepsin D	42,000	3.0–5.0	Lysosomal
Cathepsin E	100,000	2.0–3.5	Lysosomal
Metalloproteinases			
Collagenase	33,000	7.5	—

[a] Derived from Barrett and McDonald (1980).

[b] ATP-activated alkaline protease has been reported in cardiac muscle of rat (DeMartino, 1983) but not yet in skeletal muscle.

IV. NONMUSCLE CATHEPSINS

Several more cathepsins have been isolated and identified in different tissues and cells, but their presence in skeletal muscle has not yet been proved. Two of them are serine proteinases, four thiol proteinases, and one is not yet classified with respect to its active site (Table III).

A. SERINE PROTEINASES

1. Cathepsin G (EC 4.3.22)

An endopeptidase, called cathepsin G, was isolated from neutrophil leukocytes (Gerber *et al.*, 1974; Tsung *et al.*, 1977; Zimmerman and Ashe, 1977). It is composed of a single polypeptide chain with molecular weight of 30,000 (Travis *et al.*, 1978). Cathepsin G has chymotrypsin-like activity (as it hydrolyzed Bz-Phe-2-naphthyl ester and Bz-Tyr-OEt synthetic substrates), which is dependent on the serine residue (Nakajima *et al.*, 1979). The activity is maximum at pH 7.5 (Starkey and Barrett, 1976).

2. Cathepsin R

An endopeptidase, called ribosomal serine proteinase, has been isolated from 40 S polysomal subunits of liver and HeLa cells (Korant, 1977; Langner *et al.*, 1977; Bylinkina *et al.*, 1978; Bylinkina, 1986). According to Barrett and McDonald (1980) the discoverers of this enzyme used the term cathepsin R only

TABLE III

SOME PROPERTIES OF NONMUSCLE CATHEPSINS

Cathepsin	Molecular weight	pH range for activity	Mode of action
Serine proteinases			
Cathepsin G	30,000	6.5–8	Endopeptidase
Cathepsin R[a]	—	7–8	Endopeptidase
Thiol proteinases			
Cathepsin M	30,000	7.5	Exopeptidase
Cathepsin N	18,000–34,600	3–4.5	Endopeptidase
Cathepsin S	14,000–25,000	2.5–4.5	Endopeptidase
Cathepsin T	33,500–35,000	6.0–7.5	Endopeptidase
Unclassified cathepsin			
Cathepsin F	50,000–70,000	4.5	Endopeptidase

[a] Ribosomal serine proteinase, reported by Byluikina *et al.* (1978) and others, has been called cathepsin R in a verbal communication as stated by Barrett and McDonald (1980).

in verbal communication but not in writing. In the future, however, it may become the common name for ribosomal serine proteinase.

B. THIOL PROTEINASES

Four nonmuscle cathepsins, namely, cathepsins M, N, S, and T, have a cysteine residue as the active center. Cathepsin M is, in fact, an exopeptidase, whereas the remaining are endopeptidases.

1. Cathepsin M (EC 3.4.22)

Cathepsin M (MW 30,000), an exo-carboxypeptidase, was isolated from the lysosomal fraction of brains from different species (Marks, 1977; Pontremoli et al., 1982), and it resembles cathepsin B2 in some physicochemical properties. It is a Ca^{2+}-dependent thiol proteinase and needs pH 7.5 for maximal activity. According to Barrett and McDonald (1980), a few similar proteases isolated from the brain by others were given different names. For example, Oliveira et al. (1976) identified two forms with molecular weights of 71,000 and 68,000 and called them kininase A and B, respectively.

2. Cathepsin N (EC 3.4.22)

Cathepsin N, a collagenic thiol endopeptidase, has been isolated from the lysosomal fraction of granuloma, neutrophil leukocytes (Bazin and Delaunary, 1966; Gibson et al., 1976), bovine spleen (Etherington, 1980), and placenta (Evans and Etherington, 1978). Its molecular weight varied from 18,000–20,000 (bovine spleen) to 34,600 (human placenta). Like cathepsin B1, cathepsin N cleaved the telopeptide from the N terminus of tropocollagen molecules (Etherington, 1980). Its specific activity, however, was much higher than that of the former (Burleigh, 1977). Cathepsin N showed little activity, however, on synthetic substrates for cathepsin B1 and also on azocasein, which possibly distinguishes it from cathepsin L. Besides, cathepsin N required low pH (3.5) for activation.

3. Cathepsin S (EC 3.4.22)

Cathepsin S, a thiol endopeptidase, was isolated from spleen and lymph nodes (Turnsek et al., 1975; Turk et al., 1978, 1980). Different sources have shown a wide difference in its molecular weight, which varied from 14,000 to 25,000. Locnikar et al. (1981) reported the existence of multiple forms of cathepsin S whose pI values varied from 6.3 to 6.9. The pH requirement for activity ranged between 2.5 and 4.5. Cathepsin S preferably hydrolyzed hemoglobin, histones, and collagen.

4. Cathepsin T

Cathepsin T (MW 33,500–35,000), another thiol endopeptidase, was reported by Gohda and Pitot (1980, 1981) in a lysosomal fraction of rat liver. It showed no activity on synthetic substrates for cathepsins B, H, and L, but it catalyzed collagen, denatured hemoglobin and azocasein, and oxidized ribonuclease and multiple forms of tyrosine aminotransferase at neutral pH (6.0–7.5).

C. UNCLASSIFIED PROTEINASE

Cathepsin F (EC 3.4.99)

Blow (1975) and Dingle et al. (1977) isolated an endopeptidase (MW 50,000–70,000) from rabbit ear cartilage and named it cathepsin F. It showed the activity for degrading proteoglycan (Blow, 1975) at pH 4.5. Since this protease has not been characterized well for its active sites, Barrett and McDonald (1980) have cataloged it under proteinases of unknown catalytic mechanism.

V. CELLULAR AND SUBCELLULAR DISTRIBUTION OF PROTEINASES IN MUSCLE

Proteinases may be found in lysosomes, mitochondria, microsomes, nuclei, or cytosol. Those enzymes which do not require any detergent or organic solvent–water system for extraction from tissue homogenates are defined as cytosolic enzymes. They do not sediment with cytoplasmic organelles on centrifugation at forces as high as 105,000 g for 1 hr. On the other hand, those proteinases which are associated with cell organelles may be present in free state or bound with membrane. For instance, most of the lysosomal enzymes probably exist in a soluble form within lysosomes, whereas microsomal (endoplasmic reticulum) enzymes are generally membrane bound. However, the studies on the cellular and subcellular distribution of proteinases in skeletal muscle revealed somewhat conflicting results. These are considered in the following sections.

A. MUSCLE CELL AND NONMUSCLE CELL PROTEINASES

Although muscle cells (syncytia) constitute over 80% of the muscle mass, several other cells are also known to be present in the interfiber (interstitial) space (Fitton-Jackson, 1964). They include fibroblasts, adipocytes, mast cells, macrophages (histocytes), eosinophils, vascular (endothelial) cells, and nerve fibers. The fact that some of these cells, especially mast cells, are a very rich source of alkaline proteolytic enzymes (Lagunoff and Benditt, 1963; Ende et al., 1964; Budd et al., 1967; Kawiak et al., 1971; Park et al., 1973) poses a great problem in subcellular localization of proteases in skeletal muscles. The isolation of cellular organelles from muscle fibers without damage is also a difficult task.

In most of the cases, investigators have relied on a differential centrifugation procedure to determine the subcellular location of proteases. Consequently, the activity of certain serine proteinases was found in the ribosomes (Levyant et al., 1976; Langner et al., 1977; Bylinkina et al., 1978), microsomal membranes (Sogawa and Takahashi, 1978, 1979), nuclei (Garrells et al., 1972; Chong et al., 1974; Ramponi et al., 1978), and mitochondrial membranes (Ferdinand et al., 1973; Lovaas, 1974; Justić et al., 1976; Haas et al., 1977, 1978; Banno et al., 1978; Subramaniam et al., 1978) of liver or muscle from different species. However, some researchers do not consider differential centrifugation a very reliable method for this purpose as under certain extracting conditions mast cells also cosediment with myofibrils, nuclei, and mitochondria. This generally has led to incorrect interpretation of the results.

The immunohistological techniques, which are considered more reliable than the differential centrifugation method for localization of enzymes in tissue, forced many researchers to retract their earlier conclusions. For example, some serine proteinases (so-called alkaline proteases), which were first claimed to be of muscle cell origin (Katunuma and Kominami, 1977; Haas et al., 1978), were later proved by the same researchers to originate from mast cells (Woodbury et al., 1978; Haas et al., 1979; Heinrich et al., 1979; Edmunds and Pennington, 1981). Several other investigators reached the same conclusion by using compound 48/80 (a polymer of N-methylhomoanisylamine and formaldehyde) which specifically granulates the mast cells (Park et al., 1973; Drabikowski et al., 1976; McElliott and Bird, 1980; Bird et al., 1980). In the case of cardiac muscle, too, 90% of the alkaline proteinase activity was located in mast cells (McKee et al., 1979). By using the 4-aminosalicylic acid (PAS)–Alcian blue–silver staining technique (Gomori, 1954) or by staining with toluidine blue, the mast cells were found exclusively associated with connective tissue, afferent vessels, and around hilum (Heinrich et al., 1979; Kuo et al., 1981). This may explain why some alkaline protease activity was also reported in fibroblasts and leukocytes (Etherington, 1980).

Even with regard to lysosomal proteinases, the early evidence obtained by biochemical (Canonico and Bird, 1970; Stauber and Bird, 1974) and cytochemical studies (Topping and Travis, 1974; Hoffstein et al., 1975) suggested that some lysosomes in muscle may be originating from smooth sarcoplasmic reticulum. Welman and Peters (1976) separated five lysosomal populations from different subcellular fractions of guinea pig myocardial tissue, of which only three were accessible to Triton WR-1339. By using immunocytochemical techniques, Whitaker *et al.* (1983) found cathepsin D close to the sarcolemmal membrane in human muscle. It has also been located in the extracellular space (Poole *et al.*, 1973, 1974). Cathepsin D is mostly concentrated in phagocytic (Knook, 1974) and Kupffer cells (Van Berkel *et al.*, 1975; Arborgh *et al.*, 1978). Its distribution in parenchymal cells is very scanty (Brouwer *et al.*, 1979).

B. CATHEPTIC AND NONCATHEPTIC PROTEINASES

The so-called cathepsins found in the lysosomal fraction of the cytoplasm (Canonico and Bird, 1970; Iodice *et al.*, 1972; Stauber and Bird, 1974; Stauber *et al.*, 1981) are also called acid proteases because they generally require low pH for their activity. *In vivo,* the pH value of the lysosomal matrix is reported to be 4.5 (Reijngoud *et al.*, 1976; Ohkuma and Poole, 1978). Low intralysosomal pH is partly maintained passively by Donnan equilibrium and partly by energy-dependent proton pumping (Ohkuma and Poole, 1978). By now over a dozen catheptic proteases have been reported in different tissues.

Willstätter and Bamann (1929) first coined the term kathepsin (or cathepsin) to describe an acid protease (different from pepsin) which they found in gastric mucosa of different mammalian species. Since then this term has been used to define different cellular enzymes without any reservation. For example, in *in vitro* studies, the optimum pH varies with kind of substrate and with type of cathepsin. Some of the cathepsins show substantial activity even at neutral pH. In view of this, Barrett (1977) proposed that in the future catheptic numbering of proteases should be used only for endopeptidases without any restrictions of pH.

As has been discussed in Sections II–IV, over a dozen cathepsins are known to be present in lysosomal fractions of spleen, liver, and kidney. The presence of lysosomes in muscle, however, has not been universally accepted. For instance, an electron microscopic study by Pellegrino and Franzini (1963) did not find any evidence of lysosomes in healthy red and white muscles, although Tappel (1969) indicated the latency characteristics of lysosomes in chicken and rat muscles by using Triton X-100 in the extracting buffer. Several other workers isolated lysosomes containing proteolytic enzymes from muscles of different species by the density gradient centrifugation method (Romeo *et al.*, 1966; Fitzpatrick *et al.*, 1968; Stagni and De Bernard, 1968), or by zonal centrifugation (Weglicki *et al.*, 1975).

From these studies, it cannot be determined whether or not the lysosomes actually come from muscle cells per se. Somehow, the results obtained by Canonico and Bird (1970), using isopycnic zonal centrifugation in sucrose–20 m*M* KCl gradient, suggested the presence of two types of lysosomes in rat skeletal muscle. One type had an equilibrium density of 1.18, which did not change if the rats were injected with Triton WR-1339 or with dextran 500 before killing. This type was considered the true muscle cell lysosomes. The other type showed a change in density by these injections and became swollen. This represented lysosomes from macrophages and fibroblasts (connective tissue). By following this procedure, Stauber and Bird (1974) provided the evidence of the presence of cathepsins B and D in muscle fiber lysosomes. Later, this finding was not only confirmed by electron microscopy (Spanier, 1977; Bird *et al.*, 1978), but it was also demonstrated that one type of lysosomes was present in the perinuclear region close to Golgi bodies and the other was present in the interior of myofibrils. The latter type was more concentrated near I-bands (Stauber, 1981). Another isopycnic zonal centrifugation study by Stauber and Schottelius (1981) suggested that the sarcoplasmic reticulum of phasic muscle (posterior latissimus dorsi) represents a multifunctional membrane system which includes some membrane-bound lysosomal enzymes beside its specialized role in muscle contraction.

Regarding the distribution of CANP in muscle, different views have been expressed since its discovery. Initially it was shown to be present in the soluble fraction of the sarcoplasm (Busch *et al.*, 1972; Reville *et al.*, 1976). Later on immunological studies indicated its location in the vicinity of Z-disks facing the sarcolemma (Dayton and Schollmeyer, 1981; Ishiura *et al.*, 1980). However, Waxman (1981) stated that, in the case of kidney, only 50% of the CANP activity was present in the soluble cytoplasm and the remaining was associated with the microsomal fraction. This means that the other subcellular fractions did not contain any CANP activity. In contrast, Ishiura *et al.* (1980) found about 80% of CANP activity free in the sarcoplasm of skeletal muscle, and the remaining was bound to myofibrils. Barth and Elce (1981) expressed the possibility that μM-CANP may be located at the Z-band and that mM-CANP is present at the plasma membrane or in the extracellular space. A recent study by Kleese *et al.* (1985) based on double antibody reaction revealed that CANPs are distributed throughout in the sarcoplasm of skeletal muscle, while their inhibitor is localized in the I-bands.

VI. SIGNIFICANCE OF ENDOGENOUS PROTEINASES IN MUSCLE PHYSIOLOGY

Before discussing the importance of endogenous proteinases in skeletal muscle, a brief description of the updated findings on muscle proteins would be appropriate to formulate a better understanding of the subsequent sections dealing with protein turnover and postmortem changes in meat.

A. MUSCLE PROTEINS AND THEIR CLASSIFICATION

Detailed information on muscle proteins has recently been presented in another review (Asghar *et al.*, 1985), and only relevant points are summarized in this section. Skeletal muscles comprise 35–65% of carcass weight and contain 19–20% protein. Traditionally muscle proteins are divided into two main categories, intracellular and extracellular, depending on their location within or outside muscle fibers, respectively.

1. Intracellular Proteins

About 17–18% of muscle proteins are present in muscle cells (fibers). Depending on their form and function in muscle fibers, they can be classified into three groups: the sarcoplasmic, myofibrillar, and cytoskeletal (scaffold) proteins.

a. Sarcoplasmic Proteins.   Sarcoplasmic proteins are relatively low in molecular weight and mainly exist in solution form. Scopes (1964, 1968) separated over 50 proteins from the sarcoplasm. Most of them represent soluble and freely diffusible enzymes which are involved in glycolysis. Perhaps some of them are present as multienzyme complexes held together by noncovalent bonds to catalyze sequential reactions of the glycolytic pathway (Reed, 1975). Altogether sarcoplasmic proteins make up about 5.5% of skeletal muscle mass.

b. Myofibrillar Proteins.   Myofibrillar proteins constitute approximately 10–11% of muscle mass. On the basis of their functional role in muscle, myofibrillar proteins are further divided into two subgroups: contractile and regulatory proteins.

Contractile Proteins.   Myosin (MW 480,000), and actin (MW 42,000) are regarded as the contractile proteins as they are directly responsible for the muscle contraction–relaxation cycle. Myosin and actin are the major proteins of muscle and constitute, respectively, thick and thin myofilaments. By weight, myosin and actin make up 5.5 and 2.5% of muscle mass (Yates and Greaser, 1983).

Regulatory Proteins.   Regulatory proteins are associated with myofibrils. They do not directly involve the contraction–relaxation mechanism of muscle, but they play an indirect role in regulating this process, and hence are called regulatory proteins. About 18 regulatory proteins are presently known. Quantitatively, they are very low in amount and compose only about 2.5% of muscle composition. Seven of them are associated with thick (myosin) filaments, 3 with thin (actin) filaments, and about 4 with Z-disks.

Tropomyosin (MW 65,000) and troponin (MW 70,000) are the major regulatory proteins and are associated with actin filaments. Troponin is composed of three subunits, called troponin-C (Tn-C, MW 17,900), troponin I (Tn-I, MW 20,800), and troponin-T (Tn-T, MW 30,500). Another protein, β-actinin (37,000) is also suggested to be present at the free ends of actin filaments

(Maruyama *et al.*, 1977). Originally, α-actinin (Mw 95,000) was the only protein which was isolated from the Z-disk structure. Later on, several other proteins such as euactinin (MW 42,000) (Kuroda *et al.*, 1981) or Z-disk actin (Nagainis *et al.*, 1983) or stroma actin (Weber, 1984), Z-protein (MW 55,000) (Ohashi and Maruyama, 1979), and Z-nin (MW 300,000–400,000) were also thought to be the components of Z-disks. Similarly, M-protein or myomesin (MW 165,000), B-protein (MW 130,000), and two more 88,000 and 210,000 MW proteins are believed to constitute the M-line structure. The other proteins, namely, C-protein (MW 135,000), H-protein (MW 74,000), and I-protein (MW 50,000) possibly are associated with thick filaments in A-bands. Some more proteins such as F-protein (MW 121,000), X-protein (MW 152,000), γ-actinin (MW 35,000), and paratropomyosin (MW 35,000) have also been isolated from myofibrils (Starr and Offer, 1983; Takahashi *et al.*, 1983), but their location in muscle ultrastructure is yet unclear.

Cytoskeletal Protein. Cytoskeletal (Campbell *et al.*, 1979; Brinkley, 1982) or scaffold proteins are not yet as well-defined as those of skeletal muscle. However, certain superthin (McNeill and Hoyl, 1967) or intermediate (Osborn *et al.*, 1982; Price and Sanger, 1983) filaments and the so-called S- or G-filaments (Locker, 1984) which have been seen in the ultrastructure of specially prepared muscle, are believed to be composed of about six different proteins. Among them connectin (or titin) is the major one (Wang and Ramirez-Mitchell, 1984; Trinick *et al.*, 1984) which probably constitutes the G-filaments which either run from one Z-disk to another between myosin filaments or connect the ends of myosin filaments with the Z-disk (LaSalle *et al.*, 1983; Locker, 1984; Maruyama *et al.*, 1984). Another protein, nebulin (MW 500,000–600,000), possibly constitutes the N-line in the I-band (Wang, 1981, 1983). Four more proteins, desmin (MW 55,000), synemin (MW 220,000), vimentin (MW 58,000), and filamin (MW 230,000) are assumed to make up certain other superthin filaments which connect adjacent myofibrils laterally at the level of the Z-disk, A-band, and M-line (Lazarides, 1976, 1982a,b; Tokuyasu *et al.*, 1983).

A study by Fujii *et al.* (1978) indicated some similarities between connectin (titin) and collagen with respect to cross-linking characteristics. Lysine-derived cross-linkages, which are known to be specific for collagen, have been shown in connectin also (Fujii and Maruyama, 1982). On the contrary, Robins and Rucklidge (1980) did not find any evidence for the existence of such linkages in connectin. This aspect seems still an open question to be resolved.

2. Extracellular Proteins

Three fibrous proteins, namely, collagen, elastin, and reticulin, are deposited in the interstitial space and comprise about 1.5% of the insoluble connective tissue fraction of muscle. Sometimes another term, stroma, has also been used in the literature to define insoluble connective tissue. However, it seems that the stroma fraction also contained some of the cytoskeletal proteins, such as connectin (or titin) and neublin, which in fact are intracellular proteins.

   a. Collagen.   Since the latest information on collagen has recently been covered in detail elsewhere (Asghar and Henrickson, 1982a), only the pertinent points are summarized here. In skeletal muscle collagen is the principal component of connective tissue. Collagen fibrils are composed of tropocollagen molecules, and each tropocollagen molecule consists of three α chains. Until 1970, only two types of α chains, namely, α1 and α2, were known, and two chains of α1 and one chain of α2 constituted the triple helical tropocollagen molecule. Presently, more than five types of α chain have been discovered in collagen from different sources (Eyre, 1980; Miller and Gay, 1982). These chains are the product of different genes expression. Consequently, the original α1 and α2 chains are now designated as α1(I) and α2(I), respectively, and the others are called α1(II), α1(III), α1(IV), and α1(V). On this basis, at least five types of collagen have presently been recognized in mammalian tissues, and their molecular formulae are $[\alpha 1(I)_2 \alpha 2(I)]$, $[\alpha 1(II)]_3$, $[\alpha 1(III)]_3$, $[\alpha 1(IV)]_3$, and $[\alpha 1(V)]_3$, respectively. Since molecular heterogeneity in collagen types II, III, and IV has not been reported yet, their chains are homogeneous unlike that of type I.

   Very limited information is available on the collagen types in skeletal muscle. From the available results, it appears that only collagen types I, III, and IV are present in connective tissue of skeletal muscle (Bailey and Sims, 1977; Duance *et al.*, 1977), and they predominate, respectively in epimysium, perimysium, and endomysium layers.

   b. Reticulin.   On the basis of the ammoniacal silver staining method, reticulin (stains black) has been differentiated from collagen (stains brown). In view of the nonspecificity of this stain and the discovery of several collagen types, some researchers proposed that reticulin fibrils may represent one of the types of collagen (Duance *et al.*, 1977). The matter of fact is that ultrastructural periodicity and fibril cross-linking characteristics of reticulin are very similar to that of collagen. Sims and Bailey (1981) are inclined to consider collagen type III and reticulin as one and the same protein. This is exclusively found in endomysium layer (Duance *et al.*, 1977).

   c. Elastin.   Elastin is a hydrophobic protein rich in nonpolar amino acid residues (Anwar, 1982). Unlike collagen, it lacks hydroxylysine; instead, two other unique amino acids, desmosine and isodesmosine, are responsible for cross-linkages and make it resistant to acids, alkalis, and heat (Franzblau and Faris, 1982). Elastin constitutes only a very small proportion (<0.1%) of skeletal muscle in general. It is mainly found around arteries in the perimysium layers (Asghar and Yeates, 1968, 1979a). Perhaps it does not carry much significance in muscles as meat, with the exception of some muscles which contain a relatively high content of elastin (Bendall, 1967).

B. PROTEIN TURNOVER RATE IN MUSCLE

Turnover of protein, as implied in biochemistry, means the rate of renewal or the rate of replacement of a protein in the steady state of a tissue (Zilversmit, 1955) and during growth and development of animal (Fritz *et al.*, 1975). The information on protein turnover in mammalian tissues has increased enormously (Swick and Song, 1974; Waterlow *et al.*, 1978; Zak *et al.*, 1979; Millward, 1979, 1980). Protein turnover rate seems to vary widely not only between species and tissues, but also the same protein at different stages of animal growth is renewed at a different rate. For instance, the renewal rate is relatively faster in small (rat, chicken, rabbit) than in large animals such as sheep (Millward, 1980) and pigs (Garlick *et al.*, 1975). Bohley *et al.* (1979) computed the half-lives of total body protein in various species from data of different sources and found the following order: rats, 7 days; rabbits, 10 days; sheep, 21 days; and humans, 25 days. Similarly, protein turnover rate between different tissues of rat was reported to be in the following order: liver, 29 hr; kidney, 34 hr; brain, 146 hr; and muscle, 330 hr (Waterlow *et al.*, 1978).

Several workers reported a significant difference in turnover rate of protein between different muscles (Goldberg and Dice, 1974; Laurent *et al.*, 1978; Millward *et al.*, 1978). For example, fast skeletal muscles were found to have about one-half the total protein renewal rate of that in slow skeletal, cardiac, and smooth muscles. In the case of chicken, the rate of protein turnover in fast (breast) muscle was one-fifth that of cardiac muscle (Kohama, 1980). Although turnover was the fastest in white (fast) muscle in neonates, it did not hold in adults. The data quoted by Millward (1980) suggest that in red (slow) muscle of adults the turnover rate was 8–10% per day, whereas in white muscle it was merely 4–5% per day. The effect of age on protein turnover is obvious from the fact that the rate in white tensor facialatea decreased from 25% per day in 1-week-old lambs to merely 2% per day at the age of 16 weeks. Similarly, renewal rate in breast muscle decreased from 25% per day to 8% at the age of 2 weeks. It was only 3% in 35-week-old chickens.

Different proteins in a tissue have shown different rates of turnover (Serivastava, 1968; Millward, 1970; Laurent *et al.*, 1978) in that sarcoplasmic proteins were renewed at faster rates than were myofibrillar proteins. Goldberg and co-workers observed marked variation in turnover rate within sarcoplasmic proteins (Dice and Goldberg, 1975; Goldberg and St. John, 1976). Several proteins of the outer mitochondrial membrane were replaced more rapidly than was the protein of the matrix and of the inner membrane (Waterlow *et al.*, 1978). A study by Fritz *et al.* (1973) revealed different turnover rates even among isozymes of lactate dehydrogenase.

A conspicuous difference in renewal rates was also reported within myofibrillar proteins (Funabiki and Cassens, 1972, 1973; Low and Goldberg, 1973; Koizumi, 1974), varying from 5–6 days for myosin heavy chains to 50 days for actin (Kay, 1978). Ebashi and Nonomura (1973) reported that contractile proteins are synthesized at a higher rate than regulatory proteins. Based on the incorporation rate of injected labeled amino acids in rabbit (Koizumi, 1974) and in chicken breast muscle (Kohama, 1981), the renewal rate of different proteins was found in the following order: M-protein $\geq$ troponin > soluble protein (as a whole) > tropomyosin = actinin > myosin > 10 S actinin > actin. A recent study by Jones *et al.* (1983), in which they labeled isolated myofibrillar proteins with radioactive ^{14}C by reductive alkylation, showed that the susceptibility of these proteins to hydrolysis by catheptic D enzyme varied in order of their molecular weights: myosin > α-actinin > actin > tropomyosin.

With regard to collagen turnover rate, an isotopic study by Neuberger and Slack (1953) indicated that collagen is not altogether metabolically inert, although its renewal rate varied widely between different tissues. Perhaps it is the soluble fraction (monomeric form) of collagen which is mainly degraded under normal growth and development conditions (Lindstedt and Prockop, 1961; Nimni *et al.*, 1967). The major proportion of insoluble collagen (triple helical form), after being deposited in the skeletal muscles, is not renewed during the lifetime of the animal (Thompson and Ballou, 1956). A comprehensive discussion by Waterlow *et al.* (1978) on this aspect shows some controversy in the findings of different investigators, which possibly arose from the methodology in the isotopic studies. Polymeric forms of elastin and reticulin may also be metabolically inert in muscle. However, no information is yet available about the turnover rate of connectin (titin), nebulin, desmin, and other recently discovered proteins in skeletal muscle.

Many explanations have been extended to account for the variation in susceptibility of different proteins to degradation. Susceptibility of a protein has been related to its isoelectric point (Goldberg and Dice, 1974; Goldberg and St. John, 1976), glycosylation (Goldstone and Koeing, 1974; Dice *et al.*, 1978), phosphorylation (Ekman *et al.*, 1978), and age (Wiederanders *et al.*, 1981). It has also been reported that soluble proteins with high molecular weights are degraded at higher rates than those with low molecular weights (Dehlinger and Schimke, 1970; Dice *et al.*, 1973). On the other hand, Bohley and Reimann (1977) believe that surface hydrophobicity of a protein is the main factor which affects its degradation rate as this facilitates the protein's entry across the lysosomal membrane.

However, none of these generalizations hold true for myofibrillar proteins as is apparent from the findings of Koizumi (1974), Kohama (1981), and Jones *et al.* (1983). Under diabetic and starved conditions, the normal correlations between protein size and half-life and between protein charge and half-life are largely abolished, because the accelerated protein catabolism in these cases is fundamentally different from normal degradation (Dice *et al.*, 1978; Asghar *et al.*, 1986a,b). Moreover, the proportion of collagen increases in skeletal muscle of underfed animals (Asghar *et al.*, 1981), suggesting that either its synthesis is not affected adversely or it is not catabolized in the event of undernutrition to meet the energy demand.

In Table IV is summarized the average half-lives of different subcellular components and their associated enzymes. Despite some discrepancies about the turnover rate of different proteins, there is no dispute that, once a protein molecule is synthesized, it does not stay indefinitely but is catabolized in due time and replaced by a new molecule. This process serves several functions in the living cells (Goldberg and St. John, 1976; Ballard, 1977). One of the important functions of protein turnover is that it facilitates the organism to adapt to its environments. For example, adaptation to inadequate nutrition may require endogenous protein degradation to provide energy and sufficient amino acids for the synthesis of those enzymes which are required for catabolic reactions as well as to remove abnormal proteins which are formed as a result of exogenous (mutagens) or endogenous (biosynthetic error) factors.

Apart from these, proteolytic enzymes perform several other important functions in the physiology of live animals. Comprehensive coverage on these aspects is available (Reich *et al.*, 1975; Ribbons and Brew, 1976; Turk and Vitale, 1981; Havemann and Janoff, 1978; Magnusson *et al.*, 1978). Structural modification of some native enzymes by limited proteolysis seems one of the mechanisms for the regulation of their activity *in vivo* (Otto, 1971; Auricchio *et al.*, 1972; Pontremoli *et al.*, 1974; Melloni *et al.*, 1974; Nakashima and Ogino, 1974; Lazo *et al.*, 1978). For instance, the activity of 1,6-fructose-bisphosphatase (Fru-P$_2$ase) in liver and muscle is controlled by its partial hydrolysis during gluconeogensis (Nakai *et al.*, 1978; Tsolas *et al.*, 1981; Hannappel *et al.*, 1982; Katunuma *et al.*, 1983). This enzyme is one of the four which play a key role in gluconeogensis during starvation. Other enzymes are pyruvate carboxylase, phosphoenolpyruvate carboxykinase, and glucose-6-phosphatase. Since modified fructose-1,6-bisphosphatase (aldolase) is not sensitive to AMP concentration, this favors gluconeogenesis. Cathepsins B (Distelmaier *et al.*, 1972; Davidson and Poole, 1975; Melloni *et al.*, 1981), A (Pontremoli *et al.*, 1979), and L (Katunuma *et al.*, 1983; McKay *et al.*, 1984) are reported to perform the modification of aldolase. The proteolytic conversion of proinsulin (Ansorge *et al.*, 1977) and proalbumin (Quinn and Judah, 1978) to insulin and albumin, respectively, which occurs in the Golgi apparatus, is possibly brought about by cathepsin B.

TABLE IV

AVERAGE TURNOVER RATE (HALF-LIFE) OF DIFFERENT CELLULAR COMPONENTS, AND OF
INDIVIDUAL PROTEINS ASSOCIATED WITH SUBCELLULAR COMPONENTS[a]

Cellular component	Short lived ($t_{1/2} < 24$ hr)	Long lived ($t_{1/2} > 24$ hr)	Individual protein	Turnover rate ($t_{1/2}$, hours)
Plasma membranes	25	43	—	
Nuclei	8	122	RNA polymerase I	31
			Histones (mean)	430
Mitochondria	28	163	Ornithine aminotransferase	41
			δ-Aminolevulinate dehydratase	132
			Cytochrome c	216
Lysosomes	4	170	β-Glucuronidase	696
Peroxisomes	—	—	Catalase	24
Microsomes	18	72	Nucleoside diphosphatase	30
			Cytochrome b_5	55–120
			NADPH–cytochrome c reductase	70
			Carboxyesterase	96
			NADH–cytochrome b_5 reductase	115
			NAD$^+$ glucohydrolase	384
Cytosol	12	122	Tyrosine aminotransferase	1
			Tryptophan oxygenase	2
			PEP carboxylase	5
			Serine dehydratase	20
			Ferritin	31
			Acetyl-CoA carboxylase	48
			Aldolase	67
			Fatty acid synthetase	72
			Glyceraldehyde-3-phosphate dehydrogenase	74
			Arginase	108
			Lactate dehydrogenase	84–384

[a] From Bohley *et al.* (1979). Courtesy of Springer-Verlag, Berlin, Heidelberg, and New York.

Since endogenous proteases perform a vital role in the turnover of protein in muscle during normal growth and development as well as in steady state, this aspect is discussed at length in the proceeding section, with particular reference to regulation mechanisms of protein turnover and the relative contribution of different proteolytic enzymes in this process.

C. PROTEIN CATABOLISM REGULATING MECHANISMS

Gan and Jeffay (1967, 1971) demonstrated that normal skeletal muscle supplies 30% of its own amino acid requirement by intracellular metabolism. However, the overall protein turnover in muscle is rather complex, as it not only involves intracellular proteins but also includes inter- and extracellular protein turnover. When the proteins are synthesized and degraded in the same cell, this represents intracellular protein turnover. On the other hand, if a protein is synthesized in one type of cell and subsequently catabolized by other cells, this is termed intercellular protein turnover, whereas the degradation of extracellular proteins is performed by enzymes secreted from cells (Kirschke et al., 1980). Practically, however, it is not easy to distinguish these forms of protein turnover.

It is obvious from the discussion in Sections II and III that multiple proteolytic enzyme systems exist in skeletal muscle. They possibly serve discrete physiological functions within mammalian cells during the catabolism of intra- and intercellular proteins. The findings on the mechanisms which govern the degradation of protein in skeletal muscle are rather divergent. The prevalent views on this aspect can be divided into three groups which are based on the role of lysosomes, and nonlysosomal proteinases, and of calcium ions.

1. Role of Lysosomes and Lysosomal Proteinases

Since lysosomes are very rich in proteolytic enzymes, a fundamental issue in the study of protein catabolism in mammalian cells has been their possible involvement in this process. Many researchers are of the opinion that lysosomes are the primary loci for the turnover of cytoplasmic proteins (Segal et al., 1974; Segal, 1976; Dean, 1975b, 1976, 1979; Hopgood et al., 1977; Neff et al., 1979; Pearson and Kar, 1979; Ward et al., 1979; Wildenthal and Crie, 1980; Mortimore and Huston, 1981). The findings of Seglen et al. (1979) indicated that lysosomal proteases account for about 70% of total protein turnover in hepatocytes.

Intracellular macromolecules presumably enter into the matrix of secondary lysosomes by two general mechanisms: autophagocytosis (autophagy or engulfment) and fusion (Dean and Barrett, 1976). Autophagy is defined as the process by which the cell's own proteins are taken into secondary lysosomes for degradation. The lysosomal uptake of substances within cells was termed lysosomotropism by de Duve (1977). This process depends on the functional integrity of lysosomal membrane which is measured indirectly from the latency of various lysosomal enzymes. A lysosome is considered to be latent if it becomes active on exogenous substrate after the disruption of membrane by sonication or detergents.

Depending on their half-lives, cellular proteins are sometimes classified into long-lived and short-lived proteins (Mortimore, 1982). The average half-life of the latter is merely 10–12 min, and they constitute about 0.2% of the total protein in liver (Vandenburgh and Kaufman, 1980). While the long-lived proteins are believed to be degraded via the autophagocytosis pathway (Ballard and Gunn, 1982), the degradation of short-lived proteins is possibly mediated by the nonlysosomal route (Mortimore, 1982). On the other hand, the degradation of extracellular macromolecules involves a two-step mechanism (Dingle, 1973). First, the enzymes secreted in the matrix make small fragments of the macromolecules. They are then taken either into cells by endocytosis for further degradation by secondary lysosomes or into heterolysosomes where they are digested by macrophages. The latter process is called heterophagy, and the dead cells are probably degraded by this mechanism (de Duve and Baudhuin, 1966; Ten Cate and Syrbu, 1974; Dean, 1975a; Mortimore *et al.,* 1978). A study by Bigelow *et al.* (1981) also showed the possibility that some proteins are partially degraded in the cytosol and the resulting fragments then taken up by lysosomes for further degradation to amino acids.

Surprisingly, the suggestion made by some other researchers (Ehrenreich and Cohn, 1969; Goldman, 1973) about the role of cytosolic and lysosomal proteases is altogether in reverse order to that mentioned above. They think that dipeptidyl aminopeptidases in lysosomes degrade the protein into dipeptides which diffuse into cytosol where they are further hydrolyzed to free amino acids by cytosol dipeptidases. Coffey and de Duve (1968) have demonstrated that rat liver lysosomes degraded susceptible proteins mainly to dipeptides and free amino acids. Lysosomal membrane is reported to be permeable to most dipeptides (Lloyd, 1971) except those which have molecular weights greater than 200,000 (Ehrenreich and Cohn, 1969) or 290,000 (Goldman, 1973).

The concept of lysosomotropism in protein turnover sounds fancy, but it is difficult to conceive how this mechanism would explain the heterogeneity of degradation rate constants of different cellular proteins. If the native proteins are internalized by mass engulfment into lysosomes via autophagy, then different half-lives of protein (Kay, 1978) require an explanation. Naturally some other mechanisms would be needed to recognize those proteins which are to be catabolized. Schimke (1975) was of the view that the concerned proteins may be acetylated, formylated, or deaminated, or they may undergo limited proteolysis before engulfment into lysosomes. Segal (1976) considers that each protein possibly has a different susceptibility to the initial proteolytic attack inside the lysosome due to a different degree of resistance in acid conditions. Kay (1978) thought that the initial proteolysis (rate-limiting step) which occurs before internalization must be slower than the rate of uptake into lysosomes, and this may account for the differential susceptibility of proteins to proteolysis.

While reviewing the regulation and mechanisms of endogenous protein degradation in mammalian cells, Dean (1980) concluded that those organelles which exhibit unit turnover are possibly degraded by sequestration of the whole organelle by the lysosomal system. On the other hand, those organelles which show heterogeneous turnover of internal components have an internal degradation machinery which may partly be responsible for the turnover of these proteins. He considers that the lysosomal system is selective in the degrading process. In contrast, Ballard (1977) had proposed a discrete dual pathway model in which one pathway envisages the lysosomes as a system-limited nonselective route involved in the turnover of long half-life proteins. The second pathway is concerned with short half-life proteins and involves nonlysosomal proteases. Amenta et al. (1978) also believes in a dual pathway model, but they assumed that lysosomes are involved in both pathways. However, under nutritional and hormonal deprivation conditions, the lysosomal pathway was shown to be predominant, and the autophagic vacoules were conspicuous in cultured fibroblasts.

2. Role of Nonlysosomal Proteinases

Circumstantial evidence suggests that some nonlysosomal proteases are also involved in cellular degradation of proteins. Many workers are of the opinion that the degradation of so-called short-lived intracellular proteins and abnormal proteins is possibly mediated by an unregulated nonlysosomal pathway (Knowles and Ballard, 1976; Seglen et al., 1979; Mortimore, 1982). Since the catabolism of short-lived proteins was not influenced by physiological regulators (Vandenburgh and Kaufman, 1980) and lysosomotropic inhibitors (Grinde and Seglen, 1980), it was implied that different proteolytic mechanisms may be involved in these cases. In contrast to this view, Bohley et al. (1979) have reported that short-lived proteins are catabolized by lysosomal proteinases.

The findings also differ on the role of specific proteases in cytoplasm. For example, different functions seem to have been assigned to Ca^{2+}-activated neutral proteases in different tissues. They include the conversion of phosphorylase b to a by limited proteolysis (Huston and Krebs, 1968) and the transformation of some steroid hormone receptors (Vedeckis et al., 1980). Many other researchers believe that CANP is involved in myofibrillar protein turnover (Dayton et al., 1975, 1976; Reddy et al., 1975; Mykles and Skinner, 1983). The discovery of calmodulin (or parvalbumin), which acts as a Ca^{2+} receptor, provides a tentative mechanism by which Ca^{2+} requiring reactions may be regulated within cells (Cheung, 1979; Means and Dedman, 1980). The presence of calmodulin has also been indicated in skeletal muscle cells (Hartshorne, 1983), but its function is not yet clear. Besides, muscle does contain Tn-C as a Ca^{2+} receptor.

On the contrary, some studies provide evidence to refute the involvement of CANP (Gerard and Schneider, 1980; Rodemann et al., 1982) and chymotrypsin-like (serine) proteases (Libby and Goldberg, 1980b) in the catabolism of cellular proteins. These conclusions were based on the use of proteinase inhibitors such as mersalyl, leupeptin, chymostatin, and chloroquine in isolated muscle or in cultured myotubes of chicken embryonic cells. They assumed that in the presence of these inhibitors the activity of CANP, lysosomal proteinase, and serine proteinase would be completely abolished. Since protein degradation still occurred in the cultured cells in the presence of these inhibitors, they concluded that these proteinases are not involved in the degradative process. In several other studies Goldberg and associates projected the idea that yet another ATP-dependent protease system is responsible for protein catabolism in muscle (Etlinger and Goldberg, 1977; DeMartino and Goldberg, 1979). Although this enzyme has not yet been characterized in the skeletal muscle system, Wilkinson *et al.* (1980) have reported the presence of ATP-dependent protease factor I (low MW ubiquitin) in reticulocytes. Among lysosomal proteases, only cathepsins D (Watabe *et al.,* 1976) and L (Kirschke *et al.,* 1977c) are reported to be activated by ATP. The latter is also activated by reduced glutathione and coenzyme A (Kirschke *et al.,* 1981). A recent study by Kalinskii (1985) suggested a role for cAMP-dependent protein kinase in regulating cathepsin D's activity in skeletal and heart muscle of rats when they were subjected to physical load.

3.   Role of Ca^{2+}

A study by Kameyama and Etlinger (1979) showed that an increase in intracellular Ca^{2+} concentration stimulated both degradation and synthesis of proteins in skeletal muscle. They induced the increase in intracellular Ca^{2+} by injecting ionophore A23187 (a monocarboxylic acid antibiotic which increases the movement of Ca^{2+} across membranes) and by increasing K^+ content in the isolated muscle. High extracellular K^+ concentration depolarizes the muscle membrane which in turn induces the sarcoplasmic reticulum to release its Ca^{2+} into the sarcoplasm.

As to the role of Ca^{2+} in protein metabolism, two hypotheses have been extended. In one, a high level of Ca^{2+} is assumed to stimulate CANP which initiates proteolysis (Sugden, 1980; Lewis *et al.,* 1982), whereas, in others, the role of Ca^{2+} has been mediated by prostaglandin E_2 (Rodemann *et al.,* 1982). This is based on the findings that the rise in intracellular Ca^{2+} (induced by ionophore A23187) activates Ca^{2+}-dependent phospholipase A_2 which catalyzes the rate-limiting reaction in the biosynthesis of prostaglandins (Knapp *et al.,* 1977; Pickett *et al.,* 1977; Billah *et al.,* 1980; Zenser *et al.,* 1980). This enzyme releases arachidonic acid (C_{20}) from membrane-bound phospholipids to serve as the precursor for the synthesis of prostaglandin endoperoxides by cyclooxygenases. Goldberg and co-workers (Rodemann and Goldberg, 1982; Rodemann *et al.,* 1982), who are the proponents of this hypothesis, suggested that the increase in intracellular Ca^{2+} stimulates the formation of prostaglandin E_2, which in turn activates the lysosomal cathepsin B to initiate proteolysis in skeletal muscles.

D. CAUSES OF CONFLICTING RESULTS

It has been indicated in Section III that endopeptidases have been classified on the basis of certain functional groups which constitute the active site. The number of protease inhibitors of microbial origin which can inhibit the activity of each class of endopeptidase has expanded substantially in the last two decades (Umezawa and Aoyagi, 1977). However, those inhibitors which have frequently been used do not seem to be very specific between different classes (Table V). Some investigators, for instance, did not consider inhibition by EDTA or 1,10-phenanthroline as the appropriate criterion to classify a protease as metalloenzyme (McConn *et al.*, 1964; Knight, 1977). Many serine protease inhibitors

TABLE V

EFFECT OF DIFFERENT PROTEASE INHIBITORS ON THE ACTIVITY OF SERINE, CYSTEINE, ASPARTATE, AND METALLOPROTEINASES[a]

Inhibitor	Amount	Serine proteinases	Cysteine proteinases	Aspartate proteinases	Metallo-proteinases
Diisopropyl fluorophosphate (DFP)	1 mM	+	(+)	−	−
Phenylmethanesulfonyl fluoride (Pms-F)	1 mM	+	(+)	−	−
Antipain	1 mM	+	+	−	−
Leupeptin	1 mM	+	+	−	−
Chymostatin	1 mM	+	+	−	−
4-Chloromercuribenzoate	0.1 mM	−	+	−	Activates
Diazoacetylnorleucine methyl ester + Cu^{2+}	1 mM	−	+	+	−
Pepstatin	1 mg/liter	−	−	+	−
1,10-Phenanthroline	1 mM	−	−	−	+
Dithiothreitol + EDTA	2 mM each	−	Activates	−	+
Disulfites		−	+	−	−
Iodoacetate, N-ethylmaleimide	1 mM	+	+	−	+
Soybean trypsin inhibitor	100 mg/liter	+	−	−	−

[a] The information has been derived from Barrett and Dingle (1971), Barrett (1972, 1977), and Umezawa and Aoyagi (1977). +, Inhibited; −, not inhibited.

also affect the activity of thiol proteases (Whitaker and Perez-Villasenor, 1968) because of the very high nucleophilicity of sulfur. Similarly, chloromethylketone is also a strongly electrophilic reagent which reacts with the SH group, beside discriminately inhibiting serine proteases. Probably the same is true for other alkylating reagents such as iodoacetate which bring about irreversible inactivation of thiol proteases. The inhibitory effect of thiol-blocking agents like chloromercuribenzoate and Hg^{2+} can be reversed by adding an excess amount of thiol reagents. Various alkylation inhibitors fall in the following order with respect to their inhibitory power (Barrett, 1977): iodoacetate > iodoacetamide > N-ethylmaleimide > Tos-Lys-CH_2Cl > Tos-Phe-CH_2Cl.

It may also be emphasized that thiol-blocking agents do not inhibit all cysteine proteases to the same extent (Katunuma and Kominami, 1983) because the alkylating reaction depends not only on the structure of the alkylating agent but also on the charge of amino acid residues of the enzyme. Thus, the amino acid composition of the proteinase and its binding capacity would determine the magnitude of inhibition. This explains why cathepsin H was less affected by leupeptin, chymostatin, antipain, and E-64 than was cathepsins B1 and L (Davidson and Poole, 1975; Kirschke et al., 1976; Singh et al., 1978; Barrett et al., 1982). Even the proteases in different species seem to respond differently to inhibitors. For instance, Libby and Goldberg (1980b) observed a much less inhibitory effect of leupeptin and chymostatin on overall protein degradation in cultured chick muscle cells than in rat muscle.

Another important fact to note is that the inhibitory effect of in vivo injected leupeptin or E-64 on CANP (Ishiura et al., 1981) and cathepsin B and L activities started decreasing gradually soon after application and leveled off in about 24–36 hr postinjection (Pietras et al., 1978; Hashida et al., 1980, 1982). These observations weaken the validity of the finding of Goldberg and associates (Etlinger and Goldberg, 1977; Rodemann et al., 1982), who ruled out the involvement of lysosomal proteinase and CANP in cellular protein turnover because the incorporation of these protease inhibitors into muscle did not arrest the protein turnover.

E.   RELATIVE CONTRIBUTION OF DIFFERENT PROTEINASES IN PROTEIN TURNOVER

Several lysosomal proteases have been implicated in the degradation of cellular proteins. Dean (1975a) assigned the major role to cathepsin D in intracellular protein turnover. This seems to be at variance with the conclusions of others (Huisman et al., 1973, 1974b; Nakai et al., 1976; Libby and Goldberg, 1978, 1980a; Libby et al., 1979), who believe that the thiol proteinases carry much greater importance than carboxyl proteinase (cathepsin D) in the overall process of protein turnover in tissues. Although degradation of proteoglycans has also been assigned to cathepsin D in arthritis conditions (Poole *et al.*, 1973), the lack of its activity at neutral pH may preclude an important role of cathepsin D extracellularly.

Bohley *et al.* (1979) conducted an interesting study to determine the relative contribution of different cathepsins in the catabolism of short- and long-lived proteins. For that matter, they double labeled the proteins of liver cytoplasm by injecting the rats with [^{14}C]guanidine (or $NaH_3C^{14}CO_2$) and [5-^{3}H]L-arginine before killing. They observed that 90% of short-lived proteins (^{3}H labeled) were degraded only by cathepsin L, whereas long-lived proteins (^{14}C labeled because reutilization of ^{14}C is very slight) were affected by cathepsins B and D and by some unidentified nonlysosomal proteases. The relative share of different cathepsins in the total proteolytic activity at pH 6.1 was in the following order: cathepsin H, <2%; cathepsin D, <10%; cathepsin B, <20%; cathepsin L, >50%.

VII. FACTORS INFLUENCING PROTEINASE ACTIVITY IN MUSCLES

Generally speaking, the activity of an enzyme in cells is regulated by two mechanisms, namely, genetic and catalytic controls. The former implies a change in enzyme concentration, whereas the latter does not involve any change in enzyme content. The concentration of different enzymes in cells is determined by the rates at which they are synthesized and catabolized. Enzyme synthesis in prokaryotic cells is regulated at the gene level by the indirect action of certain metabolities which act either as inducers or repressors (Walsh, 1979). In eukaryotic cells, hormones regulate synthesis at the transcriptional and translational levels. This, in fact, represents a coarse or long-term metabolic regulation (Scrimgeour, 1977), whereas fine or acute controls are concerned with the activity of an enzyme rather than its concentration. The activity is controlled by allosteric activators and inhibitors present in the cells. Apart from these, several other factors which influence the activity of proteinases in skeletal muscle have been reported by different investigators and are discussed in this section.

A. ENDOGENOUS INHIBITORS

There is ample experimental evidence to show that endogenous inhibitors of serine, cysteine, aspartate, and metalloproteinases are present in mammalian tissues (Lenney, 1980). They are generally found in the cytosol fraction (Järvinen, 1979; Lenney *et al.*, 1979; Hirado *et al.*, 1981; Sasaki *et al.*, 1981; Kominami *et al.*, 1982a,b; Pagano *et al.*, 1982). The α_2-macroglobin which was first noticed by Jacobsson (1953) is now believed to be a principal circulating

TABLE VI

ENDOGENOUS INHIBITORS OF DIFFERENT PROTEINASES

Proteinase	Molecular weight of inhibitor	Reference
Serine protease	4,000	Katunuma and Kominami (1977), Noguchi and Kandatsu (1969)
Cathepsin B1	13,000	Schwartz and Bird (1977), Lenney et al. (1979)
	62,000	Schwartz and Bird (1977)
Cathepsin H	13,000	Ooyama et al. (1975), Lenney et al. (1979)
	74,000	Jarvinen and Hopsu-Havu (1975)
Ca^{2+}-activated neutral protease	300,000	Okitani et al. (1974), Waxman and Krebs (1978), Goll et al. (1978), Otsuka and Goll (1980), Takahashi-Nakamura et al. (1981)
Cathepsin D	700	Knight and Barrett (1976)
Collagenases	31,000	Welgus et al. (1979)

protease inhibitor in the mammalian body (Barrett et al., 1974; Laurell and Jeppsson, 1975). Its inhibitory effect is well documented on serine (Harpel, 1973; Venge et al., 1975), thiol (Werb et al., 1974), carboxy (Barrett and Starkey, 1973), and metalloproteinases (Abe and Nagai, 1973).

Bird et al. (1977) isolated two inhibitors (MW 13,000 and 65,000) of cathepsin B from skeletal muscle by Sephadex 75 chromatography. Many other researchers reported the presence of endogenous inhibitors of different proteinases (Udaka and Hayashi, 1965; Noguchi and Kandatsu, 1969; Järvinen and Hopsu-Havu, 1975; Ooyama et al., 1975; Knight and Barrett, 1976; Goll et al., 1978; Clark et al., 1986). The protease inhibitors found in skeletal muscle are recorded in Table VI. It may be pointed out that the ratio of an inhibitor to protease varies not only from one tissue to another but also within the same tissue depending on age, sex, or nutritional status. For instance, Spanier and Bird (1982) have shown that the content of a protease inhibitor decreased markedly in skeletal muscle of animals which were suffering from vitamin E deficiency.

Regarding the question as to how an inhibitor regulates the activity of a protease (E), the answer may be found in terms of dissociation constant (K_d). The fact that an enzyme inhibitor (I) has a dissociation constant suggests that some amount of inhibitor is present as free. The ratio [E]/[I], dissociation rate, and dissociation constant may be regulated according to the need of the cells. For instance, Leckie and McDonnell (1975) have shown that a protease (MW

55,000) and its inhibitor (MW 18,000) formed an inactive complex at high pH. On lowering the pH, the enzyme was activated again. Other studies also indicated the selective inactivation of inhibitor by a change in pH value of the system (Boyd, 1974; Loskutoff and Edgington, 1977). In any case, the fine control of enzyme catalysis is related to the alteration in the activity rather than the amount of enzyme, and the activity is regulated by allosteric activators and inhibitors present in the system (Katunuma and Kominami, 1985b; Pontremoli *et al.*, 1985).

A review by Goldberg and St. John (1976) indicates that the macrophagic role in protein degradation is regulated primarily by the concentration of certain amino acids in plasma. Most of the studies agree that only leucine, glutamine, histidine, methionine, tryptophan, and tyrosine (or phenylalanine) possess an inhibitory effect in cellular protein degradation (Hopgood *et al.*, 1977; Seglen *et al.*, 1980; Sommercorn and Swick, 1981; Pösö *et al.*, 1982; Mortimore and Pösö, 1984). However, a recent investigation by Pösö and Mortimore (1984) has indicated that, apart from the above-mentioned amino acids, a decrease in alanine content below normal levels in the amino acid pool also evoked protein degradation in liver. They argued that, although alanine has no direct inhibitory role, it possibly acts as coregulator in expressing its signals to the site of proteolytic degradation.

B. MUSCLE TYPE

The red (e.g., solenus) and white (e.g., digitorum longus) muscles, which are rich, respectively, in oxidative and glycolytic enzymes, also differ substantially in protease activity. As compared to white, red muscle contains a higher activity of cathepsin C (Goldspink *et al.*, 1970, 1971; Iodice *et al.*, 1972; Pluskal and Pennington, 1973a), cathepsin B, arylamidase (Pluskal and Pennington, 1973a), cathepsin A (Iodice *et al.*, 1972), and alkaline serine protease (Katunuma *et al.*, 1977). A study by Peter *et al.* (1972a,b) also indicated much higher activity of acid cathepsins in slow-twitch red muscle than in fast-twitch white muscle of pork. The high catheptic activity may be associated with the greater concentration of lysosomes in red than in white muscle (Stauber and Schottelius, 1975). This may explain the difference in turnover rate between red and white muscles (Arnal *et al.*, 1976; Bates and Millward, 1983).

Even during physical exercise, the red oxidative muscle fibers showed a more prominent lysosomal response than white ones, as did nonmuscle cells of rats (Vinko *et al.*, 1978). On the contrary, Iodice *et al.* (1972) had found that white skeletal muscles were affected by vitamin E deficiency relatively earlier than red muscles. This disparity could be accounted for by two possibilities: first, the protein synthesis rate is reported to be greater in red than in white muscle (Spanier, 1977), and, second, the content of endogenous protease inhibitor per unit weight is found to be higher in red than in white muscle of guinea pig (Spanier and Bird, 1982). The concentration of myoglobin, which inhibits cathepsin B activity (Bird and Schwartz, 1977) is also high in red muscles.

C. NUTRITION

The proteolytic activity in mammalian tissues increases during inadequate nutrition (Wildenthal, 1976; Millward and Waterlow, 1978; MacDonald and Swick, 1981). This accelerates catabolism of endogenous cell proteins for maintaining the amino acid pool which supplies the substrate for gluconeogenesis as well as for renewing those proteins which are essential for carrying on the vital cellular processes. However, the findings of different researchers differ as to which proteolytic enzymes play the major role. The activity of both cytosolic and lysosomal proteases seems to vary in skeletal muscle in response to the nutritional status of the animals, and this is reflected by the changes in turnover of different proteins in muscle of starved (Bates and Millward, 1983; Preedy and Garlick, 1983) or underfed animals (Asghar et al., 1985b).

Not only is the total activity of lysosomal enzymes shown to adapt according to the nutritional state of body (Desai, 1969; Filkins, 1970; Roobol and Alleyne, 1974; Wildenthal et al., 1975b; Rosochacki and Millward, 1979; Samarel et al., 1981) and to amino acid deficiency (Neely et al., 1974), but the latency of some lysosomal enzymes also changed in starved animals (Wildenthal et al. 1975a). Regarding nonlysosomal proteases, the hydrolyzing ability of leucine aminopeptidase in diaphragm muscle from 18-hr fasted rats was much higher than that from the control group (Rose et al., 1959). A severalfold increase in alkaline protease activity in gastrocnemius muscle of rats was noticed after 6 days of starvation by Noguchi et al. (1974). They also reported an increase in the content of free acid protease (cathepsin D) and a decrease in its bound form (which is released by Triton X-100). From other reports it seems that during undernutrition the activity of cathepsins A and D rises to a great extent, and that of cathepsin B and L increases only marginally (Schwartz and Bird, 1977; Katunuma and Kominami, 1983). Partially purified cathepsin D from starved mice displayed significantly higher V_{max} and K_m values than the one isolated from the control group (Lundholm et al., 1980). With regard to Ca^{2+}-activated neutral protease, Seperich and Price (1978) obtained a 3-fold greater yield of this enzyme with slightly higher specific activity from skeletal muscle of starved rabbits as compared to that from the group fed ad libitum. With the exception of cathepsin C, a marked fluctuation in the activity of cathepsins A and D in rat skeletal muscle was observed by Obled et al. (1980) even between different intervals of feeding time.

Vitamin E deficiency also leads to some changes in lysosomes (Bond and Barrett, 1974; Lin and Chen, 1982) as well as elevation of alkaline protease

(Koszalka *et al.*, 1961) and cathepsin D content (Zalkin *et al.*, 1962; Korovkin and Budniakov, 1973; Noguchi *et al.*, 1974) in skeletal muscle. Samarel *et al.* (1982) expressed the view that a decrease in the degradation of cathepsin D rather than an increase in its synthesis was responsible for the high content of this protease in cardiac muscle of rabbits suffering from nutritional deficiency. An immunofluorescence microscopic study by Decker *et al.* (1980) has shown that cathepsin D was not released into cytoplasm from lysosomes during undernutrition. Instead, there was a greater distribution of this enzyme within sarcoplasmic reticulum of cardiac muscle from starved animals. In contrast to all of this evidence Mayel-Afsher *et al.* (1983) concluded from their study that neither cathepsin D nor Ca^{2+}-activated neutral protease played any major role in catabolizing maternal skeletal muscle protein to provide amino acids for placental and fetal growth and development during protein deficiency in pregnancy.

D. ANIMAL AGE

Hajek *et al.* (1965) observed almost a doubling in the specific activity of acid proteases in extensor digitorum muscle from 2-year-old as compared to that from 3-month-old animals. A similar trend in cathepsin activity in gastrocnemius muscle from 6-month- and 3-year-old rats was reported by Torboli (1970). Several other studies have demonstrated an increase in the activity of cathepsin D in different tissues of the body with an increase in age (Lundholm and Scherstén, 1975; Platt and Gross-Fengels, 1979; Wiederanders *et al.*, 1981). This was interpreted as intracellular proteolysis increases with age. However, a study by Iodice *et al.* (1972) reveals an altogether different picture. They observed a gradual decline in the specific activity of cathepsins A, B, C, and D of chicken breast muscle with advances in age.

Those studies which have shown an increase in protease activities with age seem to be at variance with the general belief that a high concentration of proteases in the muscle of young animals is associated with a corresponding fast rate of myofibrillar protein turnover during the most rapid growth period. Etherington and Wardale (1982) also concluded that total lysosomal activity was higher in young than in old muscle cells of rats. Some age-associated changes in lysosomes have also been reported by Wildenthal *et al.* (1977) and Salminen *et al.* (1982).

E. NERVE SYSTEM

Electron micrographs of denervated skeletal muscle depicted an increase in the size of lysosomes (Pellegrino and Franzini, 1963) and in Golgi bodies (Schiaffino and Hanzlikova, 1972). Severing of the sciatic nerve of rats caused an increase in the level of acid protease and peptidases in the hind leg muscles

(Hajek et al., 1963; Syróvy et al., 1966; Banno et al., 1975). Although similar increases in the content of acid protease (Pollack and Bird, 1968), arylamidase, and alkaline protease (Pluskal and Pennington, 1973b) were observed in other rat muscles on denervation, cathepsin B displayed the largest increase. All of these changes account for the high rate of proteolysis in denervated muscles.

The observations that the ability of sarcoplasmic reticulum to sequester Ca^{2+} decreased (Duncan, 1978) and membrane permeability to Ca^{2+} increased (Joffe et al., 1981) in denervated muscles suggest the involvement of CANP in protein degradation. A study by Takala et al. (1983) in fact has proved that both lysosomal and nonlysosomal proteases play their part in neuromuscular diseases. Most of the investigations have shown an increase in the activity of such proteases as cathepsin C (Pluskal and Pennington, 1973b; Lee et al., 1984), cathepsin B2 (Hardy et al., 1977), serine proteinase (Banno et al., 1975), cathepsin D (Lukashevich and Ivanova, 1976), leucine aminopeptidase (Lee et al., 1984), and DAP IV (Kar and Pearson, 1978) in denervated muscle of different species. However, the activity of CANP (Kar and Pearson, 1976a), DAP II, and DAP III (Kar and Pearson, 1978) did not change in denervating diseases of skeletal muscle. A recent report by Tagerud and Libelius (1984) supports the hypothesis that increased endocytosis possibly initiates lysosomal activation (of cathepsin D) in denervated skeletal muscle. These findings, however, contradicted the observation of several other investigators who have shown that neurogenic stimuli such as denervation suppressed the activity of cathepsin D (McLaughlin and Bosmann, 1976; Maskrey et al., 1977; Boegman and Oliver, 1980). Gorski and Worowski (1982) also reported the influence of motor nerve activity on cathepsin D in rat skeletal muscle.

An interesting study by Rubinstein and Kelly (1978) have suggested that innervation is needed for developing slow muscles to become reprogramed for synthesizing slow myosin isozymes. Sciatic neuroectomy prevented development of fibers and synthesis of those myosin subunits which are characteristics of slow soleus muscle. The fast extensor digitorum longus muscle, however, was not affected by neuroectomy. This indicates that only the development of slow muscles is neurally controlled, while that of fast muscles is independent of it. If so, then the activity of proteolytic enzymes in fast muscle may not be influenced by denervation.

F. ENDOCRINES

Several hormones are reported to influence the activity of lysosomal proteases (Wildenthal, 1976; Flaim et al., 1978a; Goldberg, 1980; Decker and Wildenthal, 1981; Chua et al., 1978, 1983) and hence protein turnover rate in muscles. Glucocorticoids and thyroid hormones accelerate protein catabolism in muscle substantially (Mayer et al., 1976; Flaim et al., 1978b; Santidrian et al., 1981), although the response is relatively slower than in other tissues (Mortimore *et al.*, 1978; Tischler, 1981; Odedra *et al.*, 1983). An earlier study by Engel and Schwartz (1951), however, did not find any effect of adrenal cortex (ACTH) on peptidase activity of muscle; a later report showed 85% increase in the specific activity of glycyl-glycine dipeptidase in the diaphragm of rats which received adrenocorticol injections for 5 days (Schwartz *et al.*, 1956). Similarly, administration of cortisone or triiodothyroxine to rats increased the activity of leucine aminopeptidase in skeletal muscles (Rose *et al.*, 1959). The activity of cathepsin D in skeletal muscle increased by administration of thyroxine (Wildenthal and Mueller, 1974; DeMartino and Goldberg, 1978) and glucocorticoids (Goldberg *et al.*, 1980; Clark and Vignos, 1981).

Mayer *et al.* (1974b) identified a glucocorticoid receptor protein in the cytoplasmic fraction of rat muscles. They proposed that a hormone–protein complex mediates in the catabolic function of corticosteroids in inducing the protease activity. In contrast to this evidence, Bird *et al.* (1968) observed an increase in the level of free acid protease in gastrocnenius muscle from adrenalactomized rats.

The activity of alkaline proteases was found to be high in those animals which were in a state of insulin or testosterone deficiency as a result of castration (Dahlmann *et al.*, 1981). Several other investigators noted an increase in alkaline protease activity in a diabetic condition (Röthig *et al.*, 1975, 1978; Dahlmann *et al.*, 1979). McElligott and Bird (1981) obtained similar results on alkaline protease activity, but they did not find any change in lysosomal cathepsins. On the contrary, Griffin and Wildenthal (1978) observed a significant difference both in the total activity and in the latency of cathepsin D due to diabetes mellitus.

There is now ample evidence in support of the view that some growth-promoting factors (e.g., insulin) and essential nutrients (e.g., leucine) may be acting as physiological regulators of proteolysis in tissues (Jefferson *et al.*, 1974; Röthig *et al.*, 1975, 1978; Waterlow *et al.*, 1978; Chua *et al.*, 1979; Hopgood *et al.*, 1980; Morgan *et al.*, 1980; Sommercorn and Swick, 1981; Long *et al.*, 1984). Insulin may be preventing the appearance of membrane-limited autophagic vacuoles, thus increasing the latency of the lysosomal proteases. A few other hormones such as glucagon, β-agonist, and isoproterenol, which have a lipolytic effect in some tissues, also suppressed proteolysis in perfused heart (Morgan *et al.*, 1980). The level of certain free amino acids, especially of branched chain amino acids (e.g., leucine, isoleucine, valine), also contribute in the regulatory process of proteolysis in tissues (Fulks *et al.*, 1975).

G. MUSCULAR DYSTROPHIES AND OTHER MYOPATHIES

Muscular dystrophy may be a genetically transmitted disease or may be caused by vitamin E deficiency, and by some other factors (Weinstock and Iodice,

1969), which affect muscle development. Though several views have been extended to explain the molecular basis of muscle dystrophies, the hypothesis based on increased membrane permeability seems to be widely accepted (Rowland, 1980). The increase in membrane permeability may facilitate the transmission of proteolytic enzyme within and between cells to initiate degradation of intra- and intercellular proteins. Protein turnover in dystrophic muscle is substantially different from that in the normal muscle (Goldberg *et al.*, 1977). This is accompanied by an increase in endocytosis (Libelius *et al.*, 1978) and by marked changes in the activity of different proteases in dystrophic skeletal muscles (Iodice and Weinstock, 1965; Pennington and Robinson, 1968; Kohn, 1969; Aoygi *et al.*, 1981). Many investigators have shown a significant increase in the activity of such exopeptidases as cathepsin A (Weinstock *et al.*, 1958; Iodice *et al.*, 1972; Kar and Pearson, 1976b), cathepsin B2 (Bois, 1964; Montgomery *et al.*, 1974), cathepsin C (Iodice *et al.*, 1972; Lee *et al.*, 1984), dipeptidyl aminopeptidases II and IV (Kar and Pearson, 1978), and leucine aminopeptidase (Lee *et al.*, 1984) in dystrophic as compared to normal skeletal muscle.

Apart from exopeptidases, the activity of several endopeptidases has also been reported to be high in dystrophic muscles of various species. A marked increase was observed in the activity of cathepsin B (Kar and Pearson, 1977; Iodice *et al.*, 1972; Noda *et al.*, 1981a), cathepsin H (Noda *et al.*, 1981b), cathepsin D (Whitaker *et al.*, 1983; Lee *et al.*, 1984), serine proteinase (Katunuma *et al.*, 1978), and CANP (Ebashi and Sugita, 1979), Ishiura *et al.*, 1978; Dayton *et al.*, 1979; Neerunjun and Dubowitz, 1979; Sugita and Ishiura, 1980) in dystrophic muscles. A recent study by Bolli *et al.* (1983) concluded that in acute dystrophic conditions (myocardial infarction) proteolysis is largely mediated by CANP and cathepsins A, B, D, and H. Baxter and Suelter (1983) demonstrated that lysosomal enzymes in crude homogenate and lysosome-rich fractions from dystrophic muscle had short latency. However, they did not find any difference in the fragility of lysosomes from normal and dystrophic muscle by using shear, sonication, and detergents. Recently, Kuo *et al.* (1984) reported that only cathepsin D and nonlysosomal myofibrillar alkaline protease mediated the accelerated protein degradation which occurred in the late stage of diabetic cardiomyopathy in mice.

It appears that different proteases may be involved in different dystrophic conditions of muscles. For instance, Kar and Pearson (1976a) observed a significant increase in CANP activity in muscle of patients suffering from Duchenne and Becker dystrophies, but its activity remained normal in patients affected by limb girdle dystrophy or by denervating diseases. Similarly, serine protease activity increased 20–50 times in muscles inflicted by Duchenne or Becker dystrophy (Katunuma *et al.*, 1978) and by hereditary dystrophy (Sanada *et al.*, 1978b), but arylamidase activity did not change in dystrophic muscle (Kar and Pearson, 1976b). The observations made by Takala *et al.* (1983) on proteinase activity in neuromuscular diseases indicated that the activity of alkaline protease and dipeptidyl aminopeptidase IV increased in muscular dystrophy, whereas cathepsin D activity elevated in amyotrophic lateral sclerosis. Sohar *et al.* (1986) stated that Ca^{2+} content increases substantially in muscle suffering from myopathic disorders. However, under such conditions Ca^{2+}-binding proteins (e.g., troponin-C and calmodulin, are protected from digestion by chymotrypsin-like serine proteinases. They suggested a role for these proteinases in muscle wasting diseases.

H. PHYSICAL EXERCISE

Despite the early report of Åstrand and Rodahl (1970) that during exercise catabolism of protein makes little contribution to energy expenditure, several later studies demonstrated a significant increase in amino acid excretion in both human beings and animals in the course of exercise as compared to the sedentary state (Haralambie and Berg, 1976; Décombuz *et al.*, 1979). Other investigators also observed an increase in gluconeogenesis during exercise (Chang and Goldberg, 1978). The amino acids so produced originated from the breakdown of endogenous proteins (Haralambie and Berg, 1976; Dohm *et al.*, 1978), especially the myofibrillar ones (Snyder *et al.*, 1984). The catabolism of proteins naturally would involve some proteases.

However, Schott and Terjung (1979) noticed that moderate exercise neither induced any acute change in lysosomal activity nor altered the partition of lysosomal enzymes into "free" and "particulate" fractions. They considered that altered lysosomal activity was not a contributory factor in influencing fiber homeostasis during moderate running. In the case of acute exercise, Dohm *et al.* (1980) associated the increase in amino acid catabolism in muscle with free cathepsin D activity only, as they did not find any change in total activity of cathepsin D, alkaline protease, and Ca^{2+}-activated neutral protease. In contrast, Pilström *et al.* (1978) and Vihko *et al.* (1978) did observe an increase in the activity of other cathepsins during severe physical exercise.

Recently, Salminen *et al.* (1984) have shown that strenuous running by untrained animals induced necrotic lesions in muscles. This was accompanied by a 4- to 5-fold rise in the activity of several lysosomal enzymes, especially that of cathepsins C and D. The response of acid hydrolase (cathepsin D) during exercise was more prominent in red than in white skeletal muscle (Vihko *et al.*, 1978), whereas activities of alkaline proteases (alkaline and myofibrillar proteinases) were not affected in exercise myopathy. Neutral protease activity increased only slightly during severe exercises (Vihko *et al.*, 1979; Salminen and Vihko, 1983). The increase in proteolytic activity of some cathepsins was considered a part of the repair process of the injuries inflicted by exercise (Salminen and Vihko, 1980).

Generally, a muscle tends to gain weight if the work load on it is increased. This is associated with a decrease in protein catabolic rate during work-induced hypertrophy (Goldberg, 1980). Recently, Palmer *et al.* (1983) have also reported approximately 70% increase in protein synthesis rate in isolated muscle which was given intermittent stretching treatment. This increase was accompanied by the release of prostaglandin $F_{2\alpha}$. They observed a close relationship between the mechanical activity and protein synthesis in muscle. While exploring the changes in some lysosomal enzymes in soleus (red) muscle in the course of disuse atrophy, Sohar *et al.* (1979) reported an increase in the activity of cathepsins B, D, and E. Recently, Goldspink (1986) also observed high specific activities of

TABLE VII

EFFECT OF VARIOUS FACTORS ON PROTEIN TURNOVER IN ISOLATED SKELETAL MUSCLE

Factor	Anabolism	Catabolism	Reference
Nutritional			
Protein restriction	Decrease	Decrease	Li and Goldberg (1976)
Starvation	Decrease	Increase	Li *et al.* (1979), Bates and Millward (1983)
Leucine	Increase	Decrease	Fulks *et al.* (1975)
Glucose	No change	Decrease	Fulks *et al.* (1975)
Endocrines			
Insulin	Increase	Decrease	Fulks *et al.* (1975)
Growth hormone	Increase	No change	Goldberg and Griffin (1977)
Thyroid hormones	Increase	Increase	Goldberg and Griffin (1977)
Corticosteroids (normal concentration)	Decrease	Decrease	Tischler (1981)
Fed/fasted	Decrease	Increase	Tischler (1981)
Pharmacologic concentration	Decrease	Increase	Tischler (1981)
Activity			
Stimulation	No change	Decrease	Goldberg *et al.* (1975)
Passive stretch	No change	Decrease	Goldberg *et al.* (1975)
Intermediate stretch	Increase	Decrease	Palmer *et al.* (1983), Young and Munro (1980)
With age (adults)	Decrease	Increase	Munro and Young (1978)
Muscle type			
White	Slow	Slow	Bates and Millward (1983)
Red	Fast	Fast	Bates and Millward (1893)
Denervation	Increase	Increase	Goldspink (1978)
Denervation and immobilization	Increase	Increase	Goldspink (1978)
Dystrophy	Decrease	Increase	Li (1980)

cathepsins B and D (but not of H) in both tenotomized gastrocnemius and functionally overloaded soleus muscle.

I. WEIGHTLESSNESS AND *G* FORCE

Russian enzymologists Oganesyan and Eloyan (1981) explored the changes in the activity of catheptic enzymes in skeletal and myocardial muscles from rats which were flown in space on Cosmos 605 for 22 days. This study showed a significant rise in the cathepsin activity in muscles of rats which experienced weightlessness in space as compared to those of ground-based controls. However the activity of cathepsins in the test rats was restored to normal after returning to land in due course of time. They also investigated the effect of gravitational force on the cathepsin activity of skeletal and cardiac muscles. To that purpose, a group of rats was exposed to 4–5 times gravitational force for 20 min daily for 2 weeks. This operation also significantly increased the protease activity in both skeletal and myocardial tissues relative to that in control rats. In about 1 month proteolytic activity reversed to normality after termination of the experiment. These studies suggest that the changes in catheptic activity induced by weight-lessness or by gravitational force in muscles were reversible.

In Table VII is summarized information on some of the important factors which affect the synthesis and degradation of proteins in skeletal muscle systems.

VIII. SIGNIFICANCE OF ENDOGENOUS PROTEINASES IN MEAT TECHNOLOGY

The proteolytic enzymes not only play a vital role in normal growth and development, as well as in pathological conditions of live animals; they also bring about several changes in the muscle system after slaughtering the animal to convert the muscles into meat. By manipulating the postmortem handling conditions of carcasses, the desired tenderness in meat can be achieved. The available information on the biochemical events which lead to improvement in tenderness and flavor of the meat during the postmortem aging process is considered in this section.

A. POSTMORTEM GLYCOLYSIS AND RIGOR DEVELOPMENT

Although the slaughtering operation causes the death of animals within a couple of minutes with the loss of blood, the muscles remain metabolically active for many hours postmortem as long as a sufficient supply of ATP is maintained anaerobically as a source of energy. Nonspecific ATPase activity catabolizes ATP to ADP in muscle cells for maintaining their internal environment. Initially, ATP is generated from high energy reserve creatinine phosphate (Cp). As the Cp store is exhausted, an accumulation of ADP activates the catabolism of glycogen in muscle. In the absence of oxygen in postmortem muscle, the pyruvate, which is the end product of glycolysis, cannot be oxidized by mitochondria via the TCA cycle; it is rather reduced to lactic acid by $NADH^+$, whose level also increases under anaerobic conditions.

Consequently, with the anaerobic catabolism of each molecule of glucose, 3 molecules of ATP are resynthesized from ADP and 2 H^+ (lactic acids) are formed which are responsible for the progressive decrease in muscle pH value. It drops down to about 5.5 under normal conditions. At this pH, phosphofructokinase is probably inactivated (Newbold and Scopes, 1967) which causes cessation of anaerobic glycolysis, no matter if some glycogen may still be present in muscles. When the ATP content is depleted to a critical level, i.e., below 10–20% of its initial value (Bendall, 1979), the myosin and actin form a complex by cross-bridging of thick and thin filaments. The muscle loses its extensibility and stiffens. This condition of muscle, called rigor mortis development, occurs 6–24 hr postmortem depending on carcass type (Goll *et al.,* 1970; Asghar and Pearson, 1980) and on postmortem treatments of carcasses (Asghar and Henrickson, 1982b).

In normally contracting muscle only about 20% of the cross-bridges are linked to actin filaments at any one time (Huxley and Brown, 1967), but in ATP-depleted inextensible muscle 100% of the myosin cross-bridges are linked to actin filaments. Apart from these changes, an NMR study by Currie and Wolfe (1980) revealed some characteristic changes in the spin lattice relaxation time of the intrafiber water protones as the prerigor skeletal muscle entered into rigor state. These changes in intrafibril water may also be related in some way to actomyosin interactions during rigor development.

The texture of the meat, if cooked in rigor condition, is relatively tough and flat in taste. In any case, the rigor state does not persist indefinitely; its resolution occurs gradually with a further lapse of time. The rate of rigor resolution, however, again depends on the type of carcass and storage temperature. The holding of carcasses under specific conditions of storage to allow resolution of rigor mortis is referred to as "aging" or conditioning of meat.

B.   POSTMORTEM AGING TECHNOLOGY

Normally the carcasses are held at 2–3°C for a specific period of time to alleviate the effect of rigor mortis and to attain desirable tenderness in meat. Beef carcasses may require a 6-day aging period to acquire satisfactory tenderness (Martin *et al.,* 1971). Under identical conditions, the rate of postmortem tenderization in carcasses of different species falls in the order avian > porcine > ovine ≥ bovine. During the aging process, certain biochemical changes, brought about by some endogenous proteolytic enzymes in the muscle system, are believed to be responsible for converting the muscles to tender meat. Because the kinetics of enzymatic reactions are highly dependent on temperature, the aging period can be reduced significantly by holding the carcasses at high temperatures (15–40°C). The rate of tenderization, as estimated by the reduction in shear force (kg), increased by 2.4 units with each rise of 10°C (temperature coefficient, Q = 2.4) between 0 and 40°C (Etherington and Dransfield, 1981). An activation energy of about 62 kJ/mol has been worked out for beef muscle.

The hastening of rigor development and reduction in holding time of carcasses at high temperature can be achieved by electrical stimulation of the postmortem carcass. The philosophy of this unit operation and the advantages associated with it have been discussed in detail elsewhere (Asghar and Henrickson, 1982b). Since meat processing is a labor-intensive and meat distribution an energy-intensive operation, some modifications in conventional practices may be required by the meat industry to reduce the recurring expenditures. Henrickson and Asghar (1985) have recently provided elaborate information on these technological aspects of the meat industry.

C. CHANGES IN MEAT DURING AGING PROCESS

As indicated earlier in Section XIII,B, some biochemical and enzymatic changes take place during the conversion of muscles into meat in storage. Many researchers have attempted to reveal the nature of these changes and to relate them with an increase in tenderness of aged meat. The overall findings can be categorized under the following subheadings: changes in sarcoplasmic proteins, changes in contractile proteins, changes in regulatory proteins, changes in cytoskeletal proteins, and changes in connective tissue proteins.

1. Changes in Sarcoplasmic Proteins

Some earlier investigations have indicated that certain sarcoplasmic proteins were primarily degraded during the aging process (Sharp, 1963; Bodwell and Pearson, 1964; Scopes, 1964; Thompson et al., 1968). The appearance of an additional cationic band on electrophoretograms of aged meat was thought to originate from sarcoplasmic proteins (Fujimaki and Deartherage, 1964) and most likely from myoglobin (Neelin and Rose, 1964). Quite recently Patestos and Harrington (1984) also reported the degradation of a MW 15,000 sarcoplasmic protein on aging of meat extract for 72 hr at 4 and 37°C. However, Hay et al. (1973b) did not find any measurable change in sarcoplasmic proteins which could be related to increased tenderness of aged meat.

2. Changes in Contractile Proteins

Since myosin and actin are the predominating proteins in muscle systems, many studies were directed to identify the postmortem changes in these proteins in an attempt to relate them with tenderness of aged meat. These studies led to several propositions such as dissociation of the actomyosin complex, cleavage of myosin molecule, oxidoreductive changes in actomyosin, and depolymerization of F-actin during the postmortem aging process.

a. Dissociation of Actomyosin Complex. The proposition that the rigor development occurs by the association of thick and thin filaments, according to the "sliding-in" theory of Huxley and Hanson (1954), enticed some researchers to assume that the resolution of rigor may be due to slow dissociation of this complex into actin and myosin. Two types of experimental approaches were made to prove this point. One was based on the changes in sarcomere length and the other on ATPase activity of actomyosin.

For some time Stromer and Goll (1967) and Takahashi *et al.* (1967) positively believed in the complete dissociation of the actomyosin complex during aging of meat as they observed lengthening of sarcomeres in aged meat. In contrast, others did not find any significant difference in sarcomere lengths of in-rigor and postrigor muscle although these were markedly shorter than those of prerigor muscle (Gothard *et al.,* 1966; Asghar and Yeates, 1978). These observations substantiated the view that postmortem rigor development in muscle represents an irreversible contraction (Marsh, 1954; Davies, 1963). Surprisingly, however, Findlay and Stanley (1984a) recently reported that an increased interaction between actin and myosin (as monitored by changing the sarcomere length from 2.4 to 1.4 μm) caused a significant reduction in the heat of transition (ΔH) from 4 to 3 J/g as revealed by differential scanning calorimetry (DSC) study. They attributed this change to a decrease in the stability of actin when it interacted with myosin to form actomyosin.

The fact that postrigor muscle never regains its prerigor length speaks against complete dissociation of actomyosin complex during aging. It was proposed that weakening of cross-bridges may be responsible for partial dissociation of actomyosin complex in aged meat (Valin, 1968; Goll *et al.,* 1970; Arakawa *et al.,* 1976). This proposition was based on indirect experimental evidence concerned with the changes in Mg^{2+}-, Ca^{2+}-, and EGTA-activated ATPase activity of actomyosin during aging. The superprecipitation rate (development of turbidity on addition of ATP) was also found to be greater in actomyosin isolated from aged meat than that isolated from prerigor meat (Arakawa *et al.,* 1970). A relatively very low amount of ATP (0.1–0.2 mM) was required for dissociating aged actomyosin (isolated from aged meat) than for dissociating prerigor (0.6 mM ATP) actomyosin (Fujimaki *et al.,* 1965). However, Hay *et al.* (1972,

1973a) and Jones (1972) did not observe any difference in ATPase activity or reduced viscosity of actomyosin isolated from meat at different stages of postmortem aging.

Bendall (1969) reported that myosin $Mg^{2+}-Ca^{2+}$-modified activity decreased linearly with an increase in ionic concentration from the physiological level (170 mM KCl) to 1.0 M KCl. Taking advantage of this observation, a relationship was found between the changes in $Mg^{2+}-Ca^{2+}$-modified ATPase sensitivity of myosin from electrically stimulated carcasses (Valin et al., 1981) or from aged meat (Ouali, 1984) and ionic strength. This has been suggested as a biochemical index of myofibrillar aging (BIMA); however, it requires further testing for general application.

b. *Cleavage of Myosin Molecules.* Pepe (1967) expressed the view that, during aging of meat, cleavage of the myosin molecule occurs corresponding to the typsin-sensitive region which is in a nonhelical conformation (Mihalyi and Harrington, 1959). However, some researchers (Goll and Robson, 1967; Robson et al., 1967) did not consider that such cleavage occurs in myosin, since they did not observe any change in ATPase activity of myosin isolated from aged meat. This reasoning does not seem valid in view of the fact that ATPase activity resides in the S-1 subfragment of myosin (Mueller and Perry, 1962) which retains the activity even if the remaining part of the molecule is detached.

Myosin may not be affected within the initial 24 hr postmortem even at 30°C (Ouali et al., 1984; Penny et al., 1984), but a longer aging period, especially at high temperature, results in its degradation (Samejima and Wolfe, 1976; Yamamoto et al., 1979b; Ikeuchi et al., 1980). Bechtel and Parrish (1983) have shown that myosin heavy chains (MHC, MW 200,000) were degraded to MW 145,000 and 125,000 polypeptides on aging for 3 days at 37°C, although little change occurred at 4°C. Yates et al. (1983) also reported the appearance of a MW 95,000 polypeptide whose concentration increased with storage temperature, and it was thought to originate from the degradation of MHC (Koohmaraie et al., 1984). Recently, Locker and Wild (1984) also reported these changes but only in fully stretched myofibrils after a prolonged aging period (20 days). They did not observe such changes in unstretched or shortened muscle. On this ground they do not consider that degradation of myosin has any practical significance so far as mechanism of tenderization in aged meat is concerned.

c. *Oxidoreductive Changes in Actomyosin.* Weber's (1957) hypothesis on the involvement of SH groups in the mechanism of muscle contraction possibly motivated some researchers to investigate the changes in the number of SH groups during postmortem rigor development and the aging process. The results obtained from different studies were rather conflicting. While Caldwell and Lineweaver (1969) and Hay et al. (1972, 1973a) found no change in the SH group content at different stages of postmortem muscle, others observed a pronounced increase in aged meat (Chajuss and Spencer, 1962; Gawronski *et al.*, 1967). Thus, Chajuss and Spencer (1962) associated the improvement in tenderness of aged meat with the reorientation of inter- and intramolecular disulfide bonds. The ultimate end product of the reaction was shown to be the formation of sulfonates.

The disparity in results may be ascribed to the different methods employed to determine SH content in meat. For example, some investigators used the nitroferricyanide procedure (Chajuss and Spencer, 1962), whereas others applied the polarographic (Gawronski *et al.*, 1967), or the 5,5'-dithiobis(2-nitrobenzoic acid) (DTNB) (Caldwell and Lineweaver, 1969; Hay *et al.*, 1973a) method. A critical evaluation of different methods for the determination of SH content in meat/muscle suggests that they yield variable results (Hofmann and Hamm, 1978) and that only a few of them can be applied in meat to achieve reliable results. It may also be emphasized that the increase in SH groups in aged meat would carry no more significance if the meat was cooked beyond 77°C, because stable disulfide or thioester cross-linkages would form in protein on cooking to higher temperatures. The oxidoreductive reactions possibly represent nonproteolytic changes in meat during aging. Similarly, the depolymerization of F-actin which is considered in the following section also does not involve proteolytic enzymes.

d. Depolymerization of F-Actin.   King (1966) and Chaudhry *et al.* (1969) proposed that depolymerization of F-actin in aged meat may be associated with the increase in tenderness of the latter. This proposition does not seem convincing in view of the fact that postmortem conditions of the muscle system are not at all conducive for depolymerization of F-actin. The presence of ATP, absence of divalent cations (e.g., Ca^{2+}, Mg^{2+}), alkaline pH, and low ionic strength are required for depolymerization of F-actin to G-actin (Oosawa and Asakura, 1975; Pollard *et al.*, 1982). The conditions in postmortem muscle rather become more conducive for the formation of F-actin. In addition, the observation that Mg^{2+}-induced ATP activity, which depends on F-actomyosin, did not change in aged meat (Hay *et al.*, 1972; Jones, 1972) also defies the speculation of depolymerization of F-actin during the aging process. Hence, this proposition did not hold any promise.

3.   Changes in Regulatory Proteins

Among the presently known 18 regulatory proteins in skeletal muscle (Section VI,A), only a few have been found to be affected during the postmortem aging process. They are the proteins of the Z-disk structure and troponin-T (Tn-T) subunit of troponin complex. In some cases, changes in M-line proteins have also been reported.

a. Degradation of Z-Disk Proteins.   Gradual degradation of Z-disks has long been observed under the phase-contrast or electron microscope as the major consequence of postmortem aging of meat (Takahashi *et al.*, 1967; Stromer and Goll, 1967; Davey and Gilbert, 1969; Henderson *et al.*, 1970; Goll *et al.*, 1970; Asghar and Yeates, 1978). Many investigators associated the disintegration of Z-band with the loss in tensile strength of the myofibrils and an increase in tenderness of aged meat (Busch *et al.*, 1972; Penny *et al.*, 1974; Davey and Graafhuis, 1976). This relationship, however, was repealed by the fact that the degradation of Z-disks in red and white muscles was not identical. Hay *et al.* (1973b) observed substantial disintegration of Z-disks only in white (breast) muscles, whereas Z-disks of red muscles (leg) remained stable in aged chicken carcasses. These findings were supported by Dutson *et al.* (1974) and Abbott *et al.* (1977), who examined the white and red fibers from aged pork muscles. Similarly Gann and Merkel (1978) reported that Z-disks of bull red fibers remained essentially unaltered even 9 days postmortem, whereas white muscle Z-disks showed limited degradation as early as 1 hr postmortem.

In view of the potential significance of Z-band structure and myofibril fragmentation in relation to the improvement of tenderness of meat during postmortem aging, some researchers attempted to identify which particular protein is affected in the Z-disk. It has been mentioned earlier in Section VI, A,1,b,ii, that about four proteins have been claimed to be the components of Z-disks. Although some investigators expressed the possibility that α-actinin, the principal component of Z-disks, is degraded during aging (Suzuki *et al.*, 1978), others did not find any change in α-actinin content (Dayton *et al.*, 1975; Goll *et al.*, 1978). If so, then the disruption of Z-disks would arise from the degradation of some other minor proteins which are responsible for the stabilization of the lattice of the Z-disks. The presence of a KI-insoluble form of actin, which is believed to reside in Z-disks, has been reported by several investigators. Some called it euactinin (Kuroda *et al.*, 1981), while others named it Z-disk actin (Nagainis and Wolfe, 1982; Nagainis *et al.*, 1983) or stroma actin (Weber, 1984). Since Z-disk actin differed from I-band actin in proteolytic susceptibility, this led Nagainis and Wolfe (1982) to propose that it is the former actin which is possibly degraded during the postmortem aging process and which accounts for the decaying of Z-disks. However, the validity of the Nagainis–Wolfe hypothesis needs to be ascertained by examining the rate of Z-disk actin degradation *in situ* as a function of postmortem aging time of carcass.

b. Degradation of Troponin-T (Tn-T).   Some changes in the tropomyosin–troponin complex in aged meat were reported by Arakawa *et al.* (1970). Later on many investigators observed the appearance of a MW 30,000 polypeptide on SDS–PAGE of muscle protein from poultry (Hay *et al.*, 1973b; Samejima and Wolfe, 1976), beef (Penny *et al.*, 1974; MacBride and Parrish, 1977; Olson *et al.*, 1977), and rabbit (Yamamoto *et al.*, 1979b; Ouali *et al.*, 1983) with the progression of aging time. Most of the *in vitro* studies suggested that this poly-peptide originates from the proteolytic degradation of Tn-T (Dabrowska *et al.*, 1973; Dayton *et al.*, 1975; Cheng and Parrish, 1977; Ishiura *et al.*, 1979; Penny, 1980). However, the likelihood of a MW 30,000 component originating from proteolytic degradation of myosin heavy chain was also shown by Okitani *et al.* (1981). A recent study of Matsumoto *et al.* (1983) added more confusion to this issue by demonstrating that it is the tropomyosin which is degraded into the 30,000 component, whereas Tn-T is degraded into MW 33,000, 20,000, and 11,000 fragments.

A parallel increase in tenderness of meat with the increase in the level of the MW 30,000 component during the postmortem aging process has been recorded by different investigators (Moeller *et al.*, 1977; Olson *et al.*, 1977; Salm *et al.*, 1983). Penny and Dransfield (1979) considered it appropriate to use the ap-pearance of a 30,000 component in aged meat as the "biochemical index" of tenderness. However, a study by George *et al.* (1980) seems to defy any correla-tion between tenderness and the decay rate of Tn-T at least in meat from elec-trically stimulated carcasses. Parrish *et al.* (1981), who are among the propo-nents of the Tn-T decay hypothesis, also failed to find any relationship between the MW 30,000 component and tenderness of meat from E-maturity cattle.

The relevance of Tn-T degradation with the increase in tenderness of meat during the postmortem aging process was also questioned on the grounds that Tn-T was located only in the grooves of F-actin filaments at a periodicity of 38.6 nm. As it is absent from the Z-disks, Tn-T has no role in maintaining their integrity. According to the findings of Sugita *et al.* (1980) Tn-T remained intact with myofibrils on treatment with Ca^{2+}-activated factor. Perhaps the susceptible region of Tn-T was protected by binding to tropomyosin *in situ*.

4.   Changes in Cytoskeletal Proteins

As the presence of cytoskeletal proteins in skeletal muscle cells has received emphasis only relatively recently (Section VI,A,1,b,iii), very limited informa-tion is available on the fate of some of these proteins during postmortem aging process of carcasses. Marked changes only in connectin (titin), desmin, and nebulin have been reported in aged meat.

a.   Degradation of Connectin (Titin).   Takahashi and Sato (1979) first took the initiative in exploring the changes in connectin from rabbit muscle as a result of the postmortem aging process. Their SDS–PAGE profiles of connectin from fresh and aged muscle showed that the top band of the connectin doublet gradu-ally vanished with the progression of the aging period and temperature. These observations were substantiated by studies on ovine muscle (King and Harris, 1982; King, 1984) and bovine myofibrils (Penny *et al.*, 1984). Lusby *et al.*

(1983) and Wang and Ramirez-Mitchell (1983) also considered titin to be highly susceptible to endogenous proteases. Since connectin (or titin) is the major protein constituting the cytoskeletal system in muscle fibers, its degradation is likely to make a significant contribution to the increase in tenderness of aged meat. In contrast to these findings, Locker and Wild (1984) did not find any evidence of apparent degradation of connectin in beef even on aging the carcasses for 20 days at 15°C.

b. Degradation of Desmin. Another cytoskeletal protein which disappeared from meat by proteolytic degradation on aging was desmin (Young *et al.*, 1980). The N terminus of desmin, which is mainly in the form of β structure (Geisler *et al.*, 1982), is reported to be very labile to proteolysis. Robson *et al.* (1984) followed the changes in skeletal muscle desmin as a function of postmortem aging time at 15°C. They noted a 10–25% decrease in desmin content during initial 24-hr period, and the protein almost disappeared from meat after a 7-day aging period. Consequently, an unidentified MW 21,000 polypeptide appeared in the acetic acid extract of meat, and a 34,000 component appeared both in KI and acetic acid extracts. Penny *et al.* (1984) also observed the loss of desmin in aged meat.

c. Degradation of Nebulin. Recently, Locker and Wild (1984) conducted a study on postmortem changes in meat. They reported that the tenderization process is largely completed within the first 48 hr if the carcasses are aged at 15°C. Two conspicuous changes were noted in meat by SDS–PAGE during this period: first, the disappearance of nebulin and, second, an increase in polypeptide band B, which appeared between connectin and nebulin on electrophoretograms. They argued that if nebulin is located at the N-line, as indicated by Wang and Williamson (1980), then it would not be logical to find any association between tenderness and disappearance of nebulin during aging. However, Locker (1984) is now inclined to believe that both nebulin and connectin occur together in the G-filaments. If so, then the proteolytic degradation of nebulin is likely to reduce the stability of G-filaments, and hence would result in an increase in tenderness of meat on aging. Stanley (1983) also expressed the view that the improvement in tenderness, which occurs during conditioning of meat, results from the proteolytic breakdown of cytoskeletal proteins.

4. Changes in Connective Tissue

The main components of connective tissue in skeletal muscles are the collagen and the ground substance. The latter constitutes the matrix of extracellular space, where collagen is embedded. The so-called background toughness of meat is ascribed to connective tissue (Herring *et al.*, 1967). Divergent views have been expressed about the changes in connective tissue during postmortem aging of meat.

a. Degradation of Collagen. In a previous review (Asghar and Yeates, 1978), numerous studies were quoted both for and against the possible degradation of collagen during the aging process. According to Whitaker (1959), much controversy on the findings as to whether or not collagen is degraded in aged meat arose due to the lack of precision in the chemical methods used for the estimation of collagen. Despite these uncertainties, there is general agreement that the cross-linkages, present in collagen, offer different resistance toward chemical and enzymatic degradation. Some bonds are labile to acid, while others are stable.

The changes that occur in collagen during conditioning of postmortem carcasses, however, have not yet been directly characterized. Indirect evidence suggested that some alterations do occur in connective tissue and are reflected in weakening of the collagen structure. This may be merely the consequence of low pH (Asghar and Yeates, 1978) or may be the result of some limited proteolysis (Herring *et al.,* 1967; Kopp and Valin, 1981). Earlier, Clayson *et al.* (1966) suggested that postmortem changes in the cross-linkages of collagen may be caused by highly reactive nitroxyl radicals, produced from the oxidation of nitrogenous substance, possibly via hydroxylamine. The presence of lactate or succinate enhanced the effect of nitroxyl radicals on collagen. This proposition was perhaps based on the assumption that, in the presence of ATP or coenzyme A, hydroxylamine at low concentration (~ 10 mM) cleaves the ester linkages in collagen. This suggestion sounds interesting but does not hold any credibility now because the previous contention about the presence of ester-type cross-linkages in collagen has long been disproved (see review by Asghar and Henrickson, 1982a). Anyway, whatever the cause, the stability of collagen seems to decrease with postmortem aging time as revealed by DSC study by Ledward *et al.* (1975). This may partly explain the changes in the solubility characteristic of collagen during aging (Chizzolini *et al.,* 1977) and the increase in tenderness of aged meat.

b. Degradation of Mucopolysaccharides. The ground substance, which is composed of mucopolysaccharides, may not have any influence on tenderness of raw meat because the former is present in the soluble state. On cooking, mucopolysaccharides are likely to coagulate onto collagen fibrils, and hence may affect the tenderness of meat. Only a few studies were directed to explore the changes in ground substance during the postmortem aging process. Miller and Kastelic (1956) indicated that an increase in tenderness of aged meat may involve changes in mucopolysaccharides. From their study, Dutson and Lawrie (1974) also contended that a breakdown of ground substance occurred during aging of meat. Wu *et al.* (1982) ascribed the increase in collagen solubility during aging to the breakdown of proteoglycans by galactosidases and hyaluronidase. McIntosh (1967) reported that a protein cleaved off from the mucoprotein complex containing glucosamine and galactose, leaving a small fraction, high in chondroitin sulfate, in aged meat. This change commenced after 2 weeks of aging but did not become significant until 4 weeks of storage. In view of this, enzymatic degradation of polysaccharides cannot be considered an important event responsible for an increase in tenderness of aged meat, as carcasses are seldom kept in storage for such a long time.

D. ENZYMOLOGY OF POSTMORTEM AGING PROCESS

The evidence discussed in the preceding section (Section VIII,C) strongly supports the contention that proteolytic degradation of muscle proteins does occur during the postmortem aging process. This has been further substantiated by a recent DSC study (Findlay and Stanley, 1984b) which showed a significant drop in the total heat of transition (ΔH) of aged meat as compared to that of in-rigor meat. However, some discrepancies exist among the views of different investigators as to the role in the postmortem degradative process of various endogenous proteolytic enzymes which are known to be present in skeletal muscles. While some researchers consider lysosomal proteinases as instrumental in the disintegration of muscle proteins (Arakawa *et al.*, 1967; Dutson and Lawrie, 1974; Moeller *et al.*, 1976; Cohen and Trusal, 1980) others are inclined to assign this role to a nonlysosomal proteinase such as Ca^{2+}-activated neutral protease (Dayton *et al.*, 1975; Goll *et al.*, 1983; Koohmaraie *et al.*, 1984, 1986a,b). Still, some isolated studies indicated that merely a postmortem increase in Ca^{2+} causes the degradation of a specific protein in muscle without involving any proteinase (Takahashi *et al.*, 1983).

1. Role of Lysosomal Proteinases

As the lysosomal proteases are either bound with or enclosed within the lysosomal membrane, their release is prerequisite to initiate degradative changes in meat. Low pH and high temperature possibly cause rupturing of the lysosomal membrane (Weisman, 1964; Stagni and deBernard, 1968; Moeller *et al.*, 1977; Sorinmade *et al.*, 1982). Lysosomal enzymes lose their characteristic latency in postmortem muscle. It is generally assumed that catheptic proteases are released from lysosomes, which then diffuse in the intermyofilament space to begin protein degradation.

Cathepsins B (i.e., B1), D, E, H, and L are lysosomal endopeptidases whose presence has been indicated in skeletal muscle (Section III). Among these, cathepsin B (Schwartz and Bird, 1977; Ouali *et al.*, 1984), cathepsin D (Schwartz and Bird, 1977; Robbins *et al.*, 1979; Okitani *et al.*, 1981; Jones *et al.*, 1983; Ouali *et al.*, 1984), cathepsin H (Matsukura *et al.*, 1981), and cathepsin L (Matsukura *et al.*, 1981; Okitani *et al.*, 1980; Mason *et al.*, 1984; Penny *et al.*, 1984) have been viewed as the causative proteases which degrade muscle proteins during the postmortem aging process and hence improve meat tenderness. The evidence in support of the involvement of these proteinases has been obtained by treating the isolated myofibrils with the respective protease under *in vitro* conditions.

As can be seen in Table VIII, all endogenous endopeptidases have shown the ability to fragment different myofibrillar proteins in *in vitro* environments. For example, cathepsin B can degarade myosin and actin (Schwartz and Bird, 1977); according to the findings of Noda *et al.* (1981a), it also caused limited hydrolysis of myosin heavy chains and Tn-T, but had no effect on myosin light chains and Tn-C. Actin and Tn-I was degraded rather slowly. Bird *et al.* (1978, 1980) stated that both cathepsins B and D hydrolyze soluble denatured myosin more exten-sively than its insoluble native form. The ability of cathepsin D in degrading myosin heavy chains (Okitani *et al.*, 1981) and tropomyosin (Matsumoto *et al.*, 1983) to form a MW 30,000 polypeptide has also been demonstrated. A recent study of Ouali *et al.* (1984) suggests that cathepsins B and D preferably disinte-grate, respectively, low and high molecular weight myofibrillar proteins, where-as cathepsin H had no effect on such low molecular weight proteins as Tn-T and Tn-I. Okitani *et al.* (1980) have also demonstrated that cathepsin L could de-grade myosin heavy chain, actin, tropomyosin, α-actinin, Tn-T, and Tn-I.

Considering muscle pH as the limiting factor, Schwartz and Bird (1977) stated that cathepsin B has optimum activity at pH 5.2, whereas cathepsin D maintains only about 50% of its activity at this pH. Even then the degradation of actin and myosin by cathepsin D was more extensive than that by cathepsin B. Based on reaction kinetics, they derived that both can degrade all of the native myosin in about 6–9 days. In contrast to this, Goll *et al.* (1983) do not assign any signifi-cant role to cathepsin B and D in the aging process. They argued that these cathepsins require a pH between 3.5 and 4.5 for optimal activity and that the muscle milieu is not much conducive for their activity. Hence, they remarked that the role of cathepsin B (if any) is negligible, and that of cathepsin D is very unlikely. A similar opinion was expressed by Penny and Ferguson-Pryce (1979) about the contribution of cathepsin D in the postmortem aging process. This reasoning, however, also defies a major role for CANP in postmortem tenderiza-tion of meat as the CANP requires pH about 7.5 for its optimum activation.

In contrast, the observations that cathepsin D degrades myosin heavy chains (Okitani *et al.*, 1981) as well as tropomyosin (Matsumoto *et al.*, 1983) to a MW 30,000 component, and its ability to disintegrate Z-disks at pH 6.5 (Robbins *et al.*, 1979) possibly by affecting α-actinin (Matsumoto *et al.*, 1983), are sug-gestive of its role in the postmortem tenderization process of meat. Recently,

TABLE VIII

SKELETAL MUSCLE PROTEIN DEGRADING ABILITY OF
DIFFERENT ENDOGENOUS PROTEINASES

Proteinase	Labile protein	Reference
Alkaline cytoplasmic protease	Myosin	Koszalka and Miller (1960)
Myofibrillar alkaline protease	Myosin, MHC, tropomyosin, Tn-T, Tn-C	Dahlmann et al. (1981)
Myosin protease	Myosin, troponin, M- and C-protein, Z-disc, Tn-T, Tn-I, Tn-C	Murakami and Uchida (1978, 1979)
Serine protease	A-band, Z-disc, MHC, Lc-2, actin, tropomyosin, Tn-T, Tn-I	Yosogawa et al. (1978), Sanada et al. (1979)
Myosin cleaving protease	Myosin	Kuo and Bhan (1980)
Cathepsin B1	Myosin	Schwartz and Bird (1977)
	MHC,Tn-T	Noda et al. (1981a)
	Actin	Hirao et al. (1984)
	Collagen	Burleigh et al. (1974), Evans and Etherington (1978)
	Elastin	Mason et al. (1986)
Cathepsin H	Myosin	Bird and Carter (1980)
	Tn-T	Katunuma and Kominami (1983)
	Collagen	Kirschke et al. (1977b)
Cathepsin L	MHC, actin, TN-T, Tn-I, tropomyosin, α-actinin	Okitani et al. (1980), Matsukura et al. (1981)
	Myosin, α-actinin	Schwartz and Bird (1977)
	Collagen	Kirschke et al. (1977c, 1982)
	Elastin	Mason et al. (1986)
	Titin, nebulin	Penny et al. (1984)
Ca^{2+}-activated protease	Myosin	Ishiura et al. (1979)
	MHC	Pemrick et al. (1980)
	Tn-T, Tn-I, tropomyosin, C- and M-protein	Dayton et al. (1975), Goll et al. (1978)
	Desmin	O'Shea et al. (1979), Weber (1984)
	Filamin	Davies et al. (1978)
	Connectin (or titin)	Lusby et al. (1983), Wang (1983), Zeece et al. (1983)
	Nebulin	Wang (1981)
Cathepsin D	MHC, Tn-T, Tn-I, α-actinin, tropomyosin	Matsumoto et al. (1983)
	MHC, MLC, actin	Ogunro et al. (1979)
	Collagen	Woessner (1977a), Scott and Pearson (1978)

Patestos and Harrington (1984) also reported the involvement of an aspartate protease in the degradation of a MW 15,000 sarcoplasmic protein when sarcoplasmic protein extract (pH 6.0 and 5.0) was incubated for 72 hr at 4 and 37°C. They did not find any detectable proteolysis at pH 7.0. According to Bird *et al.* (1977) cathepsin B also maintains about 60–70% of its total activity at pH 5.5, which is the general ultimate pH of postmortem muscles.

While making a comparative study of the activity of different cathepsins on myosin as a substrate, Sohar *et al.* (1979) concluded that cathepsin H had 5 times greater specific activity than that of cathepsin B, whereas cathepsin L exhibited 2 times higher activity in comparison to that of H. Moreover, cathepsin L caused extensive degradation of myosin to form polypeptides with molecular weights less than 5000. Because of its maximal activity at pH 6.0–5.5, cathepsin L has been given considerable weight in the postmortem tenderization process by some workers (Okitani *et al.*, 1980; Mason *et al.*, 1984). Penny *et al.* (1984) have shown that cathepsin L degraded large protein molecules such as titin and nebulin. However, if the degradation of Tn-T to the MW 30,000 component is used as the criterion for postmortem tenderness of aged meat, then cathepsin L cannot have any important role because it did not degrade Tn-T to the 30,000 species, as shown by Penny *et al.* (1984). On the contrary, a study by Okitani *et al.* (1980) did indicate cathepsin L's ability in degrading Tn-T to MW 30,000 components.

The observations on histological changes in the endomysium layer by treatment of muscle with a liver catheptic enzymes extract (Robbins and Cohen, 1976) and the occurrence of a significant reduction in isometric tension of intramuscular collagen on incubation with lysosomal enzymes at pH 5.5 (Kopp and Valin, 1981) were suggestive of the enzymatic weakening of the collagen structure during the postmortem aging process. Beside collagenase, at least eight lysosomal enzymes, namely cathepsins H, L (Kirschke *et al.*, 1977b,c, 1982), B (Etherington, 1977), D (Woessner, 1977a), G (Starkey, 1977), and N (Etherington, 1980), β-glucuronidase, and β-galactosidase (Dutson and Yates, 1978) have also displayed collagenolytic activity in *in vitro* studies on soluble collagen under nondenaturating conditions. The nonhelical domain of tropocollagen (monomeric form) which contains the cross-linkages, was generally cleaved from the main helical segment of the molecule at pH 6.5 or less (Etherington and Evan, 1977) by catheptic enzymes. Cathepsin B is thought to act at the nonhelical segment of the N terminus, whereas cathepsin D cleaves the bond at the C-terminal domain (Woessner, 1973). The insoluble collagen was not much affected by these proteases at pH values above 4.5 (Etherington, 1980). However, Wu *et al.* (1982) assumed that the increase in collagen solubility during aging of meat was due to breakdown of proteoglycans by β-galactosidase or hyaluronidase. On the other hand, cathepsins B and D have also the ability to degrade proteoglycans (Morrison *et al.*, 1973).

As discussed in Section III, the presence of cathepsins B, D, H, and L has been shown in skeletal muscle lysosomes, whereas cathepsins G and N are in fact nonmuscle cell proteases and are not yet reported in muscle. It is likely that fibroblasts and mast cells which are associated with connective tissue may be the sources of these proteases in muscle. However, the relative contribution of cathepsins B, D, H, and L and other hydrolases in weakening the muscle collagen structure is not yet ascertained.

2. Role of Nonlysosomal Proteases

Ever since Busch *et al.* (1972) reported the evidence that Ca^{2+}-activated neutral protease (CANP) has the ability to degrade Z-disks, many investigators supported its possible role in the postmortem tenderization process of meat (Reddy *et al.*, 1975; Dayton *et al.*, 1976; Olson *et al.*, 1977; Ouali and Valin, 1981; Elgasim *et al.*, 1985; Koohmaraie *et al.*, 1987a–c; Slinde and Kryvi, 1986; Ukabaim, 1986). Dayton *et al.* (1976) have shown that CANP, beside disintegrating the infrastructure of Z-disks, can also degrade some of the regulatory proteins such as tropomyosin, Tn-T, Tn-I, and C- and M-proteins. Most of these observations were substantiated by other researchers (Goll *et al.*, 1978; Ishiura *et al.*, 1979; Azanza *et al.*, 1979; Sugita *et al.*, 1980). However, some discrepancies in results also persisted. For instance, myosin, actin, α-actinin, and Tn-C were reported to be resistant to CANP by Dayton *et al.* (1976) and Goll *et al.* (1978), but, if used at high concentration, CANP can also degrade myosin, α-actinin (Azanza *et al.*, 1979; Ishiura *et al.*, 1979), and myosin heavy chains (Pemrick *et al.*, 1980) provided the LC-2 chain present is not phosphorylated.

Sugita *et al.* (1980) reported that CANP easily removed Tn-I and Tn-C from myofibrils. Although Tn-I was also degraded, Tn-C came out intact in solution. Since Tn-I is bound to Tn-C *in situ,* the degradation of the former is likely to effect the release of the latter. As Tn-T remained intact with myofibrils, they assumed that the susceptible part of Tn-T may be protected by binding to tropomyosin. This observation was at variance with the contention of many other workers that Tn-T is degraded to a MW 30,000 component by CANP during the aging of meat (Cheng and Parrish, 1977; Olson *et al.*, 1977; Penny, 1980).

Recently, Penny *et al.* (1984) reported that both m*M*-CANP and μ*M*-CANP can degrade Tn-T to produce a MW 30,000 polypeptide. Earlier Suzuki *et al.* (1978) had indicated that postmortem decay of Z-disks in muscle was due to the removal of α-actinin by CANP. Nagainis and Wolfe (1982), however, are of the opinion that it is the Z-actin which is the possible target of CANP. This consequently results in the disappearance of Z-disks during the postmortem aging process.

Some controversy also exists as to the ability of CANP in degrading cytoskeleton proteins of muscle. Whereas Maruyama *et al.* (1981) and Penny *et al.*

(1984) consider connectin (or titin) resistant to CANP, others found it labile (Lusby *et al.*, 1983; Zeece *et al.*, 1983). However, there seems no dispute on the ability of CANP in degrading desmin (O'Shea *et al.*, 1979; Lazarides, 1980; Robson *et al.*, 1984; Penny *et al.*, 1984; Weber, 1984). It can also hydrolyze filamin (Davies *et al.*, 1978).

Despite enough *in vitro* studies in support of CANP as being the important proteolytic enzyme in the postmortem tenderizing process, some serious questions were raised regarding its activity *in situ*. For instance, CANP requires a pH of about 7.5 for its maximal activity under *in vitro* conditions and shows little activity below pH 6.0 (Dayton *et al.*, 1976). Since the pH of muscle systems drops down to about 5.5 within 24 hr postmortem, CANP cannot be expected to bring about any marked change in proteins. The fact that the pH drops down drastically within a few minutes in the case of electrically stimulated (Asghar and Henrickson, 1982b; Rashid *et al.*, 1983) carcasses and PSE pork muscles (Cassens *et al.*, 1975) especially reduces the chances for CANP to play any significant role in the postmortem tenderization process of meat.

The second limitation is that the high Ca^{2+}-requiring form, which constitutes 75% of the calcium-activated neutral protease in muscle, needs 1–5 mM Ca^{2+} for activation, as is apparent from *in vitro* studies (Dayton *et al.*, 1981; Nagainis *et al.*, 1984), and it has negligible activity at Ca^{2+} concentrations below 0.1 mM. However, the *in vivo* concentration of cytosolic Ca^{2+} in relaxed skeletal muscles from normal healthy animals is of the order of 0.01 μM (Caputo, 1978; Blinks *et al.*, 1978; Fabiato and Fabiato, 1979; Lee *et al.*, 1980). An ATP-driven Ca^{2+} pump maintains this low level of Ca^{2+} in the relaxed state. With postmortem depletion of ATP, it becomes unoperative, but, even though the cytosolic Ca^{2+} level increases to 10 μM by its release from sarcoplasmic reticulum or mitochondria, it is still far less than needed by the high calcium-requiring form for activation.

However, the low Ca^{2+}-requiring form, which is activated by micromolar Ca^{2+} and also maintains a measurable activity at pHs as low as 5.3 (Dayton *et al.*, 1981; Koohmaraie *et al.*, 1986), may be contributing to fair extent in the postmortem tenderization process of meat. Moreover, the presence of other divalent cations in muscle may modify the sensitivity of CANP to Ca^{2+}. For example, Suzuki and Tsuji (1982) have shown that 1–2 mM Mn^{2+} significantly increased the activity of CANP. Although the physiological concentration of Mn^{2+} is only about 10 μM in muscle, it is likely to exert some synergistic effect on the activity of CANP. The presence of 10 mM Mg^{2+} in muscle may also have a similar additive effect. Postmortem CANP activity also seems to be related with type of muscle. A recent study by Koohmaraie *et al.* (1987b) indicated that longissimus dorsi muscle which significantly became tender during postmortem aging had much higher CANP activity than had psoas major which showed little change in tenderness upon aging, and that postmortem increase in tenderness was attributed solely to μMCANP activity (Koohmaraie *et al.*, 1987c).

Most of the investigators generally ascribe the loss of CANP activity at low pH to denaturation of enzymes. This may partly be true, but some other mechanisms may also be operative in the case of metal-activated enzymes. The function of metal ion in such enzymes is believed to be either neutralization of the charges on the surface by preventing electrostatic repulsion of subunits or effecting of a conformational change required for the association of subunits (Schrimgeour, 1977). If so, then the metal ions must be present in a specific state to perform this function.

Generally speaking, the metallic cations in solution exist as aqua-complex ions in equilibrium with their respective hydroxo-complex (Furia, 1975):

$$M(H_2O)^{m+} \rightleftharpoons MOH^{(m-1)+} + H^+$$
Aqua-complex ion   Hydroxo-complex
(weak base)

The acid ionization constant (pK_a) of the aqua-complex ion determines whether or not the ion would form complexes with a protein. This depends greatly on the pH of the medium (Basolo and Pearson, 1956). Since the ionization constant of low charge Ca^{2+} is 12.6, they would form a stable complex only with negatively charged protein in alkaline media. They cannot bind to cationic proteins as they do not share electrons to form a covalent bond. These considerations explain why the activity of Ca^{2+}-activated protease is optimum in the alkaline pH range. Thus, a decrease in its activity at acidic pH values may partly be due to a change in the electronic state of Ca^{2+}.

Apart from CANP, several other proteinases have also shown the ability of degrading different myofibrillar proteins. A serine proteinase (called SK-protease) described by Katunuma and associates (Kobayashi et al., 1978) could degrade the A-band of myofibrils from rabbit skeletal muscle in vitro (Sanada et al., 1979). It readily cleaved the myosin heavy chain into two fragments with 100,000 and 88,000 molecular weights. Myosin light chain-2, actin, tropomyosin, Tn-T, and Tn-I were also labile to this enzyme (Yosogawa et al., 1978), but α-actinin, M-protein, and myosin light-1 and -3 were not affected. Similarly, two other serine proteinases, cytosolic and myofibrillar proteases, which were described by Dahlmann et al. (1981), could cleave myofibrillar proteins. While the former degraded myosin molecules into relatively large fragments (MW >100,000), the latter hydrolyzed it into MW 46,000 and 30,000 fragments. Myosin heavy chain, tropomyosin, Tn-T, and Tn-C were also vulnerable to myofibrillar proteinase (Dahlmann et al., 1984).

Most investigators, however, now consider that serine proteinases actually belong to mast cells rather than muscle cells per se (Section V,A). Even if some serine proteinases are present in muscle fibers, as Dahlmann et al. (1981) insist, they would not be effective in degrading proteins during the postmortem aging process because of their quite high pH (8.5) requirement for optimal activity.

Similarly ATP-activated alkaline protease, which is also a serine proteinase (Goldberg *et al.*, 1979), cannot contribute to the meat conditioning process for two reasons: first, the high pH requirement would limit its activity and, second, the AMP and ADP, whose concentration increases by hydrolysis of ATP in postmortem muscle, have no ability at all to activate this enzyme (Goldberg and St. John, 1976).

3. Role of Exopeptidases

The studies on meat flavor in model systems have revealed that derivatives of some amino acids and simple sugars are mainly responsible for the characteristic meaty aroma of cooked meats (Shibamoto and Russell, 1977; Hsieh *et al.*, 1980; Bodrero *et al.*, 1981; MacLeod and Seyyedain-Ardebili, 1981). Among the amino acids, histidine, tyrosine, and sulfur-containing amino acids (methionine and cysteine) are particularly involved in these reactions. In addition, arginine, proline, alanine, leucine, isolucine, glutamic acid, and aspartic acid also contribute significantly in the formation of flavoring compounds (Hsieh *et al.*, 1980; Bodrero *et al.*, 1981). Pearson *et al.* (1983) compared the amino acid data of different proteins of muscle, available from various reports, and concluded that myosin and actin are by far the major sources of sulfur amino acids in meat.

Prerigor meat contains only about 4.5 mmol free amino nitrogen (Asghar and Yeates, 1979b). The free amino acids and peptides each make up about 50% of free amino nitrogen (Lawrie, 1979). While reviewing the postmortem changes, Whitaker (1959) quoted several studies indicating a significant increase in the free amino acid content during aging of meat. If so, then this can be ascribed to exopeptidase activity in meat. Among the several exopeptidases present in skeletal muscle (Section II), aminopeptidases require the presence of an unsubstituted NH_2 group at the N terminus of a protein chain for catalyzing the reaction to produce free amino acids. Since the α-NH_2 group at the N terminus of the principal muscle proteins myosin (Offer, 1964) and actin (Gaetejens and Barany, 1966) is acetylated, aminopeptidases would not be capable of affecting these proteins unless they are first degraded by some endopeptidases. The same holds for dipeptidylpeptidases (e.g., cathepsin C), as they also need an unsubstituted α-NH_2 group for initiating the hydrolysis of peptide bonds to produce dipeptides sequentially, starting from the N terminus.

Even though lysosomal carboxypeptidases (e.g., cathepsins A and B2), which require an unsubstituted C terminus in a protein to commence the reaction, do not seem to face such constraints in dealing with myosin and actin as may happen with aminopeptidases and dipeptidylpeptidases, cathepsin A was shown to have no detectable action on these proteins (Bodwell and Pearson, 1964). However, it readily catabolized some sarcoplasmic proteins. On the other hand, dipeptidases are likely to hydrolyze naturally occurring peptides such as carnosine and anserine. These peptides make up about 0.35% of muscle mass (Lawrie, 1979). However, in the case of intact proteins, dipeptidases can play a part only in concert with dipeptidylpeptidases, because only the dipeptides with both N and C termini unsubstituted can be the substrate for the former. A high level of dipeptidylaminopeptidase IV (DPA IV) in fibroblasts (McDonald and Schwabe, 1977) and its tendency for cleaving those peptide bonds in which proline is involved as one of the residues are suggestive that this expopeptidase may be contributing in degrading soluble collagen. However, among exopeptidases, only acidic arylamidase, lysosomal carboxypeptidases A and B (i.e., cathepsins A and B2), DAP I (cathepsin C), and DAP II can possibly contribute in raising the free amino acid content in meat during the postmortem aging process, since they require low pH for activation. All other endogenous exopeptidases which are known to be present in muscle are active at alkaline pHs.

IX. SUMMARY AND CONCLUSIONS

The literature reviewed herein indicates the presence of about 24 proteinases in the skeletal muscle system. Half of them are exopeptidases and the other half represent endopeptidases. Some of them are distributed in the cytosolic fraction, while the others are confined in the lysosome granules of muscle fibers. However, most of the serine proteinases, the so-called alkaline proteases, whose activity had once been identified in muscle homogenate, are now believed to originate from mast cells, which are associated with skeletal muscles of some species. Some investigators, however, have insisted that the mast cells are not the only source of all alkaline protease activity in muscle (Dahlmann et al., 1981). Cellular location indeed is a prerequisite for any proteinase to have a role in inter- and intracellular protein breakdown in muscle.

Endogenous proteinases perform many vital functions in muscle physiology of live animals in the steady state, as well as during normal growth and development, thereby regulating protein turnover. However, controversy exists as to which protease or proteases play the most important role in this process. Uncertainty also exists about the mechanism by which different proteins are turned over in muscles. The activity of proteinases in the muscle system is affected by numerous factors such as endogenous inhibitors, nutrition, chronological age, nerve system, and endocrines as well as by different pathological conditions of an animal.

Endogenous proteinases also play an important role during the postmortem phase of carcasses in converting the muscle system into tender and flavorsome meat. Pearson et al. (1983) stated, ''Tenderness and flavor are undoubtedly the two characteristics of meat that contribute the most to its desirability.'' The degradative changes that occur in sarcoplasmic, myofibrillar, cytoskeletal, and connective tissue proteins during the postmortem conditioning process of meat are due, indeed, to endogenous proteinases. However, the relative contribution of endo- and exopeptidases in the overall aging process is not yet clear. Theoretically, it can be assumed that the changes brought about by endopeptidases in meat would be reflected in its tenderness, and those produced by exopeptidases may be providing precursors (free amino acids) which ultimately are involved in enhancing the aroma of cooked meat. The mechanisms of these changes are rather complex.

Among the endogenous endopeptidases, lysosomal cathepsins B1, D, H, and L and cytosolic μM-CANP are the most likely contestants which are involved in the postmortem tenderizing process in carcasses. Their activity and relative contributions in this process may be determined by the ultimate postmortem pH value of the muscle system. Other endopeptidases with alkaline pH requirements can hardly have any role in the meat tenderizing process. Similarly, lysosomal carboxypeptidases A and B (cathepsins A and B2, respectively), DAP I (cathepsin C), and DAP-II are among the endogenous exopeptidases which are likely to play a part in raising the free amino acid level in conditioned meat. The free amino acids are the precursors which are involved in the formation of flavor derivatives in meat on cooking. All other endogenous aminopeptidases, dipeptidases, and dipeptidylpeptidases are least important in the postmortem aging process as they require fairly alkaline pH for activation.

In vitro studies on the proteolytic capacity of different lysosomal and non-lysosomal endopeptidases revealed that almost all myofibrillar, cytoskeletal, and collagenic proteins are vulnerable to them. This merely reflects the potentiality of these enzymes in degrading muscle proteins under appropriate conditions and cannot be extrapolated to *in vivo* conditions, where the environments are different in several respects. Some limitations are associated with each proteinase *in vivo* as a causative factor affecting postmortem changes in meat. A particular postmortem condition might suit the activity of one proteinase and may not be conductive for the other. For this matter, it may be difficult to single out the contribution of different endogenous proteinases in the overall process of meat conditioning, although some recent studies assigned postmortem tenderizing role solely to μM-CANP.

X. RESEARCH NEEDS

The advanced information compiled very recently by Pearson and Dutson (1985) on electrical stimulation of postmortem carcasses shows a general consistency among the findings of various investigators that postmortem electrical stimulation of carcasses hastens the tenderization process in meat during the subsequent aging period. As is apparent from the discussion herein (Section VIII,D), however, opinions differ on the role of different endogenous proteinases in this process. Dutson *et al.* (1980) and Sorinmade *et al.* (1982) believe that lysosomal cathepsins are involved to a greater degree in myofibrillar protein degradation. The former investigators have shown that more than 50% of total, free, and specific activity of β-glucuronidase and cathepsin C in ovine carcasses are released within the first 60 min after electrical stimulation, possibly by rupturing of the lysosomal membrane at low pHs. In contrast, Marsh *et al.* (1981) found no evidence that rapid pH fall accelerates the tenderization process. The relation of tenderness with β-glucuronidase or cathepsin C also seems questionable. The increase in specific activity of β-glucuronidase (which affects mucopolysaccharides) and cathepsin C (which is an exopeptidase) cannot account for those degradative changes in myofibrillar and cytoskeletal proteins which have been related to the tenderization process (Section VIII,C). These discrepancies need to be resolved. The changes in the activity of such endopeptidases as cathepsins B1, D, H, L, and Ca^{2+}-activated proteases in electrically stimulated carcasses may be examined to find the answer.

Since thiol proteinases (e.g., cathepsins B1, H, L, and Ca^{2+}-activated proteinases) contain a thiol group as the active center, which should be in reduced form for the enzyme to be in the active state, the low redox potential (depletion of oxygen) in postmortem muscles is a favorable condition for their activity. However, all these proteinases cannot be expected to function equally well in postmortem muscle. In fact, some other specific requirements of each protease will determine its relative role in the overall proteolytic changes in meat. For example, pH value and various cations and anions all can modify the activity of different proteolytic enzymes differentially. Hence, the answers to some discrepancies may be explored keeping in view these variables.

A study by Penny and Ferguson-Pryce (1979) suggested that CANP was mainly responsible for degrading muscle proteins at pHs above 6.0, whereas at low pHs (5.5) the changes in meat proteins were brought about solely by lysosomal cystein proteases. As discussed in Section III,B,5, autolytic digestion of the mM-CANP form *in vitro* gave rise to the ultra μM-Ca^{2+}-requiring form on incubation (Nagainis *et al.*, 1984). In view of these observations, it is likely that, during the postmortem aging process, the mM-CANP form may be converted to μM-CANP by autodigestion *in vivo* and may be contributing to meat conditioning even at low pH. Whether or not such a conversion occurs during the aging of meat needs to be examined.

It has been discussed in Section VII,A that natural inhibitors of most of the endogenous proteinases are also present in muscle. They have an important function in regulating the enzyme activity during protein turnover in live animals. It is not known whether these inhibitors remain effective during the postmortem aging process or become ineffective due to degradation/ denaturation. It would be interesting to examine the fate of the endogenous inhibitors during the postmortem aging of carcasses in storage. A few studies have appeared dealing with this aspect. They indicate conflicting results. For example, Ducastaing *et al.* (1985) found only a marginal change in CAF's inhibitor activity during postmortem aging, but Vidalenc *et al.* (1983) and Koohmaraie *et al.* (1986b) observed a rapid decrease within 24 hr postmortem storage of meat. The inhibitor is shown to be susceptible to hydrolysis by mM-CANP (Mellgren *et al.*, 1986). However, it remains to be seen if the inhibitor is also affected by μM-CANP and what is the fate of other endogenous proteinase inhibitors during the postmortem aging process.

In addition, several more areas related to endogenous proteinases in skeletal muscle, where either the information is altogether deficient or the results are inconclusive and merit further investigations, have already been indicated at the appropriate places in the text. Hopefully, future studies on these issues will advance our understanding of the role that endogenous proteinases play in the muscle physiology of live animals and in the improvement of the tenderness and flavor of meat during the postmortem conditioning process.

ACKNOWLEDGMENTS

One of the authors (A. Asghar) is appreciative of Dr. F. H. Wolfe for his support during the writing of the manuscript. Thanks are also due to Ms. Candi Dubetz for typing the text part, and to Ms. Carol Evens for typing the bibliography.

REFERENCES

Abbott, M. T., Pearson, A. M., Price, J. F., and Hooper, G. R. 1977. Ultrastructural changes during autolysis of red and white porcine muscle. *J. Food Sci.* **42**, 1185.

Abdel-Monem, M., and Hoffmann-Berling, H. 1976. Purification and characterization of a DNA-dependent ATPase from *E. coli. Eur. J. Biochem.* **65**, 431.

Abe, S., and Nagai. 1973. Evidence for the presence of a complex of collagenases with α$_2$-macroglobin in human rheumatoid synovial fluid: A possible regulatory mechanism of collagenase activity *in vivo. J. Biochem. (Tokyo)* **73**, 897.

Abraham, R. M., Morris, M., and Smith, J. 1967. Histochemistry of lysosomes in rat heart muscle. *J. Histochem. Cytochem.* **15**, 596.

Amenta, J. S., Sargus, M. J., Venkatesan, S., and Shinozuka, H. 1978. Role of vascular apparatus in augmented protein degradation in cultured fibroblasts. *J. Cell. Physiol.* **94**, 77.

Anson, M. L. 1940. The purfication of cathepsin. *J. Gen. Physiol.* **23**, 695.

Ansorge, S., Kirschke, H., and Friedrich, K. 1977. Conversion of proinsulin into insulin by cathepsin B and L from rat liver lysosomes. *Acta Biol. Med. Ger.* **36**, 1723.

Anwar, R. A. 1982. Primary structure of insoluble elastin. *In* "Methods in Enzymology" (L. W. Cunningham and D. W. Frederiksen, eds.), Vol. 82, p. 606. Academic Press, New York.

Aoyagi, T., Wada, T., Kojima, F., Nagai, M., and Umezawa, H. 1981. Various enzyme activities in muscle and other organs of dystrophic mice. *J. Clin. Invest.* **67**, 51.

Arakawa, N., Fujiki, S., Inagaki, C., and Fujimaki, M. 1967. A catheptic protease active in ultimate pH of muscle. *Agric. Biol. Chem.* **40**, 1265.

Arakawa, N., Goll, D. E., and Temple, J. 1970. Effect of post-mortem storage on α-actinin and the tropomyosin–troponin complex. *J. Food Sci.* **35**, 703.

Arakawa, N., Inagaki, C., Kitatura, T., Fujiki, S., and Fujimaki, M. 1976. Some possible evidences for an alteration in the actin–myosin interaction in stored muscle. *Agric. Biol. Chem.* **40**, 1445.

Arborgh, B., Glaumann, H., Berg, T., and Ericsson, J. L. E. 1978. Isolation of kupffer-cell lysosomes with observation on their chemical and enzymic composition. *Exp. Cell Res.* **88**, 279.

Arnal, M., Ferrara, M., and Fauconneau, G. 1976. "Nuclear Techniques in Animal Production and Health," p. 393. International Atomic Energy Report No. 205.

Aronson, N. N., and Barrett, A. J. 1978. The specificity of cathepsin B. Hydrolysis of glucagon at the C-terminus by a peptidyldipeptidase mechanism. *Biochem. J.* **171**, 759.

Asghar, A., and Henrickson, R. L. 1982a. Chemical, biochemical, functional and nutritional characteristics of collagen in food systems. *Adv. Food Res.* **28**, 231.

Asghar, A., and Henrickson, R. L. 1982b. Post-mortem electrical stimulation of carcasses: Its effect on biophysical, biochemical, microbiological and quality characteristics of meat. *CRC Crit. Rev. Food Sci. Nutr.* **18**, 1.

Asghar, A., and Pearson, A. M. 1980. Influence of ante- and post-mortem treatments upon muscle composition and meat quality. *Adv. Food Res.* **26**, 53.

Asghar, A., and Yeates, F. M. 1968. Effect of growth rate on chemical and histological aspects of muscle. *Proc. Aust. Soc. Anim. Prod.* **7**, 89.

Asghar, A., and Yeates, N. T. M. 1978. The mechanism for the promotion of tenderness in meat during post-mortem process: A review. *CRC Crit. Rev. Food Sci. Nutr.* **8**(3), 115.

Asghar, A., and Yeates, F. M. 1979a. Muscle characteristics and meat quality of lambs grown on different nutritional planes. 3. Effect on micro- and ultrastructure. *Agric. Biol. Chem.* **43**, 445.

Asghar, A., and Yeates, N. T. M. 1979b. Muscle characteristics and meat quality of lambs grown on different nutritional planes. 2. Chemical and biochemical effects. *Agric. Biol. Chem.* **43**, 437.

Asghar, A., Pearson, A. M., Magee, C. H., and Tahir, M. A. 1981. Effect of *ad libitum* maintenance and submaintenance feeding, and of compensatory growth on some biochemical properties of muscle from weanling rabbits. *J. Nutr.* **111**, 1343.

Asghar, A., Samejima, K., and Yasui, T. 1985. Functionality of muscle proteins in gelation mechanisms of textured meat products. *CRC Crit. Rev. Food Sci. Nutr.* **22**, 27.

Asghar, A., Morita, J., Samejima, K., and Ysui, T. 1986a. The deposition of various proteins in red and white skeletal muscles of chicken as influenced by under-nutrition. 1. Proteins of subcellular fractions of sarcoplasm. *Agric. Biol. Chem.* **50**(8), 1931.

Asghar, A., Morita, J., Samejima, K., and Yasui, T. 1986b. The deposition of various proteins in red and white muscles of chicken as influenced by under-nutrition. 2. Proteins of myofibrils and connective tissue. *Agric. Biol. Chem.* **50**(8), 1941.

Åstrand, P. O., and Rodahl, K. 1970. "Textbook of Work Physiology." McGraw-Hill, New York.

Atsushi, S., and Masao, F. 1968. Studies on proteolysis in stored muscle. II. Purification and properties of a proteolytic enzyme, cathepsin D from rabbit muscle. *Agric. Biol. Chem. (Tokyo)* **32**, 975.

Aricchio, F., Mollica, L., and Liguori, A. 1972. Inactivation of tyrosine amino-transferase in neutral homogenates and rat liver slices. *Biochem. J.* **129**, 1131.

Azanza, J. L., Raymond, J., Robin, J. M., Cottin, P., and Ducastaing, A. 1979. Purification and some physiochemical and enzymic properties of a calcium-activated neutral proteinase from rabbit skeletal muscle. *Biochem. J.* **183**, 339.

Bailey, A. J., and Sims, T. J. 1977. Meat tenderness: Distribution of molecular species of collagen in bovine muscles. *J. Sci. Food Agric.* **28**, 565.

Ballard, F. J. 1977. Intracellular protein degradation. *Essays Biochem.* **13**, 1.

Ballard, F. J., and Gunn, J. M. 1982. Nutritional and hormonal effects on intracellular protein catabolism. *Nutr. Rev.* **40**, 33.

Balls, A. K. 1938. Enzyme action in food products at low temperatures. *Ice Cold Storage* **41**, 143.

Banno, Y., Shiotani, T., Towatari, T., Yoshikawa, D., Katsunuma, T., Affing, E., and Katunuma, N. 1975. Studies on new intracellular proteases in various organs of rat. *Eur. J. Biochem.* **52**, 59.

Banno, Y., Morris, H. P., and Katunuma, N. 1978. The serine protease from rat liver and hepatoma 8999. Location and role in mitochondrial protein degradation. *J. Biochem. (Tokyo)* **83**, 1545.

Barrett, A. J. 1970. Cathepsin D. Purification of isozymes from human and chicken liver. *Biochem. J.* **117**, 601.

Barrett, A. J. 1972. A new assay for cathepsin B_1 and other thiol proteinases. *Anal. Biochem.* **47**, 280.

Barrett, A. J. 1973. Human cathepsin B_1. Purification and some properties of the enzyme. *Biochem. J.* **131**, 809.

Barrett, A. J. 1977. "Proteinases in Mammalian Cells and Tissues," pp. 1, 181, 209. North-Holland, Amsterdam.

Barrett, A. J. 1980. Introduction: The classification of proteinases. *In* "Protein Breakdown in Health and Disease" (D. Evered and J. Whelan, eds.). Excerpta Medica, Amsterdam.

Barrett, A. J., and Dingle, J. T. 1971. Terminology of the proteinases. *In* "Tissue Proteinases" (A. J. Barrett and J. T. Dingle, eds.), p. 9. North-Holland, Amsterdam.

Barrett, A. J., and Dingle, J. T. 1972. Inhibition of tissue acid proteinases by pepstatin. *Biochem. J.* **127**, 439.

Barrett, A. J., and McDonald, J. K., eds. 1980. "Mammalian Proteases. A Glossary and Bibliography," Vol. 1. Academic Press, London.

Barrett, A. J., and Starkey, P. M. 1973. The interaction of α_2-macroglobin with proteinases. Characteristics and specificity of the reaction, and a hypothesis concerning its molecular mechanism. *Biochem. J.* **133**, 709.

Barrett, A. J., Starkey, P. M., and Munn, E. A. 1974. The unique nature of the reaction of α_2-macroglobulin with proteinases. *In* "Proteinase Inhibitors" (H. Fritz, H. Tschesche, L. J. Greene, and E. Truscheit, eds.), p. 72. Springer-Verlag, Berlin and New York.

Barrett, A. J., Kembhavi, A. A., Brown, M. A., Kirschke, H., Knight, C. G., Tamai, M., and Hanada, K. 1982. L-*trans*-Epoxysuccinyl-leucylamido(μ-guanidino)butane (E-64) and its analogues as inhibitors of cysteine proteinases including cathepsins B, H and L. *Biochem. J.* **201**, 189.

Barth, R., and Elce, J. S. 1981. Immunofluorescent localization of a Ca^{++}-dependent neutral protease in hamster muscle. *Am. J. Physiol.* **240**, E493.

Baskin, F. K., Duckworth, W. C., and Kitabchi, A. E. 1975. Sites of cleavage of glucagon by insulin–glucagan protease. *Biochem. Biophys. Res. Commun.* **67**, 163.

Basolo, F., and Pearson, R. G. 1956. "Mechanisms of Inorganic Reactions," p. 5. Wiley, New York.

Bates, P. C., and Millward, D. J. 1983. Myofibrillar protein turnover. *Biochem. J.* **214**, 587.

Baxter, J. H., and Suelter, C. H. 1983. Skeletal muscle lysosomes: Comparison of lysosomes from normal and dystrophic avian pectoralis muscle as a function of age. *Muscle Nerve* **6**, 187.

Bazin, S., and Delaunary, A. 1966. Charactères de cathepsines collagénolytiques présente dans les tissus enflammés du rat. *Ann. Inst. Pasteur, Paris* **110**, 192.

Bechtel, P. J., and Parrish, F. C., Jr. 1983. Effect of post-mortem storage and temperature on muscle protein degradation: Analysis of SDS gel electrophoresis. *J. Food Sci.* **83**, 294.

Beeley, J. G., and Neurath, H. 1968. The reaction of trypsin with bromoacetone. *Biochemistry* **7**, 1239.

Bendall, J. R. 1967. The elastin content of various muscles of beef animals. *J. Sci. Food Agric.* **18,** 553.

Bendall, J. R. 1969. "Muscles, Molecules and Movement," p. 29. Heinemann, London.

Bendall, J. R. 1979. Relations between muscle pH and important biochemical parameters during the post-mortem changes in mammalian muscles. *Meat Sci.* **3,** 143.

Bergmann, M., and Fruton, J. S. 1941. The specificity of proteinases. *Adv. Enzymol.* **1,** 63.

Bigelow, S., Hough, R., and Rechsteiner, M. C. 1981. The selective degradation of injected proteins occurs principally in the cytosol rather than in lysosomes. *Cell* **85,** 83.

Billah, M. M., Lapetina, E. G., and Cuatrecasas, P. 1980. Phospholipase A_2 and phospholipase C activities of platelets. *J. Biol. Chem.* **255**(10), 10227.

Bird, J. W. C., and Carter, J. 1980. Proteolytic enzymes in striated and nonstriated muscle. *In* "Degradative Processes in Heart and Skeletal Muscles" (K. Wildenthal, ed.), p. 51. Elsevier, New York.

Bird, J. W. C., and Schwartz, W. N. 1977. Intracellular protein catabolism in muscle. *In* "Intracellular Protein Catabolism II" (V. Turk and N. Marks, eds.), p. 167. Plenum, New York.

Bird, J. W. C., Berg, T., and Leathem, J. H. 1968. Cathepsin activity of liver and muscle fractions of adrenalectomized rat. *Proc. Soc. Exp. Biol. Med.* **127,** 182.

Bird, J. W. C., Schwartz, W. N., and Spanier, A. M. 1977. Degradation of myofibrillar proteins by cathepsins B and D. *Acta Biol. Med. Ger.* **36,** 1587.

Bird, J. W. C., Spanier, A. M., and Schwartz, W. N. 1978. Cathepsin B and D: Proteolytic activity and ultrastructural localization in skeletal muscle. *In* "Protein Turnover and Lysosome Function" (H. L. Segal and D. J. Doyle, eds.), p. 589. Academic Press, New York.

Bird, J. W. C., Carter, J., Triemer, R. E., Brooks, R. M., and Spanier, A. M. 1980. Proteinases in cardiac and skeletal muscle. *Fed. Proc., Fed. Am. Soc. Exp. Biol.* **39,** 20.

Bird, J. W. C., Roisen, F. J., Yorke, G., Lee, J. A., McElligott, M. A., Trimer, D. F., and St. John, A. 1981. Lysosomes and proteolytic enzymes activities in cultured striated muscle cells. *J. Histochem. Cytochem.* **29,** 431.

Blinks, H. R., Rüdel, R., and Taylor, S. R. 1978. Calcium transients in isolated amphibian skeletal muscle fibers: Detection with aeguorin. *J. Physiol. (London)* **277,** 291.

Blow, A. M. J. 1975. The detection and characterisation of cathepsin F, a cartilage enzyme that degrades proteoglycan. *Ital. J. Biochem.* **24,** 13.

Blow, D. M., and Steitz, T. A. 1970. X-Ray diffraction studies of enzymes. *Annu. Rev. Biochem.* **39,** 63.

Blow, D. M., Birktoft, J. J., and Hartley, B. S. 1969. Role of buried acid group in the mechanism of action of chymotrypsin. *Nature (London)* **221,** 337.

Bodwell, C. E., and Pearson, A. M. 1964. The activity of partially purified bovine catheptic enzymes on neutral and synthetic substrates. *J. Food Sci.* **29,** 602.

Bodrero, K. O., Pearson, A. M., and Magee, W. T. 1981. Evaluation of the contribution of flavor volatiles to the aroma of beef by surface response methodology. *J. Food Sci.* **46,** 26.

Boegman, R. J., and Oliver, T. W. 1980. Neural influence on muscle hydrolase activity. *Life Sci.* **27,** 1339.

Bohley, P., and Riemann, S. 1977. Intracellular protein catabolism. IX. Hydrophobicity of substrate proteins in a molecular basis of selectivity. *Acta Biol. Med. Ger.* **36,** 1823.

Bohley, P., Kirschke, H., Langner, J., Ansorge, S., Wiederanders, B., and Hanson, H. 1971. Intracellular protein breakdown. *In* "Tissue Proteinase" (A. J. Barrett and J. T. Dingle, eds.), p. 187. North-Holland, Amsterdam.

Bohley, P., Kirschke, H., Langner, J., Miehe, M., Riemann, S., Salama, Z., Schön, E., Weideranders, B., and Ansorge, S. 1979. Intracellular protein turnovers. *In* "Biological Functions of Proteinases" (H. Holzer and H. Tschesche, eds.), p. 17. Springer-Verlag, Berlin and New York.

Bois, P. 1964. Leucine aminopeptidase activity in muscles of dystrophic mice. *Experientia* **20,** 140.

Bolli, R., Cannon, R. D., Speir, E., Goldstein, R. E., and Epstein, S. E. 1983. Role of cellular protease in acute myocardial infraction. *J. Am. Cell. Cardiol.* **2,** 671.

Bond, J. S., and Barrett, A. J. 1980. Degradation of fructose 1,6-bisphosphate aldolase by cathepsin B. *Biochem. J.* **189,** 17.

Bond, J. S., and Bird, J. W. 1974. Effects of vitamin E-deficiency on guinea pig lysosomes. *Proc. Soc. Exp. Biol. Med.* **146,** 608.

Bouma, J. M. W., and Gruber, M. 1964. The distribution of cathepsins B and C in rat tissues. *Biochim. Biophys. Acta* **89,** 545.

Boyd, G. W. 1974. Protein-bound form of porcine renal renin. *Circ. Res.* **35,** 426.

Brinkley, B. R. 1982. The cytoskeleton: A perspective. *Methods Cell Biol.* **24,** 1.

Brocklehurst, K., and Little, G. 1972. Reactivities of the various protonic states in the reactions of papain and of L-cysteine with 2,2'- and 4,4'-dipyridyl disulphide. *Biochem. J.* **128,** 471.

Brouwer, A., Knook, D., Wiederanders, B., Riemann, S., Kirschke, H., and Bohley, P. 1979. Distribution of proteolytic enzyme activities between parenchymal-Kupffer and endothelial cells from rat liver. Unpublished report, quoted by Bohley *et al.* (1979).

Brush, J. S. 1971. Purification and characterization of a protease with specificity for insulin from rat muscle. *Diabetes* **20,** 140.

Brush, J. S. 1973. Purification and characterization of inhibitors of insulin specific protease in human serum. *Biochem. Biophys. Res. Commun.* **53,** 894.

Budd, G. C., Darzynkiewicz, Z., and Barnard, E. A. 1967. Intracellular localization of specific proteases in rat mast cells by electron microscope autoradiography. *Nature (London)* **213,** 1202.

Burghen, G. A., Kitabchi, A. E., and Brush, J. S. 1972. Characterization of a rat liver protease with specificity for insulin. *Endocrinology* **91,** 633.

Burleigh, M. C. 1977. Degradation of collagen by non-specific proteinases. *In* "Proteinases in Mammalian Cells and Tissues" (A. J. Barrett, ed.), p. 285. North-Holland, Amsterdam.

Burleigh, M. C., Barrett, A. J., and Lazarus, G. S. 1974. Cathepsin B_1. A lysosomal enzymes that degrades native collagen. *Biochem. J.* **137,** 387.

Bury, A. E., and Pennington, R. J. 1973. Arylamidases in human muscle. *Biochem. Soc. Trans.* **1,** 1306.

Bury, A. E., and Pennington, R. J. 1975. Hydrolysis of dipeptide 2-naphthylamides by human muscle enzymes. *Biochem. J.* **145,** 413.

Bury, A. E., Coolbear, T., and Savery, C. R. 1977. Separation and properties of two arylamidase from rat cardiac muscle extracts. *Biochem. J.* **163,** 565.

Busch, W. A., Stromer, M. H., Goll, D. E., and Suzuki, A. 1972. Ca^{++}-specific removal of Z-lines from rabbit skeletal muscle. *J. Cell Biol.* **52,** 367.

Bylinkina, V. S. 1986. Isolation of neutral proteinase of ribosomes (cathepsin R). *Biokhimia (Moscow)* **51,** 65 (in Russian); cited in *Chem. Abstr.* **104,** 104877y.

Bylinkina, V. S., Levyant, M. I., Gorach, G. G., and Orekhovich, V. N. 1978. Localization of neutral proteinase on the ribosomes. *Biochemistry U.S.S.R. (Engl. Transl.)* **43,** 83.

Caldwell, K. A., and Grosjean, O. K. 1971. Lysosomal cathepsins of chicken skeletal muscle. Distribution and properties. *J. Agric. Food Chem.* **19,** 108.

Caldwell, K. A., and Lineweaver, H. 1969. Sulfhydryl content of excised chicken breast muscle during post-mortem aging. *J. Food Sci.* **34,** 290.

Campbell, G. R., Chamley-Campbell, J., Groschel-Stewart, U., Small, J. V., and Anderson, P. 1979. Antibody staining of 10-nm (100 Å) filaments in cultured smooth, cardiac and skeletal muscle cells. *J. Cell Sci.* **37,** 303.

Canonico, P. G., and Bird, J. W. C. 1970. Lysosomes in skeletal muscle tissue. Zonal centrifugation evidence for multiple cellular sources. *J. Cell Biol.* **45,** 32.

Caputo, C. 1978. Excitation and contraction processes in muscle. *Annu. Rev. Biophys. Bioeng.* **2,** 63.

Cassens, R. G., Marple, D. N., and Ekeleenbloom, O. 1975. Animal physiology and meat quality. *Adv. Food Res.* **21**, 72.

Chajuss, D., and Spencer, J. V. 1962. Changes in the total sulfhydryl group content and histochemical denaturation of sulfonates in excised chicken muscle aged in air. *J. Food Sci.* **34**, 411.

Chang, T. W., and Goldberg, A. L. 1978. The origin of alanine produced in skeletal muscle. *J. Biol. Chem.* **253**, 3677.

Chaudhry, H. M., Parrish, F. C., and Goll, D. E. 1969. Effect of temperature on protein solubility of rabbit and bovine muscle. *J. Food Sci.* **34**, 183.

Cheng, C. S., and Parrish, F. C., Jr. 1977. Effect of Ca^{++} on changes in myofibrillar proteins on bovine skeletal muscles. *J. Food Sci.* **42**, 1621.

Cheung, W. Y. 1979. Calmodulin plays a pivotal role in cellular regulation. *Science* **207**, 19.

Chizzolini, R., Ledward, D. A., and Lawrie, R. A. 1977. Effect of aging on the neutral, acid-soluble and insoluble collagen from the intramuscular connective tissue of various species. *Meat Sci.* **1**, 111.

Chong, M. T., Garrard, W. T., and Bonner, J. 1974. Purification and properties of a neutral protease from rat liver chromatin. *Biochemistry* **13**, 5128.

Chua, B., Rao, R., Rannels, D. E., and Morgan, H. E. 1978. Hormonal and metabolic control of proteolysis. *Biochem. Soc. Symp.* **43**, 1.

Chua, B., Siehl, D. L., and Morgan, H. E. 1979. Effect of leucine and metabolites of branched chain amino acids on protein turnover in heart. *J. Biol. Chem.* **254**, 5388.

Chua, B. H. L., Long, W. M., Lautersack, N., Lins, J. A., and Morgan, H. E. 1983. Effects of diabetes on cardiac lysosomes and protein degradation. *Am. J. Physiol.* **245**, 91.

Clark, A. F., and Vignos, P. J. 1981. The role of proteases in experimental glucocorticoid myopathy. *Muscle Nerve* **4**, 219.

Clark, A. F., DeMartino, G. N., and Croall, D. E. 1986. Fractionation and quantification of calcium-dependent proteinase activity from small tissue samples. *Biochem. J.* **235**, 279.

Clayson, D. H. F., Beesly, J. A., and Blood, R. M. 1966. The chemistry of the natural tenderization or maturation of meat. *J. Sci. Food Agric.* **17**, 220.

Coffey, J. W., and de Duve, C. 1968. Digestive activity of lysosomes. *J. Biol. Chem.* **243**, 3255.

Cohen, S. H., and Trusal, L. R. 1980. The effect of catheptic enzymes on chilled bovine muscle. *Scaning Electron Microsc.* **3**, 595.

Currie, R. W., and Wolfe, F. H. 1980. Rigor related changes in mechanical properties (tensile and adhesive) and extracellular space in beef muscle. *Meat Sci.* **4**, 123.

Dabrowska, R., Barylko, B., Nowak, E., and Drabikowaski, W. 1973. The origin of 30,000 dalton proteins in troponin preparations. *FEBS Lett.* **29**, 239.

Dahlmann, B., and Reinauer, H. 1978. Purification and some properties of an alkaline proteinase from rat skeletal muscle. *Biochem. J.* **171**, 803.

Dahlmann, B., Schroeter, C., Herbertz, L., and Reinauer, H. 1979. Myofibrillar protein degradation and muscle proteinases in normal and diabetic rats. *Biochem. Med.* **21**, 33.

Dahlmann, B., Kuehn, L., Rutschmann, M., Block, I., and Reinaur, H. 1981. Characterization of two alkaline proteinases from rat skeletal muscle. *In* "Proteinases and Their Inhibitors" (V. Turk and Lj. Vitale, eds.), p. 163. Pergamon, Oxford.

Dahlmann, B., Kuehn, L., and Reinauer, H. 1984. Proteolytic enzymes and enhanced muscle protein breakdown. *Adv. Exp. Med. Biol.* **167**, 505.

Davey, L. C., and Gilbert, K. V. 1969. Changes in the fine structure of meat during aging. *J. Food Sci.* **34**, 69.

Davey, L. C., and Graafhuis, A. E. 1976. Structural changes in beef muscle during aging. *J. Sci. Food Agric.* **27**, 301.

Davidson, E., and Poole, B. 1975. Fractionation of the rat liver enzymes that hydrolyze benzoyl-arginyl-β-naphthylamide. *Biochim. Biophys. Acta* **397**, 437.

Davies, P. J. A., Wallach, D., Willingham, M. C., Pastan, I., Yamaguchi, M., and Robson, R. M. 1978. Filamin–actin interaction. *J. Biol. Chem.* **253**, 403.

Davies, R. E. 1963. A molecular theory of muscle contraction: Calcium-dependent contractions with hydrogen bond formation plus ATP-dependent-extensions of part of the myosin–actin crossbridges. *Nature (London)* **199**, 1068.

Dayton, W. R. 1982. Comparison of low and high-calcium-requiring form of the calcium-activated protease with their autocatalytic breakdown products. *Biochim. Biophys. Acta* **709**, 166.

Dayton, W. R., and Schollmeyer, J. V. 1981. Immunocytochemical localization of a calcium-activated protease in skeletal muscle cells. *Exp. Cell Res.* **136**, 423.

Dayton, W. R., Goll, D. E. Stromer, M. H., Reville, W. J., Zeece, M. G., and Robson, R. M 1975. Some properties of a Ca^{++}-activated protease that may be involved in myofibrillar protein turnover. *In* "Proteases and Biological Control" (E. Reich, D. E. Rifkin, and E. Shaw, eds.), p. 551. Cold Spring Harbor Laboratory, Cold Spring Harbor, New York.

Dayton, W. R., Goll, D. E., Zeece, M. G., Robson, R. M., and Reville, W. J. 1976. A Ca^{++}-activated protease possibly involved in myofibrillar protein turnover. *Biochemistry* **15**, 2150, 2159.

Dayton, W. R., Schollmeyer, J. V., Chan, A. C., and Allen, C. E. 1979. Elevated levels of a calcium-activated muscle protease in rapidly atrophying muscles from vitamin E-defficient rabbits. *Biochim. Biophys. Acta* **584**, 216.

Dayton, W. A., Schollmeyer, J. V., Lepley, R. A., and Cortes, L. R. 1981. A Ca^{++}-activated protease possibly involved in myofibrillar protein turnover. Isolation of a low calcium-requiring form of the protease. *Biochim. Biophys. Acta* **659**, 48.

Dean, R. T. 1975a. Direct evidence of the importance of lysosomes in the degradation of intracellular proteins. *Nature (London)* **257**, 414.

Dean, R. T. 1975b. Lysosomal enzymes as agents of turnover of soluble cytoplasmic proteins. *Eur. J. Biochem.* **58**, 9.

Dean, R. T. 1976. The role of cathepsin B_1 and D in the digestion of cytoplasmic proteins *in vitro* by lysosomal extracts. *Biochem. Biophys. Res. Commun.* **68**, 518.

Dean, R. T. 1979. Macrophage protein turnover. Evidence for lysosomal participation in basal proteolysis. *Biochem. J.* **180**, 339.

Dean, R. T. 1980. Regulation and mechanisms of degradation of endogenous proteins by mammalian cells: General considerations. *In* "Degrative Processes in Heart and Skeletal Muscle" (K. Wildenthal, ed.), p. 3. Elsevier, Amsterdam.

Dean, R. T., and Barrett, A. J. 1976. Lysosomes. *Essays Biochem.* **12**, 1.

Decker, R. S., and Wildenthal, K. 1981. Lysosomal alterations in heart, skeletal muscle, and liver of hyperthyroid rabbits. *Lab. Invest.* **44**, 455.

Decker, R. S., Poole, A. R., and Wildenthal, K. 1980. Distribution of lysosomal cathepsin D in normal, ischemic and starved rabbit cardiac myocytes. *Circ. Res.* **46**, 485.

Décombaz, J., Reinhardt, P., Anantharaman, K., Von Glutz, G., and Poortmans, J. R. 1979. Biochemical changes in a 100 km run: Free amino acids, urea, and creatinine. *Eur. J. Appl. Physiol.* **36**, 61.

de Duve, C. 1977. An integrated view of lysosomal function. *In* "Molecular Basis of Biological Degradative Processes" (H. Hermann and I. H. Lepow, eds.), p. 25. Academic Press, New York.

de Duve, C., and Baudhuin, P. 1966. Peroxisomes (microbodies and related particles). *Physiol. Rev.* **46**, 323.

Dehlinger, P. J., and Schimke, R. T. 1970. Effect of size on the relative rate of degradation in rat liver soluble proteins. *Biochem. Biophys. Res. Commun.* **40**, 1473.

Delange, R. J., and Smith, E. L. 1971. Leucine aminopeptidase and other N-terminal exopeptidases. *Enzymes* **111**, 81.

DeMartino, G. N. 1983. Identification of a high molecular weight alkaline protease in rat heart. *J. Mol. Cardiol.* **15**, 17.

DeMartino, G. N., and Goldberg, A. L. 1978. Thyroid hormones control lysosomal enzyme activities in liver and skeletal muscle. *Proc. Natl. Acad. Sci. U.S.A.* **75**, 1369.

DeMartino, G. N., and Goldberg, A. L. 1979. Identification and partial purification of an ATP-stimulated alkaline protease in rat liver. *J. Biol. Chem.* **254**, 3712.

Dernby, K. G. 1918. A study on autolysis of animal tissues. *J. Biol. Chem.* **35**, 179.

Desai, I. D. 1969. Regulation of lysosomal enzymes. Adaptive changes in enzyme during starvation and refeeding. *Can. J. Biochem.* **47**, 785.

Dice, J. F., and Goldberg, A. L. 1975. Relationship between *in vivo* degradative rates and isoelectric points of proteins. *Proc. Natl. Acad. Sci. U.S.A.* **72**, 3893.

Dice, J. F., Dehlinger, P. J., and Schimke, R. T. 1973. Studies on the correlation between size and relative degradation rate of soluble proteins. *J. Biol. Chem.* **248**, 4220.

Dice, J. F., Walker, C. D., Byrne, B., and Cardiel, A. 1978. General characteristics of protein degradation in diabetes and starvation. *Proc. Natl. Acad. Sci. U.S.A.* **75**, 2093.

Dingle, J. T. 1973. Role of lysosomal enzymes in skeletal tissues. *J. Bone Joint Surg. (Br.) Vol.***55**, 87.

Dingle, J. T., Barrett, A. J., Blow, A. M. J., and Martin, P. E. N. 1977. Proteoglycan-degrading enzymes. A radiochemical assay method, and the detection of a new enzyme, cathepsin F. *Biochem. J.* **167**, 775.

Distelmaier, P., Hübner, H., and Otto, K. 1972. Cathepsin B_1 and B_2 in various organs of the rat. *Enzymologia* **42**, 363.

Dohm, G. L., Puente, F. R., Smith, C. P., and Edge, A. 1978. Changes in tissue protein levels as a result of endurance exercise. *Life Sci.* **23**, 845.

Dohm, G. L., Kasperek, G. J., Tapscott, E. B., and Beecher, G. R. 1980. Effect of exercise on synthesis and degradation of muscle protein. *Biochem. J.* **188**, 255.

Drabikowski, W., Gorecka, A., and Jakubiec-Puka, A. 1976. Endogenous proteinases in vertebrate skeletal muscle. *Int. J. Biochem.* **8**, 61.

Duance, V. C., Restall, D. J., Beard, H., Bourne, F. J., and Bailey, A. J. 1977. The location of three collagen types in skeletal muscle. *FEBS Lett.* **79**, 24.

Ducastaing, A., Valin, C., Schollmeyer, J. E., and Cross, R. 1985. Effect of electrical stimulation on postmortem changes in the activities of two calcium-dependent neutral proteinases and their inhibitors in beef muscle. *Meat Sci.* **15**, 193.

Duckworth, W. C., Heinemann, M. A., and Kitabchi, A. E. 1972. Purification of insulin-specific protease by affinity chromatography. *Proc. Natl. Acad. Sci. U.S.A.* **69**, 3698.

Duckworth, W. C., Stentz, F. B., Heinemann, M., Kitabchi, A. E. 1979. Initial site of insulin cleavage by insulin protease. *Proc. Natl. Acad. Sci. U.S.A.* **76**, 635.

Duncan, C. J. 1978. Role of intracellular calcium in promoting muscle damage: a strategy for controlling the dystrophic condition. *Experientia* **34**, 1531.

Dutson, T. R., and Lawrie, R. A. 1974. Release of lysosomal enzymes during post-mortem conditioning and their relationship to tenderness. *J. Food Technol.* **9**, 43.

Dutson, T. R., and Yates, L. D. 1978. Molecular and structural altration in bovine muscle caused by high temperature and low pH incubation. *Proc. Eur. Meat Res. Workers Conf.* **24**, E6.

Dutson, T. R., Pearson, A. M., Merkel, R. A., and Spink, G. C. 1974. Ultrastructural post-mortem changes in normal and low quality porcine muscle fibers. *J. Food Sci.* **39**, 32.

Dutson, T. R., Smith, G. C., and Carpenter, Z. L. 1980. Lysosomal enzyme distribution in electrically stimulated ovine muscle. *J. Food Sci.* **45**, 1097.

Ebashi, S., and Nonomura, Y. 1973. Proteins of the myofibril. *In* "The Structure and Function of Muscle" (G. H. Bourne, ed.), Vol. 3, p. 285. Academic Press, New York.

Ebashi, S., and Sugita, H. 1979. The role of calcium in physiological and pathological processes in skeletal muscle. *In* "Current Topics in Nerve and Muscle Research" (A. J. Aguayo and G. Karpati, eds.), p. 73. Excerpta Medica, Amsterdam.

Edmunds, T., and Pennington, R. J. T. 1981. Mast cell origin of myofibrillar protease of rat skeletal and heart muscle. *Biochim. Biophys. Acta* **661**, 28.

Ehrenreich, B. A., and Cohn, Z. A. 1969. Uptake and digestion of iodinated human serum albumin by macrophages *in vitro*. *J. Exp. Med.* **129**, 227.

Ekman, P., Hermansson, U., Bergstrom, G., and Engström, L. 1978. Rapid proteolytic removal of phosphopeptides and phosphorylatable sites from protein in rat liver cell sap. *FEBS Lett.* **86**, 250.

Elgasim, E. A., Koolmaraie, M., Kennick, W. H., and Anglemier, A. F. 1985. Combined effects of the calcium-activated factor and cathepsin D on skeletal muscle. *Food Microstruct.* **4**, 55.

Ellis, S., and Perry, M. 1966. Pituitary arylamidases and peptidases. *J. Biol. Chem.* **241**, 3619.

Ende, N., Katayama, Y., and Auditore, J. V. 1964. Multiple proteolytic enzymes in human mast cells. *Nature (London)* **201**, 1197.

Engel, F. L., and Schwartz, T. B. 1951. Adrenal cortex and peptidase activity of rat tissue. *Proc. Soc. Exp. Biol. Med.* **77**, 615.

Erickson, A. H., Conner, G. E., and Blobel, G. 1981. Biosynthesis of a lysosomal enzyme. *J. Biol. Chem.* **256**, 11224.

Etherington, D. J. 1974. The purification of bovine cathepsin B_1 and its mode of action on bovine collagens. *Biochem. J.* **137**, 547.

Etherington, D. J. 1976. Bovine spleen cathepsin B_1 and collagenolytic cathepsin. A comparative study of the properties of the two enzymes in the degradation of native collagen. *Biochem. J.* **153**, 199.

Etherington, D. J. 1977. The dissolution of insoluble bovine collagens by cathepsin B_1 collagenolytic cathepsin and pepsin. The influence of collagen type, age and chemical purity on susceptibility. *Connect. Tissue Res.* **5**, 135.

Etherington, D. J. 1980. Proteinases in connective tissue breakdown. *In* "Protein Degradation in Health and Disease" (D. Evered and J. Whelan, eds.), p. 87. *Ciba Found. Symp.* (75). Excerpta Medica, Amsterdam.

Etherington, D. J., and Dransfield, E. 1981. Enzymes in the tenderization of meat. *In* "Enzymes and Food Processing" (G. G. Birch, K. J. Parker, and N. Blakebrough, eds.), p. 279. Applied Science Publ., Barking, U.K.

Etherington, D. J., and Evans, P. J. 1977. The action of cathepsin B and collagenolytic cathepsin in the digestion of collagen. *Acta Biol. Med. Ger.* **36**, 1555.

Etherington, D. J., and Wardale, R. J. 1982. The mononuclear cell population in rat leg muscle: Its contribution to the lysosomal enzyme activities of whole muscle extracts. *J. Cell Sci.* **58**, 139.

Etlinger, J. D., and Goldberg, A. L. 1977. A soluble ATP-dependent proteolytic system responsible for the degradation of abnormal proteins in reticulocytes. *Proc. Natl. Acad. Sci. U.S.A.* **74**, 54.

Evans, P., and Etherington, D. J. 1978. Characterization of cathepsin B and collogenolytic cathepsin from human placenta. *Eur. J. Biochem.* **83**, 87.

Evans, P., and Etherington, D. J. 1979. Action of cathepsin on the oxidized β-chain of bovine insulin. *FEBS Lett.* **99**, 55.

Eyre, D. R. 1980. Collagen: Molecular diversity in body's protein scaffold. *Science* 207, 1315.

Fabiato, A., and Fabiato, F. 1979. Calcium and cardiac excitation-contraction coupling. *Annu. Rev. Physiol.* **41**, 473.

Fahrney, D. E., and Gold, A. M. 1963. Problem of the serine–histidine H bond in the active site of α-chymotrypsin. *J. Am. Chem. Soc.* **85**, 997.

Ferdinand, W., Bartley, W., and Broomhead, V. 1973. Amino acid production in isolated rat liver mitochondria. *Biochem. J.* **134**, 431.

Filkins, J. P. 1970. Lysosomes and hepatic regression during fasting. *Am. J. Physiol.* **219**, 923.

Findlay, C. J., and Stanley, D. W. 1984a. Differential scanning calorimetry of beef: Influence of sarcomere length. *J. Food Sci.* **49**, 1529.

Findlay, C. J., and Stanley, D. W. 1984b. Differential scanning calorimetry of beef: Influence of postmortem conditioning. *J. Food Sci.* **49**, 1513.

Fischer, F., and Abderhalden, E. 1905. Uber das Verhalten verschiedener Polypeptide gegen Pankreassaft und Magensaft. *Z. Physiol. Chem.* **46**, 52.

Fitton-Jackson, S. 1964. Connective tissue cells. *Cell* **6**, 387.

Fitzpatrick, K., Park, D. C., Pennington, R. J., Robinson, J. E., and Worsfold, M. 1968. Further studies on muscle cathepsins. *In* "Research in Muscular Dystrophy" (Research Committee of Muscular Dystrophy Group, eds.), p. 374. Pitman, London.

Flaim, K. E., Li, J. B., and Jefferson, L. S. 1978a. Protein turnover in rat skeletal muscle: Effects of hypophysectomy and growth hormone. *Am. J. Physiol.* **234**, E38.

Flaim, K. E., Li, J. B., and Jefferson, L. S. 1978b. Effect of thyroxine on protein turnover in rat skeletal muscle. *Am. J. Physiol.* **235**, E231.

Franklin, S. G., and Metrione, R. M. 1972. Chromatographic evidences for the existance of multiple forms of cathepsin B1. *Biochem. J.* **127**, 207.

Franzblau, C., and Faris, B. 1982. Biosynthesis of insoluble elastin in cell and organ cultures. *In* "Methods in Enzymology" (L. W. Cunningham and D. W. Frederiksen, eds.), Vol. 92, Part A, p. 615. Academic Press, New York.

Fritz, P. J., White, E. L., Pruitt, K. M., and Vesel, E. S. 1973. Lactase dehydrogenase isoenzymes. Turnover in rat heart, skeletal muscle, and liver. *Biochemistry* **12**, 4034.

Fritz, P. J., White, E. L., and Osterman, J. 1975. Protein turnover during development. *In* "Intracellular Protein Turnover" (R. T. Schimke and N. Katunuma, eds.), p. 135. Academic Press, New York.

Fruton, J. S. 1980. Fluorescence studies on the active sites of proteinases. *Mol. Cell. Biochem.* **32**, 105.

Fruton, J. S., and Mycek, M. 1956. Studies on beef spleen cathepsin C. *Arch. Biochem. Biophys.* **65**, 11.

Fruton, J. S., Irving, G. W., Jr., and Bergmann, M. 1941. Classification of the cathepsins. *J. Biol. Chem.* **141**, 763.

Fujii, K., and Maruyama, K. 1982. Existance of lysine-derived cross-linking in connectin, an elastic protein in muscle. *Biochem. Biophys. Res. Commun.* **104**, 633.

Fujii, K., Kimura, S., and Maruyama, K. 1978. Cross-linking of connectin, an elastic protein in muscle. *Biochem. Biophys. Res. Commun.* **81**, 1248.

Fujimaki, M., and Deatherage, F. E. 1964. Chromatographic fractionation of sarcoplasmic proteins of beef skeletal muscle on ion-exchange cellulose. *J. Food Sci.* **29**, 316.

Fujimaki, M., Okitani, A., and Arakawa, N. 1965. The changes of myosin B during storage of rabbit muscle. *Agric. Biol. Chem.* **29**, 581.

Fulks, R. M., Li, J. B., and Goldberg, A. L. 1975. Effects of insulin, glucose and amino acids on protein turnover in rat diaphragm. *J. Biol. Chem.* **250**, 290.

Funabiki, R., and Cassens, R. G. 1972. Heterogeneous turnover of myofibrillar proteins. *Nature (London) New Biol.* **236**, 249.

Funabiki, R., and Cassens, R. G. 1973. Asynchronous turnover of the thin filaments proteins, actin, tropomyosin and troponine by a continous double isotopse method. *J. Nutr. Sci. Vitaminol. (Tokyo)* **19**, 361.

Furia, T. E. 1975. Sequestrants in foods. *In* "CRC Handbook of Food Additive," Part 1, p. 289. CRC Press, Cleveland, Ohio.

Gaetjens, E., and Barany, M. 1966. N-Acetylaspartic acid in G-actin. *Biochim. Biophys. Acta* **117**, 176.

Gan, J. C., and Jeffay, H. 1967. Origins and metabolism of the intracellular amino acid pools in the rat liver and muscle. *Biochim. Biophys. Acta* **148**, 448.

Gan, J. C., and Jeffay, H. 1971. The kinetics of transfer of plasma amino acids to tissues, and the turnover rates of liver and muscle proteins. *Biochim. Biophys. Acta* **252**, 125.

Gann, G. L., and Merkel, R. A. 1978. Ultrastructural changes in bovine longissimus muscle during post-mortem aging. *Meat Sci.* **2**, 129.

Gardell, S. J., and Tate, S. S. 1979. Latent proteinase activity of γ-glutamyl transpeptidase light subunit. *J. Biol. Chem.* **254**, 4942.

Garrells, J. I., Elgin, S. C. R., and Bonner, J. 1972. A histone protease of rat liver chromatin. *Biochem. Biophys. Res. Commun.* **46**, 545.

Garlick, J. P., Millward, D. J., James, W. P. T., and Waterlow, J. C. 1975. The effect of protein deprivation and starvation on the rate of protein synthesis in tissues of the rat. *Biochim. Biophys. Acta* **414**, 71.

Gawronski, T. H., Spencer, J. V., and Publolis, M. H. 1967. Changes in sulfhydryl and disulfide content of chicken muscle and the effect of N-ethylmaleimide. *J. Agric. Food Chem.* **15**, 781.

Geisler, N., Kaufmann, E., and Weber, K. 1982. Proteinchemical characterization of three structurally distinct domains along the protofilament unit of desmin 10 nm filaments. *Cell* **30**, 277.

George, A. R., Bendall, J. R., and Jones, R. C. D. 1980. The tenderizing effect of electrical stimulation of beef carcasses. *Meat Sci.* **4**, 51.

Gerard, K. W., and Schneider, D. L. 1980. Protein turnover in muscle: Inhibitions of the calcium activated proteinase by mersalyl without inhibition of the rate of protein degradation. *Biochem. Biophys. Res. Commun.* **94**, 1353.

Gerber, A. C., Carson, J. H., and Hadorn, B. 1974. Partial purification and characterization of a chymotrypsin-like enzyme from human neutrophil leucocytes. *Biochim. Biophys. Acta* **364**, 103.

Ghetie, V., and Mihaescu, S. 1973. The hydrolysis of rabbit immunoglobin G with purified cathepsin D and E. *Immunochemistry* **10**, 251.

Gibson, W. T., Milson, D. W., Steven, F. S., and Lowe, J. S. 1976. The subcellular location of a collagenolytic cathepsin in rabbit peritoneal polymorphonuclear leucocytes. *Biochem. Soc. Trans.* **4**, 628.

Gohda, E., and Pitot, H. C. 1980. Purification and characterization of a factor catalyzing the conversion of the multiple forms of tyrosine aminotransferase from rat liver. *J. Biol. Chem.* **255**, 7371.

Gohda, E., and Pitot, H. C. (1981). A new thiol proteinase from rat liver. *J. Biol. Chem.* **256**, 2567.

Goldberg, A. L. 1980. The regulation of protein turnover by endocrine and nutritional factors. *In* "Plasticity of Muscle" (D. Petta, ed.), p. 469. De Gruyter, New York.

Goldberg, A. L., and Dice, J. F. 1974. Intracellular protein degradation in mammalian and bacterial cells. *Annu. Rev. Biochem.* **43**, 835.

Goldberg, A. L., and Griffin, G. E. 1977. Hormonal control of protein synthesis and degradation in skeletal muscle (rat). *J. Physiol. (London)* **270**, 51P.

Goldberg, A. L., and St. John, A. C., Jr. 1976. Intracellular protein degradation in mammalian and bacterial cells. *Annu. Rev. Biochem.* **45**, 747.

Goldberg, A. L., Griffin, G. E., and Dice, J. F. 1977. Regulation of protein turnover in normal and dystrophic muscle. *In* "Pathogenesis of Human Muscular Dystrophies" (L. P. Rowland, ed.), p. 376. Excerpta Medica, Amsterdam.

Goldberg, A. L., Voellmy, R., and Swamy, K. H. S. 1979. Studies of the pathway for protein degradation in *E. coli* and mammalian cells. *In* "Biological Functions of Proteinases" (H. Helzer and H. Tschesche, eds.), p. 35. Springer-Verlag, Berlin and New York.

Goldberg, A. L., Tischler, M., DeMartino, G., and Griffin, G. 1980. Hormonal regulation of protein degradation and synthesis in skeletal muscle. *Fed. Proc., Fed. Am. Soc. Exp. Biol.* **39**, 31.

Goldberg, A. L., Etlinger, J. D., Goldspink, D. F., and Jablecki, C. K. 1975. Mechanism of work-induced hypertrophy of skeletal muscle. *Med. Sci. Sports* **7**, 248.

Goldman, R. 1973. Dipeptide hydrolysis within intact lysosomes *in vitro*. *FEBS Lett.* **33**, 208.

Goldspink, D. F. 1978. Influence of passive stretch on the growth and protein turnover of the denervated extensor digitorium longus muscle. *Biochem. J.* **174**, 595.

Goldspink, D. F. 1986. Muscle proteinase activities during compensatory growth atrophy. *Experientia* **42**, 133.

Goldspink, D. F., Harris, J. B., Park, D. C., and Pennington, R. J. 1970. Quantitative enzyme studies in extensor digitorum longus and solenus muscles of rats. *Enzymol. Biol. Clin.* **11**, 481.

Goldspink, D. F., Harris, J. B., Park, D. C., Parsons, M.E., and Pennington, R. J. 1971. Quantitative enzyme studies in denervated extensor digitorum longus and soleus muscles of rats. *Int. J. Biochem.* **2**, 427.

Goldstone, A., and Koenig, H. 1974. Synthesis and turnover of lysosomal glycoproteins. Relation to the molecular heterogeniety of the lysosomal enzymes. *FEBS Lett.* **39**, 176.

Goll, D. E., and Robson, R. M. 1967. Myofibrillar nucleosidetriphosphatase activity of bovine muscle. *J. Food Sci.* **32**, 323.

Goll, D. E., Arakawa, N., Stromer, M. H., Busch, W. A., and Robson, R. M. 1970. Chemistry of muscle proteins as a food. *In* "The Physiology and Biochemistry of Muscle as a Food" (E. J. Briskey, R. G. Cassens, and B. B. Marsh, eds.), p. 755. Univ. of Wisconsin Press, Madison.

Goll, D. E., Okitani, A., Dayton, W. R., and Reville, W. J. 1978. A Ca^{++}-activated muscle protease in myofibrillar protein turnover. *In* "Protein Turnover and Lysosome Function" (H. L. Segal and D. J. Doyle, eds.), p. 587. Academic Press, New York.

Goll, D. E., Otsuka, Y., Nagainis, P. D., Shannon, J. D., Sathe, S. K., and Muguruma, M. 1983. Role of muscle proteinases in maintenance of muscle integrity and mass. *J. Food Biochem.* **7**, 137.

Gomori, G. 1954. The histochemistry of mucopolysaccharides. *Br. J. Exp. Pathol.* **35**, 377.

Goodall, F. R. 1965. Degradative enzymes in the utrine myometrium of rabbits under different hormonal conditions. *Arch. Biochem. Biophys.* **112**, 403.

Gorski, J., and Worowski, K. 1982. Effect of motor activity on cathepsin D activity in rat muscles. *Acta Physiol. (Pol.)* **33**, 485.

Gothard, R. H., Mullins, A. M., Boulware, R. F., and Hansard, S. L. 1966. Histological studies of post-mortem changes in sarcomere length as related to bovine muscle tenderness. *J. Food Sci.* **31**, 120.

Greenbaum, L. M., and Fruton, J. S. 1957. Purification and properties of beef spleen cathepsin B. *J. Biol. Chem.* **226**, 173.

Greenbaum, L. M., and Sherman, R. 1962. Studies on cathepsin carboxypeptidase. *J. Biol. Chem.* **237**, 1082.

Griffin, W. S. T., and Wildenthal, K. 1978. Myofibrillar alkaline protease activity in rat heart and its responses to some interventions that alter cardiac size. *J. Mol. Cell. Cardiol.* **10**, 669.

Grinde, E., and Seglen, P. O. 1980. Differential effects of proteinase inhibitors and amines on the lysosomal and non-lysosomal pathways of protein degradation in isolated rat hepatocytes. *Biochim. Biophys. Acta* **632**, 73.

Guroff, G. 1964. A neutral, calcium-activated proteinase from the soluble fraction of rat brain. *J. Biol. Chem.* **239**, 149.

Gutmann, H. R., and Fruton, J. S. 1948. An intracellular enzyme related to chymotrypsin. *J. Biol. Chem.* **174**, 851.

Haas, R., Nagasawa, T., and Heinrich, P. C. 1977. The localization of a proteinase within rat liver mitochondria. *Biochem. Biophys. Res. Commun.* **74**, 1060.

Haas, R., Heinrich, P. C., Tesch, R., and Witt, I. 1978. Cleavage specificity of the serine protease from rat liver mitochondria. *Biochem. Biophys. Res. Commun.* **85**, 1039.

Haas, R., Heinrich, P. C., and Sasse, D. 1979. Proteolytic enzymes of rat liver mitochondria— Evidence for a mast cell origin. *FEBS Lett.* **103**, 168.

Hajek, I., Gutmann, E., and Syrovy, I. 1963. Proteolytic activity in denervated and reinnervated muscle. *Physiol. Bohemoslov.* **13**, 32.

Hajek, I., Gutmann, E., and Syrový, I. 1965. Proteolytic activity in muscles of old animals. *Physiol. Bohemoslov.* **14**, 481.

Hannappel, E., MacGregor, J. S., Davoust, S., and Horecker, B. L. 1982. Limited proteolysis of liver and muscle aldolases. *Arch. Biochem. Biophys.* **214**, 293.

Hara, K., Ichihara, Y., and Takahashi, K. 1983. Purification and characterization of a calcium-activated neutral protease from monkey cardiac muscle. *J. Biochem. (Tokyo)* **93**, 1435.

Haralambie, G., and Berg, A. 1976. Resting muscle levels and the influence of exercise on serum amino acid arylpeptidase activity in man. *Eur. J. Appl. Physiol.* **36**, 39.

Hardy, M. F., and Pennington, R. J. T. 1979. Separation of cathepsin B$_1$ and related enzymes from rat skeletal muscle. *Biochim. Biophys. Acta* **527**, 253.

Hardy, M. F., Parsons, M. E., and Pennington, R. J. 1975. Separation of some peptide hydrolases from skeletal muscle. *Int. Symp. Intracell. Protein Catabolism, 2nd* Ljubljana, Yugoslavia, p. 25.

Hardy, M. F., Parsons, M. F., and Pennington, R. J. 1977. Separation of some possible peptide hydrolases from skeletal muscle. *In* "Intracellular Protein Catabolism" (V. Turk and M. Marks, eds.), p. 209. Plenum, New York.

Harpel, P. C. 1973. Human plasmid α_2-macroglobin–enzyme interaction. Evidence for proteolytic modification of the subunit chain structure. *J. Exp. Med.* **138**, 508.

Harris, E. D., Jr., and Cartwright, E. C. 1977. Mammalian collagenase. *In* "Proteinases in Mammalian Cells and Tissues" (A. J. Barrett, ed.), p. 249. North-Holland, Amsterdam.

Harris, E. D., Jr., and Krane, S. M. 1974. Collagenases. *New Engl. J. Med.* **291**, 557, 605, 652.

Harris, E. D., Jr., Vater, C. A., Mainardi, C. L., and Siegel, R. C. 1980. Degradation of cartilage collegen—Factors affecting substrate and enzyme. *In* "Biology of Articular Cartilage in Health and Disease" (G. Helmuth, ed.), p. 175. Schattauer, Stuttgart.

Hartley, B. S. 1960. Proteolytic enzymes. *Annu. Rev. Biochem.* **29**, 45.

Hartshorne, D. J. 1983. Calmodulin in skeletal muscle. *J. Food Biochem.* **7**, 211.

Hashida, S., Towatari, T., Kominami, E., and Katunuma, N. 1980. Inhibitions by E-64 derivatives of rat liver cathepsin B and cathepsin L *in vitro* and *in vivo*. J. Biochem. (Tokyo) **88**, 1805.

Hashida, S., Kominami, E., and Katunuma, N. 1982. Inhibition of cathepsin B and cathepsin L by E-64 *in vivo*. *J. Biochem. (Tokyo)* **91**, 1373.

Hathaway, D. R., Werth, D. K., and Haeberle, J. R. 1982. Limited autolysis reduces the Ca^{++}-requirement of a smooth muscle Ca^{++}-activated protease. *J. Biol. Chem.* **257**, 9072.

Havemann, K., and Janoff, A., eds. 1978. "Neutral Proteases of Human Polymorphonuclear Leukocytes." Urban & Schwartzenberg, Munich.

Hay, J. D., Currie, R. W., and Wolfe, F. H. 1972. The effect of aging on physiochemical properties of actomyosin from chicken breast and leg muscle. *J. Food Sci.* **37**, 346.

Hay, J. D., Currie, R. W., and Wolfe, F. H. 1973a. Effect of post-mortem aging on chicken muscle fibrils. *J. Food Sci.* **38**, 981.

Hay, J. D., Currie, R. W., and Wolfe, F. H. 1973b. Polyacrylamide disc gel electrophoresis of fresh and aged chicken muscle proteins in sodium dodecylsulfate. *J. Food Sci.* **38**, 987.

Hedin, S. G. 1904. Investigation on the proteolytic enzymes of the spleen of the ox. *J. Physiol. (London)* **30**, 155.

Heinrich, P. C., Haas, R., and Sasse, D. 1979. Localization and some properties of a proteinase and a carboxypeptidase from rat liver. *In* "Biological Functions of Proteinases" (H. Holzer and H. Tschesche, eds.), p. 120, Springer-Verlag, Berlin and New York.

Henderson, D. W., Goll, D. E., and Stromer, M. H. 1970. A comparison of shortening and Z-line degradation in post-mortem bovine, porcine and rabbit muscle. *Am. J. Anat.* **128**, 117.

Henrickson, R. L., and Asghar, A. 1985. Cold-storage energy aspects of electrically stimulated hot-boned meat. *Adv. Meat Res.* **1**, 237.

Herring, H. K., Cassens, R. G., and Briskey, E. J. 1967. Factors affecting collagen solubility in bovine muscles. *J. Food Sci.* **32**, 534.

Hirado, M., Iwata, D., Niinobe, M., and Fujii, S. 1981. Purification and properties of thiol protease inhibitor from rat liver cytosol. *Biochim. Biophys. Acta* **669**, 21.

Hirao, T., Hara, K., and Takahashi, K. 1983. Degradation of neuropeptides by Ca^{++}-activated neutral protease. *J. Biochem. (Tokyo)* **94**, 2071.

Hirao, T., Hara, K., and Takahashi, K. 1984. Purification and characterization of cathepsin B from monkey skeletal muscle. *J. Biochem. (Tokyo)* **95**, 871.

Hoffstein, S., Gennaro, D. E., Weissman, G., Hirsch, J., Streuli, F., and Fox, A. C. 1975. Cytochemical localization of lysosomal enzyme activity in normal and ischemic myocardium. *Am. J. Pathol.* **79**, 193.

Hofmann, K., and Hamm, R. 1978. Sulfhydryl and disulfide groups in meat. *Adv. Food Res.* **24**, 1.

Holmes, D., Parsons, M. E., Park, D. C., and Pennington, R. J. 1971. An alkaline protease in muscle homogenates. *Biochem. J.* **125**, 98P.

Hook, C. W., Bull, F. G., Iwanij, V., and Brown, S. I. 1972. Purification of corneal collagenases. *Invest. Ophthalmol.* **11**, 728.

Hopgood, M. F., Clark, M. G., and Ballard, F. J. 1977. Inhibition of protein degradation in isolated rat hepatocytes. *Biochem. J.* **164**, 399.

Hopgood, M. F., Clark, M. G., and Ballard, F. J. 1980. Protein degradation in hepatocyte monolayers. Effect of glucagon, adenosine $3':5$-cyclic monophosphate and insulin. *Biochem. J.* **186**, 71.

Hsiech, Y. P. C., Pearson, A. M., and Magee, W. T. 1980. Development of synthetic meat flavor mixture by using surface response methodology. *J. Food Sci.* **45**, 1125.

Huang, J. S., Huang, S. S., and Tang, J. 1979. Cathepsin D isozymes from porcine spleens. Large scale purification and polypeptide chain arrangements. *J. Biol. Chem.* **254**, 11405.

Huang, J. S., Huang, S. S., and Tang, J. 1980. Structure and function of cathepsin D. *In* "Enzyme Regulation and Mechanism of Action" (P. Mildner and B. Ries, eds.), p. 289. Pergamon, Oxford.

Huisman, W., Bouma, J. M. W., and Gruber, M. 1973. Influence of thiols, ATP, and CoA on protein breakdown by subcellular fractions from rat liver. *Biochim. Biophys. Acta* **297**, 93.

Huisman, W., Lanting, L., Bouma, J. M. W., and Gruber, M. 1974a. Proteolysis and neutral pH in a lysosomal–cytosol system cannot be attributed to the uptake of proteins into lysosomes. *FEBS Lett.* **44**, 129.

Huisman, W., Lanting, L., Doddema, H. J., Bouma, J. M. W., and Gruber, M. 1974b. Role of individual cathepsins in lysosomal protein digestion as tested by specific inhibitors. *Biochim. Biophys. Acta* **370**, 297.

Husain, S. S., and Baqai, J. 1976. Evidence for two types of sulfhydryl groups in cathepsins B_1 and BIA. *Fed. Proc., Fed. Am. Soc. Exp. Biol.* **35**, 1460.

Huston, R. B., and Krebs, E. G. 1968. Activation of skeletal muscle phosphorylase kinase by Ca^{++}. II. Identification of the kinase activating factor as a proteolytic enzyme. *Biochemistry* **7**, 2116.

Huxley, H. E., and Brown, W. 1967. The low-angle X-ray diagram of vertebrate striated muscle and its behavior during contraction and rigor. *J. Mol. Biol.* **30**, 383.

Huxley, H. E., and Hanson, J. 1954. Changes in the cross-striation of muscle during contraction and stretch and their structural interpretation. *Nature (London)* **173**, 973.

Ikeuchi, Y., Ito, T., and Fukazawa, T. 1980. Changes in the properties of myofibrillar proteins during post-mortem storage of muscle at high temperature. *J. Agric. Food Chem.* **28**, 1197.

Inomata, M., Hayashi, M., Nakamura, M., Imahori, K., and Kawashima, S. 1983. Purification and characterization of a calcium-activated neutral protease from rabbit skeletal muscle which requires calcium ions of micro-M order concentration. *J. Biochem. (Tokyo)* **93**, 291.

Iodice, A. A., and Weinstock, I. M. 1964. Purification and properties of a proteolytic enzyme from normal and dystrophic muscle. *Fed. Proc., Fed. Am. Soc. Exp. Biol.* **23**, 544.

Iodice, A. A., and Weinstock, I. M. 1965. Cathepsin A in nutritional and hereditary muscular dystrophy. *Nature (London)* **207**, 1102.

Iodice, A. A., Leong, V., and Weinstock, I. M. 1966. Separation of cathepsins A and D of skeletal muscle. *Arch. Biochem. Biophys.* **117**, 477.

Iodice, A. A., Chin, J., Perker, S., and Weinstock, I. M. 1972. Cathepsins A, B, C, D and autolysis during development of breast muscle of normal and dystrophic chicken. *Arch. Biochem. Biophys.* **152**, 166.

Ishikawa, H., Bischoff, R., and Holtzer, H. 1968. Mitosis and intermediate-size filaments in developing skeletal muscle. *J. Cell Biol.* **38**, 538.

Ishiura, S., Murofushi, H., Suzuki, K., and Imahori, K. 1978. Studies of a calcium-activated neutral protease from chicken skeletal muscle. *J. Biochem. (Tokyo)* **84**, 225.

Ishiura, S., Sugita, H., Suzuki, K., and Imahori, I. 1979. Studies of a calcium-activated neutral protease from chicken skeletal muscle. II. Substrate specificity. *J. Biochem. (Tokyo)* **86**, 579.

Ishiura, S., Sugita, H., Nonaka, I., and Imahori, I. 1980. Calcium-activated neutral protease. Its localization in myofibril, especially at the Z-band. *J. Biochem. (Tokyo)* **87**, 343.

Ishiura, S., Hanada, K., Tamai, M., Kashiwagi, K., and Sugita, H. 1981. The effect of an *in vivo*-injected thiol protease inhibitor, E-64-C, on the calcium-induced degradation of myofilaments. *J. Biochem. (Tokyo)* **90**, 1557.

Jacoby, M. 1900. Ueber die fermentative Eiweisspaltung und Ammoniakbildung in der Leber. *Z. Physiol. Chem.* **30**, 149.

Jacobsson, K. 1953. Trypsin inhibitors in blood serum. *Scand. J. Clin. Lab. Invest.* **5**, 97.

Jansen, E. F., Nutting, M. D. F., Jang, R., and Ball, A. K. 1949. Inhibition of the proteinase and esterase activities of trypsin and chymotrypsin by diisopropyl fluorophosphate: Crystalization of inhibited chymotrypsin. *J. Biol. Chem.* **179**, 189.

Järvinen, M. 1979. Purification and some characteristics of two human serum proteins inhibiting papain and other thiol proteinases. *FEBS Lett.* **108**, 461.

Järvinen, M., and Hopsu-Havu, V. K. 1975. α-N-Benzoylarginine-2-naphthylamide hydrolase (cathespin B_1?) from rat skin. *Acta Chem. Scand.* **B9**, 772.

Jasani, B., Jasani, M. K., and Talbot, M. D. 1978. Characterization of two acid proteinases found in rabbit skin homografts. *Biochem. J.* **169**, 287.

Jefferson, L. S., Rannels, D. E., Munger, B. L., and Morgan, H. E. 1974. Insulin in the regulation of protein turnover in heart and skeletal muscle. *Fed. Proc., Fed. Am. Soc. Exp. Biol.* **33**, 1098.

Joffe, M., Savage, N., and Isaacs, H. 1981. Increased muscle calcium. A possible cause of mitochondrial disfunction and cellular necrosis in denervated rat skeletal muscle. *Biochem. J.* **196**, 663.

Jones, J. M. 1972. Studies on chicken actomyosin. Effect of storage on muscle enzymic and physicochemical properties. *J. Sci. Food Agric.* **23**, 1009.

Jones, T. L., Ogunro, E. A., Samarel, A. M., Ferguson, A. G., and Lesch, M. 1983. Susceptibilities of cardiac myofibrillar proteins to cathepsin D-catalyzed degradation. *Am. J. Physiol.* **245**, H294.

Joseph, R. L., and Sanders, W. J. 1966. Leucine amino peptidase in extracts of swine muscle. *Biochem. J.* **100**, 827.

Jusić, M., Seifert, S., Weiss, E., Hass, R., and Heinrich, P. C. 1976. Isolation and characterization of a membrane-bound proteinase from rat liver. *Arch. Biochem. Biophys.* **177**, 355.

Kalinskii, M. I. 1985. [3,′,5′-AMP-dependent regulation of cathepsin D release from skeletal muscle lysosomes and heart lysosomes during muscle activity]. *Tartu Riikliku Ulik. Toim* **702,** 115 (in Russian); cited in *Chem. Abstr.* **104,** 146252w.

Kameyama, T., and Etlinger, J. D. 1979. Calcium-dependent regulation of protein synthesis and degradation in muscle. *Nature (London)* **279,** 344.

Kar, N. C., and Pearson, C. M. 1976a. A calcium-activated neutral protease in normal and dystrophic human muscle. *Clin. Chim. Acta* **73,** 293.

Kar, N. C., and Pearson, C. M. 1976b. Arylamidase and cathepsin-A activity of normal and dystrophic human muscle. *Proc. Soc. Exp. Biol. Med.* **151,** 583.

Kar, N. C., and Pearson, C. M. 1977. Early elevation of cathepsin B_1 in human muscle disease. *Biochem. Med.* **18,** 126.

Kar, N. C., and Pearson, C. M. 1978. Muscular dystrophy and activation of proteinases. *Muscle Nerve* **1,** 308.

Kärgel, H. J., Dettmer, R., Etzold, G., Kirschke, H., Bohley, P., and Langner, J. 1980. Action of cathespin L on the oxidized B-chain of bovine insulin. *FEBS Lett.* **114,** 257.

Katunuma, N., and Kominami, E. 1977. Group-specific proteinases for apoproteins of pyridoxal enzymes. *In* "Proteinases in Mammalian Cells and Tissues" (A. J. Barrett, ed.), p. 151. North-Holland, Amsterdam.

Katunuma, N., and Kominami, E. 1983. Structure and functions of lysosomal thiol proteinases and their endogenous inhibitor. *Curr. Top. Cell. Regul.* **22,** 71.

Katunuma, N., and Kominami, E. 1985a. Lysosomal sequestration of cytosolic enzymes and lysosomal thiol cathepsin. *Adv. Enzyme Regul.* **23,** 159.

Katunuma, N., and Kominami, E. 1985b. Molecular basis of intracellular regulation of thiol proteinase inhibitors. *Curr. Top. Cell. Regul.* **27,** 345.

Katunuma, N., Kominami, E., Kobayashi, K., Banno, Y., Szukui, K., Chichibu, K., Hamaguchi, Y., and Katsunuma, T. 1975. Studies on new intracellular proteases in various of rat. *Eur. J. Biochem.* **52,** 37.

Katunuma, N., Sanada, Y., Kominami, E., Kobayashi, K., and Banno, Y. 1977. Intracellular protein catabolism and new serine proteases. *Acta Biol. Med. Ger.* **36,** 1537.

Katunuma, N., Yasogawa, N., Kito, K., Sanada, Y., Kawai, H., and Miyoshu, K. 1978. Abnormal expression of a serine proteinase in human dystrophic muscle. *J. Biochem (Tokyo)* **83,** 625.

Katunuma, N., Towatari, T., Tamai, M., and Hanada, K. 1983. Use of new synthetic substrates for assays of cathepsin L and cathepsin B. *J. Biochem. (Tokyo)* **93,** 1129.

Kaur, H., and Sanwal, B. D. 1981. Regulation of the activity of a calcium-activated neutral protease during differentiation of skeletal myoblasts. *Can. J. Biochem.* **59,** 743.

Kawashima, S., Nomoto, M., Hayashi, M., Inomata, M., Nakamura, M., and Imahori, K. 1984. Comparison of calcium-activated neutral proteases from skeletal muscle of rabbit and chicken. *J. Biochem. (Tokyo)* **95,** 95.

Kawiak, J., Vensel, W. H., Komender, J., and Barnard, E. A. 1971. Chymotrypsin-like properties from rat mast cells. *Biochim. Biophys. Acta* **235,** 172.

Kay, J. 1978. Biochemical reviews. Intracellular protein degradation. *Biochem. Soc. Trans.* **6,** 789.

Kazakova, O. V., and Orekhovich, V. N. 1972. Study of functionally active group of D cathepsins. *Biochem. U.S.S.R.* (Engl. transl.) **37,** 859.

Kazakova, O. V., Orekhovich, V. N., Pourchot, L., and Schuck, J. M. 1972. Effect of cathepsins D from normal and malignant tissues on synthetic peptides. *J. Biol. Chem.* **247,** 4224.

Keil, B. 1980. The structure–function relationship of collagenolytic enzymes. *In* "Enzyme Regulation and Mechanism of Action" (P. Mildner and B. Ries, eds.), p. 351. Pergamon, Oxford.

Keilová, H. 1971. On the specificity and inhibition of cathepsin D and B. *In* "Tissue Proteinases" (A. J. Barrett and J. T. Dingle, eds.). North-Holland, Amsterdam.

Keilová, H., and Tomásek, V. 1973. On the isozymes of cathepsin B_1. FEBS Lett. **29,** 335.

Keilová, H., and Turková, J. 1970. Analogy between active sites of cathepsin B_1 and papain. FEBS Lett. **11,** 287.

Keilová, H., Bláha, K., and Keil, B. 1968. Effect of steric factors on digestibility of peptides containing aromatic amino acids by cathepsin D and pepsin. Eur. J. Biochem. **4,** 442.

King, F. J. 1966. Ultracentrifugal analysis of changes in the composition of myofibrillar protein extracts obtained from fresh and frozen cod muscle. J. Food Sci. **31,** 649.

King, N. L. 1984. Breakdown of connectin during cooking of meat. Meat Sci. **11,** 27.

King, N. L., and Harris, P. V. 1982. Heat-induced tenderization of meat by endogenous carboxyl proteases. Meat Sci. **6,** 137.

Kirschke, H., Langner, J., Wiederanders, B., Ansorge, S., Bohley, P., and Hanson, H. 1973. Cathepsin L, and proteinases with cathepsin B_1-like activity from rat liver lysosome. In "Intracellular Protein Catabolism" (H. Hanson and P. Bohley, eds.), p. 210. Barth; Leipzig.

Kirschke, H., Langer, J., Wiederanders, B., Ansorge, S., Bohley, P., and Broghammer, U. 1976. Intrazellularer Proteinabbau. VII. Kathepsin L und H: Zwei neue Proteinasen aus Rattenleberlysosomen. Acta Biol. Med. Ger. **35,** 285.

Kirschke, H., Langner, J., Wiederanders, B., Ansorge, S., Bohley, P., and Hanson, H. 1977a. Cathepsin L and cathepsin B_3 from rat liver lysosomes. In "Intracellular Protein Catabolisms II" (V. Turk and N. Marks, eds.), p. 299. Plenum, New York.

Kirschke, H., Langner, J., Wiederanders, B., Ansorge, S., Bohley, P., and Hansen, H. 1977b. Cathepsin H: An endoaminopeptidase from rat liver lysosomes. Acta Biol. Med. (Ger.) **36,** 185.

Kirschke, H., Langner, J., Wiederanders, B., Ansorge, S., and Bohley, P. 1977c. Cathepsin L. A new proteinase from rat-liver lysosomes. Eur. J. Biochem. **74,** 293.

Kirschke, H., Langner, J., Siemann, S., Wiederanders, B., Ansorge, S., and Bohley, P. 1980. Lysosomal cystein proteinases. In "Protein Degradation in Health and Disease" (D. Evered and J. Whelan, eds.), p. 15. Ciba Found. Symp. Ser. (75). Excerpta Medica, Amsterdam.

Kirschke, H., Kargel, H. J., Riemann, S., and Bohley, P. 1981. Cathepsin L. In "Proteinases and Their Inhibitors" (V. Turk and Lj. Vitale, eds.), p. 93. Pergamon, Oxford.

Kirschke, H., Kembhari, A. A., Bohley, P., and Barrett, A. J. 1982. Action of rat liver cathepsin L on collagen and other substrates. Biochem. J. **201,** 367.

Kirschke, H., Wood, L., Roisen, F. J., and Bird, J. W. 1983. Activity of lysosomal cysteine proteinase during differentiation of rat skeletal muscle. Biochem. J. **214,** 871.

Kleese, W. C., Goll, D. E., and Shannon, J. D. 1985. Localization of the Ca^{++}-dependent proteinase and its protein inhibitor. J. Cell Biol. **106,** 42a (Abstr).

Knapp, H. R., Oelz, O., Roberts, L. J., Sweetman, B. J., Oates, J., and Reed, P. W. 1977. Ionophores stimulate prostaglandin and thromboxane biosynthesis. Proc. Natl. Acad. Sci. U.S.A. **74,** 4251.

Knight, C. G. 1977. Principles of the design and use of synthetic substrates and inhibitors for tissue proteinases. In "Proteinases in Mammalian Cells and Tissues" (A. J. Barrett, ed.), p. 583. North-Holland, Amsterdam.

Knight, C. G., and Barrett, A. J. 1976. Interaction of human cathepsin D with the inhibitor pepstatin. Biochem. J. **155,** 117.

Knook, D. L. 1974. Distribution of lysosomal enzyme activities between parenchymal and non-parenchymal cells from rat liver. Hoppe Seylers Z. Physiol. Chem. **355,** 1217.

Knowles, S. E., and Ballard, F. J. 1976. Selective control of the degradation of normal and aberrant proteins in Reuber H_{35} hepatoma cells. Biochem. J. **156,** 609.

Kobayashi, K., Sanada, Y., and Katunuma, N. 1978. Selective cleavage of peptide bonds by a serine protease from rat skeletal muscle. J. Biochem. **84,** 477.

Kohama, K. 1980. Heterogeneity of amino acid incorporation rate in adult skeletal muscle actin. J. Biochem. (Tokyo) **87,** 977.

Kohama, K. 1981. Amino acid incorporation rates into myofibrillar proteins of dystrophic chicken skeletal muscle. *J. Biochem. (Tokyo)* **90**, 497.

Kohn, R. R. 1969. A proteolytic system involving myofibrils and a soluble factor from normal and atrophying muscle. *Lab. Invest.* **20**, 202.

Koizumi, T. 1974. Turnover rates of structural proteins of rabbit skeletal muscle. *J. Biochem. (Tokyo)* **76**, 431.

Kominami, E., Wakamatsu, N., and Katunuma, N. 1982a. Endogenous thiol protease inhibitor from rat liver. *Acta Biol. Med. Ger.* **41**, 69.

Kominami, E., Wakamatsu, N., and Katunuma, N. 1982b. Purification and characterization of thiol proteinase inhibitor from rat liver. *J. Biol. Chem.* **257**, 14648.

Koohmaraie, M., Kennick, W. H., Elgasim, E. A., and Anglemier, A. F. 1984. Effect of post-mortem storage on muscle protein degradation: Analysis by SDS–polyacrylamide gel electrophoresis. *J. Food Sci.* **49**, 292.

Koohmaraie, M., Schollmeyer, J. E., and Dutson, T. R. 1986. Effect of low-calcium requiring calcium-activated factor on myofibrils under varying pH and temperature conditions. *J. Food Sci.* **51**, 28.

Koohmaraie, M., Slidman, S. C., Schollmeyer, J. E., Dutson, T. R., and Crouse, J. D. 1987a. Effect of post-mortem storage on Ca^{++}-dependent proteases, their inhibitor and myofibril fragmentation. *Meat Sci.* **19**, 187.

Koohmaraie, M., Seidman, S. C., Schollmeyer, J. E. and Dutson, T. R. 1987b. Factors associated with the tenderness of three bovine muscles. *J. Food Sci.* (submitted).

Koohmaraie, M., Babiker, A. S., Merkel, R. A., and Dutson, T. R. 1987c. Role of Ca^{++}-dependent protease and lysosomal enzymes in postmortem changes in bovine skeletal muscle. *J. Food Sci.* (submitted).

Kopp, J., and Valin, C. 1981. Can lysosomal enzymes affect muscle collagen post-mortem? *Meat Sci.* **5**, 319.

Korant, B. D. 1977. Protease activity associated with HeLa cell ribosomes. *Biochem. Biophys. Res. Commun.* **74**, 926.

Korovkin, B. F., and Budniakov, V. V. 1973. Changes in the activity of acid hydrolases in the muscle tissue of rabbits with E-avitaminosis. *Bull. Eksp. Biol. Med.* **75**, 63.

Koszalka, T. R., and Miller, L. L. 1960. Proteolytic activity of rat skeletal muscle. *J. Biol. Chem.* **235**, 665. 669.

Koszalka, T. R., Mason, K. E., and Krol, G. 1961. Relation of vitamin E to proteolytic and autolytic activity of skeletal muscle. *J. Nutr.* **73**, 78.

Krzysik, B. A., and Adibi, S. A. 1977. Cytoplasmic dipeptidases activities of kidney, ileum, jejunium, liver, muscle and blood. *Am. J. Physiol.* **233**, E.450.

Kubota, S., Suzuki, K., and Imahori, K. 1981. A new method for the preparation of a calcium activated neutral protease highly sensitive to calcium ions. *Biochem. Biophys. Res. Commun.* **100**, 1189.

Kullmann, W. 1985. Proteases as catalytic agents in peptide synthesis chemistry: Shifting the extent of peptide bond synthesis from a "quantite negligeable" to a "quantite considerable." *J. Protein Chem.* **4**, 1.

Kuo, T., and Bhan, A. 1980. Studies of a myosin-cleaving protease from dystrophic hamster heart. *Biochem. Biophys. Res. Commun.* **92**, 570.

Kuo, T. H., Giacomelli, F., Kithier, K., and Malhotra, A. 1981. Biochemical characterization and cellular localization of serine protease in myopathic hamster. *J. Mol. Cell. Cardiol.* **13**, 1035.

Kuo, T. H., Giacomelli, F., and Wiener, J. 1984. Lysosomal and nonlysomal proteolytic activities in experimental diabetic cardiomyopathy. *Exp. Mol. Pathol.* **40**, 280.

Kuroda, M., Tanaka, T., and Masaki, T. 1981. Eu-actinin, a new structural protein of the Z-line of striated muscles. *J. Biochem. (Tokyo)* **89**, 279.

Laakkonen, E., Sherbon, J. W., and Wellington, G. H. 1970. Low-temperature, long-term heating of bovine muscle. *J. Food Sci.* **35**, 181.

Laemmli, U. K. 1970. Cleavage of structural proteins during assembly of the head of bacteriophage T$_4$. *Nature (London)* **227**, 680.

Lagunoff, D., and Benditt, E. P. 1963. Proteolytic enzymes of mast cells. *Ann. N.Y. Acad. Sci.* **103**, 185.

Langner, J. 1978. The endopeptidase activity of rat liver ribosomes: Subunit distribution. *FEBS Meet. 12th, Dresden.*

Langner, J., Ansorge, S., Bohley, P., Welfle, H., and Bielka, H. 1977. Presence of an endopeptidase activity in rat liver ribosomes. *Acta Biol. Med. Ger.* **36**, 1729.

Lapresle, C. 1971. Rabbit cathepsins D and E. *In* "Tissue Proteinases" (A. J. Barrett and J. T. Dingle, eds.), p. 135. North-Holland, Amsterdam.

Lapresle, C., and Webb, T. 1962. The purification and properties of a proteolytic enzyme, rabbit cathepsin E, and further studies on rabbit cathepsin D. *Biochem. J.* **84**, 455.

LaSalle, F., Robson, R. M., Lusby, M. L., Parrish, F. C., Stromer, M. H., and Huitt, T. W. 1983. Localization of tissue in bovine skeletal muscle. *J. Cell Biol.* **97**, 258a.

Laurell, C. B., and Jeppsson, J. O. 1975. Protease inhibitors in plasma. *In* "Plasma Proteins" (F. W. Putnam, ed.), Vol. 1, p. 224. Academic Press, New York.

Laurent, G. J., Sparrow, M. P., and Millward, D. J. 1978. Turnover of muscle protein in the fowl (*Callus domesticus*). *Biochem. J.* **176**, 393, 407.

Lawrie, R. A. 1979. "Meat Science," p. 76. Pergamon, Oxford.

Lazarides, E. 1976. Two general classes of cytoplasmic actin filaments in tissue culture cells: The role of tropomyosin. *J. Supramol. Struct.* **5**, 531.

Lazarides, E. 1982a. Biochemical and immunocytological characterization of intermediate filaments in muscle cells. *Methods Cell Biol.* **25**, 333.

Lazarides, E. 1982b. Intermediate filaments: A chemically heterogenous developmentally regulated class of proteins. *Annu. Rev. Biochem.* **51**, 219.

Lazo, P. S., Tsolas, O., Sun, S. C., Pontremoli, S., and Horecker, B. L. 1978. Modification of fructose bisphosphatase by a proteolytic enzyme from rat liver lysosomes. *Arch. Biochem. Biophys.* **188**, 308.

Leckie, B., and McConnell, A. 1975. Renin inhibitor from rabbit kidney. Conversion of a large inactive renin to a smaller active enzyme. *Circ. Res.* **36**, 513.

Ledward, D. A., Chizzolini, R., and Lawrie, R. A. 1975. The effect of extraction, animal age and post-mortem storage on tendon collagen. A differential scanning calorimetric study. *J. Food Technol.* **10**, 349.

Lee, C. O., Ohm, D. Y., and Dresdner, K. 1980. Sodium–calcium exchange in rabbit heart muscle cells: Direct measurement of sarcoplasmic Ca^{++} activity. *Science* **209**, 699.

Lee, Y. B., Ashmore, C. R., and Hitchcock, L. 1984. Effect of stretch and denervation on protease activities of normal and dystrophic chicken muscle. *Exp. Neurol.* **84**, 420.

Lenney, J. F. 1980. Inhibitors associated with proteinases of mammalian cells and tissue. *Curr. Top. Cell. Regul.* **17**, 25.

Lenney, J. F., Tolan, J. R., Sugal, W. J., and Lee, A. G. 1979. Thermostable endogenous inhibitors of cathepsin B and H. *Eur. J. Biochem.* **101**, 161.

Levyant, M. I., Bilinkina, V. S., Trudolyubova, M. G., and Orekhovich, V. N. 1976. Presence of a proteinase in polyribosomes of rat liver. *Mol. Biol. U.S.S.R.* (Engl. Trans.) **10**, 634.

Lewis, S. E. M., Anderson, P., and Goldspink, D. F. 1982. The effect of calcium on protein turnover in skeletal muscles of the rat. *Biochem. J.* **204**, 257.

Li, J. B. 1980. Protein synthesis and degradation in skeletal muscle of normal and dystrophic hamsters. *Am. J. Physiol.* **239**, E401.

Li, J. B., and Goldberg, A. L. 1976. Effects of food deprivation on protein synthesis and degradation in rat skeletal muscles. *Am. J. Physiol.* **231**, 441.

Li, J. B., Higgins, J. E., and Jefferson, L. S. 1979. Changes in protein turnover in skeletal muscle in response to fasting. *Am. J. Physiol.* **236**, E222.

Libby, P., and Goldberg, A. L. 1978. Leupeptin, a protease inhibitor, decreases protein degradation in normal and diseased muscles. *Science* **199**, 534.

Libby, P., and Goldberg, A. L. 1980. Effects of chymostatin and other proteinase inhibitors on protein breakdown and proteolytic activities in muscle. *Biochem. J.* **188**, 213.

Libby, P., and Goldberg, A. L. 1980b. The control and mechanisms of protein breakdown in striated muscle. *In* "Degradative Processes in Heart and Skeletal Muscle" (K. Wildenthal, ed.), p. 201. Elsevier, Amsterdam.

Libby, P., and Ingwall, J. S., and Goldberg, A. L. 1979. Reduction of protein degradation and atrophy in cultured fetal mouse hearts by leupeptin. *Am. J. Physiol.* **237**, E359.

Libelius, R., Jirmanova, I., Lundqist, I., and Thesleff, S. 1978. Increased endocytosis with lysosomal activation in skeletal muscle of dystrophic mouse. *J. Neuropathol. Exp. Neurol.* **37**, 387.

Lin, C. T., and Chen, L. H. 1982. Ultrastructural and lysosomal enzymes studies of skeletal muscle and myocardium in rats with long term vitamin E deficiency. *Pathology* **14**, 375.

Lin, T. Y., and William, H. R. 1979. Inhibition of cathepsin D by synthetic oligopeptides. *J. Biol. Chem.* **254**, 11875.

Lindstedt, S., and Prockop, D. J. 1961. Isotopic studies on urinary hydroxyproline as evidence for rapidly catabolized forms of collagen in the young rat. *J. Biol. Chem.* **236**, 1399.

Lloyd, J. B. 1971. A study of permeability of lysosomes to amino acids and small peptides. *Biochem. J.* **121**, 245.

Locker, R. H. 1984. The role of gap filaments in muscle and in meat. *Food Microstruct.* **3**, 17.

Locker, R. H., and Wild, D. J. C. 1984. The fat of the large proteins of myofibril during tenderising treatments. *Meat Sci.* **11**, 89.

Locnikar, P., Popovic, T., Lah, T., Kregar, I., Babnik, J., Kopitar, M., and Turk, V. 1981. The bovine cystein proteinases, cathepsins B, H, and S. *In* "Proteinases and Their Inhibitors: Structure, Function, and Applied Aspects" (V. Turk and L. J. Vitale, eds.), p. 109. Pergamon, Oxford.

Logunov, A. I., and Orekhovich, V. N. 1972. Isolation and some properties of cathepsin A from bovine spleen. *Biochem. Biophys. Res. Commun.* **46**, 1161.

Long, W. M., Chua, B. H., Munger, B. L., and Morgan, H. E. 1984. Effect of insulin on cardiac lysosomes and protein degradation. *Fed. Proc., Fed. Am. Soc. Exp. Biol.* **43**, 1295.

Loskutoff, D. J., and Edgington, T. S. 1977. Synthesis of a fibrinolytic activator and inhibitor by endothelial cells. *Proc. Natl. Acad. Sci. U.S.A.* **74**, 3903.

Lovaas, E. 1974. Evidence for a proteolytic system in rat liver mitochondria. *FEBS Lett.* **45**, 244.

Low, R. B., and Goldberg, A. L. 1973. Nonuniform rates of turnover of myofibrillar proteins in rat diaphragm. *J. Cell Biol.* **56**, 590.

Lukashevich, E. F., and Ivanova, A. G. 1976. Action of acid cathepsins on the myosin and sarcoplasmic proteins of normal and denervated rat muscles. *Ukr. Biokhim. Zh.* **48**, 555 (in Russian).

Lundblad, R. L., and Stein, W. H. 1969. On the reaction of diazoacetyl compounds with pepsin. *J. Biol. Chem.* **244**, 154.

Lundholm, K., and Scherstén, T. 1975. Leucine incorpoation into proteins and cathepsin-D activity in human skeletal muscle. The influence of the age of the subject. *Exp. Gerontol.* **10**, 155.

Lundholm, K. Ekman, L., Karlberg, I., Edstrom, S., and Scherstén, T. 1980. Comparison of hepatic cathepsin D activity in response to tumor growth and to calorie restriction in mice. *Cancer Res.* **40**, 1680.

Lusby, M. L., Ridpath, J. F., Parrish, F. C., and Robson, R. M. 1983. Effect of post-mortem storage on degradation of the recently discovered myofibrillar protein titin in bovine longissimus muscle. *J. Food Sci.* **48**, 1787.

Lutalo-Bosa, A. J., and MacRae, H. F. 1969. Hydrolytic enzymes in bovine skeletal muscle. 3. Activity of some catheptic enzymes. *J. Food Sci.* **34**, 401.

MacBride, M. A., and Parrish, F. C., Jr. 1977. The 30,000 dalton component of tender bovine longissmus muscle. *J. Food Sci.* **42**, 1627.

McConn, J. D., Tsuru, D., and Yasunobu, K. T. 1964. *Bacillus subtilis* neutral proteinase. I. A zinc enzyme of high specific activity. *J. Biol. Chem.* **239**, 3706.

McDonald, J. K., and Ellis, S. 1975. On the substrate specificity of cathepsin B1 and B2 including a new fluorogenic substrate for cathepsin B1. *Life Sci.* **17**, 1269.

McDonald, J. K., and Schwabe, C. 1977. Intracellular exopeptidases. *In* "Proteinases in Mammalian Cells and Tissues" (A. J. Barrett, ed.), p. 331. North-Holland, Amsterdam.

McDonald, J. K., Ellis, S., and Reilly, T. J. 1966. Properties of dipeptidyl arylamidase I of the pituitary. Chloride and sulphydryl activation of seryltyrosyl-β-naphthylamide hydrolysis. *J. Biol. Chem.* **241**, 1494.

McDonald, J. K., Leibach, F. H., Grindeland, R. E., and Ellis, S. 1968. Purification of dipeptidyl aminopeptidase II (dipeptidyl arylamidase I) of the anterior pituitary gland. *J. Biol. Chem.* **243**, 4143.

McDonald, J. K., Callahan, P. X., Smith, R. E., and Ellis, S. 1971. Polypeptide degradation by dipeptidyl aminopeptidase I (cathepsin C) and related peptidases. *In* "Tissue Proteinases" (A. J. Barrett and J. T. Dingle, eds.), p. 69. North-Holland, Amsterdam.

McDonald, J. K., Zeitman, B. B., Callahan, P. X., and Ellis, S. 1974. Angiotensinase activity of dipeptidyl aminopeptidase I (cathepsin C) of rat liver. *J. Biol. Chem.* **249**, 234.

MacDonald, M. L., and Swick, R. W. 1981. The effect of protein depletion and repletion on muscle-protein turnover in the chick. *Biochem. J.* **194**, 811.

McElligott, M. A., and Bird, J. W. C. 1980. Effect of streptozotocin-induced diabetes on proteolytic activity in rat muscle. *Fed. Proc., Fed. Am. Soc. Exp. Biol.* **39**, 635.

McElligott, M. A., and Bird, J. W. 1981. Muscle proteolytic enzyme activities in diabetic rats. *Am. J. Physiol.* **241**, E378.

MacGregor, R. R., Hamilton, J. W., Kent, G. N., Shofstall, R. E., and Cohn, D. V. 1979. The degradation of proparathormone and parathormone by parathyroid and liver cathepsin B. *J. Biol. Chem.* **254**, 4428.

McIntosh, E. N. 1967. Effect of post-mortem aging and enzyme tenderizers on mucoprotein of bovine skeletal muscle. *J. Food Sci.* **32**, 210.

McKay, M. J., Marsh, M. W., Kirschke, H., and Bond, J. S. 1984. Inactivation of fructose-1,6-bisphosphate aldolase by cathepsin L. Stimulation by ATP. *Biochim. Biophys. Acta* **784**, 9.

McKee, E. E., Clark, M. G., Beinlich, C. J., Lins, J. A., and Morgan, H. E. 1979. Neutral–alkaline proteases and protein degradation in rat heart. *J. Mol. Cell. Cardiol.* **11**, 1033.

McLaughlin, J., and Bosman, H. B. 1976. Regulation of increased acid proteinase in denervated skeletal muscle. *Exp. Neurol.* **50**, 276.

Macleod, G., and Seyyedain-Ardebili, M. 1981. Natural and simulated meat flavors (with particular reference to beef). *CRC Crit. Rev. Food Sci. Nutr.* **14**, 309.

McNeill, P. A., and Hoyl, G. 1967. Evidence for superthin filaments. *Am. Zool.* **7**, 483.

Magnusson, S., Ottesen, M., Foltmann, B., Dano, K., and Neurath, H. (eds.). 1978. "Regulatory Proteolytic Enzymes and Their Inhibitors." FEBS, Vol. 4. Pergamon, Oxford.

Makinodan, Y., Kyaw, N. N., and Ikeda, S. 1982. Intracellular distribution of fish muscle alkaline proteinase. *Comp. Biochem. Physiol.* **73**, 785.

Marks, N. 1977. Specificity of breakdown based on the interaction of active proteins and peptides by brain proteolytic enzymes. *In* "Intracellular Protein Catabolism II" (V. Turk and M. Marks, eds.), p. 85. Plenum, New York.

Marsh, B. B. 1954. Rigormortis in beef. *J. Sci. Food Agric.* **5**, 1970.

Marsh, B. B., Lochner, J. V., Takahashi, G., and Kragness, D. D. 1981. Effects of early post-mortem pH and temperature on beef tenderness. *Meat Sci.* **5**, 479.

Martin, A. H., Fredeen, H. T., and Weiss, G. M. 1971. Tenderness of beef *L. dorsi* muscle from steers, heifers, and bulls as influenced by source, post-mortem aging and carcass characteristics. *J. Food Sci.* **36**, 619.

Maruyama, K., Kimura, S., Ishii, T., Kuroda, M., Ohashi, K., and Muramatsu, S. 1977. β-Actinin, a regulatory protein of muscle. *J. Biochem. (Tokyo)* **81**, 215.

Maruyama, K., Kimura, M., Kimura, S., Ohashi, K., Suzuki, K., and Katunuma, N. 1981. Connectin, an elastic protein of muscle. Effect of proteolytic enzymes *in situ*. *J. Biochem. (Tokyo)* **89**, 711.

Maruyama, K., Sawada, H., Kimura, S., Ohashi, K., Higuchi, H., and Umazume, Y. 1984. Connectin filaments in stretched skinned fibers of frog skeletal muscle. *J. Cell Biol.* **99**, 1391.

Maskrey, P., Pluskal, M. G., Harris, J. B., and Pennington, R. J. 1977. Studies on increased and hydrolase activities in denervated muscle. *J. Neurochem.* **28**, 403.

Mason, R. W., Taylor, M. A. J., and Etherington, D. J. 1984. The purification and properties of cathepsin L from rabbit liver. *Biochem. J.* **217**, 209.

Mason, R. W., Johnson, D. A., Barrett, A. J., and Chapman, H. A. 1986. Elastinolytic activity of human cathepsin L. *Biochem. J.* **233**, 925.

Matsubara, H., and Feder, J. 1971. Other bacterial, mold and yeast proteases. *Enzymes* **3**, 721.

Matsukura, U., Okitani, A., Nishimura, T., and Kato, H. 1981. Mode of degradation of myofibrillar proteins by an endogenous protease, cathepsin L. *Biochim. Biophys. Acta* **662**, 41.

Matsumoto, T., Okitani, A., Kitamura, Y., and Kato, H. 1983. Mode of degradation of myofibrillar proteins by rabbit muscle cathepsin D. *Biochim. Biophys. Acta* **755**, 76.

Mayel-Afshar, S., Grimble, R., Fitzsimons, J. T., and Orson, N. 1983. Cathepsin D and calcium-activated protease activities in skeletal muscle of normal and protein-deficient pregnant rats. *Ann. Nutr. Metab.* **27**, 505.

Mayer, M., Amin, R., and Shafrir, E. 1974a. Rat myofibrillar protease: Enzyme properties and adaptive changes in conditions of muscle protein degradation. *Arch. Biochem. Biophys.* **161**, 20.

Mayer, M., Kaiser, N., Milholland, R. J., and Rosen, F. 1974b. The binding of dexamethasone and triamcinolone acetonide to glucocorticoid receptors in rat skeletal muscle. *J. Biol. Chem.* **249**, 5236.

Mayer, M., Amin, R., Milholland, R. J., and Rosen, F. 1976. Possible significance of myofibrillar protease in muscle catabolism. Enzyme activity in dystrophic, tumor-bearing, and glucocorticoid-treated animals. *Exp. Mol. Pathol.* **25**, 9.

Means, A. R., and Dedman, J. R. 1980. Calmodulin—An intracellular calcium receptor. *Nature (London)* **285**, 73.

Mellgren, R. L. 1980. Canine cardiac calcium-dependent proteases: Resolution of two forms with different requirement for calcium. *FEBS Lett.* **109**, 129.

Mellgren, R. L., Lepetti, A., Muck, T. C., and Easley, J. 1982. Rabbit skeletal muscle calcium-dependent protease requiring millimolar Ca^{++}. *J. Biol. Chem.* **257**, 7203.

Mellgren, R. L., Mericle, M. T., and Lane, R. D. 1986. Proteolysis of the calcium-dependent protease inhibitor by myocardial calcium-dependent protease. *Arch. Biochim. Biophys.* **246**, 233.

Melloni, E., Salamino, F., and Accorsi, A. 1974. Degradation of rabbit liver. Fructose-1,6-biphosphatase by lysosomal proteinases. *Ital. J. Biochem.* **23**, 412, 423.

Melloni, E., Pontremoli, S., Salamino, F., Sparatore, B., Michetti, M., and Horecker, B. L. 1981. Characterization of three rabbit liver lysosomal proteinases with fructose 1,6-bisphosphatase converting enzyme activity. *Arch. Biochem. Biophys.* **208**, 175.

Metrione, R. M., Okuda, Y., and Fairclough, G. F. 1970. Subunit structure of dipeptidyl trans-ferase. *Biochemistry* **9**, 2427.

Mihalyi, E. 1972. "Application of Proteolytic Enzymes to Protein Structure Studies," p. 39. CRC Press, Cleveland, Ohio.

Mihalyi, E., and Harrington, W. F. 1959. Studies on the tryptic digestion of myosin. *Biochim. Biophys. Acta* **36**, 447.

Miller, E. J., and Gay, S. 1982. Collagen. An overview. *In* "Methods in Enzymology" (L. W. Cunningham and D. W. Frederiksen, eds.), Vol. 82, Part A, p. 3. Academic Press, New York.

Miller, M., and Kastelic, J. 1956. Chemical responses of connective tissue of bovine skeletal muscle. *J. Agric. Food Chem.* **4**, 596.

Millward, D. J. 1970. Protein turnover in skeletal muscle. *Clin. Sci.* **39**, 577, 591.

Millward, D. J. 1979. Protein degradation in muscle and liver. *In* "Comprehensive Biochemistry" (M. Florkin, L. L. M. van Deenan, and A. Neuberger, eds.), Vol. 19B, Part I, p. 153. Elsevier, Amsterdam.

Millward, D. J. 1980. Protein turnover in skeletal and cardiac muscle during normal growth and hypertrophy. *In* "Degradative Processes in Heart and Skeletal Muscles" (K. Wildenthal, ed.), Vol. 3, p. 161. Elsevier, Amsterdam.

Millward, D. J., and Waterlow, J. C. 1978. Effect of nutrition on protein turnover in skeletal muscle. *Fed. Proc., Fed. Am. Soc. Exp. Biol.* **37**, 2283.

Millward, D. J., Bates, P. C., Laurent, G. J., and Lo, C. C. 1978. Factors affecting protein breakdown in skeletal muscle. *In* "Protein Turnover and Lysosme Function" (H. L. Segal and D. J. Doyle, etds.), p. 619. Academic Press, New York.

Milson, D. W., Steven, F. S., Hunter, J. A. A., Thomas, H., and Jackson, D. S. 1972. De-polymerization of human and bovine polymeric collagen fibrils. *Connect. Tissue Res.* **1**, 251.

Mitchel, R. E. J., Chaiken, I. M., and Smith, E. L. 1970. The complete amino acid sequence of papain. *J. Biol. Chem.* **245**, 3485.

Moeller, P. W., Field, P. A., Dutson, T. R., Landmann, W. A., and Carpenter, Z. L. 1976. Effect of high temperature conditioning on subcellular distribution and levels of lysosomal enzymes. *J. Food Sci.* **41**, 216.

Moeller, L. W., Field, P. A., Dutson, T. R., Landmann, W. A., and Carpenter, Z. L. 1977. High temperature effects on lysosomal enzymes distribution and fragmentation of bovine muscle. *J. Food Sci.* **42**, 510.

Montgomery, A., Park, D. C., and Pennington, R. J. 1974. Peptide hydrolases and AMP deaminase in extensor digitorum longus and soleus muscles from genetically dystrophic hamsters. *Comp. Biochem. Physiol.* **49B**, 387.

Morgan, H. E., Chua, B., and Beinlich, C. J. 1980. Regulation of protein degradation in heart. *In* "Degradative Processes in Heart and Skeletal Muscle" (K. Wildenthal, ed.), p. 87. Elsevier, Amsterdam.

Morrison, R. I. G., Barrett, A. J., Dingle, J. T., and Prior, D. 1973. Cathepsin B$_1$ and D. Action of human cartilage proteoglycans. *Biochim. Biophys. Acta* **302**, 411.

Mortimore, G. E. 1982. Mechanism of cellular protein catabolism. *Nutr. Rev.* **40**, 1.

Mortimore, G. E., and Hutson, N. J. 1981. Internalization of cytoplasmic protein by lysosomes as the mechanism of resident protein turnover in liver. *Acta Biol. Med. Ger.* **40**, 1577.

Mortimore, G. E., and Pösö, A. R. 1984. Lysosomal pathways in hepatic protein degradation: Regulatory role of amino acids. *Fed. Proc., Fed. Am. Soc. Exp. Biol.* **43**, 1984.

Mortimore, G. E., Ward, W. F., and Schworer, C. M. 1978. Lysosomal processing of intracellular protein in rat liver and its general regulation by amino acids and insulin. *In* "Protein Turnover and Lysosomal Function" (H. L. Segal and D. J. Doyle, eds.), p. 67. Academic Press, London.

Mueller, H., and Perry, S. V. 1962. The degradation of heavy meromyosin by trypsin. *Biochem. J.* **85**, 431.

Munro, H. N., and Yound, V. R. 1978. Urinary excretion of N^+-methylhistidine: a tool to study metabolic responses in relation to nutrient and hormonal status in health and disease of man. *Am. J. Clin. Nutr.* **31**, 1608.

Murachi, T. 1985. Calcium-dependent proteinases and specific inhibitor: Calpain and calpstatin. *In* "Molecular Variants of Proteins: Biosynthesis and Clinical Relevance" (P. N. Campbell and C. R. Phelps, eds.).

Murachi, T., Hatanaka, M., Yasumoto, Y., Nakayama, N., and Tanaka, K. 1981a. A quantitative distribution study on calpain and calpastatin in rat tissues and cells. *Biochem. Int.* **2**, 651.

Murachi, T., Tanaka, K., Hatanaka, M., and Murakami, T. 1981b. Intracellular Ca^{++}-dependent protease (calpain) and its high molecular-weight endogenous inhibitor (calpastatin). *Adv. Enzyme Regul.* **19**, 407.

Murakami, U., and Uchida, K. 1978. Purification and characterization of a myosin-cleaving protease from rat heart myofibrils. *Biochim. Biophys. Acta* **525**, 219.

Murakami, U., and Uchida, K. 1979. Degradation of rat cardiac myofibrils and myofibrillar proteins by a myosin cleaving protease. *J. Biochem. (Tokyo)* **86**, 553.

Murakami, U., and Uchida, K. 1980. Ultrastructural alteration of rat cardiac myofibrils caused by a myosin-cleaving protease. *J. Biochem. (Tokyo)* **88**, 877.

Mykles, D. L., and Skinner, D. M. 1983. Ca^{++}-dependent proteolytic activity in crab claw muscle. *J. Biol. Chem.* **258**, 10474.

Nagai, Y. 1973. Vertebrate collagenase: Further characterization and the significance of its latent form *in vivo*. *Mol. Cell. Biochem.* **1**, 137.

Nagainis, P. A., and Wolfe, F. H. 1982. Calcium activated neutral protease hydrolyzes Z-disk actin. *J. Food Sci.* **47**, 1358.

Nagainis, P. A., Wolfe, F. H., and Goll, D. E. 1983. Hydrolysis of Z-disk actin by Ca^{++}-activated protease. *J. Food Biochem.* **7**, 247.

Nakai, T., Otto, P. S., and Whayne, T. F. 1976. Proteolysis of canine apolipoprotein by acid proteases in canine liver lysosomes. *Biochim. Biophys. Acta* **422**, 380.

Nakai, N., Wada, K., Kobashi, K., and Hase, J. 1978. The limited proteolysis of rabbit muscle aldolase by cathespin B_1. *Biochem. Biophys. Res. Commun.* **83**, 881.

Nakajima, K., Powers, J. C., Ashe, B. M., and Zimmerman, M. 1979. Mapping the extended substrate binding site of cathepsin G and human leukocyte elastase studies with peptide substrates related to the α_1-protease inhibitor reactive site. *J. Biol. Chem.* **254**, 4027.

Nakashima, K., and Ogino, L. 1974. Regulation of rabbit liver fructose-1,6-diphosphatase. II. Modification by lysosomal cathepsin B_1 from the same cell. *J. Biochem.* **75**, 355.

Neelin, J. M., and Rose, D. 1964. Progressive changes in starch gel electrophoretic patterns of chicken muscle proteins during aging post-mortem. *J. Food Sci.* **29**, 544.

Neely, A. N., Nelson, P. B., and Mortimore, G. E. 1974. Osmotic alterations of the lysosomal system during rat liver perfusion: Reversible suppression by insulin and amino acids. *Biochim. Biophys. Acta* **338**, 458.

Neerunjun, J. S., and Dubowitz, V. 1979. Increased calcium-activated neutral protease activity in muscles of dystrophic hamsters and mice. *J. Neurol. Sci.* **40**, 105.

Neff, N. T., DeMartino, G. N., and Goldberg, A. L. 1979. The effect of protease inhibitors and decreased temperature on the degradation of different classes of proteins in cultured hepatocytes. *J. Cell. Physiol.* **101**, 439.

Neuberger, A., and Slack, H. G. B. 1953. Metabolism of collagen from liver, bone, skin and tendon. *Biochem. J.* **53**, 47.

Neurath, H., and Schwert, G. W. 1950. The mode of action of the crystalline pancreatic proteolytic enzymes. *Chem. Rev.* **46**, 69.

Newbold, R. P., and Scopes, R. K. 1967. Post-mortem glycolysis in ox skeletal muscle. *Biochem. J.* **105**, 127.

Nimni, M. E., deGuia, E., and Bavetta, L. A. 1967. Synthesis and turnover of collagen precursors in rabbit skin. *Biochem. J.* **102**, 143.

Ninjoor, V., Taylor, S. L., and Tappel, A. L. 1974. Purification and characterization of rat liver lysosomal cathepsin B_2. *Biochim. Biophys. Acta* **370**, 308.

Nobrega, F. G., Rola, F. H., Pasetto-Nobrega, M., and Oishi, M. 1972. Adenosine triphosphatase associated with adenosine triphosphate-dependent deoxyribonuclease. *Proc. Natl. Acad. Sci. U.S.A.* **69**, 15.

Noda, T., Isogai, K., Hayashi, H., and Katunuma, N. 1981a. Susceptibilities of various myofibrillar proteins to cathepsin B and morphological alterations of isolated myofibrils by this enzymes. *J. Biochem. (Tokyo)* **90**, 371.

Noda, T., Isogai, K., Katunuma, N., Tarumoto, Y., and Ohzeki, M. 1981b. Effect of cathepsin B, H, and D in pectoral muscle of *in vivo* administration of E-64-C [*N*-(L-3-transcarboxyoxirane-2-carbonyl)-L-leucyl-3-methylbutylamine]. *J. Biochem. (Tokyo)* **90**, 893.

Noguchi, T., and Kandatsu, M. 1969. Inhibition of autolytic breakdown of muscle proteins by the sarcoplasm and the serum of rat. *Agric. Biol. Chem.* **33**, 1226.

Noguchi, T., and Kandatsu, M. 1970. Autolytic breakdown of rat skeletal muscle proteins in the alkaline pH range. *Agric. Biol. Chem.* **34**, 390.

Noguchi, T., and Kandatsu, M. 1971. Purification and properties of a new alkaline protease of rat skeletal muscle. *Agric. Biol. Chem.* **35**, 191092.

Noguchi, T., and Kandatsu, M. 1976. Some properties of alkaline protease in rat muscle compared with that in peritoneal cavity cells. *Agric. Biol. Chem.* **40**, 927.

Noguchi, T., Miyazawa, E., and Kametaka, M. 1974. Protease and protease inhibitor activity in rat skeletal muscle during growth, protein deficiency and fasting. *Agric. Biol. Chem.* **38**, 253.

Obled, C., Arnal, M., and Valin, C. 1980. Variation through the day of hepatic and muscular cathepsin A (carboxypeptidase A; EC 3.4.12.2), C (dipeptidyl peptidase; EC 3.4.14.1) and D (endopeptidase D; EC 3.4.23.5) activities and free amino acids of blood in rat: Influence of feeding schedule. *Br. J. Nutr.* **44**, 61.

Odedra, B. R., Bates, P. C., and Millward, D. J. 1983. Time course of catabolic dose of corticosterone in protein turnover in rat skeletal muscles and liver. *Biochem. J.* **214**, 617.

Offer, G. W. 1964. Myosin: An N-acetylated protein. *Biochim. Biophys. Acta* **90**, 193.

Oganesyan, S. S., and Eloyan, M. A. 1981. Cathepsin activity of skeletal muscle and myocardial myofibrils after exposure to weightlessness and G force. *Kosm. Biol. Aviakosm. Med. USSR* **15**, 38.

Ogunro, E. A., Lanman, R. B., Spencer, J. R., Ferguson, A. G., and Lesch, M. 1979. Degradation of canine cardiac myosin and actin by cathepsin D, isolated from homologous tissue. *Cardiovasc. Res.* **13**, 621.

Ogunro, E. A., Samarel, A. M., Furguson, A. G., and Lesch, M. 1982. Primary structure and similarities in canine cardiac cathepsin D polypeptide chain. *J. Mol. Cell. Cardiol.* **14**, 513.

Ohashi, K., and Maruyama, K. 1979. A new structural protein located in the Z-line of chicken skeletal muscle. *J. Biochem. (Tokyo)* **85**, 1103.

Ohkuma, S., and Poole, B. 1978. Fluorescence probe measurement of the intralysosomal pH in living cells and the perturbation of pH by various agents. *Proc. Natl. Acad. Sci. U.S.A.* **75**, 3327.

Okitani, A., Otsuka, Y., Sugitani, M., and Fujimaki, M. 1974. Some properties of neutral proteolytic system in rabbit skeletal muscle. *Agric. Biol. Chem.* **38**, 573.

Okitani, A., Goll, D. E., Stromer, M. H., and Robson, K. M. 1976. Intracellular inhibitor of a Ca^{++}-activated protease involved in myofibrillar protein turnover. *Fed. Proc., Fed. Am. Soc. Exp. Biol.* **35**, 1746.

Okitani, A., Matsukara, U., Kato, H., and Fujimaki, M. 1980. Purification and some properties of a myofibrillar protein-degrading protease, cathepsin L from rabbit skeletal muscle. *J. Biochem. (Tokyo)* **87**, 1133.

Okitani, A., Matsumoto, T., Kitamura, Y., and Kato, H. 1981. Purification of cathepsin D from rabbit skeletal muscle and its action towards myofibrils. *Biochim. Biophys. Acta* **662**, 202.

Olden, K., and Goldberg, A. L. 1978. Studies of the energy requirement for intracellular protein degradation in *E. coli. Biochim. Biophys. Acta* **542**, 385.

Oliveira, E. B., Martins, A. R., and Camargo, A. C. M. 1976. Isolation of brain endopeptidases: Influence of size and sequence of substrates structurally related to bradykinin. *Biochemistry* **15**, 1967.

Olson, D. G., Parrish, F. C., Dayton, W. R., and Goll, D. E. 1977. Effect of post-mortem storage and calcium activated factor on the myofibrillar proteins of bovine skeletal muscle. *J. Food Sci.* **42**, 117.

Oosawa, F., and Asakura, S. 1975. "Thermodynamics of Protein Polymerization." Academic Press, New York.

Ooyama, T., Sakamoto, H., and Mayumi, M. 1975. Studies on the role of proteases in the biochemical mechanism of tissue injury. *Med. Biol.* **53**, 462.

Osborn, M., Geisler, N., Shaw, G., Sharp, G., and Weber, K. 1982. Intermediate filaments. *Cold Spring Harbor Symp. Quant. Biol.* **46**, 413.

O'Shea, J. M., Robson, R. M., Huiatt, T. W., Hartzer, M. K., and Stromer, M. H. 1979. Purified desmin from adult mammalian skeletal muscle: A peptide mapping comparison with desmins from adult mammalian and avian smooth muscle. *Biochem. Biophys. Res. Commun.* **89**, 972.

Otsuka, Y., and Goll, D. E. 1980. Purification of the Ca^{++}-activated protease-inhibitor from bovein cardiac muscle. *Fed. Proc., Fed. Am. Soc. Exp. Biol.* **39**, 2044.

Otto, K. 1971. Cathepsin B1 and B2. *In* "Tissue Proteinases" (A. J. Barrett and J. T. Dingle, eds.), p. 1. North-Holland, Amsterdam.

Otto, K., and Bhaki, S. 1969. Studies on cathepsin B1: specificity and properties. *Hoppe-Seyler's Z. Physiol. Chem.* **350**, 1577 (in German).

Otto, K., and Riesenköning, H. 1975. Improved purification of cathepsin B1 and B2. *Biochim. Biophys. Acta* **379**, 462.

Ouali, A. 1984. Sensitivity to ionic strength of Mg–Ca-enhanced ATPase activity as an index of myofibrillar aging in beef. *Meat Sci.* **11**, 79.

Ouali, A., and Valin, C. 1981. Effect of muscle lysosomal enzymes and calcium activated neutral proteinase on myofibrillar ATPase activity: Relationship with aging changes. *Meat Sci.* **5**, 233.

Ouali, A., Obled, A., Cottin, P., Merdaci, N., Ducastaing, A., and Valin, C. 1983. Comparative effects of post-mortem storage and low-calcium-requiring neutral proteinase on bovine and rabbit myofibrillar proteins. *J. Sci. Food Agric.* **34**, 466.

Ouali, A., Obled, A., Deval, C., Garrel, N., and Valin, C. 1984. Proteolytic action of lysosomal proteinases on the myofibrillar structure. Comparison with the CaANP effects and post-mortem changes. *Eur. Meet. Meat Res. Workers, 30th, Bristol, U.K.* p. 126.

Pagano, M., Nicola, M. A., and Engler, R. 1982. Inhibition of cathepsin L and B by haptoglobin, the haptoglobin–hemoglobin complex and asialohaptoglobin *in vitro* studies in the rat. *Can. J. Biol. Chem.* **60**, 631.

Palmer, R. M., Reeds, P. J., Atkinson, T., and Smith, R. H. 1983. The influence of changes in tension on protein synthesis and prostaglandin release in isolated rabbit muscles. *Biochem. J.* **214**, 1011.

Park, D. C., Parsons, M. E., and Pennington, R. J. 1973. Evidence for mast-cell origin of proteinase in skeletal-muscle homogenates. *Biochem. Soc. Trans.* **1**, 730.

Parrish, F. C., Jr., and Bailey, M. E. 1966. Physiochemical properties and partial purification of porcine muscle cathepsin. *J. Agric. Food Chem.* **14**, 232.

Parrish, F. C., Jr., Selvig, C. J., Culler, R. D., and Zeece, M. G. 1981. CAF activity, calcium concentration and the 30,000 dalton component of tough and tender bovine longissimus muscle. *J. Food Sci.* **46,** 308.

Parsons, M. E., and Pennington, R. J. 1976. Separation of rat muscle aminopeptidases. *Biochem. J.* **155,** 375.

Parsons, M. E., Parsons, R., and Pennington, R. J. 1978. Peptide hydrolase activities in rat muscle cultures. *Int. J. Biochem.* **9,** 745.

Paterson, A. K., and Knowles, J. R. 1972. The number of catalytically essential carboxyl groups in pepsin. *Eur. J. Biochem.* **31,** 510.

Patestos, N., and Harrington, M. G. 1984. Proteolysis of sarcoplasmic proteins during *in vitro* incubation of bovine muscle extracts. *Proc. Eur. Meet. Meat Res. Workers, 30th,* p. 131.

Patterson, E. K., Hsiao, S. H., and Keppel, A. 1963. Studies on dipeptidases and aminopeptidases. 1. Distinction between leucine aminopeptidase and enzyme that hydrolyzes L-leucyl-β-naphthylamide. *J. Biol. Chem.* **238,** 3611.

Pauling, L. 1960. "The Nature of the Chemical Bond," p. 449. Cornell Univ. Press, Ithaca, New York.

Pearson, A. M., and Dutson, T. R., eds. 1985. "Advances in Meat Research" Vol. 1, p. 307. Avi, Westport, Connecticut.

Pearson, A. M., Wolzak, A. M., and Gray, J. I. 1983. Possible role of muscle proteins in flavor and tenderness of meat. *J. Food Biochem.* **7,** 189.

Pearson, C. M., and Kar, N. C. 1979. Muscle breakdown and lysosomal activation (Biochemistry). *Ann. N.Y. Acad. Sci.* **317,** 465.

Pellegrino, C., and Franzini, C. 1963. An electron microscope study of denervation atrophy in red and white skeletal muscle fibres. *J. Cell Biol.* **17,** 327.

Pemrick, S. M., Schneiderman, S., and Stracher, A. 1980. Ca^{++}-specific degradation of the heavy chain of unphosphorylated skeletal myosin. *Fed. Proc., Fed. Am. Soc. Exp. Biol.* **39,** 2043.

Pennington, R. J. T. 1977. Proteinases of muscle. *In* "Proteinases in Mammalian Cells and Tissues" (A. J. Barrett, ed.), p. 515. North-Holland, Amsterdam.

Pennington, R. J. T., and Robinson, J. E. 1968. Cathepsin activity in normal and dystrophic human muscle. *Enzymol. Biol. Clin.* **9,** 175.

Penny, I. F. 1980. The enzymology of conditioning. *In* "Developments in Meat Science" (R. Lawrie, ed.), p. 115. Applied Science, Barking, U.K.

Penny, I. F., and Dransfield, E. 1979. Relationship between toughness and troponin T. in conditioned beef. *Meat Sci.* **3,** 135.

Penny, I. F., and Ferguson-Pryce, R. 1979. Measurement of autolysis in beef muscle homogenates. *Meat Sci.* **3,** 121.

Penny, I. F., Voyle, C. A., and Dransfield, E. 1974. Tenderizing effect of a muscle proteinase on beef. *J. Sci. Food Agric.* **25,** 703.

Penny, I. F., Etherington, D. T., Reeves, J. L., and Taylor, M. A. J. 1984. The action of cathepsin L and calcium activated neutral proteases on myofibrillar proteins. *Eur. Meet. Meat Res. Workers, 30th, Bristol, U.K.,* p. 133.

Pepe, F. A. 1967. The myosin filament structural organization from antibody staining observed in electron microscopy. *J. Mol. Biol.* **27,** 505.

Peter, J. B., Barnard, R. J., Edgerton, E. R., Gillespie, C. A., and Stempel, K. E. 1972a. Metabolic profiles of three fiber types of skeletal muscle in guinea pigs and rabbits. *Biochemistry* **11,** 2627.

Peter, J. B., Kar, N. C., Barnard, R. J., Pearson, C. M., and Edgerton, V. R. 1972b. Distribution of acid hydrolysis in guinea pig skeletal muscle. *Biochem. Med.* **6,** 257.

Pickett, W. C., Jesse, R. L., and Cohen, P. 1977. Initiation of phospholipases A_2 activity in human platelets by the calcium ion ionophore A23187. *Biochim. Biophys. Acta* **486,** 209.

Pietras, R. J., Szego, C. M., Mangan, C. E., Seeler, B. J., Burtnett, M. M., and Orevi, M. 1978.

Elevated serum cathepsin B_1 and vaginal pathology after prenatal DES exposure. *Obstet. Gynecol.* **52**, 321.

Pilström, L., Vihko, V., Åström, E., and Arstila, A. U. 1978. Activity of acid hydrolases in skeletal muscle of untrained, trained and detrained mice of different ages. *Acta Physiol. Scand.* **104**, 217.

Planta, R. J., Gorter, J., and Gruber, M. 1964. The catalytic properties of cathepsin C. *Biochim. Biophys. Acta* **89**, 511.

Platt, D., and Gross-Fengels, F. 1979. Influence of age and spironolactone on lysosomal enzyme activities, DNA, and protein content of rat liver after partial hepatectomy. *Gerontology* **25**, 87.

Pluskal, M. G., and Pennington, R. J. T. 1973a. Peptide hydrolase activities in red and white muscle. *Int. Res. Commun. Syst.* **11**, 3.

Pluskal, M. G., and Pennington, R. J. T. 1973b. Peptide hydrolase activities in denervated muscle. *Biochem. Soc. Trans.* **1**, 1307.

Pollack, M. S., and Bird, J. W. C. 1968. Distribution and particle properties of acid hydrolase in denervated muscle. *Am. J. Physiol.* **215**, 716.

Pollard, T. D., Aebi, U., Cooper, J. A., Fowler, W. E., and Tseng, P. 1982. Actin structure, polymerization and gelation. *Cold Spring Harbor Symp. Quant. Biol.* **46**, 513.

Pontremoli, S., Accorsi, A., Melloni, E., Schiavo, E., DeFlora, A., and Horecker, B. L. 1974. Transformation of neutral to alkaline fructose 1,6-bisphosphatase. *Arch. Biochem. Biophys.* **164**, 716.

Pontremoli, S., Melloni, E., Salamino, F., Sparatore, B., Michetti, M., and Horecker, B. L. 1979. Changes in activity of function-1,6-bisphosphatealdolase in liver of fasted rabbits and accumulation of cross-reacting immune material. *Proc. Natl. Acad. Sci. U.S.A.* **76**, 6323.

Pontremoli, S., Melloni, E., Salamino, F., Sparatore, B., Michetti, M., and Horecker, B. L. 1982. Cathepsin M: A lysosomal proteinase with aldolase-inactivating activity. *Arch. Biochem. Biophys.* **214**, 376.

Pontremoli, S., Melloni, E., and Horecker, B. L. 1985. Regulation of mammalian cytosolyic calcium requiring neutral proteinases. *Curr. Top. Cell. Regul.* **27**, 293.

Poole, A. R., Dingle, J. T., and Barrett, A. J. 1972. The immunocytochemical demonstration of cathepsin D. *J. Histochem. Cytochem.* **20**, 261.

Poole, A. R., Hembry, R. M., and Dingle, J. T. 1973. Extracellular localization of cathepsin D in ossifying cartilage. *Calcif. Tissue Res.* **12**, 313.

Poole, A. R., Hembry, R. M., and Dingle, J. T. 1974. Cathepsin D in cartilage. The immunohistochemical demonstration of extracellular enzyme in normal and pathological conditions. *J. Cell Sci.* **14**, 139.

Pösö, A. R., and Mortimore, G. E. 1984. Requirement for alanine in amino acid control of deprivation-induced protein degradation in liver. *Proc. Natl. Acad. Sci. U.S.A.* **81**, 4270.

Pösö, A. R., Wert, J. J., and Mortimore, G. E. 1982. Multifunctional control by amino acids of deprived-induced proteolysis in liver. Role of leucine. *J. Biol. Chem.* **257**, 12117.

Pozzi, L. 1935. Le catepsine-esponsizione critica e ricerche sperimentali. *Mem. R. Accad. Ital. Mem. Class Sci. Fis. Mat. Nat.* **6**, 193.

Preedy, V. R., and Garlick, P. J. 1983. Protein synthesis in skeletal muscle of the perfused rat hemicorpus compared with rats in intact animal. *Biochem. J.* **214**, 433.

Press, E. M., Porter, R. R., and Cebra, J. 1960. The isolation and properties of a proteolytic enzyme, cathepsin D, from bovine spleen. *Biochem. J.* **74**, 501.

Price, M. G., and Sanger, J. W. 1983. Intermediate filaments in striated muscle. A review of structural studies in embryonic and adult skeletal and cardiac muscle. *In* "Cell and Muscle Motility" (R. M. Dowben and J. W. Shay, eds.), p. 1. Plenum, New York.

Quinn, P. S., and Judah, J. D. 1978. Calcium-dependent Golgi-vesicle fusion and cathepsin B in the conversion of proalbumin into albumin in rat liver. *Biochem. J.* **172**, 301.

Ramponi, G., Nassi, P., Liguri, G., Cappugi, G., and Grisolia, S. 1978. Purification and properties of a histone-specific protease from rat liver chromatin. *FEBS Lett.* **90,** 228.

Randall, C. J., and MacRae, H. F. 1967. Hydrolytic enzymes in bovine skeletal muscle. *J. Food Sci.* **32,** 182.

Rashid, N. H., Henrickson, R. L., Asghar, A., and Claypool, P. L. 1983. Biochemical and quality characteristics of ovine muscles as affected by electrical stimulation, hot-boning and mode of chilling. *J. Food Sci.* **48,** 136.

Réaumur, R. A. F. 1752. Sur la digestion des oiseaux. Second memoire. De la manière dont elle se fait dans l'estomac des oiseaux de proie. *Mem. Math. Phys. Acad. R. Sci.* **461.**

Reddick, M. E., Bauer, E. A., and Eisen, A. Z. 1974. Immunocytochemical localization of collagenase in human skin and fibroblasts in monolayer culture. *J. Invest. Dermatol.* **62,** 361.

Reddy, M. K., Etlinger, J. D., Rabinowitz, M., Fischman, D. A., and Zak, R. 1975. Removal of Z-lines and α-actinin from isolated myofibrils by a calcium-activated neutral protease. *J. Biol. Chem.* **250,** 4278.

Reed, G., ed. 1975. "Enzymes in Food Technology," p. 15. Academic Press, New York.

Reich, E., Rifkin, D. B., and Shaw, E., eds. 1975. "Proteases and Biological Control." Cold Spring Harbor Laboratory, Cold Spring Harbor, New York.

Reijngoud, D. J., Oud, P. S., Kas, J., and Tager, J. M. 1976. Relationship between medium pH and that of lysosomal matrix as studied by two independent methods. *Biochim. Biophys. Acta* **448,** 290.

Reinauer, H., and Dahlmann, B. 1979. Alkaline proteinases in skeletal muscle. *In* "Biological Functions of Proteinases" (H. Holzer and H. Tschesche, eds.), p. 94. Springer-Verlag, Berlin and New York.

Reville, W. J., Goll, D. E., Stromer, M. H., Robson, R. M., and Dayton, W. R. 1976. A Ca^{++}-activated protease possibly involved in myofibrillar protein turnover. Subcellular localization of the protease in porcine skeletal muscle. *J. Cell Biol.* **70,** 1.

Ribbons, D. W., and Brew, K., eds. 1976. "Proteolysis and Physiological Regulation." Academic Press, New York.

Robbins, F. M., and Cohen, S. H. 1976. Effect of catheptic enzymes from spleen on the microstructure of bovine semimembranous muscle. *J. Text. Stud.* **7,** 137.

Robbins, F. M., Walker, J. F., Cohen, S. H., and Chatterjee, S. 1979. Action of proteolytic enzymes on bovine myofibrils. *J. Food Sci.* **44,** 1672.

Robins, S. P., and Rucklidge, G. J. 1980. Analysis of the reducible components of the muscle protein, connectin: Absence of lysine-derived cross-links. *Biochem. Biophys. Res. Commun.* **96,** 1240.

Robson, R. M., Goll, D. E., and Main, M. J. 1967. Nucleoside triphosphatase activity of bovine myosin B. *J. Food Sci.* **32,** 544.

Robson, R. M., O'Shea, J. M., Hartzer, M. K., Rathburn, W. E., Lasalle, F., Scheiner, P. J., Kasang, L. E., Stromer, M. H., Lusby, M. L., Ridpath, J. F., Pang, Y. Y., Evans, R. R., Zeece, M. G., Parrish, F. C., and Huiatt, T. W. 1984. Role of new cytoskeletal elements in maintanance of muscle integrity. *J. Food Biochem.* **8,** 1.

Rodemann, H. P., and Goldberg, A. L. 1982. Arachidonic acid, prostaglandin E_2 and $F_{2\alpha}$ influence rates of protein turnover in skeletal and cardiac muscle. *J. Biol. Chem.* **257,** 1632.

Rodemann, H. P., Waxman, L., and Goldberg, A. L. 1982. The stimulation of protein degradation in muscle by Ca^{++} is mediated by prostaglandin E_2 and does not require the calcium-activated protease. *J. Biol. Chem.* **257,** 8716.

Romeo, D., Stagni, N., Sottocasa, G. L., Pugliarello, M. C., DeBernard, B., and Vittur, F. 1966. Lysosomes in heart tissue. *Biochim. Biophys. Acta* **130,** 64.

Roobol, A., and Alleyne, G. A. 1974. Changes in lysosomal hydrolase activity associated with malnutrition in young rats. *Br. J. Nutr.* **32,** 189.

Rose, H. G., Robertson, M. C., and Schwartz, T. B. 1959. Hormonal and metabolic influences on intracellular peptidase activity. *Am. J. Physiol.* **197**, 1063.

Rosochacki, S., and Millward, D. J. 1979. Cathepsin D and acid autolytic activity in skeletal muscle of protein deficient, severely protein-energy restricted and refed rats. *Proc. Nutr. Soc.* **38**, 137A.

Röthig, H. J., Stiller, N., and Reinauer, H. 1975. Proteolytic activities in skeletal muscle of diabetic rats. *Diabetalogia* **11**, 373.

Röthig, H. J., Stiller, N., Dahlmann, B., and Reinauer, H. 1978. Insulin effect on proteolytic activities in rat skeletal muscle. *Horm. Metab. Res.* **10**, 101.

Rowland, L. P. 1980. Biochemistry of muscle membranes in Duchenne muscular dystrophy. *Muscle Nerve* **3**, 3.

Rubinstein, N. A., and Kelly, A. M. 1978. Myogenic and neurogenic contributions to the development of fast and slow twitch muscle in rat. *Dev. Biol.* **62**, 473.

Salkowaski, E. 1890. Ueber Autodigestion der Organe. *Z. Klin. Med.* **17** (Suppl.), 77.

Salm, C. P., Forrest, J. C., Aberle, E. D., Mills, E. W., Snyder, A. C., and Judge, M. D. 1983. Bovine muscle shortening and protein degradation after electrical stimulation, excision and chilling. *Meat Sci.* **8**, 163.

Salminen, A., and Vihko, V. 1980. Acid proteolytic capacity in mouse cardiac and skeletal muscles after prolonged submaximal exercise. *Pflügers Arch.* **389**, 17.

Salminen, A., and Vihko, V. 1983. Exercise myopathy: Selectively enhanced proteolytic capacity in rat skeletal muscle after prolonged running. *Exp. Mol. Pathol.* **38**, 61.

Salminen, A., Kainulainen, H., and Vihko, V. 1982. Lysosomal changes related to aging and physical exercise in mouse cardiac and skeletal muscles. *Experientia* **38**, 781.

Salminen, A., Hongisto, K., and Vihko, V. 1984. Lysosomal changes related to exercise injuries and training-induced protection in mouse skeletal muscle. *Acta Physiol. Scand.* **120**, 15.

Samarel, A. M., Ogunro, E. A., Ferguson, A. G., Allenby, P., and Lesch, M. 1981. Rabbit cardiac immunoreactive cathepsin D content during starvation-induced atrophy. *Am. J. Physiol.* **240**, H222.

Samarel, A. M., Ogunro, E. A., Ferguson, A. G., Allenby, P., and Lesch, M. 1982. Regulation of cathepsin D metabolism in rabbit heart. *J. Clin. Invest.* **69**, 999.

Samarel, A. M., Worobec, S. W., Ferguson, A. G., and Lesch, M. 1984. Biosynthesis of the multiple forms of rabbit cardiac cathepsin D. *J. Biol. Chem.* **259**, 4702.

Samejima, K., and Wolfe, F. H. 1976. Degradation of myofibrillar protein components during postmortem aging of chicken muscle. *J. Food Sci.* **41**, 250.

Sanada, Y., Yosogawa, N., and Katunuma, N. 1978a. Crystallization and amino acid composition of a serine protease from rat skeletal muscle. *Biochem. Biophys. Res. Commun.* **82**, 108.

Sanada, Y., Yosogawa, N., and Katunuma, N. 1978b. Serine protease in mice with hereditary muscular dystrophy. *J. Biochem. (Tokyo)* **83**, 27.

Sanada, Y., Yosogawa, N., and Katunuma, N. 1979. Effect of serine protease on isolated myofibrils. *J. Biochem.* **85**, 481.

Santidrian, S., Moreyra, M., Munro, H. N., and Young, V. R. 1981. Effect of corticosterone and its route of administration on muscle protein breakdown, measured *in vivo* by urinary excretion of *N*-methylhistidine in rats: Response to different levels of dietary protein and energy. *Metabolism* **30**, 798.

Sapolasky, A. I., and Woessner, J. F. 1972. Multiple forms of cathepsin D from bovine uterus. *J. Biol. Chem.* **247**, 1069.

Sasaki, M., Taniguchi, K., and Minakata, K. 1981. Multimolecular forms of thiol proteinase inhibitor in human plasma. *J. Biochem. (Tokyo)* **89**, 169.

Sasaki, T., Yoshimura, N., Kikuchi, T., Hatanaka, M., Kitahara, A., Sakihama, T., and Murachi, T. 1983. Similarity and dissimilarity in subunit structures of calpains I and II from various sources as demonstrated by immunological cross-reactivity. *J. Biochem. (Tokyo)* **94**, 2055.

Schiaffino, S., and Hanzlikova, V. 1972. Studies on the effect of denervation in developing muscle. *J. Ultrastruct. Res.* **39**, 1.

Schimke, R. T. 1975. On the properties and mechanisms of protein turnover. *In* "Intracellular Protein Turnover" (R. T. Schimke and N. Katunuma, eds.), p. 173. Academic Press, New York.

Schott, L. H., and Terjung, R. L. 1979. The influence of exercise on muscle lysosomal enzymes. *Eur. J. Appl. Physiol.* **42**, 175.

Schwartz, T. B., Robertson, M. C., and Holmes, L. B. 1956. Adrenocortical influences on dipeptidase activity of surviving rat diaphragm. *Endocrinology* **58**, 453.

Schwartz, W. N., and Barrett, A. J. 1980. Human cathepsin H. *Biochem. J.* **191**, 487.

Schwartz, W. N., and Bird, J. W. C. 1977. Degradation of myofibrillar proteins by cathepsins B and D. *Biochem. J.* **167**, 811.

Scopes, R. K. 1964. The influence of post-mortem conditions on the solubilities of muscle proteins. *Biochem. J.* **91**, 201.

Scopes, R. K. 1968. Methods for starch gel electrophoresis of sarcoplasmic proteins. *Biochem. J.* **107**, 139.

Scott, P. G., and Pearson, C. H. 1978. Cathepsin D—Cleavage of soluble collagen and cross-linked peptides. *FEBS Lett.* **88**, 41.

Scrimgeour, K. G. 1977. "Chemistry and Control of Enzyme Reactions." Academic Press, London.

Segal, H. I. 1976. Mechanisms and regulation of protein turnover in animal cells. *Curr. Top. Cell. Regul.* **11**, 183.

Segal, H. I., Winkler, J. R., and Miyagi, M. P. 1974. Relationship between degradation rates of proteins *in vivo* and their susceptibility of lysosomal proteases. *J. Biol. Chem.* **249**, 6364.

Seglen, P. O., Grinde, B., and Solheim, A. E. 1979. Inhibition of the lysosomal pathway of protein degradation in isolated rat hepatocytes by ammonia, methylamine, chloroquine and leupeptin. *Eur. J. Biochem.* **95**, 215.

Seglen, P. O., Solheim, A. E., Grine, B., Gordon, P. B., Schwarze, P. E., Gjessing, R., and Poli, A. 1980. Amino acid control of protein synthesis and degradation in isolated rat heptocytes. *Ann. N.Y. Acad. Sci.* **349**, 1.

Seifter, S., and Harper, E. 1971. The collagenases. *Enzymes* **3**, 649.

Seperich, G. J., and Price, J. F. 1978. Effect of prolonged fasting upon the calcium activated sarcoplasmic factor of rabbit skeletal muscle. *Meat Sci.* **2**, 41.

Serivastava, U. 1968. Biochemical changes in progressive muscular dystrophy. *Can. J. Biochem.* **46**, 35.

Sharp, J. G. 1963. Aseptic autolysis in rabbit and bovine muscle during storage at 37°C. *J. Sci. Food Agric.* **14**, 468.

Shaw, E., Mares-Guia, M., and Cohen, W. 1965. Evidence for an active-center histidine in trypsin through use of a specific reagent. *Biochemistry* **4**, 2219.

Shibamoto, T., and Russell, G. F. 1977. A study of the volatile isolated from D-glucose–hydrogen sulfide–ammonia model system. *J. Agric. Food Chem.* **25**, 112.

Sims, T. J., and Bailey, A. J. 1981. Connective tissue. *Dev. Meat Sci.* **2**, 29.

Singh, H., Kuo, T., and Kalnitsky, G. 1978. Collagenolytic activity of lung BANA hydrolase and cathepsin B_1. *In* "Protein Turnover and Lysosome Function" (H. L. Segal and D. J. Doyle, eds.), p. 315. Academic Press, New York.

Slinde, E., and Kryvi, H. 1986. Z-Disk digestion of isolated bovine myofibrils by an endogenous calcium activated neutral proteinase. *Meat Sci.* **16**, 45.

Sliwinski, R. A., Doty, D. M., and Landmann, W. A. 1959. Overall assay and partial purification procedures for proteolytic enzymes in beef muscle. *J. Agric. Food Chem.* **7**, 788.

Smith, E. L. 1948a. The peptidase of skeletal muscle, heart and uterine muscle. *J. Biol. Chem.* **173**, 553.

Smith, E. L. 1948b. The glycylglycine dipeptidases of skeletal muscle and human uterus. *Biochem. J.* **173,** 571.

Smith, E. L. 1948c. Studies on dipeptidases. *Biochem. J.* **176,** 9, 21.

Snellman, O. 1971. A study on the reactivity of the thiol group of cathepsin B. *In* "Tissue Proteinases" (A. J. Barrett and J. T. Dingle, eds.), p. 29. North-Holland, Amsterdam.

Snoke, J. E., and Neurath, H. 1950. The proteolytic activity of striated rabbit muscle. *J. Biol. Chem.* **187,** 127.

Snyder, A. C., Lamb, D. R., Salm, C. P., Judge, M. D., Aberle, E. D., and Mills, E. W. 1984. Myofibrillar protein degradation after accentric exercise. *Experientia* **40,** 1, 69.

Sogawa, K., and Takahashi, K. 1978. Evidence for the presence of a serine proteinase(s) associated with the microsomal membrane of rat liver. *J. Biochem. (Tokyo)* **84,** 763.

Sogawa, K., and Takahashi, K. 1979. A neutral proteinase of monkey liver microsomes, solubilization, partial purification, and properties. *J. Biochem. (Tokyo)* **86,** 1313.

Sohar, I., Takacs, O., Guba, F., Kirschke, H., and Bohley, P. 1979. Degradation of myofibrillar proteins by cathepsins from rat liver lysosomes. "Szaged-Halle Symposium." Martin Luther Univ. Press, Halle.

Sohar, I., Hutter, H. J., Nagy, I., and Guba, F. 1981. Proteolytic enzymes in different kinds of muscles. *In* "Advances in Physiological Science" (J. Hideg and D. Gazenko, eds.), p. 179. Akad. Kiado, Budapest.

Sohar, I., Bird, J. W.C., and Moore, P. S. 1986. Calcium-dependent proteolysis of calcium-binding proteins. *Biochem. Biophys. Res. Commun.* **124,** 1269.

Sommercorn, J. M., and Swick, R. W. 1981. Protein degradation in primary monolayer culture of adult rat hepatocytes. *J. Biol. Chem.* **256,** 4816.

Sorinmade, S. O., Cross, H. R., Ono, K., and Wergin, W. P. 1982. Mechanism of ultrastructural changes in electrically stimulated beef longissimus muscle. *Meat Sci.* **6,** 71.

Spanier, A. M. 1977. Studies of the lysosomal apparatus in progressive muscle degeneration induced by vitamin E-deficiency. Ph.D. dissertation, Rutgers University, New Brunswick, New Jersey.

Spanier, A. M., and Bird, J. W. 1982. Endogenous cathepsin B inhibitor activity in normal and myopathic red and white skeletal muscle. *Muscle Nerve* **5,** 313.

Stagni, N., and DeBernard, B. 1968. Lysosome enzyme activity in rat and beef skeletal muscle. *Biochim. Biophys. Acta* **170,** 129.

Stanley, D. W. 1983. A review of the muscle cell cytoskeleton and its possible relation to meat texture. *Food Microstruct.* **2,** 99.

Starkey, P. M. 1977. Elastase and cathepsin G, the serine proteinases of human neutrophil leucocytes and spleen. *In* "Proteinases in Mammalian Cells and Tissues" (A. J. Barrett, ed.), p. 57. North-Holland, New York.

Starkey, P. M., and Barrett, A. J. 1976. Neutral proteinases of human spleen: Purification and criteria for homogeneity of elastase and cathepsin G. *Biochem. J.* **155,** 255.

Starr, R., and Offer, G. 1983. H-protein and X-protein. Two new components of thick filaments of vertebrate skeletal muscle. *J. Mol. Biol.* **170,** 675.

Stauber, W. T. 1981. Lysosomes and skeletal muscle atrophy. *In* "Mechanism of Muscle Adaptation to Functional Requirements" (F. Guba, G. Marechal, and O. Takacs, eds.). *Adv. Physiol. Sci.* **24,** 171. Pergamon, Elmsford, New York.

Stauber, W. T., and Bird, J. W. C. 1974. S-q zonal fractionation studies of rat skeletal muscle lysosome-rich fractions. *Biochim. Biophys. Acta* **338,** 234.

Stauber, W. T., and Ong, S. H. 1982a. Fluorescence demonstration of a cathepsin H-like protease in cardiac, skeletal and vascular smooth muscles. *Histochem. J.* **14,** 585.

Stauber, W. T., and Ong, S. H. 1982b. Fluorescence demonstration of dipeptidyl peptidase I (cathepsin C) in skeletal, cardiac and vascular smooth muscles. *J. Histochem. Cytochem.* **30,** 162.

Stauber, W. T., and Schottelius, B. A. 1975. Enzyme activities and distributions following denervation of anterior and posterior latissimus dorsi muscles. *Exp. Neurol.* **48**, 524.

Stauber, W. T., and Schottelius, B. A. 1981. Isopycnic-zonal centrifugation of plasma membrane, sarcoplasmic reticular fragments lysosomes, and cytoplasmic proteins from phasic skeletal muscle. *Biochim. Biophys. Acta* **640**, 285.

Stauber, W. T., Gauthier, F., and Ong, S. H. 1981. Identification and possible regulation of muscle cell lysosomal protease activity by exogenous protease inhibitors. *Acta Biol. Med. Ger.* **40**, 1317.

St. John, A. C., McElligott, M. A., Lee, J. A., Keaton, K. S., Yorke, G., Roisen, F. J., and Bird, J. W. C. 1981. Lyosomal proteinases in cultured muscle cells. *In* "Proteinases and Their Inhibitors" (V. Turk and Lj. Vitale, eds.). Pergamon, Oxford.

Stromer, M. H., and Goll, D. E. 1967. Molecular properties of post-mortem muscle. *J. Food Sci.* **32**, 329, 386.

Subramaniam, M., Koppikar, S. V., and Fatterpaker, P. 1978. Rapid purification of mitochondrial proteases: Use of affinity chromatography. *Indian J. Biochem. Biophys.* **15**, 214.

Suda, H., Aoyagi, T., Namada, M., Takeuchi, T., and Umezawa, H. 1972. Antipain, a new protease inhibitor isolated from actinomycetes. *J. Antibiol. (Jpn.)* **25**, 263.

Sugden, P. H. 1980. The effects of calcium ions, ionophore A23187 and inhibition of energy metabolism on protein degradation in rat diaphragm and epitrochlearis muscle *in vitro*. *Biochem. J.* **190**, 593.

Sugita, H., and Ishiura, S. 1980. Calcium activated neutral protease in Duchenne muscular dystrophy. *In* "Current Research in Muscular Dystrophy" (K. Myoshi, ed.), p. 108. Japan Society Press, Tokyo.

Sugita, H., Ishiura, S., Suzuki, K., and Imahori, K. 1980. Ca^{++}-activated neutral protease and its inhibitors: *In vitro* effect on intact myofibrils. *Muscle Nerve* **3**, 335.

Suzuki, A., and Goll, D. E. 1974. Quantitative assay for CASF (Ca^{++}-activated sarcoplasmic factor) activity, and effect of CASF treatment on ATPase activities of rabbit myofibrils. *Agric. Biol. Chem.* **38**, 2167.

Suzuki, A., Okitani, A., and Fujimaki, M. 1969. Some physiochemical properties and proteolytic specificity of rabbit muscular cathepsin D. *Agric. Biol. Chem.* **33**, 1723.

Suzuki, A., Saito, M., Sato, H., and Nonami, Y. 1978. Effect of materials released from myofibrils by Ca^{++}-activated factor on Z-disk reconstitution. *Agric. Biol. Chem.* **42**, 2111.

Suzuki, A., Ishiura, S., Tsuji, S., Katamoto, T., Sugita, H., and Imahori, K. 1979. Calcium activated neutral protease from human skeletal muscle. *FEBS Lett.* **104**, 355.

Suzuki, A., Tsuji, S., Ishiura, S., Kimura, Y., Kubota, S., and Imahori, K. 1981. Autolysis of calcium-activated neutral protease of chicken skeletal muscle. *J. Biochem.* **90**, 1787.

Suzuki, K., and Tsuji, S. 1982. Synergistic activation of calcium-activated neutral protease by Mn^{++} and Ca^{++}. *FEBS Lett.* **140**, 16.

Suzuki, K., Hayashi, H., Hayashi, T., and Iwai, K. 1983. Amino acid sequence around the active site cysteine residue of calcium-activated neutral protease (CANP). *FEBS Lett.* **152**, 67.

Swick, R. W. 1958. Measurement of protein turnover in rat liver. *J. Biol. Chem.* **231**, 751.

Swick, R. W., and Song, H. 1974. Turnover rates of various proteins. *J. Anim. Sci.* **38**, 1150.

Syròvy, I., Hàjek, I., and Gutmann, E. 1966. Factors affecting the proteolytic activity in denervated muscle. *Physiol. Bohemoslov.* **15**, 7.

Szpacenko, A., Kay, J., Goll, D. E., and Otsuka, Y. 1981. A different form of the Ca^{++}-dependent protease activated by micromolar levels of Ca^{++}. *In* "Proceedings of the Symposium on Proteinases and Their Inhibitors: Structure, Function and Applied Aspects" (V. Turk and Lj. Vitale, eds.), p. 151. Pergamon, Oxford.

Tagerud, S., and Libelius, R. 1984. Lysosomes in skeletal muscle following denervation. *Cell Tissue Res.* **236**, 73.

Takahashi, K., and Sato, H. 1979. Post-mortem changes in skeletal muscle connectin. *J. Biochem. (Tokyo)* **85**, 1539.

Takahashi, K., Fukazawa, T., and Yasui, T. 1967. Formation of myofibrillar fragments and reversible contraction of sarcomeres in chicken pectoral muscle. *J. Food Sci.* **32**, 409.

Takahashi, K., Chang, W. J., and Ko, J. S. 1974. Specific inhibition of acid proteases from brain, kidney, skeletal muscle, and insectivorous plants by diazoactyl-DL-norleucine methyl ester and by pepstatin. *J. Biochem. (Tokyo)* **76**, 897.

Takahashi, K., Isemura, M., and Ikenaka, T. 1979. Isolation and characterization of three forms of cathepsin B from porcine liver. *J. Biochem. (Tokyo)* **85**, 1053.

Takahashi, K., Hattori, A., Nakamura, F., and Yamanoue, M. 1983. Ca^{++}-induced weakening of myofibrillar structure during post-mortem storage of skeletal muscle. *Proc. World Conf. Anim. Prod. 5th, Tokyo*.

Takahashi-Nakamura, M., Tsuji, S., Suzuki, K., and Imahori, K. 1981. Purification and characterization of an inhibitor of calcium-activated neutral protease from rabbit skeletal muscle. *J. Biochem. (Tokyo)* **90**, 1583.

Takala, T. E., Myllyla, V. V., Salminen, A., Tolonen, U., Hassinen, I. E., and Vihko, V. 1983. Lysosomal and non-lysosomal hydrolases of skeletal muscle in neuromuscular diseases. *Arch. Neurol.* **40**, 541.

Tallan, H. H., Jones, M. E., and Fruton, J. S. 1952. On the proteolytic enzymes of animal tissues. X. Beef spleen cathepsin C. *J. Biol. Chem.* **194**, 793.

Tappel, A. L. 1969. Cellular degradation of proteins. *In* "Lysosomes in Biology and Pathology" (J. T. Dingle and H. B. Fell, eds.), Vol. 2, p. 167. Elsevier, Amsterdam.

Taylor, S. L., and Tappel, A. L. 1974. Identification and separation of lysosomal carboxypeptidases. *Biochim. Biophys. Acta* **341**, 99.

Ten Cate, A. R., and Syrbu, S. 1974. Relation between alkaline phosphatase activity and phagocytosis and degradation of collagen by the fibroblast. *J. Anat.* **177**, 351.

Thompson, G. B., Davidson, W. D., Montgomery, M. W., and Anglemier, A. F. 1968. Alteration of bovine sarcoplasmic proteins as influenced by high temperature. *J. Food Sci.* **33**, 68.

Thompson, R. C., and Ballou, J. E. 1956. Studies on metabolic turnover with tritium as a tracer. *J. Biol. Chem.* **223**, 795.

Tischler, M. E. 1981. Hormonal regulation of protein degradation in skeletal and cardiac muscle. *Life Sci.* **28**, 2569.

Tokuyasu, K. T., Dutton, A. H., and Singer, S. J. 1983. Immunoelectron microscope studies of desmin (skeletin) localization and intermediate filament organization in chicken skeletal muscle. *J. Cell Biol.* **96**, 1727.

Topping, T. M., and Travis, D. F. 1974. An electron cytochemical study of mechanism of lysosomal activity in the rat left ventricular mural myocardium. *J. Ultrastruct. Res.* **46**, 1.

Torboli, A. 1970. Azione di alcuni inhibitori delle proteinasi sulle catepsine nei ratti recchi e giovani. *Boll. Soc. Ital. Biol. Sper.* **46**, 845.

Towatari, T., and Katunuma, N. 1983. Selective cleavage of peptide bond by cathepsin L and B from rat liver. *J. Biochem. (Tokyo)* **93**, 1119.

Towatari, T., Tanaka, K., Yoshikawa, D., and Katunuma, N. 1978. Purification and properties of a new cathepsin from rat liver. *J. Biochem. (Tokyo)* **84**, 659.

Toyo-Oka, T., and Masaki, T. 1979. Calcium-activated neutral protease from bovine ventricular muscle: Isolation and some of its properties. *J. Mol. Cell. Cardiol.* **11**, 769.

Travis, J., Baugh, R., Giles, P. J., Johnson, D., Bowen, J., and Reilly, C. F. 1978. Human leukocytes elastase and cathepsin G: isolation, characterization and interaction with plasma protease inhibitors. *In* "Neutral Proteases of Human Polymorphonuclear Leukocytes" (K. Havemann and A. Janoff, eds.), p. 118. Urban & Schwartzenberg, Baltimore.

Trinick, J., Knight, P., and Whiting, A. 1984. Characterization of native titin. *Proc. Eur. Meet. Meat Res. Workers, 30th*, p. 137.

Tsoas, O., Crivellaro, O., Lazo, P. S., Sun, S. C., Pontremoli, S., and Horecker, B. L. 1981. Converting enzyme of fructose-1,6-biphosphatase from rat liver. *In* "Proteases and Their Inhibitors" (V. Turk and Lj. Vitale, eds.), p. 67. Pergamon, Oxford.

Tsung, P. K., Kegeles, S. W., and Becker, E. L. 1977. Some differences in intracellular distribution and properties of the chymotrypsin-like esterase activity by human and rabbit neutrophils. *Biochim. Biophys. Acta* **499**, 212.

Turk, V., and Vitale, Lj., eds. 1981. "Proteinases and Their Inhibitors," p. 376. Pergamon, Oxford.

Turk, V., Kregar, I., and Lebez, D. 1957. New observation of bovine spleen cathepsins D and E. *Iugosl. Physiol. Pharmacol. Acta* **3**, 448.

Turk, V., Kregar, I., and Lebez, D. 1968. Some properties of cathepsin E from bovine spleen. *Enzymologia* **34**, 89.

Turk, V., Kregar, I., Gubensek, F., and Lebez, D. 1969. *In vitro* transition of beef spleen cathepsin E into cathepsin D. *Enzymologia* **36**, 132.

Turk, V., Kregar, I., Gubensek, F., and Locniker, P. 1978. Bovine spleen cathepsins D and S: Purification, characterization and structural studies. *In* "Protein Turnover and Lysosome Function" (H. L. Segal and D. J. Doyle, eds.), p. 353. Academic Press, New York.

Turk, V., Kregar, I., Gubensek, T., Popovic, P., Locnikar, P., and Lah, T. 1980. Carboxyl and thiol intracellular proteinases. *In* "Enzyme Regulation and Mechanism of Action" (P. Mildner and B. Ries, eds.), p. 317. Peragamon, Oxford.

Turnsek, T., Kregar, I., and Lebez, D. 1975. Acid sulphydryl proteases from calf lymph nodes. *Biochim. Biophys. Acta* **403**, 514.

Udaka, K., and Hayashi, H. 1965. Further purification of a protease inhibitor from rabbit skin with healing inflammation. *Biochim. Biophys. Acta* **97**, 251.

Ukabaim, I. O. 1986. Neutral proteolytic activity in early post-mortem skeletal muscle. *Diss. Abstr. Int.* **846**, 3092.

Umezawa, H., and Aoyagi, T. 1977. Activities of proteinase inhibitors of microbial origin. *In* "Proteinases in Mammalian Cells and Tissues" (A. J. Barrett, ed.), p. 637. Elsevier, Amsterdam.

Valin, C. 1967. Isolement d'une fraction protéique a activité protéolytique du muscle de bovin. *Ann. Biol. Anim. Biochim. Biophys.* **7**, 475.

Valin, C. 1968. Post-mortem changes in myofibrillar protein solubility. *J. Food Technol.* **3**, 171.

Valin, C., Touraille, C., Ouali, A., and Lacourt, A. 1981. Effect of electrical stimulation on aging and eating quality of beef. *Sci. Alim.* **19**, 467.

Vallee, B. L. 1955. Zn and metallo-enzymes. *Adv. Protein Chem.* **10**, 317.

Van Berkel, T. J. C., Kruijt, J. K., and Koster, J. F. 1975. Identity and activities of lysosomal enzymes in parenchymal and non-parenchymal cells from rat liver. *Eur. J. Biochem.* **58**, 145.

Vandenburgh, H., and Kaufman, S. 1980. Protein degradation in embronic skeletal muscle. Effect of medium, cell type, inhibitors, and passive stretch. *J. Biol. Chem.* **255**, 5826.

Vanha-Perttula, T., and Kalliomäki, J. L. 1973. Comparison of dipeptide arylamidase I and II. Amino acid arylamidase and acid phosphatase activities in normal and pathological human serums. *Clin. Chim. Acta* **44**, 249.

Vedeckis, W. V., Freeman, M. R., Schrader, W. T., and O'Malley, B. W. 1980. Progestrone-binding components of chick oviducts: Partial purification and characterization of a calcium-activated protease which hydrolyzes the progestrone receptor. *Biochemistry* **19**, 335.

Venge, P., Olsson, I., and Odeberg, H. 1975. Cationic proteins of human granulocytes. V. Interaction with plasma protease inhibitors. *Scand. J. Clin. Lab. Invest.* **35**, 737.

Venugopal, B., and Bailey, M. E. 1978. Lysosomal proteinases in muscle tissue and leukocytes of meat animals. *Meat Sci.* **2**, 227.

Vernon, H. M. 1908. "Intracellular Enzymes." Murray, London.

Vidalence, P., Cottin, P., Merdaci, N., and Ducastaing, 1983. Stability of two Ca^{++}-dependent neutral proteinases and their specific inhibitor during post-mortem storage of rabbit skeletal muscle. *J. Sci. Food Agric.* **34**, 1241.

Vihko, V., and Salminen, A. 1983. Acid hydrolase activity in tissues of mice after physical stress. *Comp. Biochem. Physiol. (B)* **76**, 341.

Vihko, V., Salminen, A., and Rantamaki, J. 1978. Acid hydrolase activity in red and white skeletal muscle of mice during a two-week period following exhausting exercise. *Pflügers Arch.* **378**, 99.

Vihko, V., Salminen, A., and Rantamaki, J. 1979. Exhaustive exercise, endurance training, and acid hydrolase activity in skeletal muscle. *J. Appl. Physiol.* **47**, 43.

Walsh, C. 1979. "Enzyme Reaction Mechanisms." Freeman, San Fransisco.

Wang, K. 1981. Nebulin, a giant protein component of N_2-line of striated muscle. *J. Cell Biol.* **91**, 355a.

Wang, K. 1983. Cytoskeletal matrix in striated muscle: The role of titin, nebulin and intermediate filaments. *In* "Cross-Bridges Mechanisms in Muscular Contraction" (G. H. Pollack and H. Sugi, eds.). Plenum, New York.

Wang, K., and Ramirez-Mitchell, R. 1983. A network of transverse and longitudinal intermediate filaments is associated with sarcomeres of adult vertebrate skeletal muscle. *J. Cell Biol.* **96**, 562.

Wang, K., and Ramirez-Mitchell, R. 1984. Architecture of titin-containing cytoskeletal matrix in striated muscle. Mapping of distinct epitopes of titin specified by monoclonal antibodies. *Biophys. J.* **45**, 392a.

Wang, K., and Williamson, C. L. 1980. Identification of an N_2-line protein of striated muscle. *Proc. Natl. Acad. Sci. U.S.A.* **77**, 3254.

Ward, W. F., Chua, B. L., Li, J. B., Morgan, H. E., and Mortimore, G. E. 1979. Inhibition of basal and deprivation-induced proteolysis by leupeptin and pepstatin in perfused rat liver and heart. *Biochem. Biophys. Res. Commun.* **87**, 92.

Watabe, S., Terada, A., Ikeda, T., Kouyama, H., Toguchi, S., and Yago, N. 1976. Polyphosphate ions increased the activity of bovine spleen cathepsin D. *Biochem. Biophys. Res. Commun.* **89**, 1161.

Waterlow, J. C., Garlick, P. J., and Millward, D. J. 1978. "Protein Turnover in Mammalian Tissues and in the Whole Body," p. 481. North-Holland, Amsterdam.

Waxman, L. 1981. Calcium-activated proteases in mammalian tissues. *In* "Methods in Enzymology" (L. Lorand, ed.), Vol. 80, p. 664. Academic Press, New York.

Waxman, L., and Krebs, E. G. 1978. Identification of two protease inhibitors from bovine cardiac muscle. *J. Biol. Chem.* **253**, 5888.

Weber, A. 1984. Aging of bovine muscle: Desmin degradation observed via enzyme linked immunosorbent assay. *Proc. EM Meet. Meat Res. Workers, 30th, Bristol, U.K.*, p. 135.

Weber, H. H. 1957. The biochemistry of muscle. *Annu. Rev. Biochem.* **26**, 667.

Weglicki, W. B., Ruth, R. C., Gottwik, W. G., McNamara, D. B., and Owens, K. 1975. Lysosomes of cardiac and skeletal muscle: Resolution by zonal centrifugation. *Recent Adv. Stud. Cardiac Struct. Metab.* **8**, 503.

Weinstock, I. M., and Iodice, A. A. 1969. Acid hydrolase activity in muscular dystrophy and denervation atrophy. *In* "Lysosomes in Biology and Pathology" (J. T. Dingle and H. B. Fell, eds.), p. 450. North-Holland, Amsterdam.

Weinstock, I. M., Goldrich, A. D., and Milhorat, A. T. 1956. Enzyme studies in muscular dystrophy. *Proc. Soc. Exp. Biol. Med.* **91**, 302.

Weinstock, I. M., Epstein, S., and Milhorat, A. T. 1958. Enzyme studies in muscular dystrophy. *Proc. Soc. Exp. Biol. Med.* **99**, 272.

Weisman, G. 1964. Labilization and stabilization of lysosomes. *Fed. Proc., Fed. Am. Soc. Exp. Biol.* **23**, 1038.

Welgus, H. G., Stricklin, G. P., Eisen, A. Z., Bauer, E. A., Cooney, R. V., and Jeffrey, J. J. 1979. A specific inhibitor of vertebrate collagenase produced by human skin fibroblasts. *J. Biol. Chem.* **254**, 1938.

Welman, E., and Peters, T. J. 1976. Properties of lysosomes in guinea pig heart: Subcellular distribution and *in vitro* stability. *J. Mol. Cell. Cardiol.* **8**, 443.

Werb, Z., Burleigh, M. C., Barrett, A. J., and Starkey, P. M. 1974. The interaction of α_2-marcoglobin with proteases. Binding and inhibition of mammalian collagenases with other metal proteinases. *Biochem. J.* **139**, 359.

Wharton, C. W., Crook, E. M., and Brocklehurst, K. 1968. The preparation and some properties of bromelain covalently attached to D-(carboxymethyl)cellulose. *Eur. J. Biochem.* **6**, 565.

Wheelock, M. J. 1982. Evidence for two structurally different forms of skeletal muscle Ca^{++}-activated protease. *J. Biol. Chem.* **257**, 12471.

Whitaker, J. R. 1959. Chemical changes associated with aging of meat with emphasis on the proteins. *Adv. Food Res.* **9**, 1.

Whitaker, J. R., and Perez-Villasenor, J. 1968. Chemical modification of papain. 1. Reaction with the chloromethyl ketones of phenylalanine and lysine with phenylmethylsulfonyl fluoride. *Arch. Biochem. Biophys.* **124**, 70.

Whitaker, J. N., Bertorini, T. E., and Mendell, J. R. 1983. Immunocytochemical studies of cathepsin D in human skeletal muscle. *Ann. Neurol.* **13**, 133.

Wiederanders, B., Bohley, P., and Kirschke, H. 1981. Age-dependent changes in intracellular protein turnover. *In* "Proteinases and Their Inhibitors" (V. Turk and Lj. Vitale, eds.), p. 25. Pergamon, Oxford.

Wildenthal, K. 1976. Hormonal and nutritional substrate control of cardiac lysosomal enzyme activities. *Circ. Res.* **39**, 441.

Wildenthal, K., and Crie, J. S. 1980. The role of lysosomes and lysosomal enzymes in cardiac protein turnover. *Fed. Proc., Fed. Am. Soc. Exp. Biol.* **39**, 37.

Wildenthal, K., and Mueller, E. A. 1974. Increased myocardial cathepsin D activity during regression of thyrotoxic cardiac hypertrophy. *Nature (London)* **249**, 478.

Wildenthal, K., Poole, A. R., and Dingle, J. T. 1975a. Influence of starvation on the activities and localization of cathepsin D and other lysosomal enzymes in hearts of rabbits and mice. *J. Mol. Cell. Cardiol.* **7**, 84.

Wildenthal, K., Poole, A. R., Glauert, A. M., and Dingle, J. T. 1975b. Dietary control of cardiac lysosomal enzyme activities. *Recent Adv. Stud. Cardiac Struct. Metab.* **8**, 519.

Wildenthal, K., Decker, R. S., Poole, A. R., and Dingle, J. T. 1977. Age-related alterations in cardiac lysosomes. *J. Mol. Cell. Cardiol.* **9**, 859.

Wilkinson, K. D., Urban, M. K., and Hass, A. L. 1980. Ubiquitin is the ATP-dependent proteolysis factor I of rabbit reticulocytes. *J. Biol. Chem.* **255**, 7529.

Willstätter, R., and Bamann, E. 1929. Uber die Proteasen der Magenschleimhaut. Erste Abhandlung uber die Enzyme der Leukocyten. *Z. Physiol. Chem.* **180**, 127.

Woessner, J. F., Jr. 1977a. Specificity and biological role of cathepsin D. *In* "Acid Proteases" (J. Tang, ed.), p. 313. Plenum, New York.

Woessner, J. F., Jr. 1977b. A latent form of collagenase in the involuting rat uterus and its activation by a serine proteinase. *Biochem. J.* **161**, 535.

Woodbury, R. G., Everitt, M., Sanada, Y., Katunuma, N., Lagunoff, D., and Neurath, H. 1978. A major serine protease in rat skeletal muscle: evidence for its mast cell origin. *Proc. Natl. Acad. Sci. U.S.A.* **75**, 5311.

Woolley, D. E., Glanville, R. W., Lindberg, K. A., Bailey, A. J., and Evanson, J. M. 1973. Action of human skin collagenase on cartilage collagen. *FEBS Lett.* **34**, 267.

Woolley, D. E., Lindberg, K. A., Glanville, R. W., and Evanson, J. M. 1975a. Action of rheumatoid synovial collagenase in cartilage collagen. Different susceptibilities of cartilage and tendon collagen to collagenase attack. *Eur. J. Biochem.* **50**, 437.

Woolley, D. E., Glanville, R. W., Crossley, M. J., and Evanson, J. M. 1975b. Purification of rheumatoid synovial collagenase and its action on soluble and insoluble collagen. *Eur. J. Biochem.* **54**, 611.

Wu, J. J., Dutson, T. R., and Carpenter, Z. L. 1982. Effect of post-mortem time and temperature on bovine intra-muscular collagen. *Meat Sci.* **7**, 161.

Yamamoto, K., Katsuda, N., Himeno, M., and Kato, K. 1979a. Cathepsin D of rat spleen. Affinity purification and properties of two types of cathepsin D. *Eur. J. Biochem.* **95**, 459.

Yamamoto, K., Samejima, K., and Yasui, T. 1979b. Changes produced in muscle proteins during incubation of muscle homogenates. *J. Food Sci.* **44**, 51.

Yates, L. D., and Greaser, M. L. 1983. Quantitative determination of myosin and actin in rabbit muscle. *J. Mol. Biol.* **168**, 123.

Yates, L. D., Dutson, T. R., Caldwell, J., and Carpenter, Z. L. 1983. Effect of temperature and pH on the post-mortem degradation of myofibrillar proteins. *Meat Sci.* **9**, 157.

Yosogawa, N., Sanada, Y., and Katunuma, N. 1978. Susceptibilities of various myofibrillar proteins to muscle serine proteases. *J. Biochem. (Tokyo)* **83**, 1355.

Young, M. 1979. Proteolytic activity of nerve growth-factor: A case of autocatalytic activation. *Biochemistry* **18**, 3050.

Young, O. A., Graafhuis, A. E., and Davey, L. C. 1980. Post-mortem changes in cytoskeletal proteins of muscle. *Meat Sci.* **5**, 41.

Young, V. R., and Munro, H. N. 1980. Muscle protein turnover in human beings in health and disease. *In* "Degradative Processes in Heart and Skeletal Muscle" (K. Wildenthal, ed.), p. 271. Elsevier, Amsterdam.

Zak, R., Martin, A. F., and Blough, R. 1979. Assessment of protein turnover by use of radioisotopic tracers. *Physiol. Rev.* **59**, 407.

Zalkin, H., Tapple, A. L., Caldwell, K. A., Shibko, S., Desai, I. D., and Holliday, T. A. 1962. Increased lysosomal enzymes in muscular dystrophy of vitamin E-deficient rats. *J. Biol. Chem.* **237**, 2678.

Zeece, M. G., Robson, R. M., Lusby, M. L., and Parrish, F. C. 1983. Proteolytic disassembly of myofibrils by calcium-activated protease. *nst. Food Technol. Annu. Meet. Program Abstr.* p. 153.

Zenser, T. V., Herman, C. A., and Davis, B. B. 1980. Effect of calcium and A23187 on renal inner medullary prostaglandin E_2 synthesis. *Am. J. Physiol.* **238**, E371.

Zilversmit, D. B. 1955. Meaning of turnover in biochemistry. *Nature (London)* **175**, 863.

Zimmerman, M., and Ashe, B. M. 1977. Substrate specificity of the elastase and chymotrypsin-like enzyme of the human granulocyte. *Biochim. Biophys. Acta* **480**, 241.

Zimmerman, U.-J. P., and Schlaepfer, W. W. 1984a. Multiple forms of Ca^{++}-activated protease from rat brain and muscle. *J. Biol. Chem.* **259**, 3210.

Zimmerman, U.-J. P., and Schlaepfer, W. W. 1984b. Kinase activities associated with calcium-activated neutral proteases. *Biochem. Biophys. Res. Commun.* **120**, 767.

ADVANCES IN FOOD RESEARCH, VOL. 31

OLIVE OIL: A REVIEW

A. KIRITSAKIS* AND P. MARKAKIS

*Department of Food Science and Human Nutrition
Michigan State University
East Lansing, Michigan 48824*

I. INTRODUCTION

Olive oil is the oil extracted from the fruit of the olive tree, *Olea europea* L. The fruit itself is marketed as table or pickled olives. Most of the world supply of olive oil originates from the Mediterranean countries. Of the 1600 thousand metric tons (tmt) of olive oil produced globally in 1977, about 600 tmt were

*Present address: Technological Educational Institute, Thessaloniki, Greece.

produced in Italy, 360 tmt in Spain, and 260 tmt in Greece. Smaller quantities came from Tunisia, Turkey, Portugal, Morocco, Libya, and other countries near the Mediterranean Sea as well as from Argentina and California. Olive oil is a traditional staple food for Mediterranean people.

Olive oil of good quality is characterized by a fragrant and delicate flavor, which is appreciated by the international gourmet and cherished by the native consumer. Olive oil is almost unique among vegetable oils in that it can be consumed without any refining treatment. Its moderate degree of unsaturation is considered nutritionally preferable to the high degree of saturation or unsaturation of many other edible fats and oils. Unfortunately, not all of the olive oil marketed around the world is of very good quality. Large quantities of olive oil must be refined, mainly because it came from poor quality fruit. The refining process, however, destroys the sensory attributes which are responsible for the extraordinary quality of olive oil.

In this article we review the literature pertinent to the chemistry and technology of olive oil. We also discuss practices which may improve the quality of this fine food product.

II. THE OLIVE TREE

The olive tree (or olive, a term also used for the olive fruit) is a relatively small evergreen tree, with narrow silvery leaves and small white flowers, known for its longevity. People believe that the gnarled veteran olive trees still growing in the Garden of Gethsemane (outside Jerusalem) are living witnesses of the drama which unfolded there nearly two thousand years ago (Standish, 1960). The cultivation of the olive was probably practiced long before the time of Christ, as is surmized by the pictures on ancient Greek vases (Fig. 1) and the jars for oil storage found at the Knossos Palace in Crete, an island with long tradition in olive cultivation (Hartmann and Bougas, 1970).

The botanical progenitor of the olive is thought to be the oleaster, *Olea sylvestris,* a wild type of olive with a small, skinny fruit, still growing around the Mediterranean Sea and occasionally used as grafting stock. The cultivated type probably evolved around the eastern Mediterranean and gradually spread to Southern Europe and North Africa. The Spanish missionaries brought it to California at about 1850, and immigrants from the Mediterranean introduced it to South America. Efforts to establish an olive industry in Australia, part of which is well suited to the cultivation of this tree, were not met with enthusiasm (Hartmann, 1962).

The olive thrives in deep, drained soils, clear, dry atmosphere, and moderate temperatures, which should never fall below 15°F (-9°C), if fruit is to be produced. However, a certain degree of chilling, differing considerably among

FIG. 1. Harvesting olives by beating with sticks. From a Mycenean vase, sixth century BC.

cultivars, is necessary for the initiation of flowering (Hartmann and Porlingis, 1957). Olive production often follows a 2-year cycle, with a good crop one year followed by a medium or poor crop the following year. Such a pattern creates serious problems for the industry of olive products. The causes of alternate year fruit bearing, as well as poor fruit production in general, include insufficient irrigation, inadequate fertilization, excessively dense planting, lack of adequate pest and disease control, and use of a single cultivar over a wide area, thereby reducing the chance for cross-pollination (Hartmann and Bougas, 1970).

III. THE OLIVE FRUIT

The olive fruit, or olive, is a drupe (like the cherry or the peach), oval in shape, and consists of two main parts, the pericarp and the enclosed seed or kernel. The pericarp is composed of the epicarp, or skin; the mesocarp, or pulp; and the endocarp, or stone, or pit, which contains the seed. The pulp represents 66–85% of the weight of the fruit. The pit, including the seed, makes up 13–30% of the fruit weight, and the skin is 1.5–3.5% of the fruit weight. The seed does not exceed 3% of the weight of the fruit (Frezzotti *et al.*, 1956). The average chemical composition of the fruit (Fedeli, 1977) is as follows:

Water	50.0
Oil	22.0
Sugars	19.1
Cellulose	5.8
Protein	1.6
Ash	1.5
	100.0

The pericarp contains 96–98% of the total amount of oil; the remaining 2–4% of the oil is in the kernel.

Over the centuries, many olive cultivars have been developed, differing in size, color, and chemical composition of the fruit. The olive cultivars best suited for oil production have medium size fruits which contain 15–40% oil when ripe. Olives used for pickling at the green stage contain smaller quantities of oil, as little as 8% or even less. Some of the better known olive cultivars used for oil production are: Arauco, Corfolia, Coroneiki, Daphnolia, Fratoio, Lechin, Picual, Razzola, Rougette, Smertolia, Taggiasca, Tsunati, and Zorzalena. Cultivars preferred for table olive production include the following: Ascolano, Conservolia, Gordal, Kalamata, Manzanilla, Mission, and Sevillano. Balatsouras (1984) describes the most important olive cultivars.

IV. PRODUCTION OF OLIVES AND OLIVE OIL

There are about 805 million olive trees in the world, covering approximately 24 million acres. Almost 98% of these trees are growing in the Mediterranean area. The annual world production of olive fruit is about 9.4 million metric tons (mt). Approximately 720,000 mt of this production are consumed as table olives, and the remaining 8,680,000 mt are used for the extraction of olive oil. Nearly 1.6 million mt of olive oil are produced globally, plus 160,000 mt of olive-residue oil. About 260,000 mt of olive oil and 200,000 mt of table olives are traded in international markets.

The aggregate value of olive products is estimated to be 2.8 billion U.S. dollars, of which about $2.5 billion represent the value of olive oil and $0.3 billion the value of table olives. Olive products account for almost 25% of the farming income in the Mediterranean basin as a whole. The production and consumption of olive oil and table olives in most of the olive cultivating countries are shown in Table I.

California produces 99% of the olives grown in the United States. Arizona is the only other state with a commercial production of olives. Most of the American olive crop is used for canning. The small amount of olive oil produced in California supplies less than 3% of the olive oil consumed in the United States; the rest is imported mostly from Spain and Italy.

Olive oil is an important commodity in the daily diet of the Mediterranean people. The Greeks have the highest per capita consumption, 20.8 kg yearly,

TABLE I

WORLD PRODUCTION AND CONSUMPTION OF OLIVE OIL AND TABLE OLIVES
(AVERAGE 1978–1983)

Country	Number of olive trees (millions)	Olive oil (tmt)		Table olives (tmt)	
		Production	Consumption	Production	Consumption
Algeria	20.2	11.7	11.6	6.2	5.3
Argentina	5.0	11.1	2.0	31.0	11.9
Chile	0.8	0.2	0.3	3.2	3.3
Cyprus	2.6	1.7	1.9	3.7	4.0
Egypt	1.1	0.1	0.6	6.9	9.6
France	6.0	1.6	25.9	2.0	26.8
Greece	117.6	259.3	197.8	71.2	22.1
Israel	1.5	2.9	2.5	11.3	9.4
Italy	181.8	550.2	593.7	71.5	95.0
Jordan	2.7	8.2	9.9	7.8	8.0
Lebanon	6.0	5.2	6.9	5.6	6.0
Libya	8.0	7.1	47.8	1.7	6.6
Mexico	0.5	1.2	1.2	8.9	8.9
Morocco	30.0	23.3	21.8	48.4	16.0
Peru	0.6	0.1	0.2	14.5	14.5
Portugal	50.0	43.9	38.5	20.4	17.7
Spain	188.7	446.7	348.0	168.0	77.4
Syria	26.5	49.7	47.7	32.6	33.9
Tunisia	56.0	96.7	45.1	8.5	7.9
Turkey	82.0	111.7	88.5	123.5	117.8
United States	2.2	0.8	27.0	68.1	108.0
Yugoslavia	4.5	3.0	4.0	0.5	1.5
Rest of world	10.7	4.1	58.4	11.0	96.9
World	805.0	1,640.5	1,584.0	726.5	708.5

although it varies considerably among locations within Greece. The Spanish consumption is 10.0 kg/person/year followed by the Italian one at 8.1 kg/ person/ year (Sellianakis, 1984).

V.   FRUIT DEVELOPMENT AND OIL FORMATION

The size of the olive drupes is affected by genetic and environmental factors. At maturity, the weight of a single fruit may vary from 2 to 12 g, although the extreme values of 0.5 or 20 g may be reached, occasionally. During the growth period of the olive fruit (June to December for the northern hemisphere), along with the increase in weight, the following changes have been observed (Fig. 2). In the cultivar Gordal, as an example, and on dry weight basis, the oil content of the fruit increased continually; the reducing sugar content, after a brief rise, declined up to maturity; the crude fiber content dropped sharply initially and

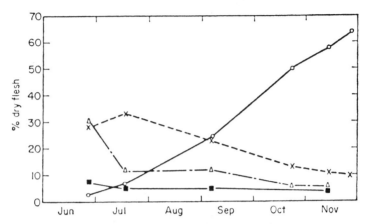

FIG. 2. Typical changes in olive flesh components for Gordal variety. ○, Crude oil; X, reducing sugars; △, crude fiber; ■, total N × 6.25. From Hernandez Diez (1971).

gradually afterward; the protein content (N × 6.25) remained low throughout the development of the fruit, as did the ash content (not shown in Fig. 2) (Fernandez Diez, 1971).

The rate of olive fruit maturation is affected by several factors including cultivar; age of the tree—the fruit of younger trees mature faster; health of the tree—sickly trees have difficulty bringing their fruit to maturity; moisture of the soil—dry spells retard fruit maturation; fertilization—properly fertilized soils allow trees to mature their fruit early; and light—abundance of sunshine shortens the time of maturation.

The biosynthesis of the oil triglycerides involves three processes: (1) Fatty acids are synthesized by successive additions of malonyl CoA to a primer mole-cule of acetyl-CoA. Since the three-carbon malonyl residue is decarboxylated after each addition, the progressive lengthening of the fatty acid chain by two carbon atoms is understandable. A multienzyme system catalyzes the condensa-tion, reduction, and dehydration reactions that are necessary for the completion of the fatty acid synthesis. (2) Glycerol phosphate is formed from the dihydroxy acetone phosphate of the glycolytic pathway. (3) Fatty acids, as CoA derivatives, are then transferred to the free hydroxy groups of the glycerol phosphate. De-phosphorylation and completion of the esterification of glycerol follow (Hess, 1975).

VI. CONSTITUENTS OF THE OLIVE FRUIT

Commercially, the mesocarp (pulp) is the most important part of the olive fruit. At maturity, water and oil account for 85–90% of the weight of the pulp.

TABLE II

PROXIMATE ANALYSIS OF THE OLIVE MESOCARP OF TWO SPANISH AND
THREE GREEK CULTIVARS (% BY WEIGHT)

Constituent	Spanish (average)	Greek (average)
Moisture	63.9	66.7
Oil	21.0	22.9
Protein (N, % $\times$ 6.25)	1.2	0.3
Ash	0.8	1.3
Sugars	3.5	8.8[a]
Crude fiber	1.6	
Other	7.1	

[a] Carbohydrate (by difference).

The proximate composition of the olive mesocarp of two Spanish (Borbolla *et al.*, 1955) and three Greek cultivars (Manoukas, 1972) used for oil extraction is shown in Table II. The main sugar of the pulp is glucose, accompanied by fructose. Sucrose, mannose, and galactose have also been detected in certain cultivars (Fedeli, 1977). Small quantities of the following organic acids have been reported as present in the olive pulp: citric, malic, oxalic, malonic, fumaric, tartaric, lactic, acetic, and tricarballelic.

A variety of phenolic compounds have been found in olive pulp. Caffeic acid and ferulic acid are among the simpler of them. Anthocyanins, specifically the glycosides of cyanidin and peonidin, are responsible for the purple and blue color of ripe olives. A phenolic glucoside typical of olives is oleuropein. It is responsible for the bitter taste of immature olives. According to Vaughn *et al.* (1961), the color of black olives is due to the oxidation products of oleuropein and other phenolics.

The results of a mineral analysis of olive pulp from a Greek cultivar are shown in Table III (Manoukas, 1972). It is worth noting that the potassium content is

TABLE III

MINERAL CONSTITUENTS PRESENT IN THE OLIVE PULP OF A GREEK
CULTIVAR (ppm)

Constituent	Content	Constituent	Content
Calcium	386	Phosphorus	188
Chlorine	683	Potassium	3642
Iron	14	Sodium	48
Magnesium	192	Zinc	7
Manganese	2		

TABLE IV

AN ANALYSIS OF THE OLIVE SEED (g/100 g fresh wt)

Constituent	Content	Constituent	Content
Lipid	37.40	Phosphorus	0.32
Carbohydrate	33.30	Calcium	0.20
Protein (% N × 6.25)	21.94	Iron	0.02
Moisture	4.60	Magnesium	0.02
Ash	2.20		

over two-thirds of the total mineral content of olive pulp. The olive pulp also contains small quantities of proteins and other nitrogenous compounds, pectins, salts, pigments, and flavor compounds. Of particular interest are the green pigments chlorophyll *a* and chlorophyll *b,* as well as the brown pheophytin *a* and pheophytin *b,* since small quantities of these pigments are carried into the extracted oil and promote its oxidation in the presence of light (Interesse *et al.,* 1971). The results of a proximate analysis along with the content in certain minerals of the olive seed appear in Table IV (Samir and Hegsted, 1974).

VII. OLIVE HARVESTING

The methods of harvesting olives remained unchanged for many centuries. Only recently have new techniques been introduced to facilitate the collection of olives. Traditionally, olives to be pickled are harvested by hand in the fall or early winter at the appropriate green–yellow stage. Olives for oil extraction are collected by beating the branches of the trees with long poles after the olive skin has darkened and the oil content has increased substantially. In Greece and other olive-producing countries, where farm labor is getting scarce in recent years, plastic nets are spread under the trees of certain cultivars and the fruits are let to fall on the nets naturally. In order to minimize the deterioration of the oil, the olives should not be left on the nets more than 15 days (Kiritsakis and Markakis, 1984). Chemical sprays helping the release of the fruit from the tree have also been introduced. Mechnical tree shakers in combination with stationary canvas or mechanized collecting frames are used in California for the harvesting of olives. Studies by Hartmann and Opitz (1977) indicate that olive harvesting represents 50–70% of the total labor cost for the production of olives in California.

Handpicking from the tree undoubtedly yields fruit of the best quality for both the table olive and the olive oil industries. At the same time, handpicking results in minimum injury to the tree. According to Jacini (1976), no more than 20% of the olive oil produced in Italy originates from olives picked by hand. For the manufacture of olive oil, the olives must be harvested at an optimum stage of maturity and when they are richest in oil. This point is not easily determined, but it is close to the time the fruit begins to darken. Subsequently, the fruit gradually loses weight as a result of dehydration, and its acidity increases (Suarez, 1975).

The time of optimum maturity may vary among years, cultivation areas, trees within the same grove, or individual fruits on the same tree. It is interesting that in practice factors such as weather, availability of labor or machines for harvesting, capacity of the olive mill, and size and health of the crop determine the harvesting time rather than optimum maturity (Frezzotti *et al.*, 1956). Of course, very early and late harvests must be avoided, as both the quantity and the quality of the crop are adversely affected by such practices.

VIII. OLIVE STORAGE

Ideally, the extraction of the oil should follow the harvesting of the olives without delay. As this is impractical, the olives must be stored for a period of time before processing. During storage, several chemical and biochemical alterations may occur leading to the deterioration of the oil. Perhaps the most serious damage is caused by the so-called fermentation of the olives. This is a term describing the reactions caused by both the enzymes indigenous to the olive tissue and those produced by bacteria, yeasts, and molds growing on it. As the olive tissue is respiring, heat is produced which, if not effectively dissipated, accelerates the enzymatic actions. Lipolysis, lipid oxidation, and other undesirable reactions occur, leading to lowering of the oil quality.

In order to minimize the effect of these activities, storage in cool buildings is recommended, with the olives piled in layers not exceeding 25 cm. Spreading the olives on perforated trays and stacking the trays leads to better utilization of storage space. It has also been suggested to store olives under water in tanks. Adding to the water mild preservatives such as salt (3%), or citric acid (0.03%) and salt (3%), or metabisulfite (2%), would result in better storage (Suarez, 1975). Partial drying of the olives with infrared radiation before storage has been tried, although such a treatment appears too costly. In recent years, plastic bags are increasingly used for transporting and storing olives. Such a use of plastic bags should be discouraged, because the conditions inside them favor microbial growth and spoilage of the fruit.

IX. OLIVE OIL EXTRACTION

Milling or crushing of the olives is the first step in oil extraction. The traditional milling machine, the edge runner, consists of a large bowl in which two heavy wheels revolve, crushing the olives. In ancient mills, the bowl and wheels were made of stone, while steel is used in modern mills. In recent years, newer types of olive crushing equipment have been introduced, such as the Riedz Disintegrator and the International Food Grinder.

In traditional mills, the olive paste obtained from the crushing is placed in cloths made of esparto grass or synthetic fibers, the cloths are folded, placed between metal or wooden racks and subjected to hydraulic pressure. One or two successive pressings are applied, and the expressed mixture of water and oil is subjected to separation either by settling or by centrifugation. In more modern mills the traditional pressing has been abandoned. Instead, the oil is separated from the aqueous phase (so-called vegetable water) and from the cake (moist solids) either by centrifugation or a combination of selective filtration and centrifugation.

Centrifugation Process. The olives are washed, milled, and the resulting paste is malaxed. The purpose of malaxation is to promote the coalescing of small oil drops into larger ones, thereby facilitating the separation of the oil and water phases. The malaxators are usually cylindrical vats with rotating blades and double walls through which circulates warm water. The heating of the paste accelerates the merging of the oil drops, but it may result in the loss of volatile aroma compounds (Mendoza, 1975). Water is added to the maxaled paste and the mixture is centrifuged through a decanter. Three fractions are obtained as a result of the centrifugation: the olive cake, the water phase, and the oil. The oil still contains a small quantity of water from which it is separated by a second centrifugation in a vertical separator.

Combination Process. In this process, also known as the Rapanelli process, the paste obtained after washing, milling, and malaxing the olives is subjected to a selective filtration which allows about 80% of the oil to be separated from the moist paste. Selective filtration is based on the property of hydrophilic filters to allow the aqueous phase to pass in preference to the oil phase. The most common filtration model is the sinolea unit. The filtered-off oil, known as the sinolea oil, still contains some water, from which it is separated by centrifugation. In order to recover the oil remaining in the paste, the latter is further moistened, malaxed again, and subjected to centrifugation in a decanter, as a result of which additional oil is obtained, the so-called decanter oil. The water that may be present in the decanter oil is separated by a final centrifugation.

Details on these processes are given by Petruccioli (1975) and Fedeli (1977). It is worth mentioning that efforts have been made to increase the yield of oil from olives by using enzymes. Pectin depolymerase, papain, cellulase, hemicellulase, and acid protease are enzymes which increase the oil yield, decrease the extraction time, or both (Montedoro and Petruccioli, 1972, 1974). Simultaneous use of enzymes and absorbing agents is reported to have increased the oil yield and improved the quality of the olive oil (Montedoro *et al.*, 1976).

The oil extracted from the sound olive fruit by mechanical means is known as *virgin olive oil* and is marketed without additional processing. If, however, poor quality olives (fermented, infested, overripe) have been used for extraction, the oil has high acidity and undesirable flavor. Oil of such quality is subjected to refining treatments, after which it is marketed as *refined olive oil*. The refining operations include (1) neutralization of the acidity by means of alkalies or ion-exchange resins; (2) deodorization by steam injection and/or application of vacuum; and (3) bleaching through use of activated carbon or diatomaceous earth.

The residue remaining after the mechanical extraction of the oil from the olives, the oil cake as it is often called, contains considerable quantities of oil. In order to gain this oil, the cake is coarsely ground, partially dried, and extracted with a fat solvent, usually hexane, in a continuous or batch process. The solvent extraction should be applied soon after the olive cake is prepared, as the latter is rich in lipolytic and oxidizing enzymes which act detrimentally on the *olive-residue oil*.

A treatment applied to olive oil less frequently than other edible oils is winterization. This is the removal of high melting point glycerides by chilling or solvent extraction (Fedeli, 1977).

X.   COMPOSITION OF OLIVE OIL

Olive oil is chiefly a mixture of glycerides, which are esters of glycerol with fatty acids. In addition, olive oil contains small quantities of free fatty acids, glycerol, phosphatides (e.g., lecithin), pigments, carbohydrates, proteins, flavor compounds, sterols, and resinous substances of uncertain identity.

A.   THE FATTY ACIDS OF OLIVE OIL

The major fatty acids present as glycerides in olive oil are oleic (18:1), linoleic (18:2), palmitoleic (16:1), palmitic (16:0), and stearic (18:0). Oleic acid is represented in much higher concentrations than the other acids. The percentage distribution of fatty acids in olive oil is shown in Table V. In a similar table prepared by Gracian (1968) and based on the analysis of about 4,000 samples originating from six countries (Spain, Italy, Greece, Tunisia, Argentina,

TABLE V

DISTRIBUTION OF FATTY ACIDS IN OLIVE OIL (%)[a]

Acid	Content	Acid	Content
Oleic acid	56.0–83.0	Myristic acid	0.0–0.1
Palmitic acid	7.5–20.0	Arachidic acid	0.8 (max)
Linoleic acid	3.5–20.0	Behenic acid	0.2 (max)
Stearic acid	0.5–5.0	Lignoceric acid	1.0 (max)
Palmitoleic acid	0.3–3.5	Heptadecanoic acid	0.5 (max)
Linolenic acid	0.0–1.5	Heptadecenoic acid	0.6 (max)

[a] Source: International Olive Oil Council (IOOC) (1984).

and the United States), the percentage ranges for the five major fatty acids are slightly wider than those of the IOOC table and the average values are as follows:

Oleic acid	67.0%
Linoleic acid	15.2%
Palmitic acid	14.0%
Palmitoleic acid	1.9%
Stearic acid	1.9%

The Codex Alimentarius Committee on Fats and Oils of the FAO/WHO (1970) has set the following low and high limits for the content of olive oil in three principal acids: oleic, 56–83%; palmitic, 7–20%; and linoleic, 3–20%. The wide ranges appearing in Table V are due to both genetic factors and environmental conditions prevailing during the development of the fruit (Amellotti et al., 1973; Christakis et al., 1980).

Colakoglu (1966) reported traces of a C_{24} fatty acid in olive oil. The presence of elaidic (i.e., trans-oleic) acid in olive oil is doubtful (Tiscornia and Bertini, 1972; Amellotti et al., 1973). Rana and Ahmed (1981) found the content of Libyan oil in oleic acid to be exceptionally low (43.7% in virgin oil and 46.4% in refined oil), while the linoleic acid content was unusually high (over 30%). It is known that delayed harvesting tends to increase the content in unsaturated fatty acids, especially linoleic, at the expense of palmitic acid.

B.   THE GLYCERIDES OF OLIVE OIL

Most of the fatty acids of olive oil are present as triglycerides (triacylglycerols). The distribution of these acids in the glycerol molecule follows the 1,3-random-2-random rule, common in most vegetable oils. Table VI shows the percentage composition of olive oil in terms of individual triglycerides.

TABLE VI

FATTY ACID DISTRIBUTION AMONG THE CHIEF TRIGLYCERIDES OF OLIVE
OIL (%)[a]

Number of double bonds per triglyceride	Fatty acid distribution[b]	Content
0	0	0.0
1	POP	2.9
	PPO	0.6
	POS	0.5
	PSO	0.3
	SOS	0.2
	N.D.	0.2
2	PPL	1.2
	POO	18.4
	PLS	0.1
	LPS	0.7
	SOO	5.1
	N.D.	2.2
3	PLO	0.2
	POL	5.9
	OPL	0.9
	SLO	2.4
	LSO	0.7
	SOL	1.3
	OOO	43.5
	N.D.	0.6
4	PLL	0.4
	LPL	0.2
	OOL	6.8
	OLO	3.5
	SLL	0.2
	LSL	0.3
	N.D.	0.1

[a] Adapted from Fedeli and Jacini (1971).
[b] P, Palmitic; O, oleic; S, stearic; L, linoleic; N.D., nondetermined acid.

C. NONGLYCERIDE CONSTITUENTS OF OLIVE OIL

As previously stated, olive oil contains small quantities (usually less than 1%) of compounds which are not glycerides of fatty acids. These minor constituents were originally studied in the unsaponifiable fraction of the oil. Saponification, however, may destroy some of the nonglyceride constituents. A more complete recovery of the nonglyceride olive oil constituents may be accomplished by means of crystallization of the glycerides from a polar solvent (acetone or ethyl acetate) at low temperatures (-15 to $-60°C$). The nonglycerides are left in the mother liquor from which they can be isolated and determined by chromatographic and other analytical methods (Fedeli, 1977). The nonglyceride fraction of olive oil comprises several groups of compounds: nonglyceride fatty acid esters; hydrocarbons; sterols; triterpene alcohols; tocopherols; phenols; phospholipids; chlorophylls; and flavor compounds.

a. Nonglyceride Esters of Fatty Acids.   Although the vast majority of fatty acids are esterified with glycerol, small quantities of fatty acids form esters with a variety of other alcoholic compounds including the following: methanol, ethanol, and certain long chain (C_{27}–C_{32}) alcohols; sterols; and triterpene alcohols. The distribution of fatty acids among the esters of different alcoholic groups is not uniform, as Table VII indicates.

b. Hydrocarbons.   Squalene, a biochemical precursor of sterols, is the main hydrocarbon of olive oil. In fact, olive oil is richer in squalene than most vegetable oils. The polycyclic aromatic hydrocarbons identified in olive oil include phenanthrene, pyrene, fluoranthrene, 1,2-benzanthracene, chrysene, and perilene (Fedeli, 1977). Both even- and odd-carbon-numbered *n*-paraffins, ranging from C_{11} to C_{30}, were found in olive oil, frequently accompanied by branched hydrocarbons (Fedeli, 1977; Nawar, 1970). The provitamin A, β-carotene is also present in olive oil, albeit in very small quantities (0.3–3.6

TABLE VII

DISTRIBUTION OF FATTY ACIDS AMONG THREE GROUPS OF
NONGLYCERIDE ESTERS IN OLIVE OIL (%)[a]

Fatty acid	Group A	Group B	Group C
14 : 0	—	2.2	0.2
16 : 0	10.6	5.9	5.5
16 : 1	3.0	1.8	0.6
18 : 0	0.5	0.7	0.4
18 : 1	49.5	41.4	89.4
18 : 2	22.9	26.8	2.5
18 : 3	0.7	0.5	0.3
20 : 0	1.4	9.0	0.5
20 : 1	8.5	9.5	0.2

[a] Esters with (A) long chain alcohols, sterols, and some triterpene alcohols; (B) most triterpene alcohols; or (C) methanol and ethanol. Source: Fedeli (1977).

mg/kg). It has been shown that β-carotene quenches singlet oxygen and thereby inhibits lipid oxidation mediated by singlet oxygen (Carlsson *et al.*, 1976; Matsushita and Terao, 1980).

c. *Sterols.* Three sterols are present in Italian olive oils: β-sitosterol accounting for about 96% of the sterol mixture; campesterol representing 3%; and stigmasterol making up the remaining 1% of the total sterols (Fedeli, 1977). Boskou and Morton (1975) found a fourth sterol, anemasterol, in considerable quantity (8% of total sterol content) in Greek olive oil. Itoh *et al.* (1981) reported the presence in olive oil of four sterolic constituents. Leone *et al.* (1976) showed that increases in the peroxide value of olive oil during storage are associated with decreases in sterol content. Olive oil contains at least four 4α-methyl sterols, the simplest of which is 4α-methyl-24-methylene-Δ^7-cholestene-3β-ol. The other three have the following groups at position 24: 24-methyl, 24-ethyl, and 24-ethylidene. The total sterol content of olive oil is in the range of 180–265 mg/100 g.

d. *Triterpene Alcohols.* Two dihydroxy triterpenes have been identified in olive oil: erythrodiol, which is 3β,17β-dihydroxy-Δ^{12}-oleane (Cucurachi *et al.*, 1975; Leone *et al.*, 1978), and uvaol, which is 3β-11β-dihydroxy-Δ^{12}-ursene (Fedeli, 1977). Quantitation of erythrodiol and uvaol by gas–liquid chromatography provides a basis for differentiation between expressed and solvent-extracted oil.

e. *Tocopherols.* The tocopherols have a special significance because of their vitamin E activity. While there is no doubt that olive oil contains α-tocopherol in quantities varying from 12 to 150 ppm (Vitagliano, 1960; Gracian and Arevalo, 1965; Colakoglu, 1966; Boatella, 1975), investigators do not agree on the presence of other tocopherols (β, γ, and δ). Since soybean oil is rich in γ- and δ-tocopherols and cottonseed oil in γ-tocopherol, quantitation of these tocopherols has been suggested as a method of determining the adulteration of olive oil with the less expensive soybean and cottonseed oils (Gutfinger and Letan, 1974). It was also found that olive seed lipids are richer in tocopherols than olive oil.

f. *Phenols.* As stated previously, the olive mesocarp contains phenolic compounds which are chiefly water soluble. Small quantities of phenolics, however, are carried into the olive oil. Among the phenolic acids worth mentioning are the caffeic and protocatechuic acids. The chief polyphenols of olive oil are tyrosol and hydroxytyrosol, derived from the hydrolysis of oleuropein (Vazquez *et al.*, 1976). Benzoic acid and cinnamic acid, probably originating from the degradation of flavonoids, are also present in olive oil (Montedoro and Can-

TABLE VIII
FLAVOR COMPONENTS OF OLIVE OIL[a]

Hydrocarbons
  Naphthalene
  Ethylnaphthalene
  Dimethylhaphthalene
  Acenaphthene
  n-Octane
  Aromatic hydrocarbons

Aliphatic hydroxy compounds
  Methanol
  Ethanol
  Methylpropane-1-ol
  Pentene-1-ol
  3-Methylbutane-1-ol
  2-Methylbutane-1-ol
  cis-3-Hexene-1-ol
  Hexane-1-ol
  trans-2-Hexene-1-ol
  Heptane-1-ol
  Octane-1-ol
  Nonane-1-ol
  2-Phenylethane-1-ol

Terpenic hydroxy compounds
  1,8-Cineole
  Linalol
  α-Terpineol
  Lavandulol

Aldehydes
  Ethane-1-al
  n-Propane-1-al
  3-Methylbutane-1-al
  2-Methylbutane-1-al
  n-Butane-1-al
  n-Pentane-1-al
  trans-2-Pentene-1-al
  Pentene-1-al
  n-Hexane-1-al
  cis-2-Hexene-1-al
  trans-2-Hexene-1-al
  n-Heptane-1-al
  2,4-Hexadiene-1-al
  Heptene-1-al
  trans-2-Heptene-1-al
  Benzaldehyde
  n-Octane-1-al

Ketones
  Acetone
  3-Methylbutane-2-one
  Pentane-3-one
  Hexane-2-one
  2-Methyl-2-hepten-6-one
  Octane-2-one
  Nonane-2-one
  Acetophenone

Ethers
  Methoxybenzene
  1,2-Dimethoxybenzene

Furan derivatives
  2-Propylfuran (two isomers)
  2-n-Pentyl-3-methylfuran
  2-n-Propyldihydrofuran

Thiophene derivatives
  2-Isopropenylthiophene
  2-Ethyl-5-hexylthiophene
  2,5-Diethylthiophene
  2-Ethyl-5-hexyldihydrothiophene
  2-Ethyl-5-methyldihydrothiophene
  2-Octyl-5-methylthiophene

Esters
  Ethyl acetate
  Ethyl propionate
  Methyl butyrate
  Ethyl 2-methylpropionate
  2-Methyl 1-propylacetate
  Methyl 3-methylbutyrate
  Ethyl butyrate
  Propyl propionate
  Methyl pentanoate
  Ethyl 2-methylbutyrate
  Ethyl 3-methylbutyrate
  1-Propyl 2-methylpropionate
  3-Methyl 1-butylacetate
  2-Methyl-1-propyl 2-methylpropionate
  Methyl hexanoate
  cis-3-Hexenyl acetate
  Methyl heptanoate
  Methyl octanoate
  Ethyl benzoate
  Ethyl octanoate

TABLE VIII (*Continued*)

2,4-Heptadiene-1-al	
(two isomers)	Methyl salicylate
trans-2-Octene-1-al	1-Octyl acetate
n-Nonane-1-al	Ethyl phenylacetate
trans-2-Nonene-1-al	Ethyl nonanoate
2,4-Nonadiene-1-al	Ethyl decanoate
trans-2-Decene-1-al	Ethyl heptanoate
2,4-Decadiene-1-al	Ethyl palmitate
(two isomers)	Methyl oleate
trans-2-Undecene-1-al	Methyl linoleate

[a] Source: Fedeli (1977).

tarelli, 1969; Vazquez *et al.*, 1976). The phenolics of olive oil decrease its oxidation rate. In fact, phenolics extracted from olive oil act as antioxidants when added to other oils (Montedoro and Cantarelli, 1969). Gutfinger (1981) observed that olive oil extracted with a solvent (chloroform–methanol mixture) was more stable to oxidation than mechanically expressed oil. He attributed this stability to the higher polyphenol content of the solvent-extracted oil (321–574 ppm versus 50–159 ppm for mechanically extracted oil). The amount of water used in the pressing of olives also affects the concentration of phenolics in the oil. Larger quantities of added water wash out more phenolics from the olive oil. Kiritsakis (1982) reported an average phenol value of 120 ppm for Greek olive oil extracted by centrifugation.

g. Phospholipids. Olive oil contains a small amount of phospholipids (phosphatidylcholine and phosphatidylethanolamine), ranging from 40 to 135 ppm. A larger quantity of phospholipids is present in the olive seed oil. Oleic acid is the dominant fatty acid in these compounds.

h. Chlorophylls. Freshly extracted olive oil contains chlorophylls *a* and *b* at a total concentration varying from 1 to 10 ppm and pheophytins *a* and *b* at about the same total concentration. Interesse *et al.* (1971) showed that in the presence of light the chlorophylls and pheophytins exert a prooxidant effect on lipids, while in the dark they act as antioxidants. Vitagliano (1960) and Kiritsakis *et al.* (1983) also observed that olive oil containing green pigments must be protected from light for the oxidation to be delayed. Apparently, these pigments facilitate the formation of singlet oxygen and thereby promote the oxidation of olive oil in the presence of light (Rawls and van Santen, 1970).

i. Flavor Compounds. Virgin olive oil has a characteristic, pleasant flavor. Gas chromatography in combination with mass spectrometry made possible the identification of many (over 70) compounds thought to contribute to the flavor of olive oil (Nawar, 1970; Flath *et al.,* 1973). Fedeli (1977) categorized the aroma compounds of olive oil into aliphatic and aromatic hydrocarbons, aliphatic and terpenic alcohols, aldehydes, ketones, ethers, esters, and furan and thiophene derivatives (Table VIII). The flavor complex changes as the oil deteriorates with storage time. According to Evans *et al.* (1971), a number of unsaturated and easily oxidized compounds are destroyed during the gas chromatographic process and must be determined otherwise. Colakoglu and Unal (1980) identified several volatile compounds (alcohols, aldehydes, and acetone) in olive oil. Table VIII shows a list of flavor compounds detected in olive oil.

XI. STORAGE AND PACKING OF OLIVE OIL

Olive oil, like all edible oils, undergoes deterioration during storage. The main type of deterioration is oxidative rancidity. Although proper storage will extend considerably the marketing life of olive oil, private and commercial stores are usually replenished every year with oil of the new season. It is recommended that olive oils extracted from olives of different cultivars be stored separately (Cucurachi, 1975). It is possible to differentiate oils of different susceptibility to oxidative rancidity by means of accelerated oxidation tests and to market them accordingly.

Storing olive oil in tanks is a common practice. Such tanks should meet the following conditions: (1) be constructed of material impermeable to oil so that they can be thoroughly cleaned before they receive new oil; (2) be inert so that they do not react with the oil, absorb odors, or contain metals accelerating the oxidation of the oil; (3) protect the oil from light and be air tight; and (4) maintain a practically constant temperature, preferably near 15°C. Higher temperatures promote oxidation, while lower temperatures cause clouding of the oil. At times metallic drums are used. Such drums may impart a metallic flavor to the oil (as soaps are formed) and catalylze the oxidation of the oil. Lining the drums and tanks with epoxy resins improves their inertness. Enameled tiles and glass are considered the best lining materials for large olive oil storage tanks (Cucurachi, 1975).

During storage, insoluble material is sedimenting out of the oil. The deposits may undergo fermentation and affect the flavor of the oil. Racking off the oil is a necessary treatment and may be repeated several times before bottling the oil. Precautions should be taken to minimize the exposure of the oil to air and avoid oxidation during decantations. Filtration supplements the decantations of the oil. Filtering removes fine, nonsedimenting particles, such as hydrated colloids. Brightening is a treatment aimed at freeing the oil from traces of humidity and other substances that may have passed the filter. Although winterization may fulfill the purpose of brightening, usually the latter is accomplished by passing the oil through paper-leaf filters (Cucurachi, 1975). Brightening is applied just before bottling.

Olive oil is packed in several types of containers: bottles made of glass or polyvinylchloride (PVC) or polyethylene; tin-plated cans; and lined cartons. Certain types of containers are provided with easy closures, nondrip openings, and other convenient features. The containers should provide protection of the oil from light and leave a minimum volume of headspace. Packing under vacuum or inert gas has been suggested, and application of use-date labeling has been considered (Gonzalez, 1975).

XII. RANCIDITY OF OLIVE OIL

The most severe quality problem of olive oil is rancidity of which there are two types: hydrolytic rancidity and oxidative rancidity (Kiritsakis and Markakis, 1978). Hydrolytic rancidity is related to the hydrolysis of the glycerides with the consequent increase in total acidity and the deterioration of the flavor caused by certain free fatty acids. Hydrolysis of the olive oil glycerides may commence while the fruit is still on the tree. The endogenous lipase (glyceride-hydrolyzing enzyme) does not manifest its activity until the fruit starts turning purple. Fruit bruised or damaged by insects displays more lipolytic activity than sound fruit. Bacteria, yeasts, and molds that may grow on the fruit elaborate their own lipases. If the fruit is stored before processing, and especially if the storage is unsatisfactory (e.g., piling in thick layers where the fruit is heated by its own respiratory activity), then the combined effect of the endogenous and microbial lipases may result in considerable rise of the acidity of the oil to the detriment of its quality.

It has already been mentioned that oxidative rancidity is the main deteriorative change of olive oil during storage. Oxidative rancidity is due to the oxidation of unsaturated fatty acids and the subsequent formation of compounds possessing unpleasant taste and odor. The oxidation affecting the stability of olive oil (and other edible oils) is often called autoxidation and involves a free radical mechanism (Dugan, 1961). Autoxidation proceeds in three stages: initiation, propagation, and termination. In the initiation stage, hydrogen is abstracted from an olefinic acid molecule (RH) and two free radicals are formed:

$$RH + O_2 \rightarrow R\cdot + HOO\cdot$$

In the propagation stage, the olefinic free radical combines with molecular oxygen to yield a peroxy free radical. The latter can abstract hydrogen from another unsaturated molecule to yield a hydroperoxide plus a new free radical, setting in motion the propagation mechanism:

$$R\cdot + O_2 \rightarrow ROO\cdot$$
$$ROO\cdot + RH \rightarrow ROOH + R\cdot$$

This chain reaction continues until either the unsaturated compound has been exhausted or the free radicals have inactivated each other. The mutual anihilation of free radicals is known as the termination stage:

$$R\cdot + R\cdot \rightarrow RR$$
$$R\cdot + ROO\cdot \rightarrow ROOR$$
$$ROO\cdot + ROO\cdot \rightarrow ROOR + O_2$$

The net result of the propagation reactions is the formation of the hydroperoxides (ROOH). The hydroperoxides are rather unstable and decompose into a variety of secondary oxidation products, some of which (such as certain aldehydes) have an unpleasant smell and taste and contribute to the rancid flavor of the oil.

Certain substances known as antioxidants (AH) may inhibit lipid oxidation by reacting with the free radicals and breaking the chain reaction:

$$R\cdot + AH \rightarrow RH + A\cdot$$
$$A\cdot + A\cdot \rightarrow AA$$

Antioxidants may be naturally present in the oil (e.g., phenols and tocopherols in olive oil) or they may be added to it. Three common synthetic antioxidants are butylated hydroxyanisol (BHA), butylated hydroxytoluene (BHT), and *tert*-butylhydroxyquinone (TBHQ). Kiritsakis *et al.* (1983) found that β-carotene and nickel chelate delay the oxidation of olive oil containing chlorophyll, in the presence of light.

It may be added that the initiation of the oxiation may occur not only through hydrogen abstraction but also through direct addition of singlet oxygen ($^1O_2$) to a double bond of an olefinic acid.

$$RH + {}^1O_2 \rightarrow ROOH$$

The hydroperoxides may then decompose into free radicals ($R\cdot$, $RO\cdot$, $HO\cdot$, among other products), which can propagate the reaction. The activation energy required for either mode of initiation (hydrogen abstraction or singlet oxygen addition) may be provided by heat or light. The light-mediated oxidation (photooxidation) is enhanced by the presence of pigments, such as the chlorophylls and pheophytins of olive oil, which act as photosensitizers. The following reaction is thought to lead to the formation of singlet oxygen in the presence of cholorophyll (chl) and light ($h\nu$) (Rawls and Van Santen, 1970; Carlsson *et al.*, 1976):

$$chl \xrightarrow{h\nu} [chl]^* \xrightarrow{{}^3O_2} chl + {}^1O_2$$

Pheophytin is supposed to act in a similar fashion. It must be made clear that it is virgin oil, which contains chlorophyll and pheophytin, that is most sensitive to photooxication. Colorless, bleached olive oil does not display the same sensitivity to photooxidation (Kiritsakis, 1982).

Strong is the catalytic effect of certain metallic contaminants, such as copper and iron, on the autoxidation of olive oil. Likely sources of these contaminants are the metallic surfaces of storage and processing equipment. Vioque (1967) proposed a mathematical relationship between olive oil stability and iron concentration of the oil:

$$k = [Fe]^a S$$

where k and a are constants, [Fe] the iron concentration, and S the stability according to the active oxygen method (AOM). Fedeli et al. (1973) correlated the oxygen absorption rate of olive oil with the concentration of metallic contaminants. Vioque (1967) reported that removal of metallic contaminants by ion exchange increased the stability of olive oil to oxidation.

In a practical way, the rancidity of olive oil may be minimized by (1) using for extraction sound olives which have not been subjected to lipolysis, as free fatty acids not only increase the acidity of the oil, but are also oxidized more readily than their glycerides; (2) avoiding contamination of the oil with metals, especially iron and copper; and (3) storing the oil under the conditions already described in the olive oil storage section (Section XI).

XIII. OLIVE OIL ADULTERATION

Olive oil commands greater prices in the international market than other vegetable, edible oils. Consequently, adulteration of olive oil with cheaper oils is a temptation. Several physical and chemical tests have been proposed for detecting such adulteration (IOOC, 1984; Ninnis and Ninni, 1966; Codex Alimentarius Commission, 1970). The purity criteria proposed by the International Olive Oil Council (IOOC, 1984) for olive oil refer to fatty acid composition, saturated fatty acid content at position 2 of the triglycerides, sterol content, saponification value, unsaponifiable matter content, the Bellier index, and the semi-drying oil test.

The fatty acid composition of olive oil, as reported by the IOOC (1984), is presented in Table V (Section X). The saturated fatty acid level (sum of palmitic and stearic acids) at position 2 should not exceed 1.5% in virgin olive oil, 1.8% in refined olive oil or in pure olive oil, and 2.2% in refined olive-residue oil. The β-sitosterol and campesterol content, as well as the ratio of β-sitosterol to campesterol + stigmasterol, are useful in detecting olive oil adulteration. Squalene, which is present in olive oil in much larger quantities than in other vegetable oils, may be used in detecting adulteration of olive oil. Systematic analysis of the entire unsaponifiable fraction will probably provide additional tests for sharpening the differentiation among vegetable oils (Ciusa and Morgante, 1974; Pallotta, 1976; Fedeli, 1977; Itoh *et al.*, 1981).

Absorption of ultraviolet light is often used in testing for olive oil adulteration. Olive oil absorbs 3–4 times less light in the region 208–210 nm than other vegetable oils. Combining the absorbance at two wavelengths, Ninnis and Ninni (1966) proposed a quantitative method for determining olive oil adulteration. Gas chromatography has also been used for estimating the admixture of olive oil with other vegetable oils (Colakoglu, 1966; Gegiou and Georgouli, 1980). A combination of gas chromatography and liquid chromatography permits the detection of as little as 5% of a foreign olive oil (Kapoulas and Passaloglou-Emmanouilidou, 1981). At times, reesterified olive-residue oils are used to adulterate olive oil. The detection of elaidic acid by infrared spectroscopy in such oils reveals the adulteration (Pallotta, 1976).

XIV. OLIVE OIL QUALITY AND THE INTERNATIONAL OLIVE OIL COUNCIL

The quality of olive oil is affected by many factors. Different cultivars may produce oil of different organoleptic characteristics under identical conditions of environment and cultivation. But also climatic and soil conditions, cultivation practices, the maturity of olives, and their health state (whether or not infested by pests) influence the quality of the oil (Suarez, 1975). Olives harvested relatively early yield oil with a fruity flavor, lower acidity, and greener color than olives harvested late in the season.

Both sensory attributes and laboratory tests are used in assessing the quality of olive oil. Based on flavor alone, the following classification of olive oil was proposed by Frezzotti *et al.* (1956):

1. Unripe oil—extracted from unripe olives
2. Bitter oil—extracted from olives mixed with leaves
3. Fruity oil—extracted from freshly picked, ripe olives (best olive oil)
4. Good flavor oil—ordinary oil with off flavors
5. Defective oil—oil with off flavors (moldy, wormy, rancid, metallic, medicinal, etc.)

The off flavors of olive oil were discussed by Cucurachi (1975).

The color of olive oil varies from light yellow, to green–yellow, to green, to green–brown depending on the maturity of the olives and the processing received by the oil. For example, the Rapanelli decanter oil is greener than the Rapanelli sinolea oil because the latter contains less chlorophyll (Kiritsakis, 1982).

Of particular interest is the categorization of olive oil and olive-residue oil into grades or qualities on the basis of criteria established by the International Olive

Oil Council (IOOC). A few words on this important organization are in order here. The IOOC was established in 1956 by parties interested in olive oil as an international trade commodity. Currently, the Council has 19 member nations accounting for 96% of the world olive oil production. The goals of this organization include the improvement of olive cultivation and olive product technology, the promulgation of quality standards for olive oil and table olives, the protection and promotion of these products in international trade, and the development and standardization of analytical methodology. At a 1984 meeting the IOOC proposed the following designations for olive oil and olive-residue oil:

1. *Olive oil* is the oil obtained solely from the fruit of the olive tree (*Olea europaea sativa* Hoff. Link), to the exclusion of oils obtained using solvents or reesterification processes and any mixture with oils of other kinds. The designation "olive oil" used alone shall not, under any circumstances, be applied to olive-residue oils.

1.1. *Virgin olive oil* is the oil obtained from the fruit of the olive tree solely by mechanical or other physical means under conditions, particularly thermal conditions, that do not lead to alterations in the oil, and which has not undergone any treatment other than washing, decantation, centrifugation, and filtration.

1.1.1. *Virgin olive oil fit for consumption as it is* includes the following:

i. *Virgin olive oil extra:* Virgin olive oil of absolutely perfect flavor and odor having a maximum acidity, in terms of oleic acid, of 1 g/100g;

ii. *Virgin olive oil fine:* Virgin olive oil of absolutely perfect flavor and odor having a maximum acidity, in terms of oleic acid, of 1.5 g/100 g;

iii. *Virgin olive oil semi-fine* (or *virgin olive oil ordinary*): Virgin olive oil of good flavor and odor having a maximum acidity, in terms of oleic acid, of 3 g/100 g, with a tolerance margin of 10% of the acidity indicated.

1.1.2. *Virgin olive oil not fit for consumption as it is,* designated *virgin olive oil lampante,* is an off flavor and/or off smelling virgin olive oil or an oil with a maximum acidity, in terms of oleic acid, of more than 3.3 g/100 g. It is intended for refining or for technical purposes.

1.2. *Refined olive oil* is the olive oil obtained from virgin olive oils by refining methods which do not lead to alterations in the initial glyceridic structure.

1.3. *Olive oil* or *pure olive oil* is the oil consisting of a blend of virgin olive oil fit for consumption as it is and refined olive oil. Blends of virgin olive oil and refined olive oil may constitute types, the characteristics of which may be determined by mutual agreement between buyers and sellers. However, these blends must meet the quality criteria as stipulated in point 4 of this standard for pure olive oil.

2. *Olive-residue oil* is the oil obtained by treating olive residue with solvents, to the exclusion of oils obtained by reesterification processes and any mixture of oils of other kinds. It can be classified as follows:

TABLE IX

DESIGNATIONS OF OLIVE OIL AND OLIVE-RESIDUE OIL AS RELATED TO SENSORY AND LABORATORY CRITERIA[a]

	Olive oil						Olive-residue oil		
	Virgin extra	Virgin fine	Virgin semi-fine	Virgin lampante	Refined	Pure	Crude	Refined	Refined and olive
Organoleptic characteristics									
Odor	Absolutely perfect	Absolutely perfect	Good	Off smelling	Acceptable	Good	—	Acceptable	Acceptable
Taste	Absolutely perfect	Absolutely perfect	Good	Off smelling	Acceptable	Good	—	Acceptable	Acceptable
Color	Light yellow to green	Light yellow to green	Light yellow to green	Yellow to brownish green	Light yellow	Light yellow to green	—	Light yellow to brownish yellow	Light yellow to green
Aspect at 20° for 24 hr	Limpid	Limpid	Limpid	—	Limpid	Limpid	—	Limpid	Limpid
Free acidity in oleic acid (%) (max)	1.0	1.5	3.3	3.3	0.3	1.5	No limit	0.3	1.5
Peroxide value, peroxide oxygen (mequiv/kg oil) (max)	20	20	20	20	10	20	No limit	20	20
Moisture and volatile matter (%) (max)	0.2	0.2	0.2	0.3	0.1	0.1	1.5	0.1	0.1
Impurities insoluble in light petroleum (%) (max)	0.1	0.1	0.1	0.2	0.05	0.05	—	0.05	0.05
Soap test	—	—	—	—	Negative	—	—	Negative	—
Flash point (min)	—	—	—	—	—	—	120°C	—	—
K_{270} [b] (max)	0.25	0.25	0.30	0.30	1.10	0.90	—	2.00	1.70
ΔK (max)	0.01	0.01	0.01	0.01	0.15	0.15	—	0.20	0.18

[a] Source: International Olive Oil Council (IOOC) (1984).

[b] K_{270} is the absorbance $E_1^{1\%}$ cm at 270 nm. $\Delta K = K_{268} - (K_{262} + K_{274})/2$.

2.1. *Crude olive-residue oil* is olive-residue oil intended for refining with a view to its use in food for human consumption or for technical purposes.

2.2. *Refined olive-residue oil* is that obtained from crude olive-residue oil by refining methods which do not lead to alterations in the initial glyceridic structure. It is intended for human consumption either as it is or else in a mixture with virgin olive oil.

2.3. *Refined olive-residue oil and olive oil* is a mixture of refined olive-residue oil and virgin olive oil fit for consumption as it is; this mixture is usually intended for domestic consumption in some producing countries.

The relationships between the aforementioned designations and certain sensory and laboratory criteria are shown in Table IX.

XV. CONSUMPTION OF OLIVE OIL AND HEALTH

In ancient times, the Mediterranean people considered olive oil not only an excellent food but also a healing agent. During the past four decades a renewed interest was generated in the nutritional and health aspects of olive oil. In the 1950s, Ancel Keys initiated a series of studies on the relationship between the degree of saturation of consumed fat and the incidence of coronary heart disease (CHD). He found (Keys, 1975, 1980a,b) that Mediterranean people (Italian and Greek in particular) who consume considerable quantities of olive oil have a much lower incidence of CHD than people elsewhere (Finland, United States), who consume more saturated fats. He also reported that the serum cholesterol level among olive oil consumers was significantly lower than among eaters of more saturated fats. He did admit, however, that the data do not prove beyond any doubt that olive oil consumption prevents CHD. Key's observations are corroborated by similar epidemiological studies conducted by Aravanis and a team of Greek physicians (1978, 1980), by Christakis alone (1966) or with co-workers (1965, 1980), and by Kuller (1976). Aravanis and Dontas (1978) noted that the number of deaths caused by myocardial infarction per 100,000 is 60 in Heraclion, the largest city of the Greek island, Crete (where 29% of the dietary calories come from olive oil), and 395 in the United States.

Christakis *et al.* (1980) and Viola (1983) contend that the high ratio of (mono) unsaturated fatty acids to saturated fatty acids imparts antiatherosclerolic properties to olive oil, while the low content in polyunsaturated fatty acids (PUFA) of this oil, in comparison to other vegetable oils, diminishes the risks associated with high PUFA intake (American Heart Association, 1982). In addition, Viola (1983) considers the ratio of vitamin E to PUFA in olive oil to be more favorable to health than the ratio in other vegetable oils (Table X). Several other authors (Carbonier and Neuman, 1969; Casares, 1969; Gyorgy, 1969; Turchetto *et al.*,

TABLE X

VITAMIN E AND POLYUNSATURATED FATTY ACIDS CONTENT OF
SEVERAL VEGETABLE OILS[a]

Oil	Vitamin E (mg/kg)	PUFA (% by weight)	Ratio of vitamin E to PUFA (mg/g)
Olive	150	8	1.88
Soybean	175	57	0.31
Peanut	100	20	0.50
Cottonseed	300	40	0.75
Sunflower	250	57	0.44
Corn	200	40	0.50
Rape	175	17	1.03

[a] Source: Viola (1983).

1969; Segovia *et al.,* 1975) attribute additional beneficial physiological effects to olive oil, such as being a eupetic, cholagoguic, and homeostatic food.

XVI. FUTURE RESEARCH NEEDS

A multilevel research approach is recommended for improvement in quality and increase in quantity of olive oil. Starting at the production level, the search for olive tree variaties best suited for each cultivation area should be continued. It is deemed desirable to consider the newer genetic engineering techniques in order to reach better health and productivity states for the trees. The search for improved ways to neutralize, and eventually eradicate, the traditional enemy of olive cultivation, the olive fly *Dacus oleae,* should be intensified.

The olive fruit harvesting methods must be modernized. As farm labor becomes increasingly scarce, the mechanical means of collecting the fruit properly and efficiently must be perfected. Improved ways of storing the fruit before processing should be also sought. The need for better fruit storage facilities is greater for olive mills of limited capacity. Although significant progress has been made in designing efficient olive processing equipment, there is room for improving the rate of oil extraction from the fruit. The use of enzymes facilitating the release of oil from the tissue should be further explored.

As antioxidants hold promise for prolonging the market life of olive oil, additional work on the application of these additives to the preservation of olive oil is indicated. The contention of a particularly beneficial effect of olive oil consumption on human health needs additional justification. The trans isomerization of oleic acid on heating olive oil for culinary purposes invites investigation.

Finally, the utilization of by-products of the olive oil industry should be further explored. An example of a potentially useful olive by-product is the anthocyanin present in the ripe olive skin. Another example is the sugars which are present in the aqueous phase of the olive tissue and which could be subjected to alcoholic fermentation after the extraction of the oil.

REFERENCES

Amellotti, G., Dachetta, A., Grieco, D., and Martin, K. 1973. Analysis of pressed olive oils in Liguria in relation to the olive harvesting period. *Riv. Ital. Sost. Grasse* **50**, 30.

American Heart Association. 1982. Diet–heart statement of AHA. *Nutr. Today* Dec.

Aravanis, C. 1980. The Greek islands heart study. *Proc. Int. Congr. Biol. Value Olive Oil, 3rd, Inst. Subtrop. Olive Trees Chanea, with IOOC Coop.*

Aravanis, C., and Dontas, A. 1978. Seventeen-year mortality from coronary heart disease in the Greek islands heart study. *Abstr. Annu. Conf. Cardiovasc. Dis. Epidemiol., 18th, Orlando, Florida.*

Balatsouras, G. 1984. "The Olive Tree" (N. Mauromatis, ed.), Vol. 1. Athens.

Boatella, R. 1975. Analysis of the tocopherols of vegetable oils by gas-phase chromatography. *J. Ann. Brom.* **27**, 287.

Borbolla y Alcala, J. M. R. de la, Fernandez Diez, M. J., and Gonzalez Pellisso, F. 1955. *Grasas Aceitas* **6**, 6 (cited in Frezzotti *et al.*, 1956).

Boskou, D., and Morton, J. M. 1975. Changes in the sterol composition of olive oil on heating. *J. Sci. Food Agric.* **26**, 1149.

Carbonnier, A., and Neuman, M. 1969. Influence de l'huile d'olive sur certaines fonctions hepatiques de l'homme. *Int. Congr. Biol. Value Olive Oil, Lucca, Italy.*

Carlsson, D. J., Suprunchuk, T., and Wiles, H. M. 1976. Photooxidation of unsaturated oils. Effects of singlet oxygen quenchers. *J. Am. Oil Chem. Soc.* **53**, 656.

Casares, R. 1969. La digestibilidad del aceite de oliva. *Int. Congr. Biol. Value Olive Oil, Lucca, Italy.*

Christakis, G. 1966. An epidemiological odyssey to Crete. *Med. Opinion Rev.* **1**, 55.

Christakis, G., Servinghaus, E. L., Maldonado, Z., Kafatos, F., and Hashim, S. 1965. A study in the metabolic epidemiology of coronary heart disease. *Am. J. Cardiol.* **15**, 320.

Christakis, G., Fordyce, M. K., and Kurtz, C. S. 1980. The biological aspects of olive oil. *Proc. Int. Congr. Biol. Value Olive Oil, 3rd, Chanea, Greece.*

Ciusa, W., and Morgante, A. 1974. Polycyclic aromatic hydrocarbons in olives. *Quad. Merced.* **13**, 31.

Codex Alimentarius Commission WHO/FAO. 1970. Recommended international standard for olive oil, virgin and refined and for refined olive-residue oil. CAC/RS-33.

Colakoglu, M. 1966. Données analytiques nourelles sur les huiles d'olive. *Rev. Fr. Corps Gras* **4**, 261.

Colakoglu, M., and Unal, K. 1980. The changes of some volatile compounds during the storage of olive oil. *Proc. Int. Congr. Biol. Value Olive Oil, 3rd, Chanea Greece.*

Cucurachi, A. 1975. Final operations. *In* "Olive Oil Technology" (J. M. M. Moreno, ed.). FAO, Rome.

Cucurachi, A., Camera, L., Angerosa, F., and Solinas, M. 1975. Erythrodiol content of "dark green" olive oil. *Riv. Ital. Sost. Grasse* **52**, 266.

Dugan, L. R., Jr. 1961. Development and inhibition of oxidative rancidity of foods. *Food Technol.* **15**, 10.

Evans, C., Helen, D., Moser, A., and List, G. R. 1971. Odor and flavor responses to additives in edible oils. *J. Am. Oil Chem. Soc.* **48**, 493.

Fedeli, E. 1977. Lipids of olives. *Prog. Chem. Fats Other Lipids* **15**, 57.

Fedeli, E., and Jacini, G. 1971. Lipid composition of vegetable oils. *Adv. Lipid Res.* **9**, 335.

Fedeli, E., Brillo, A., and Jacini, G. 1973. Metals affecting the autoxidation of vegetable oils. *Riv. Ital. Sost. Grasse* **50**, 102.

Fernandez Diez, M. J. 1971. The olive. *In* "Biochemistry of Fruits and Their Products" (A. C. Hulme, ed.). Academic Press, New York.

Flath, R. A., Forrey, R. R., and Guadagni, D. G. 1973. Aroma components of olive oil. *J. Agric. Food Chem.* **21**, 948.

Frezzotti, G., Manni, M., and Aten, A. 1956. Olive oil processing in rural mills. FAO, Rome. Agricultural Dev. paper No. 58.

Gegiou, D., and Georgouli, M. 1980. Detection of reesterified oils. Determination of fatty acids at position 2 in glycerides of oils. *J. Am. Oil Chem. Soc.* **57**, 313.

Gonzalez, Q. G. R. 1975. Bottling and canning. *In* "Olive Oil Technology" (J. M. M. Moreno, ed.). FAO, Rome.

Gracian T. 1968. The chemistry and analysis of olive oil. *In* "Analysis and Characterization of Oils, Fats and Fat Products" (H. A. Boekenoogen, ed.), Vol. 2. Wiley (Interscience), New York.

Gracian, T., and Arevalo, G. 1965. Los tocopherols en los aceites vegetales con especial referencia al aceite de oliva. *Grasas Aceites* **16**, 278.

Gutfinger, J. 1981. Polyphenols in olive oils. *J. Am. Oil Chem. Soc.* **58**, 966.

Gutfinger, J., and Letan, A. 1974. Studies of unsaponifiables in several vegetable oils. *Lipids* **9**, 658.

Gutierrez Gonsales-Quijano, R. 1975. Bottling and canning. *In* "Olive Oil Technology" (J. M. M. Moreno, ed.). FAO Rome.

Gyorgy, P. 1969. Recent developments on the nutritional role of fats. *Int. Congr. Biol. Value Olive Oil, Lucca, Italy.*

Hartmann, H. T. 1962. Olive growing in Australia. *Econ. Bot.* **16**, 31.

Hartmann, H. T., and Bougas, P. C. 1970. Olive production in Greece. *Econ. Bot.* **24**, 443.

Hartmann, H. T., and Opitz, K. W. 1977. Olive production in California. Division of Agricultural Sciences, Univ. of California. Leaflet 2474.

Hartmann, H. T., and Porlingis, J. 1957. Effect of different amounts of winter chilling on fruitfulness of several olive varieties. *Bot. Gaz.* **119**, 102.

Hess, D. 1975. "Plant Physiology." Springer-Verlag, New York.

Interesse, F. S., Ruggiero, P., and Vitagliano, M. 1971. Autoxidation of olive oil. Effects of chlorophyll pigments. *Ind. Agric.* **9**, 318.

International Olive Oil Council (IOOC). 1984. International trade standards applying to olive oils and olive-residue oils. COI/T.15/NC No. 1. IOOC, Madrid.

Itoh, T., Yoshida, K., Yatsu, T., Tamura, T., and Matsumoto, T. 1981. Triterpene alcohols and sterols of Spanish olive oil. *J. Am. Oil Chem. Soc.* **58**, 545.

Jacini, G. 1976. Problems in olive oil research. *In* "Lipids" (R. Paoletti, G. Jacini, and T. Porcellati, eds.), Vol. 2. Raven, New York.

Kapoulias, V. M., and Passaloglou-Emmanouilidou, S. 1981. Detection of adulteration of olive oil with seed oils by a combination of column and gas liquid chromatography. *J. Am. Oil Chem. Soc.* **58**, 694.

Keys, A. 1975. Mortality and coronary heart disease in the Mediterranean area. *Proc. Int. Congr. Biol. Value Olive Oil, 2nd, Toremolinos, Spain.*

Keys, A. 1980a. "Seven Countries: A Multivariate Analysis of Death and Coronary Heart Disease." Harvard Univ. Press, Cambridge, Massachusetts.

Keys, A. 1980b. Ten-year mortality and incidence of coronary heart disease in the seven countries study. *Proc. Int. Congr. Biol. Value Olive Oil, 3rd, Chanea, Greece.*

Kiritsakis, A. 1982. Quality studies on olive oil. Dissertation. Michigan State University, East Lansing.

Kiritsakis, A., and Markakis, P. 1978. The rancidity of olive oil. *Geotechnica* **4,** 54 (in Greek).

Kiritsakis, A., and Markakis, P. 1984. Effect of olive collection regimen on olive oil quality. *J. Sci. Food Agric.* **35,** 677.

Kiritsakis, A., Stine, C. M., and Dugan, L. R. 1983. Effect of selected antioxidants on the stability of virgin olive oil. *J. Am. Oil Chem. Soc.* **60,** 286.

Kuller, L. H. 1976. The epidemiology of cardiovascular disease in current perspectives. *Am. J. Epidemiol.* **104,** 425.

Leone, A. M., LaNotte, E., and Lamparelli, F. 1976. The sterolic fraction of olive oil and its analytical significance. *Riv. Tech. Alim. Nutr.* **6,** 205.

Leone, A. M., Lamparelli, F., and LaNotte, E. 1978. Sterols and terpene dialcohols in Apulian olive oil. *Riv. Ital. Sost. Grasse* **55,** 342.

Manoukas, A. G. 1972. A research report on the olive fruit fly, *Dacus oleae.* Nuclear Research Center. "Democritus," Athens (in Greek).

Matsushita, S., and Terao, J. 1980. Singlet oxygen initiation photooxidation of unsaturated fatty acid esters and inhibitory effects of tocopherols and β-carotenes. *In* "Autoxidation in Foods and Biological Systems" (M. G. Simic and M. Karel, eds.). Plenum, New York.

Mendoza, J. A. 1975. Milling, malaxation. *In* "Olive Oil Technology" (J. M. M. Moreno, ed.). FAO, Rome.

Montedoro, G., and Cantarelli, C. 1969. Phenolic compounds in olive oils. *Riv. Ital. Sost. Grasse* **46,** 115.

Montedoro, G., and Petruccioli, G. 1972. Enzymic treatments in the mechanical extraction of olive oil. *Acta Vitam. Enzymol.* **26,** 171.

Montedoro, G., and Petruccioli, G. 1974. Treatment with enzymatic preparation and tannin absorbents in extracting olive oil by single pressure and percolation processes. *Riv. Ital. Sost. Grasse* **51,** 378.

Montedoro, G., Bertucioli, M., and Petruccioli, G. 1976. The effects of treatment with enzymatic preparations and tannin phenolic absorbent agents in extracting olive oil by single process on the oil yield, and on the analytical characteristics of the oils. *Acta Vitam. Enzymol.* **30,** 13.

Nawar, W. W. 1970. The flavor of olive oil. *Natl. Meet. Am. Oil Chem. Soc., 44th, Chicago.*

Ninnis, L. N., and Ninni, M. L. 1966. L'importance pour l'analyse de l'huile d'olive de l'absorption dans l'ultra-violet (190 a 220 mμ). *Rev. Fr. Corps Gras* **60,** 1.

Pallotta, U. 1976. Analytic problems in the ascertainment of olive oil genuineness. *In* "Lipids" (R. Paoletti, G. Jacini, and R. Porcellati, eds.), Vol. 2. Raven, New York.

Petruccioli, G. 1975. Oil extraction. *In* "Olive Oil Technology" (J. M. M. Moreno, ed.). FAO, Rome.

Rana, M. S., and Ahmed, A. A. 1981. Characteristics and composition of Libyan olive oil. *J. Am. Oil Chem. Soc.* **58,** 630.

Rawls, H. R., and van Santen, P. J. 1970. A possible role for singlet oxygen in the initiation of fatty acid autoxidation. *J. Am. Oil Chem. Soc.* **47,** 121.

Samir, M., and Hegsted, D. M. 1974. Olive kernels as a source of protein. *Nutr. Rep. Int.* **9,** 117.

Segovia de Arana, J. M., Vidal, C., Sastre, A., and Bojas-Hidalgo, E. 1975. Aceite de oliva y aparato digestivo. *Proc. Int. Congr. Biol. Value Olive Oil, 2nd, Torremolinos, Spain.*

Sellianakis, G. 1984. Effects of Greek olive cultivation when Spain and Portugal will become members of European Market. Special study. Elaiourgiki, Athens (in Greek).

Standish, R. 1960. The first of trees. "The Story of the Olive." Phoenix House, London.

Suarez, J. M. M. 1975. Preliminary operations. *In* "Olive Oil Technology" (J. M. M. Moreno, ed.). FAO, Rome.

Tiscornia, E., and Bertini, G. 1972. Recent analytical data in chemical composition and structure of olive oil. *Riv. Ital. Sost. Grasse* **49**, 3.

Turchetto, E., Martinelli, M., and Formiggini, E. 1969. Lipid dieteticied omeostasi biochimical tessutale. *Int. Congr. Biol. Value Olive Oil, Lucca, Italy*.

Vaugh, R. M., Simpson, K. L., and Chicester, C. O. 1961. Compounds responsible for the color of black "ripe" olives. *J. Food Sci.* **26**, 227.

Vazquez, R. C., Del Valle, A. J., and Del Valle, J. L. M. 1976. Phenolic compounds in olive fruits. Polyphenols in olive oils. *Grasas Aceites* **27**, 185.

Viola, P. 1983. *IOOC Symp. Advantages Olive Oil, Amman*.

Vioque, A. 1967. Demetalization of edible vegetable oils. A symposium on metal catalyzed lipid oxidation. SIK—Rapport No. 240.

Vitagliano, M. 1960. Minor constituents of olive oil. *Oli Min. Grasi Saponi, Coloni Verniki* **37**, 136.

INDEX

A

Absorption
  carcinogen risk assessment and, 33, 34, 37
  chocolate and
    alkalization, 247
    cocoa bean chemistry, 229
    milk, 255, 256
  dietary fiber and, 135, 163, 166–169
Aceselfane-K, chocolate and, 271
Acetate, chocolate and, 325
Acetic acid
  chocolate and, 297, 324
    processing, 215, 216, 219, 220, 222, 223, 225
  dietary fiber and, 127, 130, 161, 180
  endogenous proteolytic enzymes and, 401
  N-nitroso compounds and, 68
  olive oil and, 459
Acetone
  chocolate and, 222–224, 279, 281
  dietary fiber and, 152, 159, 166
  N-nitroso compounds and, 60
Acetyl groups, dietary fiber and, 186, 187
Acetylation, dietary fiber and, 130, 131
Acid detergent fiber, dietary fiber and, 153, 180, 181
Acidity
  chocolate and
    cocoa butter, 278
    conching, 297
    emulsifiers, 282
    milk, 262
    processing, 215–217, 244, 246
  dietary fiber and, 137, 138, 141, 191
    analysis, 143, 148, 150, 151, 153
    dicotyledonous plants, 127, 130, 131, 133

intestinal bacteria, 172, 175
  properties, 160, 164, 165
endogenous proteolytic enzymes and
  endopeptidases, 360
  meat technology, 411
  muscle physiology, 372
  proteinase activity, 385, 386, 388
  proteinase distribution, 368
  N-nitroso compounds and, 59
  olive oil and, 460, 463, 473, 474
Acrylonitrile, chocolate and, 318
Actin, endogenous proteolytic enzymes and
  meat technology, 394, 396, 399, 404, 407, 409, 410
  muscle physiology, 370, 371
α-Actinin, endogenous proteolytic enzymes and, 404, 407
Active oxidation method, olive oil and, 473
Actomyosin, endogenous proteolytic enzymes and, 394, 396–398
ADP, endogenous proteolytic enzymes and, 393, 410
Adipose, N-nitroso compounds and, 78, 80, 83
Adsorption, dietary fiber and, 120, 142, 157, 159, 160, 163
Aging, endogenous proteolytic enzymes and, 345, 394, 395, 412, 413
  changes, 395–403
  enzymology, 403–411
AIDS, carcinogen risk assessment and, 19, 44
Air pollution, carcinogen risk assessment and, 38–41
Albumin, endogenous proteolytic enzymes and, 362, 375
Alcohol
  carcinogen risk assessment and, 17, 19, 22, 41

H